Y0-DKE-663

MATERIALS OF CONSTRUCTION

MATERIALS OF CONSTRUCTION

Their Manufacture and Properties

BY THE LATE
ADELBERT P. MILLS
Professor at Cornell University

SECOND, THIRD, AND FOURTH EDITIONS, EDITED BY
HARRISON W. HAYWARD
Late Professor of Materials of Engineering
Massachusetts Institute of Technology

FIFTH AND SIXTH EDITIONS, REWRITTEN AND EDITED BY
LLOYD F. RADER, M.S.E., Ph.D.
(University of Michigan)
Professor of Civil Engineering, The University of Wisconsin
Member American Society of Civil Engineers
Member American Society for Testing Materials

Sixth Edition

JOHN WILEY & SONS, INC.
NEW YORK · LONDON · SYDNEY

Copyright, 1915
By ADELBERT P. MILLS

Copyright, 1922, 1926, 1931
By GRACE C. MILLS
and HARRISON W. HAYWARD

Copyright, 1939
By GRACE C. MILLS
MABEL H. HAYWARD
and LLOYD F. RADER

1915 Copyright renewed 1942
1922 Copyright renewed 1949
1926 Copyright renewed 1953

Copyright, 1955
By
JOHN WILEY & SONS, INC.

All Rights Reserved

This book or any part thereof must not be reproduced in any form without the written permission of the publisher.

SIXTH EDITION

11 12 13 14 15 16 17 18 19 20

Library of Congress Catalog Card Number: 55-7368

PRINTED IN THE UNITED STATES OF AMERICA

ISBN 0 471 60654 5

Preface
TO THE SIXTH EDITION

The original purpose of Professor Mills of providing a textbook covering the manufacture, properties, and uses of materials of engineering construction has been retained as the object in the preparation of the Sixth Edition. The changes in this edition consist of the introduction of several new chapters and the treatment of certain materials not covered in previous editions, together with a revision of subject matter throughout and a rearrangement of the chapters.

In the first part of the book, fundamental properties of materials are explained and methods of testing and requirements of materials in service are described. The source and production of metals are treated in an early chapter. Most of the book consists of a detailed treatment of specific materials of construction. This arrangement and treatment is believed to be desirable from the standpoint of teaching.

This book on materials of construction is designed for use by engineers and students in the various branches of engineering. Industrial as well as structural applications are described.

The chapter on service requirements of metals has been revised to cover recent developments in the subjects of progressive fracture under repeated stresses, creep, behavior of metals under high and low temperatures, impact testing, wear, and corrosion. Descriptions of non-destructive tests have been included.

The discussion of the metallography and the constitution of metals has been amplified and brought up to date. Isothermal transformation diagrams for various steels are given and used to explain modern heat-treating methods. Additions and improvements have been made in the analysis of the various ferrous and non-ferrous metals and alloys. Particular attention has been given to modern developments in steel, alloy steels, and lightweight non-ferrous alloys. The subject of welding has been more adequately covered.

A new chapter has been written on mineral aggregates. The descriptions of the different types of cement have been brought up to date. The chapter on concrete has been revised to cover air-entrained concrete and modern methods of proportioning. Physical properties of concrete, especially durability, have been treated from a modern point of view. Concrete products have been described.

The classifications of structural-clay products have been revised to conform with present practice. The treatment of refractory and heat-insulating materials has been expanded to cover modern developments, and a new section has been written on acoustical materials. For timber, the structural values have been revised to conform to the latest practice. Timber connectors are described.

The chapters on organic protective coatings and organic plastics have been revised with attention to new developments. One of the principal contributions to the Sixth Edition is the new chapter on laminates and adhesives. Synthetic resin adhesives and various types of laminated structures are described.

The coöperation and assistance rendered to Professor Hayward in the preparation of the Second, Third, and Fourth Editions by the following members of the Massachusetts Institute of Technology faculty are acknowledged: Henry Fay, Robert S. Williams, Irving H. Cowdrey, George B. Haven, Dean Peabody, Jr., Ralph G. Adams, and Gordon B. Wilkes. The assistance rendered to me in the preparation of the Fifth Edition by Dr. Wm. Howlett Gardner, Chemical Engineer, Allied Chemical and Dye Corporation, on organic protective coatings and organic plastics is also acknowledged. It is desired to express appreciation for permission to reproduce figures in books published by John Wiley & Sons.

Acknowledgment is made to the following societies and organizations for permission to quote from their publications: American Society for Testing Materials, American Society of Civil Engineers, American Society of Mechanical Engineers, Society of Automotive Engineers, Highway Research Board, Association of State Highway Officials, American Railway Engineering Association, American Standards Association, A. M. Byers Co., American Manganese Bronze Co., Aluminum Company of America, Reynolds Metal Co., International Nickel Co., U. S. Steel Corp., Lincoln Electric Co., American Society for Metals, *Materials & Methods,* Rock Products, Public Roads, American Concrete Institute, Portland Cement Association, Vacuum Concrete Corp., National Crushed Stone Association, Harbison-Walker Refractories Co., Forest Products Laboratory, Forest Products Research Society, Wm. F. Clapp Laboratory, National Lumber Manufacturers Association, Iowa Manufacturing Co., *Metal Progress, Metals & Alloys, The Iron Age,* Carnegie-Illinois Steel Co., *Steel,* General Electric Co., and Allis-Chalmers Manufacturing Co. The material quoted from the publications of the American Society for Testing Materials is especially valuable. Government publications have been consulted on many subjects.

Care has been taken to give accurate information in this textbook; however, in a subject so varied as materials of construction, mistakes may occur. I will appreciate having errors called to my attention.

LLOYD F. RADER

MADISON, WIS.
January, 1955

Preface
TO THE FIRST EDITION

This work is an outgrowth of certain lectures and notes which have been used in the author's classes in the College of Civil Engineering, Cornell University, for the past several years. Its preparation was undertaken to meet the need which was felt for a general textbook covering the manufacture, properties, and uses of the more common materials of engineering construction in a comparatively concise and thoroughly modern manner.

Although this book is intended primarily for use as a textbook of somewhat elementary character and is not a treatise exhaustively covering the very broad field of "Materials of Construction," the treatment has been made more detailed in some respects than may be necessary for class-room purposes, and its applications as a general reference work thereby broadened.

The treatment of the various classes of materials considered follows a general systematic form which has been made uniform throughout so far as has been found practicable. The consideration of each material or class of materials is prefaced by a discussion of its ordinary applications in engineering construction, followed by a study of its manufacture or natural occurrence, and concluded by a discussion of physical and mechanical properties in their relation to its uses.

As a result of the author's experience in the teaching of this subject, the properties exhibited by a given material are, for the most part, considered as dependent phenomena closely related to certain more or less variable factors connected with the process of manufacture, natural occurrence, and conditions of service or testing, and not as independent qualities inherent in that material. It has been considered advisable to avoid the inclusion of tabulations of investigational data whenever the data could be presented graphically by curves or diagrams; discussions of conflicting empirical data on points admitting of controversy have been reduced to a minimum; and an effort has been made to present the material in a definite, concrete form, the necessity for the exercise of discriminative judgment upon the part of the student being obviated by conclusions drawn by the author, even though it is recognized that in so doing errors of judgment may be made, and the criticism of those who object to any form of dogmatic statement is invited.

The subject of testing materials has not been covered, except in so far as methods of testing are inseparable from discussions of the properties of materials revealed by laboratory tests. It is the author's conviction that this subject can be handled only in the laboratory itself, and the place for such material is therefore in a laboratory manual. It is assumed, however, that a laboratory course in testing materials will invariably parallel and supplement the textbook course in the study of materials.

The author cannot make a pretense of being a specialist in all of the fields which are covered in the various chapters of this book, and this work is therefore to a very large degree a compilation of data and opinion from a great many different sources. The author takes pleasure in acknowledging his great indebtedness to the large number of engineers and manufacturers who have privately or by their writings contributed much to make up this volume. A large number of technical books which are devoted to the consideration of some part of the ground covered by this text have been frequently consulted and freely used. An effort has been made to always acknowledge the source of information so obtained, and if any error of omission has been committed in this respect, it has been committed inadvertently, not by intention.

The following well-known textbooks and reference works have been most frequently used:

"Cements, Limes, and Plasters," by E. C. Eckel; "Portland Cement," by R. K. Meade; "Manufacture of Portland Cement," by R. C. H. West; "Masonry Construction," by I. O. Baker; "Stone for Building and Decoration," by G. P. Merrill; "Building Stones and Clay Products" and "Economic Geology," by Heinrich Ries; "The Blast Furnace and the Manufacture of Pig Iron," by Robert Forsythe; "The Metallurgy of Iron and Steel," by Bradley Stoughton; "The Metallurgy of Steel" and "Iron, Steel, and Other Alloys," by H. M. Howe; "The Manufacture and Properties of Iron and Steel," by H. H. Campbell; "Iron and Steel," by H. P. Tiemann; "Modern Iron Foundry Practice," by G. R. Bale; "Cast Iron," by W. J. Keep; "The Production of Malleable Castings," by Richard Moldenke; "The Corrosion and Preservation of Iron and Steel," by A. S. Cushman and H. A. Gardner; "The Metallography of Iron and Steel," by Albert Sauveur; and "Economic Woods of the United States" and "The Mechanical Properties of Wood," by S. J. Record.

The following periodicals and publications of various societies have also been frequently consulted:

"Engineering News," "Engineering Record," "Metallurgical and Chemical Engineering," Proceedings of the American Society for Testing Materials, Proceedings of the International Association for Testing Materials, Transactions of the American Society of Civil Engineers, Proceedings of the Institution of Mechanical Engineers, Journal of the Iron and Steel Institute, "Tests of Metals," published annually by the U. S. War Department, "Mineral Resources," published annually by the U. S. Geological Survey, Reports of the various State Geological Surveys, the publications of the Forestry Division of the U. S. Department of Agriculture, and the publications of the U. S. Bureau of Standards.

ADELBERT P. MILLS

ITHACA, N. Y.
February 20, 1915.

Contents

Section I. Definitions of Terms

CHAPTER
1. Definitions of Terms 1

Section II. Metals

2. Structure and Constitution of Metals 6
3. Tests of Metals 27
4. Service Requirements of Metals 42
5. Sources and Production of Metals 92
6. Iron Ore and Pig Iron 99
7. Steel 107
8. Wrought Iron 172
9. Cast Iron 181
10. Malleable Cast Iron 207
11. Alloy Steels 215
12. Non-Ferrous Metals and Alloys 246

Section III. Building Stones and Mineral Aggregates

13. Building Stones and Stone Masonry 301
14. Mineral Aggregates 313

Section IV. Cementing Materials

15. Gypsum Plaster 327
16. Lime 335
17. Cements 350

Section V. Concrete

18. Concrete 385

Section VI. Brick and Clay Products—Refractory, Heat-Insulating, and Acoustical Materials

19. Brick and Clay Products 457
20. Refractory, Heat-Insulating, and Acoustical Materials . . . 491

Section VII. Timber

21. Timber 508

Contents

Section VIII. Organic Plastics

CHAPTER
22. Organic Plastics 544

Section IX. Laminates and Adhesives

23. Laminates and Adhesives 571

Section X. Organic Protective Coatings

24. Organic Protective Coatings 606

Index 623

Section I Definitions of Terms

CHAPTER 1

Definitions of Terms

By LLOYD F. RADER

1.1 Introduction. The study of materials of construction is of great importance in all branches of engineering. The common materials of engineering construction are treated in this volume from the standpoint of occurrence and manufacture, properties, uses, and testing methods.

Definitions of terms relating to properties of materials and methods of testing are given in this first chapter.

1.2 Stress and Strain. *Stress* *,[1] is the intensity of the internal distributed forces or components of force which resist a change in the form of a body. Stress is measured in units of force per unit area (pounds per square inch, kilograms per square millimeter, etc.).

In many American engineering textbooks the term "stress" is defined as a force, measured in pounds; an example is the use of the term "stress" in the "stress sheet" of the structural engineer, which gives forces. The term "unit stress" may be employed to indicate that the term is used to denote force per unit of area.

There are three kinds of stress: tensile, compressive, and shearing. Flexure involves the combination of tensile stress and compressive stress. Torsion involves shearing stress.

Tensile strength * is the maximum tensile stress which a material is capable of developing. It is computed by dividing the maximum load carried during a tension test by the original cross-sectional area of the specimen.

Compressive strength * is the maximum compressive stress which a material is capable of developing.

Shear strength is the maximum shear stress which a material is capable of developing.

Strain or *deformation* * is the change, per unit of length, in a linear dimension of a body, which accompanies a stress. Strain is measured in inches per inch of length (feet per foot, millimeters per millimeter, etc.).

---

[1] Definitions marked by an asterisk are from the "Standard Definitions of Terms Relating to Methods of Testing," *ASTM Designation* E6–36.

In many American engineering textbooks the term "strain" is used in the sense of total deformation and is measured in inches; change of dimension per unit length is called "unit strain" or "unit deformation."

A *stress-strain diagram* * is a diagram plotted with values of stress as ordinates and values of strain as abscissas. (See Fig. 1.1.)

Elastic limit * is the greatest stress which a material is capable of developing without a permanent deformation remaining upon complete release of stress.

Proportional limit * is the greatest stress which a material is capable of developing without a deviation from the law of proportionality of stress to strain (Hooke's law). Point A in Fig. 1.1 is the proportional limit. For many metallic materials the values found for elastic limit by means of observations of permanent deformation after release of stress do not differ widely from the values found for proportional limit.

Yield point * is the stress in a material at which there occurs a marked increase in strain without an increase in stress. The yield point defines the stress beyond which structural damage is likely to occur. Ductile irons and steels and a few non-ferrous metals have well-defined yield points. (See Fig. 3.1, p. 28.) The yield point may be readily determined by the "drop of beam" method in the tension test.

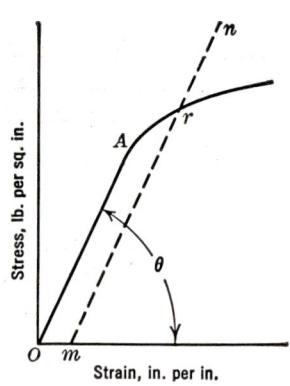

Fig. 1.1. Stress-strain diagram.

Most metals do not have well-defined yield points but have smooth stress-strain curves of gradual curvature in the yield range. Therefore, some other method must be employed to determine the limiting stress above which structural damage is likely to occur. The method of yield strength is recommended by the American Society for Testing Materials to meet this requirement.

Yield strength * is the stress at which a material exhibits a specified limiting permanent set. The specified value of the permanent set is laid off as Om on the stress-strain diagram (Fig. 1.1). The line mn is drawn parallel to the straight part of the stress-strain diagram OA. The intersection of mn with the stress-strain diagram at point r gives the stress which is the yield strength. The specified value of the offset in per cent should be reported.

1.3 Elasticity. *Elasticity* is that property of matter by which a body, if deformed by the action of forces, will endeavor to resume its original shape when the disturbing forces are removed. The elasticity of a number of engineering materials is practically perfect provided that they are not stressed above the elastic limit.

Hooke's law states that in elastic bodies stress is proportional to strain provided that the elastic limit is not exceeded. Most materials show slight variations from Hooke's law, but the common metals adhere to it so closely as to justify its assumption from a practical standpoint.

1.4 Modulus of Elasticity. *Modulus of elasticity* is the ratio, within the elastic limit of a material, of stress to corresponding strain. It is a measure of the *stiffness* of a material. Modulus of elasticity is expressed in pounds per square inch. As there are three kinds of stress, so are there three moduli of elasticity for any elastic material: the modulus in tension, in compression, and in shear.

The modulus of elasticity in tension has nearly the same value, for most metals, as the modulus of elasticity in compression. The modulus of elasticity in shear is smaller than the modulus of elasticity in tension. The modulus of elasticity in shear may be determined by means of a torsional test. The modulus of elasticity in flexure can also be obtained in connection with the flexure test. The modulus of elasticity is the slope of the stress-strain curve within the elastic range; i.e., $E = \tan \theta$ (Fig. 1.1).

Strictly speaking, the modulus of elasticity should be considered only within the range where the stress-strain relation is practically constant for materials of a truly elastic nature.

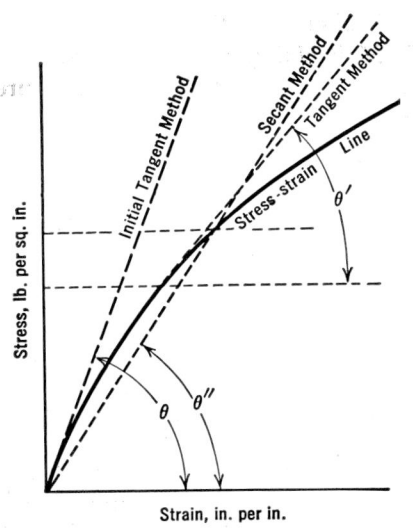

Fig. 1.2. Three methods of determining modulus of elasticity of a material having a curved stress-strain diagram.

It is common practice, however, to determine the modulus of elasticity for materials whose stress-strain graph is a curved line and whose elastic limit is relatively low in value, as, for example, concrete. The modulus of elasticity for such materials is determined by an arbitrary method. Three such methods in common use are illustrated in Fig. 1.2: (1) the initial tangent method, (2) the tangent method, and (3) the secant method. Suitable stresses are chosen in the tangent and in the secant method. The values of E for each method may be determined by finding the tangents of the angles θ, θ', and θ'' respectively.

1.5 Physical Properties of Materials. *Resilience* is that property of an elastic body by which energy can be stored up in the body by loads applied to it and given up in recovering its original shape when the loads are removed.

Plasticity is the property by which a body, when deformed by the application of forces, remains in the deformed shape without recovering its original shape when the forces are removed. Some materials are partly elastic and partly plastic since they recover a part of the deformation when the load is removed. Some metals become partly plastic at elevated temperatures. Materials stressed above the elastic limit so as to produce some permanent set are partly plastic. Plasticity of metals is usually determined by means of a tensile-strength test.

Ductility is the property of a material of being deformed by stretching, without recovery of shape upon removal of the stretching force. Ductility of metals is ordinarily determined by measuring the elongation and reduction of cross-sectional area of a tensile-strength-test specimen.

Malleability refers to the ability of a material to withstand hammering into a thinner sheet without fracture. It depends on the ductility and softness of the material.

Hardness is resistance to plastic deformation. Thus a hard material may have a high elastic limit or a high value of stress below which there is no permanent set. Other meanings are given to the term, however, such as resistance (1) to abrasion, (2) to scratching, or (3) to indentation of a cone or ball.

Toughness may be defined as resistance to impact. Toughness is also considered to mean resistance to fracture when the material is deformed above the elastic limit. A tough material can withstand appreciable permanent deformation before fracturing.

Brittleness is the opposite of toughness and ductility and refers to small resistance to a sudden blow. A brittle metal breaks suddenly without appreciable permanent deformation or warning of approaching failure.

Durability refers to resistance of a material to deterioration in quality during its period of use.

1.6 Stress-Concentration Factor. The term "stress-concentration factor" may be defined as the ratio between the stress actually occurring at a section of localized stress (such as at a notch, at the edge of a hole, at the root of a screw thread, at a shoulder in a shaft, or other sudden change in cross-section) and the stress at that point as calculated by the formulas of mechanics of materials.

1.7 Statistical Properties of Materials. The subject of mechanics of materials, which is based on Newtonian mechanics, implies definite relations in the physical world between cause and effect. That these relations may be predicted only on the basis of probability is the viewpoint of modern physics. These probabilities when considered in terms of a great number of atoms become exact laws in the same sense that actuarial tables of life insurance based upon the records of many persons are exact. The results obtained by the application of these laws of probability to an individual case may differ greatly from the actual value. Or if only a small section of material is considered, as, for example, the material near a small notch, the probable stress calculated by mechanics may not agree with the actual stress.

Definitions of Terms

But if the section of material is large enough so that it contains almost an infinitude of atoms, there are many paths through which action may take place and the most probable or "statistical" value should be close to the actual value.

The engineer in dealing with the properties of materials should keep in mind that natural phenomena just happen and that there is no controlling law that predicts the details of that occurrence exactly. Any physical phenomenon which may be observed is controlled by chance, and prediction may be made only in terms of probability or statistically. Furthermore, mechanics of materials formulas are based on the supposition that the material is homogeneous, isotropic, and elastic, and that it satisfies Hooke's law; although most materials of construction satisfy these assumptions closely enough for most practical purposes, stresses and strains calculated by mechanics of materials formulas are in reality only statistical approximations.

Questions

1.1. Define the following terms: stress, strain, deformation, elastic limit, proportional limit, yield point, and yield strength.

1.2. What is the significance of the modulus of elasticity?

1.3. Distinguish between elasticity and plasticity.

1.4. Define: ductility, malleability, toughness, and brittleness.

1.5. State four different meanings given to the term "hardness."

References

1.1. American Society for Testing Materials: "Standard Definitions of Terms Relating to Methods of Testing." *Designation E6, Book of Standards,* 1952.

1.2. Clapp, W. H., and Clark, D. S.: *Engineering Materials and Processes.* Scranton, Pa., International Textbook Co., 1938; Chap. 1, pp. 1–46.

1.3. Laurson, P. G., and Cox, W. J.: *Mechanics of Materials.* John Wiley & Sons, 3rd ed., 1954.

1.4. Maurer, E. R., and Withey, M. O.: *Strength of Materials.* John Wiley & Sons, 2nd ed., 1940; Chap. 2, pp. 39–70.

1.5. Roark, R. J.: *Formulas for Stress and Strain.* McGraw-Hill Book Co., 3rd ed., 1953.

1.6. Seely, F. B.: *Resistance of Materials.* John Wiley & Sons, 3rd ed., 1947; Chap. 1.

1.7. Seely, F. B., and Smith, J. O.: *Advanced Mechanics of Materials.* John Wiley & Sons, 2nd ed., 1946; Chap. 1.

1.8. Seitz, F.: *The Physics of Metals.* McGraw-Hill Book Co., 1943; Chap. 1.

1.9. Swain, G. F.: *Structural Engineering-Strength of Materials.* McGraw-Hill Book Co., 1924; Chap. 4, pp. 48–86; Chap. 24, pp. 557–562.

Section II · Metals

CHAPTER 2

Structure and Constitution of Metals
Originally Written by ROBERT S. WILLIAMS *
Rewritten by LLOYD F. RADER

2.1 Metallography in General. *Metallography* [1] is that branch of science which relates to the constitution and structure, and their relation to the properties, of metals and alloys. Since metallography deals with the relationship between structure of metals and their physical properties, the subject is sometimes called physical metallurgy. It should be distinguished from *process metallurgy* which deals with the study of extraction of metals from their ores and of refining metals and preparing them for use.

Metallography includes the study of microstructure and macrostructure of metals, space lattice arrangements of the atoms, thermal critical points, heat treatment, and examination by the X-ray beam, with particular reference to the physical properties such as tensile strength, elastic limit, ductility, hardness, toughness, resistance to fatigue, and magnetic properties.

The meanings of the terms *composition* and *constitution* should be distinguished. Composition is the term employed to indicate the proportions of the different elements of a material; constitution refers to the state or structure in which those elements or their combinations are found. For example, two metals may have the same composition but different constitutions and physical properties depending upon thermal and mechanical treatments. On the other hand, two metals may have a similar arrangement of atoms, but the properties may be different owing to differences in composition.

2.2 History of Development of Metallography. Sorby in 1864 in England reported the results of his studies of the microstructure of meteoric irons. In 1886 and 1887 he presented two papers, illustrated by photomicrographs of iron and steel, before the British Iron and Steel Institute. Pioneer work on the use of the microscope in studying the structure of metals was

---

* Professor of Physical Metallurgy, Massachusetts Institute of Technology.
[1] Definitions of Terms Relating to Metallography, *ASTM Designation* E7–27.

also carried on by Martens in Germany, Osmond in France, Stead and Arnold in England, and Howe and Sauveur in the United States. By 1910 metallographic methods were in common use in industrial laboratories in the United States. The science of metallography has been developed in recent years by means of X-ray methods and electron diffraction. Atoms in space lattices reflect X-rays and electron waves, and, from such reflections, the interatomic distances and the arrangement of atoms in space lattices can be determined. Since electron waves penetrate only the surface layers, they are utilized for the study of thin films, whereas X-rays may be used for thicker sections. Such research has revealed important information concerning space lattices and crystal structures.

2.3 Use of the Microscope. The microscope is of great value in determining the nature of an alloy, both as to its heat treatment and as to its possible defective condition. A small section of the metal to be examined is polished with a series of abrasive materials, each finer than the preceding one, until a scratch-free, highly polished surface is obtained. In most cases the polished surface is treated with a chemical reagent that will attack one constituent more readily than the other and so disclose the internal structure of the alloy. This operation is called etching.

Since metals are opaque, the microscope is provided with a device that throws a spot of light on the polished surface, and the specimen is examined by the reflected light, instead of transmitted light as is usual in the microscopic examination of transparent materials. It is often desirable to have a photographic record of the structure of an alloy. For this purpose a camera may be attached to the microscope, and the magnified image is transmitted to a photographic plate. An instrument especially designed for this work is known as a metallograph, and the pictures taken are photomicrographs. These are used frequently in connection with specifications and as a check on the condition of an alloy.

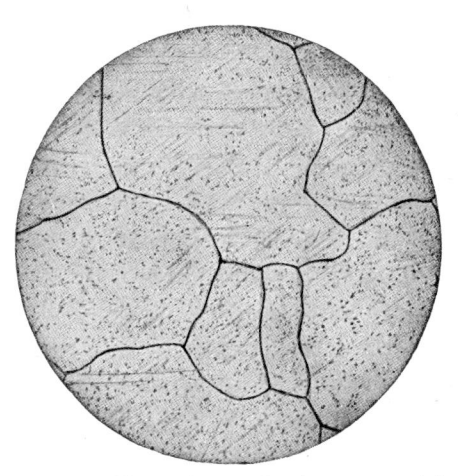

Fig. 2.1. Photomicrograph of a pure metal (copper) 100×. (Homerberg.)

Photomicrographs of non-ferrous alloys are commonly taken at magnifications of 75 to 100 diameters. Magnification is the ratio of the size of the image to that of the object and is generally expressed in "diameters," thus "100×" or 100 diameters. The finer structure of steel alloys often needs a

8   Materials of Construction

magnification of 250 diameters, and, for special work, very high magnifications up to several thousand diameters are sometimes used.

A pure metal when seen under the microscope is found to consist of a number of grains, polygonal in shape, separated by fine boundary lines (Fig. 2.1). The experienced observer can distinguish readily between coarse-grained and fine-grained metal.

2.4   The Macro-Examination of Metals.   Macro-examination refers to a study of materials either with the unaided eye or at a low magnification, not exceeding 10 diameters. The surface to be examined need not be so highly

Fig. 2.2. Macroetch of steel forging showing fiber. Etched with Humphrey's reagent. (Homerberg.)

polished as for microscopic study but should be smooth. The prepared surface is treated with a suitable chemical to make the structure visible. This type of treatment often discloses ingotism, carbon or phosphorus segregation, blowholes, and slag inclusion. It may also indicate the direction of the *fiber* in wrought material. Figure 2.2 shows a macroetch of a steel forging.

2.5   Examination of Metals in Polarized Light.   The examination of metals by a polarizing microscope is a special development. In polarized light the true colors of metallic oxides become visible. Applications are made in the identification of metallic compounds, phases in alloys, and coatings on metals, and in studies of grain size.

2.6   Crystallization of Metals.   A metal is any of the metallic elements, either of very high purity or of ordinary commercial grades.[2] Metals generally crystallize when they pass from the liquid to the solid state. Crystallization is the arranging of the atoms of the material in a space lattice to form small solids of regular geometric outlines, such as cubes, tetragons, or hexagons.

[2] "Definitions of Terms Relating to Metallography," *ASTM Designation* E7–27.

Structure and Constitution of Metals

Solid substances which do not have a geometric arrangement of their atoms are termed "amorphous." Asphalt is an example of an amorphous material.

Crystallization of metals usually begins simultaneously at many centers. Each crystal grows by successive additions of crystalline matter in a regular pattern, but each crystal center is differently oriented. The crystals generally develop so that they meet in irregular surfaces. Such crystals of regular space lattice but irregular form are termed *allotriomorphic* crystals. The crystals are commonly called "crystalline grains" or merely "grains." Allotriomorphic crystals of a pure metal are illustrated in Fig. 2.1.

Crystals developing under conditions that permit the forming of regular geometric exterior surfaces are termed *idiomorphic* crystals. These are rarely found.

2.7 Space Lattice of Crystals. Space lattice is the pattern of arrangement of atoms in a material. There are three types of space lattices of

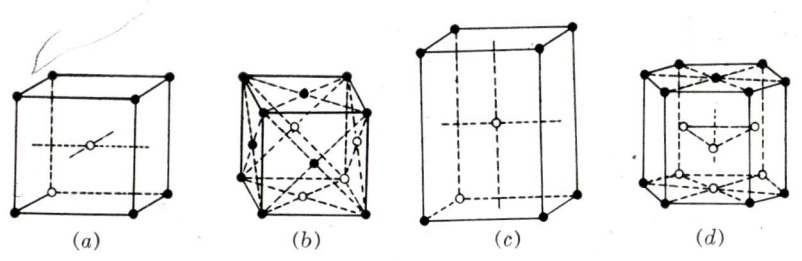

(a) (b) (c) (d)

Fig. 2.3. Space lattices of crystals.

importance in metallography: cubic, tetragonal, and hexagonal. The cubic system of space lattice is by far the most common and occurs in two forms, viz., the body-centered cubic and the face-centered cubic structure. The *body-centered cubic structure* has an atom at each of the corners of a cube, shared, of course, with adjoining cubes, and an atom at the geometric center of the cube which is not shared with any other cube. (See Fig. 2.3a.) The *face-centered cubic structure* has an atom at each corner and an atom at the center of each of the six faces, making fourteen atoms in all for a single cube. (See Fig. 2.3b.)

Alpha iron is a good example of a metal having a body-centered cubic structure. The face-centered cubic arrangement is possessed by most of the common ductile metals such as gold, silver, gamma iron, nickel, copper, and lead.

Tin has a body-centered tetragonal lattice structure which is similar to the body-centered cubic lattice but has the dimension in one axis lengthened or shortened. (See Fig. 2.3c.)

Zinc has a close-packed hexagonal structure which consists of an atom at each corner of the hexagonal lattice and at the center of the hexagonal faces and also an atom at the geometric center of each alternate triangular prism, as shown in Fig. 2.3d. Magnesium also has a hexagonal structure.

The planes of least resistance to movement are different in the various crystal forms; this accounts to some extent for differences in physical properties.

2.8 Crystalline Grains. The size and shape of crystalline grains depend upon the rate of solidification and may be altered by heat treatment or mechanical working of the solidified metal. Typical grain shapes are described. *Equiaxed* grains have approximately the same dimensions along each axis; they are produced by heat treatment or mechanical working of hot metal. Fine equiaxed grains are strong and have good mechanical properties. (See Fig. 2.6a.) *Acicular* grains are needlelike in appearance and are found in hardened metals. For an example see Fig. 7.13 which shows grains of martensite. *Columnar* grains are elongated in shape with the long axis perpendicular to the outer surface. They are common in the exterior portion of castings where the metal cools at a rapid rate with solidification proceeding to the center. Such grains are brittle and somewhat weak. *Dendritic* structure consists of grains of many branches with grain growth developing along the axes of the space lattice and has the appearance of a fir tree. (See Fig. 7.4.) This structure is weak and is not desirable. *Lamellar* or thumbprint structure comprises thin platelike grains composed of two constituents. (See Fig. 7.9 which shows the lamellar structure of pearlite.) *Spheroidal* structure consists of grains of globular shape interspersed throughout the other materials; it has good machinability. Spheroidized cementite illustrated in Fig. 7.18 is a good example. *Banded* structure has bands of distorted grains produced by cold working. (See Art. 7.40 and Fig. 7.3.)

2.9 Slip Lines. Many metals that have been stressed beyond their elastic limit show a number of fine black lines or bands across the polished surface

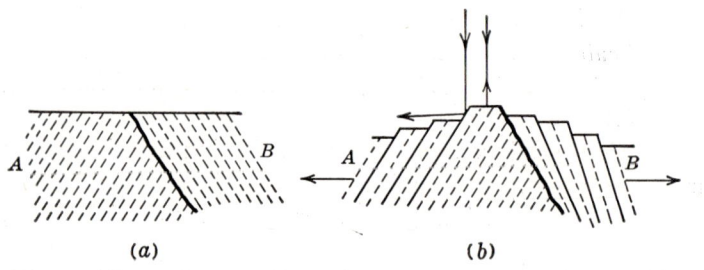

Fig. 2.4. Diagram illustrating the formation of slip lines: (a) before straining and (b) after straining.

when viewed under a microscope. The lines change their direction at each grain boundary but are parallel within the grains. These lines are not cracks in the surface but are steps caused by slips along the gliding planes of the crystals. Figure 2.4 illustrates the formation of slip lines: in (*a*) the surface of two crystals *AB* has been polished smooth prior to straining; in (*b*) the steps in the surface have been produced by slips along gliding planes due to application of force in the direction of the arrows.

The steps appear as black bands because the light beams passing through the microscope are not reflected from these oblique surfaces back into the microscope but outside the microscope's field. Slip bands are illustrated in Fig. 2.5. When the amount of straining due to cold work has been extreme, the crystal grains become distorted in the direction of the force applied. Such distortions in Fig. 2.5 should be compared with normal metal as illustrated in Fig. 2.6. The smaller the grain size, the shorter are the uninterrupted slip planes. It is for this reason that fine-grained metals are generally stronger than coarse-grained metals.

Fig. 2.5. Cold-worked cartridge brass showing slip bands 100×. (Homerberg.)

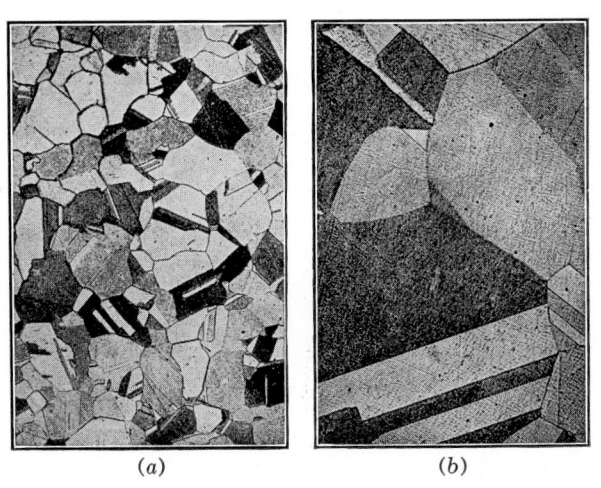

(*a*)   (*b*)

Fig. 2.6. 70-30 Brass worked and annealed 100×. (Homerberg.)
a. Annealed at 650° C. (1202° F.).   *b.* Annealed at 800° C. (1472° F.).

2.10 Twinning. Slip lines should be distinguished from *twinning*. Twinning or twin crystals appear as broad bands parallel in a single grain when viewed under the microscope. (See Fig. 2.6.) Two parts of the crystal become symmetrical along the twinning plane owing to rotation of the parts of the crystal. Each part of the crystal becomes the mirror image of the other and hence is termed a twin. Twinning is due to straining of the metal. Mechanical twins are produced by straining; annealing twins are formed by straining followed by annealing.

Neumann bands are parallel lines across crystalline grains usually produced by impact or shock and are considered to be mechanical twins by most metallurgists. Since slip lines are due to steps in the surface, they may be distinguished from twinning or Neumann bands by repolishing the strained metal and again observing under the microscope to see whether the lines have been removed.

2.11 Cohesion and Adhesion. The strength of a crystalline structure depends upon cohesion between atoms in the space lattice structure within individual crystalline grains and upon adhesion between crystalline grains at the grain boundaries. Failure of ductile metals under tensile or compressive loads at ordinary temperature usually occurs by distortion of the crystalline grains and formation of slip lines within the grains. Resistance to distortion is affected by grain shape. Equiaxed grains have equal resistance in each direction and in general give the greatest strength.

Grain boundaries are stronger than the crystalline grains at ordinary temperatures and constitute a reinforcing network. Structures of small-size grains are stronger than those of large-size grains owing to the greater proportion of grain-boundary material in the metal. (For effects of high temperatures, see Art. 4.35.)

Some alloys have structures consisting of two or more phases. The theory is explained in Art. 2.21. The properties of such alloys may depend not only upon the individual properties of each phase but also upon the distribution of the phases. For example, if a phase of hard metal has a network into which a phase of soft metal is distributed, the alloy will be relatively hard. But if crystalline grains of a hard phase are dispersed throughout the mass of a soft phase, the alloy will have properties characteristic of the soft phase. The strength of a crystalline structure therefore depends on space lattice structure, grain size and shape, type of phases, and distribution of phases.

At elevated temperatures creep may occur and failure may result from the crystals pulling apart at the grain boundaries. This failure may occur suddenly without appreciable permanent set, indicating brittleness. These types of failures are illustrated in Fig. 4.8.

Elasticity of metals is due to the attraction between atoms in the space lattice. The application of a force causes a distortion in the atomic arrangement, but the attraction or bond between the atoms causes the original space lattice to be resumed when the force is removed. Modulus of elasticity,

Structure and Constitution of Metals

which is a measure of stiffness, may be thought of as the measure of resistance of the cohesion between the atoms against change in shape of the space lattice in crystalline grains.

2.12 Constitution of Metals and Alloys. An alloy is a metallic substance produced by the combination of two or more elements. For example, an alloy may consist of the combination of two metals, or of the combination of a metal with a non-metallic element.

The properties of many metals and alloys, both non-ferrous and ferrous, are determined by their behavior on cooling from the melted state and by the internal structure of the solid alloys. Some of the relationships existing between alloyed metals are fairly complex, but a knowledge of the general behavior of metals is of real service to the engineer.

The types of solids which may result from crystallization due to freezing may be classified into six groups:

1. Pure metal.
2. Chemical compound.
3. Two-layer alloy.
4. Eutectic.
5. Solid solution.
6. Eutectoid.

2.13 The Freezing of a Pure Metal. If a pure metal, aluminum for example, solidifies under such conditions that the changes taking place dur-

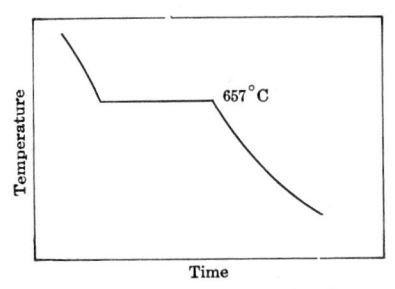

Fig. 2.7. Cooling curve for aluminum.

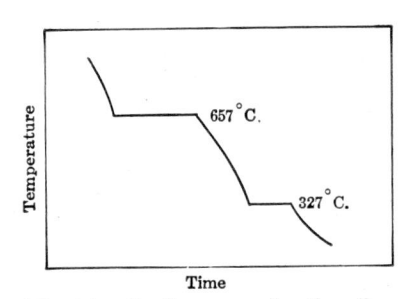

Fig. 2.8. Cooling curve for the alloy aluminum 90%, lead 10%.

ing the cooling can be studied, the following facts will be observed. The temperature will fall at a regular rate, depending on the cooling conditions, until the freezing point of the metal is reached. The temperature then stays constant until the metal has completely solidified, after which the normal cooling is resumed. These facts are shown by Fig. 2.7, in which the ordinates represent temperature, and the abscissas, time intervals.

In this figure the sloping lines indicate the cooling rate and the horizontal line represents the number of seconds taken for the metal to solidify. The

14   Materials of Construction

length of this horizontal line depends, therefore, on the cooling conditions and the amount of metal solidifying. Other conditions being equal, the length of the horizontal line will be proportional to the amount of metal present.

2.14 The Chemical Compound. A chemical compound contains its elements in single definite proportions by weight, is a single definite substance, and usually has properties entirely different from those of its constituents. The cooling curves for chemical compounds are essentially the same in characteristics as those for pure metals.

2.15 The Two-Layer Alloy. If a mixture containing 90 per cent of aluminum and 10 per cent of lead is melted, and heat effects during the

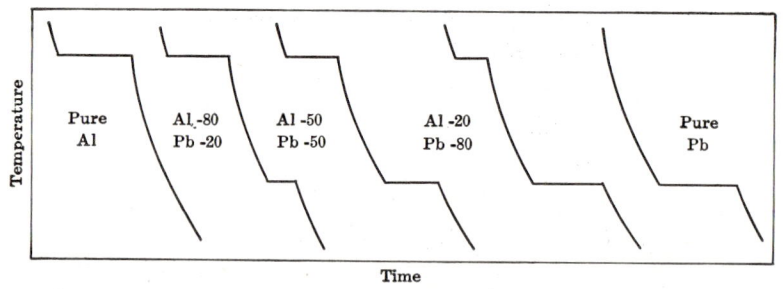

Fig. 2.9. Cooling curves for a series of aluminum-lead alloys.

cooling of the melted mass are determined as before, the curve showing the relation between temperature and time of cooling has the form shown in Fig. 2.8.

Here again the sloping lines indicate the cooling rate and the horizontal lines represent the intervals of time for the two heat effects which take place during the solidifying process. If several mixtures of aluminum and lead are allowed to solidify, the total weight of each mixture being the same but the proportions of the two metals varying in each, the series of curves shown in Fig. 2.9 will be obtained.

It will be noticed that in the alloys the two temperature effects are at the same temperatures regardless of the composition. The difference between the curves is that, although the total weight of metal was the same in each of the three alloys, the time at the higher temperature decreases with the proportion of aluminum, whereas the time at the lower temperature increases, corresponding to an increase in the proportion of lead. It is seen, further, that the temperature at the upper horizontal corresponds to the melting point of pure aluminum and that the lower horizontal break occurs at the melting point of pure lead. This means that neither metal changes the melting point of the other and suggests that the two metals do not mix. That this is the fact can be shown by melting lead and aluminum together

Structure and Constitution of Metals

in a glass tube. The melted mass will be found to consist of a layer of melted aluminum floating on melted lead; and, as no change takes place on cooling, the resulting mass is composed of two solid layers, one of lead, the other of aluminum.

2.16 The Equilibrium Diagram. It is easy to see the relation between the two metals in the simple case illustrated by the series of curves shown in Fig. 2.9, but it becomes difficult, if not impossible, with more complex alloy systems. Another method of showing the relationships between alloyed metals has, therefore, been developed and is shown in Fig. 2.10, which is known as the *equilibrium* or *alloy diagram*.

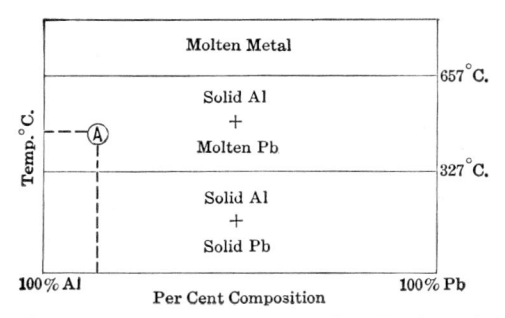

Fig. 2.10. Equilibrium or alloy diagram for aluminum-lead alloys.

This diagram is made by combining the curves shown in Fig. 2.9 and differs from that figure in that, whereas the ordinates represent temperatures as before, the abscissas no longer indicate time intervals but correspond to varying percentage relations of the alloying metals. The intersection of the horizontal line at a given temperature with the vertical line corresponding to the percentage composition indicates the conditions existing at the given temperature for the alloy of given composition and may be applied equally well to any composition or any temperature. An alloy having the composition corresponding to point A on the abscissa line and at a temperature A on the ordinate line consists, therefore, of a mixture of solid aluminum and melted lead. The condition at any other temperature or with any other mixture may be determined from the alloy diagram in the same way. Alloy diagrams have been worked out for all the common alloys of two metals (binary alloys) and for a few alloys with three or more constituents.

The alloys of aluminum and lead, which were used to illustrate the construction of the alloy diagram, show under the microscope the two layers of aluminum and lead, respectively, each layer having the characteristic appearance of a pure metal.

The aluminum-lead alloys are of no industrial importance and were selected only because they give the simplest possible alloy diagram. A very similar industrial alloy is found in the copper-tin-lead bronzes. Tin is dissolved in copper to make a solid solution (Art. 2.18) which behaves in many respects like a simple metal. Lead does not dissolve in the copper-tin alloy (bronze) but forms an emulsion with it. If the alloy is properly made, the drops of lead should be uniformly distributed through the bronze matrix. Figure 2.11 shows a properly mixed alloy and a badly mixed one,

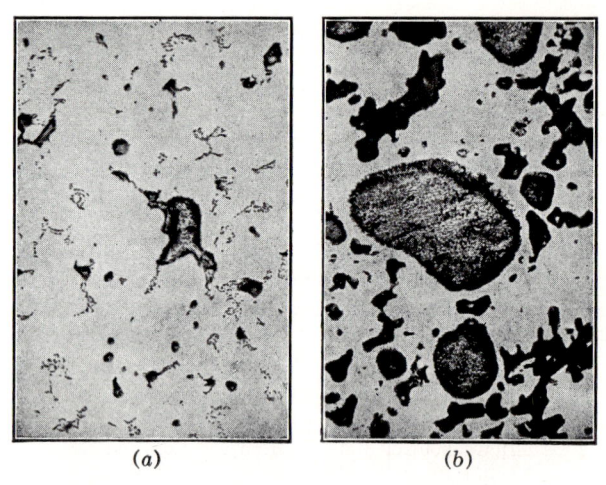

(a)   (b)

Fig. 2.11. Leaded bronze 100×. (Homerberg.)
a. Good distribution of lead.   b. Poor distribution of lead.

as seen under the microscope. The leaded phosphor bronze is discussed in Art. 12.29.

2.17 The Eutectic Alloy. If a small amount of lead is added to tin and the changes which take place on cooling are plotted as before, a curve similar to that shown in Fig. 2.12 results.

If still more lead is added, the curve is similar in form but differs from that shown in Fig. 2.12 in that the temperature of the first break is somewhat lower than before. Conversely, if tin is added in increasing quantities to lead, the melting point of the resulting alloy becomes lower with each addition. Since the addition of tin to lead lowers the melting point of the lead and since the addition of lead to tin lowers the melting point of the tin, it follows that a certain mixture of lead and tin melts lower than any other mixture of the two metals. This alloy is called the *eutectic mixture*, or, more commonly, simply the *eutectic*. The conditions existing in a series of alloys of the eutectic type are shown in Fig. 2.13. This has been constructed from cooling curves of the type shown in Fig. 2.12.

The meaning of this diagram is readily understood from a consideration of one or two definite examples. If an alloy having the composition indicated by (1) is cooled from the liquid state, no change takes place until the "liquidus" line Sn–E is reached. Here pure tin separates. Owing to the separation of tin, the remaining melted alloy becomes richer in lead. Tin continues to separate until the remaining melted mass has the composition E. Since this composition represents that mixture of lead and

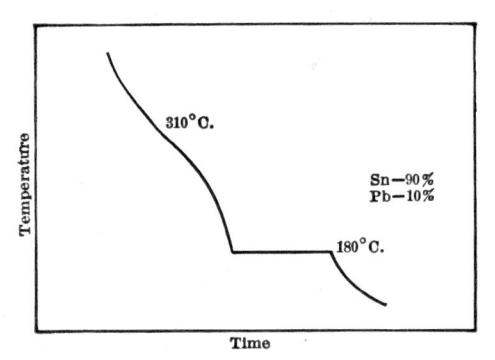

Fig. 2.12. Cooling curve for the alloy tin 90%, lead 10%.

tin which has the lowest melting point (the eutectic), the alloy becomes wholly solid at this temperature (the eutectic temperature). The line AEB is called the "solidus." The final alloy is found by microscopic examination to consist of crystals of tin imbedded in a ground mass of eutectic mixture composed of very fine interlocked plates or needles.

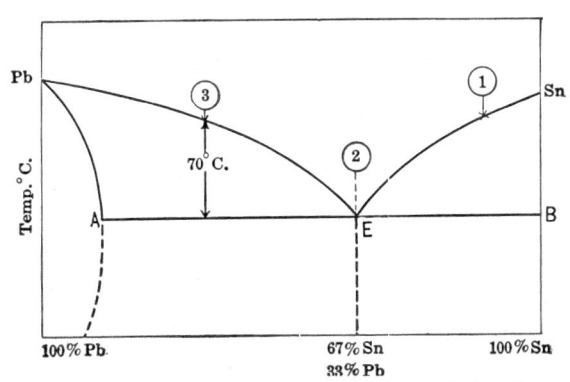

Fig. 2.13. Equilibrium diagram for the lead-tin alloys.

An alloy of the composition (2) stays in the melted condition until the temperature E is reached, when it solidifies at a constant temperature. The microscope shows the granular eutectic structure which is composed of very fine interlocked plates and which is often referred to as the "thumbprint" structure (Fig. 7.9). The eutectic is not a solution or a compound but an extremely intimate mixture of the two (or more) metals of which it is composed. There is no indication of the tin crystals seen in alloy (1).

All alloys in the range between E and pure tin show but two structure elements, pure tin crystals and the eutectic. The difference between alloys in this group are differences in the relative amounts of tin and eutectic; those at the tin end consist largely of tin with small quantities of eutectic, and those near E are composed largely of eutectic with a small number of tin crystals. *Pewter* is an alloy in this group corresponding to (1), composed of 80 per cent tin and 20 per cent lead. It is a hard metal with a silvery color that is extensively used as a decorative metal especially for household utensils.

Various solders are members of this alloy group. Of these the two most common are *tin solder,* corresponding to (2), and *plumbers' solder,* of the composition (3). The first is useful because of its low melting point, and the second, alloy (3), because it solidifies through a long temperature range (70° C.) owing to the continuous separation of solid lead along the line Pb–E, thus giving the plumber time to wipe joints and close up holes. The existence of the solid crystals in the melted metal makes it possible to use such an alloy in the making of a wiped joint.

The addition of a third metal to the eutectic of the two others often causes further lowering of the melting point due to the formation of a ternary eutectic. These low-melting eutectics are used commercially in the manufacture of fusible plugs in automatic sprinkler systems.

2.18 The Solid Solution. The line Pb–A in Fig. 2.13 illustrates another condition in which two metals may exist after solidification from the molten state. When lead is added to tin and the melted alloy allowed to cool, the eutectic E always forms along the line EB no matter how small the amount of lead present. If, however, tin is added to lead in an amount less than about 14 per cent, a separation of the eutectic does not take place at the temperature E but the tin stays in solution in solid lead. This condition is known as the formation of a *solid solution,* and the resulting alloy has the appearance, under the microscope, of a pure metal, with no indication of the existence of the eutectic mixture. The two metals forming the solid solution are intimately dissolved in each other, and the crystals are so nearly homogeneous that the constituent metals cannot be distinguished even under the microscope.

Alloys having less than 14 per cent of tin with lead are unsaturated solid solutions. When the amount of tin present is more than 14 per cent, the lead is no longer able to hold it in solid solution and the excess tin separates as a constituent of the eutectic. The alloy of composition (3) in Fig. 2.13 has a microstructure consisting of solid-solution particles of tin in lead imbedded in a mass of eutectic mixture. Since lead dissolves

Structure and Constitution of Metals 19

tin to only a limited extent, the alloy is known as a partial solid solution. In other alloys the solubilities may vary with the constituent metals.

2.19 Types of Equilibrium Diagrams. These relations are indicated by the general alloy diagrams shown in Fig. 2.14. The simple eutectic alloy in which neither metal dissolves in the other in the solid state is

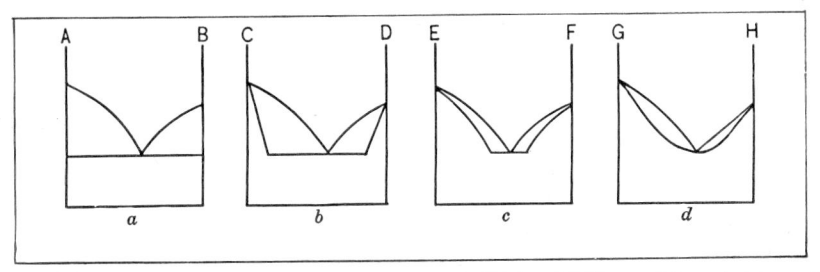

Fig. 2.14. Types of equilibrium diagrams. (a) Solid-insolubility. (b) and (c) partial solid-solubility. (d) Complete solid-solubility.

represented by (a). In (b) metal C dissolves to a limited extent in D, and D also dissolves somewhat in C. (c) is similar to (b) except that the mutual solubilities of the two metals E and F are much greater. In (d) the metals G and H are soluble in each other in all proportions in the solid state. This is known as complete solid-solubility. In this case metal G lowers the melting point of H, and H lowers that of G. The solution having the lowest melting point is called the *solid-solution minimum* and differs radically from the eutectic in that although it is the lowest-melting alloy it is perfectly homogeneous, whereas the eutectic is as non-homogeneous as possible.

2.20 Alloys of Complete Solid-Solubility. When two metals dissolve in each other in all proportions, each does not necessarily lower the melting point of the other. Quite commonly, one melting point is raised and the other lowered. This leads to the diagram shown in Fig. 2.15 and is characteristic of the alloys of copper and nickel and several other alloys of industrial importance.

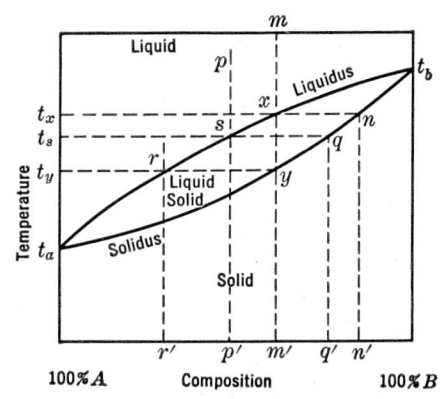

Fig. 2.15. A type of equilibrium diagram indicating complete solid-solubility.

Referring to Fig. 2.15, if an alloy mm' at temperature t_m is slowly cooled to the liquidus at temperature t_x, freezing begins by the separating out of crystals of composition nn'. Since the crystals nn' are richer in constituent B than the original melt mm', the remaining liquid metal is leaner in constituent B. Suppose that the composition of the remaining liquid metal is pp'. Then, as the temperature is further lowered, the liquid pp' is brought to the liquidus at s and more crystals of composition qq' are formed. This process continues until the liquid metal reaches composition rr' and is cooled to the liquidus at temperature t_y. The solid with which this last portion of melt is in equilibrium has the composition mm' since the composition of the solid phrase moves also to the left. The two extreme limits of composition of the solid solution are nn' and rr', but if the rate of cooling is slow enough to maintain conditions of equilibrium constantly, diffusion takes place between the liquid and solid metal so that the composition of the crystals becomes uniformly the same as that of the original liquid metal.

If the rate of cooling is not slow enough to maintain equilibrium conditions, diffusion between liquid melt and crystals will not take place, and consequently the remaining liquid will become progressively leaner in composition of B until crystals of pure A are formed at a temperature t_a. Although the crystals are formed with different compositions, diffusion between crystals tends to make the mass uniform in composition provided that sufficient time is allowed.

2.21 Alloys of Partial Solid-Solubility. A typical equilibrium diagram illustrating mutual partial solid-solubility is shown in Fig. 2.16. The components of the seven characteristic areas are as follows: I, liquid solution; II, liquid solution and solid solution of B in A (called alpha solid solution or alpha phase); III, liquid solution and solid solution of A in B (called beta solid solution or beta phase); IV, alpha solid solution; V, beta solid solution; VI, alpha solid solution and eutectic mixture of solid solutions of compositions D and F; VII, beta solid solution and eutectic mixture of solid solutions of compositions D and F.

An alloy of composition pp' will crystallize in a manner similar to that described for complete solid-solubility (Fig. 2.14). Under equilibrium conditions freezing will take place between temperatures z and w as the composition of the liquid solution changes from pp' to rr'. By diffusion the beta solid-solution crystals tend to become uniform in composition.

The alloy mm' begins to crystallize at temperature x, the first crystals having a composition yy'. The remaining liquid metal becomes richer in B, and further lowering of temperature is required to cause additional freezing. The solid-solution composition moves from yy' to D. Diffusion between liquid and solid solutions causes the solid-solution crystals to attain a composition D provided that equilibrium conditions are maintained. Some liquid solution is left at this stage; it solidifies at the eutectic temperature E into a eutectic mixture composed of an alpha solid solution of composition D and a beta solid solution of composition F. It will be noted that the eutectic is not merely a mixture of A and B, but is a heterogeneous mixture of alpha and beta solid solutions. The micrograph will show a mixture of alpha solid-solution crystals of composition D imbedded in a granular mass of eutectic mixture of alpha and beta solid solutions of compositions D and F respectively.

An alloy EE' of eutectic composition will solidify at temperature E forming a granular mass of alpha and beta solid solutions (phases) of compositions D and F respectively.

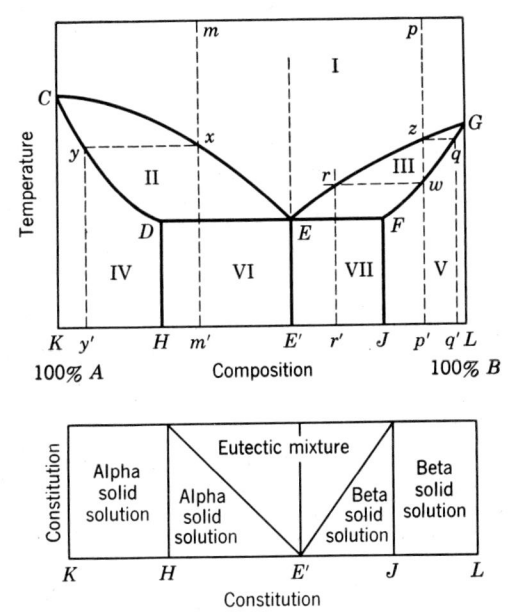

Fig. 2.16. A type of equilibrium diagram indicating partial solid-solubility and corresponding constitution diagram.

The constitution diagram in Fig. 2.16 shows graphically the constitution of the different alloys.

The solid-solution alloys, whether partial or complete, are of great importance. Most of the better-known alloys, brass, bronze, Monel metal, steel, and some others, are found in this class.

2.22 Crystal Structure of Solid Solutions. Having considered the equilibrium diagrams of solid solutions, we will now discuss their crystal structures. In a solid solution, there is a dispersion of atoms of one element into the space lattice of another element. Solid solutions have four types of dispersions of solute atoms among solvent atoms: (1) substitutional, (2) interstitial, (3) intermetallic compound, and (4) superlattice.

In the *substitutional* solid solution, the solute atoms are substituted for one or more atoms of the solvent. This is the most common type.

Second, in the *interstitial* solid solution, the solute atoms are placed in the spaces between atoms of the solvent. Ordinarily in this case, the solute atoms are much smaller than the solvent atoms.

Third, reference is made to *intermetallic compounds*. Solid solutions not only may be composed of homogeneous mixtures of elements with dispersion of the atoms of one element in the space lattice of another, but also may be formed in phases containing intermetallic compounds. Intermetallic compounds are so named because they are combinations of elements at least one of which is always a metallic element as for example Fe_3C, Ca_3Mg_4, $CuAl_2$, Cu_3P, Cu_2Zn_3, Mg_2Sn, and $NaZn_{11}$. These intermetallic compounds are not true chemical compounds because they do not always conform to rules of valence. Intermetallic compounds have complex space lattices which differ significantly from those of the constituent elements. The phases formed may be variable in characteristics ranging from an ideal solid solution to a true chemical compound. In some cases, a single alloy may resemble a true solid solution at a high temperature and yet at a low temperature be made up of intermetallic compounds. Intermetallic compounds are hard, and their formation in combinations of metals when properly controlled may assist in producing desirable physical properties in alloys.

Fourth, the *superlattice* is a rare phenomenon in which solid solutions that have a random arrangement of atoms at high temperatures become rearranged when cooled to low temperatures so that solute atoms place themselves in the solvent lattice in specific and periodic positions. Two good examples of superlattices with periodic structure are $CuAu$ and Cu_3Au. The attraction between atoms is weaker for superlattices than for intermetallic compounds, and the crystals are less stable.

2.23 Formation of the Eutectoid. In considering the solid solutions it must be remembered that the general nature of such a solid solution is in most ways exactly like that of a liquid solution. On this account it is not hard to imagine that changes which take place when a liquid solution cools may also occur during the cooling of a solid solution. In Art. 2.17, the formation of the eutectic due to the decomposition of a liquid solution was considered. An analogous situation is often found in connection with solid solutions. An alloy that exists as a perfectly homogeneous solid solution at one temperature may decompose into its constituents at some lower temperature. Such a decomposition leads to the formation of an alloy the structure of which is like that of the eutectic. As this structure is the result of the decomposition of a solid solution rather than of a liquid solution, it has been called a *eutectoid*. The formation of the eutectoid is shown in Fig. 2.17.

The metals A and B dissolve in each other in all proportions in the solid state and at temperatures above the line CED. If the cooling of alloy (1) takes place very slowly, as, for example, in cooling with the furnace in which the metals were melted, there is no difference whatever between the resulting eutectoid and the eutectic coming from a liquid melt. It has not been found possible to cool a melted alloy quickly enough to prevent the formation of the eutectic, but by rapid cooling of the alloy (1) the separation of the constituent metals may be completely or partly prevented and the alloy retained at room temperature in the solid-solution condition

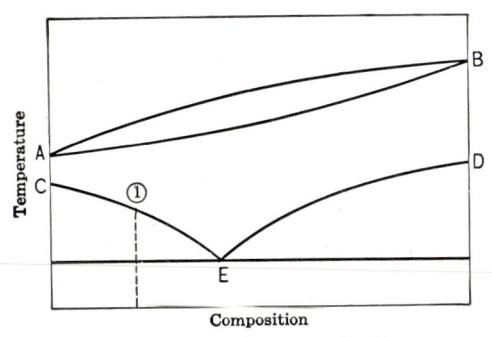

Fig. 2.17. The simple eutectoid diagram.

normally existing at a much higher temperature. This operation, commercially known as "quenching," is the basis of the heat treatment of steel which is an iron-carbon solid solution decomposing with falling temperature into the eutectoid.

The four types of diagram (1) the two-layer, (2) the eutectic, (3) the solid solution, and (4) the eutectoid, or combinations of two or more of them are those found in most of the industrially important alloys.

2.24 Properties of the Alloys. *Hardness.* The hardness of the eutectic alloys is practically the average of the hardness of the component metals. The eutectic itself and alloys close to it in composition are slightly harder than would be calculated from the average values. The hardness of solid solutions is always greater than that of the constituent metals; and, when the metals are completely soluble, the hardness is greatest when the metals are present in approximately equal proportions. Compounds between metals are always extremely hard but correspondingly brittle. A metal or alloy may be hardened by being subjected to cold mechanical work, as rolling, drawing, or pressing. A metal that has been work-hardened can be restored by annealing to its original soft condition. The brittleness accompanying mechanical hardening makes necessary the annealing to which a metal or alloy is always subjected if it is to undergo a series of operations during its fabrication.

Electrical Conductivity. The conductivity of an alloy is determined to a considerable extent by the relations of the alloying elements as shown in their alloy diagrams. The important general relations are as follows:

1. In eutectic alloys the conductivity is practically the average of the conductivities of the constituent metals based on the weight percentages of the alloying elements.

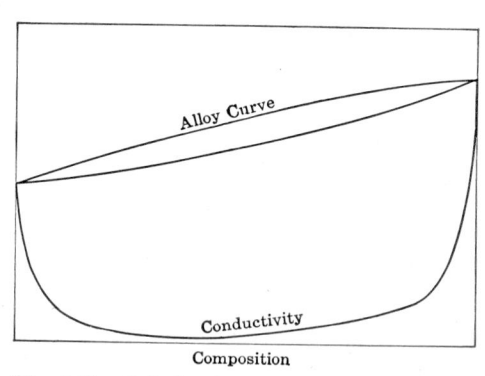

Fig. 2.18. Relation between conductivity and the solid-solution diagram.

Fig. 2.19. Equilibrium diagram. (Refer to question 2.13.)

2. The formation of solid solutions causes a marked decrease in the electrical conductivity of the resulting alloys. The general effect is shown in Fig. 2.18.

Questions

2.1. Define the following terms: metallography, photomicrograph, macro-examination, allotriomorphic crystal, and space lattice.
2.2. Distinguish between the terms "composition" and "constitution."
2.3. State the type of space lattice possessed by the following metals: copper, iron, lead, nickel, tin, and zinc.
2.4. Discuss the significance of "slip lines."
2.5. What is "twinning"? What are Neumann bands?
2.6. Discuss the relation between strength of metals and their cohesive and adhesive properties.
2.7. Name six types of solids which may result from crystallization.
2.8. Distinguish between a mixture, a chemical compound, and a solution.
2.9. Distinguish between a liquid solution and a solid solution.
2.10. Distinguish between a eutectic and a eutectoid.
2.11. What is meant by complete solid-solubility?
2.12. What is the meaning of the term "solid-solution minimum"?
2.13. Referring to Fig. 2.19, state the microscopic structure of each of the four cooled alloys whose compositions are represented by the vertical lines *M, N, P,* and *R*. Draw

Structure and Constitution of Metals

a constitution diagram showing graphically the constitution of these alloys. Draw cooling curves for these alloys.

2.14. Distinguish between substitutional and interstitial solid solutions.

2.15. What are intermetallic compounds? Of what significance are they?

References

2.1. American Society for Testing Materials: "Preparation of Micrographs of Metals and Alloys." *Designation E2, Book of Standards,* 1952, and "Preparation of Metallographic Specimens," *Designation E3, Book of Standards,* 1952.

2.2. Bragg, W. H., and Bragg, W. L.: *The Crystalline State.* London, G. Bell & Sons, 1949, 352 pages.

2.3. Bullens, D. K.: *Steel and Its Heat Treatment.* John Wiley & Sons, 5th ed., 1948; v. 1, 489 pages.

2.4. Chalmers, B.: *The Structure and Mechanical Properties of Metals.* London, Chapman & Hall, 1951, 132 pages.

2.5. Clapp, W. H., and Clark, D. S.: *Engineering Materials and Processes.* Scranton, Pa., International Textbook Co., 1938; Chaps. 2 and 3, pp. 47–88.

2.6. Clark, G. L.: *Applied X-Rays.* McGraw-Hill Book Co., 3rd ed., 1940.

2.7. Davey, W. P.: *A Study of Crystal Structure and Its Application.* McGraw-Hill Book Co., 1934.

2.8. Desch, C. H.: *Chemistry of Solids.* Cornell University Press, 1934.

2.9. Desch, C. H.: *Metallography.* London, Longmans, Green & Co., 5th ed., 1942, 408 pages.

2.10. Doan, G. E., and Mahla, E. M.: *The Principles of Physical Metallurgy.* McGraw-Hill Book Co., 2nd ed., 1941, 388 pages.

2.11. Dowdell, R. L., Jerabek, H. S., Forsyth, A. C., and Green, C. H.: *General Metallography.* John Wiley & Sons, 1943, 292 pages.

2.12. Epstein, S.: *The Alloys of Iron and Carbon.* McGraw-Hill Book Co., 1936, v. 1, Constitution, 476 pages.

2.13. Greaves, R. H., and Wrighton, H.: *Practical Microscopical Metallography.* D. Van Nostrand Co., 3rd ed., 1940, 272 pages.

2.14. Gwiazdowski, A. P.: *Engineering Metallurgy.* Appleton, Wis., C. C. Nelson Publishing Co., 1950, 247 pages.

2.15. Jeffries, Z., and Archer, R. S.: *The Science of Metals.* McGraw-Hill Book Co., 1924, 500 pages.

2.16. Kehl, G. L.: *The Principles of Metallographic Laboratory Practice.* McGraw-Hill Book Co., 1943, 2nd ed., 453 pages.

2.17. Kingston, W. E.: *The Physics of Powder Metallurgy.* McGraw-Hill Book Co., 1951, 404 pages.

2.18. Liddell, D. M., and Doan, G. E.: *The Principles of Metallurgy.* McGraw-Hill Book Co., 1933; Chaps. 15, 16, and 17, pp. 341–534.

2.19. March, J. S.: *Principles of Phase Diagrams.* McGraw-Hill Book Co., 1935.

2.20. Moore, H. F.: "Correlation between Metallography and Mechanical Testing." *Trans. Am. Inst. Mining Met. Engrs.,* v. 120, 1936, pp. 13–35.

2.21. Mott, N. F., and Jones, H.: *The Theory of the Properties of Metals and Alloys.* Oxford, Clarendon Press, 1936, 326 pages.

2.22. Newton, J.: *An Introduction to Metallurgy.* John Wiley & Sons, 2nd ed., 1947, 645 pages.

2.23. Rosenhain, W.: *Introduction to the Study of Physical Metallurgy.* Revised by J. L. Haughton. London, Constable & Co., 1935.

2.24. Sauveur, A.: *The Metallography and Heat Treatment of Iron and Steel.* McGraw-Hill Book Co., 5th printing, 1938.
2.25. Seitz, F.: *The Physics of Metals.* McGraw-Hill Book Co., 1943.
2.26. Twyman, F.: *Metal Spectroscopy.* London, Charles Griffin & Co., 1951, 569 pages.
2.27. Williams, R. S., and Homerberg, V. O.: *Principles of Metallography.* McGraw-Hill Book Co., 4th ed., 1939, 339 pages.
2.28. Young, J. F.: "The Nature of Pure Metals." *Mech. Eng.,* Nov., 1943, p. 795.

CHAPTER 3

Tests of Metals

By LLOYD F. RADER

3.1 Purpose of Physical Tests of Materials. Physical tests are conducted on materials of construction in order to determine their quality and their suitability for specific uses in machines and structures. It is necessary for both the consumer and the producer to have tests for determining quantitative properties of materials in order that materials may be properly selected and specified. Tests are also needed to duplicate materials and to check up on the uniformity of different shipments. In fact, in describing materials of construction, quantitative data obtained by testing are necessary in order to describe adequately the properties of materials produced from different raw materials and by different processes.

3.2 Physical Tests of Metals. Tests employed in determining the physical properties of metals include: tension, ductility, compression, flexure, torsion, hardness, endurance to repeated stresses or fatigue, creep, and impact tests. These methods of testing pertaining to metals are briefly described in this chapter, but the values of physical properties of metals are given in the chapters pertaining to the different metals. The service requirements of metals as measured by resistance to repeated stresses (fatigue), impact, creep, wear, and corrosion are discussed in more detail in Chapter 4.

3.3 Physical Tests of Non-Metallic Materials. Common physical tests of non-metallic materials of construction such as mortar, concrete, building stone, structural clay products, and timber include compression, tension, and flexure tests. Endurance to repeated stresses or fatigue, resistance to abrasion, resistance to impact, and permeability are determined in special cases. The methods of testing each non-metallic material are described, and typical test values are given in the chapters on the various materials.

3.4 Tensile-Strength Test. Most commercial specifications for metals have requirements for physical properties as determined by the tensile-strength test. The properties determined include ultimate tensile strength, yield strength or yield point, elongation, character of fracture, and reduction of area In order to obtain complete information concerning the tensile properties of a metal, a stress-strain curve should be determined experimentally. Strains corresponding to definite stresses imposed upon the specimen are measured by means of an extensometer. The extensometer is attached to the specimen so as to measure elongations between two gauge points. The procedure may consist of taking a series of load readings on the testing machine with corresponding readings of the extensometer, or the stress-strain diagram may be drawn directly by an autographic attachment to the testing machine.

For metals having no well-defined yield point (Fig. 1.1), the yield strength is ordinarily determined, as explained in Art. 1.2. Ductile carbon steel has a well-defined yield point. Owing to the importance of steel, the methods of testing steel in tension are described in some detail in the following articles.

3.5 The General Behavior of Steel under Tensile Stress. The behavior of steel under tensile stress is best studied with the aid of the *stress-strain*

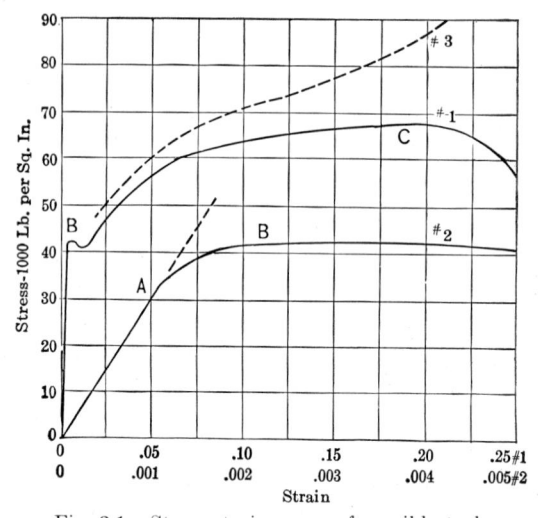

Fig. 3.1. Stress-strain curves for mild steel.

diagram. Curve 1 of Fig. 3.1 presents a typical stress-strain diagram for a mild steel. Curve 2 shows the portion of curve 1 between O and B to an enlarged horizontal scale. This second curve to such a scale is necessary in order that the *limit of proportionality* or the point of departure of the curve from the straight line at A can be accurately located. For steel the elastic limit and proportional limit are usually considered to be identical. The *yield point* B is easily detected either by making a test (by the drop of the weighing lever or halt of the gauge of the testing machine) or from the stress-strain diagram where a more or less sharp break appears in the curve when the yield point is reached The *ultimate strength* is represented by the maximum ordinate to the stress-strain curve at C.

The stress-strain diagram for steel in compression is essentially similar to the curve as described for tension, and the elastic limit is approximately the same in both cases.

The modulus of elasticity can be determined from the slope of the first portion of the stress-strain diagram but is usually computed from the observed values of stress and strain. The modulus of elasticity is unaffected by the factors which influence other properties of steels and is about 29,000,000 pounds per square inch for practically any class of carbon steel.

3.6 Routine Commercial Tension Test of Steel. In this test the ultimate tensile strength, the yield point, the per cent elongation, and the character

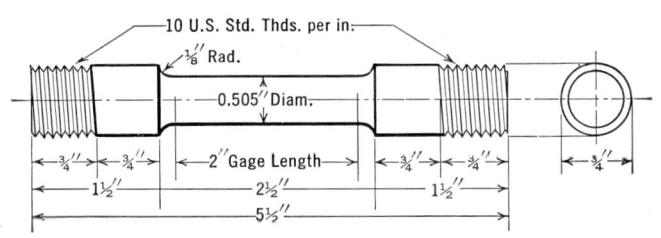

Fig. 3.2. Standard tensile-strength test specimen.

of the fracture are determined. Sometimes the per cent reduction of area is also determined. The standard tensile-test specimen, shown in Fig. 3.2, has a diameter of 0.505 inch and a cross-sectional area of 0.2 square inch.

All these values can be obtained by a single operator. It is not customary to determine deformations of the specimen for plotting the stress-strain curve in the routine commercial tension test of ductile carbon steel since a great deal of additional labor and cost would be required.

Ultimate Tensile Strength. This value is determined by dividing the maximum load registered on the testing machine by the nominal cross-sectional area of the specimen. Maximum load occurs simultaneously with the beginning of the "necking down" in ductile steel and with rupture in brittle materials.

Yield Point. Yield point may be obtained on ductile carbon steel by the drop-of-the-beam method which consists of reading the load on the weighing beam of the screw-power type of testing machine when the beam drops as the load on the specimen decreases just after the yield point is reached. This load divided by nominal cross-sectional area is the yield point. Care should be taken to apply the load at a low rate when approaching the yield point, and the poise on the weighing beam should be moved carefully to keep the beam in balance in order to secure accurate results.

As an aid in determining the yield point, a divider pointer may be inserted in the gauge marks of the specimen for the purpose of indicating the large deformations that occur after the yield point is reached. Frequently the loosening of scale on the steel specimen indicates these large deformations.

Elongation. Elongation of the specimen after fracture may be determined by placing the parts of the broken specimen closely together and holding them in place by means of a vise. The distance between gauge marks may be measured to the nearest 0.01 inch by means of dividers.

$$\text{Per cent elongation} = \frac{\text{Final length} - \text{Original length}}{\text{Original length}} \times 100$$

Character of the Fracture. Valuable information concerning the characteristics and composition of metals may be obtained by observing the character of the fracture of the test specimens. Necking down of the cross-section of the specimen near the fracture accompanied by a fracture in the form of a cup and cone indicates ductility and is typical of low-carbon steel. A square break normal to the longitudinal axis with little or no necking down indicates a non-ductile metal such as high-carbon steel or gray cast iron.

The texture of the metal at the fracture is commonly recorded. The texture of low-carbon steel is usually "silky"; of high-carbon steel, finely crystalline; of cast iron, finely or coarsely crystalline. By observing the extent of necking down and the type and texture of the fracture, the carbon content of steels can be estimated approximately.

A rosette or serrated fracture is typical of heat-treated high-strength alloy steel. Many non-ferrous metals exhibit considerable elongation over the length of the specimen without appreciable necking down. Wrought iron may be distinguished by the fibrous structure of its fracture.

Reduction of Area. Reduction of area can usually be determined if the specimen is circular in cross-section. The area of the smallest cross-section after fracture may be measured by means of thin pointed calipers to the nearest 0.01 inch. If the section is slightly irregular, the maximum and minimum diameters may be measured and the cross-sectional area computed as a circle, taking the mean of the observed values as diameter. Such an irregular section may be computed as an ellipse.

It is difficult to measure the cross-sectional area of rectangular sections when fractured since necking down tends to produce a section composed of four concave surfaces. The cross-sectional area of deformed reinforcing bars is also difficult to determine. Reduction of area is ordinarily not reported for such specimens.

Tests of Metals

$$\text{Per cent reduction of area} = \frac{\text{Original area} - \text{Area after fracture}}{\text{Original area}} \times 100$$

3.7 Distribution of Elongation. The distribution of elongation of a steel specimen in tension is illustrated by Fig. 3.3. If uninfluenced by any local cause, a bar of homogeneous steel subjected to axial tension should fail near the center of the distance between the points of application of the load, because there the flow of the metal will be least impeded. The maximum ordinate to the curve of Fig. 3.3 represents the point where neck-

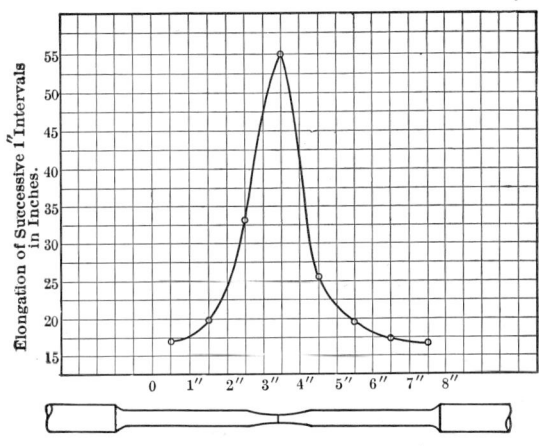

Fig. 3.3. Distribution of elongation.

ing down occurred, since the point of maximum reduction in area must necessarily coincide with the point of maximum elongation. The fact that steel test specimens are reduced in cross-section as they are elongated under stress, and finally neck down, accounts for the fact that the breaking load, according to the stress-strain diagram, is below the ultimate strength. If the stress at all loads was computed upon the basis of the actual section then existing, instead of being computed (as it usually is) upon the basis of the original section, the stress-strain curve would follow such a course as is indicated by the dotted-line curve 3 of Fig. 3.1.

3.8 Ductility Testing. Ductility of metals is usually determined in the tension test by noting the percentage elongation and in some cases the percentage reduction of area.

The indication of the ductility of steel which is afforded by a simple *cold-bending test* is also very valuable and significant. Cold-bending is accomplished either in a special bending machine or by blows or pressure. According to the severity of the test desired, the bend may be made over a sharp edge or about a pin or template of any desired radius.

The *drift test* is used to determine ductility of metal plates. A hole of a given size is bored into the metal plate and expanded by driving a drift pin into it until the metal is fractured. The ratio of sizes of holes before and after the test is a measure of ductility.

3.9 Compressive Strength. The compressive strength should be determined on cylinders with a height equal to about two times the diameter. The ends of the cylinders should be carefully prepared to insure parallel and plane surfaces. Load should be applied concentrically, using spherical-seated bearing blocks.

For steels it is possible to determine the ultimate compressive strength only for brittle steels since all ductile steels are greatly deformed under load and show no well-defined fracture.

The compressive strength of metal is quite closely allied with the tensile strength, the properties revealed under one kind of stress being practically identical with those revealed under the opposite kind. It is not necessary, therefore, to consider tensile strength and compressive strength separately, except to a slight extent. One fact which must not be overlooked in this connection is that soft or medium steel is often subjected to compressive loading under such circumstances that the stress induced does not remain purely compressive but becomes a combination of compressive stress with bending stresses. The behavior of the material in this event is manifestly not that which is characteristic of steel in compression. When, for instance, compressive load is applied to a steel test specimen whose length is more than three or four times its diameter, or to a steel column whose length bears a large ratio to the least radius of gyration of its cross-section, complete failure occurs under a load which has induced an average compressive stress only slightly in excess of the yield point. Flow of the ductile metal at the yield point has caused eccentricity of stress, and failure ensues almost immediately owing to lateral flexure and the concentration of stress in the extreme fiber on one side of the section.

3.10 Flexural Strength. In the flexure test, the beam may be tested on simple supports or as cantilevers with one end fixed. The flexural strength is commonly expressed by the term "modulus of rupture," meaning the apparent extreme fiber stress under the load which produces rupture as computed from the flexure formula,

$$f = My \div I$$

wherein f is the extreme fiber stress, M is the bending moment, y is the distance from the neutral axis to the extreme fiber, and I is the moment of inertia of the section.

As a matter of mechanics, this procedure is not warranted, since it involves the assumption that the neutral axis remains a constant distance from the extreme fiber and the further assumption that a constant proportionality of strain to stress obtains for all stresses up to the breaking stress.

The proportion of strain to stress is not a constant, and the neutral axis shifts as the material deforms. Therefore the actual extreme fiber stress is less than this value of f computed by the rule for the bending moment which exists under the load which produces rupture, and, indeed, the actual fiber stress for cast iron is not more than 50 to 60 per cent of the modulus of rupture.

The modulus of rupture, however, is a good index for comparing different grades and classes of materials. The beams tested in flexure in a given series of tests should be of the same shape and size so that the modulus-of-rupture values can be compared directly.

The flexural strength of a metal directly depends upon the tensile and compressive properties of that metal. Whether one or the other is the controlling factor depends upon the form of the beam and the location of the neutral axis. If the section is symmetrical the failure will usually occur on the tension side if the metal is not ductile, and on the compression side if it is ductile. Absolute rupture in cross bending is not possible with any grade of mild or medium steel, since these steels may be bent 180 degrees without fracture.

The modulus of elasticity as obtained from bending tests is slightly lower than the values obtained from tensile or compression tests because the slight deflection due to the shear introduces a small error into the formulas for deflection from which the flexural modulus of elasticity is usually calculated.

3.11 Torsion Test. The torsion test is conducted by twisting a solid cylindrical specimen. The torque and the angle of twist are measured.

The intensity of the shearing stress due to torsion on any section of a cylindrical shaft is not uniform but varies directly as the distance from the axis of the shaft (assuming that the section is circular), and the maximum intensity of shearing stress is therefore found at the circumference. The mathematical expression for the maximum shearing stress in the extreme fiber of circular shafts is:

$$s = \frac{2Pa'}{\pi r^3}$$

where Pa is the torque, r is the radius of the section, and s is the shearing stress in the extreme fiber of the shaft.

The shearing modulus of elasticity E_s is expressed by the equation

$$E_s = \frac{sl}{r\theta}$$

where l is the distance between the planes of the external forces, and θ is the angle of torque or twist.

The shearing strength as determined by torsion tests appears higher than it does in the case of direct shear. This is because the expression for s given above is true only as long as the material behaves elastically. When computed for the torque that produces rupture it may be called the "torsional modulus of rupture" and corresponds to the true value of the shearing strength of the material in about the same way as the modulus of rupture for cross breaking corresponds to the actual extreme fiber stress.

3.12 Hardness Tests of Metals. Hardness of metals is usually determined by measuring the resistance to penetration of a ball, cone, or pyramid.

The *Brinell* method is based upon determining the resistance offered to indentation by a hardened sphere that is subjected to a given pressure. The pressure used in testing steel is usually 3000 kilograms, and the diameter of the ball is 10 millimeters. When testing softer materials a pressure of 500 kilograms is used. Brinell numbers can be computed by the formula

$$BHN = \frac{2P}{\pi D(D - \sqrt{D^2 - d^2})}$$

where P is pressure in kilograms; D and d, respectively, the diameters of the ball and of the impression in millimeters. The harder the steel, the smaller the indentation under the load and the greater the Brinell hardness number. Hardened steel balls of the regular ball-bearing type are employed for testing steels from 70 to 500 Brinell hardness, and carbide balls are used for hard steels up to 800 Brinell hardness.

The *Rockwell* method employs either a ball or a diamond cone in a precision-testing instrument that is designed to measure depth of penetration accurately. Two superimposed impressions are made, one with a load of 10 kilograms and the second with a load of 100 kilograms. The depth to which the major load drives the ball or cone below that depth to which the minor load has previously driven it is taken as a measure of the hardness. The size of the ball generally used is $1/16$ inch in diameter, but for hardened steels greater accuracy is obtained by use of a diamond cone (120 degrees with slightly rounded tip) applied under a major load of 150 kilograms. The method employing the ball is designated the Rockwell B test, and that using the cone the Rockwell C test. The Rockwell C test can be utilized to measure the hardness of thin pieces since the depth of penetration of the cone is about 0.005 inches.

The Rockwell Superficial hardness tester is capable of measuring hardness of very thin hard surfaces such as those on nitrided steel since the depth of penetration required is only 0.002 inches approximately. The initial load applied on the Superficial tester is 3 kilograms, and the common major

Tests of Metals

load is 30 kilograms; a sensitive depth measuring device is provided on the tester. For the regular Rockwell test, smooth, clean machined surfaces are desired, but, for the Superficial test, the surfaces must be smoothly finished and clean, though polishing is unnecessary.

Concerning hardness conversions, Rockwell C values using the diamond cone are about one-tenth of the Brinell hardness for metals within the range of 300 to 600 Brinell. (For a hardness conversion chart for steels for various hardness tests, refer to *American Society for Metals Handbook*, 1939 Edition, page 127.)

The *Vickers* method is a plastic indentation method similar to the Brinell but uses a square diamond pyramid as an indenter which eliminates the errors due to deformation of the steel ball and places practically no limits on the hardness of metals that can be accurately determined. The impressions may be small and shallow owing to the fact that light pressures may be employed, making it possible to determine, satisfactorily, the hardness of fairly thin material and to test finished work without serious injury. The values obtained approximate those obtained by the Brinell apparatus, but are not subject to the variations in accuracy of that method. The Vickers hardness number is computed from the formula

$$\text{Hardness} = \frac{1.8544 \text{ Load}}{(\text{Diagonal})^2}$$

in which the load is in kilograms and the diagonal of the impression is in millimeters.

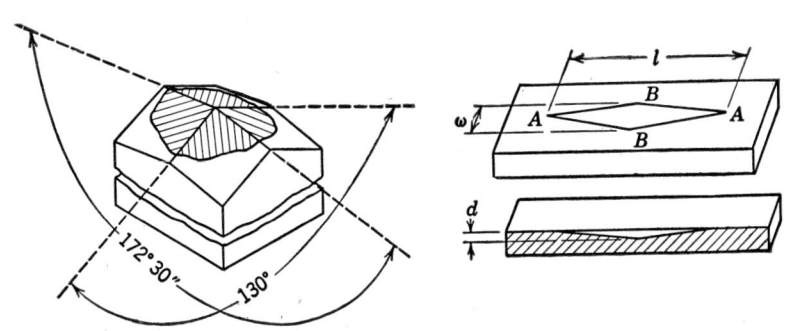

Fig. 3.4. Knoop indenter and diamond-shaped indentation. (*Courtesy* Bullens.)

The *Knoop* pyramidal indenter makes a diamond-shaped or rhomb impression, the diagonals having a ratio of 7:1 approximately. (See Fig. 3.4.) Knoop hardness is calculated by the formula

$$I = \frac{L}{A_p} = \frac{L}{l^2 C_p}$$

in which I = indentation hardness.
L = load applied to the indenter, in kilograms.
A_p = unrecovered projected area of the indentation, in square millimeters.
l = measured length of the long diagonal of the indentation, in millimeters.
C_p = constant relating l to the projected area. For indenter shown in Fig. 3.4, $C_p = 0.07028$.

The long diagonal of the indentation does not change its dimension appreciably upon removal of load, but, owing to elastic recovery of the metal, the short diagonal becomes shorter. By measuring the indentation and knowing the dimensions of the indenter, both recovered and unrecovered dimensions of the indentation can be computed. Because the Knoop test is sensitive to small depths of indentation and the loads applied are less than one kilogram, it is utilized for thin specimens and for brittle materials such as glass which might fracture under heavy loads required by standard hardness testers such as Brinell and Rockwell.

The *Monotron* test is an indentation type in which an impression to a standard depth of 9/5000 inch is made by means of a micrometer indicator, and the force required to produce this penetration is taken as the hardness of the metal. A small diamond hemisphere, 0.75 mm. in diameter, is used. Results are read on the scales of the Monotron machine in kilograms and also in terms of equivalent Brinell numbers. Because of small depth of penetration, thin materials can be tested; also because of the diamond hemisphere, hard steels can be tested more precisely than by means of the steel ball in the Brinell test.

The *Shore scleroscope test* is made by means of a pointed hammer which is allowed to fall through a guiding glass tube upon the metal being tested. The hardness is expressed by the height of rebound of the hammer after falling from a specified height. The hammer of the instrument becomes slightly changed in form after a certain number of tests and must then be recalibrated. The indications of the instrument must certainly depend in some measure upon the resiliency of the material tested as well as upon that of the hammer itself, but the extent of the permanent deformation of the metal is also a factor. A very smooth surface is required for precise results. For ordinary steels the Brinell number is approximately the sclero-scope number multiplied by 5¾ to 6¼.

The *Herbert test* for hardness operates on a different principle. A heavy balanced pendulum rests, through a small steel or diamond ball, on a leveled surface of the material to be tested; and the amplitude or the period of the swing of the pendulum after starting from a given position is taken as the Herbert hardness number.

The hardness test is finding a constantly widening field of application. It can be used to test castings, forgings, etc., without impairing their subsequent availability for use. It can also be used advantageously in exploring different portions of a finished article to ascertain the varying effect of cooling conditions, working, etc., upon the properties of the metal.

3.13 Fatigue Tests. Fatigue tests, or tests to determine endurance to repeated stresses, are commonly conducted on metals by means of a rotating beam machine such as the R. R. Moore machine in which bending moment is applied to the specimen through holders. This apparatus produces alternating or *reversed stress* where stress in the specimen changes from tension to compression with each half revolution.

Some fatigue-testing machines produce stress of only one type, either tensile or compressive, which is termed *swelling stress*. *Repeated stress* is a general term including both this type and reversed stress. The behavior of metals under repeated stress is discussed in Chapter 4.

3.14 Impact Tests. Impact tests may be performed for two purposes: (1) to determine the ability of the material to resist impact under service conditions and (2) to determine the quality of the metal from a metallurgical standpoint. Impact tests may be classified into two groups: (1) utility impact tests and (2) standard impact tests.

Utility Impact Tests. Utility impact tests for detecting the presence of brittleness or determining the comparative toughness of materials are applied to steel rails, pipes, tubing, gear teeth, and tire chains, as well as to non-metallic materials such as concrete, stone, wood, fiber board, enamels, and organic plastics. Such tests are conducted with machines and specimens of various types, shapes, and sizes.

Standard Impact Tests. The Charpy and the Izod impact-testing machines are the two most common machines for conducting standard impact tests on metals. These machines determine the amount of work in foot-pounds necessary to fracture a small test specimen by impact. They consist essentially of a weighted pendulum, suitable holders or supports for the specimen, and a device for recording the angular swing of the pendulum. The work done in fracturing the specimen must be absorbed from the energy of the swinging pendulum. Consequently, the pendulum rises to a smaller angle than it would for a free swing. The energy absorbed by the specimen may be computed from the angle to which the pendulum actually rises after fracturing the specimen.

The specimens tested are generally notched in order to secure uniformity of results by localization of the fracture. Either tensile or transverse type specimens can be tested in the Charpy machine. The transverse type shown in Fig. 3.5 is well adapted for examining metals that break with a relatively low absorption of energy, since the notch is not sufficiently sharp to make the spread of foot-pound values too narrow. The depth of the notch eliminates the influence of surface effects. For tough metals the notched Izod type of specimen tested as a cantilever is frequently used.

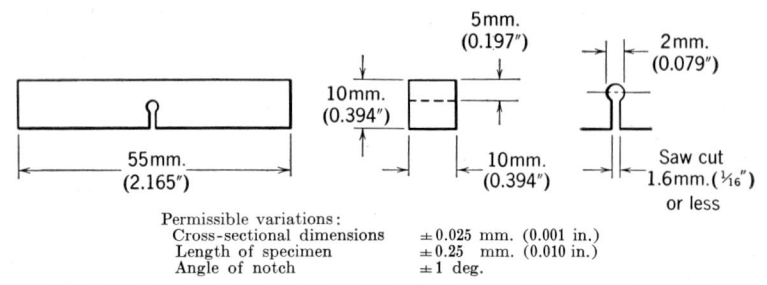

Permissible variations:
Cross-sectional dimensions ±0.025 mm. (0.001 in.)
Length of specimen ±0.25 mm. (0.010 in.)
Angle of notch ±1 deg.

Fig. 3.5. Standard keyhole notch specimen. (*Courtesy* ASTM.)

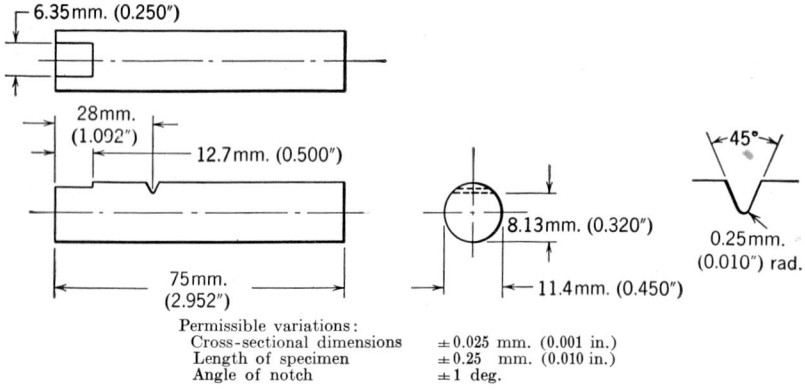

Permissible variations:
Cross-sectional dimensions ±0.025 mm. (0.001 in.)
Length of specimen ±0.25 mm. (0.010 in.)
Angle of notch ±1 deg.

Fig. 3.6. Izod V-notch round type specimen. (*Courtesy* ASTM.)

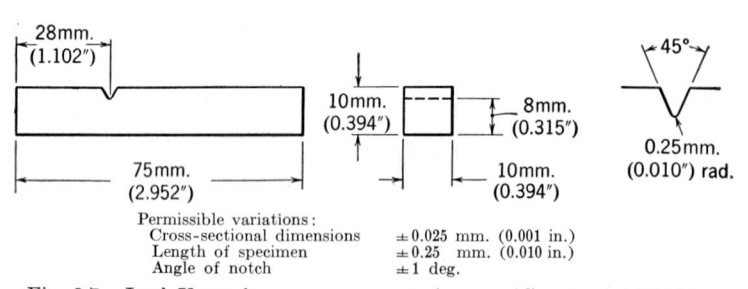

Permissible variations:
Cross-sectional dimensions ±0.025 mm. (0.001 in.)
Length of specimen ±0.25 mm. (0.010 in.)
Angle of notch ±1 deg.

Fig. 3.7. Izod V-notch square type specimen. (*Courtesy* ASTM.)

(See Figs. 3.6 and 3.7.) For extremely brittle metal the test specimen requires no notch because the first suddenly applied stress causes a brittle failure.

Tests of Metals

Impact tests are not limited in application to metals that are to be subjected to impact in service but are also employed to determine whether metals are metallurgically satisfactory. The theory of impact tests and their use in selection of metals are described in Chapter 4.

3.15 Creep-Testing Equipment. Long-time creep tests of metals under sustained stress at high temperatures are conducted in tubular electric-resistance furnaces on tension specimens. Maximum temperatures of 1600, 1800, or 2200° F. may be obtained in standard machines with temperatures controlled either $\pm 5°$ F. or $\pm 2°$ F. Three thermocouples are employed, one at each end and one at the middle of the specimen. Test specimens are 0.505 inch in diameter with 2-inch gauge length for bar stock and are rectangular for sheet and plate stock. The testing equipment is designed to maintain a constant tensile stress on the specimen at a given temperature as elongation takes place over a long period of time. Loads are applied on the specimen by means of dead weights on a lever arm. A minimum capacity of 12,000 pounds with a loading accuracy within 1 per cent of load is typical of creep machines. Creep measurements are obtained by means of extensometers reading directly to 0.000025 inch with precision to approximately 0.00005 inch.

For creep-rupture tests the lever-arm creep machine is used. The same procedure is employed as for creep testing, but higher loads may be applied to produce rupture at an earlier time. For higher rates of elongation a screw-driven testing machine is employed in which the test specimen is loaded by a screw jack through a stiff spring in series with the specimen. The load is maintained by keeping a constant deflection of the calibrated spring. A continuous elongation-time curve up to rupture is automatically recorded without the use of an extensometer on the test specimen. Creep characteristics of metals are described in Chapter 4.

Questions

3.1. Draw a stress-strain diagram for structural steel showing thereon approximate average values of yield point, proportional limit, ultimate strength, and modulus of elasticity.

3.2. Name and briefly describe the principal observations made in the routine commercial tension test of structural steel. Which of these observations are indications of the ductility of the steel? Briefly describe the form of a test specimen commonly used in this test.

3.3. What gauge length is usually specified in the commercial tension test of steel?

3.4. For what purpose is an extensometer test conducted on a specimen of structural steel?

3.5. What is meant by a "cup and cone" fracture?

3.6. What is the purpose of the cold-bend test of steel? of the drift test?

3.7. Why should beams of a given material tested in flexure be of the same dimensions?

3.8. Describe the torsion test of metal.

3.9. Describe how the hardness of steels is determined by various methods.

3.10. Which hardness test would be affected the least by surface roughness, scales, scratches, and pits? Why? Which hardness test would be affected the most? Why?

3.11. Which indentation hardness test would be most applicable to a variety of metals ranging from very hard to very soft? Why?

3.12. For what purposes may impact tests be conducted on metals?

3.13. Compare the Charpy and Izod impact-test specimens.

3.14. Describe briefly the testing of metals in fatigue.

3.15. The results of a tension test on a specimen of high-carbon steel 0.505 inch in diameter is given as follows:

Load, lb.	*Total Elongation in 2 in.*, in.
1,990	0.0007
4,005	0.0013
6,010	0.0020
8,120	0.0027
10,250	0.0034
11,780	0.0039
14,230	0.0047
15,620	0.0053
16,150	0.0056
16,700	0.0110
17,840	0.0171

Determine the yield strength for an offset of 0.2 per cent, and compute the value of the modulus of elasticity.

References

3.1. American Society for Testing Materials: "Standard Methods of Tension Testing of Metallic Materials." *Designation* E8, *Book of Standards,* 1952. Also "Symposium on Significance of the Tension Tests of Metals in Relation to Design." *Proc. ASTM,* v. 40, 1940, pp. 501–609.

3.2. American Society for Testing Materials: "Standard Methods of Brinell Hardness Testing of Metallic Materials." *Designation* E10, *Book of Standards,* 1952.

3.3. American Society for Testing Materials: "Standard Methods of Rockwell Hardness Testing of Metallic Materials." *Designation* E18, *Book of Standards,* 1952.

3.4. Campbell, R. F., Henderson, Q., and Donleavy, M. R.: "A New Microhardness Tester and Some Factors Affecting the Diamond Pyramid Hardness Number at Light Loads." *Proc. ASTM,* v. 40, 1948, p. 954.

3.5. Clark, D. S., and Duwez, P. E.: "The Influence of Strain Rate on Some Tensile Properties of Steel." *Proc. ASTM,* v. 50, 1950, pp. 560–576.

3.6. Cowdrey, I. H., and Adams, R. G.: *Materials Testing.* John Wiley & Sons, 3rd ed., 1944, 156 pages.

3.7. Davis, E. A.: "The Effect of the Speed of Stretching and the Rate of Loading on the Yielding of Mild Steel." *Trans. Am. Soc. Mech. Engrs.,* v. 60, 1938, p. 137.

3.8. Findley, W. N.: New Apparatus for Axial-load Fatigue Testing, *Bull. ASTM,* 147, Aug., 1947, pp. 54–56.

3.9. Grossman, M. A.: "Toughness and Fracture of Hardened Steels." *Metals Technol. Tech. Paper* 2020, Apr., 1946, 41 pages.

3.10. Kahn, N. A., Imbembo, E. A., and Ginsberg, F.: "Effect of Variations in Notch Acuity on the Behavior of Steel in the Charpy Notched-bar Test." *Proc. ASTM,* v. 50, 1950, pp. 619–648.

Tests of Metals

3.11. Lea, F. C.: *Hardness of Metals.* London, C. Griffith & Co., 1936, 141 pages.

3.12. MacGregor, G. W.: "Tension Test." *Proc. ASTM,* v. 40, 1940, pp. 508–534; also "True Stress-Strain Tension Test." *J. Franklin Inst.,* v. 238, 1944, pp. 111–135, 159–176.

3.13. Mack, D. J.: "Young's Modulus, Its Metallurgical Aspects." *Am. Inst. Mining Met. Engrs. Tech. Publ.* 1936, 1945, 17 pages.

3.14. Moore, H. F., and Moore, M. B.: *Materials of Engineering.* McGraw-Hill Book Co., 8th ed., 1953; Chaps. 18 and 19.

3.15. Muhlenbruch, C. W.: *Testing of Engineering Materials.* D. Van Nostrand Co., 1944, 200 pages.

3.16. Murphy, G.: *Properties of Engineering Materials.* Scranton, Pa., International Textbook Co., 2nd ed., 1946, 459 pages.

3.17. National Bureau of Standards: Mechanical Properties of Metals and Alloys, *Circular* C447, Dec. 1, 1943.

3.18. O'Neill, H.: *Hardness of Metals and Its Measurement.* London, Chapman & Hall, 1934, 292 pages.

3.19. Sauveur, A.: "The Torsion Test." *Proc. ASTM,* v. 38, part II, 1938, pp. 3–20.

3.20. Unckel, H. A.: "Microhardness of Constituents in Steel Tested." *The Iron Age,* Aug. 30, 1951, p. 68.

3.21. Williams, S. R.: *Hardness and Hardness Measurements.* Am. Soc. Metals, 1942, 558 pages.

CHAPTER 4

Service Requirements of Metals
By LLOYD F. RADER

4.1 General. Requirements of metals in various types of service and under different conditions of exposure will be considered in this chapter. The resistance of metals to failure due to slip, progressive fracture under repeated stresses (fatigue), impact, creep, stress rupture, wear, and corrosion are described. Non-destructive testing methods are also discussed.

Slip

4.2 Action of Slip. Slip is the phenomenon of movement along gliding planes of crystals due to the application of stress above the elastic limit. Slip is an inelastic action that does not continue indefinitely under sustained static stress but reaches a state of equilibrium after a short time. The occurrence and appearance of slip lines were described in Art. 2.9.

Slip-Interference Theory. The hardening and increase in elastic limit of metals by cold-working can be explained by the slip-interference theory of Jeffries and Archer.[1] This theory states that, during the motion of slipping, the grains are broken down into thin plates whose surfaces tend to gouge into each other, causing increased resistance. Also slip planes in different crystalline grains have different orientations so that slip in one grain interferes with slip in adjacent grains. Cold-working tends to increase the number of points of contact and thus hardens the metal and raises the elastic limit. This theory explains why slipping stops after a time when the metal is subjected to a stress above the elastic limit.

In metals containing hard crystals interspersed in softer ones, the hard crystals act as "keys," tending to reduce movements along slip planes in the weaker grains. The size of these hard crystals is important. With large crystals, many slip planes would not be intercepted. For extremely small particles, resistance is small because slipping can take place past the particles without much change in path. For small grains of "critical" size, the movement along slip planes is restricted to an optimum degree.

Slip developed by repeated stresses is discussed in Art. 4.3.

[1] Jeffries and Archer: *The Science of Metals.* McGraw-Hill Book Co., 1924.

Fracture of Metals under Repeated Stresses

4.3 Behavior of Metals under Repeated Stresses. All metals may ultimately fail through repetition of stresses below the elastic limit. Such failures have often been observed in the case of axles, machine parts, shafts, etc., and the phenomenon has frequently been demonstrated in a scientific manner since the pioneer work reported by Wöhler in 1870. If the repeated stress approaches anywhere near the ultimate strength, failure may, in steels, be induced by very few repetitions, but, with a maximum stress not far from one-half the ultimate strength, rupture, if ever attained, will usually be produced only by millions of repetitions.

This phenomenon was once ascribed to a general deterioration of the cohesion between crystalline constituents of the metal when subjected to many repetitions or reversals of comparatively low stresses. Owing probably to this idea of deterioration, the phenomenon came long ago to be known as the *fatigue* of metals, and the use of the term has persisted in spite of the fact that it is now known to be a process of gradual or *progressive fracture* of the crystals themselves.

Examination under the microscope and the electron microscope of the behavior of the crystalline constituents of metals under repeated stress has shown that failure of crystals is caused by a succession of shear slips on parallel planes of least strength. The failure of the piece as a whole is due to the successive failure of individual crystals and the development of cracks. Failure very seldom occurs at crystalline boundaries.

Slip in crystals is likely to occur at points where high localized stresses are set up. These stresses depend chiefly upon the distribution of stress between crystals, which in turn depends upon the homogeneity of the structure. Thus flaws and cracks in the internal structure, sudden changes in cross-section, sharp corners, especially reëntrant angles, irregularities in surface finish, poor fitting of pins, rivets and bolts at connections, etc., may cause high localized stresses. The preëxistence of internal stresses, originating during cooling, heat treatment, or mechanical working, may cause concentrations of stress under service conditions. In general, these high localized stresses tend to increase as the average computed stress across a section is increased. Localized stresses do not ordinarily affect the static structural strength but tend to produce slip in crystals when the metal is subjected to repeated stress.

The localized nature of slip in crystals under repeated stress has been verified by studies made by Professor W. J. Craig [2] using the electron microscope. These studies indicate that alpha brass and ingot iron under static

[2] W. J. Craig: "An Electron Microscope Study of the Development of Fatigue Failures." *Proc. ASTM*, v. 52, 1952.

tension deform by slip throughout the crystals of the specimen whereas under repeated loading the deformation is extremely localized and the extent of the deformation varies within the individual crystals as well as throughout the specimen. Spacings of deformations or slip as revealed by the electron microscope are similar for both static tension and repeated stress for alpha brass and ingot iron. For aluminum, however, statically produced slip has rather uniform spacings of deformation, but repeated stressing causes irregular spacings of deformations and great distortion at localized points.

4.4 Character of Fracture. Test specimens of cylindrical shape rotated under reversed bending have fatigue cracks formed around the circumference. As the application of stress is continued, these cracks tend to increase in number and to extend inward until only a central core of uncracked metal is left. When the cross-section of this core becomes too small to withstand the load upon it, the core suddenly fractures at right angles to the direction of stress in a manner similar to the rupture of a brittle metal. The surface of the fracture of the core is rough and "crystalline" in texture and similar to that obtained by nicking the specimen and breaking by a sudden blow. The walls of the cracks are worn smooth by the alternate opening and closing of the cracks under reversed bending, thus producing a smooth surface on the exterior portion of the fractured cross-section.

4.5 Endurance Limit. The stress below which a material can withstand an indefinitely large number of repetitions of stress is defined as the *en-*

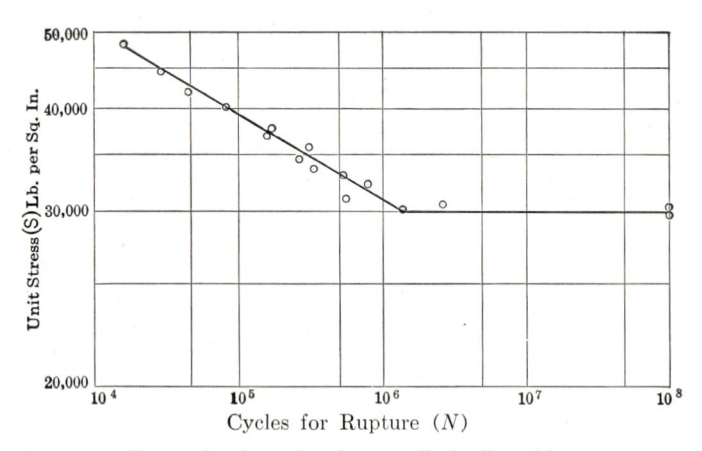

Fig. 4.1. Determination of endurance limit (logarithmic scale).

durance limit of that material. The endurance limit is determined by testing specimens in special testing machines for a number of cycles of stress of different magnitudes. The values are plotted with stress S as ordinates against cycles for rupture N as abscissas. A typical curve plotted to loga-

Service Requirements of Metals

rithmic scale is shown in Fig. 4.1. Such a curve is commonly called an *S-N* diagram. The unit stress for which the curve becomes horizontal is designated as the endurance limit. Most metals have a fairly definite endurance limit, but some metals as, for example, aluminum alloys have curves which do not become horizontal.

4.6 Fatigue-Testing Methods. Metals are usually tested under alternating or *reversed stress* where stress changes from one direction to the opposite one. Stresses may be applied wholly in one direction, however, either in tension or in compression. These stresses are called *swelling* stresses. *Repeated stress* is a general term covering both cases.

Both notched and unnotched specimens are used in testing. The notched specimens have a lower endurance limit.

A large amount of data has been obtained on fatigue properties of metals by using the R. R. Moore rotating-beam machine with the bending moment applied through holders at operating speeds of 1725 and 3450 cycles per minute. Oberg and Johnson[3] employed a similar type of machine with ball-bearing housings supporting nitrided-steel spindles for holding the specimen which can be rotated at a speed of 10,600 cycles per minute. Tests at this speed gave endurance limits for a number of metals comparable with those obtained at lower speed. The rate of speed may affect the shape of the *S-N* diagram at stresses above the endurance limit. A speed of 10,000 cycles per minute makes it possible to obtain endurance limits of satisfactory precision for most metals in a moderate length of time.

Special testing machines are used for fatigue testing at elevated and low temperatures.

During testing it is sometimes desired to detect the presence of fatigue cracks. One method consists of placing oil in the cracks by applying oil to the metal surface and then rubbing the surface free from oil. A coating of thin white paste is applied. The piece is set up on supports and subjected to a sudden blow to set up bending stresses which will close the cracks, squeeze out the oil, and discolor the white coating. Another method is to magnetize the steel and sprinkle fine iron dust over it. A thin line of dust is formed by the magnetic poles at a crack. Some cracks can be observed by visual inspection or by means of a magnifying glass.

4.7 Machine Parts Subjected to Repeated Stress. Endurance limits are determined for metals that are to be used in the manufacture of machine parts subjected to rotation, bending, vibration, etc. Typical examples are axles, shafts, piston rods, connecting rods, well-drilling rods, steam turbine blades, and springs. Structural members in airplanes are subjected to repeated stress due to vibration.

[3] T. T. Oberg and J. B. Johnson: "Fatigue Properties of Metals Used in Aircraft Construction at 3,450 and 10,600 Cycles." *Proc. ASTM,* v. 37, Part II, 1937.

4.8 Effects of Overstressing and Understressing in Fatigue. The effects of repeated stress above and below the endurance limit have been reported by Professor J. B. Kommers.[4] These effects are of importance because materials in service are frequently subjected to overstress, which is stress above the endurance limit, and are commonly subjected to understress, which is stress below the endurance limit.

Overstressing for a number of cycles may initiate cracking that will weaken the metal. The procedure of testing the metal for a number of cycles at an overstress and then reducing the load on the specimen to determine the value of the new endurance limit quite commonly reduces the endurance limit below that of the virgin metal. In general, the amount of damage due to overstress tends to increase with increase in the percentage of overstress and the cycle ratio. Cycle ratio is defined as the ratio of the number of cycles applied at a given overstress to the number of cycles at which the material would fail at that stress.

Understressing of carbon steel, annealed ingot iron, and cast iron by Kommers for cycles ranging from 5 million to 60 million produced increases in endurance limit from 6 to 25 per cent.

A still greater increase in the endurance limit of annealed ingot iron was obtained by Kommers when the understressing was followed by a "coaxing" process in which the endurance limit is said to be "coaxed" to higher values by a procedure of gradually increasing the applied load in small increments and allowing a relatively large number of cycles of stress to occur after each new increase in load. Great increases in fatigue life (number of cycles which a material can endure at the higher stresses) have also been obtained by understressing plus coaxing of annealed ingot iron.

Results of coaxing tests of SAE 1045 steel obtained by Professor G. M. Sinclair are given in Fig. 4.2. The S-N diagram which was obtained by testing specimens to failure at a single stress level is represented by the dashed line. Coaxing followed a period of understressing. The stress increment used in coaxing was 1000 pounds per square inch. Results plotted in curve 1 were obtained for a cycle increment of 2 million, whereas curve 2, which indicated a higher coaxing failure-stress, was the result when a longer time of testing was employed by increasing the cycle increment to 10 million. This coaxing effect in fatigue may be due to cold working the metal during the understressing period; however, it has been explained on the basis of strengthening of the metal by strain-aging in the local regions where fatigue damage is initiated.

Kommers found that progressively increasing cyclic understress, applied to a specimen after overstress, not only may repair the damage that has been

---

[4] J. B. Kommers: "The Effect of Overstressing and Understressing in Fatigue." *Proc. ASTM*, v. 38, Part II, 1938, pp. 249–268; v. 43, 1943, pp. 749–762.

done but sometimes may augment the original endurance limit by a substantial percentage.

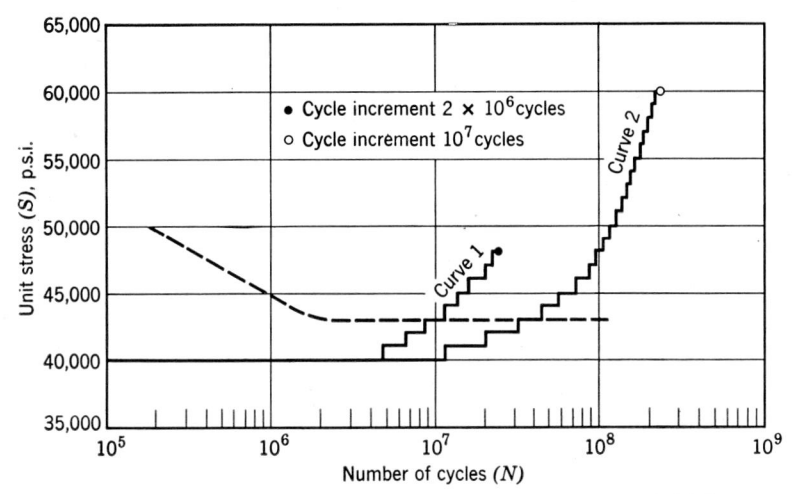

Fig. 4.2. Influence of cycle increment on coaxing failure stress of SAE 1045 steel. (G. M. Sinclair: "An Investigation of the Coaxing Effect in Fatigue of Metals," *Proc. ASTM*, v. 52, 1952.)

4.9 Statistical Nature of Fatigue Properties. Considerable scatter of results occurs in fatigue testing of many metals. In view of no conclusive proof that experimental factors contribute to the scatter, the conclusion has been reached by a number of investigators [5] that variability is an inherent characteristic of fatigue properties and that fatigue (progressive fracture) involving both nucleation and growth of cracks is a statistical phenomenon. This statistical variability affecting both fatigue life and endurance limit should be taken into account in planning and interpreting fatigue tests.

4.10 Endurance Ratios. The ratios of endurance limit to tensile strength, torsional strength, etc., are known as *endurance ratios*. Tests have led to the establishment of endurance ratios for many of the ferrous metals after conditioning by various workings and heat treatments, and for most of the commercially important non-ferrous metals and alloys. The endurance ratios for the worked ferrous metals vary considerably, but a fair value seems to be 0.5 of the ultimate tensile strength. For cast steel and cast iron this endurance ratio is about 0.4. For the non-ferrous metals this value varies between wide limits but is, as an average, lower.

4.11 Effects of Heat Treatment and Cold Working. The endurance limit of steel is increased by proper heat treatment. Annealing generally

---

[5] J. T. Ransom, and R. F. Mehl: "The Statistical Nature of the Fatigue Properties of SAE 4340 Steel Forgings." *Proc. ASTM*, v. 52, 1952.

decreases the endurance of steel. Cracks formed by repeated stresses cannot be healed by annealing. The endurance limit of metals is increased by cold working.

4.12 Effect of Surface Finishing of Steels. Professor P. G. Fluck [6] has reported that the fatigue life of specimens of two steels was greatly increased by reducing the size of circumferential scratches. A tenfold increase in the fatigue life of hardened and tempered SAE 3130 steel was accomplished by grinding and polishing the lathe-formed specimens. The fatigue life of the annealed SAE 1035 specimens was increased by a factor of 5. Longitudinal scratches, even though relatively large, did not greatly reduce the fatigue life of these two steels.

Shot peening of steels increases endurance limit. For example, shot peening of automotive rear-axle shafts of NE 8650 steel with decarburized surface gave about three times the endurance limit of axles not shot peened.[7]

4.13 Effect of Carbon Content of Steels. As the percentage of carbon is increased, the proportion of relatively coarse crystals of ferrite decreases, and the endurance of steels under repetitions of stress normally tends to increase until the carbon content approaches the eutectoid ratio. The relation of carbon content to the endurance of steels is very often masked, however, by the effect of other factors. Thus any heat treatment that tends to increase the size of crystals formed is very detrimental to endurance, and the presence of comparatively large amounts of phosphorus, manganese, etc., or the existence of internal stresses caused by the conditions of cooling, heat treatment, or mechanical working, may be factors whose influence outweighs that of carbon content.

4.14 Endurance Limits at Elevated and Low Temperatures. For temperatures up to about 300° C. (572° F.) a number of metals show an increase in endurance limit as compared with that developed at normal temperature. The fatigue strength of practically all metals drops off at temperatures above 500° C. (932° F.). Some alloy steels, as, for example, 12 per cent chromium steel, some tempered carbon steels, and some non-ferrous alloys such as aluminum alloys show a decrease in endurance limit for all elevated temperatures.

The endurance limit of certain carbon steels at low temperatures has been found by Professor O. H. Henry of the Polytechnic Institute of Brooklyn to be greater than at normal temperature.

4.15 Fatigue Strength of Welds. Henry and Amatulli found an endurance limit of 35,000 pounds per square inch for a joint of 0.18 per cent carbon steel welded with steel of an original endurance limit of 35,000 pounds

---

[6] P. G. Fluck: "The Influence of Surface Roughness on the Fatigue Life and Scatter of Test Results of Two Steels." *Proc. ASTM,* v. 51, 1951, pp. 584–592.

[7] O. J. Horger and C. H. Lipson: "Automotive Rear Axles and Means of Improving Their Fatigue Resistance." *ASTM, Tech. Publ.* 72, 1946.

per square inch. The welding was carefully executed by the electric-arc method using a coated electrode rod which gave off a non-oxidizing gas that protected the weld metal from oxidation. Additional tests at 300° C. (572° F.) on the same weld gave an increased endurance limit of 41,000 pounds per square inch, but fatigue resistance was reduced at 500° C. (932° F.). Somewhat lower fatigue strengths may be expected for field welds and particularly for welds made with plain electrodes.

4.16 Pitting Resistance. Closely related to fatigue resistance is resistance to pitting of surfaces in connection with surface wear of gears and rollers. Case-hardening treatments such as carburizing and nitriding markedly improve resistance to such pitting. For example, NE 8615 case-carburized steel, SAE 4615 eutectoid-carburized steel, SAE 4615 carbo-nitrided steel, and nickel-chrome-molybdenum-vanadium steel nitrided 100 hours at 524° C. (975° F.) have showed exceptional resistance to pitting under high stress conditions.[8]

Impact Testing

4.17 General. The methods of impact testing are described in Chapter 3. In this section the theory of impact tests and their use in selecting and inspecting metals are described.

4.18 Object of Impact Testing. The object of an impact test should be to determine whether a metal has resistance to failure due to brittleness under service conditions in a machine or structure. An impact test of metals should not be considered merely as a simulation of shock in service but should be used as a control test even for metals that will not be subjected to impact stresses in service.

4.19 Cold Brittleness. Failure due to brittleness often occurs when ferrous metals become cold brittle. *Cold brittleness* refers to the change from a ductile fracture having a "silky" texture to a fracture exhibiting a granular structure that takes place in ferrous metals; it is accompanied by a decrease in the work required to cause failure. Cold brittleness does not refer to any particular temperature range since it is a condition dependent upon state of stress, velocity of deformation of the specimen, size of specimen, influence of notches in the specimen, carbon content of the steel, heat treatment, and cold work, as well as temperature.

Most non-ferrous metals do not exhibit cold brittleness to the same degree as steel. This is probably due to the different space lattice of non-ferrous metals as illustrated by the face-centered cubic arrangement compared to the body-centered cubic structure of alpha iron. Tin and zinc, however,

---

[8] M. R. Gross: "Laboratory Evaluation of Materials for Marine Propulsion Gears." *Proc. ASTM,* v. 51, 1951, pp. 701–720.

show cold brittleness; this is probably associated with an allotropic change in the metal.

4.20 Type of Specimen. Impact tests are made both in flexure and in tension. The standard notched bars for the flexure type of test as used in the Charpy and Izod machines are illustrated in Figs. 3.5, 3.6, and 3.7. Unnotched bars are seldom used in flexure. In tension impact testing, both notched and unnotched specimens are employed. These tension impact specimens have not been standardized but are preferred to the flexure type by many investigators because errors in machining are usually smaller than for the flexure test bars. When errors are made in machining notches, the resultant energy values become more a measure of local structural conditions than of the true dynamic properties of the metal.

Kahn and Imbembo [9] recommend for unnotched tension-impact specimens that the gauge section be proportioned with a length to diameter ratio of between 3 and 5, preferably 4. Also, the diameter of the gauge section should not be made too large in proportion to the diameter of the shoulders in order to avoid plastic deformation of the shoulders. These investigators further suggest that the results be expressed in terms of unit energy absorption, that is the number of foot-pounds of energy absorbed per cubic inch of metal contained in the gauge section. The use of this unit permits comparison of tests made on specimens of appreciably different size.

4.21 Notched-Bar Impact Testing. The effect of notches in bars is to modify the stress distribution and to set up a highly localized concentration of stress at the root of the notch. The notch localizes the stress and accentuates the need for the metal to flow and distribute the stress. Steels with high yield strengths, which can not yield or flow over any appreciable volume at the tip of a notch or the point of an advancing crack to distribute the stress and prevent rapid advancement of the crack, are termed "notch sensitive." Thus hard steels with high yield strengths are more notch sensitive than mild steels with lower yield points.

However, notched bars of certain ductile steels break off sharply when tested by impact, exhibiting a brittle fracture of crystalline appearance, whereas in the ordinary tension test the same steels fail with the usual silky texture of the fracture characteristic of a ductile steel. Other ductile steels are tough and deform appreciably in the same notched-bar impact test. The type, sharpness, and depth of notches have a direct bearing on brittleness as indicated both by fractures and by impact resistance.

4.22 Effect of Temperature upon Brittleness. Temperature has a much more marked effect on the cold brittleness of steel than upon tensile properties. Brittleness as determined in notched-bar impact tests may change abruptly with temperature change. The temperature corresponding to this

---

[9] N. A. Kahn and E. A. Imbembo: "A Study of the Geometry of the Tension-Impact Specimen." *Proc. ASTM,* v. 46, 1946, pp. 1179–1197.

Service Requirements of Metals

abrupt change depends both upon the form and size of notch as well as upon the properties of the steel. Some steels show this sudden decrease in impact resistance at normal room temperature, which explains why it is often difficult to check results of energy absorbed on duplicate specimens. Tests are readily reproducible, however, in those ranges of temperature where no sudden changes in impact resistance occur.

If the steel is to be used at a low temperature, the impact tests should be performed at this temperature because a high impact value at normal temperature is no insurance of ductile behavior at lower temperatures.

Cold brittleness exhibited by tests on notched specimens of steel at subnormal temperatures may not be shown by tests on unnotched specimens. This phenomenon has been observed by Professor O. H. Henry in the testing of welded unnotched steel specimens in tensile impact.

4.23 Low-Temperature Notch-Impact Tests. Low-temperature notch-impact tests are employed to measure effects of exposure at elevated tem-

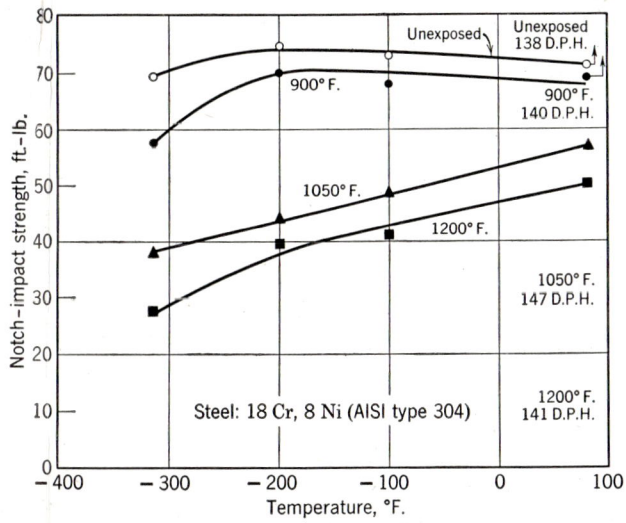

Fig. 4.3. Effect of 10,000-hr. exposure at 900, 1050, and 1200° F. on hardness and notch-impact strength at room and low temperatures for chrome-nickel steel. (U. S. Steel Co.)

peratures for long duration periods. Fig. 4.3 shows the results of tests at room and low temperatures on standard keyhole-notch Charpy impact specimens of austenitic chrome-nickel steel (AISI type 304; Cr, 18.53%; Ni, 10.72%) which has been exposed to high temperatures of 900, 1050, and 1200° F. for 10,000 hours. The unexposed specimens show approximately the same notch-impact strength at low temperatures as at room temperature.

The exposed specimens had somewhat lower notch-impact strengths at room temperature than the unexposed, the strength decreasing with increase of exposure temperature. With decreasing temperature of the notch-impact test, some further decreases in notch-impact strength occurred for the exposed specimens. There is, however, a striking difference between the above results for an austenitic steel and those obtained for a ferritic steel (Mo, 0.5%; C, 0.13%) as shown in Fig. 4.4. For the ferritic steel for decreasing temperatures of the notch-impact test, the values for the unexposed speci-

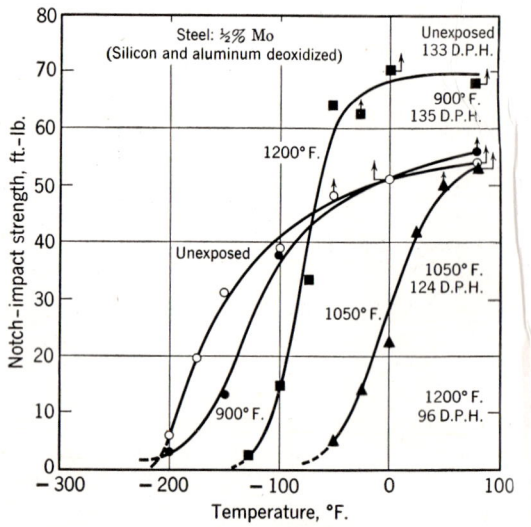

Fig. 4.4. Effect of 10,000-hr. exposure at 900, 1050, and 1200° F. on hardness and notch-impact strength at room and low temperatures for ½% Mo ferritic steel. (U. S. Steel Co.)

mens decreased, and the notch-impact strengths of the exposed specimens were significantly impaired.

Vickers diamond-pyramid-hardness (20-kilogram load) test values at room temperature are also indicated in Figs. 4.3 and 4.4.[10] Softening of the ferritic steel by exposure at high temperatures was due to decarburization; the hardness changes for the austenitic steel were of small magnitude.

4.24 Effect of Velocity of Deformation. The pendulum of the ordinary impact-testing machine strikes the specimen with a relatively low velocity of deformation. It has been found that increasing the velocity of deformation affects the energy absorbed at different temperatures. It has been shown that high-velocity tests are essential to reveal the true dynamic properties of metals. For example, it has been found by Jenks, Mann, and Haskell at the Watertown Arsenal that steels which are similar in

[10] G. V. Smith, W. B. Seens, H. S. Link, and P. R. Malenock: "Microstructural Instability of Steels for Elevated Temperature Service." *Proc. ASTM*, v. 51, 1951, pp 895–917.

impact properties at low velocities may behave differently at high velocities, some showing extreme brittleness.

4.25 Selection of Ferrous Metals. Steels from different mill heats of the same typical chemical composition and almost duplicate tensile-strength properties may possess strikingly different notched-bar impact values as shown in Table 4.1, which gives results reported by Riegel and Vaughn.

Table 4.1

STEEL QUALITY SHOWN BY IMPACT TESTS *

	Carbon, %	Manganese, %	Sulfur, %	Phosphorus, %	Silicon, %	Nickel, %
Mill heat A	0.46	0.61	0.031	0.016	0.20	3.57
Mill heat B	0.47	0.70	0.036	0.018	0.24	3.55

Physical Properties (Drawn at 425° F. for 1½ hr.)

	Rockwell Hardness, "C" scale	Tensile Strength, p.s.i.	Yield Point, p.s.i.	Elongation in 2 in., %	Reduction of Area, %	Charpy Impact, ft.-lb.	Tension Impact (Notched Specimen), ft.-lb.
Mill heat A (good)	52	278,000	214,000	11.5	44.3	18.0	62
Mill heat B (poor)	53	288,500	214,500	11.5	34.1	5.5	9

* Riegel and Vaughn: *Proc. ASTM*, v. 38, Part II, 1938.

These authors have reported that notched-bar impact testing made it possible to select between satisfactory and unsatisfactory steels for heavily stressed gears and pinions of tractors when tensile strength and chemical composition showed no appreciable differences. Freedom from failures of tractor parts in service closely paralleled the classification made on the basis of notched-bar impact tests. Riegel and Vaughn conclude that the notched-bar impact test is useful in evaluating the quality of ferrous metals, even though the material is not called upon to resist impact stresses in service, and that it is a discriminating proof of the quality of heat treatment of ferrous metals.

It is questionable whether, at this stage in the development of the impact test, selection between different classes of ferrous metals can properly be made on the basis of energy values obtained in impact testing. Furthermore, actual notched-bar impact results are of no direct value in designing.

The type of fracture obtained, whether crystalline or ductile, is considered to be of more importance than the actual value of energy absorbed in fracturing the specimen in foot-pounds.

Creep

4.26 Action of Creep. Creep is the slow flow which takes place in solid materials under sustained stress at elevated temperature. This phenomenon occurs in materials such as lead and zinc at normal temperatures under relatively low stresses, but most metals have to be at a high temperature before appreciable flow occurs. Creep may continue indefinitely under sustained stress tending to distort the material and may cause failure by rupture. Creep affects the entire body of the material under stress instead of producing a localized rupture, which occurs under repeated loading.

Four variables are involved in creep testing: stress, temperature, deformation, and time. Usually creep tests are conducted on tensile specimens under constant stress and temperature conditions so that the relations between deformation and time can be determined.

4.27 Creep of Steel. The influence of time on the creep characteristics of carbon steel at 538° C. (1000° F.) as determined by the Department of

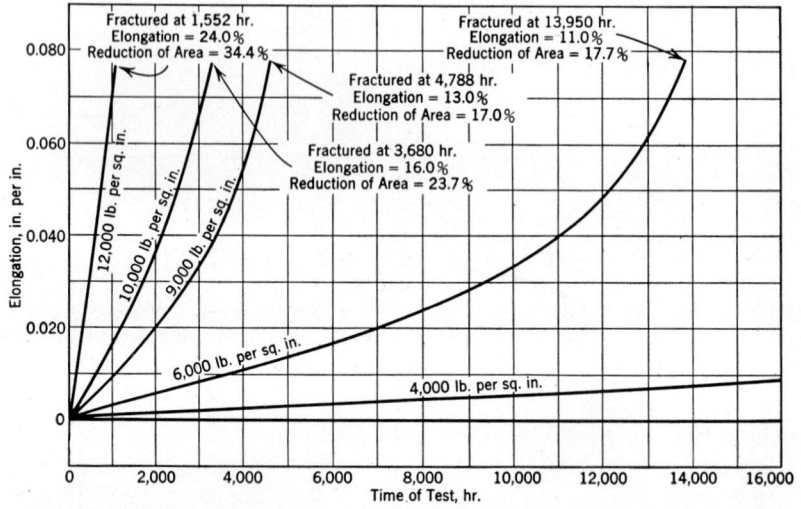

Fig. 4.5. Time-elongation curves at 538° C. (1000° F.) for annealed electric-furnace carbon steel. (*Courtesy* A. E. White, C. L. Clark, and R. L. Wilson.)

Engineering Research, University of Michigan, for different stresses, is shown in Fig. 4.5.[11] The slope of the time-elongation curve is a measure of the rate of flow. The rates of creep may be divided into three stages; the creep rate is rapidly decreasing in the first stage, is rather constant in the

[11] A. E. White, C. L. Clark, and R. L. Wilson: "Influence of Time at 1000° F. on the Characteristics of Carbon Steel." *Proc. ASTM,* v. 36, Part II, 1936.

second stage, and is rapidly increasing in the third stage. These stages are illustrated in Fig. 4.6. Increase in stress increases the elongations and the rates of creep. The curves show that the duration of each stage of creep tends to decrease with increasing stress but that fracture will not necessarily occur soon after the third stage of creep is entered. The specimen under 4000-pounds-per-square-inch stress was still in the second stage at 14,000 hours.

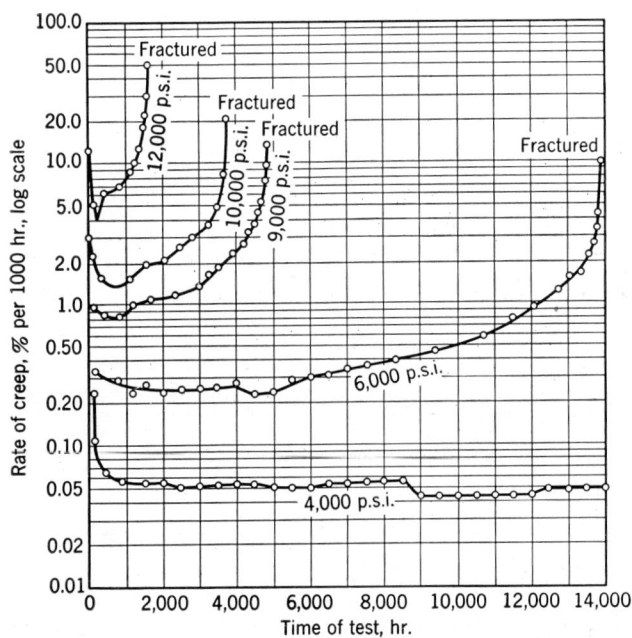

Fig. 4.6. Influence of time of test on the observed creep rate of annealed electric-furnace carbon steel at 538° C. (1000° F.). (Semilogarithmic coördinates.) (*Courtesy* A. E. White, C. L. Clark, and R. L. Wilson.)

4.28 Effect of High Temperature on Ductility. The reduced ductility of 0.15 per cent carbon steel subjected to a temperature of 538° C. (1000° F.) is shown in Table 4.2. This low ductility of carbon steel is explained by the formation of oxide between the grains at the surface of the specimens which is illustrated in the photomicrograph of Fig. 4.7. Progressive deterioration of the surface due to this intergranular oxidation with respect to time was noted.

A similar decrease in ductility of chromium-silicon-molybdenum alloy steel was not observed, however, as is shown by the results in Table 4.2. None of the fractured creep specimens possessed as high ductility as the short-time tension specimen, but the amount of decrease was not so pronounced as for carbon steel. Furthermore, the ductility of this alloy steel

Table 4.2

INFLUENCE OF TIME AT 538° C. (1000° F.) ON DUCTILITY OF STEELS

Type of Steel	Ultimate Tensile Stress, p.s.i.	Time for Rupture, hr.	Elongation, % in 2 in.	Reduction of Area, %
Annealed 0.15% C electric-furnace steel	Short-time tension specimen	—	42.5	76.9
	12,000	1,552	24.0	34.4
	10,000	3,680	16.0	23.7
	9,000	4,788	13.0	17.0
	6,000	13,950	11.0	17.7
Alloy steel ⎡Cr 1.25⎤ ⎢Si 0.72⎥ ⎢Mo 0.52⎥ ⎢C 0.07⎥ ⎣Mn 0.42⎦	Short-time tension specimen	—	32.5	78.6
	34,000	2,625	25.0	70.3
	30,000	3,250	21.0	67.9
	24,600	6,151	28.5	72.8

did not decrease progressively as the testing time was increased. This alloy steel did not show intergranular oxidation.

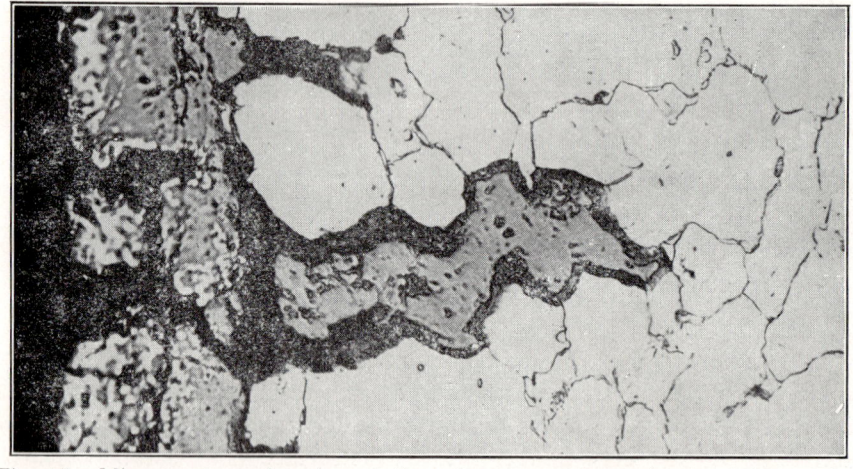

Fig. 4.7. Microstructure of surface section of creep specimen showing intergranular oxidation (1000×). (Annealed 0.15 C electric-furnace steel. 12,000 p.s.i., 1552 hr. for rupture.) (*Courtesy* C. L. Clark.)

4.29. Type of Fracture. Fracture at 538° C. (1000° F.) in the short-time tension test of 0.15 per cent carbon steel is transcrystalline as shown in Fig. 4.8*a*. Both the ferrite and pearlite grains are distorted and elongated parallel with the axis of the specimen. This indicates that considerable strain hardening occurred during the test with little if any recrystallization.

Service Requirements of Metals

The fracture of the carbon-steel specimen subjected to creep for 4788 hours at 538° C. (1000° F.) showed a lack of strain hardening as illustrated in Fig. 4.8b. The fracture is intercrystalline, and the grains are small and equiaxed and are thus free from strain. This type of fracture would be expected only when the temperature is above the lowest temperature of recrystallization of the metal.

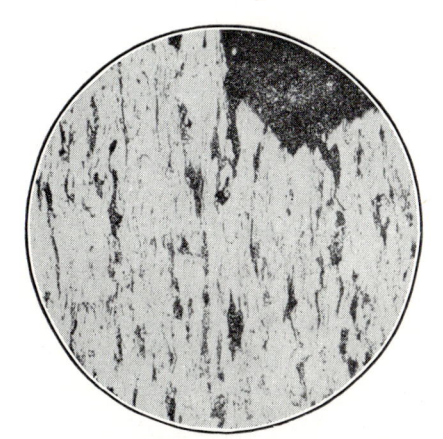

Fig. 4.8a. Short-time tension specimen. Note strain hardening and transcrystalline fracture.

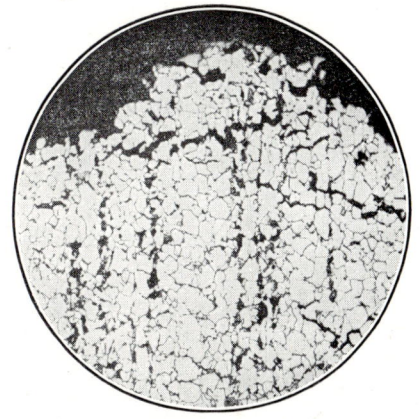

Fig. 4.8b. Creep specimen. 9000 p.s.i., 4788 hr. for rupture. Note intercrystalline fracture and lack of strain hardening.

Fig. 4.8. Microstructures of short-time tension and creep specimen fractures showing influence of time on type of fracture obtained on annealed 0.15% C electric-furnace steel (100×). (*Courtesy* C. L. Clark.)

4.30 Strain Hardening and Annealing in Creep. During the first stage of creep, the creep rate decreases rapidly owing to strain hardening. "Strain hardening" means elongating a metal beyond its yield point and then allowing it to rest which increases the yield point; subjecting the metal to extremely slow straining as in creep testing has the same effect. In the third stage, the rate of deformation increases as the time of exposure to the high temperature is increased, with a resulting cumulative effect. In the second stage, the two opposing forces of strain hardening and annealing are approximately balanced, and a period of time at a nearly constant creep rate results. Thus, the phenomenon of creep may be considered as the net effect of the two opposing forces of strain hardening and annealing.

4.31 Creep Limit. Creep limit is the stress allowable in a metal when subjected to a given temperature which will keep the deformation within a given limit in a certain number of years. Since it is not feasible to conduct creep tests at various temperatures and stresses over periods of a number of years on all metals before using them, the determination of a creep limit by extrapolation of data extending into the second stage is proposed by P. G. McVetty.[12] Referring to Fig. 4.6 it may be seen that the rate of creep in the second stage is practically constant for the stress of 4000 pounds per square inch. Since this creep curve is typical of creep curves for actual working stresses for many metals, the assumption that the creep curve in the second stage approaches a straight line is sufficiently accurate for many purposes, according to McVetty. He proposes the formula $\epsilon = \epsilon_0 + Vt$, where ϵ = final deformation in inches per inch, ϵ_0 = deformation at end of first stage in inches per inch, V = rate of creep during the second stage in inches per inch per hour, and t = time in second stage in hours. Tests conducted at different stresses for a given temperature can be thus extrapolated, and a series of curves can be drawn for the benefit of designers so that the creep limit corresponding to a maximum deformation for an expected service life under a certain temperature condition can be readily found.

4.32 Creep under Combined Stresses. In addition to investigations of creep-time relations under conditions of simple stress, there have been experimental investigations of creep properties of materials subjected to combined stresses. Marin [13] and associates have subjected aluminum thin-walled tubular specimens of circular cross-section to combinations of axial tension and torsion. The creep rates for various principal stresses were found to be in approximate agreement with values predicted theoretically using simple tension creep-test results.

Stress Rupture of High-Temperature Metals

4.33 General. Developments in jet propulsion and aircraft gas turbines have focussed attention on the manufacture of metals to withstand stresses at high temperatures up to 982° C. (1800° F.). Laboratory testing procedures at high temperatures have been formulated and have proven to be reliable indications of the performance of metals, serving to eliminate many time-consuming engine tests. In determining the life of any alloy under continued high-temperature loading, the property of greatest significance is the stress to cause rupture at given time and temperature (called *stress rupture*).

In the operation of jet engines and aircraft gas turbines, however, severe localized overheating or overstressing may occur for short durations. For example, for a jet engine at idling speed, a blast of gas at 410° F. roars out at about 700 feet per second velocity; at military power, the temperature

---

[12] P. G. McVetty: "The Interpretation of Creep Tests." *Proc. ASTM*, v. 34, Part II, 1934, pp. 105–122. "Interpretation of Creep Test Data." *Proc. ASTM*, v. 43, 1943, pp. 707–734.

[13] J. Marin, J. H. Faupel, and L. W. Hu: Combined Tension-Torsion Creep-Time Relations for Aluminum Alloy 2S-O, *Proc. ASTM*, v. 50, 1950, pp. 1054–1072.

Service Requirements of Metals

increases to 770° F. and the velocity to 1350 feet per second; and, when the pilot cuts in the afterburner, 1800° F. temperatures with 1830 feet per second velocities are common. Designs must provide for short-time strengths of alloys at temperatures somewhat higher than expected operating levels as well as sufficient stress rupture strengths at the anticipated operating temperature level. Since sheet-metal structural parts are required in the combustion and exhaust systems and particularly in the reheat system and hollow fabricated buckets of gas turbines where their performance may be the limiting factor in service life of an engine, data are given in this section for high-temperature sheet metals rather than for bar stock.

4.34 Stress Rupture. Stress rupture tests at high temperature are conducted in the same manner as creep tests, but higher loads are placed on

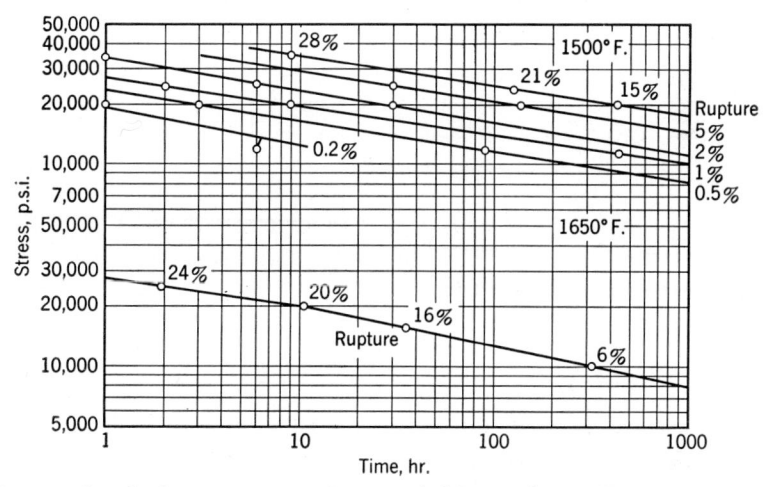

Fig. 4.9. Standard rupture curves for annealed L 605 sheet. (Preston; *Courtesy* ASTM.)

the specimen to cause rupture; creep data are also obtained. A standard rupture curve obtained by the General Electric Company [14] for annealed L 605 sheet is given in Fig. 4.9. L 605 sheet is a cobalt-base alloy that was hot rolled, solution annealed at 2200° F. for 10 minutes, air cooled, and pickled. Log stress is plotted versus log time. For a temperature of 1500° F. the top curve is the rupture curve and the others are creep curves for different percentages of elongation. Specimens were stressed at 35,000, 25,000, 20,000, and 12,000 pounds per square inch. Plotted points indicate time required to produce elongations of 0.2, 0.5, 1, 2, and 5 per cent on the specimens (creep data) as well as the time to produce rupture. The percentage

[14] D. Preston: "Exploratory Investigation of High-Temperature Sheet Materials, Symposium on Strength and Ductility of Metals." *ASTM Special Tech. Publ.* 128, 1952.

total elongations at failure are given adjacent to the rupture points. A similar rupture curve is shown for a temperature of 1650° F.

From the data given in Fig. 4.9, a stress-to-rupture versus temperature curve for a duration of 100 hours can be plotted as shown in Fig. 4.10 for

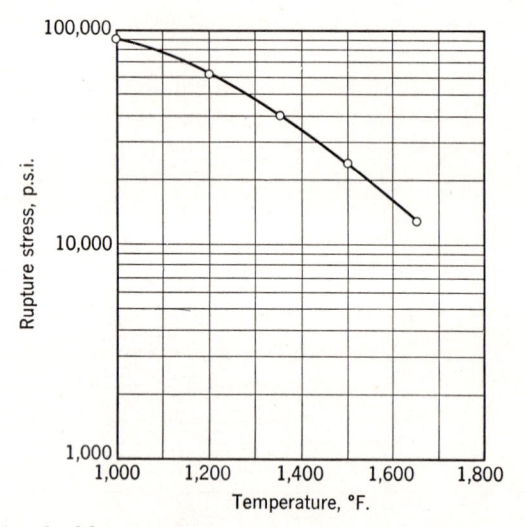

Fig. 4.10. One-hundred-hour rupture stress versus temperature curve for annealed L 605 sheet. (Preston.)

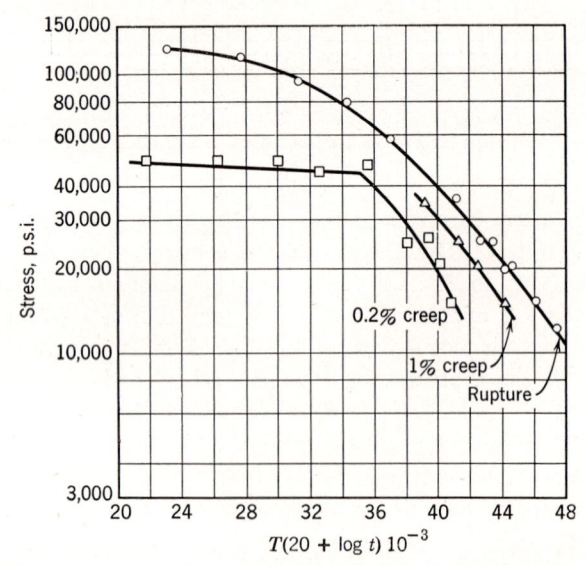

Fig. 4.11. Master rupture curve for annealed L 605 sheet. (Preston; *Courtesy* ASTM.)

L 605 sheet. Similar rupture curves can be drawn for other duration times. Creep curves can also be plotted in a similar manner. Comparisons between different alloys can be made by means of such diagrams, but a better over-all picture of rupture and creep properties of different alloys can be obtained by

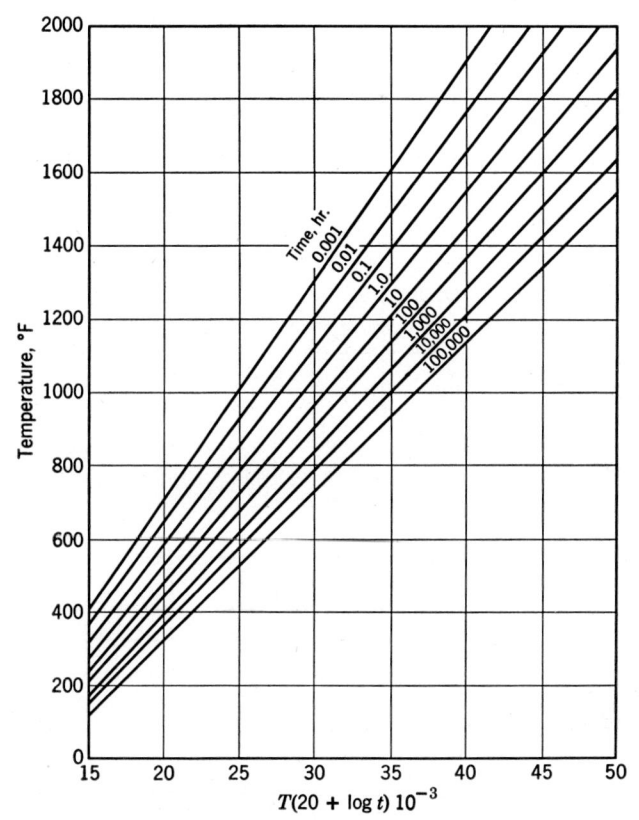

Fig. 4.12. Plot relating the parameter $T\,(20 + \log t)\,10^{-3}$ to various time temperature combinations. (Miller and Larson.)

preparing master rupture curves. Figure 4.11 is the master rupture curve for L 605 sheet on which rupture and creep points are plotted by means of a time-temperature parameter. This parameter is $T\,(20 + \log t)\,10^{-3}$ in which T = temperature in degrees absolute, and t = time in hours.[15] (Note: 0° F. corresponds to plus 460 degrees absolute.) Figure 4.12 can be utilized to convert time and temperature to parameter reading. Figures 4.13 and 4.14 are master rupture curves for two other alloys having good high-tem-

[15] F. R. Larson and J. Miller: "A Time-Temperature Relationship for Rupture and Creep Stresses." *Am. Soc. Mech. Engrs.*, meeting, Nov., 1951.

62   Materials of Construction

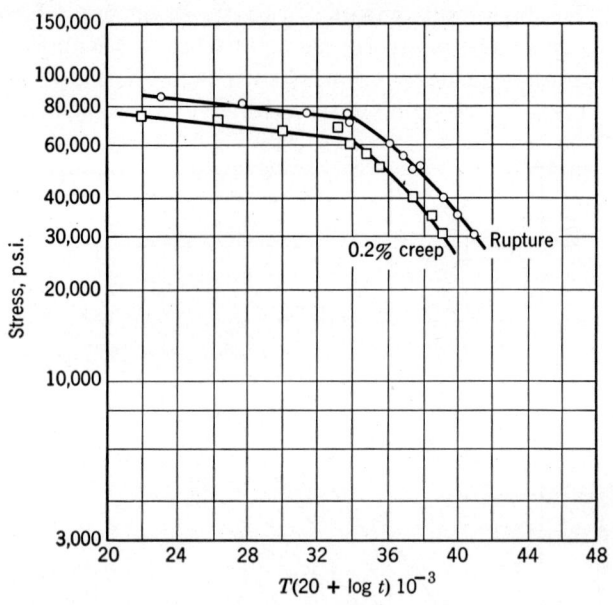

Fig. 4.13. Master rupture curve for hot cold-rolled HS No. 88 sheet. (Preston; *Courtesy* ASTM.)

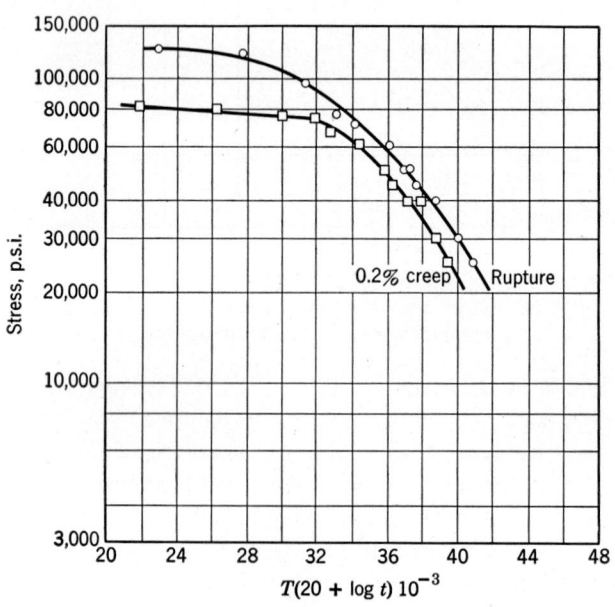

Fig. 4.14. Master rupture curve for Discaloy 24 sheet (aged). (Preston; *Courtesy* ASTM.)

Service Requirements of Metals

perature properties. HS No. 88 alloy is an iron-base alloy that obtains its high-temperature properties from strain hardening. Discaloy 24 is an iron-base alloy which secures its high-temperature properties from precipitation hardening. Table 4.3 gives the chemical composition of these three alloys,

Table 4.3

CHEMICAL COMPOSITIONS OF SHEET ALLOYS *

Alloy	C	Cr	Ni	Mo	Co	Cb	Ti	Si	S	P	Mn	W	Fe	Others
L-605	0.08	21.11	10.84	—	bal.	—	—	0.61	0.006	0.010	1.64	15.54	1.60	N_2 = 0.03
HS No. 88	0.07	12.62	15.04	2.42	—	—	0.50	0.52	0.006	0.013	1.40	0.84	bal.	B = 0.14
Discaloy 24	0.036	13.50	26.20	3.91	—	—	1.61	1.00	—	—	1.38	—	bal.	Al = 0.11

* Courtesy ASTM

and Table 4.4 records the results of short-time mechanical tests at various temperatures up to 1800° F.

Table 4.4

EFFECT OF TEMPERATURE ON MECHANICAL PROPERTIES OF SHEET ALLOYS *

Effect of Temperature on Tensile Strength

Alloy	Room	750° F.	1000° F.	1200° F.	1350° F.	1500° F.	1650° F.	1800° F
L-605	160,700	138,000	130,550	94,000	83,750	55,250	34,200	29,175
HS No. 88	101,750	87,450	82,725	71,850	59,700	45,800	33,650	17,200
Discaloy 24	142,500	125,200	119,350	95,800	71,300	33,030	18,800	11,175

Effect of Temperature on Elongation

Alloy	Room	750° F.	1000° F.	1200° F.	1350° F.	1500° F.	1650° F.	1800° F.
L-605	47.0	47.0	40.0	29.0	11.0	16.0	30.0	37.0
HS No. 88	23.0	14.5	14.0	15.5	18.0	16.0	26.0	26.5
Discaloy 24	22.5	17.0	14.5	15.0	17.5	56.0	84.5	81.5

Effect of Temperature on 0.0002 In. per In. Yield Strength

Alloy	Room	750° F.	1000° F.	1200° F.	1350° F.	1500° F.	1650° F.	1800° F.
L-605	60,950	47,450	51,900	53,060	48,250	39,800	27,600	25,775
HS No. 88	78,275	62,000	58,600	50,600	44,425	34,625	31,550	15,750
Discaloy 24	75,625	67,950	66,000	65,250	59,750	26,400	17,400	10,225

Effect of Temperature on 0.002 In. per In. Yield Strength

Alloy	Room	750° F.	1000° F.	1200° F.	1350° F.	1500° F.	1650° F.	1800° F.
L-605	85,800	55,900	53,900	54,900	51,300	44,850	31,900	27,475
HS No. 88	90,200	74,600	70,900	67,350	56,200	43,750	33,350	17,100
Discaloy 24	91,200	82,150	79,700	77,500	67,350	30,200	18,275	10,825

* Courtesy ASTM.

4.35 Equicohesive Strength. The "hot strength" of high-temperature alloys can be explained, at least in part, by reference to the term "equicohesive strength." Crystalline grains have different strengths than grain boundaries. At ordinary temperatures, the grain boundary strength exceeds grain strength, but for high temperatures this relationship is reversed. This is illustrated in Fig. 4.15. The point where the grain boundary and grain strengths are equal is called the "equicohesive strength." The dashed line is a representation of the strength of the combined structure of grains and grain boundaries. The equicohesive temperature corresponds to the lowest temperature of recrystallization which is considered to be the critical temperature insofar as "hot strength" of an alloy is concerned. At temperatures above the equicohesive point, continuous creep of measurable magnitude

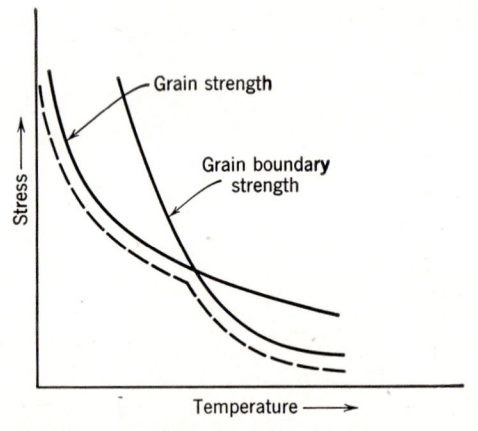

Fig. 4.15. Equicohesive strength (variable temperature).

occurs even under small applications of stress, whereas, at temperatures below this point, alloys exhibit less creep for the same stress.

HS No. 88 alloy is austenitic in structure; its good high-temperature strength may be explained on the basis that austenite has a high equicohesive point.

4.36 Effect of Periodic Overstressing on Creep and Creep Rupture. In operating aircraft gas turbines, occasional demands for very high accelera-

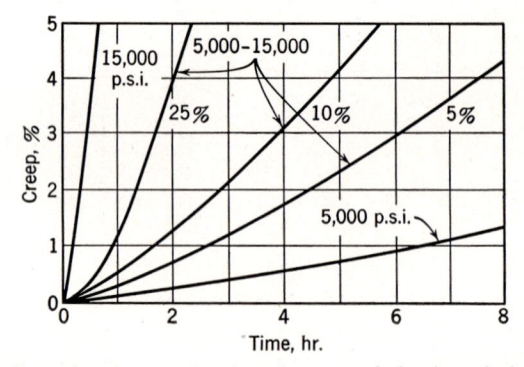

Fig. 4.16. Time-elongation curves showing the creep behavior of chrome-nickel Type 347 stainless steel at 1500° F. for 5, 10, and 25% times of overstressing. (Overstress to Normal Stress Ratio = 3.) (Guarnieri and Yerkovich; *Courtesy* ASTM.)

tion cause abnormal stressing of parts at high temperatures. Such overstressing has been shown by laboratory experiments to be quite detrimental to creep rates and creep-rupture life of typical high-temperature alloys. For example, the creep-time curves in Fig. 4.16 show the results of overstress-

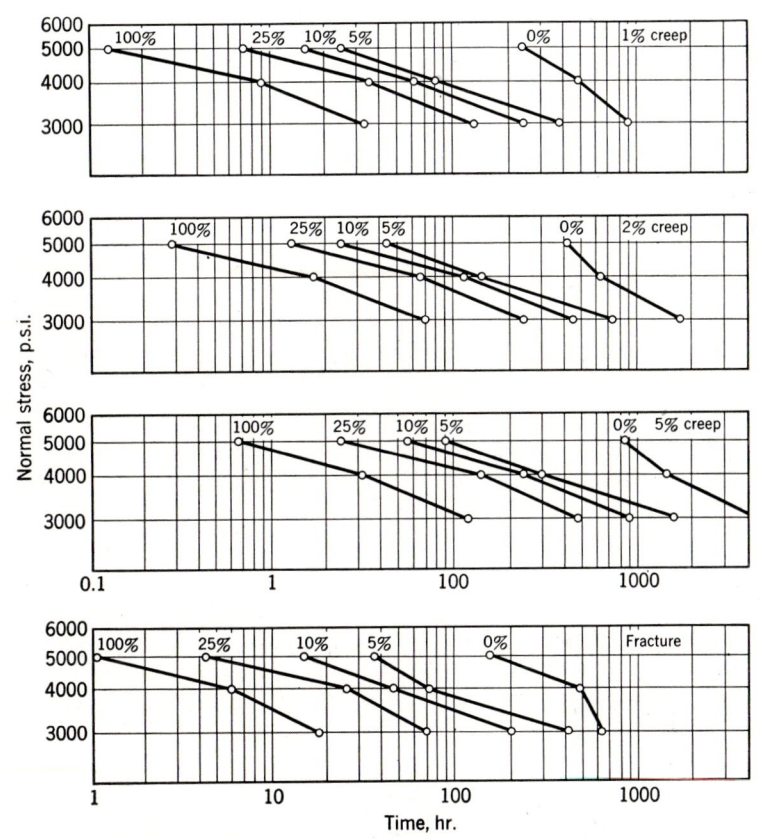

Fig. 4.17. Type 347 stainless steel normal stress versus time design curves for overstress to normal stress ratio of 3.0, overstressed 5, 10, and 25% of the time at 1500° F. (The 0 and 100% lines represent the static stress-time curves for the normal and overload stresses, respectively.) (Guarnieri and Yerkovich; *Courtesy* ASTM.)

ing chrome-nickel austenitic stainless steel (AISI type 347: Cr, 17.60%; Ni, 11.03%; Cb, 0.77%) on creep at 1500° F.[16] The overstress of 15,000 pounds per square inch applied only 5 per cent of the time considerably increased the creep rate. A high percentage of the total creep occurred during the overstressing periods. For application of this overstress 25 per cent of the time, the creep rate approached that obtained by overstress

[16] G. J. Guarnieri and L. A. Yerkovich: "The Influence of Periodic Overstressing on the Creep Properties of Several Heat Resistant Alloys." *Proc. ASTM*, v. 52, 1952.

for 100 per cent of the time. For a given ratio of overload time to normal load time, the creep characteristics are not critically affected by various timing patterns of overload application. Figure 4.17 indicates the effect of overstressing on creep and rupture life of chrome-nickel type 347 steel at 1500° F.; these curves may be employed in designing.

4.37 Notched-Bar Creep-Rupture Tests. In gas turbines there are structural members such as turbine rotors and bolts in which particularly severe stress concentrations occur owing to abrupt changes in section, slots, and sharp threads. The selection of materials for such structural members for high-temperature service is related to the subject of "notch sensitivity." See Art. 4.21. Two research projects on notched-bar creep-rupture testing are referred to in this article. First, tests at 1000° F. and 1200° F. on the heat-resistant alloy Discaloy whose hardness was increased by additions of small percentages of titanium as a hardener. These specimens had a 60-degree V notch with reduced section equal to one-half the full bar area. The ratio of the radius of curvature at the base of the notch to the full bar diameter was 0.020, and the stress concentration factor for these proportions was 3.9. Two or three specimens were tested in creep rupture at different stresses until a rupture time of 100 hours had been bracketed; then on a log-log plot of stress versus rupture time the 100-hour rupture stress was obtained by interpolation. These 100-hour rupture strengths were plotted against diamond pyramid hardness as is illustrated in Fig. 4.18.[17] Titanium contents corresponding to the specimens of different hardness are marked on the abscissa. The percentage elongation measured by the machine at rupture is marked beside each point. Notched-bar specimens showed a maximum in rupture strength at a much lower hardness than did the plain-bar specimens. For 1200° F. notched-bar strength is greater than plain-bar strength at hardness values less than 315 (associated with a creep-rupture ductility greater than 5 per cent elongation). Notched-bar strength decreases rapidly as hardness is increased above that at the maximum rupture strength.

In a second project,[18] notched-bar creep-rupture tests were conducted on a Cr-Mo-V alloy (Timken "17-22A" S) at temperatures from 900 to 1200° F. and compared to plain-bar rupture tests up to 1000 hours. These notched-bar specimens had a 60-degree V notch with reduced section equal to 40 per cent of the full bar area. The ratio of notch to unnotch rupture-strength varied a great deal for both temperature and time. More research on notch-bar creep-rupture testing is needed. The weakening effect caused by notches

[17] F. C. Hull, E. K. Hann, and H. Scott: "Effect of a Notch and of Hardness on the Rupture Strength of 'Discaloy,' Symposium on Strength and Ductility of Metals." *ASTM Special Tech. Publ.* **128**, 1953.

[18] G. Sachs and W. F. Brown, Jr.: "A Survey of Embrittlement and Notch Sensitivity of Heat-Resisting Steels, Symposium on Strength and Ductility of Metals." *ASTM Special Tech. Publ.* **128**, 1953.

in creep loading is believed to be related to the phenomenon of embrittlement of steels after heating for long periods of time.

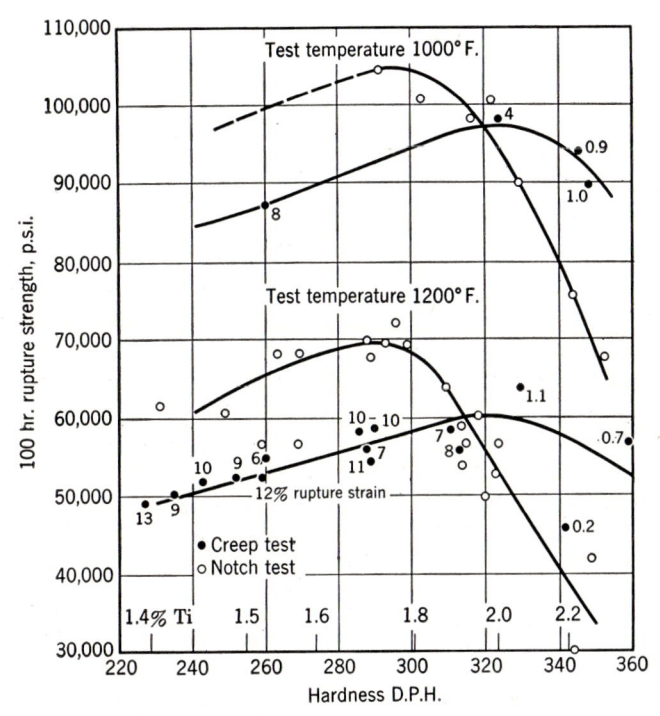

Fig. 4.18. One-hundred-hour rupture strength of Discaloy solution treated 1 hr. at 1950° F. aged 20 hr. at 1350° F. and 20 hr. at 1200° F. (Hull, Hann, and Scott; *Courtesy* ASTM.)

Rate of Strain Tests

4.38 Effect of Rate of Strain on Flow Stress of High-Temperature Alloys. In the gas turbine there are stationary and rotating parts which are subjected to great variations in stress and impact over a range of high temperatures. For design purposes it is necessary to know the maximum flow stress and strain the metal can withstand when deformed at different rates at high temperatures. Flow stress is a stress under which the material will deform plastically; the term customarily refers to the stress corresponding to the maximum load. In creep tests the flow stress is constant. Figure 4.19 gives results of rate of strain tests conducted by the Westinghouse Electric Corporation [19] for Inconel (nickel-chromium alloy)

[19] M. J. Manjoine: "Effect of Rate of Strain on the Flow Stress of Gas Turbine Alloys at 1200 and 1500° F." *Proc. ASTM*, v. 50, 1950, pp. 931-950.

68   Materials of Construction

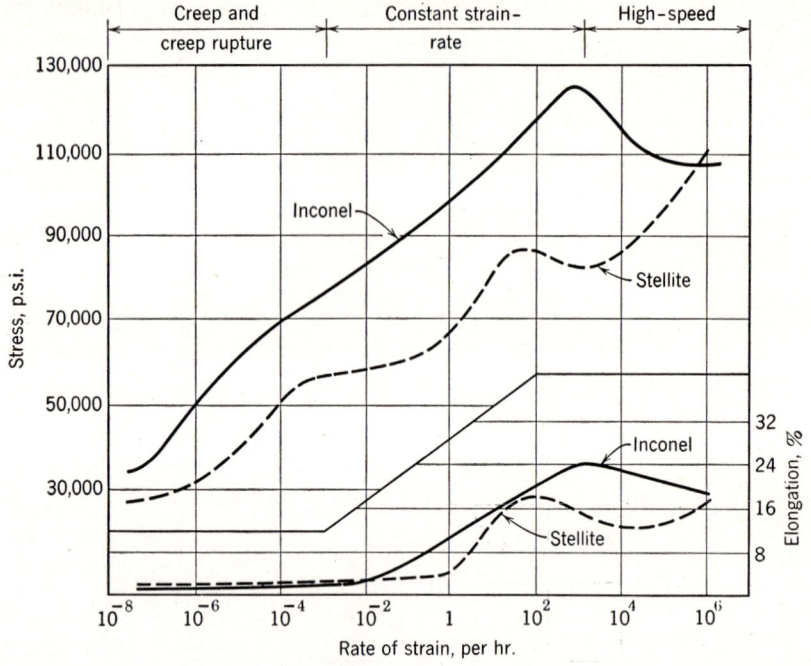

Fig. 4.19. Flow stress versus strain-rate of wrought age-hardening Inconel and cast Stellite at 1200° F. (Manjoine; *Courtesy* ASTM.)

and Stellite (cobalt-base alloy). Stresses are shown for strain rates per hour ranging from 6.0×10^{-8} to 7.2×10^5. The strength of Inconel in general increases with rate of strain, reaching a peak at about 10^3 per hour and then dropping off; the precision-cast Stellite has lower strength than the wrought Inconel, but the curve has the same general shape. The solution treatment of Inconel was 1975° F., 6 hours, water quenched; its aging treatment was 1300° F., 16 hours, air cooled. Stellite was not heat treated.

The high-speed (impact) tests were made on a tension machine equipped with a recording oscillogram and a flywheel to store the energy necessary to pull a specimen to rupture in about 1 millisecond. An oscillogram of high-speed stress-elongation curves at a strain rate of 200 per second or 7.2×10^5 per hour for Stellite is reproduced in Fig. 4.20. This curve indicates that the load increases from the yield strength to fracture; from this it is concluded that the alloy strain-hardens and stretches uniformly throughout the test. The intermediate range of strain rates were obtained

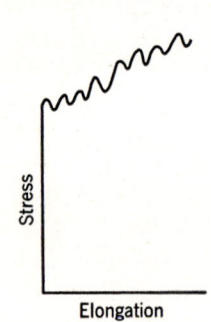

Fig. 4.20. Oscillogram of high-speed load-elongation test of Stellite No. 23 at strain-rate of 7.2×10^5 per hr. (Manjoine; *Courtesy* ASTM.)

Service Requirements of Metals

by means of a screw-driven constant strain-rate tension machine with autographic recording equipment. Creep-testing machines were employed for the low range of strain rates. Table 4.5 records the creep and creep-rupture test data.

Table 4.5

CREEP AND CREEP RUPTURE TEST DATA AT 1200° F. (Manjoine)*

Stress p.s.i.	Total Strain Intercept, %	Creep Rate, per hr.	Transition Point † Time, hr.	Transition Point † Total Strain, %	Rupture Time, hr.	Rupture Total Strain, %	Diamond Pyramid Hardness, 100 kg., No Stress Original	Diamond Pyramid Hardness, 100 kg., No Stress Final	Reduction of Area, %
Wrought Inconel (Ni, 74%; Cr, 14%; Ti, 2.5%)									
63,000	0.4	1.2×10^{-5}	88	0.51	89	2.3	—	308	5
55,000	—	—	—	—	310	1.23	—	328	5
50,000	—	—	—	—	650	1.20	—	350	1
45,000	0.26	4.3×10^{-7}	910	0.30	915	0.30	284	340	—
40,000	—	1.5×10^{-7}	—	—	540	—	286	329	—
40,000	0.24	2.6×10^{-7}	—	—	1,168	0.27	301	353	1.8
35,000	0.145	6.0×10^{-8}	1,340 ‡	0.16	1,455 ‡	0.24	298	336	—
Cast Stellite No. 23 (Co, 66%; Cr, 28%; W, 5.6%)									
50,000	1.77	8.0×10^{-5}	157	3.05	186	3.66	336	351	8.3
40,000	0.86	1.1×10^{-5}	1,150	2.07	1,475	2.76	350	434	4.6
31,500	0.28	7×10^{-7}	1,600 §	0.35 §	—	—	347	462	0.5

* *Courtesy* ASTM.
† Transition from second to third stage of creep where creep rate has increased 10% over the minimum rate.
‡ Broke at fillet.
§ Test was interrupted before this point was reached.

4.39 Elongation Curves. The per cent elongation versus strain-rate curves at the bottom of Fig. 4.19 have a similar pattern to the stress curves. Inconel and Stellite have good ductility at the higher values of strain rate but are somewhat brittle when deformed at the low rates of strain.

4.40 Characteristic Strain-Rate Curve. The stress versus strain-rate curves in Fig. 4.19 for Inconel and Stellite conform to the characteristic flow-stress versus strain-rate curve illustrated in Fig. 4.21. The characteristic curve is divided into five zones. In zone 5 for extremely high strain rates, the stress increases nearly as a power function of the log of strain rate. In zone 4, the dotted line for non-aging or pure metals such as copper and aluminum is fairly uniform, but the solid line for age-hardening alloys has a peak in the curve; an increase in strength occurs as the strain rate is decreased until the "aging" is complete, and then, as the strain rate is further decreased, overaging takes place and the strength decreases. In zone 3, the stress is practically linear with respect to the log of creep rate. In zone 2, metallurgical changes take place causing instability with an accompanying loss of strength when the strain rate is decreased. The mechanism of flow

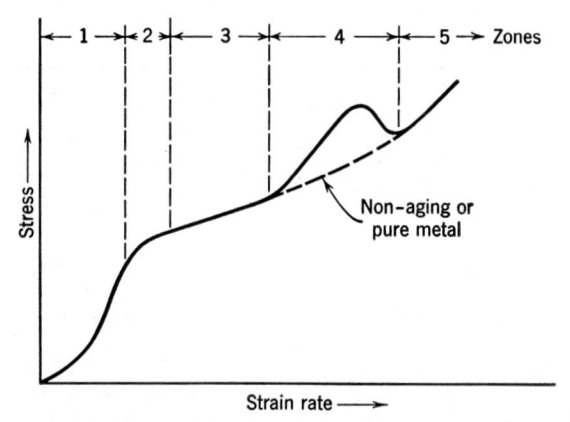

Fig. 4.21. Characteristic flow-stress curve for metals. (Manjoine; *Courtesy* ASTM.)

may also change in this zone as well as the relative strength of the grains and grain boundaries. This can be explained on the basis of "equicohesive strength" as illustrated in Fig. 4.22 where stress is plotted against strain

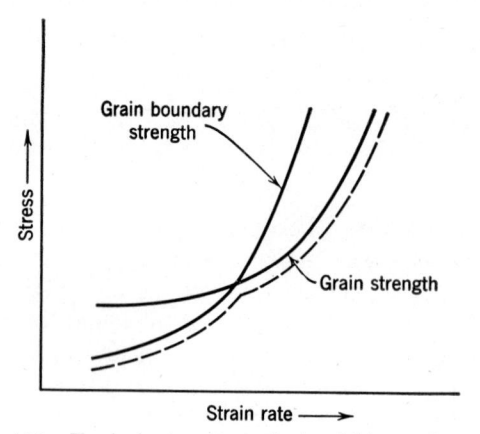

Fig. 4.22. Equicohesive strength (variable strain rate).

rate. (These curves are similar to those of Fig. 4.15 in which stress is plotted versus temperature.) The strengths of the grains and grain boundaries are given by the solid curves and their combined strength by the dashed curve. There is a reversed position of grain strength and grain boundary strength at low strain rates as compared to high strain rates. The equicohesive point lies in zone 2. The similarity between the curve in Fig. 4.21 and the dashed curve of Fig. 4.22 should be noted. In zone 1 for extremely low rates of strain, the stress decreases further with decreasing strain rate. For many materials, the stress in zone 1 can be expressed as a hyperbolic function of the rate of strain.[20] In zone 4, Inconel and Stellite curves conform to the solid line for age-hardening alloys. Mild carbon steel at 400° C. (752° F.) also conforms to the characteristic curve with the age-hardening feature in zone 4 (called "blue brittleness").

Relative superiority of individual wrought and cast alloys at a given high temperature depends on the rate of strain at which they are compared since the curves for different alloys may cross several times.

Relaxation Test

4.41 Relaxation Test. The relaxation test at high temperature is a modification of the creep test. It might be termed a flow-rate test at

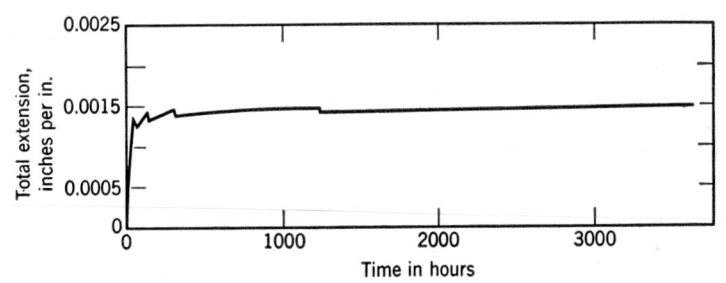

Fig. 4.23. "Step-down" type of relaxation curve for 0.35 C steel at 850° F. (E. L. Robinson.)

constant extension as distinguished from the creep test which is conducted under constant stress. Relaxation tests at high temperature give direct information on the permanent tightness of *bolted joints*. Relaxation tests may be conducted in the same furnaces and with the same testing equipment as for creep tests; however, automatic relaxation-testing machines have been built which maintain the gauge length of the test specimen at a constant extension by automatically decreasing the load. In conducting the relaxation test with equipment for creep tests, a large load is first applied producing creep at a rapid rate; care is taken not to exceed a given total extension (elastic plus plastic). The loading is then reduced, causing an immediate reduction in elastic extension, and further creep takes place but at a slower rate. The total load is reduced each time the total extension

[20] A. Nadai and P. G. McVetty: "Hyperbolic-Sine Chart for Estimating Working Stresses of Alloys at Elevated Temperatures." *Proc. ASTM*, v. 43, 1943, pp. 735–748.

reaches the specified limit, and further creep readings are obtained. The slower creep rates resulting from reduction of loadings are caused at least partly by progressive strengthening of the metal by strain hardening. Plotting total extension versus time in hours gives a "step-down" type of curve as shown in Fig. 4.23; [21] comparison may be made with creep curves for constant stress in Fig. 4.5.

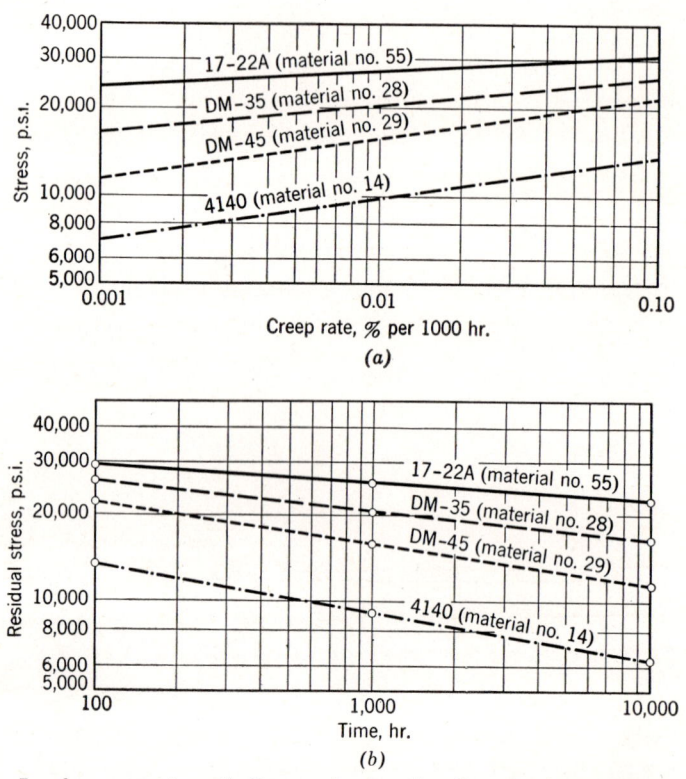

Fig. 4.24. Log-log creep strength lines and relaxation lines for four different materials at 482° C. (900° F.). (University of Michigan; *Courtesy* ASTM.)

Figure 4.24a gives the log-log plot of relaxation test results of stress versus creep rate for four steels. (The composition and mechanical properties of these steels are given in Tables 4.6 and 4.7.) These lines are straight over a long range of stresses and may be extrapolated for not to exceed ten times the duration of the tests.

4.42 Residual Stress in Bolts. Application of the results of the relaxation test is made in the design of bolts in flanges for high-temperature service. The high initial loading of the test specimen corresponds to the

[21] E. L. Robinson: "A Relaxation Test on 0.35 C. Steel K20." *Trans. Am. Soc. Mech. Engrs.*, v. 59, 1937, pp. 451–452.

Table 4.6

CHEMICAL COMPOSITION AND HEAT TREATMENT OF LOW-ALLOY BOLTING STEELS FOR HIGH-TEMPERATURE SERVICE
(University of Michigan) *

No.	Material (Timken)	C	Mn	Si	Cr	Mo	P	S	Other
14	SAE 4140 (Cr-Mo)	0.40	0.70	0.21	0.97	0.19	0.016	0.022	Ni-0.15
29	DM-45 (Cr-Mo)	0.45	0.57	0.70	1.26	0.57	0.018	0.018	
28	DM-35 (Cr-Mo)	0.35	0.47	0.75	1.20	0.57	0.001	0.016	
55	17-22A (Cr-Mo-V)	0.29	0.46	0.75	1.27	0.54	—	—	V-0.24

No.	Heat Treatment
14	1550° F. oil quench, drawn 1100° F. to 269 BHN
29	1650° F. oil quench, drawn 1250° F. to 285 BHN
28	1650° F. oil quench, drawn 1250° F. to 269 BHN (7-8 grain)
55	Normalized 1725° F., drawn 1225° F., 6 hr. to 285 BHN

* *Courtesy* ASTM.

initial tightening of a bolt; care should be taken not to exceed a specified total extension. As time proceeds, bolts in an unyielding flange stretch or "relax," and their initial stress is decreased by relaxation to a "residual" stress. This residual stress may be calculated by the following equation:

$$(n - 1)tr_o ES^{(n-1)} = bS_o^n$$

where n = the percentage increase in creep rate per percentage increase in stress. This is the slope (reciprocal) of the line on the log-log plot of stress versus rate of creep.

S = the residual stress in pounds per square inch after an elapsed time t in hours.

S_o = the creep stress in pounds per square inch for a nominal creep rate r_o.

E = the modulus of elasticity in pounds per square inch.

b = the ratio of the total elasticity to that of the bar or bolt which is subject to creep.

Table 4.7
MECHANICAL PROPERTIES OF LOW-ALLOY BOLTING STEELS FOR HIGH-TEMPERATURE SERVICE (University of Michigan) *

Room Temperature

No.	Tensile Strength, p.s.i.	Proportional Limit, p.s.i.	Elongation in 2 in., %	Reduction of Area, %
14	131,000	105,000	22.0	54.1
29	139,500	100,000	22.0	54.1
28	128,250	100,000	24.0	65.4
55	133,500	110,000	17.5	58.2

Temperature of 900° F.

No.	Initial Strain, in. per in.	Initial Stress, p.s.i.	Modulus of Elasticity, p.s.i. $\times 10^{-6}$	n
14	0.00158	37,690	25.3	6.97
29	0.00158	38,540	22.0	7.86
28	0.00173	42,270	23.8	10.5
55	0.00176	40,850	25.0	18.07

* *Courtesy* ASTM.

Figure 4.24b shows the log-log plot of residual stress versus time for the same steels given in Fig. 4.24a. These curves are straight lines whose slope is $(n - 1)$. By these lines the strength characteristics of each metal may be visualized. The residual stress for a given duration time is useful in comparing bolting materials for high-temperature service. An extensive tabulation of data of relaxation tests of different metals is given in the final report of the Subcommittee for Project No. 16 on High-Temperature Bolting Materials, *Proc. ASTM*, v. 48, 1948, pp. 214–238.

Comparisons by means of residual stresses are not valid unless the metals have been subjected to approximately the same total strain. Materials elongated to greater total extension will exhibit a greater creep rate for a given stress on the specimen; this in turn will by computation give greater residual stresses for a given time. The effect of different initial stresses (causing different total strains) on creep strength and residual stress is illustrated in Fig. 4.25. Tests are usually run at 0.1 to 0.2 per cent limiting strain which corresponds to initial stresses of 20,000 to 60,000 pounds per square inch, depending upon modulus-of-elasticity values. If the specimen is pulled out to a greater limiting strain than this, the resulting residual stress will be higher than that which will probably develop in service unless the bolt is tightened more than desirable. If an initial stress of only 10,000 pounds per square inch is applied, the residual stress may be so low that the capabilities of the metal will not be shown; by analogy, this corresponds to not tightening up the bolt enough to stress it up to its capability. Therefore, residual stresses of different bolting materials should be compared on the basis of the same total extension in the relaxation tests.

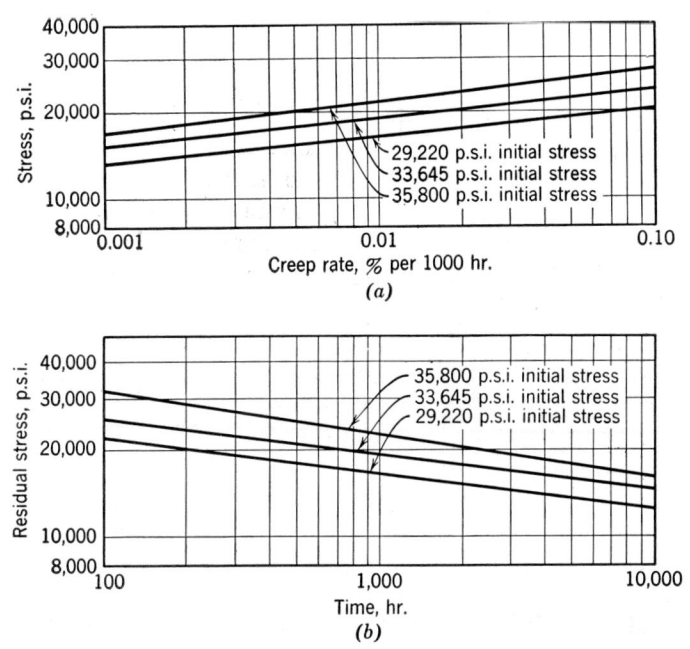

Fig. 4.25. Log-log creep strength lines and relaxation lines at 538° C. (1000° F.) for material 17-22A. (University of Michigan; *Courtesy* ASTM.)

4.43 Design of Bolts. To obtain permanent tightness of bolted joints, the bolts should be provided large enough (in other words low design stresses should be selected) so that they will not relax down to the design stress value. Bolts that perform as intended and stay tight do so because they are strong enough to resist relaxation. Bolts always tend to relax somewhat, reducing the stress down from the initial stress, and, at any time before the next overhaul when the bolts are tightened, the residual stress should be well above the design value to preclude the possibility of leakage. A unique feature of bolt design is that bolts are always expected to be stressed *above* design values and to *stay* so stressed. The remedy for a loose bolt is to tighten it, but, if it does not hold on tightening, it is not properly functioning and should be replaced by a bolt of material possessing better high-temperature properties.

4.44 Application to Stress-Relief Anneal. Relaxation tests are quantitative measurements of stress relief, and in their early stages if run at annealing temperatures they constitute direct measurements of the effectiveness of the anneal.

4.45 Correlation between Relaxation and Creep Tests. Results from relaxation tests do not replace those from creep tests run at constant stress. No satisfactory correlation between data from the two methods has been established.

Wear

4.46 Characteristics of Wear. Wear of metal is produced by contact with other materials. Usually the term "wear" is associated with abrasion. A worn metal part many times appears to have small fractures on its surface and if the metal is ductile may have its shape distorted owing to plastic flow. Oxide films formed on metallic surfaces may be worn off by abrasion.

When ductile steels rub against each other, particles of soft metal may come into contact and become displaced, causing the formation of pits in the surfaces. (Refer to Art. 4.16.) Pitting is not so likely to occur when steel is in contact with brittle metal or when steel shafts are in contact with a bearing metal such as babbitt metal. Increased wear and pitting may be caused by increase in temperature of the rubbing metals.

4.47 Accelerated Wear Tests. Attempts have been made many times to determine the wearing properties of materials by means of accelerated tests. Such tests usually consist of abrasion tests where one material is rubbed against another under given conditions of load and velocity. Poor correlation has been found to exist between the results of many of these accelerated tests and actual service results. Furthermore, when materials are tested by various wear tests, some materials show up well under some tests and poorly in others.

These difficulties are due in part to the difficulty in simulating service conditions of load application, velocity, and nature of abrading surface in accelerated wear tests. For example, grit between metal wearing surfaces may act as a cleaner removing film from both mating surfaces so that true contact is made, resulting in seizure or galling. Elimination of the grit in testing would give erroneous results compared to service conditions. There is need for research on wear tests for many materials of construction.

Corrosion

4.48 Corrosion in General.[22] *Corrosion* may be defined as the conversion of metals by natural agencies into compound forms. *Rusting* refers to the corrosion of iron and steel.

[22] F. N. Speller: Corrosion-Resistant Metals, *Mech. Eng.*, December, 1936.

Service Requirements of Metals

Corrosion of metals is a problem of great industrial importance not only on account of the wastage involved but also because of the limited services rendered under certain conditions of exposure by several common metals, particularly iron and steel, which otherwise have good physical properties.

The common metals are relatively unstable in that they tend to revert with a decrease in free energy of the system to the more stable compounds such as oxides and carbonates, in which form they are found in nature.

The different types of corrosion may be classified according to environment as atmospheric, underwater, soil, chemical, and electrolysis due to stray electric currents. In atmospheric corrosion there is an excess of oxygen available so that the predominant factor is moisture. In underwater corrosion the concentration of dissolved oxygen is the predominant factor. In soil corrosion the principal factors are electrical conductivity, total acidity, and water content. Chemical corrosion depends largely upon the chemical compounds in contact with the metal surfaces. Electrolysis due to stray electric currents may cause severe corrosion.

4.49 Electrolytic Theory. The electrolytic theory of corrosion of metal is generally accepted. According to this theory, metal passes into solution as ions, and the metallic ions give up their electric charge in escaping from solution and forming metal again. This theory extends the operation of Faraday's law as applied to the voltaic cell to the corrosion of metals. In a voltaic cell the passing of an electric current through an electrolyte is associated with the dissolving of a certain amount of material from the anode and the depositing of a chemically equivalent amount at the cathode. In the process of corrosion, adjacent areas on the surface of the metal become anodes and cathodes. Electrolytes such as water, aqueous solutions, or moist air in contact with the metal connect the anodes and cathodes and establish numerous small cells. The driving force in these cells is the solution pressure of the corroding metal.

Anodic and cathodic areas may be caused by differences in metal composition, structural homogeneity, surface finish, mechanical strain, inherent power to form surface films, and by unequal concentration of oxygen on different parts of the surface.

4.50 Primary and Secondary Reactions. There are two main steps in the reactions which occur when corrosion takes place on metal in contact with water: first, the primary reactions due to the initial tendency of the metal to enter solution; and second, the secondary reactions which control the rate of deterioration. The initial rate of reaction is likely to be quite rapid but is soon retarded by the formation of films of hydrogen or other corrosion products on the surface of the metal. The formation of these protective films may in time render the metal passive. The secondary reactions have to do with the breaking down of these protective films and hence tend to cause corrosion.

In the presence of water, the metal enters the solution at anodic areas and an equivalent amount of hydrogen is deposited at adjacent cathodic areas, forming a polarizing film and thus in time making the metal passive. If free oxygen or oxidizing compounds combine with hydrogen, the polarizing film of hydrogen on the cathodic areas is removed and corrosion will occur since the primary reaction can continue.

Many illustrations of the effect of dissolved oxygen upon corrosion can be given. Iron which is alternately wet and dry tends to corrode faster than iron which is continually wet because both water and oxygen are present in plentiful amounts. Plumbing systems tend to corrode owing to the changing of the water and consequent replenishment of the oxygen. The flow of water in open channels in a hydraulic laboratory increases the supply of oxygen and causes increased corrosion in pipes and tanks through which the water flows.

If oxygen is not available for this depolarization, corrosion is reduced to a negligible amount in water that is alkaline or only slightly acid, but, if the acidity is sufficient to cause evolution of gaseous hydrogen, more metal can be dissolved.

4.51 Galvanic Corrosion. Galvanic corrosion is a bimetal electrochemical function which takes place when an electrolyte connects two dissimilar metals forming a shorted galvanic couple. The energy force is the potential difference between the two metals expressed in terms of the concentration of the connecting electrolyte. Weak solutions such as waste water, sewage, and condensation water containing residual corrosive materials act as electrolytes between dissimilar metals. Table 4.8 is a practical listing of dis-

Table 4.8

DISSIMILAR METAL CHART

Practical Arrangement of the Usual Metals of Construction in Corrosive Galvanic Relationship

	Metals	*Volts*
Ignoble (base) metals	Magnesium and alloys Aluminum and alloys Zinc Cadmium	↑ Increasing Positive
	Iron Nickel Tin	
	(Hydrogen)	Zero
Noble metals	Copper and alloys Chromium and stainless steel Silver Gold Platinum	Increasing Negative ↓

similar metals in corrosive galvanic relationships. The "base" metals are rapidly destroyed when in galvanic connection with the "noble" metals in the lower part of the table. The less noble (base) metal acts as the anode and the more noble metal as the cathode. The anodic metal (such as zinc) goes into solution and the cathodic metal (such as copper) is unaffected. Pits are formed on the surface of the anodic metal.

Not only will direct contact between two different metals such as stainless steel and "Alclad" aluminum sheet set up galvanic action, but condensate dripping from a copper bus bar on to a magnesium casting can be corrosive to the magnesium owing to the copper ion in the condensate. The engineering design of parts should include consideration of the place they will have in assemblies in order to avoid dissimilar metal relationships.

4.52 Pitting. Pitting is caused mainly by contact with dissimilar metals or other material on the surface. Blisters of rust are formed, and the pits under the blisters are kept anodic since no oxygen can come in contact. The relatively large cathodic areas have their hydrogen films rapidly depolarized by oxygen which causes the metal in the pits to go into solution with increased intensity. Such action can cause rusting completely through thin sections of metal in a short time.

The presence of mill scale on steel, deposits of corrosion products or of foreign matter, cracks or angles in the structure which interfere with diffusion are likely to cause the formation of active cells at such spots on the metal due to variations in oxygen concentration. The metal surface should be kept clean to prevent this form of corrosion.

4.53 Corrosion of Pipes. A thin stationary film of water is maintained on the surface of pipes carrying water. It is necessary for free oxygen to penetrate this stationary film in order to depolarize hydrogen films. Corrosion is less for laminar flow conditions when the velocity of the water is low than for turbulent flow conditions at velocities above the critical velocity. It is thought that this is due to the decreased thickness of the stationary film of water at the higher velocities. At high velocities in turbulent flow the formation of ferric protective films may be promoted, causing a decrease in corrosion.

A continuous coating on the inside surface of pipes reduces corrosion since oxygen has to penetrate the coating in order to react with hydrogen on the cathodes. Coatings such as sodium silicate, mud, ferric hydrogel deposited from dissolved ferrous hydroxide, and deposits from sulfates and bicarbonates in water may tend to prevent depolarization of hydrogen films by oxygen.

4.54 Intergranular Corrosion. Intergranular corrosion is corrosion of grain-boundary material. Intergranular corrosion occurs in some metals at high temperatures (see Art. 4.28) and in others such as aluminum alloys develops very rapidly even under normal temperatures. Such corrosion is caused by a combination of corroding effect of contacting liquid and of stress conditions in the metal. In appearance it can be compared to the rotting of wood; the metal may be easily loosened by digging with a sharp tool. Utilization of "Alclad" aluminum alloys reduces intergranular corrosion in aluminum construction.

4.55 Transcrystalline Corrosion. Transcrystalline corrosion is galvanic in type and develops through slip planes and planes of precipitated constituents across crystalline grains. It occurs in magnesium alloys containing small percentages of aluminum.

4.56 Corrosion Fatigue. Metals subjected to reversed stresses are more apt to develop fatigue cracks when subjected to corrosive influences. Pits formed by corrosion are good beginning points for development of corrosion-fatigue cracks. The rate of failure increases as the stress is increased. Failure occurs in fibers under tensile stress which ruptures protective films and allows the corrosive liquid to come into contact with unprotected metal.

4.57 Effect of Corrosion on Endurance Limit. Even a small degree of corrosion is sufficient to reduce the endurance limit of metals. Water corrosion has been known to reduce the endurance limit of carbon and alloy steels from one-half the tensile strength to as low as 12,000 pounds per square inch. Special precautions should be taken to protect parts from corrosion when under high cyclic stresses.

4.58 Effect of Temperature on Corrosion. At high temperatures, all metals have an increased tendency to react with their environment. Copper forms a black oxide film in air at high temperatures from 200 to 1800° F. which tends to scale off. Aluminum forms a protective film at high temperatures which is stable in dry air until the aluminum becomes molten at 1220° F. Stainless 18–8 chrome-nickel steel tarnishes somewhat at high temperatures, but the film is stable up to 1600° F. Intergranular oxidation may occur at elevated temperatures by direct chemical reaction between air and metal (Art. 4.28). Water corrosion is increased as the temperature is increased owing to decreased viscosity of water which tends to increase oxygen diffusion. In pressureless containers the worst condition is reached at about 185° F.

4.59 Preventive Measures. Preventive measures against corrosion may be divided into four classifications according to the principle employed: (1) paints, varnishes, lacquers, and other applied coatings (see Chapter 24); (2) the use of metals that have the power to form self-healing protective films with the particular environment under consideration; (3) treatment of liquids coming into contact with the metals as by the addition of chemicals to the liquids to assist in forming a natural protective layer on the metal surface; and (4) cathodic protection of underground structures.

Cathodic protection refers to the prevention of galvanic corrosion of underground cables, pipes, and storage tanks owing to electrolysis by stray electric currents. This protection consists in connecting of a base metal such

Service Requirements of Metals 81

as magnesium, aluminum, or zinc with the structural metal such as iron or steel which is to be protected. The base metal acts as an anode and thus protects the structural metal which acts as a cathode. The anodic metal is buried in the soil adjacent to the conduit or tank and is connected to the cathodic metal by means of an insulated copper wire. Thus the potential of the structure is lower than that of the grounded base metal, insuring electrical drainage. Cathodic protection is also provided for propeller shafts, rudders, and condensers on ships by attaching zinc plates.

Behavior of Metals at Low Temperatures

4.60 Low-Temperature Requirements. The service requirements of metals under low-temperature conditions have created a need for metals with suitable physical properties at low temperatures. Such service requirements include the expanding use of low-temperature operations in the chemical processing industries and the increased need for operation of aircraft and military and construction equipment under subfreezing conditions. In the upper air, the lowest ambient temperature is about *minus* 130° F. In the Arctic and Subarctic regions, temperatures as low as *minus* 70° F. are encountered. The mean temperature during the coldest months of the year, January and February, is approximately *minus* 53° F. in the coldest places in the Arctic. In the chemical industries, extremely low temperatures may be employed down to as low as *minus* 320° F.

4.61 Properties of Metals at Low Temperatures. In considering the low-temperature properties of metals, the conditions of loading are important; shock loading is much more selective than static loading. Under static loading, the strength and hardness of steels increase with falling temperatures. For carbon steels, the ductility as measured by the tension test shows only a small amount of change or decreases slightly down to a temperature of about *minus* 250° F. below which a sharp drop may occur. However, under shock loading where the specimen is notched as in the Charpy impact test, steels react in a much different manner. Some steels become embrittled at temperatures only slightly below freezing, whereas other steels retain their toughness to very low temperatures. For example, certain carbon steels are brittle at temperatures below *minus* 40° F. and have lowered resistance to shock, whereas austenitic chrome-nickel stainless steel retains toughness to a temperature as low as *minus* 314° F. (see Table 4.9). Both metallurgical and mechanical factors affect the low-temperature properties of metals.

Metallurgical Factors. Body-centered cubic and hexagonal close-packed structures are embrittled at some low temperature, whereas face-centered cubic metals retain their ductility and toughness to extremely low temperatures. The austenitic chrome-nickel stainless steel has a face-centered cubic

Table 4.9

LOW-TEMPERATURE PROPERTIES OF STEELS *

Type	Condition	Tempera-ture, °F.	Tensile Strength, p.s.i.	Yield Strength, p.s.i.	Elonga-tion in, 2 in., %	Reduc-tion of Area, %	Impact Strength, ft.-lb.
SAE 30304	Cold-rolled	77	212,000	149,000	12.0	54	24.7
18.5% Cr		(−)108	241,000	180,000	14.5	62	34.5
8.8% Ni		(−)314	296,000	189,000	23.5	45	30.3
stainless steel							
SAE 30316	Annealed	32	90,000	39,000	60	75	110
16-18% Cr		(−) 40	104,000	41,000	59	75	110
10-14% Ni		(−) 80	118,000	44,000	57	73	110
2- 3% Mo		(−)320	180,000	70,000	46	64	110
stainless steel							
Carbon steel	Normalized at	(−)106					53
0.10% C	1700° F.	(−)148					60
		(−)184					42
		(−)229					39
		(−)292					4

* John L. Everhart: "How to Select Steels for Low-Temperature Service." *Materials & Methods*, Jan., 1952, p. 75.

structure and is unique in that its toughness is not reduced at very low temperatures; and tensile strength and yield strength are greatly increased without appreciable loss of ductility. It is too expensive, however, to use austenitic stainless steel for all low-temperature applications, so ferritic steels must be utilized in many applications.

The ferritic steels, possessing the body-centered cubic structure, are sensitive to embrittlement at some temperature. The temperature at which embrittlement occurs is termed "transition temperature." Some ferritic steels have transition temperatures above room temperature and are brittle at 32° F. Melting practice affects the transition temperature. Thoroughly killed steels containing residual aluminum have the lowest transition temperatures and in general retain their toughness better at low temperatures; in order of decreasing toughness at low temperatures come the semikilled steels with aluminum additions, the silicon-killed steels, the rimmed steels, and the ordinary Bessemer steels, although some overlapping may occur.

In ferritic steels, fully hardened martensite and tempered martensite are the structures having the lowest transition temperatures. Hardenability is an important property since it determines the facility of producing martensite. In order to avoid temper brittleness, the steels should be water quenched from the highest tempering temperature which will yield the desired strength. For ferritic steels in order of decreasing toughness (increasing transition temperatures) are the normalized and tempered steels, bainitic steels, and slowly cooled steels containing lamellar pearlite. Steels in the "as-rolled" condition are erratic in low-temperature behavior.

Service Requirements of Metals

Concerning composition, an increase in carbon content raises the transition temperature and reduces toughness at low temperatures. Least damaging is carbon in a fully dispersed form of iron carbide. Silicon is beneficial to toughness up to 0.25 per cent, but high amounts of silicon are detrimental to carbon steels and high-strength low-alloy steels for all structures from martensite to pearlite. Manganese up to 1.5 per cent is beneficial to low-temperature properties in that the transition temperature is lowered; however, in large amounts manganese may cause reduced toughness. Increasing the phosphorus content definitely increases the transition temperature. Sulfur in normal amounts is not detrimental. Both phosphorus and sulfur should be kept to minimum values.

Fine-grained steels have lower transition temperatures than coarse-grained steels for the same level of tensile strength. Overheating of steel, even though it may not change the appearance of the grain size, can produce much lower toughness at low temperatures.

Mechanical Factors. Ferritic steels are increasingly sensitive to embrittlement with falling temperatures and are notch sensitive at low temperatures. Because of this, notches and sharp changes in section should be avoided. Surface imperfections may serve as the points where failure begins in highly stressed steels at low temperatures because of decreased toughness and ductility. Geometrical shapes that restrict the straining of a metal during stressing tend to produce brittleness as compared to shapes which do not prevent the part deforming and bending. Thus heavy sections tend to be brittle whereas thin sections fail in a ductile manner owing to the greater restraint in the heavy sections.

As to metals other than steel, wrought copper and aluminum alloys have improved mechanical properties at low temperatures. Solders of lead and tin alloys with lead contents from 65 to 97 per cent increase in toughness and retain ductility at low temperatures. The mechanical properties of lead are not appreciably affected by low temperatures. Cast iron has similar properties at room temperature and at low temperatures except that it has decreased toughness at extremely low temperatures. Pearlitic malleable cast iron has lower toughness at low temperatures than standard malleable cast iron.

Non-Destructive Testing Methods

4.62 Non-Destructive Testing. The most important non-destructive devices used in inspecting and testing structural and machine parts will be described.

4.63 Oil-Powder Inspection. This method is utilized to locate surface cracks. A penetrating oil colored by means of a dye is sprayed on the metal part and is later wiped off. Clean talcum powder is sprinkled on to the surface or a thin white paste is applied to absorb oil deposited in cracks, thus producing colored lines.

4.64 Magnetic-Particle Inspection. Magnetic-particle inspection makes possible the detection of invisible cracks and imperfections on or near the surface. The part is magnetized, and a light application of dry magnetic powder (Magnaflux) is made, or a liquid suspension of a magnetic powder is applied. The magnetic particles tend to congregate in regions of magnetic non-uniformity associated with discontinuities in the metal. North and south magnetic poles are formed at a defect producing a build-up of particles which is termed an "indication." The strongest indication of a fault is produced when the part is magnetized so that the direction of the magnetic field is at right angles to the crack. Thus in checking railroad-car axles, if the coil is wrapped around the axle, the magnetic field runs lengthwise through the axle which is the proper direction to detect transverse cracks running around the axle. Such transverse cracks may be fatigue cracks, corrosion fatigue cracks, and heat checks in journals. If, on the other hand, the current is passed longitudinally through the axle, the magnetic field is set up circularly and makes possible the indication of defects running lengthwise along the axle such as seams, laps, and splits. Direct current has to be used for locating subsurface discontinuities because alternating current is limited to detection of defects at or very near the surface.

Magnetic-particle inspection is extensively employed to detect incipient fatigue failures and for checking machine parts in service. It is also used in foundries and forge shops for quality control of castings and forgings. In machine shops, it is applied in order to discard defective pieces before beginning work and to inspect finished machine parts. A disadvantage of this method is that in some instances stress concentrations give the same indications as cracks.

4.65 Fluorescent Magnetic-Particle Inspection. A new development in the wet method is the use of fluorescent magnetic particles which glow visibly when activated under near-violet ("black") light in a darkened enclosure. By this method (called "Magnaglo") indications are shown in better contrast, which is particularly useful in investigating roughened surfaces and parts of intricate shape.

4.66 Fluorescent-Penetrant Inspection. Another fluorescent method of inspection (called Zyglo) is available for testing non-magnetic metals, especially austenitic stainless steel, carbides, brass, bronze, and aluminum. The fluorescent penetrant is suspended in oil. The part such as a ball bearing is dipped in the fluorescent penetrant which penetrates any fine cracks. The penetrant is removed from the surface by wiping or washing. A developer is applied to help draw the penetrant from the depth of the crack and spread it on the surface of the piece on each side of the defect. The process makes cracks visible when viewed under near-violet or black light.

Service Requirements of Metals

4.67 Magnetic-Analysis Inspection. Electrical and magnetic properties of iron and steel are affected by changes in physical structure. Variations in structure due to defects such as cracks, cupping, and seams can be detected by a magnetic-analysis machine. This machine has primary and secondary windings. Introduction of a test bar distorts the sine wave of the voltage induced in the secondary winding. The machine is adjusted to a standard piece. If production pieces vary from the standard, their variations in magnetic properties will cause the sine wave to shift. The altered wave form may be viewed by the operator in an oscilloscope. Stock up to 4 inches thick can be handled. A defect 0.012 inches in depth can be discovered. The magnetic-analysis machine is used in rough inspection of bars, tubes, and manufactured parts to find defects, sort mixed stock, and detect underannealing to avoid tool breakage in automatic machines.

The *Cyclograph* is another magnetic-analysis machine and consists of a two-stage oscillator. The test coil, which is part of the tuned circuit, controls the operating frequency of the oscillator. Core losses occurring in the field of the test coil decrease the output of the oscillator. This output is viewed on a cathode-ray-tube screen. Variations in the amplitude of the indication on the screen are related to the amount of core loss. The Cyclograph is built to operate at frequencies from 2,000 to 200,000 cycles per second. Variations in heat treatment in different pieces can be determined, and abnormally high internal stresses which might cause early failure can be detected. This instrument is employed in controlling the manufacture of bolts, screw-machine products, and springs. It can also be utilized to measure thickness of case depth from 0.010 to 0.040 inches within a few thousandths and plating thickness within ±10 per cent. A limitation of the Cyclograph is that it does not indicate cracks and surface discontinuities.

The General Electric *metals comparator* is an electronic unit including an oscillator, a balancing network, and an indicator that is designed to detect variations in hardness of metals by measuring differences in magnetic characteristics. One application is the testing of automotive universal trunnion yoke bearings.

4.68 X-Ray Radiography. X-ray radiography utilizes X-rays to detect invisible deep-seated defects such as cracks, holes, and voids in metals. Whereas magnetic-particle inspection is used to locate discontinuities at or near the surface, radiography makes possible the determination of defects in the interior of the piece. X-rays have short wavelengths (about 1/10,000 the wavelength of visible light), which permits them to penetrate through metals if enough power and sufficient time is provided. The part such as a forging is placed between the source such as an X-ray tube and a photographic plate. After exposure and development of the plate, cracks, holes, and inclusions will appear as dark spots against a light background representing the sound metal. The following operating voltages are required for penetration of X-rays through sections of different metals:

3,000 to 50,000 volts	Thin sections of aluminum and magnesium
30,000 to 150,000 volts	4-inch sections of aluminum
	5- to 6-inch sections of magnesium
60,000 to 250,000 volts	Heavy sections of light alloys
	1½- to 1¾-inch sections of steel
	1-inch sections of copper alloys
400,000 volts	2- to 2½-inch sections of cast and rolled steel
1,000,000 volts	4½- to 5-inch sections of steel
2,000,000 volts	8- to 12-inch sections of steel by means of special techniques.

X-ray equipment should be operated in lead-lined or concrete-lined chambers for protective purposes. X-ray radiography is used for light metals and steel principally, with some applications to other metals and plastics. Its applications include the checking of welds, castings, and forgings. It is employed to examine final assemblies where internal parts can not be viewed and where it is desired to check the fusion in brazed or soldered joints. As to sensitivity, cavities as small as 0.5 to 1.0 per cent of the total section thickness can be revealed on the radiograph by careful control, and by ordinary control 2.0 per cent sensitivity is readily attained. The latter percentage meets the requirements of the ASME boiler code. A difficulty of this method is that thin laminations and elongated discontinuities may not be easily discovered.

4.69 Gamma-Ray Inspection. Gamma-rays are emitted from radium salts. They have shorter wavelengths than X-rays and hence have greater penetrating power. However, the intensity of radiation is smaller so that longer exposure times are required. Capsules containing from 25 to 500 milligrams of radium salts are used in examining large castings. Gamma-ray radiation is used for inspecting structural welds, especially in shipbuilding. The sensitivity is about 3 per cent. Advantages of gamma-ray radiation are that great thicknesses of metal can be penetrated, given sufficient time, and the cost of installing the source is less than for X-ray radiation. The capsules are portable, hence assemblies in shops and ships can be inspected without dismantling.

4.70 Fluorescent Inspection. If a fluorescent screen is substituted for X-ray film or plates, the observer can see the shadow pattern directly. Fluorescent inspection is used extensively for light alloys, die castings, and plastics. It is installed for checking finished articles moving on assembly lines.

4.71 X-Ray Diffraction. X-rays have short wavelengths capable of penetrating between atoms in a space lattice. The X-rays are bent or redirected in passing through a space lattice into a series of emergent rays whose intensities and separations are typical of the metal. By X-ray diffraction, a photographic negative is obtained which shows the arrangement and intensity of the diffracted rays. No two metals have the same diffraction pattern, hence each photographic record may be considered to provide a "fingerprint" identification. X-ray diffraction is employed to study residual stresses in both riveted and welded structures. It is a routine inspection tool in checking case hardening, annealing, welding, and other processing. X-ray diffraction is also used in production research to predict properties of materials developed by different treatments.

4.72 Supersonic Inspection. Supersonic inspection makes use of equipment capable of sending a high-frequency sound beam through metal. Longitudinal sound waves of very short wavelength travel through a material at a velocity corresponding to the elastic characteristics and density of the material. The time for a reflected beam to come back to the transmitter is determined. When the supersonic impulses strike a defect such as a blowhole, inclusion, or crack, a change in velocity of the impulses takes place. The differences in time required for the impulses to penetrate sound material and be reflected as compared to material containing a defect can be determined. Such differences can be viewed by the operator on an oscilloscope on which the impulses from the reflected vibrations are indicated. A great disadvantage is that this method requires a very smooth finish on specimens to obtain suitable transmission of impulses to the material. Metal plates up to about 25 feet thick can be examined, but the method can not be used for plastics thicker than 3 inches because of the damping-out effect of plastics. Since the supersonic equipment does not generate waves, it is not hazardous to personnel.

Sperry Supersonic Reflectoscope. The sound waves are sent out by a quartz crystal about ¾-inch square which is moved over the specimen. The Reflectoscope is utilized to detect subsurface defects such as voids, ruptures, and inclusions at depths up to 28 feet. Defects to depths of 10 feet can be readily located in steel, iron, aluminum, and magnesium.

Brush Hypersonic Analyzer. The Hypersonic Analyzer (Brush Development Co.) has two crystal units: one is a transmitter, and the other is a receiver. Materials to be tested are passed through a water bath between the crystals while a supersonic beam is being projected. The sound energy picked up by the receiver is converted into electrical energy for operation of a recorder. Changes in energy received cause the recording pen to indicate by means of a peak. This method locates flaws but does not give a direct indication of the depth of a defect. It is used for rejecting parts with flaws. Separations as thin as 0.001 inch can be detected. It is used for steel, iron, aluminum, brass, phosphor bronze, beryllium-copper alloy, and plastics.

Sperry Supersonic Thruray. This is similar to the Brush Supersonic Analyzer in that two crystals immersed in oil or water are used. It is useful in checking soundness of spot welds and in inspecting bonds in clad and plated materials. It provides a quick, inexpensive method of inspection of manufactured products.

4.73 Hydrostatic Pressure Tests. Hydrostatic pressure tests are applied to tanks and pipes to determine the existence of leaks. Usually a much greater pressure than the normal working pressure is employed in testing.

Questions

4.1. What is meant by "slip"?

4.2. Describe the behavior of metals under repeated stresses.

4.3. What is the character of the fracture of steel cylindrical shafts which fail under alternating cycles?

4.4. Sketch an *S-N* diagram.

4.5. How is the endurance limit of steels determined? Is it a definitely fixed value? Explain.

4.6. How may the presence of fatigue cracks be ascertained?

4.7. What is meant by "overstressing" in fatigue? By "understressing"? By "coaxing"?

4.8. May overstressing in fatigue cause damage to a metal? Explain.

4.9. State typical endurance ratios for rolled steel, wrought iron, cast steel, and cast iron with respect to ultimate tensile strength.

4.10. For what purposes may impact tests be conducted on metals?

4.11. What is "cold brittleness"?

4.12. What is the significance of the term "notch sensitivity"?

4.13. Describe the characteristics of the three stages of creep.

4.14. What is the effect on ductility caused by stressing carbon steel under high-temperature conditions for long periods of time? How may this effect be explained?

4.15. Describe the differences in type of fracture obtained in instantaneous tension tests and long-time creep tests at an elevated temperature of 538° C. (1000° F.) for a 0.15 per cent carbon steel.

4.16. Describe the essential features of McVetty's method of determining creep limit.

4.17. Referring to Fig. 4.13, master rupture curve for HS No. 88 sheet, calculate stresses for 100-hour duration for temperatures of 1000, 1200, and 1350° F. Plot a curve for log rupture-stress versus temperature.

4.18. Referring to Fig. 4.14, master rupture curve for Discaloy 24 sheet, compute stresses for 100-hour duration for temperatures of 1000, 1200, and 1350° F. Plot a curve for log rupture stress versus temperature.

4.19. Solve questions 4.17 and 4.18 for a 1000-hour duration time. For a temperature of 1350° F. which alloy has the greater rupture stress? Which alloy has the greater tensile strength at 1350° F.? (See Table 4.4.)

4.20. A specification requires that a creep rate of 0.002 per cent per hour at a temperature of 1500° F. under a stress of 10,000 pounds per square inch shall not be exceeded. Does alloy L 605 sheet (Fig. 4.9) meet this specification?

4.21. What is the significance of "equicohesive strength"?

4.22. Under what conditions may grain boundaries be weaker than crystalline grains? Discuss.

4.23. Discuss the influence of rate of strain upon flow stress of high-temperature alloys.

4.24. How does a relaxation test differ from a creep test?

4.25. Discuss the characteristics of wear of metals.

4.26. Discuss briefly the correlation of accelerated wear tests with actual service conditions.

4.27. Discuss the importance of preventing corrosion of metals.

4.28. Describe the electrolytic theory of corrosion of metal.

4.29. Discuss the effect of secondary reactions upon corrosion.

4.30. Why may aeration of water in a hydraulic laboratory increase corrosion in pipes?

4.31. What causes pitting?

4.32. Describe the corrosion of pipes carrying flowing water.

4.33. What is the effect of corrosion on fatigue resistance of carbon steel?

4.34. Discuss the prevention of corrosion of metals.

4.35. How may underground pipelines be protected from electrolysis?

4.36. Describe in detail a suitable non-destructive testing method for detecting fatigue cracks in railroad-car axles.

4.37. Machine parts of austenitic chrome-nickel stainless steel require inspection for small surface cracks. What non-destructive testing method would be most suitable?

4.38. It is desired to select a non-destructive testing method for checking the contours of steel-splined shafts for possible defects. What method would you recommend?

4.39. It is necessary to check the sternpost on a ship for deep-seated defects. What method would you suggest?

References

4.1. American Society for Metals: "Symposium on Effect of Surface Stressing Metals on Endurance under Repeated Loadings." *Proc. Am. Soc. Metals*, Cleveland, Ohio, 1946.

4.2. American Society for Testing Materials: *Symposium on Wear and Wear Materials*. Philadelphia, 1937, 105 pages.

4.3. American Society for Testing Materials: "Manual on Fatigue Testing." *Special Tech. Publ.* 91, 1949, 82 pages; and "Symposium on Statistical Aspects of Fatigue." *Special Tech. Publ.* 121, 1951, Philadelphia.

4.4. Battelle Memorial Institute: *Prevention of the Failure of Metals under Repeated Stress*. John Wiley & Sons, 1941, 264 pages.

4.5. Boyvey, H. O.: "Fatigue Tests of Parts Made Basis of Design." *Product Eng.*, v. 15, July, 1944, pp. 444–448.

4.6. Buckingham, E.: "Qualitative Analysis of Wear." *Mech. Eng.*, v. 59, 1937, pp. 576–578.

4.7. Bullens, D. K.: *Steel and Its Heat Treatment*. John Wiley & Sons, 5th ed., 1948, 3 vols.

4.8. Clark, C. L., and White, A. E.: "Creep Characteristics of Metals." *Trans. Am. Soc. Metals*, v. 24, 1936, pp. 831–864.

4.9. Clark, D. S., and Wood, D. S.: "The Time Delay for the Initiation of Plastic Deformation at Rapidly Applied Constant Stress." *Proc. ASTM*, v. 49, 1949, pp. 717–737.

4.10. Clark, D. S., and Wood, D. S.: "The Influence of Specimen Dimension and Shape on the Results in Tension Impact Testing." *Proc. ASTM*, v. 50, 1950, pp. 577–586.

4.11. Copson, H. R.: "Atmospheric Corrosion of Low-Alloy Steels." *Proc. ASTM*, v. 52, 1952.

4.12. Cross, H. C., and Lowther, J. G.: "Study of Effects of Manufacturing Variables on the Creep Resistance of Steels." *Proc. ASTM*, v. 38, Part I, 1938, pp. 149–171.

4.13. Davis, E. A., and Manjoine, M. J.: "Effect of Notch Geometry on Rupture Strength at Elevated Temperatures, Symposium on Strength and Ductility of Metals." *ASTM*, 1952.

4.14. Ellinger, G. A., Waldron, L. J., and Marzolf, S. B.: "Laboratory Corrosion Tests of Iron and Steel Pipes." *Proc. ASTM*, v. 48, 1948, pp. 618–627.

4.15. Grover, H. J., and Jackson, L. R.: "Fatigue Tests on Some Spot-welded Joints in Aluminum-alloy Sheet Materials." *Welding J.*, v. 26, 1947.

4.16. Henry, O. H.: "Tensile Impact Tests on Welds at Low Temperatures." New York, *Welding Research Committee of The Engineering Foundation*, v. 3, 8, Aug., 1938, pp. 23–27.

4.17. Herzig, A. J., and Parke, R. M.: "Low Temperature Impact Properties of Some SAE Steels." *Metals & Alloys*, v. 9, 1938, pp. 90–93.

4.18. Hetenyi, M.: *Handbook of Experimental Stress Analysis*. John Wiley & Sons, 1950, 1077 pages.

4.19. Hoover, Helen D.: "The Measurement of Directional Strength in Straight- and Cross-Rolled Strip Steel by the Navy Tear Test (developed by Kahn and Imbembo)." *Proc. ASTM*, v. 53, 1953.

4.20 Hoppman, W. H.: "The Velocity Aspect of Tension-Impact Testing." *Proc. ASTM*, v. 47, 1947, pp. 533–554.

4.21. Hull, F. C., Hann, E. K., and Scott, H.: "Effect of a Notch and of Hardness on the Rupture Strength of 'Discaloy,' Symposium on Strength and Ductility of Metals." *ASTM*, 1952.

4.22. Karry, R. W., and Dolan, T. J.: "Influence of Grain Size on Fatigue Notch-Sensitivity." *Proc. ASTM*, v. 53, 1953.

4.23. Kommers, J. B.: "The Effect of Overstressing and Understressing in Fatigue." *Proc. ASTM*, v. 43, 1943, pp. 749–764.

4.24. LeGrand, R.: "Non-destructive Testing Methods." *Am. Machinist*, May 23, 1946, pp. 119–142.

4.25. McVetty, P. G.: "The Interpretation of Creep Tests." *Proc. ASTM*, v. 34, Part II, 1934, pp. 105–122. "New Equipment for Creep Tests at Elevated Temperatures." *Ibid.*, v. 37, Part II, 1937, pp. 235–257. "Interpretation of Creep Test Data." *Ibid.*, v. 43, 1943, pp. 707–727.

4.26. Moore, H. F., and Moore, M. B.: *Materials of Engineering*. McGraw-Hill Book Co., 8th ed., 1953.

4.27. Moore, H. F.: "A Study of the Size Effect and Notch Sensitivity in Fatigue Tests of Steels." *Proc. ASTM*, v. 45, 1945, pp. 507–531.

4.28. Murphy, G.: *Properties of Engineering Materials*. Scranton, Pa., International Textbook Co., 2nd ed., 1946, 459 pages.

4.29. Nadai, A., and McVetty, P. G.: "Hyperbolic Sine Chart for Estimating Working Stresses of Alloys at Elevated Temperatures." *Proc. ASTM*, v. 43, 1943, pp. 735–748.

4.30. Peterson, R. E.: "Relation between Life Testing and Conventional Tests of Materials." *ASTM Bull.* 133, Mar., 1945, pp. 9–16.

4.31. Roberts, I.: "Prediction of Relaxation of Metals from Creep Data." *Proc. ASTM*, v. 51, 1951, pp. 811–831.

4.32. Russell, H. W., and Welcker, W. A., Jr.: "Damage and Overstress in the Fatigue of Ferrous Metals." *Proc. ASTM*, v. 36, Part II, 1936, pp. 118–138.

4.33. Russell, H. W.: "Resistance to Damage by Overstress of Precipitation-Hardened Copper-Steel and Copper-Malleable." *Metals & Alloys*, v. 7, 1936, pp. 321–323.

4.34. Schuster, L. W.: "Some Aspects of the Notched-Bar Test." *Manchester Assoc. Engrs., Symposium on Notched-Bar Impact Testing*, Oct. 29, 1937, pp. 15–54.

4.35. Sinclair, G. M., and Dolan, T. J.: "Some Effects of Austenitic Grain Size and Metallurgical Structure on the Mechanical Properties of Steel." *Proc. ASTM,* v. 50, 1950 , pp. 587–618.

4.36. Southwell, R. V.: "Impact Testing from a Physical Standpoint." *Manchester Assoc. Engrs., Symposium on Notched-Bar Testing,* Oct. 29, 1937, pp. 1–14.

4.37. Thum, E. E.: "Factors Relating the Impact Strength of Metals with Their Service." *Metal Progr.,* v. 32, Aug., 1937, pp. 138–141.

4.38. Uhlig, H. H.: *The Corrosion Handbook.* John Wiley & Sons, 1948, 1188 pages.

CHAPTER 5

Sources and Production of Metals
By LLOYD F. RADER

5.1 General. Metals are classed into two groups: ferrous and non-ferrous. A ferrous metal is one whose principal element is iron; examples are cast iron, wrought iron, and steel. Non-ferrous metals comprise all metals and alloys whose principal constituent is not iron.

5.2 Sources of Metals. There are more than 30 metals of industrial importance. They are found in the lithosphere which is the solid crust of the earth's surface approximately 850 miles thick. Only aluminum (8.1 per cent), iron (5.1 per cent), magnesium (2.1 per cent), and titanium (0.6 per cent) occur in appreciable percentages of the composition of the earth's crust; all the other commercial metals comprise less than 1 per cent of the lithosphere. Only a small portion of these are near the earth's surface where they are available for mining. Some copper is found in a free (native) state, but, in general, industrial metals occur in nature as minerals which are chemical compounds or mechanical mixtures with other materials.

An *ore* is such a chemical compound or mechanical mixture from which industrial metals can be extracted on an economic basis. *Gangue* is the associated material in the ore of no commercial value and may be either acid or basic in character. The more common type is acid gangue which is composed largely of clay or sand; basic gangue consists mainly of calcareous or dolomitic stone.

5.3 Classes of Ores. There are six classes of ores: (1) native metals—copper and precious metals only; (2) oxides; (3) sulfides; (4) carbonates; (5) chlorides; and (6) silicates.

Oxide ores are the most important, comprising iron, aluminum, and copper ores and many others. The sulfides include ores of copper, lead, zinc, and nickel as well as others. The carbonates constitute important sources of iron, copper, and zinc. Chlorides are a source for magnesium, and silicates for copper, zinc, and beryllium.

5.4 Strategic Importance of Metals. Possession of ores of industrial metals in the territory of a nation is of strategic importance to a country especially in times of war. Not only are the principal industrial metals

Sources and Production of Metals 93

needed in war for manufacture of military weapons and supplies, but also they are required in large quantities for increased industrial activity which accompanies mobilization. Although the United States is self-sufficient in supplies of many metallic ores, a deficiency exists in a number of important metals such as tin, chromium, manganese, antimony, platinum, and tungsten. Owing to increased demands for aluminum during World War II, high-grade bauxite ores were imported even though the United States has extensive deposits of this commercial ore of aluminum. Likewise to meet increased requirements, lead, zinc, copper, and iron ores were imported.

A great deal of the high-grade iron ore in the Mesabi range in Minnesota was depleted during World War II. Large rich deposits in Venezuela and in Labrador and Quebec in Canada are being developed, which will make it possible to retain a comparatively large stockpile of high-grade iron ore in Minnesota. Owing to depletion of high-grade iron ores, it is now economic to recover iron oxide from a low-grade iron ore called "taconite," composed of iron oxide and silica, which is being mined in Minnesota from sedimentary rock deposits.

5.5 Production of Metals. For the production of most metals, the following operations are required:

1. Mining the ore.
2. Preparing the ore.
3. Extracting metal from the ore.
4. Refining the metal.

5.6 Mining. Mining is carried on in both open-pit and underground mines. Two examples of large open-pit operations are the iron mine in the Mesabi Range in Minnesota and the copper mine at Bingham, Utah. Underground metal mines are of the room and pillar type for working horizontal veins or of the stoping type for working vertical veins by cutting a series of steps (stopes). Some underground mines are quite deep as for example certain copper mines in Upper Michigan which are over 5000 feet deep.

5.7 Preparation of the Ore. The preparation of ores consists of crushing, followed by concentration. Concentration has for its purpose the removal of large quantities of gangue, and may be accomplished by gravity operation, by magnetic separation, or by flotation. Passing streams of water over crushed ore, called "dressing," is a common method of gravity separation, the lighter gangue being washed away and the heavier metallic particles being separated. In magnetic separation, the crushed ore is transported on belts or conveyors under magnets which attract the magnetic metal-bearing particles. The flotation method is extensively employed for sulfide ores; finely ground ore is mixed with water, and a frothing agent is added. The gangue settles to the bottom, but the metallic particles are attracted by the froth, which causes them to rise to the surface where they are removed from the tank.

Preparation of the ore may in some cases involve roasting or calcining. Roasting consists of heating sulfide ores to remove sulfur; calcining comprises heating carbonate ores to remove carbon dioxide and water.

5.8 Extraction of Metal from the Ore. Extraction of metal from the ore is accomplished by chemical processes. These processes reduce the chemical compounds such as oxides, releasing oxygen from chemical combination and freeing the metal. Three general processes of extraction are used: (1) pyrometallurgy, (2) electrometallurgy, and (3) hydrometallurgy. The first, *pyrometallurgy* (commonly called "smelting"), comprises the application of heat in a furnace to form a molten solution from which the metal can be obtained by chemical separation. Two general types of furnaces are employed: (1) the blast furnace and (2) the reverberatory furnace; these are described in detail later. (See Arts. 6.6 and 9.5.) *Electrometallurgy* consists in reducing metals from ores by electrical processes utilizing either the electric furnace (Art. 7.29) or the electrolytic process (Art. 12.15). *Hydrometallurgy* is a chemical process (commonly called "leaching") that involves subjecting the ore to an aqueous solution by means of which the metal is dissolved and recovered.

5.9 Refining the Metal. Metals reduced from ores by extraction methods contain impurities; such impurities are removed by *refining*. Metals extracted by methods of pyrometallurgy are more commonly refined by oxidizing the impurities in a furnace (example: steel from pig iron); however, other methods such as liquation (tin), distillation (zinc), electrolysis (copper), and addition of a chemical reagent (manganese to molten steel) are utilized.

Introduction to Non-Ferrous Metals

5.10 History of Copper. Copper was the first metal developed by man for utilitarian purposes. This early availability was due to the existence of copper in a comparatively pure state in nature and also because certain oxide minerals can be readily reduced to yield copper by heating in a fire in contact with carbon and carbon monoxide. Later, man learned to mix different metals to form alloys. Copper and its alloys, brass and bronze, have a long history of domestic, military, and industrial service, and extensive use is made of them today in various phases of science and industry. Copper and its alloys possess a great range in physical properties. Historically, the first important non-ferrous alloy produced in the United States, in 1885, was naval brass (also called Tobin bronze after its inventor); naval brass resists corrosion by sea water quite well and is utilized for marine parts and shafting.

5.11 History of Aluminum and Magnesium. Also of great importance are the light metals aluminum and magnesium and their alloys. Aluminum and magnesium are young metals historically. Aluminum was first produced as a metal by H. C. Oersted in 1825. Only 2 tons had been produced by 1852. The modern process of reduction of aluminum from its ore, bauxite, was discovered by Charles M. Hall of Oberlin, Ohio, in 1886; this made possible the manufacture of aluminum on a commercial basis. Magnesium was first isolated by Sir Humphry Davy in 1808, but it was not produced commercially until the twentieth century. These light metals have properties of light weight, moderate strengths, and good machinability. Aluminum is resistant to corrosion and possesses high thermal and electrical conductivity. These properties account for the extensive use of these light metals and alloys in structures, machines, ships, aircraft, and automotive equipment.

Introduction to Ferrous Metals

5.12 General. The ferrous metals comprise three general classes of material, cast iron, wrought iron, and steel. All these are produced by the reduction of iron ores into pig iron and subsequent treatment of the pig iron by various metallurgical processes.

5.13 Classification of Iron and Steel. Iron products may be grouped under the following heads:

Pig iron is the product obtained by the reduction of iron ores in the blast furnace. Carbon is present in amounts not usually below 2.5 per cent or above 4.5 per cent. The iron may be cast into rough bars called "pigs."

Cast iron is remelted pig iron after being cast or about to be cast in final form. It does not necessarily differ from pig iron in composition. It is not malleable at any temperature.

Malleable cast iron is a form of cast iron which, by a special annealing treatment after casting or rolling in final form, has been rendered malleable or semimalleable.

Wrought iron is a form of iron which is aggregated from pasty particles without subsequent fusion. Wrought iron contains slag enclosures and is initially malleable but normally possesses so little carbon that it will not harden when rapidly cooled.

Ingot iron is a form of iron or extremely low-carbon steel that has been cast from a molten condition.

Steel is an iron-carbon alloy which has been cast from a molten mass, whose composition is such that it is malleable at least in some one range of temperature, and which may or may not harden upon sudden cooling. Steel that owes its distinctive properties chiefly to carbon is called "carbon steel"; its carbon content is less than 2.0 per cent and is generally below 1.5 per cent. Steels of which the distinctive properties are due chiefly to the presence of elements other than carbon are called "alloy steels."

History of Development of Iron and Steel Manufacture

5.14 Early Furnaces. Little information is available regarding the early methods of manufacturing iron other than that crude furnaces were used and the finished material was made directly from the ore mixed with charcoal in one operation. The product was a small pasty mass of red-hot iron which could be hammered into shape. Natural draft and crude forms of artificial draft were used in early days.

5.15 Catalan Forge. A major change took place when the Catalan forge was developed by the iron workers in Catalonia, in Spain, for manufacturing wrought iron. This forge consisted of a furnace 2 feet high with a crucible about 1 foot deep to hold the heated lump of iron. The blast was derived by water power and entered the furnace through tuyères in the bottom. The increased efficiency of this furnace over previous methods was due mainly to the improved air blast. The fuel was charcoal, burned in direct contact with the metal.

5.16 Two-Stage Process. In the fourteenth century the method of producing wrought iron direct from the ore began to be replaced by a two-stage process. The principal difficulty with single-stage operations was encountered in reducing the carbon in the iron. The charcoal fuel was an excellent carburizing agent, and every precaution had to be taken to keep the wrought iron from recarburizing to the point where it was no longer malleable and ductile. The first heating was in a shaft-type forge furnace, called a stückofen in Germany, and the second heating, carried out in a Catalan furnace, reduced the material which had been overcarburized. The wrought iron produced by this additional working was more uniform and superior in physical properties to the product of the single-stage operation.

5.17 Blast Furnace. During the fifteenth century the shaft-type furnace was increased in size and the draft improved so that higher temperatures were attained. The iron was heated to a point where it absorbed carbon from the fuel, and thus its fusion temperature was lowered from 1500°C. to between 1130° C. and 1200° C. Since this was below the working temperature of the furnace, the product was a molten metal which was hard, brittle, and relatively weak. This marked the beginning of production of pig iron in a *blast furnace.*

Coal was employed in 1619 in England in the smelting of iron ore, but coke was not used in the blast furnace until 1735. Steam engines were employed for blowing air into the blast furnace during the eighteenth century. Neilson invented the hot blast in 1828 by devising a means of preheating the air blown into the blast furnace. This greatly increased the production of pig iron and reduced fuel requirements. The hot-blast stove based upon the regenerative principle was developed by Cowper in 1857.

5.18 Reverberatory Furnace. The development of equipment and methods of making wrought iron and steel from pig iron was a slow process. The reverberatory or air furnace was perfected and patented in 1784 by Henry Cort in England. Its principal feature was that the fuel was burned on a grate adjacent to the hearth where the iron was worked, the hot gases passing over and fusing the charge of iron, thereby removing most of the impurities by oxidation. Coke or coal could be substituted for charcoal as fuel in this furnace in producing wrought iron since the fuel was not in direct contact with the metal. The puddling process utilizing the reverberatory furnace was developed, making possible increased production of wrought iron of good quality.

5.19 History of Steel Making. Cementation steel was the earliest form of steel. It was manufactured by heating wrought iron in contact with charcoal so that carbon was absorbed by the iron.

Crucible steel was first produced by Huntsman in England in 1740. The crucible process consisted essentially in the melting of wrought iron in closed crucibles of refractory material, the carburizer being placed in the crucible with the iron, together with any special alloying element desired. The crucibles were heated in a furnace, and the temperature gradually was brought to a melting heat. The process was divided into two stages called "melting" and "killing." The melting required from 2 to 4 hours; killing consisted in holding the steel at a melting temperature until it did not evolve gases, but would pour dead and produce sound ingots. The manufacture of crucible steel was discontinued in industrial plants in the United States in 1948. The crucible process has been supplanted by the electric furnace.

William Kelly in 1847 in Kentucky developed a process of refining pig iron in a converter by blowing air through the molten iron. This was the beginning of modern methods of making steel. Sir Henry Bessemer a few years later developed independently the same process which he patented in England in 1855. Kelly was issued a patent in the United States, but he later sold the rights to his invention to Bessemer. The process is commonly called the Bessemer process. The modern process consists of blowing air through a bath of molten pig iron to remove carbon, silicon, and manganese by oxidation. It is used to produce a low grade of steel.

Beginning in 1856, the open-hearth process was developed by the Siemens brothers in England and by the Martin brothers in France. This process is in general use today for quantity production of the better grades of ordinary steel. The process consists of removing impurities by oxidation in a reverberatory regenerative type of furnace.

Experiments on an electric melting furnace were carried on by Sir William Siemens in 1878. Electric furnaces for smelting iron ores and refining steel were developed for industrial operation in 1898. They are used today for production of special alloy steels and steels for special purposes.

Questions

5.1. Discuss the sources of important industrial metals.
5.2. Discuss briefly the subject of strategic importance of metals.
5.3. Where are iron ores obtained for iron and steel manufacture in the United States?
5.4. What is "taconite"?
5.5. What is meant by concentration of ores?
5.6. Distinguish between electrometallurgy and hydrometallurgy.
5.7. Discuss briefly the history of development and use of copper, aluminum, and magnesium.
5.8. Describe the essential features of the Catalan forge.
5.9. Describe the history of the blast furnace.
5.10. Discuss the development of wrought-iron manufacture.
5.11. Discuss the history of steel making.
5.12. Describe briefly the crucible process for manufacturing steel.

References

5.1. Boylston, H. M.: *An Introduction to the Metallurgy of Iron and Steel.* John Wiley & Sons, 2nd ed., 1936; Chaps. 1 and 2, pp. 1–34.
5.2. Hadfield, Sir Robert: *Metallurgy and Its Influence on Modern Progress.* London, Chapman & Hall, 1925.
5.3. Newton, J.: *An Introduction to Metallurgy.* John Wiley & Sons, 2nd ed., 1947, 645 pages.
5.4. Nord, M.: *Textbook of Engineering Materials.* John Wiley & Sons, 1952, 534 pages.
5.5. Richard, T. A.: *A History of American Mining.* McGraw-Hill Book Co., 1932 (A.I.M.E. Series).
5.6. Richard, T. A.: *Man and Metals.* McGraw-Hill Book Co., Whittlesey House, 1932.
5.7. Sullivan, J. W. W.: *The Story of Metals.* Am. Soc. Metals, Cleveland, Ohio, 1951, 290 pages.
5.8. U. S. Naval Academy: *Engineering Materials.* U. S. Naval Institute, Annapolis, Md., 1949.

CHAPTER 6

Iron Ore and Pig Iron

The Raw Materials of the Iron Industry

6.1 Ores of Iron. Ores of iron consist essentially of compounds of iron, usually oxides, mixed with gangue (silica, clay, etc.). Those of commercial importance contain from 25 to 70 per cent metallic iron.

Iron is extracted from ores by a process known as smelting, which consists primarily in heating the ore to a high temperature under strongly reducing conditions in the presence of a flux. The reducing agent serves to remove the oxygen from the oxides of iron, leaving metallic iron together with such elements as carbon, silicon, manganese, phosphorus, and sulfur, which are invariably present either in the ore or in the fuel used in melting. The flux, usually limestone, combines with the gangue of the ore and the ash of the fuel, producing a fusible slag which may be separated from the metallic iron. The forms of iron ore of greatest commercial importance are as follows:

Hematite, sometimes called red hematite or red iron ore, is anhydrous ferric oxide, Fe_2O_3, containing when pure 70 per cent iron. It is the most important iron ore commercially.

Limonite, also called brown iron ore or bog iron ore, is hydrated ferric oxide, $Fe_2O_3 + [n]H_2O$, containing about 60 per cent iron.

Magnetite is the magnetic oxide of iron, Fe_3O_4, containing when pure 72.4 per cent iron. It occurs in a state of high purity in Sweden where it is extensively used.

Iron carbonate, commonly called siderite or spathic iron ore, $FeCO_3$, contains when pure 48.3 per cent iron.

The Lake Superior district is the largest iron-ore-producing region in the world, a soft red hematite of high grade being obtained.

Taconite ore, also found in the Lake Superior region, contains 25 to 35 per cent iron in the form of magnetite. Taconite is still in the development stage. It is crushed by jaw crushers to ¾-inch size, mixed with water, and crushed again in a rod mill into small pebbles. The pebbles are run past large magnets which draw off a sandy mass containing about 35 per cent iron. This mixture is then ground in a ball mill to a flour which is subjected to magnetic separation again. The iron powder in moist condition is fed into a rotating drum where it forms into pellets. The pellets are run through a furnace at 1260° C. (2300° F.) where they are fused into hard balls. The fused pellets are then used as a charge for the blast furnace together with regular iron ore in the production of pig iron.

All ores of iron in which the phosphorus content does not exceed one-thousandth part of the iron content are classed as Bessemer ores, and all ores carrying a higher percentage of phosphorus as non-Bessemer ores. This division is due to the fact that acid Bessemer steel must contain less than 0.1 per cent phosphorus, and neither the blast-furnace reduction of the ore nor the acid Bessemer steel process is able to reduce the phosphorus content.

6.2. Special Preliminary Treatment of Ores. Practically all the hematite is charged into the furnace without any preliminary treatment. Some ores, however, behave more satisfactorily in the furnace after having been subjected to concentration, roasting, or calcining.

6.3. The Flux. The function of the flux is to provide a fusible slag in which the non-metallic portion of the ore may be carried off. In general, it may be said that a basic flux is required for acid gangues (high in silica, alumina, etc.), whereas an acid flux may be required where the gangue is basic (high in lime, magnesia, or alkaline matter). As a rule, gangues are acid in character and therefore the fluxes are usually basic in character.

The most common form of basic flux is limestone, which should be very pure. Pure or high-calcium limestones are not always available and magnesian or dolomitic limestones are sometimes used.

The flux serves another purpose, besides taking care of the gangue and ash. The sulfur in the charge, whether in the ore or in the fuel, combines with the lime of the flux, forming calcic sulfide, which is removed in the slag.

6.4 The Fuel. Coke is the most commonly employed fuel for the blast furnace. Coke is porous in structure, thereby exposing a large amount of surface to oxidation. Hard, well-made cokes withstand the pressure of the charge very well and possess sufficient firmness while being heated so as not to fill up the interstices of the charge, thereby impeding the flow of the gases. The fuel for a blast furnace serves as a reducing agent as well as a source of heat.

Manufacture of Pig Iron

6.5 The Blast-Furnace Process in General. Practically all the iron used commercially, whether as cast iron, wrought iron, or steel, is first reduced from the ores in a blast furnace to form pig iron. The process of smelting iron in the blast furnace consists essentially of charging a mixture of fuel, ore, and flux into the top of the furnace, and simultaneously blowing in a current of air at the bottom. The air burns the fuel, forming heat for the

Iron Ore and Pig Iron

chemical reactions and for melting the products; the gases formed by this combustion remove the oxygen from the ore, thereby reducing it to metallic form; and the flux renders the earthy materials fluid. The gaseous products of the operation pass out at the top of the furnace; the liquid products, pig iron and slag, are tapped off at the bottom.

6.6 The Blast Furnace and Its Mechanical Equipment. The blast furnace, Fig. 6.1, consists of a vertical shaft built of steel and lined with

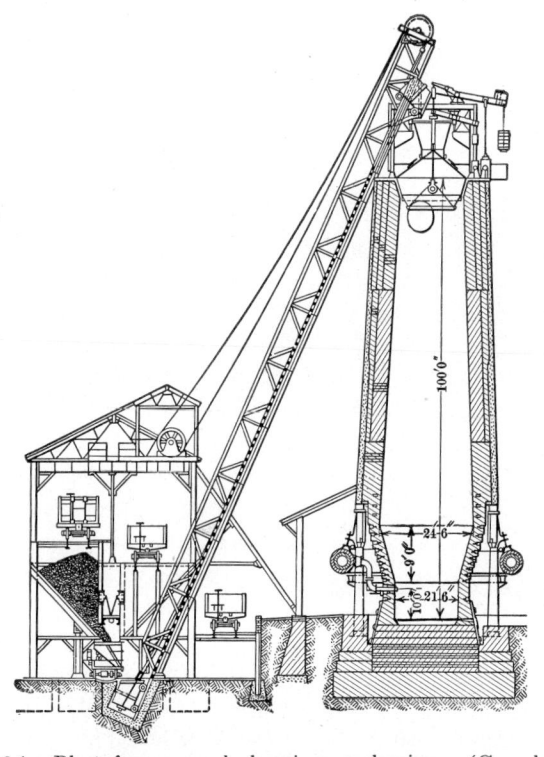

Fig. 6.1. Blast furnace and charging mechanism. (Campbell.)

firebrick. The lower portion, called the hearth or crucible, is cylindrical, about 10 feet high, and 21 to 22 feet in diameter. It contains the tuyères, the cinder notch, and the iron notch, and serves as a crucible in which the molten products of the operation are collected. Above the hearth the walls diverge, forming an inverted truncated cone called the bosh, which is 8 to 12 feet high and 24 to 25 feet in diameter at the widest point. Above the bosh extends the stack, converging to a diameter of about 17 to 18 feet at the throat at a height of 45 to 60 feet above the bosh.

The top of the stack is equipped with two cone-shaped bells and two hoppers for charging the materials without losing hot gases from the furnace.

The materials are dumped into the upper hopper and the upper bell is lowered, causing them to fall into the lower hopper. The upper bell is closed and the lower bell opened, permitting the materials to flow into the stack.

An inclined track or skipway is used to haul the buckets or skips of materials from the ground to the top of the furnace. The engines are located and operated on the ground.

The ring of tuyères through which the hot blast of air is driven pierces the hearth lining just below the bosh. Both the tuyères and the tuyère blocks are protected from burning by being of hollow metal construction and cooled by water circulating through them. Air is forced through the tuyères under a pressure of approximately 15 pounds per square inch.

The bustle pipe is an annular steel pipe lined with firebrick, encircling the bosh, which conducts the hot blast from the hot-blast main to the tuyères.

The hole for tapping off the liquid slag, called the cinder notch, is located on the side of the hearth about 3 feet below the tuyères. This also is protected by a water-cooled casting. It is closed by stopping up the hole by an iron bar having an enlarged end, until the slag itself has solidified and plugged the hole.

The iron notch is at the front of the furnace and about 2 feet above the furnace bottom. It consists of an opening in the brickwork several inches square which is closed by means of a semiplastic clay that burns solidly into place. The clay is drilled out when it is desired to tap the furnace. The opening is closed by means of a steam or air reciprocating clay gun or an electric rotary clay gun; with the rotary gun the clay is forced in continuously under a high pressure against the full blast pressure of the furnace, thus permitting continuous operation of the furnace.

Each furnace is equipped with three to five hot-blast stoves. A stove consists of a vertical steel cylinder, 20 to 22 feet in diameter and 80 to 110 feet high, containing two firebrick chambers. The central chamber is open; the outer annular chamber is divided into a large number of small flues. Gas from the blast furnace and a definite proportion of air are admitted at the bottom of the open chamber and burned. The products of combustion rise to the top of the furnace and pass downward through the small flues and thence to the stack. The greater part of their heat is taken up by the brickwork of the flues. After gas has been burned in a stove for about 3 hours, the stove is hot enough to heat the blast.

Air from the blowing engines is now admitted at the bottom of the small flues in the outer chamber and passes upward, taking up the heat stored in the brickwork and attaining a temperature of about 538° C. (1000° F.). Thence it passes downward through the central flue to the hot-blast main leading to the furnace.

6.7 The Operation of the Blast Furnace. The blast furnace has five distinct duties to perform:

Deoxidation of the iron ore.
Carburization of the iron.
Melting the iron.
Conversion of the gangue to fusible slag.
Separation of the molten iron and the slag.

Deoxidation of the Iron Ore. The recovery of iron would be impossible without deoxidation, because of the operation of the general principle that oxidized bodies in a state of fusion will not unite with unoxidized ones. The application of this principle to the metallurgical processes in iron and steel making may be stated as follows:

First, when an element such as carbon, silicon, or phosphorus, existing in chemical union with a metal, combines chemically with oxygen, the resulting oxidized product must, when melted, separate itself from the remaining metallic portion.

Second, if oxidized metal parts with its oxygen and becomes reduced to the metallic state, the newly liberated portion joins the metal in the furnace.

If, therefore, the iron were not reduced, the iron oxide would not be recovered, but would be lost with the slag.

Carburization of the Iron. Carburization of the iron is essential because at the temperature attained in at least the greater part of the melting zone it would be impossible to melt free iron, whereas iron saturated with carbon is sufficiently superheated beyond its melting point to make it very fluid, so that it easily becomes separated from the slag in the hearth.

Melting the Iron. When fusion takes place, all oxidized bodies unite to form the slag and expel therefrom all fused unoxidized bodies. It is, therefore, essential that the iron be fused in order that it may be expelled from the slag. The molten iron will necessarily absorb all deoxidized substances such as silicon, manganese, and phosphorus, which exist as free metals or metalloids in the lower portion of the furnace. Carbon will also be absorbed until the saturation point is reached.

It is further essential that the iron be not only fused but also superheated, in order that it may remain fluid until drained from the furnace and cast into pigs or transported to steel furnaces.

Conversion of Gangue to Fusible Slag. The function of the slag formed in the blast furnace is primarily the elimination of all non-volatile matter, in the gangue of the ore and in the fuel, that does not properly belong in pig iron. This can be accomplished only by giving to the slag such a composition that it will offer a greater attraction to the impurities than the metal offers.

The slag-making materials consist of the gangue of the ore, the ash of the fuel, and the lime of the flux. The chemical nature of the slag and consequent metallurgical action are controlled by varying the relation of lime to the other slag-making constituents in the furnace charge. The slag-making materials upon fusion form a molten silicate of lime, together with magnesia and alumina. The alumina and earthy and alkaline bases naturally enter into the slag, since they exist as oxides and are not reduced in the furnace. In addition, the bulk of the silicon will enter the slag as silica (SiO_2), and most of the sulfur, by an entirely chemical action, enters the slag as sulfide of calcium, which, although an unoxidized body, does not unite with the molten iron, but appears to dissolve in the slag.

Separation of Iron and Slag. The two substances are chemically mutually repellent, and both are very fluid and of different specific gravities. The slag floats upon the molten iron in the hearth of the furnace and may be readily tapped off through the cinder notch above the level of the iron.

Capacity. Blast furnaces are built in sizes for a daily capacity of 100 to 1000 tons of iron. The blast furnace of the dimensions shown in Fig. 6.1 would have a capacity of about 800 tons of pig iron per 24-hour day. Such a furnace would require about 2700 tons of charge material per day consisting of ore, 1500 tons; coke, 800 tons; and limestone, 400 tons. Approximately 3000 tons of air would be required and about 6,000,000 gallons of water per 24 hours. About 300 tons of slag would be produced.

Handling the Products. The iron when tapped from the furnace is handled in one of two general ways: by casting into pigs, or, still molten, in ladles. Casting into pigs is accomplished usually by a pig-molding machine. One type of pig-molding machine consists essentially of a continuous series of pressed-steel molds carried on an endless chain. The iron runner of the furnace delivers the molten iron into a ladle which is discharged into a spout, whence the metal is poured into the molds as they slowly travel past. The iron quickly chills and is discharged into a car when the mold passes over a sheave at the end of the run. On the return the molds are immersed or sprayed with limewater to prevent the pigs' adhering. The cooling of the pigs is usually facilitated by depressing the chains and running them through a tank of water.

The blast furnace is so often operated in direct conjunction with a steel plant that the iron is very commonly not cast into pigs at all, but is run directly into ladles which transport it to the steel furnaces. The ladle is built of steel, mounted on trunnions on a car-truck, and lined with firebrick. Its capacity is usually 20 tons or more.

The slag which accumulates above the level of the cinder notch is tapped off at intervals of about two hours, while the iron notch is closed.

Iron Ore and Pig Iron

6.8 Classification of Pig Irons. Pig irons are classified according to method of manufacture, the purpose for which they are intended, and composition.

Method of manufacture.
   Coke pig: smelted with coke and hot blast.
   Charcoal pig: smelted with charcoal, with either hot or cold blast.
   Anthracite pig: smelted with anthracite coal and coke, with hot blast

Purpose for which intended.
   Bessemer pig: for Bessemer process.
   Acid pig: for acid open-hearth process.
   Basic pig: for basic open-hearth process.
   Malleable pig: for malleable cast iron.
   Foundry pig: for cast iron.
   Forge pig: a foundry pig used for manufacture of wrought iron.

Chemical composition.
   High-phosphorus pig.
   Low-phosphorus pig.
   Intermediate low-phosphorus pig.
   Special low-phosphorus pig.
   Special cast irons (spiegeleisen, ferromanganese, ferrochrome, etc.).

The second of these classifications is most commonly used.

The composition of the different grades of pig iron is usually specified within the limits indicated in Table 6.1. Pig iron as such has no structural

Table 6.1
RANGE IN COMPOSITION OF PIG IRONS

Percentages

Grade of Pig Iron	Carbon	Silicon	Sulfur, max.	Phosphorus	Manganese
Bessemer, acid	3.50–4.00	1.00– 3.00	0.05	0.076–0.10	1.25 max.
Acid, open-hearth	——	0.50– 3.00	0.035	0.035 max.	0.75–1.25
Basic, northern	3.50–4.00	1.00– 1.50	0.05	0.400 max.	1.01–2.00
Basic, southern	3.50–4.00	1.00– 1.50	0.05	0.700–0.900	0.40–0.75
Malleable	3.75–4.50	0.75– 5.00	0.05	0.101–0.300	0.50–1.25
Foundry					
Intermediate low-phosphorus	4.00–4.50	1.00– 3.00	0.05	0.036–0.075	0.75–1.25
Northern low-phosphorus	4.00–4.50	1.00– 5.00	0.05	0.30 –0.50	0.50–1.25
Northern high-phosphorus	4.00–4.50	1.00– 5.00	0.05	0.501–0.700	0.50–1.25
Southern	3.50–4.00	1.00– 5.00	0.05	0.700–0.900	0.25–0.75
Silvery	0.75–1.00	5.00–17.00	0.05	0.300 max.	0.50–1.25
Forge, gray	4.15–4.40	1.20– 1.75	0.05	0.10 –0.35	0.50–1.00

uses, but a considerable amount is used after remelting, in the form of cast iron. By far the greater part of all the pig iron made is converted into steel either by the Bessemer process or the open-hearth process, or into wrought iron.

6.9 Direct Reduction Method. A direct reduction process was developed by Ploro, Inc., in 1946, in a pilot plant in Brooklyn, N. Y. In this process, iron ore is finely ground, and impurities are separated from the ore by a magnetic method. The powdered iron is blown by nitrogen gas into an electric furnace which is lined with graphite and has a hydrogen atmosphere, and is quickly transformed into liquid ferrous metal. The inventor, Mr. René Planiol, claims that steel of excellent quality can be manufactured directly, and by adding alloying materials that alloy steels can also be produced.[1]

Questions

6.1. Name the common iron ores and state their chemical formulas.

6.2. Discuss briefly the characteristics of ore obtained from the principal iron-ore region in the United States.

6.3. What is a flux? What materials are used as flux in reducing iron ore?

6.4. Sketch a blast furnace, naming the principal parts and showing approximate dimensions.

6.5. Describe how hot-blast stoves are used in connection with the blast furnace.

6.6. What is the "regenerative principle"?

6.7. What would be the charge for a blast furnace of a daily capacity of 800 tons of pig iron?

6.8. In blast-furnace operation why is it necessary to carburize the iron?

6.9. Classify varieties of pig iron according to the purpose for which they are intended.

References

6.1. American Society for Metals: *Metals Handbook.* Cleveland, Ohio, 1948 ed.

6.2. Boylston, H. M.: *An Introduction to the Metallurgy of Iron and Steel.* John Wiley & Sons, 2nd ed., 1936; Chaps. 3 and 4, pp. 36–127.

6.3. Bray, J. L.: *Ferrous Production Metallurgy.* John Wiley & Sons, 2nd ed., 1947, 587 pages.

6.4. Cammen, L.: *Principles of Metallurgy of Ferrous Metals.* New York, Am. Soc. Mech. Engrs., 3rd ed.

6.5. Camp, J. M., and Francis, C. B.: *The Making, Shaping, and Treating of Steel.* Pittsburgh, Pa., Carnegie-Illinois Steel Corp., 5th ed., 1940.

6.6. Moore, H. F., and Moore, M. B.: *Textbook of the Materials of Engineering.* McGraw-Hill Book Co., 8th ed., 1953.

6.7. Nord, M.: *Textbook of Engineering Materials.* John Wiley & Sons, 1952.

[1] *New York Times,* June 17, 1949.

CHAPTER 7

Steel

7.1 Definition. Steel is an iron-carbon alloy having a carbon content less than 2.0 per cent and generally below 1.5 per cent. It is usefully malleable as cast and exhibits properties of toughness as well as strength.

Professor Albert Sauveur gives the following definition: "Steel is a malleable alloy of iron and carbon, usually containing substantial quantities of manganese."

7.2 Classifications of Steel. Steels are classified according to method of manufacture as:

Bessemer steel, open-hearth steel, electric steel, and *duplex steel.*

Wrought steels are further roughly classified according to carbon content as:

Soft, mild, or *low-carbon steel,* containing from 0.05 to 0.15 per cent carbon.
Medium or *medium-carbon steel,* containing 0.15 to 0.30 per cent carbon.
Half-hard or *medium-high-carbon steel,* containing from 0.30 to 0.60 per cent carbon.
Hard or *high-carbon steel,* containing from 0.60 to about 1.50 per cent carbon.

There are five classes of commercial steel castings:

Low-carbon steel castings, containing less than 0.20 per cent carbon.
Medium-carbon steel castings, containing 0.20 to 0.50 per cent carbon.
High-carbon steel castings, containing over 0.50 per cent carbon.
Low-alloy steel castings, containing alloy content totaling less than 8 per cent.
High-alloy steel castings, containing alloy content totaling more than 8 per cent.

Steels are also classified according to the uses for which their properties fit them, such as:

Rivet steel, structural steel, machinery steel, rail steel, spring steel, and *tool steel.*

The Manufacture of Steel

7.3 Steel-Making Processes. The three principal methods of steel making by the refining of pig iron (with or without the admixture of iron and steel scrap) are the *Bessemer process*, which produces Bessemer steel by blowing finely divided air currents through molten pig iron contained in a retort-shaped furnace called a "converter," the impurities being oxidized and thus removed in the slag, carbon being subsequently added; the *open-hearth process*, which produces open-hearth steel by subjecting pig iron and scrap to the oxidizing flame of gas and air burned in a reverberatory regenerative furnace, carbon being restored after the removal of the oxides in the slag; and the *electric-furnace process* which is used in the direct melting and refining of selected steel scrap to produce electric steel.

7.4 Acid and Basic Steel Processes. Both the acid and basic processes are employed in connection with the Bessemer converter, the open-hearth furnace, and the electric furnace. In the acid process the slag has a high silica content, whereas the slag in the basic process is made basic by the addition of lime or limestone as a flux.

The refractory lining of an acid furnace is made of acid material such as silica or ganister in order to prevent scouring, since any unsatisfied silica in the slag would tend to reach saturation by attacking any bases in the lining with which it might come into contact at high temperature.

Silicon, manganese, and carbon may be removed by means of the acid process, but phosphorus and sulfur cannot be eliminated from the steel. Phosphorus is an especially undesirable ingredient in steel because it greatly reduces shock resistance. Low-phosphorus pig iron must be used in the acid process to produce good-quality steel.

The furnace in the basic process must have its lining composed of basic refractories such as magnesite or dolomite, since any excess base in the slag would tend to neutralize itself by scouring an acid lining.

The basic process can be so conducted as to accomplish the removal of phosphorus and sulfur as well as silicon, manganese, and carbon. Therefore, pig iron produced from low-grade ores may be utilized. In general, it is possible in the basic process to utilize materials for the charge that vary considerably in chemical composition.

In the steel-casting industry, the acid open-hearth and acid electric processes are used mainly, whereas in the wrought-steel industry, basic linings in open-hearth and electric furnaces are in more common use. The Bessemer converter process in the United States is acid exclusively; it is used for the production of wrought products primarily.

7.5 Characteristics of Steel-Making Processes. Table 7.1 indicates the principal characteristics of steel-making processes as operated in the United

Table 7.1
CHARACTERISTICS OF STEEL-MAKING PROCESSES

Process	Rank with respect to			Typical Products
	Low Cost	Quality	Tonnage	
Basic Bessemer (not used in U.S.A.)	—	—	—	
Acid Bessemer	1	5	2	Pipes, tubes, sheet, wire, free-machining steels
Basic open-hearth	2	4	1	Structural shapes, plates, sheet, wire, rails, castings
Acid open-hearth	3	3	4	Large castings and forgings, armor plate, high-strength wire
Acid electric	4	2	5	Special alloy steels, small castings of carbon and alloy steels
Basic electric	5	1	3	Special alloy steels, tool steels, high-speed steels, high-grade carbon steels

States. The different processes are listed in order of low cost of finished product, although differences in cost are in some instances small. The quality of steels produced by the different processes is indicated to be in inverse order to that of low cost. As to tonnage, the bulk of steel production in the United States is by the basic open-hearth process. The basic and acid electric-furnace processes are utilized for producing high-quality carbon steels and special alloy steels.

THE BESSEMER PROCESS

7.6 General. The Bessemer process consists of the removal of most of the impurities in pig iron, by oxidation, through the agency of finely divided air currents blown through a bath of molten iron contained in a vessel known as a converter. The addition of a recarburizer after blowing is generally necessary to give the blown metal the required carbon content.

7.7 Acid Bessemer Process. The following operations constitute the essential features of the acid Bessemer process:

Molten pig iron is brought from the blast furnace in hot-metal ladles and discharged into a large reservoir called the mixer. The mixer supplies molten iron as required to charging ladles, which in turn discharge into the converters, the latter being rotated into a horizontal position during charging. The air blast of the converter is started, and the vessel is elevated into a vertical position. The finely divided air currents pass up through the molten metal for a period of about 10 minutes, by which time the impurities will have been practically eliminated by oxidation.

The converter is again turned into a horizontal position, the wind is cut off, and the recarburizer is added in order to obtain a steel of any desired carbon content. The molten steel is poured from the converter into a ladle which is swung by a crane over a series of cast-iron ingot molds into which the metal is teemed.

The Pig Iron Used. Since it is impossible to remove either phosphorus or sulfur from the iron in the acid process, a grade of pig iron specially low in these elements is required. The usual limits of composition of "Bessemer pig iron" are given in Table 6.1.

At least 1.0 per cent of silicon is required in order to insure the production of a sufficient quantity of satisfactory slag and also to provide heat. The oxidation of the silicon is the principal source of heat in the converter, the amount so derived being much greater than that derived from the oxidation of the carbon and the manganese.

7.8 The Bessemer Converter. The Bessemer converter consists of a heavy steel pear-shaped shell supported upon two trunnions upon which it can be rotated. The upper portion of the shell may be either concentric or eccentric. A section of a concentric converter showing a hollow trunnion connected by a pipe and slip ring with the windbox in the bottom is shown in Fig. 7.1. The bottom of the converter is pierced with a large number of small holes, called tuyères, through which the air blast is forced by means of a blower from the windbox up through the molten metal.

Converters have capacities from 1 to 40 tons. For a converter of 15-ton capacity, the clear opening at the converter mouth is from 2 to 2½ feet in diameter, the inside diameter of the cylindrical portion is about 8 feet, and the height from inside of bottom to "mouth" is about 15 feet.

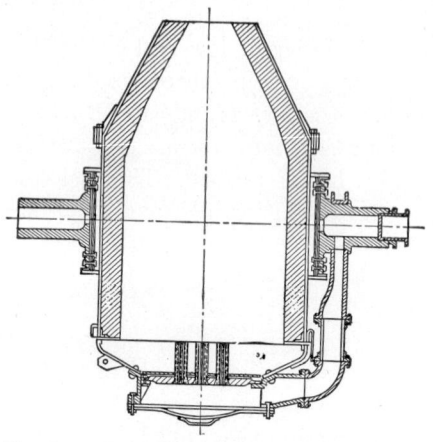

Fig. 7.1. Bessemer converter, 12-to-15-ton concentric type.

The lining of the converter is usually from 12 to 15 inches thick and is made of refractory material of strongly acid character, silica being the principal constituent. In American practice, ganister blocks or bricks laid with thin fireclay joints are usually employed. Under average conditions a lining may last for several months—perhaps 10,000 to 12,000 heats—before it need be entirely replaced.

The lining of the bottom which is 24 to 30 inches thick is made up of damp siliceous material bound together with clay in which the molded tuyère brick are set. Each tuyère brick is about 30 inches long and has about 10 blast holes each approximately ¼ inch in diameter. On account of the fact that uncombined iron oxide has a strongly corrosive action on the lining, the bottom is corroded very rapidly, especially in the vicinity of the tuyères, where the air encounters the molten iron. This limits the life of the bottom lining to about 20 or 25 heats, even though repairs are made between heats. On this account the bottom of the converter is made easily detachable, the fastenings to the body being links secured by keys which can be quickly removed.

7.9 Operation of the Acid Bessemer Process. The converter is tilted to a horizontal position while receiving its charge. The blast is turned on after charging and before righting, in order to prevent the metal from entering the tuyères. The bath of metal occupies only a small portion of the volume of the converter, on account of the increase in volume of the bath caused by the violent ebullition of the metal during the blow.

As soon as the blow is on, the silicon and manganese begin to burn to SiO_2 and MnO and are reduced to mere traces before the oxidation of the carbon becomes appreciable. After 2 or 3 minutes, the carbon begins to oxidize and a reddish-yellow flame makes its appearance at the mouth of the converter. This becomes rapidly augmented until a white-hot flame 20 to 30 feet in height pours out with a loud, roaring sound, and a shower of sparks appears. Soon the flame begins to flicker and shorten, indicating that the carbon is practically burned out, whereupon the converter is turned down, the blast shut off, and the recarburizer added.

Photoelectric cells are used in some modern installations to determine accurately the completion of the blow. The total time required for the blow is about 10 minutes for a 15-ton charge and about 15 minutes for a 40-ton charge.

The phosphorus and the sulfur will not have been affected by the standard process, but the percentage in the blown metal will be slightly higher than in the pig iron because of the loss of other elements which have been carried away in the slag. About 0.01 to 0.02 per cent nitrogen is present in the steel after blowing; such nitrogen increases the tendency of the steel to "age."

7.10 Recarburizers and Recarburizing. The principal recarburizers are spiegeleisen and ferromanganese. Spiegeleisen is a special pig iron, high in manganese and carbon. The manganese content varies from 16 to 28 per cent and the carbon from 4 to 6.5 per cent. Standard ferromanganese contains about 80 per cent manganese and 7.5 per cent carbon maximum. Spiegeleisen is always added in a molten state because large amounts are necessary, and the bath would otherwise be cooled too much before pouring. For this reason small auxiliary spiegel-melting cupolas are a necessary feature of Bessemer plants. Other recarburizing agents which are used include ferrosilicon, silicomanganese, and powdered coal or coke.

7.11 Deoxidation. The addition of the desired amount of carbon to the blown metal is by no means the only important function served by the spiegeleisen or ferromanganese. Blown metal invariably contains considerable amounts of oxides of carbon and iron. The carbon monoxide gas is somewhat soluble in the molten metal, and, even though a great part of it is removed when the spiegel is added, it continues to be evolved until the metal becomes solidified. The imprisoned carbon monoxide means the presence of blowholes in the ingots of steel.

Iron oxide is reduced principally by the manganese of the recarburizer. It is also reduced by the carbon and the silicon of the recarburizing agent. The silicon, too, is very effective in reducing the carbon monoxide gas, thereby becoming an important factor in the prevention of blowholes. Usually a small amount of aluminum is added as a deoxidizing agent to the mold. Sometimes especially strong deoxidizing agents such as ferrosilicon are used in addition to the recarburizer to eliminate the last traces of oxides in the steel.

7.12 Carbon-Deoxidized Acid Bessemer Steel. This class of steel is produced by adding molten iron containing about 4 per cent carbon to the converter at the end of the blow; oxygen is removed from the molten metal as carbon monoxide. The removal of oxygen as a gas rather than with silicon or a similar deoxidizer which form inclusions, improves the cleanliness of the steel. Such a steel can be pierced in manufacturing operations. After carbon deoxidation, manganese and silicon are added to either the converter or the ladle, and aluminum is added to the ladle. The silicon combines with oxygen remaining after carbon deoxidation, and aluminum further deoxidizes the steel and combines with the nitrogen present. Manganese is added to enhance forgeability. The phosphorus content of Bessemer steel may be used to replace part of the carbon or manganese required to meet certain tensile properties. This practice results in a fully killed Bessemer steel; it is used extensively for seamless pipes and tubes whose production calls for a difficult forging operation.

7.13 Dephosphorized Bessemer Steel. The raw materials are controlled to form a "dry" slag by holding the silicon to manganese ratio to 2.5:1.0 closely. Careful manipulation of the blow causes a viscous slag which can be raked off the top of the metal in the converter, thus entirely separating slag and metal. A dephosphorizing mixture of lime, flux, and mill scale is added to the stream of metal run from the Bessemer converter into the ladle. A phosphorus content as low as 0.02 to 0.04 per cent can be attained.

7.14 Casting the Ingots. When the reaction between the blown metal and the recarburizer is complete, the steel is poured from the converter into a teeming ladle which is suspended from a crane. The teeming ladle consists of a bucket-shaped steel shell, lined with refractory material and provided with a valve in the bottom through which the molten metal is teemed. The ladle is suspended by a bail and mounted in such a manner that it may be tipped over to pour out the slag which remains in the vessel after the steel has been teemed off.

The ingots are cast in cast-iron molds mounted on cars which are moved along a track through the mill. The ingot produced is about 7 feet high, has an average cross-section of about 21 by 23 inches, and is about 3 inches thicker at the base than at the top in order to facilitate the stripping off of the mold. Ingots of this type are sometimes cast with the large ends up. A special head of refractory material, called a "feeder" head, on the top of the latter type of ingot mold serves as a reservoir to keep the mold full during shrinkage of the hot steel as it cools. The largest big-end-down mold has a bottom 29 by 48 inches in size for forming ingots of 15 tons.

The mold cars are moved along in such a manner as to bring each mold in succession under the nozzle of the ladle. The plunger is raised, allowing a thin stream of metal to flow into the mold, then dropped while a new mold is brought into place. The slag floats on top of the steel, and the valve is closed when slag begins to flow and the ladle is swung over a slag car and dumped.

The mold cars are drawn outside the steel mill, where the molds are stripped off by a crane, which engages the lugs provided on the molds and lifts them off, leaving the ingots standing on the iron stools which form the bottom to the mold. The ingots are then taken to the pit-furnaces, while the molds are washed with clay water, allowed to cool somewhat, and run back into the mill for another cast.

7.15 The Basic Bessemer Process. The basic Bessemer process differs from the acid Bessemer process only because of the different class of iron used. The basic Bessemer process has not been used to any extent in America but is the principal Bessemer process in Europe. The basic converter differs from the acid converter only in being considerably larger than the acid converter of the same capacity, on account of the increased amount of slag formed, and in having a basic lining. This lining is much less durable than an acid lining, its average life being commonly from 100 to 200 heats, whereas the bottoms are good for from 20 to 40 heats.

The Pig Iron Used. Basic Bessemer pig iron is relatively high in phosphorus, manganese, and usually sulfur and relatively low in silicon. The usual limits of composition are as tabulated.

Phosphorus	Sulfur	Manganese	Carbon	Silicon
1.9–2.5%	Under 0.20%	1.5–2.5%	3.50–4.00%	0.5–1.0%

If the phosphorus is not high the charge is likely to blow cold after the elimination of carbon. High manganese is desired to aid the silicon in producing heat at the beginning of the blow and to facilitate the removal of sulfur which is likely to be high because of the low silicon content.

7.16 Operation of Basic Bessemer Process. The basic Bessemer process is divided into two more or less distinct stages. The first, called the "fore-blow," is characterized by the oxidation of silicon, manganese, and carbon and corresponds to the ordinary blow of the acid Bessemer process. The phosphorus and most of the sulfur are removed and absorbed by the slag during a later period called the "after-blow."

The time required for the conversion process with the basic converter is much longer than that for the acid process. The fore-blow requires from 9 to 12 minutes, and the after-blow from 5 to 6 minutes.

7.17 Recarburization. The manner of using a recarburizer in the basic process differs from that in the acid process, because, if the spiegel is added to a bath containing a great quantity of basic slag, the carbon, silicon, and manganese of the recarburizer will reduce phosphorus from the slag and restore it to the metal.

As much as possible of the basic slag is therefore poured out of the converter first, and, later, as the metal is poured into the teeming ladle, a further quantity of the slag is held back and retained in the vessel. The recarburizer is then added in the ladle, and its action is thereafter similar to that noted for the acid process. The deoxidizing effect of the recarburizer is no less important in the basic than in the acid process, for the oxidation of iron in the basic converter is likely to be excessive.

The Open-Hearth Process

7.18 General. The open-hearth process is so called because it consists in the oxidation and removal of impurities contained in a bath of metallic iron lying on the hearth of a reverberatory regenerative furnace, the bath being exposed to the action of the flame which sweeps across above the hearth.

The rate of oxidation is so slow in the open-hearth process that insufficient heat is generated by oxidation to maintain the metal in the bath in a molten condition. Consequently, heat must be applied to the metal during the process. This additional heat is usually derived from the combustion of gas fuel.

The open-hearth process differs from the Bessemer process in the rate of oxidation of the impurities, requiring about 12 hours as compared with about 10 minutes. The furnace capacity is much greater than that of the converter, however, being from 50 to 250 tons.

In America the open-hearth method is conducted either as an acid or as a basic process, but the basic process greatly predominates.

The open-hearth furnace is charged with pig iron (either solid or molten) and scrap steel (always solid), and the operation is started by admitting a current of preheated natural or producer gas and air which burn within the hearth chamber. Much heat is reflected from the arched roof and the walls. A certain amount of ore is added during the process to provide additional oxides.

The furnace is tapped through a spout either by opening a taphole or by tilting the furnace, the spout in the latter case being located above the normal level of the bath of metal.

7.19 The Furnace and Its Operation. The arrangement of an open-hearth furnace to utilize the regenerative principle is shown in the diagram

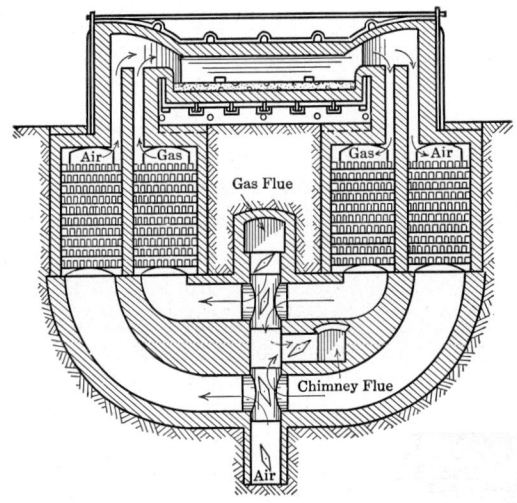

Fig. 7.2. Diagram of regenerative furnace. (Stoughton.)

of Fig. 7.2. The regenerative principle makes possible increased thermal efficiency. The melting chamber, or hearth, is shown in the upper central portion of the figure. On either side are the openings called "ports," through which the gas and air enter the melting chamber, and the vertical flues which lead to the regenerative chambers. Two regenerative chambers, or "regenerators," are provided on each side of the furnace, the larger and outermost one preheating the air required for combustion and the smaller inner chamber heating gas. Each regenerator is filled with a checkerwork of brick through which the gas and air pass.

By reversal of the valves, the direction of flow of the air and gases may be reversed, so that, as soon as one set of regenerators begins to be cooled too much, the incoming gas and air may be sent through the other set, which has just been heated by the burned gases. By reversing the direction of the currents about every 20 minutes the temperature of the melting chamber may be maintained at a fairly constant point, in the neighborhood of 1600° C. (2912° F.) to 1700° C. (3092° F.).

The two common forms of the open-hearth furnace, both of which find wide application in the steel industry, are the stationary furnace and the tilting or rolling furnace.

Stationary Open-Hearth Furnace. The melting chamber is a rectangular structure built of brick masonry and supported upon either a solid masonry foundation or on beams and piers. It is reinforced with buck stays, bearing plates, and tie rods, and is lined with refractory material of suitable chemical nature to resist the attack of the materials which come in contact with it. The hearth is built in the form of a shallow dish and has a capacity of 50 to 250 tons of metal.

If the furnace is intended for the acid process, the hearth is built of fire-clay bricks overlaid with a layer of silica about 18 inches thick. The silica is applied as silica sand, which is spread in thin layers, each layer being exposed to the full heat of the furnace and brought to the sintering point before the application of the next layer.

The basic furnace is built of magnesite bricks overlaid with a mixture of calcined magnesite and about 10 per cent of anhydrous tar. The lining is placed in layers and burned in place as in the acid furnace.

One or more large charging doors are provided in the front wall of the furnace just above the level of the top of the hearth lining, and an inclined spout leads from the lowest portion of the hearth to the back or pouring side of the furnace.

The side walls of the melting chamber and the arched roof are made of silica bricks, the most refractory material that can be obtained, laid with almost no mortar in the joints. The roof is arched from front to back, and its skewbacks are supported upon steel channels, which practically carry the weight of the roof independently of the side walls. In lining the basic furnace a layer of neutral chromite brick is usually placed between the silica bricks of the side walls and the basic hearth.

The ports are designed with great care in order that the flames may impinge neither upon the bath, thereby oxidizing it excessively, nor upon the roof, which would quickly be burned out. The gas ports are always located beneath the air ports, in order that the bath may not be oxidized excessively by direct contact with the air, and also to promote a better mixing of gas and air, since the gas is lighter and therefore rises. The masonry of the ports is built of silica bricks, and the floor is commonly covered with a layer of neutral chrome ore. The port area required for air is about twice that required for gas.

In order to prevent the carrying of dust and slag into the regenerators, the vertical flues from the ports do not lead directly to the regenerators, but to chambers called *slag pockets* which are located on a level with the regenerators below the melting chamber.

Steel

The regenerators are very large in proportion to the melting chamber and are nearly filled with the checkerwork of bricks which serves to absorb heat from the outgoing gases and preheat the incoming gas and air.

Tilting or Rolling Furnace. A furnace of the tilting or rolling type consists of a heavy steel casing of rectangular form, lined with masonry like the stationary furnace, but mounted on two steel rockers which rest upon heavy bed-castings. Two large hydraulic cylinders on the pouring side of the furnace serve to rock the furnace forward or backward during the operation of pouring. The design and arrangement of the slag pockets, regenerators, valves, and flues for the rolling furnace differ in no essential respect from those of the stationary furnace above described.

Zebra Roof. The Zebra roof for basic open-hearth furnaces comprises rings of silica brick alternated with rings of basic brick in areas of greatest wear such as occur along back and front skews. This type has been in use since 1947. It is intermediate in cost and serviceability between all-silica and all-basic roofs. In Zebra roofs, the high hot-strength silica brick insures a mechanically stable roof despite the relatively low hot-strength of the magnesite brick. The basic brick, superior in resistance to chemical attack by iron oxide and other basic fluxes, wears away more slowly than the adjacent silica brick. Thus, the basic brick protrudes beyond the silica brick most of the time, thereby protecting it from the erosive effect of flame and furnace gases.

7.20 The Basic Open-Hearth Process. The basic open-hearth process differs from the acid process mainly in that it utilizes stock higher in phosphorus and sulfur, and a basic slag must be produced by the addition of strong bases to the charge in order to effect the removal of this excess phosphorus and sulfur. Table 6.1 gives the compositions of northern and southern basic pig irons. The pig iron may be charged either solid or molten.

The substitution of scrap iron for pig iron results in shortening the time required for the operation, since there will be a lower percentage content of impurities to eliminate. When the pig iron is entirely replaced by scrap, insufficient reducing material is present to prevent excessive oxidation of the iron in melting, and it becomes necessary to supply carbon in some form as a reducing agent.

The "pig-and-scrap" process is the most common, the exact proportions in a given charge being largely a question of relative costs. Very often a small proportion of ore or mill scale is added to hasten the process.

The flux is commonly lime, the amount required depending upon the contents of phosphorus, sulfur, and silicon in the charge.

Melting on the basic hearth is attended by oxidation of the metalloids, the most easily oxidized ones being eliminated first. The silicon, manganese, and carbon are all considerably reduced in amount during the period of melting (the first 4 or 5 hours). The phosphorus, however, remains practically unaffected until the end of this period, when it begins to be oxidized rapidly.

It is necessary, in order to prevent the bath from becoming too cool and to prevent oxidation of the iron toward the end of the operation, to eliminate the carbon last. If the carbon is disappearing too early it is the practice of the melter to add pig iron to provide additional carbon. Sometimes, when the phosphorus burns out rapidly and the carbon too slowly, it is necessary to hasten the oxidation of carbon by adding ore. The progress of the operation is tested from time to time by ladling out a small amount of metal, casting a small test billet, breaking it, and examining the fracture. Billet tests are usually supplemented by chemical analysis of frequent samples.

The slag performs several very important offices in the operation of the basic hearth. Its chief function is to take up and retain the oxides of silicon, manganese, phosphorus, and sulfur. It must also act as a protection to the bath from excessive oxidation by the furnace gases, and, by virtue of its contained oxides, assist in the oxidation of the impurities. For efficient action as a deoxidizing agent it must be very fluid in order that it may mix intimately with the bath.

7.21 Turbo-Hearth Process. In 1950 the turbo-hearth process was introduced. It consists in blowing jets of air over the surface of the charge. Oxidation is greatly increased, and the output enlarged.

7.22 Recarburization. Recarburization of basic steel cannot be accomplished in the furnace because the carbon, silicon, and manganese of the recarburizer would reduce the phosphorus in the slag and restore it to the metal. On this account the recarburizer, in the form of ferromanganese, ferrosilicon, or silicomanganese together with coal, charcoal, or coke, is added to the stream of metal as it flows into the ladle. Provision is made for the removal of the greater part of the slag by overflowing at the top of the ladle. In manufacturing high-carbon steels, spiegeleisen is sometimes added in a molten state.

7.23 The Acid Open-Hearth Process. The acid open-hearth process differs from the basic open-hearth process principally in the kind of iron used, the omission of the flux, and the time required for the operation. Since the slag formed is acid, it is unable to retain oxides of phosphorus and sulfur, and a pig iron low in these elements is required. Thus the limits of composition of the charge are more restricted in the acid than in the basic process. An acid lining of the hearth is necessary to prevent rapid corrosion by the acid slag. The time required for the operation is shorter than that required for the basic process, as the iron contains less impurities to be removed and because no part of the heat is consumed in melting and accomplishing the function of the flux.

The charge of the acid furnace usually consists of approximately one-third pig iron and two-thirds scrap. The pig iron is fairly low in silicon and manganese and low in phosphorus and sulfur. (See Table 6.1.)

Ore is not usually charged initially in the acid furnace, but it may be added during the process to hasten the removal of carbon. In some plants, the pig iron is charged into the furnace before the scrap in order to prevent the scorification of the hearth, which would occur if the scrap were charged first. In other plants, scrap is charged first so that pig iron on top will be partly refined as it melts and drips over the practically molten steel scrap.

The melting operation is in the main an oxidizing action. The metalloids (impurities) are largely eliminated during the melting-down stage, which requires some 3 to 4 hours, the silicon usually disappearing first, closely followed by the manganese. The amount of carbon oxidized during melting depends largely upon the amounts of the more easily oxidized elements (silicon and manganese) present. The lower the content of the latter elements, the greater will be the proportion of carbon oxidized. In any event, two-thirds of the carbon will be removed very soon after the charge is completely melted. The balance will be oxidized only very slowly, its disappearance usually being accelerated by the addition of ore to the bath. The slag in the acid process never constitutes the important oxidizing agency that it does in the basic process.

7.24 Recarburizing. Recarburizing in the acid process is accomplished in the furnace, rather than in the ladle. The practice as to the degree of recarburization varies, but, in general, the carbon is reduced to the practical minimum for mild or medium steel, and the recarburizer is added 20 to 40 minutes before the heat is tapped. In melting for high-carbon steel, the carbon is usually reduced only slightly below the desired amount before the recarburizer is added. In this event, the addition to the bath is rather more a deoxidizer than a recarburizer. The recarburizer or deoxidizer is, in this process, ferromanganese and ferrosilicon, as a rule. Coal is sometimes added in the ladle as in the basic process. The addition of the recarburizer necessarily largely increases the content of silicon and manganese in the steel, as well as the carbon content.

7.25 Alloy Additions. In manufacturing alloy steels by the acid open-hearth process, various alloys are added to the furnace or ladle at the time recarburizers are added. Vanadium in the form of ferrovanadium is added to the ladle. Added to the furnace are the following: nickel in the form of nickel scrap; chromium in the form of ferrochromium; and, in manufacturing molybdenum steels, ferromolybdenum or calcium molybdate.

7.26 Comparisons of Bessemer and Open-Hearth Processes. The Bessemer process has the following advantages as compared with the open-hearth process: the operation is comparatively simple, the conversion period is short, no fuel is required, and the plant cost is small per unit of output.

The open-hearth process has a small conversion loss, the heats are relatively large, more accurate control of the product is possible, and in the basic process considerable variation in the composition of the materials of the charge is permissible. Open-hearth steel is of better quality than Bessemer steel. Under proper conditions of operation an excellent grade of steel can be produced by the acid open-hearth process.

7.27 Duplex Processes. There are several methods by which the acid Bessemer and the basic open-hearth processes may be combined in a so-called "duplex process," whereby the silicon, manganese, and part of the carbon are eliminated in the converter, the phosphorus and the remainder of the carbon being removed in the open hearth.

In one duplex process the pig iron is blown in the acid converter until the silicon and manganese are practically eliminated and the carbon reduced to about 1 per cent, after which the converter charge is transferred to a mixer and thence to the basic open-hearth furnace. Sufficient carbon is added to the hot metal charge so that the period in the open-hearth furnace will be long enough to eliminate nitrogen brought in by the metal from the converter, and to eliminate impurities to about the same amount as by the regular open-hearth process.

The advantage of the duplex over the Bessemer process lies in the fact that lower-grade, high-phosphorus pig iron may be used and yet produce a satisfactory grade of open-hearth steel.

The advantages of the duplex over the open-hearth process are the saving of about one-half the time ordinarily required in the open-hearth, and the saving effected in cost of renewals of the hearth lining, because of the fact that the silica is removed before the metal enters the hearth.

Electric Refining of Steel

7.28 Electric Refining Processes in General. The part which electricity plays in electric steel-refining processes is simply that of a source of heat. Electric furnaces for refining steel may be of either the arc or resistance type. Historically, the arc type of furnace may be traced from Davy's experiments with Volta's battery in 1800 in which an arc was produced between carbon points. The principle of the resistance furnace was developed by Pepys in 1815 by his experiments on heating an iron wire to a red heat by passing an electric current through it. The invention of the dynamo made possible increased experimentation and use of electric furnaces for steel making.

The main use of electric furnaces is in the production of alloy steels and of highly refined steel from steel scrap and Bessemer and open-hearth-process steels.

7.29 Electric Steel-Refining Furnaces. Electric furnaces have hearths constructed of steel plates and lined with refractory materials. Electrodes

Steel

are inserted through holes in an arched roof of firebrick. Doors for charging and a taphole for drawing off the refined steel are provided. The tilting type of furnace is in common use since the operations of tapping the steel and drawing off the slag are more conveniently handled than in the stationary type. The hearth in the basic process is lined with burned magnesite or dolomite and is bonded with tar. Acid hearth linings are of silica.

Three quite distinct types of electric steel-refining furnaces have been developed:

1. Furnaces employing an open arc between electrodes above the bath, the bath being heated by radiation alone. Owing to radiation losses of the arc to the roof, this type is not so popular as the other types.

2. Furnaces employing an arc between electrodes and the bath, the bath forming a part of the electric circuit. The metal is heated largely by conduction from the slag bath, which carries much of the current and is heated both by radiation and by reason of its electrical resistance. The Héroult furnace is an example of this type and is the most extensively used electric steel-making furnace. The arcs are operated in series, and hence this furnace is known as a series-arc type. Three-phase alternating current and three electrodes are commonly used. The capacity of this type ranges from 2 to 100 tons. Large arc furnaces are used for producing low-alloy steels with either acid Bessemer or basic open-hearth steel as the charge.

3. Electric induction furnaces, wherein the bath forms the secondary of a transformer. The transformer consists of a primary winding of insulated copper wire of many turns, a core of laminated iron sheets, and a closed circuit with but a single turn which is the metal in the bath. Metal must be placed in the secondary in starting up the furnace, and at the end of a heat some of the metal is left in the furnace to form the secondary circuit. Its capacity ranges from 1 to 5 tons. It is employed largely to melt high-alloy steels without loss of expensive alloying materials. Ordinarily no slag is used.

Current is usually brought to the furnace at high voltage and transformed into a current of low voltage and high amperage. Automatic devices are commonly provided to control the rate of heating by regulating the distance between the electrodes and the metal in the bath.

7.30 Basic Electric Refining Process. Slags, which are strongly oxidizing, must be added to the bath in order to effect any refinement. In practice, the slag is a strongly basic iron oxide slag, because such a slag will oxidize phosphorus as well as retain the oxide formed. If much phosphorus is to be removed, or if it is to be reduced to a very low point, it is necessary to use two slags, skimming off the first after it becomes highly phosphorized. The second slag is composed of lime, fluorspar, and silica. This second slag, consisting essentially of calcium silicate, is deoxidized, and strongly reducing conditions are maintained in the furnace by adding ferrosilicon or coke to the slag. The slag and metal are in equilibrium so that the removal of iron oxide from the slag also deoxidizes the metal. Sulfur can also be reduced by removing the iron oxide slag. The presence of manganese favors the removal of sulfur, because manganese sulfide is more readily taken up by the slag than iron sulfide, thus making possible the formation of calcium sulfide, in which form the sulfur is retained in the slag.

Recarburization is accomplished by adding carbon or ferromanganese to the steel in the furnace after the slag has been removed.

The basic electric-furnace process is used to manufacture special alloy steels, tool steels, high-speed steels, and high-grade carbon steels. By this process the highest quality steel is produced.

7.31 Acid Electric Refining Process. Generally small electric-arc acid furnaces of 3- to 10-ton capacity are employed in foundries. The acid refining process is well suited for intermittent operation and is used for melting steel for small high-grade castings. Acid electric steel is not as well deoxidized as basic electric steel, but it is cheaper.

7.32 Limitations and Advantages of Electric Refining Processes. The electric processes have the advantages of rapid heating to very high temperatures under accurate control. Sound metal can be produced because harmful gases are not formed. Oxidizing, reducing, or neutral conditions can be maintained in the furnace. Loss of elements can be avoided, thus making possible control of the composition of steel to low tolerances. Working conditions are more pleasant around electric furnaces. Overhead costs tend to be low for electric furnaces, but the cost of melting is greater.

In the production of special alloy steels, the electric furnace has a special advantage over other steel processes in that it need not be operated under oxidizing conditions, but may be worked under either neutral or reducing conditions. This is an important consideration in using certain valuable alloying elements which are very easily oxidized and lost in other furnaces.

The electric furnace is not a competitor of the Bessemer converter and the open-hearth furnace in the production of mild and medium steel of ordinary quality. It is an important adjunct of both these processes, however, taking their product and superrefining it to produce steel for special purposes.

7.33 Killed or Rimmed Steel. A *killed* steel is one which has been deoxidized by additions of ferrosilicon or aluminum so that there is no evolution of gas, thus permitting the steel to "lie quiet" in the ingot. Killed steel is characterized by few blowholes and the normal formation of pipe (shrinkage cavity) in the top of the ingot. The carbon content of killed steel is generally over 0.25 per cent. Castings and forgings are made of killed steel as is practically all the steel that is heat-treated by quenching and tempering. A killed-steel ingot has a thin skin of fine-grained crystals; inside this skin, a layer of columnar crystals form perpendicular to the mold wall; in the central core, the crystals are equiaxed.

Rimmed steel is produced by only partly deoxidizing the steel by addition of manganese or other deoxidizers and permitting evolution of gases which upon solidification of the metal cleanses the surface of growing crystals thus forming a skin of clean metal with low carbon content. Rimmed steel contains blowholes and has a rather porous structure. Rimming is confined to steels low in manganese and silicon and of carbon content not exceeding 0.15 per cent. Careful control is required since it is desirable to balance the volume contraction of the steel from liquid to solid state against the volume of gas entrapped as bubbles. Blowholes should be well distributed and must be deep seated so they will not break through but will remain clean and weld during rolling of the ingot. Rimmed steel is used for wrought products such as sheet, plate (including ship plate), and wire. Because the skin of good purity is ductile, rimmed steel can be deep drawn and stamped. Bars rolled from rimmed steel usually have good surfaces.

Semikilled steel is not deoxidized as completely as killed steel. Pipe is formed in the top of the ingot. Semikilled steel usually has a carbon content from 0.15 to 0.25 per cent.

7.34 Continuous Casting of Steel. A continuous casting process for steel was developed in 1947 by the Republic Steel Corporation and the Babcock and Wilcox Tube Company at a pilot plant at Beaver Falls, Pennsylvania.[1] A vertical flow of steel is a unique feature of the plant design. The process begins on the sixth floor of the plant where molten steel is poured from an electric reheating furnace through a slag separator into a water-jacketed brass mold. Oxygen contamination is eliminated by shooting compressed inert gas from an injecter around the stream of flowing metal. The steel is solidified in the brass mold and then extruded downward in the form of a red-hot rod. Vertical descent of the rod is controlled by rolls. An acetylene cutting torch mounted on the second floor cuts off sections of steel rod into 15-foot lengths. The rod sections are assembled on the ground floor and transported to a rolling mill for rolling into structural shapes. The continuous process simplifies the operations from the furnace to the rolling mills by eliminating casting into ingots, stripping, soaking, and initial rolling of ingots into blooms. Less loss of steel in processing is claimed for the method. The process can be readily installed by small steel companies.

Rolling Mill Operations

7.35 Reheating Furnaces. An ingot cannot be sent to a rolling mill and rolled immediately after the ingot mold has been removed, because at that time the interior is still molten. If, on the other hand, the ingot is allowed

---

[1] *Iron Age,* Aug. 19, 1948; *Life,* Oct. 4, 1948.

to stand until the interior has solidified, the exterior will be too cold to be worked. It is therefore necessary to place the ingots, immediately after stripping, in a furnace or pit where the interior may be solidified and the exterior kept at the required temperature for working.

The process of rolling finished steel sections from ingots requires many passes of the metal through the rolls. It is necessary, at one or more stages in the reduction of the section, to reheat the bloom or billet or slab which has been formed by the initial reduction of the ingot, when it has cooled below the proper working temperature.

Two classes of reheating furnaces are therefore a necessary part of the equipment of a rolling mill: first, a pit-furnace for heating ingots, and, second, a furnace wherein billets or unfinished shapes may be reheated at any stage in the rolling process.

The regenerative gas-fired *pit-furnace* is a vertical furnace, built below the floor level, and charged through the top. A typical fuel is a mixed gas composed of 6 parts of blast-furnace gas to 1 part of non-desulfurized coke-oven gas, having a heating value of 155 British thermal units. A typical pit-furnace can hold 70 tons of ingots at one time. Attention should be given to the time and temperature of soaking. Undersoaked ingots have a great difference in temperature from the surface to the center. This temperature differential will lead to cracks and tears in rolling. Prolonged soaking in the oxidizing atmosphere of the pit may contribute to decarburization in the finished steel. The maximum soaking time must be closely controlled for steel helical springs because the total decarburization permissible is very small. Certain alloy steels must be withdrawn after a given soaking period. A high pit temperature may result in burnt steel which must be scrapped. Overheating encourages the growth of large grains which may cause cracking in rolling.

Billet-heating furnaces are commonly of the reverberatory type, gas-fired, and recuperative in principle. The billets are charged at the cool end of the furnace, and are pushed along through the length of the furnace by a hydraulic ram mounted at the charging end. Water-cooled pipes laid in the bed of the heating chamber and extending throughout its length provide a sort of track along which the billets are pushed. The billets encounter hotter temperatures as they approach the end where the gas and air ports are located and are there discharged and conveyed back to the rolls. The burned gases, upon leaving the heating chamber, are caused to pass through a series of pipes in a chamber below the working chamber, and the air which is to be used for combustion is caused to circulate through this chamber, thus becoming preheated.

7.36 Rolling Mills. The most essential parts of a rolling mill are the rolls. Cast-iron rolls, which have been chilled to produce a hard exterior and turned in a lathe to produce a smooth surface of the desired form, are very commonly used, especially for finishing rolls. High-carbon and alloy steels are also used. All the rolls except those for finishing have their surface roughened in order to increase their grip on the metal.

Rolls are turned in a great variety of shapes, varying from the plain cylinders for plates and some rectangular shapes to the rolls for structural shapes, rails, corrugated bars, etc., which may be quite intricate in form. All rolls except plain cylindrical rolls make provision for several passes of the metal, each pass approximating the final form of the section desired more closely than the last.

Rolling mills may be in general classed under one of three heads: "two-high" mills, "three-high" mills, and "universal" mills.

Two-high mills consist of a single pair of rolls mounted in the same vertical plane. One variation of the two-high mill is the "pull-over" mill, whose rolls always run in the same direction, so that the metal after each pass must be pulled back over the top of the rolls to be fed in for the next pass. This is the simplest form of mill and the cheapest, but its operation is slow, and it is adapted only for rolling small shapes which can be readily handled. A more important type of two-high mill is the "reversing" mill, the rolls of which may be made to run in either direction by reversing the engines which drive them. Successive passes are therefore made in opposite directions through the rolls. The two-high reversing mill is often used in "cogging" ingots.

The *three-high mill* has three rolls geared together, so that the metal may make one pass between the lower and the middle roll, and the next pass in the opposite direction between the middle and upper roll, without reversing the rolls. A very large proportion of all steel shapes are rolled or at least finished by a three-high mill.

The *universal mill* is provided with four auxiliary rolls mounted vertically one in front and one behind at each end of the horizontal rolls. The distance between the axis of these rolls is adjustable horizontally, and they are designed simply to keep the edges of the metal smooth without effecting any reduction. Universal mills are made with vertical rolls on only one side of the horizontal rolls or on both sides, and they may be either two-high or three-high mills.

All rolling mills that handle anything except very light material must be provided with a series of rollers in front of and behind the rolls, known as the "roll tables." The roll tables for three-high mills must be capable of being raised or lowered at the end next the rolls, in order that the metal may be directed between either the upper or the lower set of rolls.

7.37 Examples of Rolling Practice. *Steel Rails.* The ingot, after reheating in a pit-furnace, is cogged down to a bloom the cross-sectional dimensions of which are about one-half those of the original ingot. This operation is accomplished by a series of about 8 or 10 passes through a set of cogging rolls. The bloom is now sheared at each end to remove the pipe and the ragged end formed by the rolls, cut in two, returned to the reheating furnace, and brought again to the proper temperature for rolling. The next series of 4 to 6 passes are made in one or more trains of roughing rolls, and the last 8 or 10 passes in a train of finishing rolls. (The figures given here are merely representative of average practice. The number of passes in each roll train varies considerably in the different rail mills.)

Structural steel sections are rolled in the same manner as rails. The different sectional areas for a given size of any structural shape, such as angles, I-beams, and channels, may be produced with the same set of rolls by simply changing slightly the axial distance between the finishing rolls.

Plates are rolled from slabs. The successive reduction in the thickness of the plate is accomplished by bringing the rolls slightly nearer together between passes. Plates that are rolled in an ordinary mill and then sheared are known as sheared plates. Plates rolled in a universal mill are known as universal mill plates. *Sheets* and *strip* are rolled from sheet bars.

Rods are rolled in a manner similar to that described for steel rails except that the original bloom is usually cut up into a number of small sections before reheating and rolling. A mill called a guide mill is used, the material after each pass being bent around and guided into the next pass by a device specially attached to the mill for the purpose.

Wire-making is only a rolling operation so far as the making of the wire-rod is concerned. A considerable portion of the reduction of the section is accomplished by a special operation known as cold drawing. The wire-rod is rolled in the manner above noted, its final diameter being usually from $\frac{1}{4}$ to $\frac{1}{2}$ inch. The wire-rod is then wound into coils and pickled in a dilute solution of sulfuric acid, which removes the scale. Water is next sprayed on to wash off the acid, and this is followed by immersion in a bath of limewater, which removes the last traces of acid. The coils are now dried in an oven and sent to the wire-drawing mill.

Cold drawing consists in successively reducing the section, and extending the length, by repeatedly pulling it cold through tapered holes in a die or "draw-plate." Each hole through which the metal is drawn is somewhat smaller than the preceding hole, the average amount of reduction being from 20 to 25 per cent. Some thick lubricant is applied to the draw-plate to reduce friction and prevent too rapid wear on the hole.

The wire must be annealed by heating to a low red heat in a closed receptacle after each three to ten passes, because of the hardening of the metal caused by drawing. The finished wire is also annealed unless it is to be sold as hard-drawn wire.

Lap-Welded Pipes. The metal is first rolled into flat strips called "skelp," of the desired thickness, then bent to a U-shaped section and, by another pass, to a circular section with the edges overlapping. (Small pipe may be bent to the circular section by drawing the skelp through a die.) The metal is now brought to a welding heat and is passed through a pair of welding rolls over a mandrel which is supported between the rolls on the end of a long rod. A second pass through sizing rolls is made to insure accuracy of size.

Butt-welded pipes are made by drawing the skelp at a welding heat through a die or "bell" which welds the edges together without lapping.

Seamless tubes are made either by forcing a flat plate through a cylindrical die by means of a mandrel or by piercing a billet longitudinally, expanding the hole by forcing larger and larger tapered expanders through it and finally rolling over mandrels until the section desired is attained.

Cold-rolled steel is steel in which the last few passes through the rolls are made with comparatively cold metal. Pickling is necessary before cold-rolling to remove the scale, the result being a great gain in accuracy in size and form and in surface finish.

Thin-Gauge Steel. *Cold pressing* of steel sheets and strip into thin-gauge structural-steel shapes is extensively employed in 1954 because of the economy gained in building construction. The flat sheets (up to $3/16$ inch thick) are blanked into desired shapes and sizes, and then cold pressed by bending and stamping into structural shapes such as angles and channels. Built-up sections such as H-sections are formed by spot-welding channels back to back.

7.38 Mechanical Work. Steel is said to be mechanically worked when it undergoes the operations of forging, rolling, or drawing. If the operation is carried out above the critical range the steel is *hot worked* and if below the critical range *cold worked*.

Forging under the Steam Hammer. The steam hammer now finds little application in the steel industry except in the forging of high-grade steel, where the value of the product and the especial desirability of giving the metal the fine grain attained by hammering justify the higher cost as compared to rolling, and in the production of that large class of articles called "drop forgings." This class of articles includes a great variety of machine parts, small tools, automobile parts, etc.

Drop forgings are made by the use of dies, between which the metal is worked into the desired form by the blows of a steam hammer. The dies are made of hardened steel, the impressions formed in the faces of the dies corresponding to the impressions formed in the mold for a casting. The metal is placed upon the lower die, which is made fast to the anvil, and the upper die is carried by the head of the hammer. Very often a series of dies are necessary to complete a forging, each set approximating more closely the final form required.

Pressing. The effect of pressing steel, by the action of large hydraulic presses, differs from that produced by the action of a hammer in that the force applied acts for an appreciable interval of time and the distortion produced extends deeper into the metal. In consequence, the press produces a better crystalline structure than the hammer for all except very thin sections and is therefore preferred to the hammer for all heavy forging.

The hydraulic press consists essentially of a hydraulic cylinder in which a plunger or ram moves vertically and is forced down upon the metal supported on an anvil block or bed as for hammers. Presses vary in size from a few tons capacity up to 14,000-ton armor-plate presses which will handle ingots weighing 50 tons or more.

Hydraulic presses are used to a great extent not only in the reduction of ingots in place of a cogging mill and in the pressing of heavy plates but also in the production of forgings pressed between dies, as in the case of the steam hammer, and in the production of a large class of articles made of thin plate steel which is pressed cold between dies.

7.39 Effects of Hot Mechanical Working. The first effect of hot mechanical working is the benefit derived from the elimination of flaws, blowholes, etc. The coarse crystalline structure of steel slowly cooled from a high temperature is also improved by working, since the crystals are broken up and mix intimately, the continuity of their cleavage planes thus being destroyed and their cohesive and their adhesive power being increased.

In the ordinary practice of steel mills the finished section is not more than 10 per cent of the ingot section, and it is commonly not more than 2 or 3 per cent, often being much less than 1 per cent.

The temperature at which working is finished ("finishing temperature") is a very important consideration, since, if this temperature is much above Ar_3, the crystals grow to a certain extent, thus diminishing strength and especially lowering the elastic limit of the steel. In the ordinary practice of rolling structural steel, the finishing heat is above Ar_3 and the elastic limit is therefore comparatively low. If the working be continued until the metal is not above Ar_3, large crystals cannot reform, and strength and especially the elastic limit are increased. The lower the finishing temperature, the better the effect of mechanical work, so long as Ar_3 is not passed.

7.40 Effects of Cold Mechanical Working. Cold working of steels, i.e., the mechanical distortion of the metal below the critical range of temperatures, cannot be practiced except with low- or medium-carbon steels. The effect of cold working upon the existing structure is to elongate the crystalline elements in the direction of working. Cold working does not improve the crystalline structure as does working above the critical range, and the primary effect of cold working upon physical properties is a marked decrease in ductility and an increase in hardness and brittleness. One other effect, which constitutes a great practical advantage for steels used for certain purposes, is the very material extent to which the elastic limit of steel may be raised by cold working. This fact is taken advantage of in the manufacture of certain grades of hard wire and in the finishing of steel rods intended for particular purposes. The extent of the effect of cold working depends directly upon how far below the critical range working is continued and is most marked when working is done at atmospheric temperatures.

Cold working breaks up and distorts the crystalline grains. The grains will remain deformed if kept below the temperature of recrystallization, but, if "annealed" (Art. 7.51) at a temperature slightly higher than the critical temperature, a "rebirth" of the grains occurs and they become equiaxed. This phenomenon is called "recrystallization."

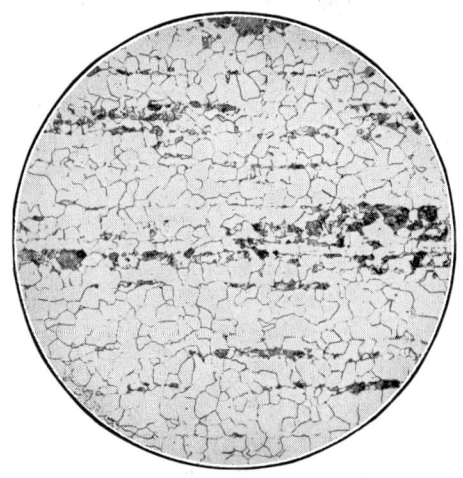

Fig. 7.3. Bands of pearlite in 0.15% open-hearth steel cold-worked and annealed at 843° C. (1550° F.) 100×. (*Courtesy* C. L. Clark.)

Banded Structure. In cold-working hypoeutectoid steel, the ferrite grains may become elongated and bands of distorted pearlite grains may be formed parallel to the direction of cold rolling. The ferrite grains may be recrystallized by annealing, but the bands of pearlite grains are not changed, as may be seen in Fig. 7.3. Steel with banded structure has pronounced directional properties.

7.41 Defects in Ingots and Their Correction. *Blowholes.* Blowholes are caused by the presence of gases, such as hydrogen, nitrogen, and oxygen, which are held in solution by the metal when molten but released as the metal solidifies, and they are also caused by the presence in the metal of iron oxide, which, upon encountering carbon, forms carbon monoxide gas.

The gas in blowholes is usually reducing in effect, and therefore the surfaces of the holes do not become oxidized and will weld together when the ingot is subjected to pressure in the operation of rolling or pressing. Blowholes near the surface of an ingot, however, are likely to break through to the exterior, allowing oxidation, preventing perfect welding in the rolls, and producing "seamy" steel.

Pipe. Another defect in ingots, which cannot be corrected in rolling, is the occurrence of the pipe or shrinkage cavity which forms during solidification. Since the metal cools first in contact with the walls of the mold, the interior will remain molten after an outside solid shell has formed. The interior metal contracts as it solidifies progressively from the outside inward, causing the formation of a cavity which becomes filled with gases evolved during solidification. Since the hottest metal is at the top of the ingot, the upper portion remains molten longer and acts as a feeder to fill the shrinkage cavity in the bottom portion. The pipe is thus localized in the upper third of the ingot. This portion must be cut off in the rolling mill, and it goes back to the steel furnace as scrap.

Ingotism, the formation of large crystals of steel, caused by too-slow cooling or casting at too high a temperature, is a serious defect in ingots which causes the steel to be weak and low in ductility. The bad effects of ingotism may be largely or entirely corrected by careful rolling or forging. The compression of the metal crushes and reduces the size of the crystals, imparting to the steel a much superior degree of strength and ductility. Care must be taken in the initial rolling or forging to avoid the formation of cracks which cannot subsequently be welded.

Segregation of the impurities in steel ingots is caused by the fact that most impurities, notably carbon, phosphorus, and sulfur, are less soluble in iron when solidified than while molten. In consequence, a part of the impurities in the iron are progressively rejected by each layer of metal as it solidifies, being absorbed by the still molten portion, the net result being a tendency toward concentration of the impurities in the part or parts of the ingot which solidify last. Segregation cannot be altogether prevented, but it may be lessened by the addition of elements such as aluminum or titanium, which have the effect of quieting the steel. Casting in narrow ingots is also effective, but is not always practicable because it would take so long to cast many small ingots from one large ladle that the first metal would be too hot if the last metal were not too cold.

7.42 Dendritic Structure. During the crystallization of steel, elongated crystals known as "dendrites" are many times formed (Fig. 7.4). The growth of dendrites in steel is associated with the segregation of phosphides and possibly sulfides and oxides. During hot working, the dendritic structure is rolled into ribbons; in hypoeutectoid steel, banded structures are formed which when suitably etched and viewed under the microscope have phantom-like structures called "ghost lines." These ghost lines are lines of ferrite with small inclusions of impurities (Fig. 7.5). Carbon is probably expelled from these bands by the action of segregated phosphorus. The formation of such dendritic lines affects the directional properties of steel since the tensile strength is reduced across the bands.

Fig. 7.4. Macroetch showing dendritic structure. Etched with Stead's reagent. (Homerberg.)

Fig. 7.5. Macroetch showing phosphorus segregation in steel bar. Etched with iodine. (Homerberg.)

Structure and Constitution of Iron and Steel

7.43 The Iron-Carbon Equilibrium Diagram. The iron-carbon equilibrium diagram shown in Fig. 7.6 gives essential information concerning the constitution of iron, steel, and cast iron. It might more properly be termed the iron-iron carbide diagram since it is generally considered that the carbon exists in the stable phase as iron carbide, Fe_3C, which is called *cementite*. The equilibrium diagram shown in Fig. 7.6 is plotted for amounts of carbon up to 5 per cent, which is sufficient for practical purposes. The diagram is sometimes shown extended up to 6.67 per cent carbon, which corresponds to 100 per cent cementite, since 1 per cent carbon corresponds to 15 per cent cementite.

Figure 7.7 is an iron-carbon equilibrium diagram which shows the temperatures for various heat-treating operations.

7.44 Classification of the Ferrous Alloys. Alloys containing very small amounts of carbon (not exceeding 0.008 per cent) are classed as *irons;* alloys in which the carbon ranges from small amounts up to the point of maximum solubility in iron (up to about 2.0 per cent) are usually classed as *steels*; and the iron alloys containing above 2.0 per cent carbon are generally classed as *cast irons*. A further subdivision may be made in which those steels having less than 0.80 per cent carbon (the eutectoid composition) are known as the *hypoeutectoid* steels, whereas those varying in carbon content from 0.80 per cent up to 2.0 per cent are called *hypereutectoid* steels. A similar division is made in the iron class. Irons from 2.0 per cent carbon up to the eutectic at 4.3 per cent carbon are known as *hypoeutectic* irons and those from 4.3 per cent carbon upward are called *hypereutectic*.

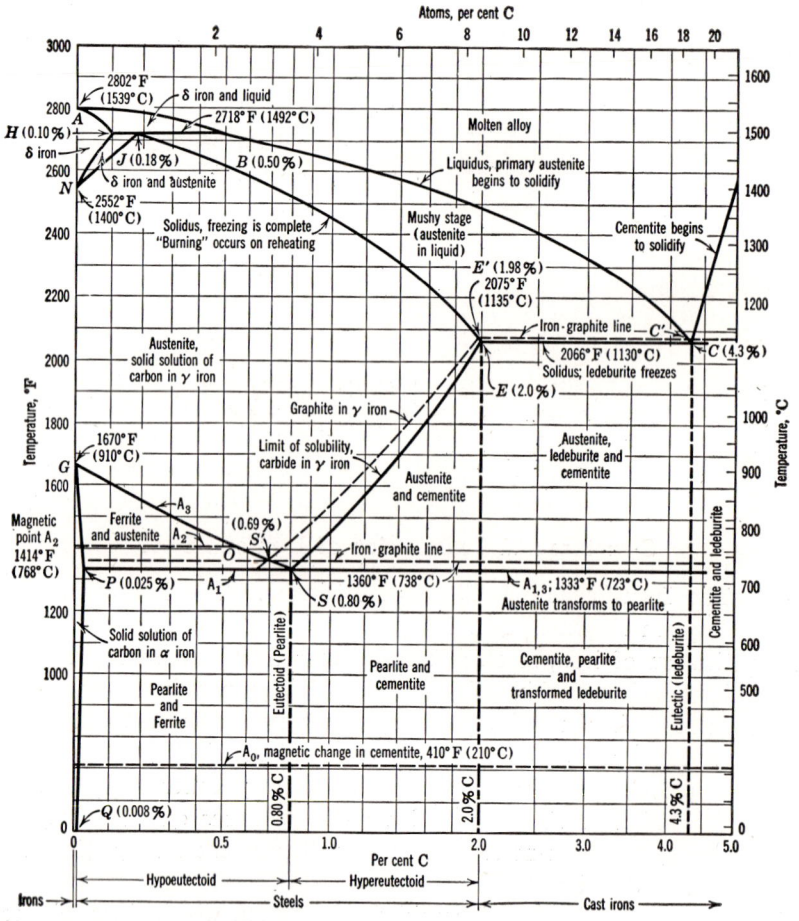

Fig. 7.6. Equilibrium diagram for iron-carbon alloys. (*Courtesy* American Society for Metals.)

7.45 Constitution of Iron. The constitution of iron is shown at the left side of Fig. 7.6. Ingot iron which contains small amounts of impurities (Art. 7.65) is a commercial iron that is typical of this class. Iron completely free from impurities has never been obtained. However, the constitution of iron of 0 per cent carbon, as shown in Fig. 7.6, has been obtained experimentally from iron containing extremely small amounts of impurities.

Steel

When pure iron is cooled from the liquid state, a temperature effect is noticed at 1539° C. (2802° F.) (the melting point of iron), a second at

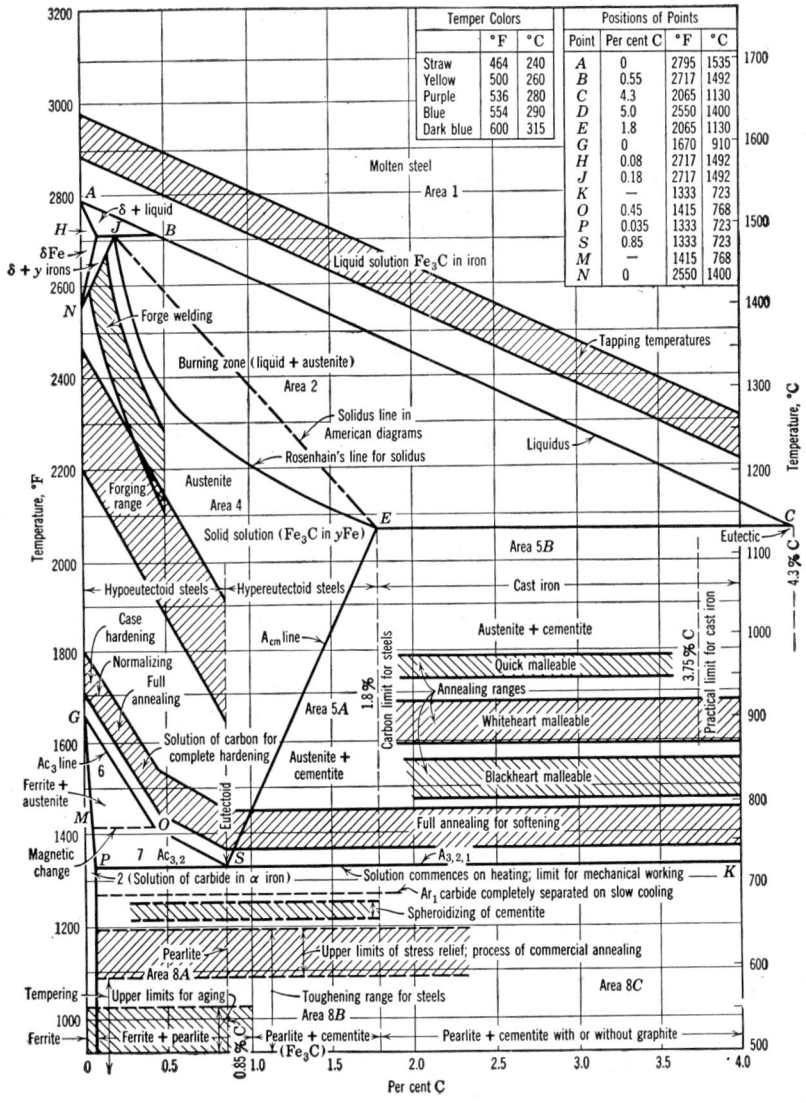

Fig. 7.7. Iron-carbon equilibrium diagram modified for shopmen. (*Courtesy* American Society for Metals.)

1400° C. (2552° F.), a third at 910° C. (1670° F.), and a fourth at 768° C. (1414° F.). The last three temperature effects correspond to retardations in the cooling curve which are due to allotropic changes in the metal. Such allotropic changes are due to rearrangement of the atoms in the solidified metal and are accompanied by evolution of heat. The four allotropic forms of pure iron are in order: delta, gamma, beta, and alpha iron. Delta iron is not of much practical importance since, as the diagram indicates, it is stable only above the top forging temperature. Gamma iron has a face-centered cubic space lattice, is paramagnetic, and is stable above 910° C. (1670° F.) in the range of forging and hot working. Much doubt has been expressed as to the existence of beta iron (below 910° C. [1670° F.] and above 768° C. [1414° F.]), especially since the methods of X-ray examination of metals have been so greatly improved. From the viewpoint of the engineer it makes little difference whether beta iron exists or not, as the valuable properties of steel are associated with the alpha and gamma forms. Beta iron has a body-centered cubic space lattice. Alpha iron forms below 768° C. (1414° F.), has a body-centered cubic arrangement, and is ferromagnetic.

On heating iron from a low temperature, the heat effects take place in the reverse direction at very closely the same temperatures as for cooling if the heating and cooling operations are carried on very slowly; for ordinary rates of temperature change, the heat effects take place on heating at slightly higher temperatures than on cooling.

As these changes were first studied in detail by the French metallurgist Osmond, the names and abbreviations corresponding to the temperature effects have been taken from the French. The symbols used are A (*arrêt*) meaning stop (arrest), c (*chauffage*) referring to a temperature rise, and r (*refroidissement*) applied to the falling temperature. For example, Ar_3 indicates the change at about 910° C., when iron is cooled, and Ac_1 is applied to the heat evolution occurring at a temperature of about 723° C. when iron is heated. These points are referred to as the *critical points* in iron. Since the Ac and Ar points are very close for very slow rates of heating and cooling, the letter A without either symbol c or r is used in Fig. 7.6 to denote the average temperature. The symbol A_e is employed to denote arrests on the equilibrium diagram (e for equilibrium) for infinitely slow cooling or heating and from a practical standpoint may be considered as averages of A_r and A_c temperatures.

A change in magnetism of iron on heating occurs at A_2 (768° C.); ferrite loses its magnetism upon heating above this temperature.

7.46 Constitution of Steel. Steel is essentially an alloy of iron and carbon, although various other elements are usually present. In the "plain carbon" steels, sulfur, phosphorus, manganese, and silicon are present in small amounts, whereas chromium, nickel, or other elements are found in the alloy steels.

A comparison of the iron-carbon equilibrium diagram in Fig. 7.6 with those previously considered in Chapter 2 shows it to be a combination of various simple types. The area *ABJHN* dealing with transformations of delta iron will not be considered in this volume since these are not of primary importance for engineers.

Molten alloy when cooled to the liquidus line BC begins to solidify as austenite, which is the solid solution of carbon in gamma iron. Austenite has a face-centered space lattice, is soft and ductile, and has considerable strength. It is non-magnetic. Austenite in carbon and low-alloy steels is not stable at room temperature but exists in certain high-alloy steels such as manganese steel or 18-8 chromium-nickel steel. See Fig. 7.8 for a photo-

Fig. 7.8. Rolled manganese steel, water-quenched from 1925° F. 100×. (Battelle.) Carbon, 1.36%, manganese, 14.2%, silicon, 0.36%. The bands and wrinkles across the crystals are due to deformations from rolling, not to local composition differences. (*Courtesy* Bullens.)

micrograph of austenite in manganese steel. No carbides are visible since the Fe_3C is in solution in the austenite. Austenite is a single phase, all the grains appearing alike.

Carbon is soluble in austenite up to 2.0 per cent. Molten alloys containing up to 2.0 per cent carbon solidify along the solidus line JE into austenite. Molten alloys containing from 2.0 to 4.3 per cent carbon solidify as austenite and a eutectic mixture, called ledeburite, composed of saturated austenite and cementite. Molten alloys containing 4.3 per cent carbon solidify as ledeburite (point C). Above 4.3 per cent carbon, the diagram shows a line along which cementite begins to solidify; below 1130° C., cementite and ledeburite are formed. The constitution of those alloys containing more than 2.0 per cent carbon is discussed further in Chapter 9, "Cast Iron."

Further slow cooling of austenite for those alloys classed as steels (below 2.0 per cent carbon) causes transformation from the solid-solution state into the eutectoid state. Austenite containing exactly 0.80 per cent carbon will be transformed into the eutectoid at S (Fig. 7.6). The eutectoid S is an intimate mixture of pure iron (called *ferrite*) and iron carbide (*cementite*)

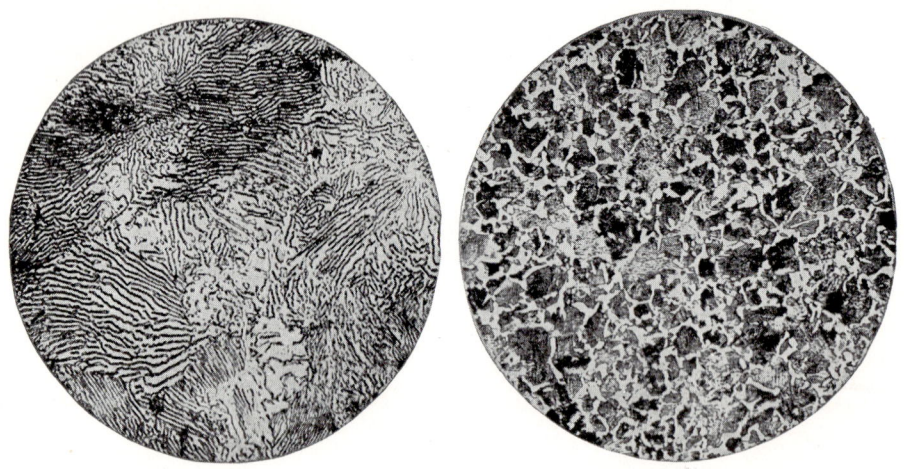

Fig. 7.9. Pearlite 250×. (Homerberg.)

Fig. 7.10. Microstructure of slowly cooled 0.4% carbon steel 250×. (Homerberg.)

which, because of its resemblance to mother of pearl under certain forms of lighting, has been called the pearly constituent, or *pearlite*. Pearlite has the characteristic laminated or thumbprint structure shown in Fig. 7.9.

Fig. 7.11. Microstructure of slowly cooled 1.6% carbon steel 250×. (Homerberg.)

When austenite containing 0.15 per cent carbon is slowly cooled, pure iron (called ferrite) separates along the line GS, the remaining solid solution becoming increasingly richer in carbon until it contains 0.80 per cent carbon and so corresponds to the eutectoid S, which then forms. The iron has changed from gamma iron through beta iron and into alpha iron. The resulting structure is a mixture of ferrite crystals with pearlite crystals and is typical of hypoeutectoid steels (Fig. 7.10).

When austenite containing 1.6 per cent carbon is slowly cooled, separation occurs along the line ES. The austenite then decomposes into *cementite*, and the remaining austenite becomes poorer in carbon as the cooling proceeds until it contains only 0.80 per cent carbon at S, where the eutectoid is formed. The resulting hypereutectoid structure consists of a mixture of cementite and pearlite (Fig. 7.11).

Consideration of the diagram indicates, then, that, if a steel is cooled so slowly that all changes have taken place, only three combinations of constituents are possible: (1) in the hypoeutectoid steels (below 0.80 per cent carbon), ferrite and pearlite will be found in varying amounts; (2) at 0.80 per cent carbon the eutectoid pearlite occurs alone; and (3) in the hypereutectoid steels (above 0.80 per cent carbon), cementite and pearlite will be found. The relative amounts of the three constituents are shown graphically in Fig. 7.12.

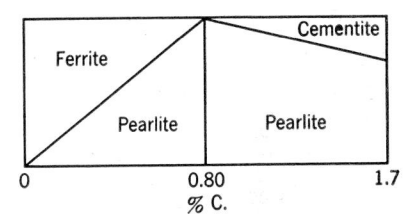

Fig. 7.12. Constitution diagram for slowly cooled steels.

7.47 Properties of Ferrite, Cementite, and Pearlite. The physical properties of the three constituents are approximately as follows:

Ferrite is soft and ductile.
    Tensile strength, 40,000 pounds per square inch (commercially pure).
    Elongation, 40 per cent in 2 inches.
    Brinell hardness, about 90.
    Diamond hardness, 170. (Microhardness measured by H. A. Unckel on ferrite in low and medium carbon steel containing 0.25 per cent manganese and 0.50 per cent silicon. See reference 7.40.)

Pearlite is harder and less ductile.
    Tensile strength, 125,000 pounds per square inch.
    Elongation, 15 per cent in 2 inches.
    Brinell hardness, 250 to 300.
    Diamond hardness, 310. (Pearlite in commercial steel of 0.35 per cent carbon.)

Cementite is hard and brittle. Its tensile strength is not known because it has been obtained only in fine crystals.
    Brinell hardness, about 650.
    Diamond hardness, 760. (Cementite in 0.35 per cent carbon steel carburized.)

Pearlite is characteristic only of slowly cooled, fully annealed steel. If the mechanical properties of the microconstituents are known, it is possible to estimate with a fair degree of accuracy the properties of any slowly cooled steel by a calculation of its microstructure from its chemical composition. This can be done most readily by means of Fig. 7.12.

If the three constituents, ferrite, cementite, and pearlite, were the only possible ones, steel would be limited in its properties. It is known that many changes in the physical properties can be produced by the operations of quenching, tempering or drawing, annealing, and similar forms of heating and cooling classified under the general name of "heat treatment."

7.48 Hardening or Quenching. Whenever a solid solution decomposes with falling temperature into the eutectoid, this decomposition may be more or less complete depending on the cooling rate. The hardening of steel is an illustration of this phenomenon. If the steel is cooled slowly from above *GSE* (Fig. 7.6), the changes just considered will take place. If, however, the steel is cooled as quickly as possible, decomposition into the eutectoid will be prevented; in carbon steel, rapid cooling produces a structure called *martensite*.

Successful hardening of steel is an art which requires much experience, but a few general principles apply.

1. Steel should always be annealed before hardening, to remove forging or cooling strains.
2. Heating for hardening should be slow.
3. Steel should be quenched on a rising and not on a falling temperature. The reason for this suggestion is that, as the temperature of heating increases above the Ac_3 line, the grains tend to increase greatly in size with a corresponding decrease in the physical properties of the material.

Many quenching mediums have been proposed, but practically any desired degree of hardness can be produced by means of one of the following: (1) brine for maximum hardness, (2) water for the rapid cooling of the common steels, and (3) light, medium, or heavy oil for use with common steel parts of irregular shape or for alloy steels. The rate of cooling, and therefore the hardness of the steel, decreases with the increasing density of the quenching oil. Increase in size of steel part decreases the rate of cooling in given quenching mediums; for example, steels which harden satisfactorily in oil baths when in small bars, require water quenching when in larger sections.

The quenching power of coolants depends on their temperatures, the higher the temperature the lower the cooling velocity. For uniform results, the coolant temperature must be controlled, as by means of cooling coils; circulation of the quenching medium is necessary to avoid adherence of gas

Steel

films on the metal surfaces which results in soft spots owing to non-uniform heat transfer.

All hardened steel is in a state of strain, and steel pieces with sharp angles or grooves sometimes crack immediately after hardening. For this reason tempering must follow the quenching operation as soon as possible. Quenching strains due to water hardening are always more severe than those caused by oil hardening.

In order to obtain maximum hardness in quenching hypoeutectoid steels, it is necessary to dissolve all the ferrite; this can be accomplished by heating above GS (Fig. 7.6). On the other hand, hypereutectoid steels need only to be heated above A_1 to obtain great hardness because the cementite is quite hard itself and does not need to be entirely dissolved in austenite.

If the steel is cooled somewhat less rapidly than would naturally lead to the formation of martensite, as, for example, if it is cooled in heavy oil, bainite or a pearlitic structure may be produced.

7.49 Martensite. Martensite is the usual product of water quenching. It is magnetic and has an interlacing needlelike (acicular) structure. (See Fig. 7.13.) Martensite is an extremely hard substance, but it is not as hard as cementite, however, since its diamond hardness ranges from about 400 to 500. It is wholly lacking in ductility.

Martensite is defined as ferrite supersaturated with carbon. It occurs in two phases, alpha and beta. Alpha martensite has the carbon atoms arranged in a tetragonal structure. Beta martensite has a body-centered cubic arrangement. Alpha martensite is under internal stress; beta martensite has internal stress relieved. These structures are further explained as follows. In alpha martensite, the structure is a rectangular prism with its height slightly longer than the sides of the square base; the presence of carbon in an orderly arrangement is considered to be the cause of the stopping of the transformation from austenite before a perfect cubical structure is formed. Slight heating (tempering) or standing for a long time causes the crystals to expel the trapped carbon into random orientation (forming Fe_3C), which relieves internal stresses, and to contract to the perfect cubical structure.

Fig. 7.13. Martensite 1000×.

The hardness of martensite is due to the presence of many fine hard carbon particles being dispersed throughout the matrix of ferrite. When the small hard particles are close together, the entire mass acts as a hard and brittle substance. The hard particles may also be considered as keys in the mass of the metal tending to prevent "slip."

7.50 Tempering of Steel. *Tempering* may be defined as the process of reheating a hardened steel to a definite temperature below the critical temperature, holding it at that point for a time, and cooling it usually by quenching for the purpose of obtaining toughness and ductility in the steel. This operation is commonly called "drawing" if carried out below 400° C. (752° F.), and "toughening" if temperatures higher than 400° C. are used.

7.51 Annealing. *Annealing* is the process of heating a metal above the critical temperature range, holding at that temperature for a proper period of time, and then slowly cooling. The metal is ordinarily allowed to cool slowly in the furnace. The three chief functions of annealing are: (1) to soften the steel to meet definite specifications or to make machining easier; (2) to relieve internal strains caused by quenching, forging, cold working or in other ways; and (3) to refine the grain.

Another operation which is very similar to annealing is called *normalizing*. This may be defined as heating above the upper critical range and cooling to below that range in still air at ordinary temperature. Normalizing is employed to obtain uniform conditions in metals previously treated in different ways and is often applied to alloy steels and machined parts, especially if they are later to be heat treated.

7.52 Example of Heat Treatment. The heat treatment of a 0.40 per cent carbon steel is given as an example. This is a medium-high-carbon steel of fair machining properties and good hardening characteristics, suitable for small and medium-sized forgings. The part would be normalized or annealed at a temperature of 871 to 927° C. (1600 to 1700° F.) to give a structure of suitable machining properties. (See Fig. 7.7.) After machining it would be hardened by heating to 830 to 857° C. (1525 to 1575° F.) and quenching in water or oil, depending upon the section.[2] The hardened piece of martensitic structure is then tempered to desired hardness. For example, the steel might be reheated to 600° C. (1112° F.), held at that temperature for a time, and then quenched.

7.53 Isothermal Transformation Diagrams. Isothermal transformation diagrams plot the time required for the transformation of austenite into ferrite and iron carbide at a constant temperature. The experimental work necessary to develop such a diagram for a given steel will be described. Early work on the decomposition of austenite was done by Davenport and Bain. Small specimens of the given steel are heated to austenitic state and then are immersed in a liquid bath at a constant temperature. At the end of a definite period of time a specimen is withdrawn and quenched in brine

[2] *SAE Handbook*, 1952, Table 2, p. 85.

Steel 141

or cold water to preserve the existing structure. Each specimen is polished, etched, and examined under the microscope to ascertain the extent of the decomposition and the character of the structure produced. Quenching causes any untransformed austenite remaining at the end of the time the specimen is immersed to appear as martensite; in this way the time required for austenite to be completely transformed into ferrite and iron carbide at

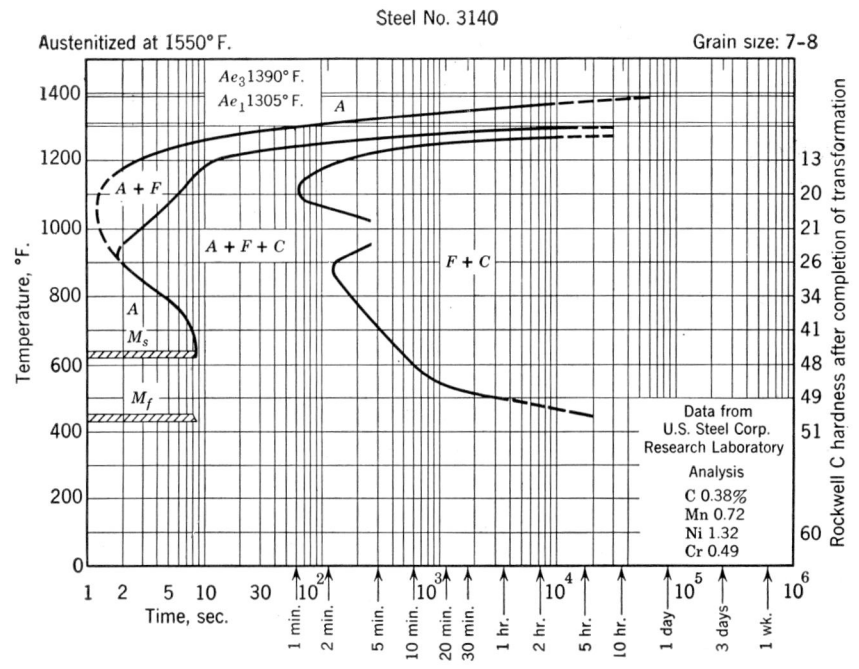

Fig. 7.14. Isothermal transformation diagram for SAE 3140 nickel-chromium steel austenitized at 1550° F. (*Courtesy* Research Laboratory, U. S. Steel Corp. and International Nickel Co.)

a given temperature can be determined. This procedure is followed for various temperatures. Transformation data for a number of temperature levels are plotted on the diagram, which has the time plotted logarithmically as abscissas versus temperature as ordinates.

Figure 7.14 is an isothermal transformation diagram for SAE 3140 nickel-chromium alloy steel (a hypoeutectoid steel). Such diagrams are generally referred to as TTT (transformation-temperature-time) diagrams, or may be called IT (isothermal transformation) diagrams; they are also frequently called "S" curves (from their shape for carbon steels). The logarithmic scale for time is necessary for the purpose of showing the short periods of time for the reactions to begin as well as the long periods required for the completion of the reactions. At the left is the ordinate scale for temperature. On the right of the diagram, Rockwell C hardness values are plotted for the steel when cooled to room temperature immediately after completion of transformation of the austenite at the temperature shown. The maximum hardness for the SAE 3140 steel obtained by quenching in brine from the austenitizing temperature of 70° F. is indicated by the bottom number (60). For these curves, the samples were heated to 1550° F. initially and completely austenitized. Above the temperature Ae_3 (1390° F.), the austenite is stable and will remain so indefinitely without transformation. Below Ae_3 but above Ae_1 (1305° F.), the austenite becomes unstable, and in the course of time precipitates ferrite, leaving the remaining austenite approaching the composition of the eutectoid. The Ae_3 line is the asymptote of the top curve, and the Ae_1 line is the asymptote of the second curve from the top. The area A at the top and at the left of the diagram (Fig. 7.14) is the region where austenite only occurs. The various regions have constituents as tabulated:

Region	Constituents
A	Austenite
A + F	Austenite plus ferrite
A + F + C	Austenite plus ferrite plus carbide (cementite)
F + C	Ferrite plus carbide (cementite)

If a sample of SAE 3140 steel is rapidly quenched from 1550° F. to a temperature of 1320° F. (slightly above Ae_1) and held at this temperature, the austenite will remain without change for about 5 minutes until the top heavy line is crossed; ferrite separates; and the carbon content of the austenite is increased. The resulting products are ferrite and austenite since at this temperature only ferrite separates.

If the same steel is quickly quenched from 1550° F. to 1200° F. and held at that temperature, ferrite will start to precipitate at 2½ seconds, and this precipitation will proceed until approximately 13 seconds have elapsed. Here at the second curve the austenite will commence to decompose into pearlite (ferrite plus cementite); this decomposition will continue until the third curve is reached at about 150 seconds. To the right of the third curve, no further change will take place and the final product will consist of coarse-grained lamellar pearlite and ferrite. Rockwell C hardness will be 13.

At a temperature of 1100° F., similar phenomena would occur, but the resulting steel will have a structure of fine-grained lamellar pearlite and ferrite. Rockwell C hardness would be 20. (See Fig. 7.14.)

The two upper curves merge at 920° F. If a sample of this steel is quenched from 1550° F. to 920° F., the austenite will transform directly to pearlite (ferrite plus cementite) without the separation of any excess ferrite. The resulting pearlite will contain only 0.38 per cent carbon corresponding to the carbon content of this SAE 3140 steel instead of 0.80 per cent carbon corresponding to the eutectoid. This pearlite will have a uniformly fine-grained lamellar structure.

Below a temperature of 920° F. for this SAE 3140 steel, the structure formed by transformation of the austenite is *bainite* which has an acicular structure. Bainite is harder than pearlite, but tougher and softer than martensite.

The M_s temperature represents the temperature at which austenite begins to transform to martensite, and the M_f temperature corresponds to the temperature at which the transformation is substantially complete. (Note that the lengths of the bars marking these temperatures have no significance.) When austenite is cooled to a temperature just below the M_s point, a small amount will transform immediately to martensite; with time (at this temperature) some or all of the remaining austenite will transform finally to bainite. However, continuous cooling down to the M_f temperature will result in continuous formation of martensite as the temperature is reduced, so that the structure will be entirely martensitic at the M_f temperature. This operation of sudden cooling or quenching to produce a martensitic structure is called *hardening*.

The above discussion pertains to small specimens where the temperatures in the interior and exterior of the piece do not vary greatly. If a piece of large section is cooled, it is possible when the exterior temperature is at M_f causing formation of martensite, that the interior temperature will be above M_s and austenite at the center will not be transformed. Warping or cracking of the piece frequently occurs owing to such non-uniform transformation. As a matter of fact carbon steels will retain a small percentage of austenite even when very rapidly quenched; however, tempering usually transforms the remaining austenite and equalizes the stresses.

Summarizing the above discussion, it is noted that for transformation of austenite at progressively lower temperatures, the character of the structure of the steel would be:

1. Coarse-grained lamellar pearlite plus ferrite.
2. Fine-grained lamellar pearlite plus ferrite.
3. Uniformly fine-grained lamellar pearlite.
4. Bainite.
5. Martensite.

7.54 Hardenability. In hardening steels by quenching, the critical cooling rate from the austenitic state must be sufficiently rapid to pass to the left of the pearlite and bainite "noses" in the isothermal transformation diagram. For plain carbon steels, the nose of the pearlite curve is close to the left of the diagram which means that the transformation of austenite begins in a very short interval of time; consequently in order to produce martensite by quenching, the critical cooling rate must be very fast, particularly through the temperature range from 1200° F. to 800° F. (See Fig. 7.15 for SAE 1050 carbon steel.) The introduction of alloys into steels in many instances moves the pearlite nose to the right which means that the transformation of austenite is delayed; such incorporation of alloys into steels also may cause the bainite nose to be shifted to the right in some instances. A good example of this action is shown in Fig. 7.16 which is an

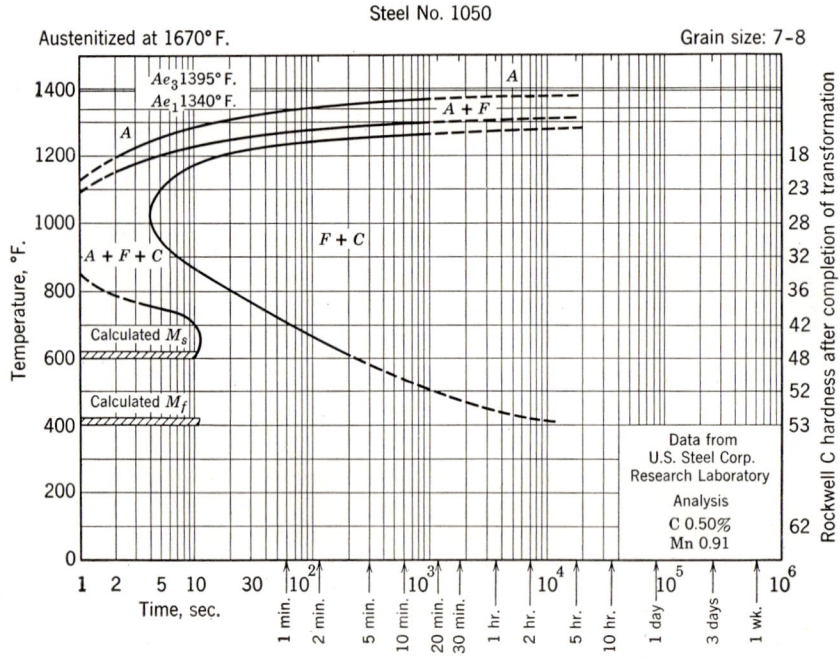

Fig. 7.15. Isothermal transformation diagram for SAE 1050 carbon steel austenitized at 1670° F. (*Courtesy* Research Laboratory, U. S. Steel Corp. and International Nickel Co.)

isothermal transformation diagram for SAE 4330 nickel-chromium-molybdenum steel. SAE 4330 steel has high hardenability, since the pearlite and bainite noses lie well to the right. The hardenability of a steel is expressed as a function of the required rate of cooling in quenching to avoid transformation of austenite into pearlite or bainite, the lower the rate the greater the hardenability. SAE 4330 steel is deep hardening even in rather large sections; a slow rate of cooling makes possible more uniform temperatures throughout the piece and hence more uniform hardening from surface to center.

Figure 7.17 illustrates deep hardening. A plain carbon steel SAE 1045 is shown at the left, and a chromium-vanadium steel SAE 6140 at the right. Steel bars of different diameters were quenched in water, and then the Rockwell C hardness test was conducted at various points across the diameter. Hardness values plotted from outside to center of the bars are given. The carbon steel bars have low hardness values at the center. The outer layers of only the two smallest carbon steel bars attain maximum hardness, and for the larger carbon steel bars, the outer surfaces have low hardness values. On the other hand, the chromium-vanadium steel bars have a greater hard-

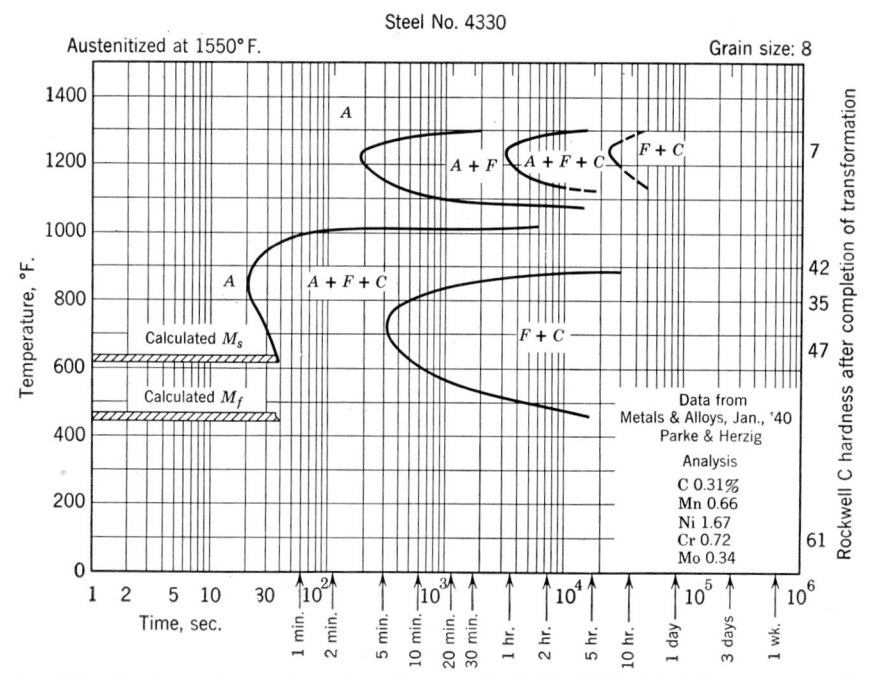

Fig. 7.16. Isothermal transformation diagram for SAE 4330 nickel-chromium-molybdenum steel austenitized at 1550° F. (*Courtesy* Parke and Herzig, *Metals & Alloys*, Jan., 1940, and International Nickel Co.)

ness than the carbon steel bars, particularly in the interior of the bars. The alloy steel is termed deep hardening.

7.55 Tempered Martensite. Reheating a hardened steel of martensitic structure to a temperature of 260° C. (500° F.) or higher causes the iron carbide particles to increase in size. Small carbide particles coalesce to form bigger ones, thus producing larger volumes of ferrite matrix free from carbide. This tempering action has the effect of making the steel tougher and more ductile but lower in strength and hardness. This may be explained by noting that the tempered steel has fewer keys in the mass to prevent slip action, hence it is weaker and softer. The resulting condition is called "tempered martensite"; its structure is nodular or globular. Both temperature and time of tempering affect the change. The time a piece is held at a given tempering temperature is usually at least 30 minutes for each inch of cross-section. An increase in tempering temperature lowers the tensile strength and elastic limit but increases the ductility and resistance to shock. The maximum resistance to shock is obtained by heating to about 40° F.

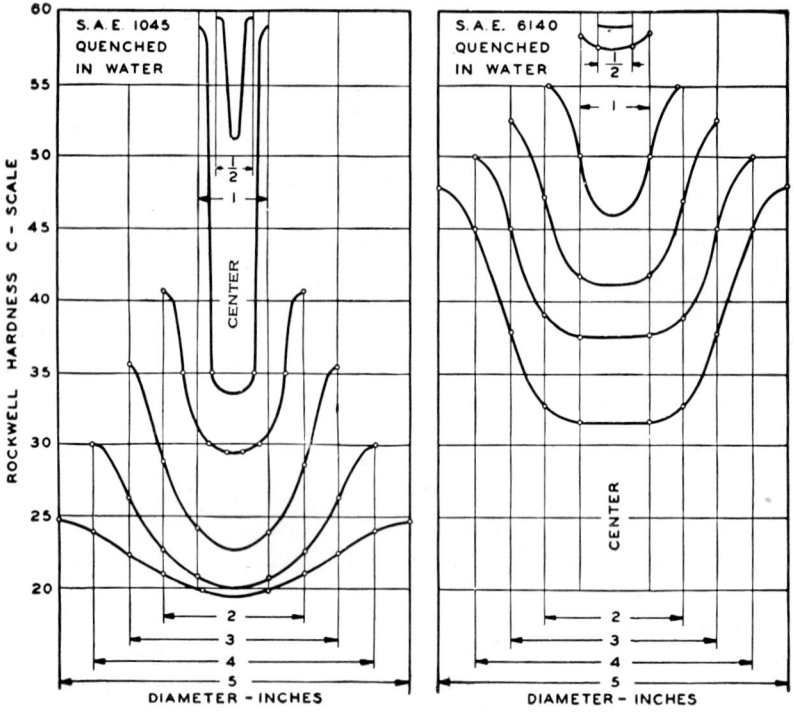

Fig. 7.17. Hardness values from outside to center of steel bars quenched in water. (*Courtesy* Carnegie-Illinois Steel Co. From Campbell, *The Working, Heat Treating, and Welding of Steel,* 2nd ed., John Wiley & Sons.)

below the Ac_1. Modern tempering is effected by heating the hardened steel in a furnace which is gas or oil fired or is electrically heated, or it is accomplished by means of salt baths or melted lead.

7.56 Spheroidized Cementite. Pearlite cannot be formed by reheating hardened steel. That temperature which might be expected to produce lamellar pearlite forms instead the structure known as "spheroidized cementite" (Fig. 7.18). The reheating temperature is about 700° C. (1292° F.) or slightly below the Ac_1. Holding at this temperature for a period of time, agglomeration of carbides occurs, the carbide particles becoming rounded or "spheroidized." Steel in this condition has excellent machining qualities. This is the condition sought in properly annealed tool steel.

7.57 Austempering.

Austempering is a heat-treating process of interrupted quenching of high-carbon and low-alloy steels from a temperature above the transformation range in a coolant having a suitably high rate of heat abstraction and having an intermediate temperature below that of pearlite formation and above that of martensite formation. The steel is kept in the coolant at the intermediate temperature until transformation is completed. Austempering comprises isothermal transformation at a suitable temperature within the bainite transformation range; this is graphically illustrated in Fig. 7.19. Thus it may be seen that austempering is a method of hardening steels without cooling to atmospheric temperature; high internal stresses caused by rapid quenching to atmospheric temperature are avoided so there is less likelihood of cracking or

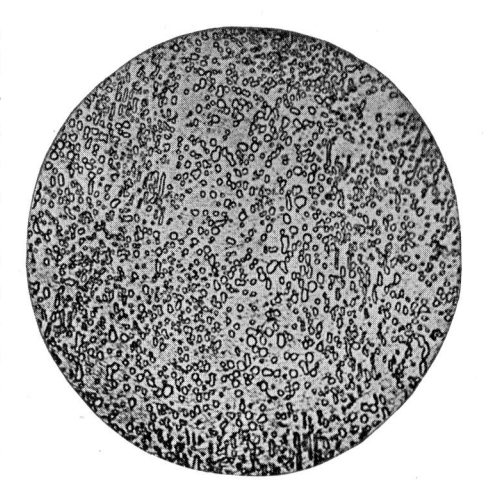

Fig. 7.18. Spheroidized cementite 500×. (Zavarine.)

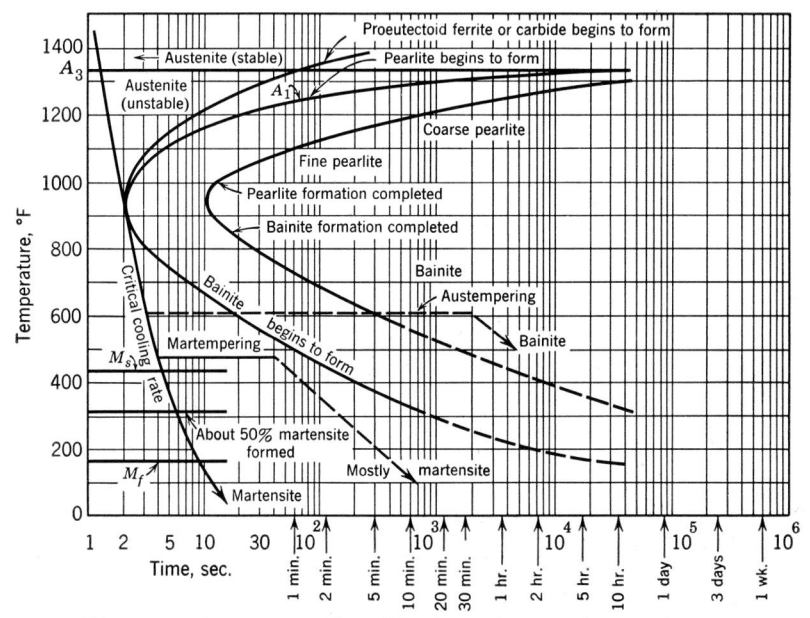

Fig. 7.19. Diagrammatic representation of isothermal curves for a carbon steel showing pearlite formation, bainite formation, critical cooling rate, M_s, M_f, austempering, and martempering. (*Courtesy* F. J. McMulkin, *Iron Age*, v. 157, June 27, 1946, p. 58.)

warping. Physical properties can be varied by choosing the intermediate temperature of the coolant for austenitic transformation (usually from 260° C. [500° F.] to 425° C. [797° F.] for carbon steel).

The purpose of austempering is to obtain a relatively hard structure by direct transformation of the austenite instead of by quenching to martensite with subsequent tempering. Austempered high-carbon steel is generally more ductile and more resistant to impact at hardness level of Rockwell C 50 than steel quenched and tempered by the ordinary procedure, but tensile strength and hardness are not changed appreciably. The explanation advanced for improved ductility is that rapid quenching to atmospheric temperature causes microcracks in the martensitic structure which may not be fused by tempering. Austempering is utilized commercially in the manufacture of wire.

7.58 Martempering. *Martempering* or "time quenching" is a form of interrupted quenching whereby austenite is transformed to martensite. A diagrammatic representation of martempering is given in Fig. 7.19. Martempering consists in quenching high-carbon or low-alloy steel at a critical rate (to the left of the pearlite nose) in a bath held at a temperature slightly above M_s (about 232° C. [450° F.] for a high-carbon steel) and holding it there for a short time until the temperature throughout the piece is equalized. Reference to Fig. 7.19 indicates that this time must be controlled so that the bainite curve will not be crossed. The steel is then cooled at a slow rate to room temperature. The principle of martempering is that if austenite can be retained by rapid quenching down to the temperature of martempering, then hard martensite can be transformed from austenite at a slower cooling rate than in the usual quenching.

The purpose of martempering is to produce hard martensite by transformation of austenite without setting up high internal stresses caused by rapid quenching to atmospheric temperature. Instead of a bath, air at the desired temperature above M_s may be used, and the time period may be utilized for straightening or forming the steel while it is in the soft austenitic condition. Nickel alloy steels have an advantage of extending the bainite transformation curve to the right, hence increasing the time for forming operations. Martempering was developed by B. F. Shepherd.[3] It is utilized for heat treatment of large pieces with reëntrant angles which tend to crack by ordinary quenching.

7.59 Jominy End-Quench Hardenability Test. The Jominy test is employed for determining the depth of hardening of steel. (See *ASTM, Designation:* A255-48T.) The quenching conditions are standardized, and the steel tested is the variable. The comparative ability of a steel to harden under heat treatment becomes apparent in the degree to which the material

---

[3] *Product Eng.*, July, 1945, p. 438; Aug., 1945, p. 515.

Steel

hardens when quenched at different cooling rates. It may be measured by observing the "depth of hardening" of a test specimen of standard shape and size in a standardized quenching procedure. The test specimen is shown in Fig. 7.20. The test consists of water-quenching one end of the cylindrical specimen and measuring the extent of the hardening from the quenched end. Quenching is done by a water spray from an orifice located below the bottom of the specimen. After the quenching is completed, two flat surfaces are ground running parallel to the length of the test specimen 0.015 inches deep and 180 degrees apart for a series of hardness readings. Rockwell C hardness readings are taken at $\frac{1}{16}$-inch intervals for a distance of 2 inches beginning at the water-quenched end. Results on the two sides of the specimen are averaged, and the results plotted with hardness as ordinate versus distance from the water-quenched end as abscissa. (See Fig. 7.21 for curves for steels SAE 5140 and 2340.) Table 7.2 gives the chemical analyses of these two steels.

The structure and hardness of the cold 1-inch Jominy bar corresponds to cooling rates varying from 490° F. per second at $\frac{1}{16}$ inch from the water-quenched end to 3.5° F. per second at

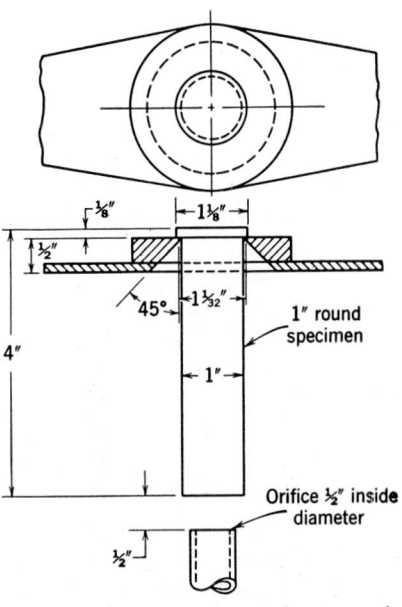

Fig. 7.20. Jominy end-quench test specimen in support for water quenching.

2 inches from the quenched end. (See Fig. 7.21.) These cooling rates correspond approximately to those at the center of a 4-inch cylindrical bar quenched in oil or of a ½-inch cylindrical bar quenched in stirred cold water.

7.60 Index of Hardenability. An index is employed to designate the hardenability of a given steel. For example, an alloy steel such as SAE 5140 containing 0.36 per cent carbon could be specified to have a hardenability of $J_{40} = 8$ which means that the minimum requirement for this steel would be a Rockwell C hardness of 40 at a distance of $\frac{8}{16}$ inches from the water-quenched end of the Jominy bar. If both minimum and maximum limits are required, the index may be specified as $J_{40} = 6$ to 10; this would mean that 40 Rockwell C hardness should lie between $\frac{6}{16}$- and $\frac{10}{16}$-inch positions on the Jominy bar. See curve for SAE 5140 steel in Fig. 7.21. As an alternate method, the code $J_{35/45} = 8$ may be used which specifies a minimum hardness of 35 Rockwell C hardness and a maximum hardness of 45 at $\frac{8}{16}$ inches distance from the water-quenched end. This specification

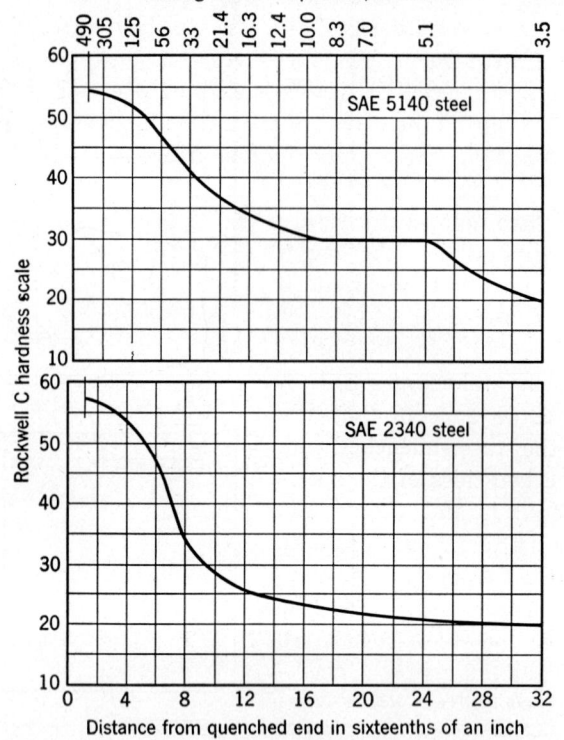

Fig. 7.21. Hardness survey of SAE 5140 and 2340 steels as determined by standard Jominy end-quench test. (*Courtesy* E. J. Eckel, *Univ. Illinois Eng. Exp. Sta. Bull. Ser. 389.*)

Table 7.2

CHEMICAL ANALYSES OF TWO ALLOY STEELS

(*Courtesy Univ. Illinois Exp. Sta. Bull. Ser. 389*)

Percentages

Steel	C	Mn	P	S	Si	Ni	Cr
SAE 5140	0.36	0.76	0.015	0.027	0.170	——	1.05
SAE 2340	0.41	0.62	0.017	0.02	0.204	3.44	——

is also met by steel SAE 5140 as may be seen by referring to Fig. 7.21. In addition, the minimum and maximum hardness values at the distance $\frac{1}{16}$ inch from the end may be specified.

7.61 Selection of Steel by Hardenability. The selection of steels to give a desired hardness may be done by means of curves published in the *SAE*

Handbook, 1952, p. 114, Fig. 10. These curves give a correlation of identical cooling rates in the Jominy test bar and quenched round bars of various diameters. The cooling rates are given for various bar diameters at the surface, at the center, and at ½ and ¾ radius positions of the bar cross-sections.

The American Iron and Steel Institute and the Society of Automotive Engineers have established specifications for hardenability upon quenching of certain steels for heat treatment, called H steels; steel numbers suffixed with an H indicate the steel will meet the hardenability limits as well as the chemical specifications. Hardenability limits are based on the Jominy end-quench test. (See *SAE Handbook,* 1952, p. 48.)

7.62 Grain-Size Control. Grain-size control of steel is an important factor in heat treatment, forging, case hardening, and mechanical working. A test for determination of grain size was originated by McQuaid and Ehn. The American Society for Testing Materials has a standard method of test for grain size. Steel of a given grain size is specified for many applications in order to give greater latitude for safe heat treatment and mechanical operations.

It is well established that grain size affects the physical properties of steels. (See Table 7.3.) For example, of two mild steels of the same com-

Table 7.3

RELATION OF GRAIN SIZE TO THE PHYSICAL PROPERTIES OF CARBON STEELS

Effect of Grain Size

Property	*Coarse-Grained Steels*	*Fine-Grained Steels*
Hardenability	Deeper	Shallower
Ductility for same hardness	Lower	Higher
Resistance to impact	Lower	Higher
Finish	Fair	Good
Condition of surface after deformation	Poorer	Better
Warping after quenching	More	Less
Cracks produced by quenching	Frequent	Generally free from cracks
Carburized steels	Uniform surfaces of good hardness	Soft spots may occur

position and tensile strength, one may have a low impact value due to coarseness of grain. By subjecting this steel to a normalizing treatment at 900° C. (1652° F.), the grain can be refined and the full impact value obtained. However, it is desirable to be able to obtain proper fine grain size consistently after the usual heat treatment and mechanical working. This can be accomplished by specifying suitable fine grain size so that the size of grain will be unchanged by any of the heat-treating operations except uncontrolled overheating. An ordinary steel of coarse grain size may have grain growth beginning at about 730° C. (1346° F.), which is within the range of everyday operations, but a controlled fine-grained steel will not begin to grow until 1000° C. (1832° F.) is reached, which is above the temperature of most operations except those for high-speed tool steel and high-alloy steels.

Forgings of greater strength and density can be formed from coarse-grain-size steel on account of its tendency to produce sounder metal and more uniformly flowing metal than fine-grain-size steel.

Shearing is an important operation in flash trimmings of forgings or stamping for automobile connecting rods, front axles, etc. Steel of fine grain size is tougher and offers greater resistance to shearing but shows less tendency to crack at the edges. Since any fine cracks develop on subsequent heat treatment, the selection of suitable fine-grain-size steel is important in decreasing cracking.

7.63 Case Hardening. An operation closely allied to the heat treatment of steel is that known as case hardening or case carburizing. Case hardening is a form of cementation applied to low- or medium-carbon steels in order to impregnate them with carbon to a depth of a few hundredths to one-fourth of an inch, thus securing a high-carbon case which may subsequently be hardened by quenching. The advantage gained by this treatment is that a surface is produced which will withstand wear, abrasion, cutting, or indentation, and at the same time the core is left soft and tough so that the shock resistance of the material is not impaired.

Usually, the steel for case hardening is one originally containing from 0.1 to 0.2 per cent carbon, and the operation is generally applied to the finished casting, forging, or otherwise fabricated object, so that no machine work need be done on the hardened surface.

Steel for case hardening should have an intermediate grain size for ordinary practice. With coarse-grained steel, quicker, deeper, and more even penetration of carbon is obtained, producing a harder and more even case, but the coarseness is limited by the greater tendency to crack, warp, and check on grinding. Fine-grained steel causes more shallow hardening but freedom from the above defects.

The general method of case hardening consists in heating the steel in contact with carbonaceous matter such as potassium ferrocyanide, charcoal, barium carbonate, bone dust, or charred leather. The usual temperature of heating is about 900° C. (1652° F.). A more rapid penetration of the carbon may be secured by means of higher temperatures, but this practice is attended by the danger of the growth of coarse grains in the interior at the temperature of carbonization, resulting in loss of toughness and strength unless the steel is subsequently reheated to restore the grain size. Enfoliation, which is the splitting off of case from the core, may also occur at high temperatures. Furthermore, more heat units are required and furnaces deteriorate more rapidly at high temperatures. A time of 2 to 12 or more hours is required for the process, depending upon the temperature of the furnace and the class of carburizer. Many special or alloy steels are often treated by a case-hardening process with very beneficial results. Nickel and chrome steels are especially valuable for case hardening.

Because of the duplex character of case-hardened steel (the core has about 0.2 per cent carbon while the case has 0.8 per cent or more) a double heat treatment is common. The material is:

1. Annealed at Ac_3 to refine the grain of the core.
2. Annealed at Ac_1 and quenched to refine the grain of the case.
3. Tempered to meet the conditions required.

A method of surface hardening known as "nitriding," is discussed under "Alloy Steels" (Art. 11.41).

Steel Castings

7.64 Steel Castings. Steel castings comprise cast steel objects which do not require further mechanical working. They are made by pouring molten steel into sand molds in a manner similar to that employed for iron castings.

Foundry Practice. Molds for steel castings are similar to those for iron castings. Both green-sand and dry-sand molds are used for steel castings. (See Art. 9.10.) The molding sands should have a high fusion point since steel is cast at a higher temperature than cast iron. The shrinkage of ordinary carbon steel is about ¼ inch per foot.

Steel for castings may be produced in steel foundries by means of the Bessemer, open-hearth, electric-furnace, or duplex processes. For the Bessemer process, a side-blown converter of 1 or 2 tons capacity, called a Tropenas converter, is the vessel used. Its advantage is in heating steel to a high temperature so that the molten steel will be fluid enough for pouring light castings. The open-hearth furnace of 20 to 50 tons capacity is most used, however. Both electric-arc and electric-induction furnaces of small capacity are employed. Steel for castings is poured hotter than steel for ingots. Killed steel is required.

Heat Treatment. In recent years there has been a considerable development in heat-treating practices in the cast-steel industry. Research by the Battelle Memorial Institute has shown that, in general, steel castings can have their properties improved by heat treatment in a manner similar to that for wrought steels. Improved tensile strengths in steel castings are obtained by the process of normalizing, hardening by water quenching, and tempering as compared with those developed by annealing, by normalizing, or by normalizing and tempering. (See Table 7.4 for tensile strengths of carbon cast steels for typical compositions and heat treatments.)

Table 7.4

TENSILE STRENGTHS OF CARBON CAST STEELS

(*Courtesy Metals Handbook*, 1948 ed.)

Type of Steel	\multicolumn{3}{c}{Composition, %}	\multicolumn{4}{c}{Heat Treatment, °F.}	Tensile Strength, p.s.i.
	C	Mn	Si	Anneal	Normalize	Quench	Temper	
Low-carbon	0.17	0.74	0.40	1,650	—	—	—	65,900
					1,650	—	—	66,000
					1,650	—	1,250	64,500
					1,650	1,550	1,250	67,000
Medium-carbon	0.30	0.60	0.36	1,650	—	—	—	74,200
					1,650	—	1,250	73,000
					1,650	1,550	1,250	78,800
					1,650	1,550	1,100	89,400
Medium-carbon	0.42	0.72	0.41	1,650	—	—	—	84,250
					1,650	—	1,250	83,900
					1,650	1,550	1,250	93,800
					1,650	1,550	1,100	105,500

The process of isothermal quenching is preferred from the standpoint of reducing cracking and distortion in the quenched casting. In isothermal quenching the castings are quenched in a molten salt bath whose temperature is slightly above M_f temperature and are held there long enough to equalize the temperatures in the center and exterior portions of the piece. The castings are then put into the tempering furnace which is at the desired temperature for tempering. The martensitic structure is changed by tempering to tempered martensite. In commercial tempering, temperatures between 900 and 1275° F. are commonly employed. Castings, hardened by quenching, should be tempered without delay in order to relieve stresses and reduce the tendency toward cracking.

Defects. Defects that often occur in steel castings are blowholes, shrinkage cavities, ingotism, segregation, and cracks.

Mechanical Properties. Tensile strengths of carbon cast steels are given in Table 7.4 for typical compositions and heat treatments. Mechanical properties are given in Table 7.5. Low-carbon steel in "as cast" condition is extensively utilized for railroad castings. Annealing this steel relieves internal stresses and is beneficial, but it does not affect the mechanical properties much except to increase the Izod impact value from 25 up to 39 foot-pounds. The mechanical tests are conducted on specimens machined from test coupons which are cast attached to the main casting such as a

Steel

Table 7.5
MECHANICAL PROPERTIES OF CARBON CAST STEELS

	\multicolumn{4}{c}{Type of Steel}
Property	Low-Carbon	Medium-Carbon	Medium-Carbon	High-Carbon
Carbon, %	0.19	0.30	0.30	0.60
Condition	As cast	As cast	Annealed	Annealed
Tensile strength, p.s.i.	64,500	80,000	78,000	105,000
Yield point, p.s.i.	34,700	42,000	41,000	57,000
Elongation in 2 in., %	33	19	27	13
Reduction of area, %	53	31	41	17
Brinell hardness	130	162	150	205

locomotive frame and are heat treated with the casting. Steel castings are tougher and stronger than castings of gray iron or malleable iron.

Uses. Typical uses of steel castings are locomotive castings and frames, draw-bars for railroad cars, machinery and automotive castings, annealing boxes, hot-metal ladles, pressure containers, and rolling-mill equipment. Steel products of intricate shape can usually be manufactured more cheaply by casting than by rolling or forging processes, especially in small quantities.

Ingot Iron

7.65 Ingot Iron. Ingot iron is a commercially pure iron. It has a very low percentage of impurities, the total content of carbon, silicon, manganese, phosphorus, and sulfur usually being less than 0.08 per cent. From a practical standpoint it can be classified as ferrite. In photomicrographs, the grains have a polygonal shape. The chief characteristic of ingot iron is its resistance to corrosion as compared with low-carbon steel.

Manufacture. Ingot iron is manufactured by the basic open-hearth process. Production of an iron low in impurities requires careful selection of raw materials, an additional period of time in the furnace for purification, and careful control of the operation. The process is more expensive than for steel because of extra fuel needed to maintain longer heats and the high-grade refractories needed for the furnace lining in order to withstand the longer heating and the corrosive action of the slag which is high in iron oxide. Pouring into ingots and rolling into shapes require special care to secure sound metal. Ingot iron is readily galvanized and corrugated.

Tensile Properties. Ingot iron has a tensile strength of about 40,000 pounds per square inch, a yield point of about 25,000 pounds per square inch, a minimum elongation in 8 inches of 22 per cent for ½-inch plate, and a reduction of area of at least 65 per cent. Brinell hardness varies from 80 to 100.

Uses. Ingot iron is used extensively for culverts, gutters, eaves troughs, fencing, wire, furnace metal, and galvanized sheet metal of various types.

The Physical Properties of Steels

7.66 Principal Factors. The principal factors influencing the strength, ductility, and elastic properties of steel are: (1) the carbon content; (2) the percentage of silicon, sulfur, phosphorus, manganese, and other alloying elements; and (3) the heat treatment and mechanical working. The factors are not necessarily independent, and their effects are usually combined. The nature and extent of the effect of heat treatment and mechanical working depend inevitably upon the amounts of carbon and other elements present.

7.67 Effect of Carbon upon Physical Properties. The distinctive properties of the different grades of plain carbon steel are due to variations in carbon content more than to any other single factor. Carbon always acts as a hardener and strengthener, but at the same time it reduces the ductility The effect of carbon upon the mechanical properties of carbon steels is shown in Fig. 7.22.

7.68 Effects of Silicon, Sulfur, Phosphorus, and Manganese. The direct effect of *silicon*, in the ordinary proportions commonly encountered in steels (usually not over 0.2 per cent), upon strength and ductility is very slight. Increasing the silicon content intentionally to 0.3 or 0.4 per cent has the effect of raising the elastic limit and ultimate strength of the steel considerably, without reducing the ductility greatly. This is sometimes done in the production of steel castings.

Sulfur, within the limits common to ordinary steels (0.02 to 0.10 per cent), has no appreciable effect upon the strength or ductility of steels. It has, however, a very injurious effect upon the properties of the hot metal in lessening its malleability and weldability, thus causing difficulty in rolling, called "red-shortness." If it were possible that the steel might contain an excess of sulfur over that which is neutralized by manganese, the effect would certainly be to reduce both strength and ductility.

Phosphorus is the most undesirable of all the elements commonly found in steels. Its effect upon the properties of steels is very capricious, but it is always detrimental to toughness or shock resistance, and often detrimental to ductility under static load. Campbell states that the strength of steel under static load is increased by 1000 pounds per square inch for each 0.01 per cent of phosphorus so long as the total phosphorus does not exceed 0.12 per cent. Beyond this limit even static strength is diminished. High-phosphorus steels are apt to break under very slight stress (called "cold-shortness") at ordinary temperature, if this stress is suddenly applied or if vibration is encountered, and this fact alone is sufficient to bar such steels from most uses in construction.

Manganese has a tendency to improve the strength of plain carbon steel. With less than 0.3 per cent manganese the steel is likely to be impregnated

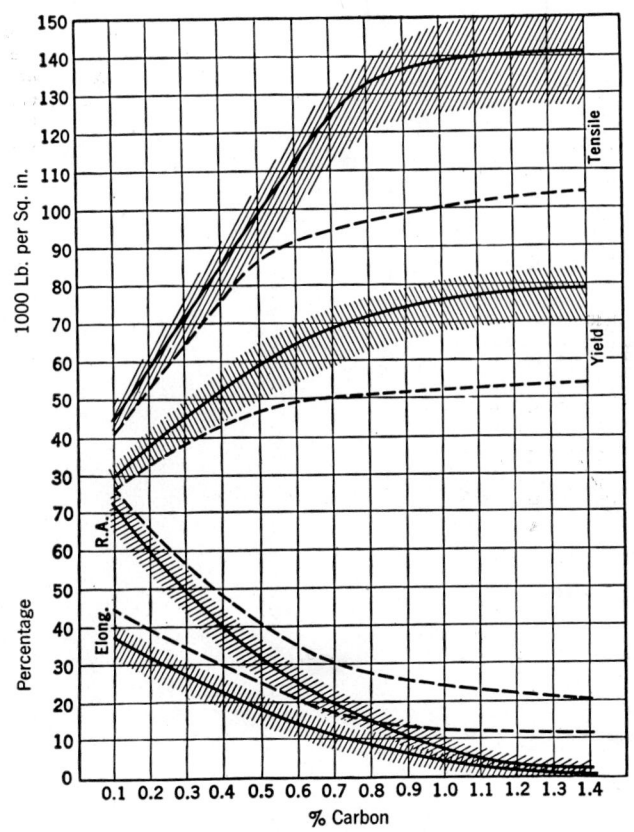

Fig. 7.22. Variation in properties of normalized and annealed carbon steels with carbon content. Hatched bands, normalized steels; dashed lines, average for annealed steels. Specimens 0.505 in. in diameter, from bars approximately 1 in. in diameter. (*Courtesy* D. K. Bullens and Battelle Memorial Institute.)

with oxides the harmful effect of which outweighs any beneficial effect due to the manganese. Between 0.3 per cent and about 1.0 per cent manganese, the beneficial effect depends upon the amount of carbon present. (See reference 7.8, Fig. 11.16, p. 420.) As the content of manganese rises above 1.5 or 2.0 per cent, however, the metal becomes so brittle as to be worthless.

7.69 Effects of Heat Treatment upon Physical Properties. The effects of different heat treatments upon the mechanical properties of wrought or rolled carbon steels of various compositions are shown in Table 7.6.

Table 7.6
MECHANICAL PROPERTIES OF HEAT-TREATED WROUGHT OR ROLLED CARBON STEELS *

Carbon, %	Manganese, %	Heat Treatment	Yield Point, p.s.i.	Tensile Strength, p.s.i.	Elongation in 2 in., %	Reduction of Area, %	Brinell Hardness
0.14	0.45	Hot-rolled	45,000	59,500	37.5	67.0	112
		Annealed	31,000	54,500	39.5	67.0	107
		Quenched in water	——	90,000	21.0	67.0	170
		Quenched in oil	56,500	71,500	34.0	75.5	134
0.32	0.5	Hot-rolled	49,500	75,000	30.0	51.9	144
		Annealed	41,000	70,000	30.5	51.9	131
		Quenched in water	——	135,000	8.0	16.9	255
		Quenched in oil	67,500	101,000	23.5	62.3	207
		Quenched in oil, tempered at 650° F.	61,500	84,000	30.0	71.4	163
0.46	0.40	Hot-rolled	52,500	86,500	22.5	30.7	160
		Annealed	48,000	79,500	28.5	46.2	153
		Quenched in water	——	220,000	1.0	0.0	600
		Quenched in oil	87,500	126,500	20.5	51.9	255
		Quenched in oil, tempered at 560° F.	81,500	111,500	24.0	57.2	——
		Quenched in oil, tempered at 650° F.	73,000	98,000	25.5	59.8	192
0.57	0.65	Hot-rolled	57,000	106,500	19.0	27.4	220
		Annealed	50,000	95,000	25.0	40.3	183
		Quenched in water	——	215,000	0.0	0.0	578
		Quenched in oil	105,000	152,000	16.5	40.3	311
		Quenched in oil, tempered at 460° F.	97,500	145,000	16.0	46.2	293
		Quenched in oil, tempered at 650° F.	79,500	113,000	24.0	62.3	228
0.71	0.67	Hot-rolled	66,000	128,000	15.0	20.5	240
		Annealed	46,500	111,500	16.5	24.0	217
		Quenched in oil	100,000	184,500	1.5	0.0	364
		Quenched in oil, tempered at 460° F.	115,500	177,000	10.0	34.0	340
		Quenched in oil, tempered at 560° F.	106,000	148,500	17.0	43.0	311
		Quenched in oil, tempered at 650° F.	91,000	125,500	19.5	57.2	269

* Data from American Society for Steel Treating.

7.70 Tensile Properties. The tensile properties of various carbon steels called for in the standard specifications of the American Society for Testing Materials are summarized in Table 7.7. The modulus of elasticity of all grades is about 29,000,000 pounds per square inch.

7.71 Structural Steel for Bridges and Buildings. Table 7.8 gives ASTM specifications for the chemical composition of this structural steel. The carbon content is not specified; the manufacturer is permitted to vary the carbon percentage to meet the tensile strength requirements given in Table

Steel

Table 7.7
TENSILE PROPERTIES OF VARIOUS STEELS

Kind and Use of Steel	Tensile Strength, p.s.i.	Yield Point, min. p.s.i.	Elongation, min. in 8 in., %	Elongation, min. in 2 in., %	Reduction of Area, min., %.
Structural steel for bridges and buildings					
Structural	60,000–72,000	33,000	21	22	
Rivet	52,000–62,000	28,000	24		
Structural steel for ships					
Structural	58,000–71,000	32,000	21	22	
Rivet	55,000–65,000	30,000	23		
Carbon steel forgings for locomotives and cars					
Annealed or normalized	75,000 min.	37,500		20	33
Normalized quenched, and tempered	115,000 min.	75,000		16	35
Carbon-steel bolting material heat treated					
Grade B0	100,000 min.	75,000		16	45
Boiler and firebox steel					
Flange	55,000–65,000	0.5 u.t.s *	1,500,000/u.t.s	1,750,000/u.t.s	
Firebox, grade A	55,000–65,000	0.5 u.t.s.	1,550,000/u.t.s	1,750,000/u.t.s.	
Firebox, grade B	48,000–58,000	0.5 u.t.s.	1,550,000/u.t.s	1,750,000/u.t.s	
Boiler-rivet steel					
Grade A	45,000–55,000	0.5 u.t.s.	1,500,000/u.t.s.		
Grade B	58,000–68,000	0.5 u.t.s.	1,500,000/u.t.s.		
Billet-steel-concrete reinforcing bars					
Plain bars					
Structural grade	55,000–70,000	33,000	1,400,000/u.t.s		
Intermediate grade	70,000–90,000	40,000	1,300,000/u.t.s.		
Hard grade	80,000 min.	50,000	1,100,000/u.t.s.		
Deformed bars					
Structural grade	55,000–75,000	33,000	1,200,000/u.t.s.		
Intermediate grade	70,000–90,000	40,000	1,100,000/u.t.s.		
Hard grade	80,000 min.	50,000	1,000,000/u.t.s.		
Concrete reinforcing bars from rerolled steel rails					
Plain bars	80,000 min.	50,000	1,100,000/u.t.s.		
Deformed bars	80,000 min.	50,000	1,000,000/u.t s.		

* u.t.s. stands for "ultimate tensile strength."

7.7. The usual carbon content ranges from approximately 0.15 to 0.30 per cent.

Structural rivet steel has a carbon content ranging from approximately 0.05 to 0.15 per cent and is softer than structural steel. Its chemical composition requirements are given in Table 7.8.

7.72 Torsional Shear. The strength of steel in torsional shear is shown in Table 7.9. The modulus of elasticity for shear is about two-fifths of the tensile modulus or about 12,000,000 pounds per square inch.

M. C. Fetzer found the torsional strength of solid bars of carbon steel to be an average of 68 per cent of the true tensile strength, that is, of the

Table 7.8
CHEMICAL COMPOSITION OF STRUCTURAL STEEL FOR BRIDGES AND BUILDINGS, ASTM SPECIFICATIONS

Open-Hearth and Electric-Furnace Structural and Structural-Rivet Steel

Element	Maximum Per Cent Ladle Analysis	Maximum Per Cent Check Analysis
Phosphorus, acid process	0.06	0.075
Phosphorus, basic process	0.04	0.05
Sulfur	0.05	0.063
Copper (when specified)	0.020	0.18

Acid Bessemer Structural Steel

(Not permitted in bridges nor in building members subject to dynamic loads)

Element	Maximum Per Cent Ladle Analysis	Maximum Per Cent Check Analysis
Phosphorus	0.11	0.138

Table 7.9
STRENGTH OF STEEL IN TORSIONAL SHEAR

Class of Steel	Computed Extreme Fiber Stress, p.s.i.	Shearing Modulus of Elasticity, p.s.i.
Mild Bessemer	64,200	11,320,000
Medium Bessemer	68,300	11,570,000
Hard Bessemer	74,000	11,700,000
Cold-rolled	79,900	11,950,000

strength per square inch not of the original cross-section, but of the reduced cross-section.

7.73 Magnetic Properties of Steel. Large quantities of steel are consumed in the construction of electrical machinery, motors, generators, transformers, etc., where the magnetic properties of the material used are of supreme importance.

Relation between Magnetic Properties and Chemical Composition. The following conclusions have been arrived at by de Nolly and Veyret as the result of an investigation of the hysteresis and eddy-current losses of dynamo sheet metals of varying chemical composition.

Carbon. "The carbon percentage should be as low as possible and always remain below 0.1 per cent." A 0.15 per cent carbon steel is greatly inferior to one containing 0.10 per cent carbon.

Silicon. "The presence of silicon diminishes the hysteresis losses considerably."

Manganese. Manganese appears to be detrimental to magnetic properties if present in amounts exceeding about 0.3 per cent.

Sulfur and Phosphorus. Both sulfur and phosphorus were found to be elements whose presence in amounts exceeding about 0.3 per cent (for both combined) constitutes a distinct injury to magnetic properties.

Sperry Transverse Fissure Test. Transverse fissures in steel railroad rails can be detected by means of the Sperry transverse fissure test. The detector is mounted on a railroad car which can be run over the track at a low speed. Since transverse fissures obstruct the flow of the current in the rails, the presence of fissures is automatically determined by noting variations in electric current passing through the head of the rail.

Welding

7.74 Pressure Welding. There are two general processes of welding: (1) the pressure process and (2) the fusion process. Pressure welding is carried on by heating the edges to be united to a temperature below fusion, cleaning the surfaces by adding flux to remove oxide, and hammering or pressing the surfaces together so that there is diffusion between the space lattices of the metal on each side of the joint. In pressure welding, the heat is usually applied by the electric-resistance method; the metals to be welded are placed between two low-resistance conductors and a high-amperage low-voltage current is applied. The various types of electric-resistance welding comprise: seam welding, projection welding, butt welding, flash-butt welding, percussion welding, and spot welding. These are manufacturing methods for large volume production. Spot welding will be described.

A *spot weld* is made by passing an electric current through a localized area of the parts to be joined in sufficient quantity that the heat generated in these parts will fuse them together. Alternating current, supplied at low voltage by a transformer, passes through conductors and electrodes to the metal pieces to be welded. The electrodes are pressed against the metal to restrict the flow of current through the metals to be joined and thus localize the heat in a small spot. Spot welding is suitable for joining metals which do not have to transmit heavy stress.

An improved form of spot welding, called "shot welding," provides for mechanical control of the time of application of the current to insure sufficient heat for a satisfactory weld without danger of damaging the metal by overheating. This process has made possible the welding of alloy steels such as 18-8 chromium-nickel stainless steel without precipitation of chromium carbide near the weld zone, which robs the parent metal of some of its chromium, rendering it less resistant to corrosion. The amount of heat applied in a shot weld can be checked by an ammeter with an automatic recording device.

An improvement in electric-resistance welding is possible by utilizing a pulsating electric current. A higher-quality weld may be obtained with less expelling of weld metal; also thicker materials can be welded. The theory is that by alternating the current, a better distribution of heat throughout the weld is obtained, whereas a continuous current heats irregular and high spots quickly, causing excessive agitation of the metal and even expulsion at such points.

7.75 Fusion Welding. Fusion welding consists of depositing molten metal at the joint at a temperature sufficiently high to fuse together the deposited metal with that of the edges of the pieces to be joined. Fusion welding is carried on by one of the following methods: (1) the electric-arc method, (2) the gas-flame method, (3) the combination of gas and electric-arc method, and (4) the Thermit process.

7.76 Electric-Arc Method. In this method heat is supplied by an electric arc which passes between the joint and an electrode. Metal-arc welding is the common process, but carbon-arc welding is used to a limited degree.

Metal-Arc Welding. In metal-arc welding the electrode is of metal which is melted by the heat of the arc and deposited at the joint. An intense but concentrated heat is imparted to the base metal. Globules of molten metal forced across the arc do not drop, making it possible to perform overhead and vertical welding. Both alternating current and direct current are used for arc welding. Advantages of alternating-current welding are a faster rate of deposition and a better quality of weld. For direct current, either straight or reversed polarity is used. With straight polarity, the metal to be welded is made the positive terminal; and the electrode, the negative terminal. For straight polarity, the positive pole is the hotter, and for bare electrodes and some covered electrodes, a more stable arc is formed. Some covered electrodes require reversed polarity for efficient results.

Covered electrodes may have light coatings or heavy coverings. Light coatings are composed of metal oxides and carbonates; heavy coatings are composed of metal oxides and silicates or organic materials containing up to 30 per cent carbohydrates with the remainder of inorganic slag-forming materials. Better physical properties are obtained with heavy coatings because nitrogen and oxygen are excluded from the arc stream. Light-coated electrodes give a minimum tensile strength of 45,000 pounds per square inch in non-stress-relieved condition, whereas heavy-covered electrodes are arranged in five groups having minimum tensile strengths of 60,000, 70,000, 80,000, 90,000, and 100,000 pounds per square inch, respectively. (See *ASTM Designation* A233–45T.) Electrode coverings are required to have sufficient electrical resistance to insulate effectively against a difference of potential of 100 volts, 60 cycles alternating current. Metal electrodes range in size from $\frac{1}{32}$ to $\frac{1}{2}$ inches in size and contain less carbon ordinarily than the base metal. A typical core wire is manufactured from

SAE 1010 rimmed steel with carbon content ranging from 0.05 to 0.15 per cent, which has been carefully heat treated to insure good arc stability.

One end of the electrode is first brought in contact with the base metal and then raised to a position about $\frac{1}{8}$ inch above the base metal. Electrons are emitted across the arc, generating sufficient heat to raise the temperature of both base metal and electrode to the fusion point. Metal from the electrode is deposited in small drops into a crater formed in the base metal. The passage of each drop produces a brief short circuit of the arc. Drops from bare electrodes are smaller than from covered electrodes and cause short circuits about 15 per cent of the time as compared with about 4 per cent for covered electrodes.

Carbon oxides escape as gases, or, if the welding is carried on too fast, the gases are entrapped in the metal, producing porous welds. Silicon and manganese oxides rise to the surface of the weld as slag. Phosphorus and sulfur are not greatly affected. Absorption of nitrogen reduces ductility.

Automatic Arc Welding. Automatic welding machines are available for metal-arc welding. The differences between the manual method and automatic welding consist of methods in controlling the equipment and the arc. A welding head holding light-coated filler materials takes the place of hand-operated electrodes. A travel mechanism either for moving the machine or feeding the pieces to be welded is a part of the machine.

Shielded-Arc Welding. When exposed to the air, molten steel enters into chemical combination with nitrogen and oxygen to form nitrides and oxides in the steel. These impurities embrittle the steel and reduce its strength as well as lessen its resistance to corrosion. If the metal during the welding process is protected from contact with the air, such detrimental chemical combination can not occur. Such protection is achieved by shielding with an inert gas such as hydrogen. This can also be accomplished by using coatings on the electrodes with an excess of carbon so as to form carbon monoxide. In addition electrodes can be used which produce an easily removable slag which covers the weld during cooling. Shielded arcs produce welds of superior physical properties. However, the shielded-arc process requires power of considerably higher voltage and amperage; greater heat is attained which permits a higher welding speed in comparison with welding with an unshielded arc.

Carbon-Arc Welding. The electrode is of carbon or graphite. A large amount of heat is generated across the arc, fusing the base metal. Filler metal is supplied from a welding rod held in the arc. Sometimes no filler metal is used, the base metal being fused together at the joint.

Applications. Electric-arc welding, generally conducted with a metal electrode, is used for welding structural members of various types, joints in ships' hulls, joints in pipe lines, and for repairing steel and iron castings.

7.77 Gas-Flame Method. In the gas-flame method, welding-rod metal is fused and deposited on the joint by means of a gas flame. Oxyacetylene gas is required for welding steel in order to get a high enough temperature. Oxyhydrogen gas or oxygen with city gas are sometimes used for welding non-ferrous metals which require only low temperatures. Oxyacetylene gas welding is used for joints in light plating, butt joints of pipes, manufacture of fittings, and repair of steel and iron castings. A large amount of heat is expended in gas flame welding, which causes buckling of plates and shapes. For this reason gas welding is not used much for joints in hulls of ships. The oxyacetylene gas torch operated with an excess of oxygen is an effective burning or cutting tool for steel and iron.

7.78 Combination of Gas and Electric-Arc Method. This method is a combination of gas and electric-arc welding. Two examples are atomic-hydrogen electric-metal-arc welding and inert-gas electric-metal-arc welding.

Atomic-Hydrogen Electric-Metal-Arc Welding. An alternating-current arc changes hydrogen gas from the molecular to the atomic form. The reverse process takes place just outside of the arc on the joint, the recombining of the hydrogen atoms into molecules generating intense heat which melts a thin rod of filler metal held in an atmosphere of hydrogen. The deposited weld metal is surrounded by hydrogen gas which protects it from oxidation. Welds of good quality can be produced by this method.

Inert-Gas Electric-Metal-Arc Welding. This method (called Heliarc) involves the utilization of tungsten electrodes in an atmosphere of helium or argon. It makes possible the welding of stainless steel and aluminum without damage to surface finish. Alternating current may be used, or direct current with either straight or reversed polarity.

7.79 Thermit Method. The Thermit process consists of producing an extremely hot molten steel by ignition of iron oxide in contact with aluminum in a crucible. The reaction gives very hot steel and Al_2O_3 as slag. The hot steel is poured into a mold placed about the joint, producing a solid casting at the joint. Thermit welding is used for joining of trolley rails and repair of large broken parts such as sternposts of ships and side frames of locomotives.

7.80 Inspection and Testing of Welds. It is important to inspect and test welds for the purpose of detecting defects that might impair the serviceability of welded structures. Inspection of the work while in progress is desirable. In order to determine quality of welding, it is common practice to require operators to make up weld samples that can be subjected to destructive tests.

Common tests of welds of the destructive type are the bending, the nick-break, and the tension tests. The fatigue, the impact, and the compression and drift tests are also sometimes conducted. Non-destructive tests for locating defects in the interior parts of welds have the advantage of not destroying the weld. Specific gravity of some welds can be obtained to locate cavities and inclusions of iron oxide. Pure iron has a specific gravity of 7.85, iron oxide of about 6.0. A specific gravity of 7.8 is required for welds. Cavities and cracks can be detected by noting with a stethoscope the sound of metal when struck with a hammer. The X-ray test has been successful in locating defects, but the weld may have to be cut into samples to get X-ray penetration. A hydrostatic internal-pressure test for pipes is used for testing welded pipes. Hardness tests can be performed on the surface of welded joints without injuring them.

7.81 Comparison of Welding with Riveting. The following advantages of welding as compared with riveting may be stated:

1. Greater continuity of strength and greater stiffness are obtained.
2. Welded structures are lighter, since riveted connections require wide laps and gusset plates.
3. Joints have improved tightness.
4. Structures of greater simplicity and better symmetry can be obtained by welding.

Welding has the following disadvantages:

1. Defects in welds may not be discovered and corrected.
2. Deposited metal is similar to cast metal and may be low in ductility, shock resistance, and endurance limit.
3. Stresses due to non-uniform heating and to shrinkage may cause difficulties in assembling.
4. Base metal adjacent to weld may be injured by high temperatures, producing coarse grain size.
5. High-carbon steel cannot be used since welds are brittle and unreliable.
6. Sudden changes in section may cause stress concentrations.

7.82 Flame Hardening. This is a process in which the surface of a hardenable ferrous metal is heated locally by an oxyacetylene flame and then quenched. The metal has its surface raised rapidly to a high temperature by the intense heat of the flame and is then cooled quickly, generally by a stream of water. The surface can be hardened without changing the ductile properties of the core of the metal. No change takes place in the chemical composition. The most desirable steels for flame hardening are 0.35 to 0.70 per cent carbon steels and low-alloy steels; plain and alloy cast irons and malleable cast iron can also be flame hardened. Scleroscope hardness for water-quenched flame-hardened surfaces ranges from 50 to 90 which is equivalent approximately to 350 to 700 Brinell hardness. Stress relieving at about 204° C. (400° F.) is desirable for flame-hardened pieces. Applications include hardening of teeth of large gears and pinions, camshafts, ball-bearing raceways, and cast-steel chain-conveyor rails which because of large size and irregular shape would be difficult to heat-treat.

7.83 Resurfacing. An oxyacetylene-welding torch can be utilized with melt rods of ferrous alloy or of bronze to resurface old parts and bring them up to their original size. Ferrous surfaces can subsequently be flame hardened and tempered. Steel parts in the chemical industry can be resurfaced with chrome-nickel stainless-steel melt rods to obtain resistance to corrosion. Cast-iron pieces can be resurfaced by means of cast-iron rods. Many machine and automotive parts such as pistons, shafts, spindles, and gear teeth are resurfaced with bronze which is easy to machine.

7.84 Hard Facing. Hard facing or hard surfacing consists of welding a hard metal as a facing on a metal that is softer. The purpose is to give a certain area or part a greater wear resistance; in some instances, it is desired to obtain greater resistance to corrosion. The method is applicable to refacing worn parts as well as to manufacturing new machinery. Oxyacetylene-gas welding and electric-metal-arc welding are the two most used methods.

Types of Welding Rod. For hard facing, the following five types of welding rod are extensively used:

1. High-carbon steel rod (class 3), electric-arc method, for moderately hard abrasion-resisting welds.

2. Manganese-steel rod (class 9), electric-arc method, for high-manganese steel.

3. Low-alloy hard-facing steel rod (class 8), electric-arc method, for impact-resisting welds.

4. Tungsten-carbide tube rod (class 4), oxyacetylene method (such as Haystellite tube) for hard-facing parts subjected to severe abrasion.

5. Hard-facing rod to resist heat, corrosion, and impact (class 3), oxyacetylene method (such as Stellite 6 or Stoody 6).

Methods of Handling Parts during Hard Facing. The following procedures are in common use for four different classes of steel:

1. Low- and medium-carbon steel castings should be preheated to 300 or 400° F. Where parts are badly worn, a high-carbon (class 3) build-up deposit is applied prior to the final overlay of hard-facing rod (class 8) to resist wear. Peening the hard-facing deposit while hot is recommended to relieve welding stresses and give a smoother surface.

2. Manganese steel parts are rebuilt to size using manganese rod (class 9) followed by a final overlay of hard-facing rod (class 8).

3. High-carbon steel parts are usually built up with tungsten-carbide tube rod (class 4, oxyacetylene) to prolong the life and operating efficiency. Large pieces such as grader blades should be annealed to 1500° F. before

welding to prevent fracture of the part due to welding stresses. Subsequent to welding, large parts should be normalized to 1500° F. with cooling in still air.

4. Alloy-steel parts to be hard faced with heat- and corrosion-resistant material (class 3, oxyacetylene) should be preheated to 1000° F. or 1100° F. (dull red) before welding to minimize shrinkage stresses. After welding the part should be slowly cooled in an insulated chamber.

Applications. Examples of hard facing commonly encountered on machinery and construction equipment include: crusher jaws and rolls, sheepsfoot tampers, grader blades, dipper fronts, scarifier teeth, track pads and driving tumblers on shovels, and idler wheels and drive sprockets on tractors.

7.85 Hard Setting. Hard setting is the process of welding tungsten-carbide shapes or small castings to wearing surfaces. After hard setting, the entire wearing surface is generally hard faced which produces a built-up surface with great abrasion resistance and extremely great cutting qualities at the edges. The method is used for parts such as oil-well-drilling bits which are subjected to very severe abrasion.

7.86 Brazing. Brazing is a process of joining metals coördinate with welding. In brazing, the metals to be joined are heated to temperatures below their respective melting points and a non-ferrous filler metal having a considerably lower melting point is applied in molten state to the metal surfaces. Four methods of applying heat are used in brazing.

1. Torch brazing, where an open flame or radiant burner is employed.

2. Furnace brazing, in which the electric furnace is preferred because it prevents oxidation of the parts.

3. Dip brazing, in which the metals are covered with flux and dipped into molten brazing alloy.

4. Induction brazing, which requires the use of high-frequency generators to supply current to the induction coil that surrounds the joint to be brazed. The coil induces a voltage that in turn produces current within the part which causes its temperature to increase. Its advantages are rapid temperature rise and extremely localized heating. Better-appearing and more completely filled joint is obtained by induction brazing.

Brazing is used for steel, cast iron, brass, and bronze. Aluminum is brazed by the torch, furnace, or dip methods. The torch method is the most versatile and economical for fabrication and repair of aluminum.

Questions

7.1. What is steel?
7.2. Sketch a Bessemer converter, indicating approximate dimensions.
7.3. Describe the Bessemer process, and state how impurities in the charge are removed.

168 Materials of Construction

7.4. In American practice what are the usual limits of composition of Bessemer pig iron? Why should at least 1.0 per cent of silicon be required? Why is a low phosphorus content necessary?

7.5. Why does the metal not cool off considerably during an acid Bessemer blow?

7.6. What is the function of a recarburizer?

7.7. How is steel deoxidized?

7.8. State some important differences between the acid and basic Bessemer processes.

7.9. What is the fundamental distinction between the open-hearth and the Bessemer processes?

7.10. Draw a diagram of a regenerative open-hearth furnace which utilizes producer gas as a fuel.

7.11. Describe the essential steps in the reduction of pig iron to steel in the basic open-hearth process.

7.12. Compare, in tabulated form, iron and steel making by: blast furnace, acid Bessemer process, basic open-hearth process, and basic electric refining process as to the following particulars:
  a. Materials of the charge.
  b. Order in which materials of charge are placed in furnace.
  c. Which flux is used.
  d. How impurities are removed.
  e. How recarburized.
  f. Characteristics of resultant product.

7.13. Compare the advantages and disadvantages of the acid Bessemer process and the basic open-hearth process.

7.14. Discuss the applications and limitations of electric-refining processes.

7.15. A pig iron has the following impurities: carbon 4.2 per cent, silicon 0.8 per cent, manganese 1.2 per cent, phosphorus 0.8 per cent, sulfur 0.04 per cent. State the process you would choose to produce good steel of 0.5 per cent carbon content from this pig iron.

7.16. Indicate (a) the steel process that would give the cheapest structural steel, (b) the steel process that would give the best structural steel, (c) the cheapest method of producing a small amount of tool steel of a special analysis, and (d) the cheapest method of producing a good-quality carbon steel from scrap steel and iron of varying composition. State the reasons for your choices.

7.17. Distinguish between killed and rimmed steels.

7.18. Describe the steps in making rolled-steel shapes from the casting of the ingots to the finished product.

7.19. Name and describe three types of rolling mills.

7.20. Compare the action of the steam hammer with that of the hydraulic press for mechanical working of steel.

7.21. Discuss in general terms the effects on the mechanical properties of hot working and of cold working of steels.

7.22. Describe the characteristics of dendritic structure.

7.23. Name and describe four defects in ingots.

7.24. Sketch from memory the iron-carbon equilibrium diagram.

7.25. Distinguish between delta, gamma, and alpha iron.

7.26. a. Explain what takes place when a 0.4 per cent carbon steel is cooled slowly from austenite at about 1000° C. to room temperature. Sketch the microstructure of this steel at ordinary temperature.
  b. Do the same for a 1.2 per cent carbon steel.
  c. Do the same for a 0.80 per cent carbon steel.
  d. What percentage of pearlite would each of these steels have?

7.27. Discuss the principal characteristics of steels of the following structures: austenite, martensite, ferrite, cementite, pearlite, and spheroidized cementite.

7.28. Distinguish between hardening, tempering, annealing, and normalizing. What are the chief functions of each?

7.29. Discuss the importance of control of grain size of steel.

7.30. How does the structure of bainite differ from that of tempered martensite?

7.31. Describe the essential features of an isothermal transformation diagram.

7.32. What are the differences in microscopic structure and physical properties between a steel of 1.0 per cent carbon content heated to 750° C. (1382° F.) for 30 minutes and cooled slowly and a similar steel heated to 1000° C. (1832° F.) for the same length of time and cooled in a similar manner?

7.33. How would you heat-treat a 0.4 per cent carbon steel casting to refine the grain and produce a soft steel that would be easy to machine?

7.34. How would you heat-treat a steel forging of 0.6 per cent carbon content to produce a tempered-martensitic steel of good grain structure?

7.35. What is martempering? How does martempering differ from austempering?

7.36. What is the significance of the term "deep hardening"?

7.37. Describe the Jominy end-quench hardenability test.

7.38. An oil-quenched 1.8-inch circular shaft must have a Rockwell C hardness of 50 at the surface and 35 at the center. The cooling rate in oil for this bar at the surface is 125° F. per second and 20° F. per second at the center. Referring to Fig. 7.21 for the Jominy end-quench-test curves, does SAE 2340 steel meet these hardness requirements? Does SAE 5140 steel? Explain.

7.39. An oil-quenched 1.8-inch circular shaft must have a Rockwell C hardness of 43 at a point in the cross-section corresponding to ¾ radius. The cooling rate for this bar in oil at this point is 42° F. per second. Referring to Fig. 7.21, does SAE 2340 steel meet this hardness requirement? Does SAE 5140 steel? Explain.

7.40. Describe the process of case hardening, and state the chief characteristics of case-hardened steels.

7.41. Describe the manufacture and uses of steel castings.

7.42. What are the properties of ingot iron? How is it manufactured? What are its uses?

7.43. What are the ASTM specifications for composition and tensile strength of basic open-hearth structural steel for bridges and buildings?

7.44. State in general terms the effects of carbon on the strength, ductility, hardness, and elastic properties of steel.

7.45. What are the effects of silicon, manganese, phosphorus, and sulfur on the mechanical properties of steel?

7.46. Discuss the magnetic properties of steel.

7.47. How can transverse fissures in steel rails be detected?

7.48. Describe the electric arc and the oxyacetylene methods of welding.

7.49. What method of welding would you choose for the following types of construction: (*a*) hull of a steel ship, (*b*) structural-steel frame of a building, (*c*) repair of a broken sternpost of a ship, (*d*) butt welds in steel pipe, and (*e*) exterior surfaces of streamlined railroad cars consisting of sheets of 18-8 chromium-nickel alloy steel?

7.50. State the advantages and disadvantages of welding as compared with riveting.

7.51. Describe the methods used in inspecting and testing welds.

7.52. How does flame hardening differ from case hardening?

7.53. Describe the process of hard facing.

7.54. Describe the procedure in rebuilding and hard-facing carbon-steel sheepsfoot tampers on a roller. What classes of welding rods are needed?

7.55. Manganese-steel crusher jaws have become worn. Describe the procedure in building up and hard-facing the crusher jaws, stating what welding rods are required.
7.56. Describe a process for resurfacing a worn automotive piston.
7.57. How does brazing differ from welding?

References

7.1. American Institute of Steel Construction: *Steel Construction—A Manual.* New York, 5th ed., 1947.
7.2. American Society for Metals: *Metals Handbook.* Cleveland, Ohio, 1948 ed.
7.3. American Society for Metals: *Carburizing.* Cleveland, Ohio, 1938, 339 pages.
7.4. American Society for Testing Materials: "Standard Classification of Austenite Grain Size in Steels." E19, *ASTM Book of Standards,* 1952.
7.5. American Society for Testing Materials: "Electron Microstructure of Steel." Progress Report, Committee E-4, *Proc. ASTM,* v. 50, 1950, pp. 444–492.
7.6. American Welding Society: *Welding Handbook.* New York, 2nd ed., 1942.
7.7. Antia, D. R., Fletcher, S. G., and Cohen, M.: "Structural Changes during the Tempering of High-Carbon Steel." *Trans. Am. Soc. Metals,* v. 32, 1944, pp. 290–324.
7.8. Bateman, J. H.: *Materials of Construction.* New York, Pitman Publishing Corp., 1950, 568 pages.
7.9. Bates, A. A.: *Fundamentals of Ferrous Metallurgy.* Cleveland, Ohio, Am. Soc. Metals.
7.10. Bethlehem Steel Co.: *Modern Steels and Their Properties.* Handbook 268, Bethlehem, Pa., 1949, 228 pages.
7.11. Bitter, F.: *Introduction to Ferromagnetism.* McGraw-Hill Book Co., 1937, 314 pages.
7.12. Bullens, D. K.: *Steel and Its Heat Treatment.* John Wiley & Sons, 5th ed., 1948, 3 vols.; v. 1, *Principles,* 489 pages; v. 2, *Tools, Processes, Control,* 293 pages.
7.13. Camp, J. M., and Francis, C. B.: *The Making, Shaping, and Treating of Steel.* Pittsburgh, Pa., Carnegie-Illinois Steel Corp., 5th ed., 1940.
7.14. Campbell, H. L.: *The Working, Heat Treating, and Welding of Steel.* John Wiley & Sons, 2nd ed., 1940.
7.15. Davenport, E. S., Roff, E. L., and Bain, E. C.: "Microscopic Cracks in Hardened Steel, Their Effects and Elimination." *Trans. Am. Soc. Metals,* v. 22, 1934, pp. 289–310.
7.16. Digges, T. G.: "Effect of Carbon on the Hardenability of High Purity Iron-Carbon Alloys." *Trans. Am. Soc. Metals,* v. 25, 1938, pp. 408–424.
7.17. Eckholm, L. E.: " 'H' Steels and Their Specification." *Metal Progr.,* v. 48, Oct., 1945, pp. 673–683.
7.18. Grigsby, C. E.: "A Survey of Zebra Roof Practice." *J. Metals,* Feb., 1952, pp. 132–139.
7.19. Herty, C. H., Jr., McBride, D. L., and Hollenback, E. H.: "Which Grain Size?" *Trans. Am. Soc. Metals,* v. 25, 1937, pp. 297–314. Also: *Steel,* v. 100, Mar. 15, 1937, pp. 46–50, 80.
7.20. Hilton, B. R.: *Welding Design and Processes.* London, Chapman & Hall, 1950, 342 pages.
7.21. Hipperson, A. J., and Watson, T.: *Resistance Welding in Mass Production.* London, Iliffe & Sons, 1950, 278 pages.
7.22. Jominy, W. C.: "The Surface Decarburization of Steel at Heat-Treating Temperature." *Univ. Mich. Dept. Eng. Research, Eng. Research Bull.* 18, 1931, 49 pages.

7.23. Larsen, B. M.: "Origin and Effect of Inclusions in Steel." *Metals & Alloys*, v. 1, 1930, pp. 703–713, 763–769, 819–825.
7.24. Lincoln Electric Co.: *Procedure Handbook of Arc Welding Design and Practice.* Cleveland, Ohio, 9th ed., 1950.
7.25. Lipson, H., and Parker, A. M. B.: "The Structure of Martensite." *J. Iron & Steel Inst.* (London), v. 149, 1944, pp. 123–418.
7.26. Lytle, C. W., and Gould, A. F.: *Manufacturing Equipment and Processes.* Scranton, Pa., International Textbook Co., 3rd ed., 1951, 759 pages.
7.27. Morris, J. L.: *Welding Principles for Engineers.* Prentice-Hall, 1951, 511 pages.
7.28. Rosenholtz, J. L., and Oesterle, J. F.: *The Elements of Ferrous Metallurgy.* John Wiley & Sons, 2nd ed., 1938, 251 pages.
7.29. Rowland, E. S., Welchner, J., Hill, R. G., and Russ, J. J.: "The Effect of Carbon Content on Hardenability." *Trans. Am. Soc. Metals*, v. 35, 1945, pp. 46–72.
7.30. *SAE Handbook.* New York, Society of Automotive Engineers, 1952, 946 pages.
7.31. Sauveur, A.: *The Metallography and Heat Treatment of Iron and Steel.* McGraw-Hill Book Co., 5th printing, 1938.
7.32. Schane, P., Jr.: "Effects of McQuaid-Ehn Grain-Size on the Structure and Properties of Steel." *Trans. Am. Soc. Metals*, v. 22, 1934, pp. 1038–1050.
7.33. Sims, C. E., and Boulger, F. W.: "Cast Steels, Low Temperature Properties." *Am. Foundryman*, v. 10, July 1946, pp. 49–66.
7.34. Sisco, F. T.: *Modern Metallurgy for Engineers.* New York, Pitman Publishing Corp., 2nd ed., 1948.
7.35. Slottman, G. F., and Roper, E. H.: *Oxygen Cutting.* McGraw-Hill Book Co., 1951, 407 pages.
7.36. Steel Founders' Society of America: *Steel Castings Handbook.* Cleveland, Ohio, 1950, 511 pages.
7.37. Stoughton, B., and Butts, A.: *Engineering Metallurgy.* McGraw-Hill Book Co., 3rd ed., 1938.
7.38. Swanger, W. H., and Wohlgemuth, G. F.: "Failure of Heat-Treated Steel Wire in Cables of the Mt. Hope, R. I., Suspension Bridge." *Proc. ASTM*, v. 36, Part II, 1936, pp. 21–84.
7.39. Teichert, E. J.: *Ferrous Metallurgy.* McGraw-Hill Book Co., 2nd ed., 1944.
7.40. Unckel, H. A.: "Microhardness of Constituents in Steel Tested." *Iron Age*, Aug. 30, 1951, p. 68.
7.41. U. S. Steel Corp.: *Atlas of Isothermal Transformation Diagrams.* Research Lab., Kearny, N. J., 1943, 103 pages.
7.42. Webber, J. A.: "Furnace Atmospheres and Decarburization." *Am. Soc. Metals*, "Carburizing Symposium," Oct. 18 to 22, 1937, pp. 89–114. Also *Trans. Am. Soc. Metals*, v. 26, 1938, pp. 515–540.
7.43. Wilder, A. B., Kennedy, W. B., and Crouch, F. W.: "Welding Characteristics of Open-Hearth and Bessemer Seamless Steel Pipe." *Proc. ASTM*, v. 50, 1950, pp. 763–788.
7.44. Zener, C.: "Kinetics of the Decomposition of Austenite." *Am. Inst. Mining Met. Engrs. Tech. Publ. 1925, Metals Technol.*, v. 3, Jan., 1946, 34 pages.

CHAPTER 8

Wrought Iron

8.1 General. The definition of wrought iron given by the American Society for Testing Materials is: "A ferrous material, aggregated from a solidifying mass of pasty particles of highly refined metallic iron, with which, without subsequent fusion, is incorporated a minutely and uniformly distributed quantity of slag."

Wrought iron is a two-component metal composed of high-purity iron and iron silicate, which is an inert glasslike slag. Wrought iron usually contains less than 0.12 per cent carbon. The slag is associated physically with the iron in contrast to chemical or alloy relationships which generally exist between the constituents of other metals.

The slag content varies from about 1 to 3 per cent in finished wrought iron. The slag is distributed throughout the iron in the form of threads or fibers which extend in the direction of rolling and are so thoroughly distributed throughout the iron that there may be 250,000 or more per square inch of cross-section.

8.2 Wrought Iron as a Material of Engineering Construction. Wrought iron has certain properties, among which are resistance to corrosion and repeated stress, that will always class it as a material of importance in engineering construction. A perfected process for its production has been developed which has reduced its cost. Its principal uses are as a material for general forging operations, particularly where welding is involved, as rolled rods and bars, as wire, as welded pipe, and as a metal for buildings and tanks.

The Manufacture of Wrought Iron

8.3 The Puddling Process. The puddling process consists in the melting of a grade of pig iron known as forge pig, in the hearth of a reverberatory furnace which is lined with iron oxides, resulting in the elimination of most of the carbon, silicon, manganese, phosphorus, and sulfur present in the charge by oxidation. The oxidizing reaction, coupled with the basic conditions maintained by the furnace lining, produces a refined metal approaching virtually pure iron.

The metal becomes pasty toward the end of the process, owing to the decreased fusibility of the purer iron, and is removed as a plastic ball from which the slag must be removed as completely as possible by squeezing or hammering. The resultant puddled bloom is rolled into large "muck bars." The bars are cut into short lengths, piled up in bundles which are wired together, heated to a white heat, and rolled down to a smaller size called "merchant bars."

The puddling process has been largely supplanted by the Aston (Byers) process which was placed in commercial operation in 1930.

8.4 The Aston Process. This process has three essential steps:

1. Melting and refining the base metal.
2. Producing a molten slag of proper composition.
3. Granulating or disintegrating the base metal and mechanically incorporating with it the desired amount of slag.

Bessemer pig iron is melted in a cupola, tapped into ladles where it receives a special desulfurizing treatment, and is then refined in a Bessemer converter until most of the oxidizable impurities have been removed. The refined metal is not recarburized. It is then poured into the ladle of the processing machine.

Iron oxide and sand are fused in an open-hearth furnace to form an iron silicate slag. The molten slag is poured into a ladle which is placed on a ladle car and moved directly below the processing machine.

The key operation which is called "shotting" consists of pouring the molten refined iron at a temperature of about 1540° C. (2804° F.) from the ladle of the processing machine into the ladle containing the molten slag at a temperature of about 1260° C. (2300° F.), as is shown in Fig. 8.1. The processing machine is oscillated as well as moved forward and backward to insure a uniform distribution of the refined metal into the slag. The refined iron has a freezing point of about 1480° C. (2696° F.) while the slag solidifies at about 1120° C. (2048° F.). Since the slag is maintained at a temperature considerably lower than the freezing point of the iron, the iron is continuously and rapidly solidified. The liquid iron contains large quantities of gases in solution, but, when the metal solidifies, the gases are no longer soluble in it and escape. The solidification of the iron when it strikes the slag occurs so swiftly that the gases go off in the form of many small explosions of sufficient force to shatter the metal into small fragments which settle to the bottom of the slag ladle. Since the iron is at a welding temperature of about 1370° C. (2498° F.), and owing to the fluxing action of the siliceous slag, these fragments cohere to form a spongelike "puddle ball" of large size (6000 pounds or more), consisting of pea-sized globules of pure iron coated with silicate slag.

174   Materials of Construction

The resulting mixture is similar to that formerly produced by the puddling process but is much more uniform as regards the character and distribution of the slag. The Aston process makes it possible to produce high-grade wrought iron in large quantities and at a much lower cost than by the puddling process.

Fig. 8.1. Key operation of pouring molten iron from ladle into the ladle containing molten slag.

8.5 Removal of Slag. The puddle ball produced in the Aston process is a very loosely agglomerated mass of pasty iron and slag. This slag must be removed as far as possible by mechanical means, and the iron compacted and welded together by squeezing or shingling. In the squeezing method, the ball is squeezed in a specially designed press of large dimensions.

The puddle ball may also be shingled, i.e., forged down by some type of power hammer. The steam hammer is usually employed in shingling. Between blows, the puddle ball is turned by the operator until it is thoroughly welded together and the slag largely excluded.

The compression of the porous mass of metal, either in squeezing or shingling, results in a considerable rise in temperature of the mass, which favors the expulsion of the slag by retaining it in a very fluid condition.

8.6 Rolling-Mill Operations.

The puddled blooms from the squeezer (press) or the shingling are immediately transferred to the rolling mill wherein the finished bar or shape is produced. The solid rectangular bloom is immediately rolled to the desired billet size. These billets are then reheated and rolled into plate, skelp, bars, rods, etc.

Properties and Uses of Wrought Iron

8.7 Composition and Constitution.

The composition of wrought iron approaches that of pure iron very closely. The usual impurities—carbon, silicon, phosphorus, sulfur, and manganese—are always present in small amounts, in addition to the slag which is invariably present. Wrought iron is a composite material consisting of an intermingling of high-purity iron base metal and siliceous slag, and the impurities are distributed between the metal and the slag. Table 8.1 gives the limits which are seldom exceeded

Table 8.1

ANALYSES OF WROUGHT IRONS

	High-Quality Wrought Iron, Upper Limit, %	High-Quality Wrought Iron, Typical Analysis, %	Very Pure Swedish Charcoal Iron, %
Carbon	0.10	0.04	0.050
Silicon	0.20	0.10	0.015
Phosphorus	0.25	0.10	0.055
Sulfur	0.05	0.03	0.007
Manganese	0.10	0.05	0.006
Slag	3.25	2.75–3.25	0.610

in high-quality wrought iron and also shows typical analyses of high-quality wrought iron and very pure Swedish charcoal iron.

The constitution of wrought iron is quite simple as compared with that of cast iron, because of the very low percentages of carbon and other impurities in the iron. The great bulk of the material is nearly pure ferrite with small amounts of silicon, phosphorus, etc.

The appearance of a longitudinal section of wrought iron under high magnification is shown in the photomicrograph of Fig. 8.2. The slag appears as many irregular black lines of varying thickness, and the crystalline nature of the pure iron can also be plainly seen. The photomicrograph of Fig. 8.3 shows the appearance of the transverse section of wrought iron. The structure is in every way similar to that seen in the longitudinal section except that the slag here appears as irregular dark areas corresponding to the cross-section of the slag fibers.

Fig. 8.2. Longitudinal section of wrought iron showing duplex structure of slag 100×. (Homerberg.)

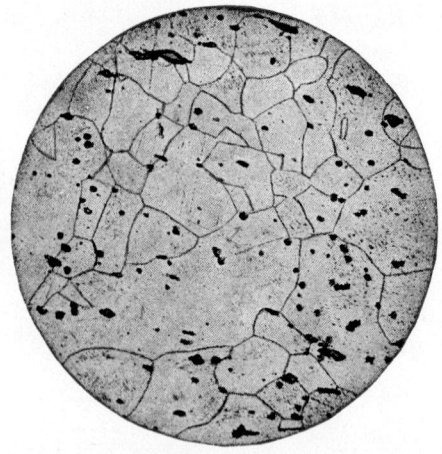

Fig. 8.3. Transverse section of wrought iron 100×. (Homerberg.)

8.8 Tensile Strength. The tensile strength of a given wrought iron depends to a considerable extent upon the direction of stress with respect to the "grain" of the iron. This is to be expected, since the continuity of the metal in a direction transverse to the direction of rolling is interrupted by numerous strands of slag which are comparatively weak. The tensile strength of wrought iron in a transverse direction has usually been found to be between 0.6 and 0.9 of the strength in a longitudinal direction. The ductility is also appreciably greater in a longitudinal direction than in a transverse direction, but the yield point is practically the same in either direction. Typical physical properties of wrought iron in the longitudinal and transverse directions are given in Table 8.2.

Table 8.2

LONGITUDINAL AND TRANSVERSE TENSILE PROPERTIES OF WROUGHT IRON

Property	Longitudinal	Transverse
Tensile strength, p.s.i.	48,000–50,000	36,000–38,000
Yield point, p.s.i.	27,000–30,000	27,000–30,000
Elongation in 8 in., %	18–25	2–5
Reduction of area, %	35–45	3–6

The specifications of the American Society for Testing Materials prescribe the tensile properties as given in Table 8.3.

During recent years the development of rolling procedure has tended to equalize tensile strength and ductility in the two directions. This development has an important bearing on the use of wrought-iron plates for appli-

Table 8.3

ASTM SPECIFICATIONS FOR TENSILE PROPERTIES OF WROUGHT IRON

Longitudinal Properties—Minimum Requirements

Property	Pipe	Refined Bars	Double-Refined Bars	Forgings	Rivet Rounds	Plates	Special Forming Plates (maximum transverse ductility)	Rolled Shapes and Bars
Tensile strength, p.s.i.	40,000	45,000–48,000	46,000–54,000	45,000	47,000	48,000	39,000	46,000–48,000
Yield point, p.s.i.	24,000	25,000	23,000–32,400	22,500	28,200	27,000	27,000	23,000–28,800
Elongation in 8 in., %	12	16–20	22–28	24 *	22–28	14	8 (either direction)	20–25
Reduction of area, %			35–45	33				30–40

* Four-inch gauge length

cations where the metal must be formed in more than one direction, as in flanged and dished tank heads.

The modulus of elasticity of wrought iron is about 29,000,000 pounds per square inch for all the different grades.

8.9 Effect of Overstrain and Cold Work. The effect of previous straining of wrought iron upon the elastic limit and ultimate strength, as revealed by subsequent test, is to raise the elastic limit and increase the ultimate strength provided the metal has been allowed to rest after strains.

Cold working of wrought iron, i.e., deforming it by rolling, hammering, or pressing, at temperatures below about 690° C. (1274° F.), affects the structure and the mechanical properties of iron in much the same way as straining it beyond the elastic limit. The elastic limit is considerably raised, the ultimate strength is slightly raised, and the elongation or ductility is usually lowered.

8.10 Compressive Strength of Wrought Iron. The properties shown by wrought iron in compression do not differ materially from its tensile properties. Its elastic limit, ultimate strength, and modulus of elasticity are about the same in compression as in tension, provided that the ratio of length to radius of gyration of the cross-section of the test specimen does not approach the point where lateral flexure occurs.

The compressive strength of wrought iron is between 45,000 and 60,000 pounds per square inch if the length is short in proportion to the radius of gyration. Usually, however, this proportion is too great to make it possible to disregard flexure, and the ultimate compressive strength must be taken to be only equal to the stress at the yield point, or from 25,000 to 35,000 pounds per square inch, according to the character and condition of the iron.

8.11 Shearing Strength of Wrought Iron. The resistance of the material to shearing stresses will be less on a plane parallel to the direction of the "grain" than on one that cuts the fiber of the iron transversely.

The actual shearing strength shown by tests is variable, but in general it will be from 20,000 to 35,000 pounds per square inch on a longitudinal plane and from 30,000 to 45,000 pounds per square inch on a transverse plane.

8.12 Wrought Iron vs. Steel. The fibrous character of wrought iron is often used as a basis for differentiating wrought iron from low-carbon steel

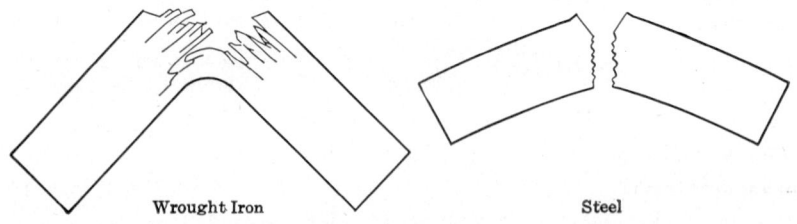

Fig. 8.4. Nick-bend test.

in the *nick-bend* test, wherein the bar to be tested is nicked with a sharp chisel and bent cold with the nick at the outside of the bend. Steel snaps sharply after a small bend, but wrought iron tears gradually with a distinctly fibrous or "woody" fracture as shown in Fig. 8.4.

Wrought iron may also be distinguished from steel by means of the fact that steel nearly always contains an appreciable amount of manganese whereas wrought iron usually contains very little of this element. The presence of slag in its characteristic lines (see Figs. 8.2 and 8.3) also distinguishes wrought iron, as steel should contain practically no slag. The presence of slag can also be determined by a deep acid etch since the slag fibers cause the surface to become black.

8.13 Fatigue Resistance. Wrought iron shows good resistance to fatigue fracture, or progressive failure of the crystals. It is claimed that the slag fibers serve to minimize stress concentration and to deflect the path of the slip lines. Wrought iron has a good service record with respect to resistance to the effects of constant vibration and sudden shock.

8.14 Resistance to Corrosion. Corrosion resistance of wrought iron is attributed to the purity of the iron base metal, to freedom from segregated impurities, and to the presence of the glasslike slag fibers. Wrought iron has a good record of durability under actual operating conditions in various kinds of service.

Under some conditions where corrosion is a factor, the life of metals can be increased by the application of a protective coating such as paint or galvanizing. The surface of wrought iron is microscopically rougher than that of most metals and consequently provides good anchorage for paints. Because of the slag fibers, the natural roughness of a wrought-iron surface is accentuated by pickling with acid prior to galvanizing with molten zinc. As a result, wrought iron will take on a heavy zinc coating.

8.15 The Welding of Wrought Iron. One of the valuable properties of wrought iron is the comparative ease with which it may be welded. Its superiority is due largely to its comparative purity, since all impurities, especially carbon, silicon, and sulfur, reduce weldability in a marked degree. The general use of welding as a means of fabrication makes this an important characteristic. Any of the methods of welding, such as oxyacetylene, electric-arc method, or hammer-welding, may be employed for wrought iron.

The high degree of purity of the base metal in wrought iron makes its fusion temperature somewhat higher than that of other common ferrous metals, and for that reason it should be worked hotter for best results. The slag content acts as a natural flux, thus serving as an important factor in producing a strong, uniform weld.

In gas welding, the procedure to employ with wrought iron is the same as that for mild steel, except that heating should be continued for a slightly longer period in order to attain the proper temperature. When using the electric-metal-arc process, the best results are obtained when the welding speed is decreased slightly below that suitable for the same thickness of mild steel. In welding light sections where there is a possibility of burning through the material, it also may be necessary to employ a slightly lower current value. Excessive penetration into the face of the parent metal is unnecessary and undesirable. The penetration should be no greater than that required to secure a sound bond between the deposited metal and the parent metal. The slight modifications in the procedure for electric fusion welding that have been indicated fall well within the normal operating range of standard equipment. Any good-quality welding rod, either coated or bare, can be used in welding wrought iron.

8.16 Forming, Machining, and Threading. Forming of wrought iron may be done either hot or cold, depending on the severity of the operation. Threading and machining operations are readily accomplished with wrought iron on account of its fibrous structure and the softness of the base metal.

8.17 Uses. For about 25 years prior to the introduction of the Aston process in 1930, the principal uses of wrought iron were for standard pipe, tubular products, bars, and forging stock; since then wrought iron has been used for structural shapes, plates, sheets, welding fittings, rivets, and special pipes and tubes. Wrought-iron products are used in building construction, public-works construction, and for the railroad, marine, and petroleum industries.

8.18 Nickel-Alloy Wrought Iron. The development of the Aston process has made possible the manufacture of nickel-alloy wrought iron. Up to 5 per cent nickel may be used, but for most practical purposes 1.5 to 3 per cent nickel is satisfactory. The nickel is added to the molten wrought iron.

The comparative typical physical properties of unalloyed and 3 per cent nickel wrought iron in the same class of product are given in Table 8.4.

Table 8.4
TENSILE PROPERTIES OF NICKEL WROUGHT IRON

Property	Unalloyed Wrought Iron	Nickel Wrought Iron
Tensile strength, p.s.i.	48,000	60,000
Yield point, p.s.i.	30,000	45,000
Elongation in 8 in., %	25	22
Reduction of area, %	45	40

It will be noted that the addition of nickel increases the tensile strength 25 per cent and the yield point 50 per cent without a marked decrease in the ductility. In these respects nickel-alloy wrought iron is similar to nickel-alloy steel. (See Art. 11.8.) The properties of nickel-alloy wrought iron can be improved by heat treatment. Nickel-alloy wrought iron has good impact strength at subzero temperatures.

Questions

8.1. Distinguish between wrought iron and steel.
8.2. Distinguish between wrought iron and ingot iron.
8.3. Describe briefly the puddling process of producing wrought iron. Was the puddling-furnace operation acid or basic? Why did the wrought-iron metal form in a pasty condition?
8.4. Describe the Aston process of producing wrought iron.
8.5. Give a typical analysis of high-quality wrought iron.
8.6. Sketch the photomicrograph of a longitudinal section of wrought iron.
8.7. Discuss the relationship between the strength of wrought iron in tension and also in shear with respect to the direction of rolling.
8.8. Discuss the fatigue-resistance and corrosion-resistance properties of wrought iron.
8.9. What is the significance of the nick-bend test?
8.10. What tensile strength value is typical of nickel-alloy wrought iron? what yield point value?
8.11. Compare the welding processes for wrought iron with those employed for mild carbon steel.
8.12. State typical uses of wrought iron.

References

8.1. Aston, J., and Storey, E. B.: *Wrought Iron: Its Manufacture, Characteristics, and Applications.* Pittsburgh, Pa., A. M. Byers Co., 2nd ed., 1939, 97 pages.
8.2. Bateman, J. H.: *Materials of Construction.* New York, Pitman Publishing Corp., 1950; Chap. 14, pp. 475–483.
8.3. Sauveur, A.: *The Metallography and Heat Treatment of Iron and Steel.* McGraw-Hill Book Co., 5th printing, 1938.

CHAPTER 9

Cast Iron

9.1 General. Cast iron differs considerably both in chemical composition and in physical characteristics from wrought iron and steel. It possesses a very complex constitution. It is comparatively coarsely crystalline in structure, possesses considerable hardness but lacks toughness, melts readily, and passes suddenly into a very fluid state, in which it will take a good impression of a mold.

Cast iron is used to a certain extent for columns and posts in buildings, for column bases, bearing plates, and innumerable minor structural parts. In machine construction it finds a wide field of application, for it can be cast in complex forms at a comparatively low cost.

A small number of iron castings are made by running the metal into molds as it comes from the blast furnace. Ingot molds, for instance, are made in this way at steel works. The variability of the blast-furnace product, however, limits the use of these direct castings. The bulk of all the iron used as cast iron is processed either in the *cupola furnace,* the *air furnace,* or the *electric-melting furnace* before being cast in molds.

Manufacture of Cast Iron

9.2 Raw Materials. *Foundry Pig Iron.* Nearly all pig irons for foundry purposes are bought by analysis, the content of silicon and sulfur being specified, and sometimes also the total carbon, manganese, and phosphorus.

In addition to the irons properly classed as foundry pig irons, Bessemer pig, ferrosilicon, and a few other special pig irons are used at times to bring the composition of the cast iron within the required limits.

Scrap Iron. The term "scrap iron" designates that considerable portion of the iron charged into the furnace which has been remelted one or more times. It consists mainly of castings discarded after having been in service, but includes also defective castings, gates, sprues, etc.

Steel Scrap. Steel scrap is also added to the charge in modern foundries.

Ferrosilicon and *ferromanganese* may be added to adjust the composition of the resulting metal.

The Flux. The office of a flux in the melting of iron is to absorb and carry off in a slag the non-metallic residue of the iron and the ash of the fuel, and to assist in the removal of sulfur. The requirements vary greatly, but in general they will average in the neighborhood of $\frac{1}{2}$ to $1\frac{1}{2}$ per cent of the weight of the metal.

The flux is calcium carbonate, usually in the form of limestone, but oyster shells, marble chippings, dolomite, etc., are sometimes used, and a portion of fluorspar (CaF_2) is often added to obtain a more liquid slag.

The Fuel. The fuel in iron melting serves simply as a source of heat. Coke is the most common fuel in the cupola. The air furnace requires a long-flaming bituminous coal or gas.

The fuel requirements depend upon the character of the castings being made, small and thin castings requiring a hotter metal than large ones.

THE CUPOLA

9.3 The Cupola Furnace and Its Equipment. The cupola in its essential arrangement is really a small blast furnace, operated under a very much lower blast pressure, and intended only to melt the charge without any attempt being made to attain reducing conditions. The cupola is used for most foundry purposes in the production of gray-iron castings.

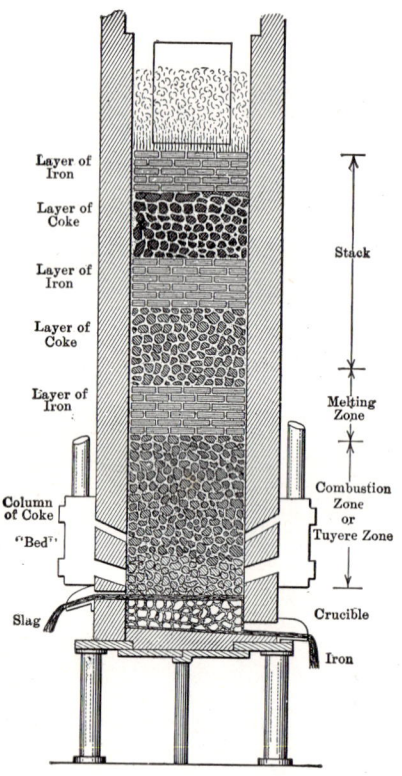

Fig. 9.1. Zones in cupola. (Stoughton.)

The type of cupola shown in Fig. 9.1 is representative of those used in foundries. It consists of a vertical cylindrical shell of wrought iron or steel, lined with firebrick set in fireclay grout. The size of the cupola is quite variable, ranging from about 22 to about 100 inches inside diameter. The height depends upon the diameter.

The air blast enters the crucible through tuyères leading from the wind belt, or air chamber, which surrounds the lower portion of the furnace. The tuyères are usually arranged in two horizontal rings some 12 or 15 inches apart vertically, the area of the upper tuyères being, as a rule, only a small fraction of that of the lower ones.

The slag hole is situated just below the tuyères at a height above the bottom plate governed by the amount of metal required per heat. The taphole, or spout, is located just at the level of the bed of sand which covers the bottom doors.

9.4 Operation of the Cupola. *Charging.* The bed of fuel having been properly prepared and leveled off, the charge of broken pig and scrap is carefully placed, an effort being made to fill up the interstices as far as possible and keep the charge level. The next charge of fuel is now placed on the iron, and alternate charges of iron and fuel continue until the height of the charging door is reached. When a flux is required, the proper proportion is charged on top of each bed of iron, except at the start and at the end of the heat, when it may be omitted.

When the furnace is properly operated, it shows the following distinct zones of action, beginning at the bottom and proceeding upwards: The crucible zone or hearth, the tuyère zone, the melting zone, and the stack. These four zones are indicated in Fig. 9.1.

The crucible zone extends from the bottom up to the level of the tuyères. It serves the sole purpose of collecting and holding the molten metal and slag until tapped out.

The tuyère zone is the zone of combustion. The blast here comes in contact with the red-hot coke and rapidly oxidizes it. A column of coke always extends from the melting zone to the bottom of the crucible, and combustion occurs from the level of the molten metal to a point above the tuyères, the height of which depends upon the pressure of the blast.

The melting zone is situated directly above the tuyère zone. During the melting, the iron is supported on a column of coke, extending to the bottom of the cupola, which is the only solid material below the melting zone. The iron as it melts trickles down to the bottom over the column of coke. Each layer of iron requires about 5 to 10 minutes to melt, and the column of coke is constantly sinking, so that the last of the iron melts several inches lower than the first. If the charges of iron and coke and the pressure of the blast are properly proportioned, each charge of iron will enter the top of the melting zone just before the last charge is completely melted at the bottom.

The stack extends above the melting zone to the level of the charging door. Its function is to contain material that will absorb heat to bring it into good condition for action in the melting zone, and to keep the heat in the melting zone as much as possible.

Duration of the Cupola Run. A foundry cupola is never run continuously, but is started anew for each casting and is "dumped" at the conclusion of the run. As a general rule, the duration of the run does not exceed 3 or 4 hours, and it cannot exceed this period if no provision is made for draining off the slag.

Tapping Out and Stopping In. The taphole is usually left open until the iron begins to run after the blast is started, at which time it is closed if an accumulation of metal is desired. The "stopping in" is accomplished by means of the "bod" and "bod-stick." The bod is a plug made of fireclay, sand, or molding sand, molded in the shape of a cone that adheres to the enlarged end of the "bod-stick," which is simply an iron bar with an upset end. The bod is thrust in quickly to stop the flow of metal. It bakes hard enough to withstand the pressure.

Tapping consists simply in piercing the bod with a round iron bar provided with a pointed end. It is an operation requiring great care, since the danger of causing molten iron to spill and burn those near at hand is ever present.

The Air Furnace

9.5 The Reverberatory or Air Furnace. The reverberatory or air furnace has natural draft and employs the principle of utilization of heat derived by reflection from the roof upon the bath of the metal.

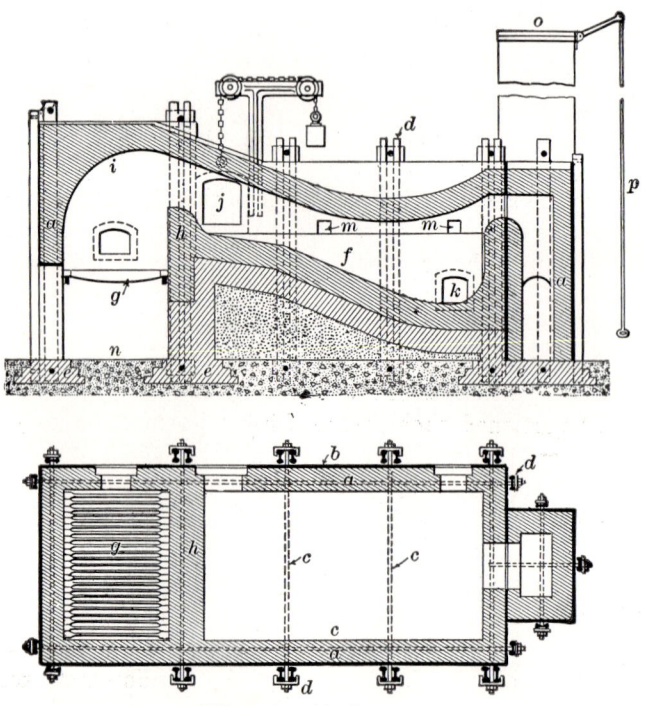

Fig. 9.2. Air furnace.

The air furnace is principally confined to the production of white iron for malleable cast iron, but it is also used to produce irons of particular composition for special purposes.

The design of air furnaces shows many variations, but Fig. 9.2 shows a typical form in which coal is burned as fuel. The main portion of the furnace, the hearth (*f*), is flanked on one end by a firebox (*g*), and on the other by a flue leading to a stack (*o*). The walls of the furnace (*a*) are of very heavy brick masonry incased in iron plates (*b*) and reinforced both ways by tie rods (*c*) between buck stays (*d*).

The hearth bottom is a mixture of sand and fireclay supported by brickwork built to slope downward from the fire bridge (*h*) to the flue bridge. The crown of the furnace is similarly inclined downward toward the stack in order to deflect the heat of the flames downward on the iron in the hearth.

The firebox is provided with iron grate bars, and fuel is introduced through a fire door in one side wall of the firebox. Pig iron and scrap are charged in through the charging door (*j*), and holes (*m*) are provided to facilitate the skimming of the bath of metal. The spout is not shown in the figure, but is so placed as to drain the metal from the lowest part of the hearth.

In some modern air furnaces the hand-fired iron-grate firebox is replaced by a burner using powdered coal or fuel oil.

9.6 Operation. *The Charge.* The charge is placed in the furnace hearth. The furnace is either still hot from the last melt, or it is heated for some hours before charging, so that melting begins soon after the charge is placed.

Control of Melting. The temperature of the furnace is controlled by the regulation of the draft by means of a damper in the stack or stack flue, and one in the firebox. The bituminous coal burns with a long flame which sweeps through the melting chamber, the conditions being strongly oxidizing rather than reducing. A slag soon forms and covers the metal as it accumulates, so protecting it in a measure from oxidation.

The time required for melting is much greater than in the cupola, the actual time depending upon the capacity of the furnace. The fuel requirement is about one-fourth the weight of the charge. The metal is tapped as rapidly as possible, and, since the hottest metal is at the top of the bath, a series of tapholes at different levels are sometimes used successively. The loss of metal due to oxidation amounts to 2 to 5 per cent of the charge.

Oxidation can be more carefully controlled by means of fuel oil or powdered coal burners. No regulation of air from the draft is required. The composition of the finished cast iron and the temperature of pouring can be accurately controlled.

9.7 Advantages and Disadvantages. The product of the air furnace is purer than cupola iron, since the metal does not come in contact with the fuel. This means less absorption of sulfur and less absorption of carbon, resulting in general in a higher grade and stronger iron. The process being much slower than the cupola process, it is under better control and any desired composition can be more closely approached.

The cupola, on the other hand, is a cheaper installation, requires less skilful management and is therefore cheaper to operate; the heat is more uniform, so that all the metal of a melt has more nearly the desired temperature; very hot iron is more easily obtained; the furnace can be started and stopped more readily; the fuel efficiency is greater; and there is less loss of metal through oxidation and consequent removal in the slag.

The Electric-Melting Furnace

9.8 The Electric-Melting Furnace. The electric furnace is employed in modern foundries for melting cast iron. A common type is the Detroit rocking furnace. Its advantage is that temperature and composition can be accurately controlled. It is used particularly for producing high-strength cast iron and alloy cast iron. Scrap metals such as borings can sometimes be used in the charge, which may compensate for the higher heating cost of the electric furnace. In some cases in manufacturing alloy cast iron, the cast iron is first melted in a cupola and then tapped into an electric-melting furnace where the alloying elements are added.

Iron Founding

9.9 Iron Founding in General. The art of founding consists in pouring molten metal into a mold of any desired special form, which the metal assumes and retains when cold. Provision must be made for elimination of gases evolved when the iron solidifies and for shrinkage of the iron upon cooling.

The most important part of iron founding is making the molds, a process which demands considerable mechanical skill and no small amount of manual labor. Sand, the material generally used for molds, cannot be molded into any conceivable shape, but has certain practical limitations. For the most part, the impression in the sand of the mold is made by a pattern which must be so designed that its removal from the mold is possible. Another consideration is that sand, when confined, is a comparatively unyielding material, and therefore the shape of castings must be such that the shrinkage which invariably occurs as the metal cools will not induce dangerously high internal stresses.

9.10 Molds and Molding. The various methods of making sand molds may be divided into the following three classes of greatest importance: (1) "green-sand molding" involves the making of an impression of the desired form, by means of a pattern, in a mold composed entirely of sand in a damp state; (2) "dry-sand molding" involves the making of molds in damp sand by means of a pattern as in green-sand molding, after which the mold is dried in an oven until the moisture is expelled and the sand is baked hard (molds made of foundry sand coated with a thin film of clay and colloidal iron hydroxide retain their form after drying); (3) "loam molding" does not involve the use of patterns, but its application is largely confined to articles whose surfaces are surfaces of revolution, the molds being built up of brickwork covered by a layer of loamy sand in which the desired imprint is made by a "sweep." Machine molding may replace hand work in any of these methods.

A mold is usually made in two parts, the upper part being called the *cope* and the lower part the *drag*. The rectangular frame commonly used to hold the mold is called the *flask*. Patterns are many times divided into two parts. The lower part is placed at proper height in the sand in the drag, and the sand is tamped and struck off evenly at the top. The pattern is then carefully withdrawn from the sand, leaving an imprint of the pattern in it. The upper part of the pattern is similarly employed in the cope, and the cope is inverted and placed on top of the drag so that a hollow space corresponding to the casting will be formed. A passage called a *gate* is formed in the cope for pouring the metal into the cavity, and at least one passage of relatively large cross-section called a *riser* is provided to the upper surface to serve as a vent for gases and to form a reservoir of excess molten metal for the purpose of filling the casting cavity completely as the metal shrinks in cooling.

9.11 Patterns and Cores. *Patterns* may in general be divided into two classes, the first of which are used to produce solid castings, the second to produce hollow ones. Usually, however, the pattern is solid, the hollow portion being formed by a core which is placed in the mold after the removal of the pattern.

The great majority of all patterns are made of wood. Brass or other metals are sometimes used for the sake of greater durability when a great many molds are to be made from the same pattern. The simplest patterns are merely solid-wood duplicates of the desired castings except that an allowance of about $\frac{1}{8}$ inch per foot is made in dimensions to compensate for the shrinkage of gray-iron castings in cooling and about $\frac{1}{4}$ inch per foot for white-iron castings. A slight tapering known as draft is given the vertical plane surfaces in order to facilitate the withdrawal of the pattern from the mold.

The *cores* are usually made from a mixture of fine siliceous sand with clay or loam, which is packed in the core-box while damp. Some binder, such as flour and water, starch, molasses, linseed oil, rosin, or glue-water, is usually required to give the core strength enough to permit handling, and holes are commonly left running lengthwise through the core for the purpose of venting. When the cores are dried in an oven prior to use in a mold they are called dry-sand cores. The great majority of all cores are of this class. If a core is long, particularly if it is supported horizontally over a considerable span, it is necessary to stiffen the core by insertion of iron or steel wires or even skeleton frames of metal. A core maintains its shape while the molten metal flows around it, but the heat carbonizes the binder, destroying the bond between the sand grains and thus permitting the core to be crushed by the shrinkage of the metal without damage to the casting. Cores that are adjacent to thick parts of a casting are apt to be fused before the metal is solidified, unless protected from the heat of the slowly cooling molten metal. They are therefore often daubed with an insulating coating of blackening. For this purpose pulverized graphite or plumbago is either applied wet as a wash, dry with a brush, or shaken from a cloth bag.

9.12 Chilled Castings. A chilled casting is one made in a mold, some parts of which, at least, are made of iron, such portions of the mold being called "chills." The purpose of introducing chills into a mold is to convey away the heat of the molten metal rapidly, a treatment which has the effect of causing the carbon in the iron to remain in chemical combination, instead of separating therefrom in the form of graphite, as it normally does in slowly cooled castings of gray iron. The physical effect of chilling on the character of the iron is to harden it greatly for a certain depth, giving to the exterior of the iron the characteristic appearance of white iron, while the body of the casting remains a gray iron. Chilling is principally used for wearing surfaces of such castings as iron rolls and treads of car wheels.

9.13 Designing Castings. The following rules should be observed by the designer: (1) avoid sudden changes in thickness, (2) avoid sharp corners, and (3) avoid sharp reëntrant angles. Changes in thickness should be gradual, and sharp corners should be rounded. Reëntrant angles are particularly bad since the flow of heat at such angles is greater than on plane surfaces, causing crystals to grow slowly on a line bisecting the reëntrant angle and thus producing initial tension there. The remedy is to round off the angles. The designer should make use of fillets to avoid sharp edges. Parts of a casting should be arranged so that it can shrink without restraint.

9.14 Pouring the Iron. For small work the metal is caught in hand ladles at the cupola taphole and conveyed to the molds by one or two men. Practically all foundry ladles are top pouring (i.e., the metal is poured by tipping the ladle), rather than teeming ladles, which are provided with a valve in the bottom. This necessitates the use of a bar to keep back the slag which floats on the metal and would otherwise enter the mold. Care is exercised by the molder to hold the ladle as near the pouring gate as possible to lessen the impact of the stream of metal upon the sand of the mold. The proper time to cease pouring is indicated by the appearance of the metal at the top of the riser. Large foundries employ traveling cranes and large teeming ladles holding perhaps a ton or more of metal.

The flasks are removed soon after the completion of the pouring, and the molds are dumped off the bottom boards in piles, from which the hot castings are hooked out and allowed to cool. The gates and runners are now broken off by a few sharp blows with a hammer, and the castings are removed for cleaning.

9.15 Cleaning the Castings. The sand that adheres to the castings is usually removed by one of three methods: rattling them in a tumbling barrel, pickling, or sand blasting.

Rattling is most commonly practiced with small castings. The tumbling barrel is simply a short horizontal cylinder mounted on trunnions. The castings are piled into the barrel, together with a quantity of abrasive material in the shape of small, irregularly shaped, hard iron stars or picks. The barrel is rotated slowly, and the falling about of the castings and the stars gradually knocks the burned sand and scale off the surfaces of the castings. This method has the disadvantage of producing a hard skin upon the castings which causes difficulty if they are subsequently to be machined.

Rattling will never completely clean any but very simple castings, and a better method consists in pickling the castings by immersion in a dilute sulfuric or muriatic acid solution. The acid attacks the iron somewhat, thereby loosening the sand and scale. Pickling in a 15 per cent solution of sulfuric or muriatic acid requires about 12 hours and must be followed by a careful washing in water. Hydrofluoric acid sometimes replaces sulfuric or muriatic acid. The former attacks the sand itself, instead of the iron, and with only about a 5 per cent solution castings may be cleaned in an hour or less.

The sand blast is the most convenient method of cleaning large castings, especially those of very irregular form, such as gears, etc. Very often the sand blast is followed by pickling.

The final operation in the preparation of castings for use consists in smoothing up the irregularities left by breaking off the gates, the "fin" formed where the metal has run between the two portions of a mold, etc. With small castings this is most readily done with an emery wheel. With larger castings chipping with a cold chisel is often necessary, and a pneumatic chipping tool is most efficient. Portable emery wheels fitted with a flexible drive are also used for this purpose.

9.16 Centrifugal Casting. Centrifugal casting involves rotation of a metal mold or a sand-lined mold during pouring and cooling of the cast iron. The rotation produces a centrifugal force toward the outside, giving greater density and purity to the casting. The method is applied to piston rings, cylinder liners, pipes, and gears. Centrifugally cast gears are stronger than forged gears. Cast-iron pipe can be cast hollow by rotation at about 1500

Materials of Construction

revolutions per minute; the metal is forced to the outside against a metal shell which is lined with a refractory material.

Properties of Cast Iron

CONSTITUTION

9.17 Essential Constituents of Cast Iron. Referring to the iron-carbon diagram, Fig. 7.6, Art. 7.43, it will be noted that only up to about 2.0 per cent carbon will dissolve in iron in the solid solution. This marks the limit of the steel range; beyond is the series of alloys known as cast iron, the usual carbon content of which is from 2.5 to 4.5 per cent. Neglecting the effects of other elements, the constitution of iron-carbon alloys in the cast-iron range is described.

A liquid iron-carbon alloy containing from 2.0 to 4.3 per cent of carbon separates during solidification along line AC into austenite (solid solution of carbide in gamma iron having a maximum of 2.0 per cent carbon at 1130° C. [2066° F.]) and a residual liquid which becomes increasingly richer in carbon. At the eutectic temperature (1130° C. [2066° F.]) the liquid contains 4.3 per cent of carbon and solidifies as the eutectic mixture, called ledeburite, which consists of a mixture of saturated austenite and cementite. When the alloy is cooled below the eutectic temperature, cementite is separated from austenite along the line ES. At the eutectoid (723° C. [1333° F.]) the remaining austenite is transformed into pearlite. Below the eutectoid the iron has a complicated microstructure of cementite and pearlite.

Iron-carbon alloys containing above 4.3 per cent of carbon separate during solidification into cementite and a residual liquid. At the eutectic the remaining liquid solidifies into ledeburite. The austenite in the ledeburite is transformed into cementite and pearlite as above described. Below the eutectoid this iron also has a complex microstructure of cementite and pearlite.

The discussion above refers to iron-carbon alloys, but the composition of cast iron is that of a complex alloy containing usually six important elements, together with other elements of less frequent occurrence. The elements invariably present are, in the approximate order of their importance, iron, carbon, silicon, phosphorus, sulfur, and manganese.

The constitution of cast iron is much more complex than the composition, because of the variety of compounds which the elements present combine to form. The most important consideration affecting the character and properties of cast iron is the carbon content and, in particular, the form assumed by the carbon, i.e., whether free as graphite, or in chemical combination with the iron as a carbide. The importance of the elements other than the iron and carbon is chiefly due to their influence upon the state assumed by the carbon.

Before the essential constituents of cast iron can be stated even in a general way the existence of three principal classes of cast iron must be recognized, the differences being due to the different states in which the carbon occurs.

Gray cast iron is that in which the carbon occurs chiefly in the graphite state.

White cast iron is that in which the carbon occurs chiefly as the carbide of iron.

Mottled cast iron is a mixture of particles of gray iron with particles of white iron. It has no special adaptation, and its production is largely unintentional.

9.18 Carbon in Cast Iron. When cast iron solidifies from the molten state the carbon probably remains in the combined conditions as carbide of iron, Fe_3C, which is partly free as cementite, and partly in solid solution in the iron as austenite. The Fe_3C is an unstable compound, however, and when formed at a high temperature is readily decomposed into graphite and iron.

The decomposition of the carbide with the consequent formation of graphite carbon is facilitated particularly by a slow rate of cooling and by the presence of silicon. It is retarded, on the other hand, by rapid cooling or by the presence of much sulfur or manganese.

9.19 Gray Cast Iron. Cast irons containing considerable amounts of graphite carbon are known as gray cast irons, because of the grayish or blackish, coarsely crystalline appearance of their fractures. This appearance is caused by the presence of many irregular and generally elongated and curved plates of graphite imbedded in the matrix of ferrite and cementite. These plates of graphite are made up of smaller plates, somewhat like sheets of mica, and may be split apart with ease. The individual sheets of graphite vary in size from microscopic proportions to one-eighth of a square inch or more in area. The characteristic structure of gray cast iron is shown in Fig. 9.3. The irregular dark bands are graphite plates, the intermediate area being the ferrite-cementite matrix. The actual amount by weight of graphite in gray cast iron is between 2 and 4 per cent, the combined carbon being under 1½ per cent. The volume content of graphite is much higher, however, since iron has a specific gravity about 3½ times that of graphite.

Since the strength of gray iron depends almost entirely on the matrix in which the graphite is imbedded, it follows that the strongest and hardest gray iron is that in which the matrix is wholly pearlitic. The constitution of the matrix may be varied from pearlite, through mixtures of pearlite and ferrite in different proportions, down to a practically pure ferrite. The graphite-ferrite mixture is the softest and weakest iron; the strength and hardness increase, reaching the maximum with the pearlitic gray iron.

The American Society for Testing Materials jointly with the American Foundrymen's Association has developed a recommended practice (A247)

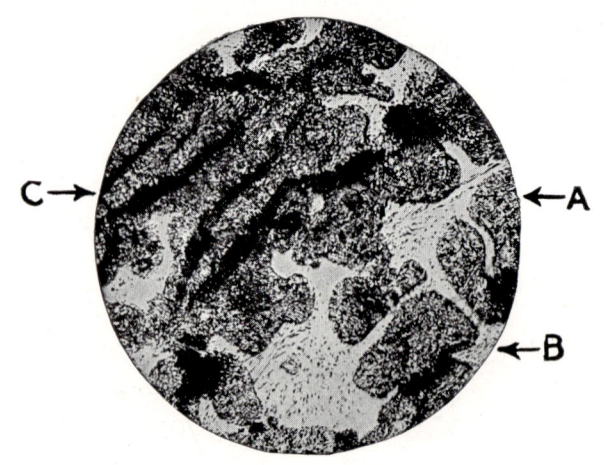

Fig. 9.3. Gray cast iron 150×. A, pearlite; B, ferrite; C, graphite (dark streaks). (Homerberg.)

for evaluating the microstructure of graphite in gray cast iron. A graphite-flake-size chart illustrates eight graded flake lengths photographed at 100 diameters. Five different types of flakes are illustrated in a flake-type chart.

9.20 White Cast Iron. Cast iron in which most of the carbon is present in chemical combination with iron as carbide of iron (Fe_3C), or cementite, is called white cast iron because of the white, highly metallic fracture which

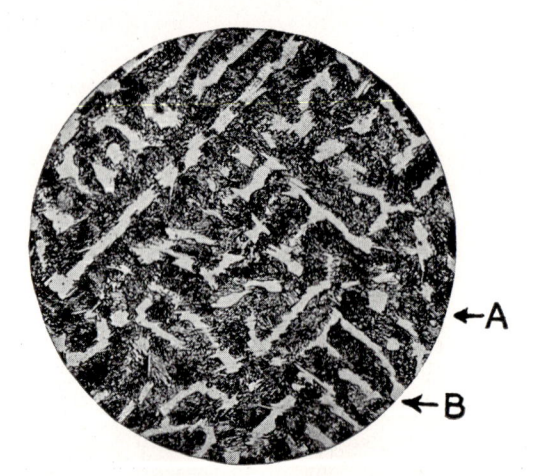

Fig. 9.4. White cast iron 100×. A, pearlite; B, cementite. (Homerberg.)

characterizes it. The ferrite and a portion of the cementite together form pearlite, so that the ultimate constitution of an iron free from graphite will be a mixture of cementite and pearlite. The appearance of white cast iron is shown in Fig. 9.4, in which the light areas are free cementite and the dark banded areas are pearlite. The thumbprint structure of the pearlite is shown in the 1000× photomicrograph of white cast iron given in Fig. 9.5.

The dividing line between high-carbon steel and white cast iron lies at about 2.0 per cent carbon, but, as a matter of fact, most steels do not approach 2.0 per cent carbon, and few white cast irons have less than 2.25 per cent or even 2.50 per cent carbon. The chief industrial use of white iron is as a starting point in making malleable iron (Art. 10.5).

9.21 Silicon in Cast Iron. After iron and carbon, silicon is, in its effects upon the character of the iron, the most important element present in cast iron. Silicon combines with a part of the iron to form the silicide (Fe_2Si), which forms a solid solution with the ferrite. The primary effect of silicon upon the carbon is as a precipitant, driving

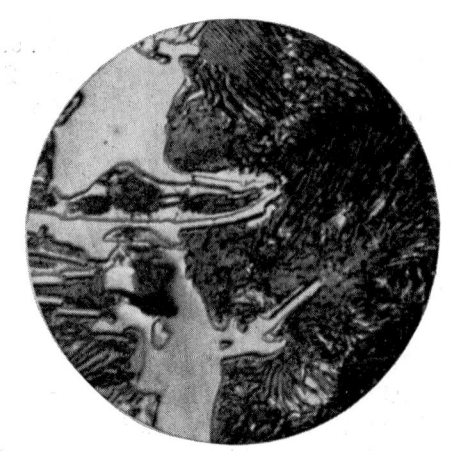

Fig. 9.5. White cast iron 1000×.

the carbon out of combination into the graphite form. The maximum precipitation of graphite seems to occur with about 2.5 to 3.5 per cent of silicon.

The presence of silicon causes the eutectic to consist of austenite and graphite instead of austenite and cementite. Final solidification occurs above the eutectic temperature for plain iron-carbon alloys. Further slow cooling after solidification decomposes the austenite along the lines $E'S'$ (Fig. 7.6), causing graphite to be formed. At the eutectoid the remaining austenite decomposes into alpha iron and cementite, forming a pearlitic structure. Very slow cooling below the eutectoid will transform the cementite into alpha iron and graphite.

Silicon in percentages below about 2.5 per cent acts, therefore, as a pronounced softener, producing soft gray iron, but larger percentages result in the formation of hard and brittle iron due to the excess of the hard, brittle iron silicide, Fe_2Si. Small percentages also produce freedom from oxides and blowholes, promote fluidity, and decrease shrinkage and depth of chill.

9.22 Sulfur in Cast Iron. The influence of sulfur upon the form assumed by the carbon in cast iron is the reverse of the influence of silicon. The higher the sulfur content, the higher will be the proportion of combined carbon. This tendency upon the part of sulfur is much greater than is the opposite tendency exhibited by silicon, however, a given amount of sulfur being able to neutralize about 15 times as much silicon. Sulfur, therefore, tends to produce hard, brittle, white iron.

Aside from the effect of sulfur upon the properties of iron on account of the fact that the carbon is driven into combination as the carbide, sulfur, if present as iron sulfide, FeS, possesses the power materially to affect the behavior of iron in solidifying and cooling. Only a few tenths of 1 per cent of sulfur suffice to render iron very tender at a red-heat ("red-short"), and therefore likely to check or crack if in solidifying the shrinkage causes the casting to tend to crush the sand of the mold, thus resulting in the setting up of internal stresses in the iron. Sulfur also causes solidification to become very rapid, and often is responsible for the presence of blowholes and sandholes.

Manganese, because of its great affinity for sulfur, will tend to rob the iron sulfide, FeS, of its sulfur, forming MnS, a compound which is less potent than FeS in affecting the proportion of combined carbon. A given percentage of sulfur may, in general, be neutralized by the presence of about twice as much manganese. Specifications usually limit the maximum sulfur content of gray cast iron to not more than 0.10 per cent, and often the maximum allowance does not exceed 0.05 per cent.

9.23 Phosphorus in Cast Iron. Chemically, phosphorus tends to increase the proportion of combined carbon, especially when the silicon is low and the phosphorus high. On the other hand, phosphorus lengthens the time of solidification, thereby affording opportunity for the precipitation of graphite. When the silicon is high, therefore, the presence of moderate amounts of phosphorus actually increases the precipitation of graphite, but when the proportion of phosphorus is very large, the chemical effect is great enough to retain the carbon in the combined form in spite of the longer period of solidification.

The presence of phosphorus in considerable amounts tends therefore to produce a hard white iron, lacking in toughness and workability, and especially lacking in shock resistance when cold. Phosphorus reduces the melting point of iron and makes it very fluid. It is therefore useful in making very thin castings where a less fluid iron will not take a perfect impression of the mold. Not more than 0.05 per cent of phosphorus is allowed in the best gray iron, though from 1.0 to 1.5 per cent is sometimes used when fluidity is more important than toughness.

9.24 Manganese in Cast Iron. Manganese increases the tendency for iron to hold carbon in solution and therefore increases the proportion of combined carbon, though it is much less potent in this respect than sulfur.

If no more manganese is present than is required to combine with the sulfur, forming MnS, its effect will not be to increase the proportion of combined carbon, but just the reverse, because the sulfur is taken from the sulfide, FeS, which is so powerful in causing the carbon to assume the combined form. Any additional manganese unites with carbon to form the carbide, Mn_3C, and this carbide unites with the Fe_3C, causing the cementite to be made up in part of the double carbide of iron and manganese $(FeMn)_3C$.

It appears, therefore, that manganese, up to the amount which combines with sulfur to form MnS, tends to lower the proportion of combined carbon and consequently decreases the hardness and brittleness of the iron. Any additional manganese, however, has a marked effect in causing the carbon to assume the combined form and is therefore a hardener.

Physical Properties

9.25 Behavior of Iron in Cooling. *Shrinkage.* The shrinkage of cast iron is an important consideration for the pattern maker, because due allowance for shrinkage must be made in the dimensions of the pattern if the casting is to conform to the size called for by the drawings. It is also an important consideration for the designer and the founder, because the stresses set up in cooling and the consequent danger of checking depend directly upon the degree of shrinkage if the casting is of such a shape that its shrinkage tends to crush the sand in the mold.

With few exceptions, all metals expand upon heating and contract when cooling. The total expansion in melting a metal will correspond to its total shrinkage in solidifying and cooling. Pure iron shrinks about 0.3 inch per foot; a less pure iron usually shrinks less, because impurities, particularly carbon, in general lower the melting point.

The separation of carbon as graphite exerts a powerful influence upon the total net shrinkage of iron because of the expansion which its separation causes.

The factors that chiefly determine the amount of shrinkage are therefore the factors that chiefly control the separation of graphite, i.e., the silicon content and the rate of cooling. Moreover, since the rate of cooling largely depends upon the size of the castings, the shrinkage becomes largely a function of silicon content and size. The shrinkage is inversely proportional to the percentage of silicon, and for an iron of given composition the shrinkage decreases as the size of casting increases.

Other elements whose presence affects the separation of graphite, either directly or by affecting the rate of cooling, naturally have an effect upon shrinkage. Sulfur, which drives carbon into combination with iron, therefore increases shrinkage unless neutralized by other elements. Phosphorus, by lowering the rate of cooling, tends to promote the separation of graphite and decrease the shrinkage.

Checking. The tendency of iron to check (develop small cracks) while cooling depends upon the magnitude of the stresses caused by the contracting of the metal upon the sand and upon the weakness of the metal at a temperature slightly above a black heat. The factors that govern shrinkage, therefore, determine the stresses to which the cooling metal will be subjected, if the casting is of such a shape as to compress the sand in shrinking.

Sulfur is the most deleterious element affecting the strength of iron at a temperature just above a black heat. Phosphorus, by decreasing shrinkage, should decrease the checking of the metal, but this effect may be more than offset by the tendency of phosphorus to cause the metal to assume a coarsely crystalline structure. Manganese somewhat counteracts this last tendency upon the part of the phosphorus and therefore tends to prevent checking.

Segregation. Segregation in castings is the collecting together of impurities in spots. The primary cause of segregation is the effect of impurities in lowering the freezing point of iron. This results in forming a fluid solution which remains molten after the remainder of the metal has solidified and runs to that part of the casting which has the loosest texture. These spots, often called "hot spots," are likely to occur in the middle of the larger sections of the casting. They are often porous, and are usually hard and brittle.

The tendency to segregation is proportional to the amount of impurities present. Phosphorus is especially likely to cause segregation, and manganese and sulfur have the same effect to a less marked extent. Segregation is not commonly encountered in iron founding, however, since other considerations usually require a degree of freedom from excessive amounts of phosphorus, sulfur, or manganese which will minimize the danger of segregation.

9.26 Hardness. The principal factor in determining the hardness of cast iron is the amount of combined carbon. This is due, first, to the hardness of cementite itself, and second, to the fact that increase in combined carbon usually means a decrease in graphite carbon, which is very soft. Graphite has a further effect in increasing the ease with which cast iron may be worked.

The influence of elements other than carbon upon the hardness of iron, with the exception of manganese, directly depends upon their power to vary the amount of combined carbon. Silicon, therefore, acts as a softener, unless its percentage exceeds about 3 per cent, when the effect is reversed. Sulfur and phosphorus act as hardeners in all percentages, and manganese, in addition to its indirect effect on combined carbon, has a direct hardening influence owing to the hardness of the compound $(FeMn)_3C$.

For the purpose of insuring good machinability, Navy Department Specification 46-I-5C requires that a maximum value of Brinell hardness shall not be exceeded for a minimum tensile strength of gray cast iron as tabulated:

Tensile Strength, Minimum, p.s.i.	Brinell Hardness, Maximum
30,000	250
35,000	260
40,000	270
45,000	280

J. T. MacKenzie developed the following equation (of best fit calculated by least squares from 1553 individual values) expressing the relationship between Brinell hardness number and tensile strength of gray cast iron:

$$\text{Tensile strength} = 1.82(\text{B.H.N.})^{1.85}$$

(See reference 9.11.)

9.27 Tensile Strength. The tensile strength of cast iron depends upon the founding methods, the design, and the size of castings. In addition, the

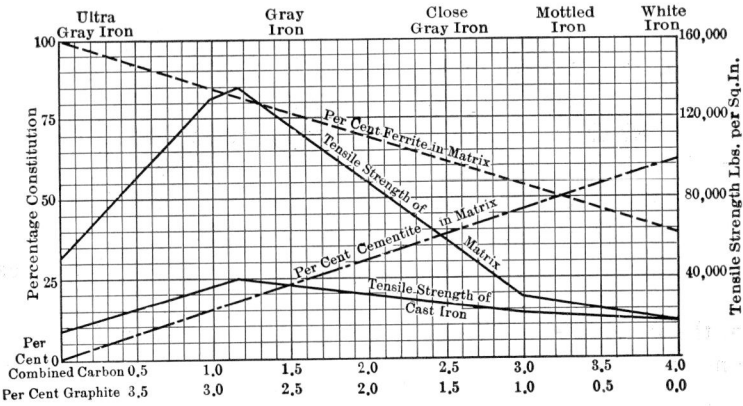

Fig. 9.6. Approximate relationship between tensile strength of cast iron and state of carbon. (Howe.)

composition, and more particularly the constitution, exert a great influence upon strength.

The presence of graphite plates in any proportion must necessarily decrease the strength of the iron as a whole. This injurious effect of graphite is not necessarily directly proportional to the degree of continuity of the graphite mesh.

Any diminution in the proportion of graphite will, in general, diminish in some degree the continuity of the graphite mesh and will, therefore, lessen its detrimental effect upon strength. This increase in the proportion of cementite in the matrix means a proportionate increase in its strength until the percentage of cementite in the iron reaches a certain point, which is in the neighborhood of 1.2 per cent for an iron containing about 4 per cent total carbon. Further increases in the percentage of cementite beyond this point increase hardness and brittleness at the expense of toughness, ductility, and strength. It is evident, therefore, that the strength of an iron will be greater when the percentage of combined carbon does not exceed about 1.2 per cent than it will be if any higher percentage is present. Whether the highest strength is found with about 1.2 per cent cementite or when the percentage of cementite is below this point will depend upon whether the loss of strength due to increase in graphite, on the one hand, or the gain in strength due to the higher carburization of the steel matrix, on the other hand, is the more influential factor.

The approximate relation between tensile strength and state of carbon is shown graphically by the diagram of Fig. 9.6, which is abstracted from the original of Professor Henry M. Howe. In this diagram it has been assumed that the iron possesses a constant total carbon content (4 per cent).

9.28 Influence of Metalloids and Rate of Cooling upon Strength. The influence of the metalloids and the rate of cooling upon the strength of castings is largely an indirect one, depending upon the extent to which the separation of graphite is facilitated or retarded.

Silicon in small amounts, by favoring the precipitation of graphite, exerts an influence which is beneficial to strength, provided that an excessive amount of combined carbon would otherwise be present. In this event the gain in strength of the matrix which accompanies the relief of brittleness more than compensates for the injurious effect of the increase of graphitic carbon. If, on the other hand, the additional graphite precipitation caused by silicon produces an iron whose matrix possesses too little combined carbon, the iron is weakened both because of the lowering of the strength of the matrix and because of the weakening and softening influence of the graphite.

The influence of sulfur, when present as FeS, is always as a weakener of cast iron, not only because it prevents the separation of graphite chemically and by hastening solidification, but also because it promotes the inclusion of flaws (blowholes, sandholes, or shrinkage cracks), induces internal stresses, and causes coarse crystallization and brittleness. The harmful influence of sulfur may, of course, be more or less completely neutralized by much larger percentages of silicon or by the presence of about twice as much manganese.

Phosphorus usually tends to weaken cast iron. When the silicon is high, however, a moderate amount of phosphorus may, by increasing the time of solidification, promote the separation of graphite as above explained, thereby improving strength. The presence of more than about 0.05 per cent phosphorus will, however, always be detrimental to strength.

The effect of manganese upon strength always depends upon the relative amounts of sulfur and manganese present. If the manganese content does not exceed twice the sulfur content, the manganese simply neutralizes the tendency of sulfur to decrease the proportion of graphite, and therefore the manganese increases strength. When the content of manganese exceeds the amount required to neutralize the sulfur, however, the excess manganese has a marked effect detrimental to strength because of the resultant excessive increase in the proportion of combined carbon.

9.29 Stress-Strain Diagram for Cast Iron. Cast iron exhibits a great variation in elastic properties, since so many factors affect its strength.

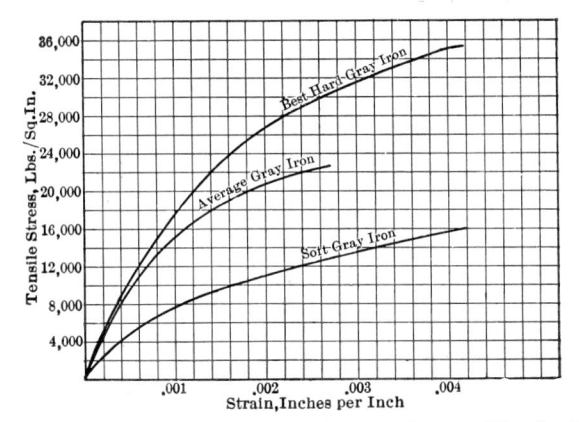

Fig. 9.7. Stress-strain diagrams for cast irons. (Tension.)

In Fig. 9.7 typical stress-strain diagrams for three radically different cast irons are presented in order to illustrate their usual behavior under tensile stress.

It will be observed that there is no well-defined elastic limit or yield point. For the typical irons shown, the ultimate strength falls at 35,500 pounds per square inch for the hard gray iron, 22,500 pounds per square inch for the average gray iron, and 16,000 pounds per square inch for the soft gray iron.

No constant proportionality of stress to strain exists for any considerable load interval, and therefore the modulus of elasticity must be determined by an arbitrary method. The value of E as determined by the initial tangent method is about 30,000,000 pounds per square inch for hard cast iron, 24,000,000 pounds per square inch for average iron, and 14,000,000 pounds per square inch for soft iron. The values of E as determined by the tangent method at 5000-pounds-per-square-inch stress have decreased to about 20,000,000 pounds per square inch, 15,000,000 pounds per square inch, and 7,000,000 pounds per square inch, respectively; and at 10,000-pounds-per-square-inch stress, the values of E are about 15,000,000 pounds per square inch for hard iron and about 14,000,000 pounds per square inch for average iron.

The percentage elongation is small for all cast irons, rarely exceeding from 3 to 4 per cent for any grade, and the reduction of area is usually too slight to be appreciable.

9.30 Transverse Strength. The transverse or flexural strength of cast iron is very valuable as the criterion by which the quality of the material going into gray-iron castings may be judged. Transverse strength is affected by the same factors as tensile strength, since failure under transverse loading is really failure by tension on the tension side of the beam. Three sizes of cylindrical transverse test bars are commonly employed (Table 9.1).

Table 9.1

ASTM REQUIREMENTS FOR CAST IRONS

Controlling section of casting	0.50 in. and under	0.51 to 1.00 in.	1.01 to 2.00 in. and over
Transverse test bar	A	B	C
Diameter of transverse test bar, in.	0.875	1.20	2.00
Span length, in.	12	18	24
Length of bar, in.	15	21	27

Class No.	Tensile Strength, min., p.s.i.	Breaking Load at Center, lb.	Breaking Load at Center, lb.	Breaking Load at Center, lb.
20	20,000	900	1,800	6,000
25	25,000	1,025	2,000	6,800
30	30,000	1,150	2,200	7,600
35	35,000	1,275	2,400	8,300
40	40,000	1,400	2,600	9,100
50	50,000	1,675	3,000	10,300
60	60,000	1,925	3,400	12,500

9.31 Specifications for Gray Cast Iron. The specifications of the American Society for Testing Materials classify gray cast irons with respect to tensile strength into seven classes, numbers 20, 25, 30, 35, 40, 50, and 60, as shown in Table 9.1. Each class corresponds to the minimum tensile strength required in thousands of pounds per square inch. The tension-test specimens are machined from test bars that are cast separately from the casting. The requirements of transverse strength for these classes of irons are also given in Table 9.1.

Classes 20, 25, and 30 cover the ordinary grades of gray cast iron. Classes 35, 40, 50, and 60 are considered to be high-strength irons, particularly in medium and heavy sections. Since, in general, the higher-strength irons are more difficult to produce in heavy sections, and more difficult to machine, the specification of a stronger cast iron than is needed may result in unnecessarily increased costs in producing the casting and in machining.

The specifications of the Society of Automotive Engineers for automotive-type cast iron are summarized in Table 9.2. Suggested usage is:

Cast Iron

SAE 110: Miscellaneous soft iron castings (as cast or annealed) in which strength is not a primary consideration.

SAE 111: Small cylinder blocks, cylinder heads, transmission cases, and gear boxes.

SAE 120: Automobile cylinder blocks, flywheels, truck-brake drums, and pistons.

SAE 121: Truck and tractor cylinder blocks and heads, heavy flywheels, and heavy gear boxes.

SAE 122: Diesel-engine castings, cylinders, pistons, and heavy parts in general.

Table 9.2

MECHANICAL PROPERTIES OF AUTOMOTIVE-TYPE CAST IRON *

SAE Number	Brinell Hardness Number	Transverse Load, min., lb.	Deflection, min., in.	Tensile Strength, min., p.s.i.
110	187 max.	1,800	0.15	20,000
111	170–223	2,200	0.20	30,000
120	187–241	2,400	0.24	35,000
121	202–255	2,600	0.27	40,000
122	217–269	2,800	0.30	45,000

* *SAE Handbook, 1952*, page 147. Properties determined from arbitration test bar (1.2-in. diameter as cast or stress relieved at 1050° F. max.).

9.32 High-Strength Cast Iron. Cast irons of classes 35, 40, 50, and 60 are usually produced by the addition of steel to the iron, thus decreasing the percentages of carbon and silicon and consequently increasing the strength through reducing the formation of graphite. Such iron can be produced without the addition of alloys but requires careful control of melting, molding, and pouring. The high-strength cast irons are harder and more difficult to machine, requiring the use of cemented carbide tools with much coolant solution.

9.33 Properties at High Temperatures. The most significant high-temperature characteristic of cast iron is its tendency toward "growth" when subjected to temperatures over 500° F. for long periods of time. This expansion is due to separating out of graphite. If subjected to successive periods at high temperatures as for example in steam fittings, the casting will become misshapen. The presence of silicon tends to promote "growth" in gray iron castings.

9.34 Heat Treatment of Gray Cast Iron. The tensile strength and hardness of gray cast iron can be increased by quenching in oil from about 871° C. (1600° F.) and tempering at about 427° C. (800° F.). If the iron is quenched only and not tempered, the metal will be under such internal strain that the tensile strength will be reduced, but, if the heat treatment is properly conducted, an increase of about 10 per cent will be obtained. Hardening and tempering are particularly beneficial to iron with a total carbon content of 3 per cent or less; the silicon content should not exceed 2 per cent. A cast iron so treated is extremely wear resistant and can be used for cams, dies, and other parts subjected to wear.

The machinability of high-strength cast iron can be greatly improved by tempering conducted at a temperature below 705° C. (1300° F.) to soften the matrix of iron. Hardness can be reduced from 300 to 240 Brinell with only a moderate reduction in tensile strength. In general, the higher the temperature of tempering and the longer the heat treatment, the more the tendency for carbon combined in cementite to go to the graphitic form, thus reducing the tensile strength and hardness.

Careful control and good technique are required to obtain good results in heat-treating cast iron, for two reasons: (1) cast iron has a higher critical temperature than steel because of its higher silicon content (871° C. [1600° F.] is usually adequate); and (2) cast iron has a high carbon content. Castings must be allowed to soak sufficiently to reach a uniform temperature throughout. In hardening, castings must be quenched quickly before the surfaces can cool during removal and handling. Surface layers which have been air cooled will not harden even though the core may reach a satisfactory hardness. In order to prevent decarburization of the graphite exposed on the surfaces of the castings during heat treatment, the atmosphere should be controlled artificially, preferably by packing the castings in carburizing boxes with partly spent carburizing compounds or with cast-iron borings.

Heat-treated cast iron expands during the hardening process. This growth can be diminished by first annealing the castings by heating at 732° C. (1350° F.) for about 4 hours. After annealing, the castings can be machined with great ease and the heat treatment will cause a much smaller amount of growth and distortion.

9.35 Alloy Cast Irons. Nickel, chromium, or a combination of nickel and chromium is often used with beneficial effect in the preparation of so-called "alloy" cast irons. The effect of these alloying elements is somewhat variable, depending on the percentages of the other elements present, and particularly on the proportions of graphite and combined carbon.

In general, the effect of nickel is to harden the iron and thereby increase its resistance to wear, without materially decreasing its machinability. The resilience of cast iron is also improved and considerable grain refinement is caused by addition of nickel.

The addition of 0.5 to 1.0 per cent of chromium counteracts the tendency for combined carbon to be changed to graphite during heat treatment.

Chromium carbide is formed, which is very stable. Such alloy iron can be heat treated into an extremely tough, high-strength material by holding at about 705° C. (1300° F.) for a period of time. This treatment converts the pearlite in the cast matrix into a mixture of ferrite and cementite particles in a manner similar to the spheroidizing of tool steel for the purpose of increasing toughness and improving machinability. The resultant iron has high strength, excellent toughness, and some ductility; it is easily machined and has good wear resistance.

If chromium and nickel are used in proper proportions (1 to 2 parts nickel to 1 part chromium), and if the percentages of carbon, silicon, and phosphorus are carefully controlled, a casting will result which, in addition to good grain refinement, high strength, and hardness, will be uniform, even in heavy sections, and will also show excellent machining qualities and resistance to wear.

Nickel is added either in the cupola charge or in the ladle, generally in amounts between 2 and 5 per cent. Irons containing both chromium and nickel may be prepared by using Mayari pig iron in the charge. This pig iron is smelted from Cuban ores containing chromium and nickel.

The alloy cast irons are used in the manufacture of chilled rolls, chilled car wheels, grinding machinery, sand-blast nozzles, rolling-mill guides, engine cylinders, pistons, etc.

9.36 Inoculated Cast Iron. Inoculated cast iron is cast iron to which an inoculant has been added for the purpose of modifying the structure and changing the mechanical properties. Inoculants cause considerable changes in mechanical properties without appreciably affecting the chemical composition. Typical inoculants comprise ferrosilicon, nickel-silicon, calcium-silicon, zirconium-silicon, ferromanganese-silicon, chromium, and a group of commercial materials called graphitizing inoculants which are sold under trade names. Inoculants are useful in producing high-quality castings, but they must be added under carefully controlled conditions to obtain good results.

The addition of ferrosilicon may be cited as an example. The iron is melted with a low silicon content, and the ferrosilicon is added to the ladle. This inoculation improves the structure and tends to eliminate chilling of corners and edges; mechanical properties are bettered except for hardness which is less for an equivalent tensile strength. See Table 9.3. For low-carbon cast iron, inoculation reduces the formation of dendritic graphite; the effect of this change in structure is brought out by the increased arbitration-bar Izod impact value for the inoculated iron.

9.37 Controlled Cast Iron. Superior qualities may be obtained by carefully controlling the melting and pouring of cast iron. *Meehanite* cast iron

Table 9.3

EFFECT OF INOCULATION ON MECHANICAL PROPERTIES OF GRAY CAST IRON *

Composition	Gray Cast Iron	Inoculated Gray Cast Iron
Inoculation, %	None	0.5 Ferrosilicon (Fe 85 Si)
Total carbon, %	2.93	2.93
Silicon, %	1.92	2.3 approx.
Manganese, %	1.0	1.0
Sulfur, %	0.1	0.1
Phosphorus, %	0.04	0.04
Arbitration-bar Izod impact, ft.-lb.	22	40
Transverse load on 12-in. span, lb.	4,210	5,110
Deflection, in.	0.13	0.21
Tensile strength, p.s.i.	43,700	50,300
Brinell hardness number	235	228

* J. T. Eash and A. P. Gagnebin: "An Arbitration Bar Izod Impact Test for Cast Iron." *Proc. ASTM*, v. 51, 1951, pp. 1061–1071.

is a proprietary cast iron produced by careful control which can be heat treated to produce a strong casting and which can be flame hardened. It is similar in composition and structure to tool steel. Meehanite contains no free ferrite. Its matrix consists entirely of pearlite (91.50 per cent); it has graphite (7.25 per cent) and iron phosphide (1.25 per cent). One application of Meehanite is for matched molds for manufacture of reinforced plastics.

9.38 Nodular Graphite Cast Iron. This iron is a recent development. Additions of small amounts of magnesium or cerium to the ladle may produce a casting with the graphite in *nodular* form instead of in flake form. Magnesium additions in alloy form (20 to 50 per cent magnesium, 80 to 50 per cent copper or nickel) are typical of practice in the United States; in Great Britain misch metal (50 per cent cerium, 50 per cent other rare earths) is added to the ladle. In nodular graphite cast iron, the graphite particles are of spherical form in a matrix of pearlite. The combined carbon gives high strength, and the nodular graphite contributes toward good ductility. Thus, tensile strength and ductility of nodular cast iron is greatly improved as compared to plain gray cast iron. For example, annealed nodular cast iron containing 3.5 per cent carbon has a tensile strength of about 75,000 pounds per square inch, an elongation in 2 inches of 15 per cent, and a Brinell hardness number of 185. Its modulus of elasticity varies from 20,000,000 to 26,000,000 pounds per square inch. (See reference 9.9.) Nodular cast iron can be heat treated by quenching, tempering, annealing, and normalizing to develop different mechanical properties. Section thickness has but small effect on the mechanical properties of nodular graphite cast iron. It is much less susceptible to growth at high temperatures than gray cast iron.

Questions

9.1. Describe the cupola and the air-furnace methods of manufacturing cast iron, and state the advantages of each method.
9.2. What are the advantages of the electric-melting furnace?
9.3. Describe the essential steps in iron founding.
9.4. Describe the method of centrifugal casting.
9.5. In what state is the carbon in gray cast iron; in white cast iron?
9.6. Sketch the microstructure of gray cast iron; of white cast iron.
9.7. Briefly discuss the effects of carbon, silicon, phosphorus, sulfur, and manganese on the properties of cast iron.
9.8. Discuss the relationship between tensile strength and the state of carbon in cast iron.
9.9. What are the SAE specifications for mechanical properties of automotive-type cast iron suitable for automobile cylinder blocks?
9.10. Give typical values of the ultimate tensile strength and modulus of elasticity in tension of commercial gray cast iron of a good grade.
9.11. Describe the heat treatment of gray cast iron.
9.12. Distinguish between inoculated cast iron and nodular graphite cast iron.

References

9.1. American Foundrymen's Association: *Cast Metals Handbook.* Chicago, 3rd ed., 1944.
9.2. American Society for Metals: *Metals Handbook.* Cleveland, Ohio, 1948 ed.
9.3. Bolton, J. W.: *Gray Cast Iron.* Cleveland, Ohio, Penton Publishing Co., 1937.
9.4. Boylston, H. M.: *An Introduction to the Metallurgy of Iron and Steel.* John Wiley & Sons, 2nd ed., 1936; Chap. 5, pp. 128–186.
9.5. Campbell, H. L.: *Metal Castings.* John Wiley & Sons, 1936, 318 pages.
9.6. Draffin, J. O., and Collins, W. L.: "The Tensile Strength of Cast Iron." *Proc. ASTM*, v. 37, Part II, 1937, pp. 88–101.
9.7. Eash, J. T., and Gagnebin, A. P.: "An Arbitration Bar Izod Impact Test for Cast Iron." *Proc. ASTM*, v. 51, 1951, p. 1061.
9.8. Fisher, J. C.: "A Criterion for the Failure of Cast Iron." *ASTM Bull.* 181, Apr., 1952, p. 74 (TP76).
9.9. Gagnebin, A. P.: "INCO Writes Specifications for Ductile Iron." *Iron Age,* May 4, 1950, p. 89.
9.10. Kommers, J. B.: "The Effect of Under-Stressing on Cast Iron and Open-Hearth Iron. *Proc. ASTM,* v. 30, Part II, 1930, pp. 368–381.
9.11. MacKenzie, J. T.: "The Brinell Hardness of Gray Cast Iron and Its Relation to Some Other Properties." *Proc. ASTM*, v. 46, 1946, pp. 1025–1038.
9.12. Maxwell, H. L.: "Cast Iron in Chemical Equipment." *Mech. Eng.,* Dec., 1936, pp. 803–808 and 845.
9.13. Morrogh, H., and Williams, W. J.: "The Production of Nodular Graphite Structures in Cast Iron." *J. Iron Steel Inst. (London),* v. 158, 1948, pp. 306–322.
9.14. Nord, M.: *Textbook of Engineering Materials.* John Wiley & Sons, Inc., 1952, 534 pages.

9.15. *SAE Handbook.* New York, Society of Automotive Engineers, 1952, 946 pages.

9.16. Schneidewind, R., and Hoenicke, E. C.: "A Study of the Chemical, Physical, and Mechanical Properties of Permanent Mold Gray Iron." *Proc. ASTM,* v. 42, 1942, pp. 622–638.

9.17. Valenta, E.: "Electric-Furnace and Alloy Cast Irons for Corrosion Resistance." *Iron Age,* v. 125, 1930, p. 532.

9.18. Wickenden, T. H.: "Production of Nodular Structure in Cast Iron." Discussion at meeting of American Foundrymen's Society, May, 1948.

CHAPTER 10

Malleable Cast Iron

10.1 General. Malleable cast iron is iron of special composition which, after having been cast or rolled to its final form, is rendered malleable by a process of annealing. It is essential that the iron used be a white iron before malleablizing, in order that the carbon may be almost wholly in the combined form. The malleablizing process will then result in the conversion of the combined carbon into free carbon in an amorphous condition, not resembling free carbon in the crystalline form as graphite. This amorphous carbon will exist as isolated particles in a continuous mesh of metal. Through this circumstance the casting is rendered very much tougher than white or gray cast iron, and its ductility and malleability are increased to such an extent that it may be bent or twisted to a considerable degree even when cold.

Malleable iron combines the advantages of ordinary cast iron, with respect to the ease with which complicated forms may be cast, with a considerable degree of toughness, ductility, and strength. Its physical properties approach those of mild carbon-steel castings, and from the standpoints of uniformity, soundness, and machinability it surpasses steel.

This material is especially valuable in the manufacture of that large class of articles whose form is too complicated for economical forging, but which must possess a strength and toughness not attainable in gray castings.

Among the more common applications of malleable iron may be especially mentioned its use in automobile construction for rear-axle housings, differential cases, brake supports, steering-gear housings, hubs, pedals, etc., which must withstand severe service, yet permit of rapid manufacture in large quantities. In railroad equipment manufacture, couplers are commonly made of malleable iron, as are the journal boxes, brake fittings, and many other small fittings for rolling stock. Other uses include many parts of agricultural machinery, all manner of pipe fittings, elbows, unions, valves, etc., and household hardware such as parts of locks, hinges, and window and door fittings.

Another class of articles is made of malleable iron that has been casehardened after prolonged annealing. The material then closely resembles cast steel and is often sold as such. These articles include many carpenter tools, such as hammers, hatchets, chisels, and planer irons.

Manufacture of Malleable Castings

10.2 The Materials Used. The charge of the furnace of a malleable-iron foundry includes pig iron, sprues, annealed malleable-iron scrap, and steel scrap.

The pig iron should contain not more than 0.60 per cent manganese, not more than 0.225 per cent phosphorus, not more than 0.05 per cent sulfur, and not less than 2.75 per cent total carbon. The silicon requirement varies according to the castings made. Heavy castings require from 0.75 to 1.50 per cent silicon; light castings, from 1.26 to 2.00 per cent.

The sprues or "hard scrap" include the gates and scrap castings that have not been annealed. Thorough cleaning of the sprues to remove the burned sand is very necessary.

Malleable scrap is difficult to melt because of the comparative infusibility of the skin of malleable castings. It contributes greatly to the strength of the castings made, however, and if the large scrap is broken up before charging, it may be handled without serious difficulty.

Steel scrap of any sort may be used as a part of the charge with beneficial results, if added after the balance of the bath is molten.

10.3 Melting Malleable-Iron Mixtures. Three types of furnaces are used in melting iron for malleable casting: the cupola, the air furnace, and the open-hearth furnace. The cupola process for melting iron for malleable-iron castings differs in no respect from ordinary gray-iron foundry practice, except in the higher proportion of fuel charged. The advantages of the cupola process lie in the cheapness of installation and operation, the comparative ease with which the furnace is controlled, and the small loss of silicon in melting. The disadvantages are the great danger of burning, owing to the direct contact of metal and fuel, and the extremely close structure of the hard castings produced, which causes trouble in annealing.

The advantages of the air furnace as compared wtih the cupola are principally the better grade of castings produced, the wider range of scrap material possible, the shorter time required for pouring, the less serious consequences of a breakdown, and the better control over process and product. The disadvantages of the air-furnace process are the greater expense of equipment, the greater skill required in operation, and the longer time for melting.

The open-hearth furnace is operated in the malleable-iron foundry in almost exactly the same manner as in the production of open-hearth steel. Its advantages over the air furnace are the saving of time required for melting, the very exact control of the process, and the resultant high efficiency and gain in the percentage of first-grade castings. The disadvantages are the high cost of installation, the heavy repair bill, the necessity of having gas fuel, and the necessity of continuous operation.

10.4 Foundry Methods for Malleable Castings. Molds for malleable castings are made in the same manner as gray-iron castings in green sand.

Particular care must be exercised to furnish proper gating in handling white-iron mixtures, and risers or feeders must be provided where thin sections are encountered, to prevent cooling of the metal at these points before the mold is completely filled.

Chills are very commonly used in molds for malleable castings, particularly for the sake of cooling the larger parts of castings rapidly, thereby preventing the possibility of graphite separating out, as it tends to do with slow cooling.

Molten white iron is a very different material from molten gray iron. The former must be poured very hot, and as rapidly as possible, to insure proper complete filling of the mold.

Hard castings for malleable iron are cleaned by any of the methods common to the gray-iron foundry. Very careful inspection of the cleaned castings is necessary, and all defective castings are rejected before being annealed.

10.5 Graphitization by Heat Treating. The castings are graphitized or malleablized by means of a suitable heat treatment which converts the hard white iron into a ductile, strong, tough, and easily machinable product. The treatment consists of heating to a temperature above the critical point, maintaining this malleablizing temperature, cooling to the critical point, maintaining at a temperature slightly below the critical point, and finally cooling to room temperature.

White cast iron consists of pearlite and cementite; its structure is illustrated in the photomicrographs of Figs. 9.4 and 9.5. Heating to a point just above the critical temperature (about 760° C. [1400° F.] for iron of usual silicon content) transforms the pearlite into austenite, the cementite remaining unchanged. Austenite is a constituent of indefinite composition with respect to carbon, capable of dissolving carbon in amounts proportional to its temperature. Accordingly, when in the process the temperature is raised to about 871° C. (1600° F.), the austenite absorbs as much carbon from the cementite as it can hold at that temperature. As the temperature is maintained, the austenite gives up some of the absorbed carbon which is precipitated in the form of "temper" carbon. As this precipitation takes place, the austenite absorbs more carbon from the cementite until all the carbon in the cementite has been dissolved. At this stage some carbon has been precipitated and the remainder is in the austenite. Then the temperature is slowly lowered to the critical temperature and more temper carbon is precipitated from the austenite. At the critical temperature, however, the austenite still contains the amount of carbon originally present in the pearlite of the white iron. To prevent reversion to the relatively hard pearlite in passing through the critical temperature, and to effect complete precipitation of the carbon, it is slowly cooled to about 590° C. (1275° F.), where the temperature is maintained to permit the breaking up of the austenite into ferrite and temper carbon.

In brief, the malleablizing process converts hard, brittle white cast iron with a structure of pearlite and cementite into malleable cast iron with a structure of relatively soft ferrite and carbon in the free amorphous form called "temper" carbon. This structure, known as ferritic malleable cast iron, is shown in the photomicrograph of Fig. 10.1.

In order to prevent oxidation during the process, and also warping of the castings, the castings must be packed in annealing pots surrounded by a proper packing material. This packing material might be sand, clay, or other inert material, and the heat alone would effect the desired change in the state of the carbon and produce malleable castings. Higher-grade and stronger castings are produced, however, when the packing material is a decarbonizing agent such as iron oxide. This results in the migration of carbon from the outer shell of the casting, producing a layer resembling steel about $\frac{1}{16}$ inch thick, encased in a skin of almost carbonless iron on the surface. This skin may subsequently be enriched in carbon by a case-hardening process, and, if the reduction of carbon has previously been carried to the maximum depth possible (about $\frac{1}{4}$ inch), the resultant material will greatly resemble cast steel. It may even be hardened and tempered.

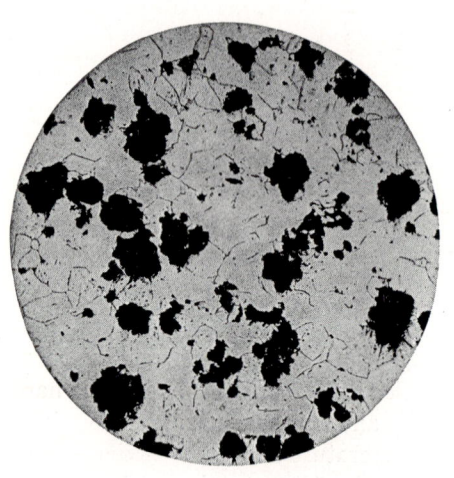

Fig. 10.1. Malleable cast iron 100×.

When one pot has been filled, another pot is superimposed on it and filled in a similar manner. Several pots in such a stack constitute what is known as a stand. The top of the stand is covered with flat cast-iron pieces and sealed with clay to prevent the access of oven gases to the castings.

10.6 Types of Malleablizing Furnace. Malleablizing or annealing furnaces are of either the periodic or continuous types. The periodic type predominates in general usage; this type of oven is ordinarily of rectangular box form with a fire pot at one end on the outside, the products of combustion passing from it to the oven proper over a communicating bridge

Malleable Cast Iron

wall. It may be heated with powdered coal, oil, gas, or electricity, though the first two are most generally used because of their lower cost. The regenerative principle is not employed in this type of oven, since the castings must cool slowly in the oven itself. The capacity varies from about 25 to 45 tons of castings charged, and the total time for the process averages about 7 days.

The muffle oven, which is also of periodic type, consists of an insulated rectangular brick shell supported on the outside by steel plates and buck stays. Within this shell, a firebrick muffle is constructed with a space between it and the brick shell sufficient for proper combustion of the fuel, and so arranged with flues as to enable the flame to heat the entire surface of the muffle. In most such ovens oil or natural gas is the fuel. Since the products of combustion do not come in direct contact with the castings, the necessity of packing the castings in pots is avoided.

Tunnel kilns of the continuous type vary from 200 to 350 feet in length. The stands are loaded on short cars which when in the kiln form its bottom. The cars on passing through the tunnel are subjected to a gradation of temperature so timed as to correspond to the heating cycle required. In the continuous kiln the malleablizing time is shortened about 2 days.

10.7 Malleablizing Period. The complete malleablizing or annealing cycle may be subdivided into five distinct intervals. First, the temperature is slowly increased in about 2 days' time to about 871° C. (1600° F.); second, this annealing temperature is maintained for 48 to 60 hours; third, the castings are slowly cooled to the critical temperature (approximately 704° C. [1300° F.]) and are held just under the critical point for about 35 hours, after which they are cooled to permit handling. About 6 days are required.

The annealed castings must be cleaned to remove the scale which has formed. This is accomplished in tumbling barrels.

In order to test the quality of the annealed iron, "test plugs," which are simply small projections, about ¾ by ½ by 1 inch long, are cast on the more important work. These are broken off and the fracture examined. If normal, the fracture should have a black velvety surface in the interior, surrounded by a band of dark gray about $\frac{1}{16}$ inch thick, and this in turn should be encased in a band of white not more than $\frac{1}{64}$ inch thick.

10.8 Types of Malleable Cast Iron. There are two types of malleable cast iron, namely, black-heart and white-heart. *Black-heart* malleable iron, so called because a fractured surface has a black appearance, is usually produced in American practice. The descriptions in this chapter pertain to black-heart iron. *White-heart* malleable iron is usually produced in European foundries; the process requires the maintenance of a higher annealing temperature for a longer time, the effect of which is not only to break down the combined carbon (Fe₃C) into temper carbon and ferrite but also to decarburize the iron very markedly, producing a white heart of nearly pure iron.

Properties of Malleable-Iron Castings

10.9 Chemical Composition and Constitution. The percentage composition of malleable cast iron may vary considerably depending upon the properties desired, especially tensile strength. Also, carbon at the center of a thick section may be nearly the initial total carbon while very thin sections may be almost completely decarburized. The accompanying tabulation presents average values of chemical composition of good malleable iron:

	Per Cent
Carbon	2.00–2.65
Silicon	0.60–1.30
Manganese	0.25–0.50
Phosphorus	0.08–0.18
Sulfur	0.06–0.16
	(usually about 0.10)

It is important that the different elements be adjusted properly in relation to each other. Since there is no combined carbon in malleable cast iron, phosphorus may be present up to 0.20 per cent without danger of cold shortness. A sulfur content as indicated is not objectionable since malleable cast iron is not hot worked.

The constitution of malleable iron is extremely variable, even in a single casting, because the effect of the annealing process depends largely upon the thickness of the casting. The outermost skin is practically carbonless iron. The intermediate gray portion of black-heart malleable castings consists largely of ferrite but contains scattered particles of free carbon in the amorphous state, called temper carbon. The black interior consists of ferrite in which many isolated particles of temper carbon are interspersed.

10.10 Physical Properties. The average physical properties of American malleable cast irons are as tabulated:

Tensile strength	54,000 p.s.i.
Yield strength	36,000 p.s.i.
Elongation in 2 in.	18%
Modulus of elasticity in tension	25,000,000 p.s.i.
Brinell hardness number	115; range, 100–140
Izod impact value	9.3 ft.-lb.
Charpy impact value	7.75 ft.-lb.
Fatigue endurance limit	25,000 p.s.i.
Ultimate shearing strength	48,000 p.s.i.
Yield point in shear	23,000 p.s.i.
Specific gravity	7.15 to 7.45
Average coefficient of thermal expansion	0.0000066 per °F.

The specifications of the American Society for Testing Materials for two grades of malleable iron castings, numbers 32510 and 35018, require minimum tensile strengths of 50,000 and 53,000 pounds per square inch, minimum yield strength of 32,500 and 35,000 pounds per square inch, and minimum elongations in 2 inches of 10 and 18 per cent, respectively.

Malleable cast iron has no well-defined yield point. Its yield strength is ordinarily determined as the stress under which the specimen has an elongation in 2 inches of 0.01 inch. (See reference 10.7.)

10.11 Pearlitic Malleable Cast Iron. Pearlitic malleable cast iron contains both temper carbon and combined carbon. The matrix containing cementite can vary in a manner similar to steel from almost a completely ferritic structure to an almost completely pearlitic structure. The combined carbon can be in the form of pearlite or in the form of martensite and, under certain conditions, austenite. Tensile strength will range from 54,000 pounds per square inch for ordinary malleable iron to 120,000 pounds per square inch for martensitic "pearlitic malleable" iron. The ductility is similar to that of cast steel but somewhat lower owing to the presence of temper carbon.

Pearlitic malleable cast iron is produced by two processes. In the first the castings are completely malleablized and afterwards are reheated above the critical temperature to redissolve a portion of the temper carbon as combined carbon. This cementite is retained by rapid cooling with the formation of a pearlitic matrix. In the second process the castings are incompletely malleablized so that the castings as cooled contain both temper carbon and combined carbon which has never been decomposed. In this process two variations are possible: (a) white iron of normal analysis is used but is incompletely malleablized, and (b) white iron is used of an analysis which will not completely malleablize under normal conditions. Pearlitic malleable cast iron produced by the above methods may be heat treated to produce martensitic structure.

Questions

10.1. Describe the materials and methods used in producing white-iron castings.
10.2. Describe the malleablizing process.
10.3. Sketch the microstructure of malleable cast iron, labeling each constituent.
10.4. How is decarburization accomplished?
10.5. Distinguish between black-heart and white-heart malleable iron.
10.6. State average values of the chemical composition of a good grade of malleable cast iron.
10.7. Discuss the physical properties of malleable cast iron.
10.8. Name typical articles manufactured from malleable cast iron.
10.9. What is pearlitic malleable iron? How may it be produced?

References

10.1. American Foundrymen's Association: *Cast Metals Handbook*. Chicago, 3rd ed. 1944.
10.2. Bryce, J. T., and Schwab, H. G.: "Faster Annealing of Malleable Cast Iron." *Metal Progr.*, Jan., 1938, pp. 35–41.
10.3. Campbell, H. L.: *Metal Castings*. John Wiley & Sons, 1936, 318 pages.
10.4. Forbes, D. P.: "New Cast Irons, Heat Treated, Rolled." *Metal Progr.*, Feb., 1938, p. 137.
10.5. Heine, R. W.: "Some Effects of Deoxidizing Additions on Foundry Malleable Irons." *Univ. Wisconsin, Eng. Exp. Sta Reprint* 156, 1950.
10.6. Kanter, J. J., and Guarnieri, G.: "Some Creep Studies on Cupola Malleable Cast Iron." *Proc. ASTM*, v. 42, 1942, pp. 659–667.
10.7. Landon, R. D.: "Stress-Strain Relations for Malleable Cast Iron in Tension with Special Attention to Yield Point Determination." *Proc. ASTM*, v. 40, 1940, pp. 849–863.
10.8. Lansing, J. H.: "Production of Malleable Castings." Cleveland, Ohio, Malleable Founders' Society, *Malleable Iron Facts* 37.
10.9. Lansing, J. H.: *Malleable Iron Castings, Their Production and Use*. Cleveland Engineering Co., 1946.
10.10. Lorig, C. H.: "Properties of Commercial Pearlitic Malleable Iron." *ASTM Bull.* 105, Aug., 1940, p. 29.
10.11. Malleable Founders' Society: *American Malleable Iron*. Cleveland, Ohio, 1944.
10.12. Ruff, W.: "The Running Quality of Liquid Malleable Iron and Steel." *Iron Steel Inst. (London), Carnegie Schol. Mem.*, v. 25, 1936, pp. 1–39.
10.13. Schneidewind, R., and White, A. E.: "The Malleabilization of White Cast Iron." Ann Arbor, Mich., *Univ. Michigan, Eng. Research Bull. 24*, 1933, 76 pages.
10.14. Schneidewind, R., and White, A. E.: "Properties of Fully Annealed and Heat-Treated Malleable Castings." *Trans. Am. Foundrymen's Assoc.*, v. 45, 1937, pp. 1–28.
10.15. White, A. E., and Schneidewind, R.: "The Metallurgy of Malleabilization." *Trans. Am. Foundrymen's Assoc.*, v. 40, 1932, pp. 88–124.

CHAPTER 11

Alloy Steels

11.1 Definition and Classification. An alloy steel may be defined as a steel that owes its distinctive properties chiefly to some element or elements other than carbon. *Ternary steels,* or three-part alloy steels, are those whose properties chiefly depend upon the presence of one element other than iron and carbon. *Quaternary steels* contain two influential elements other than iron and carbon.

All alloy steels bear names that indicate the alloying element present. The principal classes of alloy steels are those listed below:

Ternary Alloys	Quaternary Alloys
Nickel steel	Chrome-nickel steel
Silicon steel	Chrome-vanadium steel
Copper steel	Chrome-molybdenum steel
Manganese steel	Chrome-tungsten steel
Chromium steel	Chrome-silicon steel
Tungsten steel	Manganese-silicon steel
Molybdenum steel	Aluminum-chromium steel
Vanadium steel	Nickel-molybdenum steel

The special elements may be divided into two classifications: (1) those like nickel, silicon, and copper which do *not* combine with carbon to form carbides; and (2) those like manganese, chromium, tungsten, molybdenum, and vanadium which do combine with carbon to form carbides.

Alloying elements such as titanium, aluminum, and vanadium are sometimes used to act as scavengers and otherwise facilitate manufacture. In such cases the alloying element is absent, or nearly so, in the final analysis, and steels so prepared are known as alloy-treated steels. Alloy steels are also manufactured which contain more than two alloying elements such as nickel-chrome-molybdenum steels and alloy tool steels.

The benefit from the alloying elements and the valuable properties of an alloy steel can be obtained only by proper heat treating. As a general rule, alloy steels when untreated are little, if at all, superior to plain carbon steel. Structural nickel and silicon steels and high-strength low-alloy steels may be mentioned as exceptions.

11.2 SAE Steel Numbering System. The Society of Automotive Engineers has developed a convenient classification of steels by means of a numeral index system which makes it possible to indicate by numerals on shop drawings and blueprints partial descriptions of the composition of the metals. The first digit indicates the type to which the steel belongs; thus "1—" indicates a carbon steel; "2—" a nickel steel; "3—" a nickel-chromium steel. The approximate percentage of carbon, expressed in hundredths of 1 per cent, is shown by the last two digits. For simple alloy steels the second digit generally indicates the approximate percentage of the predominant alloying element. Thus 1020 indicates a plain carbon steel of approximately 0.20 per cent carbon; 2350 indicates a nickel steel of 3.25–3.75 per cent nickel and 0.45–0.55 per cent carbon. Table 11.1, giving the basic

Table 11.1

SAE NUMERAL INDEX SYSTEM FOR STEELS

Type of Steel and Average Chemical Content	Numerals and Digits
Carbon steels	1xxx
Plain carbon	10xx
Free cutting (screw stock)	11xx
Manganese steels (Mn, 1.75)	13xx
Nickel steels	2xxx
Ni, 3.50	23xx
Ni, 5.00	25xx
Nickel-chromium steels	3xxx
Ni, 1.25; Cr, 0.65 or 0.80	31xx
Ni, 3.50; Cr, 1.55	33xx
Corrosion- and heat-resisting	303xx
Molybdenum steels (Mo 0.25)	40xx
Chromium	41xx
Chromium-nickel	43xx
Nickel	46xx and 48xx
Chromium steels	5xxx
Low-chromium	50xx and 51xx
Bearing	501xx, 511xx and 521xx
Corrosion- and heat-resisting	514xx and 515xx
Chromium-vanadium steels	61xx
Nickel-chromium-molybdenum steels	86xx and 87xx
	93xx and 94xx
	97xx and 98xx
Silicon-manganese steels	92xx
Low-alloy, high-tensile steels	950

numerals for the various types of SAE steel, is taken from the *SAE Handbook*, 1952 edition.

The SAE has established specifications for hardenability upon quenching of certain steels for heat treatment, called H steels; steel numbers suffixed with an H indicate that the steel will meet the hardenability limits as well

Alloy Steels

as the specifications for chemical composition. Hardenability limits are based on the Jominy end-quench test. (See Art. 7.61.)

11.3 AISI Steel Numbering System. The American Iron and Steel Institute steel numbering system is practically identical with the SAE steel numbering system. The AISI has also designated "treated" steels by the symbol T which is inserted between the first and second pairs of digits; a treated steel is one to which ferroboron has been added, or it is a deoxidizing-type alloy containing boron together with a combination of elements such as silicon, aluminum, vanadium, titanium, calcium, and zirconium to produce quench hardenability. The AISI further employs letters as prefixes to denote the process of manufacture as follows:

A, basic open-hearth alloy steel.
B, acid Bessemer carbon steel.
C, basic open-hearth carbon steel.
D, acid open-hearth carbon steel.
E, electric-furnace steel.

Thus, the designation "E46T20H" refers to 4620 nickel-molybdenum steel made in the electric furnace (E), treated with boron (T), and manufactured to meet the hardenability specification (H).

11.4 General Classification. Alloy steels may be classed in three general groups:

1. High-strength low-alloy steels.
2. Standard alloy steels.
3. High-alloy and special-purpose steels.

High-strength low-alloy steels are structural steels possessing good mechanical properties and good corrosion resistance.

Standard alloy steels have medium percentages of alloys and are used in construction of machines, hence they are sometimes called "constructional alloy steels."

High-alloy and special-purpose steels include corrosion-resisting and heat-resisting steels such as "stainless," tool and die steels, wear-resisting steels, and other special-purpose steels possessing particular properties.

11.5 High-Strength Low-Alloy Steels (SAE 950 Series). This group of structural and equipment steels has improved mechanical properties and corrosion resistance as compared to carbon steels. These steels are furnished as rolled or in normalized condition and do not require heat treatment. They are utilized to obtain savings in weight and greater durability than carbon steels. Typical elements added comprise copper, chromium, molybdenum, nickel, phosphorus, and silicon. One or more elements in small percentages are added to low-carbon steel which may contain varying amounts of manganese. Typical compositions are given in Table 11.2.

Table 11.2
COMPOSITION OF TYPICAL HIGH-STRENGTH LOW-ALLOY STEELS
(Courtesy Materials & Methods)

Element	Chemical Composition, %		
Trade name	Aldecor	Cor-Ten	Hi-Steel
Carbon	0.12 max.	0.12 max.	0.12
Manganese	0.15–0.40	0.20–0.50	0.50–0.90
Sulfur	0.05 max.	0.05 max.	0.05 max.
Phosphorus	0.08–0.15	0.07–0.15	0.05–0.12
Silicon	0.35–0.75	0.25–0.75	0.15 max.
Copper	0.35–0.60	0.25–0.55	0.95–1.30
Chromium	—	0.50–1.25	—
Nickel	—	0.65 max.	0.45–0.75
Molybdenum	0.16–0.28	—	0.08–0.18
Aluminum	—	—	0.12–0.27

Mechanical Properties. Minimum properties as specified by the SAE for thicknesses up to ½ inch are:

Tensile strength	70,000 p.s.i.
Yield point	50,000 p.s.i.
Elongation in 2 in.	22%
Elongation in 8 in.	$\dfrac{1,500,000}{\text{Tensile strength}}$ per cent
Bend test, 180°	$D = 1T$ (ASTM A242)

Ductility as well as increased tensile strength is required in order to insure workability. High-strength low-alloy steels also have better notch toughness than ordinary carbon steels.

Corrosion Resistance. The resistance to atmospheric corrosion of high-strength low-alloy steels has been demonstrated to be superior to ordinary carbon steels both by test and by results of service.

Fabrication. High-strength low-alloy steels are readily welded by methods regularly employed for carbon steels. In riveted construction, high-strength rivets should be selected. Drilling, punching, shearing, sawing, and milling procedures are essentially the same as for carbon steel. These steels are available in the standard forms and shapes as for ordinary carbon steel.

Applications. High-strength low-alloy steels are used in large quantities for highway and railway bridges, railroad freight and passenger cars, truck, trailer, and bus bodies, agricultural equipment, earth-moving equipment such as power shovels, cranes, conveyors, bulldozers, and graders, concrete mixers, and asphalt-paving plants.

Standard Alloy Steels

11.6 Standard Alloy Steels. These steels have medium percentages of alloying elements and are usually ferritic or pearlitic in structure. They are generally heat treated to improve mechanical properties. There are three grades of heat-treated standard alloy steels: (1) carburizing grades (case-carburized, see Art. 7.63); (2) semithorough-hardening grades; and (3) thorough-hardening grades. The latter two types may be produced by either oil hardening or water hardening.

11.7 Manganese Steel (SAE 1300 Series). Manganese steel has high tensile strength, fair ductility, and excellent abrasion resistance. The manganese content ranges from 1.60 to 1.90 per cent with carbon from about 0.30 to 0.50 per cent. The structure is pearlitic. The effect of manganese is to strengthen and harden the steel. These steels are utilized most often in the semithorough-hardening and thorough-hardening grades. They are generally oil quenched.

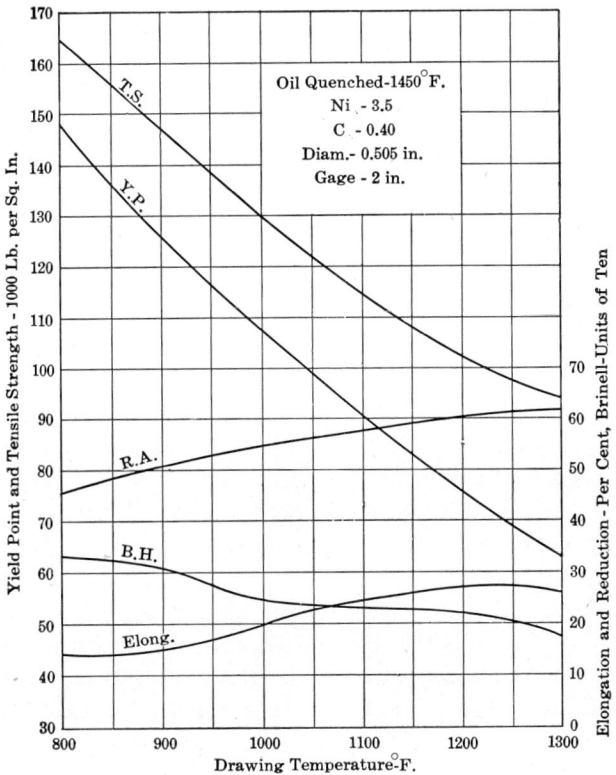

Fig. 11.1. 3½% nickel steel, 0.4% carbon, oil quenched.

220   Materials of Construction

Applications. Applications include heavy forgings because of good forgeability. This steel is used for shafts, gears, automotive and tractor parts, springs, and forgings for aircraft and locomotives.

11.8 Nickel Steel (SAE 2300 Series). The nickel content is 3½ per cent with carbon content ranging from 0.15 to 0.50 per cent. This nickel steel combines great tensile strength and hardness with a high elastic ratio, good ductility, and relatively high resistance to corrosion and to fatigue. It is pearlitic in constitution. This steel is produced in carburizing, semi-thorough-hardening and thorough-hardening grades. The effect of heat treatment on 3½ per cent nickel steel is illustrated in Fig. 11.1. The tensile properties specified by the American Society for Testing Materials for structural nickel steel to contain from 3.0 to 4.0 per cent nickel are listed in Table 11.3.

Table 11.3

ASTM SPECIFICATIONS FOR STRUCTURAL NICKEL STEEL

	Rivet Steel	Plates, Shapes, and Bars	Eyebars, Flats, and Rollers, Unannealed	Eyebars, Flats, and Pins, Annealed
Tensile strength, p.s.i.	70,000–80,000	90,000–115,000	95,000–110,000	85,000–100,000
Yield point, min., p.s.i.	45,000	55,000	55,000	48,000
Elongation in 8 in., min., %	$\frac{1{,}500{,}000}{T.S.}$	$\frac{1{,}600{,}000}{T.S.}$	$\frac{1{,}500{,}000}{T.S.}$	20
Elongation in 2 in., min., %	—	$\frac{1{,}700{,}000}{T.S.}$	16	20
Reduction of area, min., %	40	30	25	30

Applications. Uses of this nickel steel include gun and tank parts, propeller shafts, aircraft engine parts, and truck and tractor transmission and differential gears. This steel is valuable as a structural steel because of its high elastic and endurance ratios. The use of this steel has been specified in the construction of many large bridges.

(*SAE 2500 Series.*) This series of nickel steel has 5.0 per cent nickel with carbon content from 0.10 to 0.20 per cent. It comes in the carburizing grade. Its application is for truck, tractor, and bus transmission and differential gears, and airplane engine crankshafts.

11.9 Chrome-Nickel Steel (SAE 3100, 3200, and 3300 Series). Nickel-chromium steels are of the first order of importance. Typical compositions of three SAE series chrome-nickel steels are given in Table 11.4. These steels are available in carburizing and thorough-hardening grades. When properly heat treated, they have a very high tensile strength and elastic limit, together with great toughness and considerable ductility. They are

Alloy Steels

Table 11.4

CHEMICAL COMPOSITION OF CHROME-NICKEL STEELS

SAE and AISI Designation	Chromium, %	Nickel, %	Carbon, %
A3120	0.55–0.75	1.10–1.40	0.17–0.22
A3240	0.90–1.20	1.65–2.00	0.38–0.43
E3316	1.40–1.75	3.25–3.75	0.14–0.19

markedly resistant to repeated stress and impact. Their structure is pearlitic.

Thermal Critical Points. The combined effect of the two alloying elements is slightly to lower the critical temperature on heating and to depress

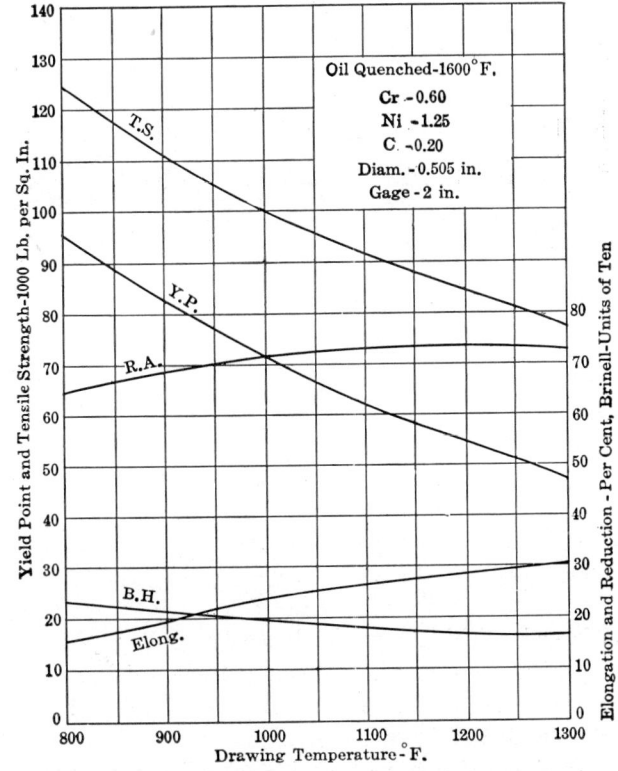

Fig. 11.2. Chrome-nickel steel (oil quenched 1600° F.).

the critical temperature on cooling very greatly, enough under certain conditions to produce an air-hardening steel as for example in the SAE 3300 series. (See Art. 7.53 and Fig. 7.14 for isothermal transformation diagram for SAE 3140.)

Mechanical Properties. The tensile properties of this group of steels are excellent, as will be noted from Figs. 11.2, 11.3, and 11.4. The analysis of the steel in Fig. 11.2 is typical of a low-carbon case-carburizing steel (SAE 3100 Series), where core toughness is of more importance than high tensile strength. The steel in Fig. 11.3 is adaptable for oil-hardened parts, either

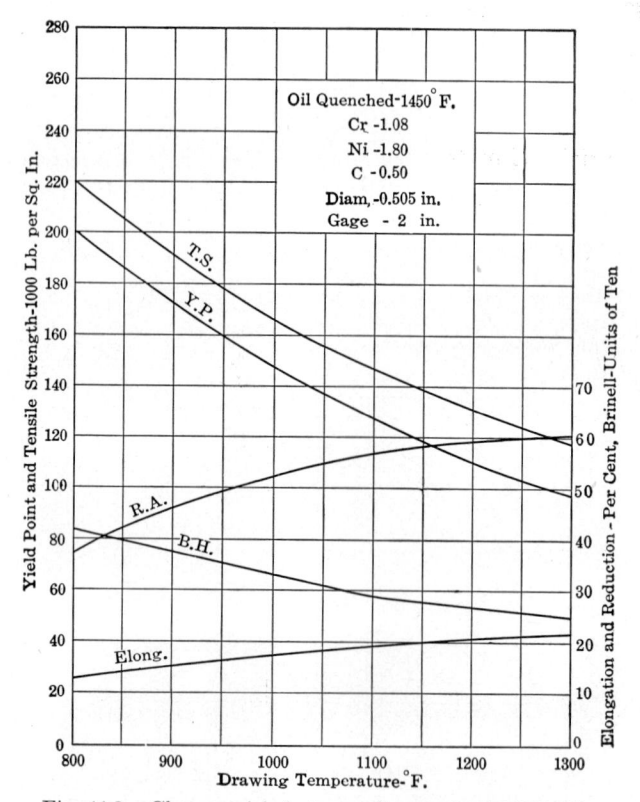

Fig. 11.3. Chrome-nickel steel (oil quenched 1450° F.).

machined or forged, which require high mechanical properties (SAE 3200 Series). The properties of an air-hardening chrome-nickel steel (SAE 3300 Series) are shown in Fig. 11.4. This steel is possessed of remarkably high strength, toughness, and resistance to dynamic stresses.

Castings. Castings of chrome-nickel steel, with its characteristic high strength and toughness, are sometimes made. Heat-treated steel castings containing 0.30 per cent carbon, 2.50 per cent nickel, and 0.50 per cent chromium have developed a tensile strength of 110,000 pounds per square inch and an elastic limit of 80,0000 pounds per square inch, with percentage reduction of area and elongation of 30 and 20, respectively.

Alloy Steels 223

Applications. Chrome-nickel steels of the 3100 and 3200 series are used for tractor transmission gears, aircraft engine parts such as crankshafts and connecting rods, automotive knuckles, steering arms, drive shafts and pinions, and rear axles. The 3300 series steels are selected for heavy-duty shafting, truck and tank gears, bearings, and pneumatic tools.

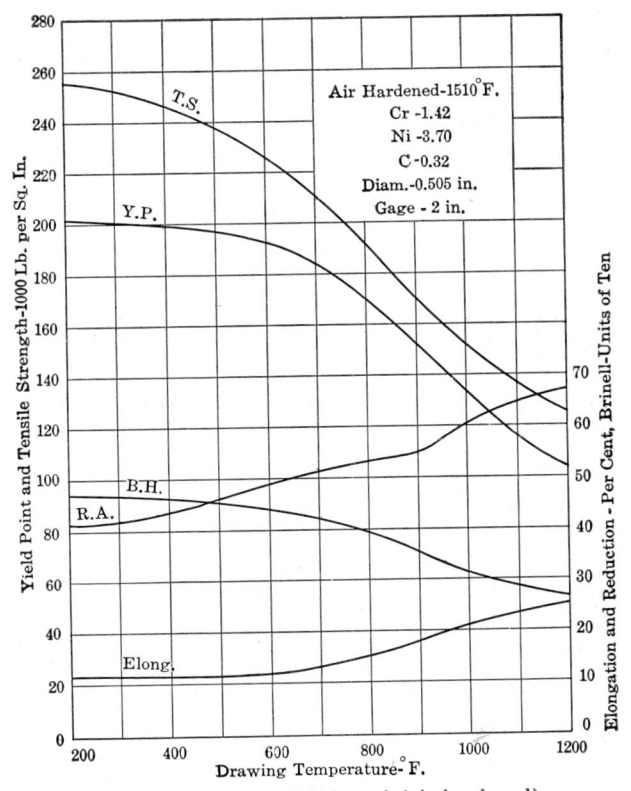

Fig. 11.4. Chrome-nickel steel (air hardened).

11.10 Molybdenum Steel (SAE 4000 Series). This steel has a composition of molybdenum ranging from 0.20 to 0.30 per cent; carbon ranging from 0.20 up to 0.70 per cent; and manganese ranging from 0.70 to 1.00 per cent. Molybdenum combines with carbon to form carbides; it also becomes dissolved in ferrite. This steel has comparatively high-quenching and normalizing temperatures over a wide range which facilitates commercial heat-treating operations. The steels of this series are deep hardening and are available in semithorough-hardening and thorough-hardening grades.

Mechanical Properties. High strength, good hardness, and relatively high resistance to impact are characteristic of molybdenum steels of the 4000 series. Molybdenum steels retain their mechanical properties well at ele-

224 Materials of Construction

vated temperatures. Welding of molybdenum steels is not more difficult than of carbon steels.

Applications. Uses are for hand tools, scraper blades, pneumatic tool bits, and automotive gears, axles, springs, drive pinions, and bolts.

(*SAE 8000 Series.*) This series of molybdenum steels have a composition of molybdenum, 0.10 to 0.40 per cent; carbon, 0.22 to 0.45 per cent; and manganese, 1.00 to 1.60 per cent. This steel is manufactured in carburizing grade and has good depth of hardness. This steel has excellent mechanical properties including high impact resistance and resistance to fatigue, easy machining and weldability, and good ductility. Its uses include machine tools, drive pinions, transmission shafts and gears, tread chains, and parts for lathes.

11.11 Chrome-Molybdenum Steel (SAE 4100 Series). Molybdenum is more effective as an alloying element when used in combination with chromium. The composition of 4100 series steel is: chromium, 0.40 to 1.10 per cent; molybdenum, 0.20 to 0.40 per cent; and carbon, 0.20 to 0.50 per cent. This type of steel has great hardness as its outstanding feature, and it

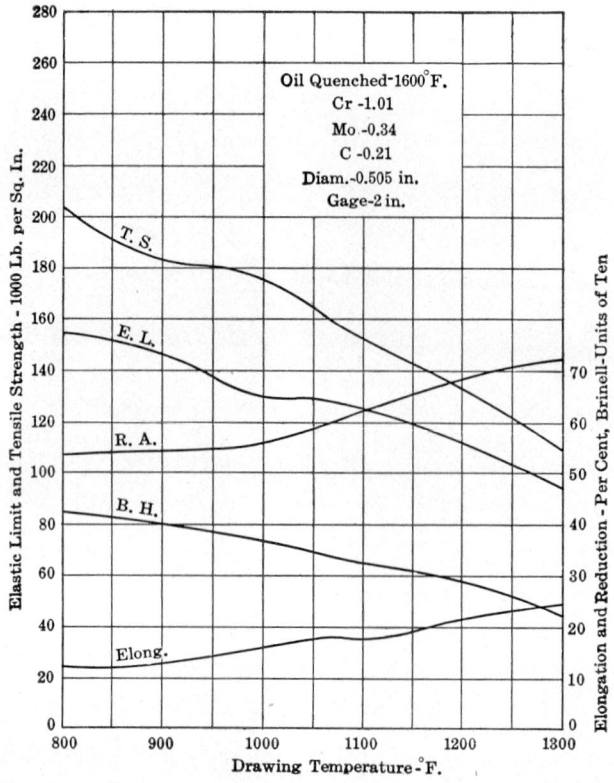

Fig. 11.5. Chrome-molybdenum steel (oil quenched 1600° F.).

Alloy Steels

possesses great strength and toughness. Semithorough-hardening and thorough-hardening grades are manufactured. Mechanical properties of heat-treated chrome-molybdenum steel are shown in Fig. 11.5.

Applications. Chrome-molybdenum steel is used for heat-treated forged or machined parts which require high strength and elastic limit, coupled with toughness, ductility, and shock resistance. This steel is of value in the aircraft industry for tubing, bars, and sheets on account of its freedom from scale and good resistance to abrasive wear. Other examples of use are scarifier teeth, oil-industry shafting and collars, and rams, impellers, and shafts in hydraulic machinery.

11.12 Nickel-Chromium-Molybdenum Steel (SAE 4300 Series). This steel has the highest hardenability of any of the standard alloy steels. It is selected for heavy and medium-size sections where high strength coupled with suitable ductility is required. It has excellent depth-hardness properties; consequently it is suitable for large shafts subjected to torque. (See Art. 7.54 and Fig. 7.16.) The composition of SAE 4335 steel is given in Table 11.5. This series of steel is furnished in carburized grade, or it is

Table 11.5

CHEMICAL COMPOSITION OF NICKEL-CHROMIUM-MOLYBDENUM STEELS

Element	Composition, %	
Designation	SAE 4335 Steel	SAE 8630 Steel
Nickel	1.50–2.00	0.40–0.70
Chromium	0.45–0.90	0.40–0.60
Molybdenum	0.20–0.30	0.15–0.25
Carbon	0.28–0.40	0.28–0.33
Manganese	0.60–0.90	0.70–0.90
Phosphorus	0.05 max.	0.05 max.
Sulfur	0.04 max.	0.05 max.
Silicon	0.20–0.35	0.20–0.35

heat-treated either by normalizing and tempering, or by oil or water quenching and tempering.

Mechanical Properties. The mechanical-property chart for SAE 4335 cast steel is given in Fig. 11.6. This steel has high fatigue resistance. The presence of molybdenum makes this steel resistant to softening at high temperatures. It is somewhat difficult to weld, however.

Applications. This steel is used for aircraft and automotive parts where unusually high stresses are involved and for oil-well tools, die-casting dies, and dredge-bucket teeth.

(*SAE 8600 Series.*) Type SAE 8600 nickel-chromium-molybdenum steel is similar in mechanical properties and uses to the SAE 4300 series but is

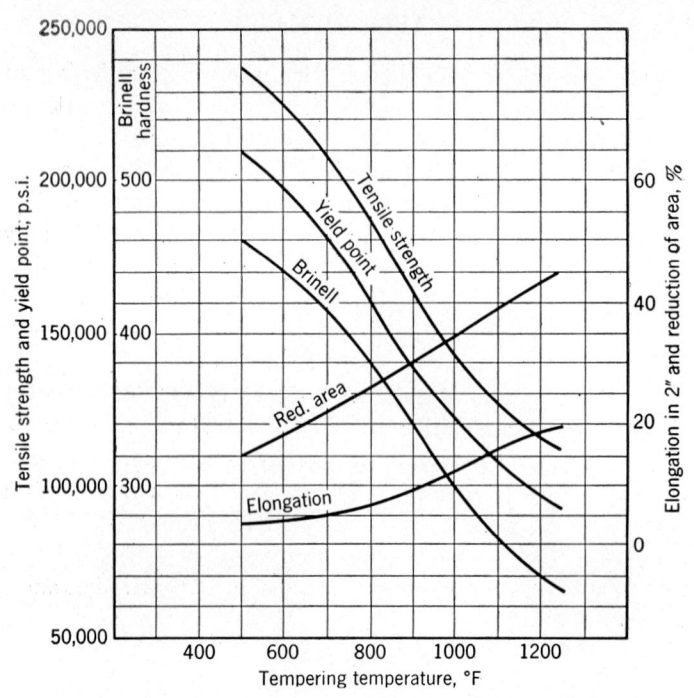

Fig. 11.6. Mechanical properties of oil-quenched cast 4335 nickel-chromium-molybdenum steel in sections up to 1½". (*Courtesy* International Nickel Co.)

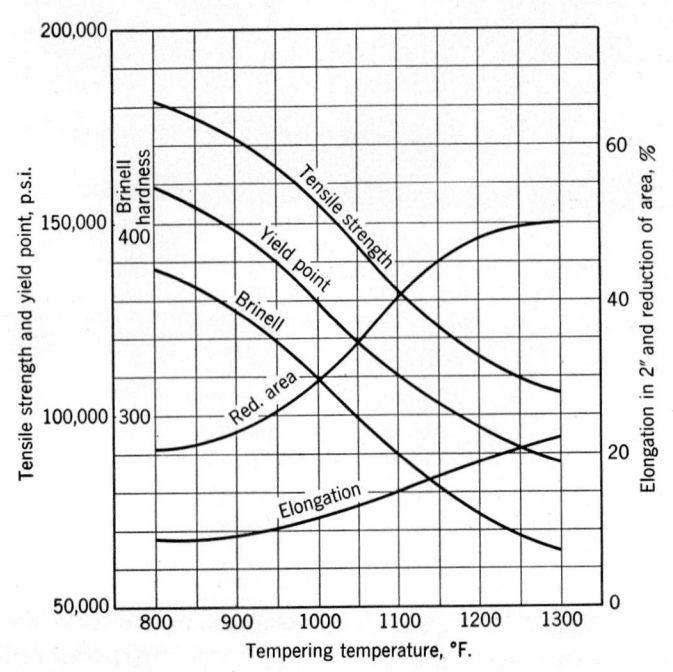

Fig. 11.7. Mechanical properties of water-quenched cast 8630 nickel-chromium-molybdenum steel in 1 in. section. (Juppenlatz; *Courtesy* International Nickel Co.)

Alloy Steels

utilized for sections under 1½ inches in size. The composition of SAE 8630 steel is listed in Table 11.5. This type is available in carburizing, semi-thorough hardening, and thorough-hardening grades. The 8600 series steel is readily welded; however, welding should be done before final heat treatment. The mechanical-property chart for SAE 8630 cast steel is shown in Fig. 11.7. Mechanical properties of heat-treated rolled 8600 series steel are tabulated in Table 11.6.

Table 11.6
MECHANICAL PROPERTIES OF HEAT-TREATED ROLLED NICKEL-CHROMIUM-MOLYBDENUM STEELS (SAE 8600 SERIES) *

SAE Designation	Heat Treatment	Tensile Strength, p.s.i.	Yield Strength, p.s.i.	Elongation in 2 in., %	Reduction of Area, %	Brinell Hardness	Izod Impact, ft.-lb.
8620	Normalized	94,000	61,000	29	61	190	—
	As-rolled	91,000	65,000	29	56	185	—
	Annealed	77,000	51,000	32	64	163	—
	Hardened and tempered at 800° F.†	122,000	98,000	21	63	245	76
	Hardened and tempered at 1200° F.†	96,000	76,000	26	70	193	105
8630	Normalized	112,000	73,000	23	52	225	—
	As-rolled	109,000	78,000	25	48	220	—
	Annealed	86,000	58,000	29	59	174	—
	Hardened and tempered at 800° F.†	162,000	142,000	14	54	325	42
	Hardened and tempered at 1200° F.†	111,000	92,000	23	66	225	91
8640	Normalized	130,000	85,000	18	45	262	—
	As-rolled	126,000	90,000	20	40	244	—
	Annealed	95,000	63,000	27	55	193	—
	Hardened and tempered at 800° F.†	208,000	183,000	13	43	420	18
	Hardened and tempered at 1200° F.†	130,000	110,000	21	60	262	68
8650	Normalized	149,000	96,000	11	36	300	—
	As-rolled	143,000	101,000	17	31	290	—
	Annealed	105,000	70,000	23	50	210	—
	Hardened and tempered 800° F.†	214,000	194,000	12	41	423	—
	Hardened and tempered at 1200° F.†	136,000	116,000	21	61	271	—

* Prepared by International Nickel Co., published in *Materials & Methods*, Mar., 1951, p. 105.
† Properties after heat treatment based on oil quench and 1-in. round bar.

Applications. SAE 8620 and 8630 steels are used for medium-duty carburized parts such as cams, gears, and bearing races. SAE 8640 and 8650 steels are utilized for medium-duty high-strength applications in sections up to 2 inches thick such as shafts, gears, forgings, and aircraft tubing.

(*SAE 8700 Series.*) This steel is similar in properties to SAE 8600 series but is somewhat deeper hardening and is used in heavier sections. Other series 9300, 9400, 9700, and 9800 of nickel-chromium-molybdenum steels are similar to the 8600 series.

11.13 Nickel-Molybdenum Steel (SAE 4600 and 4800 Series). Nickel-molybdenum steel has uniformity of case and is usually used in case-carburized grade, but is available in semithorough-hardening and thorough-hardening grades. It is readily heat treated, and is comparatively free from distortion when quenched. The composition of typical steels is given in Table 11.7. This steel has good toughness. It is used in the petroleum

Table 11.7

CHEMICAL COMPOSITION OF NICKEL-MOLYBDENUM STEEL

Element	Composition, %	
Designation	SAE 4620 Steel	SAE 4820 Steel
Nickel	1.65–2.00	3.25–3.75
Molybdenum	0.20–0.27	0.20–0.30
Carbon	0.17–0.22	0.18–0.23
Manganese	0.45–0.65	0.50–0.70
Phosphorus	0.025	0.040
Sulfur	0.025	0.040
Silicon	0.20–0.35	0.20–0.35

industry for brake drums, sheaves, and valves, in the aircraft industry for gears, pins, and forgings, and in the automotive industry for transmission and differential gears.

11.14 Chromium Steel (SAE 5100 Series). Chromium steel of the 5100 series, more commonly termed chrome steel, generally contains from 0.70 to 1.20 per cent chromium, with a variation in carbon content of 0.17 to 0.55 per cent. It is pearlitic in structure. Its value is due principally to its property of combining intense hardness after quenching with very high strength and extremely high elastic limit. It is therefore especially well able to withstand abrasion, cutting, or shock. It is rather lacking in ductility, but this is often unimportant in view of its high elastic limit. The standard chromium steels corrode less rapidly than carbon steels.

Thermal Critical Points. Chrome steels possess distinct transformation temperatures corresponding to those of ordinary carbon steels. The effect of the chromium, however, is to raise slightly the critical temperature in heating and to lower considerably the critical temperature on cooling. Maximum hardness and grain refinement are not attained by quenching from slightly above the critical temperature, 830–843° C. (1525–1550° F.), but by quenching from a much higher temperature, usually between 982 and 1038° C. (1800 and 1900° F.).

Manufacture. Chrome steel of the 5100 series is made in the basic open-hearth furnace. Chromium may be added in the form of ferrochrome just before the end of the process in the open hearth so as to avoid loss by

Alloy Steels

oxidation. Additions may also be made in the form of exothermic chromium ferroalloys in which case the alloy would be added to the final tapping ladle.

Applications. This chrome steel is used where an extremely hard surface and shock resistance are desired. It is used in the manufacture of gears, shafts, steering worms, and leaf and coil springs for automobiles, of scarifier teeth, power-shovel buckets, and wearing parts of rock-crushing machinery. Among constructional steels, 5100 steel is relatively cheap. Low-chromium steel is used for safes and vaults; chrome steel is welded with alternate layers of wrought iron into a composite 3- or 5-ply plate. The chrome steel resists cutting by drills while the wrought iron introduces an element of toughness so that it is better able to withstand concussion.

11.15 Chromium Bearing Steel (SAE 50100, 51100 and 52100 Series). These bearing steels have a high carbon content of 0.95 to 1.10 per cent (1.02 per cent mean carbon content) with chromium ranging from 0.40 to 0.60, 0.90 to 1.15, and 1.30 to 1.60 for the three different series, respectively. SAE 50100 is a low-hardenability steel, and the other two are medium-hardenability steels. These steels are exceptionally hard and have excellent wear resistance. A surface hardness of Rockwell C 65 with high endurance limit can be obtained by heat treatment of SAE 52100 steel. Uses are for high-grade balls, rollers, races, and antifriction bearings. They are electric-furnace steels.

11.16 Chromium-Vanadium Steel (SAE 6100 Series). The composition is as follows: chromium, 0.70–0.90 per cent; vanadium, 0.10–0.15 per cent; and carbon, 0.17–0.55 per cent. This steel has high strength, high ductility, and good machinability. It is fine grained and is readily weldable. When the lower-carbon grades are case carburized, the core has good properties, not flaking or flowing when subjected to pressure, and the case is hard and resistant to wear and impact. Medium-carbon grades are used for hardening. The hardening grades of this steel retain high-strength properties up to temperatures as high as 510° C. (950° F.). Typical uses of the hardening grades include aircraft propeller blades, locomotive springs, bolts for high-temperature service in oil refineries, hot-work die blocks, pistons, pneumatic bits, automotive gears and springs, and marine-engine crankshafts.

High-Alloy and Special-Purpose Steels

11.17 General. The following types of high-alloy and special-purpose steels will be described.

1. Corrosion- and heat-resisting steels.
2. Tool and die steels.
3. Wear-resisting steels.
4. Free-cutting steels.

5. Structural silicon steel.
6. Electrical steels and iron alloys.
7. Miscellaneous special-purpose steels and iron alloys.

11.18 Corrosion- and Heat-Resisting Steels. Because heat-resisting steels must be corrosion resisting at high temperatures, they are grouped for convenience with corrosion-resisting steels. All heat-resisting steels contain chromium since their resistance to oxidation is achieved primarily by alloying with chromium. The stainless corrosion-resisting steels all contain chromium or chromium and nickel. Thus the stainless steels SAE 30300 (chrome-nickel), 51400 (chromium), and 51500 (chromium) series are designated as corrosion- and heat-resisting steels. However, copper steel which is corrosion resisting at ordinary temperatures under atmospheric conditions is not heat resistant.

The main groups of corrosion-resisting steels comprise:

1. Chrome-nickel stainless steel.
2. Chrome stainless steel.
3. High nickel steel.
4. Copper steel.

The main groups of heat-resisting steels comprise:

1. Chrome-nickel stainless steel.
2. Chrome stainless steel.
3. Special heat-resisting steels.

11.19 Chrome-Nickel Stainless Steel (SAE 30300 Series). This steel is of first-order importance. Its corrosion resistance is its most important characteristic. Other qualities such as tensile strength, ductility, hardness, and resistance to creep and oxidation at high temperatures are possessed to a varying degree by individual steels of this group. Compositions of three typical chrome-nickel stainless steels are given in Table 11.8. Chrome-nickel stainless steel is sold under various trade names, as 18-8, "Enduro Nirosta," K.A. 2, and "Alleghany metal."

SAE 30302 is a general-purpose stainless steel of 18-8 composition and is the one most widely used. It is selected where excellent corrosion resistance is wanted together with high tensile strength and good forming properties. Its mechanical properties are listed in Table 11.9. This steel is austenitic in all temperature ranges and, therefore, cannot be heat treated in the same manner as ordinary steels but must be altered in physical properties by cold working. In this manner the tensile strength may be varied from 90,000 (annealed) to 168,000 (cold reduction 30 per cent) pounds per square inch. Corresponding ductilities are 60 per cent elongation in 2 inches (annealed) to 15 per cent (cold reduction 30 per cent). This strength-

Alloy Steels

Table 11.8
CHEMICAL COMPOSITION AND HEAT-RESISTING PROPERTIES OF STAINLESS STEELS *

SAE Designation	AISI Designation	Composition, % Cr	Ni	C	Maximum Temperature without Excessive Scaling, °F.	Creep Strength 1000-Hr Life, 1% Elongation At 1000° F.	At 1500° F.	Short-Time Tensile Strength, p.s.i. at 1700° F.
30302	302	17–19	8–10	0.08–0.20	1,650	18,300	850	12,000
30309	309	22–24	12–15	0.20 max.	2,000	15,000	1,000	16,000
30316	316	16–18	10–14	0.10 max.	1,650	25,000	3,000	18,000
51410	410	11.5–13.5	0	0.15 max.	1,300	13,000	700	8,000
51430	430	14–18	0	0.12 max.	1,550	8,500	600	7,000

* *Materials & Methods*, Manual 59, May, 1950, p. 88.

ening by cold working is explained by the decomposition of austenite resulting in the formation of ferrite which is supersaturated with carbon in the same condition as in martensite; also strain hardening of the ferrite and of that austenite which remains undecomposed may produce increased strength. If cold working is followed by low-temperature stress-relieving heat treatment, the tensile strength and yield strength are improved with practically no lowering of ductility. This steel may be forged, welded, brazed, and soldered, and is available in any of the usual shapes and wire sizes. For effects of exposure at high temperatures, see Art. 4.23 and Fig. 4.3 for AISI 304 (SAE 30304) which has similar properties to SAE 30302. For low-temperature properties of SAE 30304, see Art. 4.61 and Table 4.9.

High-chromium-nickel steel of the 18-8 type is utilized in light-weight high-strength structural applications. Light weight is obtained by utilizing its high tensile strength and by simplification of structural parts and connections by employing welding, particularly spot welding (Art. 7.74), instead of riveting. Resistance to corrosion of this steel makes it durable and attractive as a surfacing material. Thin sheets can be used without fear that corrosion subsequently will reduce effective sections. An important application is in the construction of streamline, light-weight railroad cars. The exterior surfaces and the major portion of the car structures are fabricated from this high-chromium-nickel steel. This steel has also been employed in the construction of airplane structures in competition with light-weight alloy materials.

SAE 30309 stainless steel (called 25-12) has better corrosion resistance and resistance to scaling than 30302 since it will withstand a maximum temperature of 2000° F. without excessive scaling. (See Table 11.8.) SAE 30316 chrome-nickel stainless steel contains 2.0–3.0 per cent molybdenum which improves high-temperature strength, creep resistance, and resistance to corrosion. It is particularly resistant to sea-water corrosion, and many types of chemical corrosion particularly of a reducing nature. (See Tables 11.8 and 11.9.) The latter two stainless steels are used for high-temperature

Table 11.9

MECHANICAL PROPERTIES OF STAINLESS STEELS *

SAE Designation	Heat Treatment	Tensile Strength, p.s.i.	Yield Strength, p.s.i.	Elongation in 2 in., %	Reduction of Area, %	Brinell Hardness	Izod Impact, ft.-lb.
30302	Annealed	90,000–100,000	35,000– 45,000	55–65	60–70	140–150	115–140
	Cold-worked	100,000–180,000	50,000–150,000	—	—	180–375	—
30309	Annealed	95,000–105,000	35,000– 45,000	40	50	170–200	—
30316	Annealed	90,000–100,000	35,000– 45,000	50–60	60–75	170–200	70–120
51410	Annealed	100,000–120,000	80,000–100,000	25–35	50–75	135–155	20–45
	Heat-treated	100,000–185,000	60,000–170,000	10–30	—	160–400	—
51430	Annealed	75,000– 85,000	35,000– 45,000	30–40	50–60	150–190	20–60
	Cold-worked	—	—	2–20	—	185–270	—

* *Materials & Methods*, Manual 59, May, 1950, p. 88.

installations such as heat exchangers and for chemical-processing equipment. Low-temperature properties of SAE 30316 are given in Table 4.9.

11.20 Chromium Stainless Steel (SAE 51400 and 51500 Series). Chromium ranges from 10 to 30 per cent in the 51400 series; there are two types: martensitic and ferritic. The martensitic type contains up to 18 per cent chromium whereas the ferritic type has from 14–18 per cent chromium on up to 30 per cent maximum. SAE 51410 is the general-purpose martensitic stainless steel. By heat treatment its mechanical properties can be varied to give a range of values. (See Table 11.9.) Its corrosion resistance is also improved by heat treatment. It can withstand oxidation satisfactorily up to 1300° F. It is air hardening. This steel is selected for parts requiring high strength with moderate resistance to corrosion.

SAE 51430 is a non-hardenable ferritic chromium steel which has excellent corrosion resistance and heat resistance, being able to resist destructive oxidation up to 1550° F. Its strength is less than that of the 51410 martensitic steel, however. This is the most-used ferritic stainless steel. It is sufficiently ductile to be roll formed, hence it is used for automobile fender guards and body trim. Other applications are for heat-control valves and shafts.

SAE 51501 stainless steel contains from 4 to 6 per cent chromium and is martensitic. It is corrosion resistant and has good strength at elevated temperatures. A typical use is for tubing in oil stills and heat exchangers.

11.21 High-Nickel Steel. High-nickel steels containing from 18 to 40 per cent nickel are notable because of their marked resistance to corrosion. Comparative tests conducted at the U. S. Bureau of Standards on 36 per cent nickel steel and electrolytic iron showed a loss in weight of the latter of nearly four times that of the high-nickel steel. High-nickel steels are used

Alloy Steels

where exposure to corrosion is very severe, as in parts of pumps, salt-water connections, and spark plugs. They are austenitic in structure.

11.22 Copper Steel. Copper steel containing from about 0.15 to 0.25 per cent copper has increased resistance to atmospheric corrosion as compared to ordinary carbon steel. No noticeable change in the other properties of the steel is effected by the additions of these small percentages of copper. Copper-bearing steel is used for culverts.

11.23 Special Heat-Resisting Steels. There are a great number of special heat-resisting steels, but reference will be made to only two examples. HS No. 88 alloy and Discaloy 24 are described in Art. 4.34, and their compositions and mechanical properties are given in Tables 4.3 and 4.4. Their rupture curves are shown in Figs. 4.13, 4.14, and 4.18.

Tool and Die Steels

11.24 Characteristics of Tool and Die Steels. *Tool steels* comprise carbon and alloy steels capable of being hardened and tempered and possessing special properties that are utilized for machine tools. The term tool steel does not include steels for hand tools such as hammers, chisels, and picks. The special properties required of cutting and shearing tools comprise high hardness, high wearing resistance, toughness to overcome breakage and chipping, and ability to withstand the softening effect of heat produced by friction of the tool against the piece. Tool steels are ordinarily produced in the basic electric furnace.

Die steels are steels utilized for dies for forming metal shapes, such as cold-heading dies, forging dies, and die-casting dies, and for dies for manufacturing plastics. The properties required for dies are similar to many of those needed for tools, hence the same composition may in some instances be employed for both tools and dies. Dies require a tough center with hardened surfaces to withstand impact and pressure, and to be resistant to heat softening and cracking when subjected to extreme changes in temperature. Die steels must be able to resist warping and checking during heat treatment, particularly if the dies are of varying cross-section.

Tool steels may be divided into four general classes:

1. High-carbon tool steels.
2. Medium-alloy tool steels.
3. High-alloy tool steels.
4. High-speed tool steels.

11.25 High-Carbon Tool Steels. These plain carbon steels are suitable for mild cutting. They have a carbon content ranging from 0.6 to 1.4 per cent. The relative toughness and hardness of these steels is given in Table

11.10. Data for four grades of high-carbon tool steels as specified by the Department of the Navy are given in Table 11.11. Classes I, II, and III

Table 11.10

PROPERTIES OF PLAIN HIGH-CARBON TOOL STEELS

Carbon, %	Properties
0.60	Good toughness; steel can be readily hardened and tempered.
0.70	Excellent toughness and cutting edge.
0.80	Excellent toughness and good resistance to shock.
0.90	Very good toughness and good cutting edge.
1.00	Very good toughness and very good cutting edge.
1.20	Great hardness, very good cutting edge with fair toughness.
1.30	Great hardness, excellent cutting edge, but poor toughness.
1.40	Extreme hardness, excellent cutting edge, but toughness only a slight factor.

Table 11.11

HIGH-CARBON TOOL STEELS

U. S. Navy Specification 4659a

Composition, %

Class	Carbon	Silicon	Manganese	Phosphorus	Sulfur
I	1.20–1.35	0.10–0.45	0.15–0.45	0.015 max.	0.025 max.
II	1.05–1.15	0.10–0.40	0.15–0.35	0.015 max.	0.025 max.
III	0.81–0.90	0.10–0.40	0.15–0.35	0.02 max.	0.03 max.
IV	0.71–0.80	0.10–0.40	0.15–0.35	0.02 max.	0.03 max.

Applications and Properties

Class	Description
I	Drills, taps, reamers, and screw-cutting dies. Keen cutting edge combined with great hardness.
II	Mandrels, milling cutters, trimmer dies, and threading dies. Keen cutting edge combined with hardness.
III	Shear blades, punches, and pneumatic chisels. Hard surface with considerable toughness.
IV	Hot-drop-forge dies, cupping tools, and rivet sets. Great toughness with necessary hardness on surface.

are hypereutectoid steels and are composed of pearlite and cementite in the annealed state. When hardened, these hypereutectoid steels may be 100 per cent martensite in the hardened portion on the surface, and they usually have fine pearlite in the core. Class IV is hypoeutectoid steel. Plain carbon steels are shallow hardening and do not harden throughout the section. The core is tough and forms a resilient backing for the hardened case and cutting tip. This type of tool with the same chemical composition throughout the section is preferred to one made of surface-carburized soft steel for mild forms of cutting and for many dies.

Graphitic Tool Steels. This type of carbon tool steel contains free carbon in the form of graphite. Uniformly distributed flakes of graphite increase machinability and resistance to wear and abrasion. The carbon content is about 1.5 per cent, and silicon is increased to the range of 0.65 to 1.25 per cent to control precipitation of carbon during heat treatment. This steel is moderately high in toughness and in resistance to distortion during heat treatment. Rockwell C hardness of the surface is 60–66, but the interior has a much lower hardness because of low to moderate hardenability. Applications are for gauges, rolls, molds, and dies.

11.26 Medium-Alloy Tool Steels. The medium-carbon tool steels meet needs which can not be met by high-carbon tool steels; they are deeper hardening and more resistant to wear and to softening at high temperatures. These steels utilize alloying elements such as chromium, tungsten, molybdenum, and vanadium which are carbide formers. There are three general classes of these steels: water-hardening, oil-hardening, and air-hardening. Chemical compositions of each of these classes are given in Table 11.12.

Table 11.12

COMPOSITION OF ALLOY AND HIGH-SPEED TOOL AND DIE STEELS *

Chemical Composition, %

Class	Type	Carbon	Manganese	Silicon	Chromium	Tungsten	Molybdenum	Vanadium
Medium-alloy	Water-hardened	0.55	0.50	0.80	—	—	0.45	—
	Water-hardened, semihigh speed	1.30	—	—	0.75	3.75	—	—
	Oil-hardened	0.90	1.25	0.25	0.50	0.50	—	—
	Oil-hardened	0.92	0.30	0.35	3.80	—	0.55	0.55
	Air-hardened	0.30	—	1.00	5.00	1.25	1.36	—
	Air-hardened	0.40	—	1.05	5.00	—	1.35	0.35
High-alloy	Hot-work die steels	0.37	0.30	0.30	3.00	13.50	—	0.30
		1.50	—	—	11.50	—	0.80	0.20
High-speed	18-4-1	0.73	0.28	0.28	4.00	18.00	—	1.00
	18-4-1 plus 5% Co	0.75	—	—	4.00	18.00	0.75	1.15
	M-1	0.83	—	—	4.00	—	8.0	2.0
	W-Cr-Mo	0.83	—	—	4.15	6.40	5.00	1.90
Die steel for forming plastics	Plus 1.25% Ni	0.10	0.50	—	0.60	—	—	—
	Plus 3.5% Ni	0.10	0.40	—	1.50	—	—	—

* Selected from *Materials & Methods.*

Heat treatment of alloy tool steels must be performed with precision to obtain desired properties.

11.27 High-Alloy Tool and Die Steels. These steels are highly resistant to wear, abrasion, and effects of heat. They contain over 5 per cent of any one alloying element and generally are composed of several alloying elements such as chromium, tungsten, molybdenum, and vanadium. Compositions of representative steels of this class are shown in Table 11.12. An important application is for hot-work die steels.

11.28 High-Speed Tool Steels. The outstanding characteristic of high-speed tool steel is its ability to retain cutting hardness up to temperatures of a red-heat; carbon steels under these conditions would rapidly become soft. Compositions of typical high-speed tool steels are listed in Table 11.12. It will be noted that the percentages of alloying materials are relatively high. The 18-4-1 type is the well-known tungsten-chromium-vanadium high-speed tool steel. Applications are for metal-cutting tools such as drills, taps, and reamers.

11.29 Effects of Chromium, Tungsten, Molybdenum, Vanadium, and Cobalt as Alloying Elements. *Chromium* combines with carbon to form hard carbides. Up to 1.8 per cent chromium increases the hardenability by heat treatment. Chromium from 5 to 15 per cent promotes air hardening. Chromium contributes toward red-hardness and wear resistance.

Tungsten is a carbide former and hence gives strength and hardness to steels. It produces high red-hardness. After moderately rapid cooling from high temperatures, tungsten steel exhibits remarkable hardness which is still retained upon heating to temperatures considerably above the ordinary tempering heats of carbon steels. It is this property of tungsten which makes it a valuable alloy in conjunction with chromium or manganese for production of high-speed tool steel.

Molybdenum in steels produces action similar to that of tungsten so far as the influence of the alloy upon transformation temperatures, hardening power, and physical properties are concerned, but the effect of molybdenum differs in magnitude from that of tungsten, 1 per cent of molybdenum being apparently equivalent to 2 or 3 per cent of tungsten.

Vanadium is a powerful element for alloying in steel. It forms stable carbides and improves the hardenability of steel. In high-speed tool steels, vanadium promotes a fine-grain structure and assists in maintaining their hardness at high temperatures.

Cobalt in amounts from 5 to 8 per cent increases red-hardness of high-speed tool steels. Small percentages of cobalt may be added to hot-work die steels which are subjected to high temperatures.

11.30 Die Steels for Forming Plastics. Compositions of two typical die steels for forming plastics are given in Table 11.12. They are case hardened. The 1.25 per cent nickel steel has a core with good mechanical properties: tensile strength, 110,000; yield strength, 80,000 pounds per square inch; and Rockwell C hardness of 62. It has good wear resistance. The cavity in the mold can be shaped by die-sinking methods (called "hobbing"). The die steel with 3.5 per cent nickel is used for molds which have their cavities formed by machining. It has higher core strength of 165,000 pounds per square inch, yield strength of 135,000 pounds per square inch, but the same hardness. It is used for high molding pressures, large cavities, and abrasive plastics.

Wear-Resisting Steels

11.31 High-Manganese Steel. High-manganese steel is an important wear-resisting steel. It usually contains from 11 to 14 per cent manganese and from 0.8 to about 1.5 per cent carbon. Its structure is austenitic. The outstanding properties of manganese steel are its extreme tough hardness and resistance to wear by abrasion, rather than its tensile properties.

When cast in the ingot, manganese steel is brittle and so hard that it is extremely difficult to machine. Reheating to about 1000° C. (1832° F.), followed by quenching in water, has the remarkable effect of rendering the material very much tougher and very much more ductile without materially altering its hardness. No treatment will materially soften manganese steel when cold, and it is therefore usually cast to as nearly its final form as possible and subsequently finished by grinding. Manganese steel is very fluid when molten, and sound castings are produced, although the shrinkage is excessive. The metal may be worked or forged with great difficulty through a short range of temperatures above a red-heat. It is practically non-magnetic under all circumstances.

The mechanical properties of high-manganese steel are approximately: tensile strength, 130,000 pounds per square inch; proportional limit, 35,000 pounds per square inch; elongation in 2 inches, 50 per cent; and Brinell hardness, 190. The proportional limit is very low in proportion to the tensile strength, but the ductility is high.

Large quantities of manganese steel are used as steel castings, particularly where great hardness and strength combined with great toughness are called for. It finds a special application in the construction of those parts of crushing and grinding machinery which are subjected to severe shock and abrasion. It is also used for curve rails, frogs, and crossings where hardness and freedom from brittleness constitute a great advantage and to a limited extent for axles and treads of wheels of railway rolling stock. Its principal limitation in machine construction is the practical impossibility of machining it to final form by ordinary methods, on account of its excessive hardness.

11.32 High-Chromium Steels. High-chromium steels with 12 to 14 per cent chromium and 1.5 to 2.5 per cent carbon have high resistance to wear. Their value is due principally to the property of combining intense hardness after quenching with very high strength and elastic limit. The value of the high-chromium steels is greatly enhanced by their resistance to corrosion. Applications are in shear blades, dies, and lathe centers.

Other chromium steels have wear-resisting properties. See Art. 11.14 for description of the SAE 5100 series chromium steel. Also see Art. 11.15 for chromium bearing steels. Chromium-vanadium steels are described in Art. 11.16.

11.33 Free-Cutting Steels (SAE 1100 Series). Free-cutting steels are produced for stock for automatic-screw machines. Small chips are formed in the machining of parts made of free-cutting steels; this characteristic is important because long stringy chips interfere with high-speed operation of automatic-screw machines. Both Bessemer and open-hearth processes are employed in manufacturing free-cutting steels.

Composition. Free-cutting steels contain comparatively large percentages of sulfur and manganese. Manganese sulfides are formed as well as iron sulfides. Sulfides harden the steel and make it brittle. Hardness results in a smaller force being required to cut chips from the steel, and brittleness tends to cause the chips to break into smaller pieces.

Applications. Parts made from free-cutting steels are usually small; examples are screws, studs, nuts, and rivets.

11.34 Structural Silicon Steel. Structural silicon steel is used for structural purposes because of its high yield point, high tensile strength, and good ductility. It has been utilized particularly in long-span bridges in order to reduce dead weight. The average chemical composition and physical properties of silicon steel and carbon structural steel used in the towers of the George Washington Bridge are given in Table 11.13. Structural silicon steel is less expensive than structural nickel steel (SAE 2300 Series).

Table 11.13

AVERAGE PROPERTIES OF SILICON AND CARBON STEELS IN TOWERS OF GEORGE WASHINGTON BRIDGE *

Property	Silicon Structural Steel	Carbon Structural Steel
Carbon, %	0.35	0.21
Silicon, %	0.27	—
Manganese, %	0.78	0.50
Phosphorus, %	0.022	0.018
Sulfur, %	0.037	0.037
Tensile strength, p.s.i.	88,800	63,600
Yield point, p.s.i.	50,800	38,200
Elongation in 8 in., %	22	28
Reduction of area, %	43	52

* H. J. Baker: *Trans. Am. Soc. Civ. Eng.*, v. 97, 1933, p. 340.

11.35 Electrical Steels and Iron Alloys. Electrical steels and iron alloys are utilized because of their magnetic properties. There are two main classes of these materials: (1) magnetically soft materials, and (2) magnetically hard materials.

Magnetically Soft Materials. Magnetically soft metals are employed in electrical machinery for poles of dynamos and cores of transformers and electromagnets. These materials have high permeability. Permeability defines the magnetic value of a material and is a measure of its reaction to a magnetizing force. Permeability, μ, may be expressed by the following equation:

$$\mu = B/H$$

where B = flux density (number of magnetic lines per unit of area).

H = magnetizing force (flux density produced in air per unit of area).

Air has a permeability of 1; non-magnetic materials from a practical standpoint have a permeability of 1. Ferromagnetic materials have permeabilities much greater than 1. An understanding of the significance of permeability may be obtained from the following. If a wire coil is wound around a closed circular ring of magnetic steel or iron, and a current is circulated around its coils, a magnetic circuit is set up with a given number of magnetic lines of force. If the magnetic metal is replaced by air, the number of magnetic lines of force passing through the air inside the coil would be reduced. Permeability is the ratio of the number of lines of force in the metal ring as compared to air.

Commercial magnetically soft metals comprise ingot iron, silicon steel, and certain nickel-iron alloys. Ingot iron (Armco) is commercially pure iron (99.9 per cent Fe); it has a high permeability of 4300 corresponding to a magnetizing force $H = 1$ gilbert per centimeter and also has high permeability for stronger magnetizing forces. However, its resistivity is low, which makes it necessary to roll the ingot iron in thin sheets to reduce eddy currents, and when this is done, the magnetic properties are relatively poor. It is unsuitable for alternating-current applications. It is of interest to note that the addition of carbon to iron reduces permeability a great deal. Thus carbon steel containing 0.1 per cent carbon has a permeability of about 275, and 0.3 per cent carbon, a permeability of about 200.

Silicon steel is very valuable for electrical machinery. It contains about 3 to 4 per cent of silicon and the smallest possible amounts of carbon, manganese, and other impurities. It has a very high permeability of about 10,000 corresponding to a magnetizing force $H = 1$ gilbert per centimeter. Silicon steel has a resistivity about 5 times that of magnetic iron; consequently, eddy currents are greatly reduced. This steel acquires its remarkable magnetic properties of very high permeability and low core loss only after a special heat treatment. It is heated to between 900° C. (1652° F.) and 1100° C. (2012° F.), cooled quickly to atmospheric temperatures, reheated to between 700° C. (1292° F.) and 850° C. (1562° F.), and cooled very slowly. Sometimes it is again heated and cooled very slowly from about 800° C. (1472° F.). Silicon steel is available in castings and sheet metal stampings. It is used for poles of dynamos and cores of transformers, and is suitable for both alternating-current and direct-current circuits.

Certain nickel-iron alloys have magnetic properties which are especially useful for communications equipment. *Permalloy*, containing 78.5 per cent nickel, 21 per cent iron, and small additions of other elements, has very high initial and maximum permeability when air quenched. Applications are as thin tape wrapped around the conductors of continuously loaded submarine cable, and as cores of loading coils placed at intervals in land long-distance telephone lines to make the electrical impulses distinct. This alloy shows only a small amount of hysteresis. A similar alloy is *Supermalloy* with 79 per cent nickel, 5 per cent molybdenum, and 16 per cent iron which, when carefully melted, poured, and annealed, increases the band width of communications transformers.

Perminvar is a nickel-cobalt-iron alloy with 45 per cent nickel, 25 per cent cobalt, and 30 per cent iron, which has a constant permeability of about 400 up to a flux density of 1000 gausses. It is an excellent material with respect to the amount of speech distortion produced, and hence is used in loading coils in long-distance telephone transmission lines, and in filter coils in radio and telephone circuits.

Magnetically Hard Materials. The magnetically hard metals are used for permanent magnets. An approximate measure of the magnetic energy that can be stored in a material is the product of B and H as defined above. The *tungsten steel* which contains about 4.5–6 per cent of tungsten and 0.5–0.7 per cent carbon possesses remarkable magnetic reluctance. When suitably hardened, it has a maximum BH product of 250,000 to 300,000. This steel requires special care during heat treatment to avoid cracking and distortion.

Chromium steel containing about 0.6–1.0 per cent carbon and chromium ranging from 1 to 6 per cent has a maximum BH product of about 230,000.

Cobalt steel containing 34 per cent cobalt, 5 per cent chromium, 4–6 per cent tungsten, and 0.9 per cent carbon when oil-quenched from 1700° F. has a maximum BH product of about 1,000,000.

Alnico is an aluminum-nickel-cobalt-iron alloy of exceptional magnetic properties. Alnico V alloy containing 8 per cent aluminum, 14 per cent nickel, 24 per cent cobalt, 3 per cent copper, and the remainder iron has a maximum BH product of about 5,000,000. Several grades of Alnico are available, each possessing somewhat different properties. Alnico alloys are hard and brittle and must be cast to shape and finished by grinding.

Cunife is a ductile magnetic alloy which can be cold rolled to wire or strip and can be punched and machined. Its magnetic properties are not quite

Alloy Steels

as good as Alnico II. The composition of Cunife is 60 per cent copper, 20 per cent nickel, and 20 per cent iron. *Cunico* is a copper, nickel, cobalt alloy similar to Cunife.

Miscellaneous Special-Purpose Steels and Iron Alloys

11.36 Boron-Treated Steels. Boron is added in very small amounts to standard (constructional) alloy steels; this produces a greater hardenability, or tendency to increase the depth to which the steel will harden when quenched. The effect of boron is greater in steels of low-carbon content than in those of high-carbon content. The addition of a very small amount of boron to manganese steel makes it possible to obtain a reduction in manganese content and yet reach the desired hardenability. Since boron does not modify the properties of high-strength low-alloy steel used in as-rolled or normalized condition, it is not added to this type of steel. Boron has been used as an alloying element in special steels such as stainless and high-speed steels.

In the United States, boron, a domestic product, is used as a conservation measure to reduce the amount of other alloys that may be imported or are critical during war. An example of boron-treated steel used as an alternate for scarce or critical material is boron-treated lean triple-alloy steel (80BXX) which can be substituted for SAE 8600 nickel-chromium-molybdenum steel for automotive axle pinions, driving gears, pinion shafts, and universal joint spiders.

11.37 Silicon-Manganese Steel (SAE 9200 Series). This is a spring steel. SAE 9260 is typical; it contains 1.80–2.20 silicon, 0.70–1.00 manganese, and 0.55–0.65 per cent carbon. It is used for flat and leaf springs, cold-coiled small helical springs, and hot-coiled large helical springs. This steel is ordinarily supplied in annealed condition for hardening and tempering after forming into springs.

11.38 Nickel-Copper Steel. Nickel-copper steel has good fabricating characteristics, and structural shapes can be welded from it. A typical composition is 0.45–2.25 per cent nickel and 0.60–1.50 per cent copper with carbon not exceeding 0.12 per cent. Minimum yield points are 50,000 pounds per square inch in sections ½–¾ inch thick, 45,000 pounds per square inch in sections ¾–1½ inches thick, and 40,000 pounds per square inch in sections 1½–3 inches thick. Such higher yield points are advantageous as compared with those for carbon steels, especially in the thicker sections. Nickel-copper steel is more resistant than carbon steel to corrosion in marine and industrial atmospheres.

11.39 Special Nickel-Iron Alloys. Certain nickel-iron alloys are remarkable for their low coefficient of temperature expansion; one containing 36 per cent nickel called *Invar* has a coefficient approaching zero and is used for tapes for geodetic measurements. This alloy is also used for the low expansion side of thermostatic bimetal which consists of compound bars of a low expansion alloy and a more expansive one. Bending of the bar is induced by differential expansion or contraction of the two alloys when heated or cooled, making possible actuation of temperature regulating devices.

Elinvar, composed of 36 per cent nickel, 8–12 per cent chromium, and balance iron with small amounts of molybdenum and tungsten, has a unique property of a constant modulus of elasticity for different temperatures. Most metals lose stiffness when heated, but this alloy has a modulus of elasticity of 21,000,000 pounds per square inch that is practically independent of temperature over the range of (−)101° C. [(−)150° F.] to 149° C. (300° F.). It is used for hairsprings for time pieces, tuning forks, and scale springs.

The nickel-iron alloy called *Dumet* containing 42 per cent nickel with a borated copper coating is suitable for sealing metal to glass in vacuum-tight joints for electric light bulbs and radio tubes since it has about the same coefficient of expansion at different temperatures as glass; the copper coating produces a strong bond.

11.40 Aluminum Steels. This group of steels contains about 1.25 per cent of aluminum, 1.5 to 1.6 per cent of chromium, and about 0.2 per cent of molybdenum. These steels have excellent mechanical properties and, in the annealed condition, show a tensile strength of about 90,000 pounds per square inch and an elongation of 30 per cent in 2 inches. They may be heat-treated to show a tensile strength of more than 200,000 pounds per square inch with an elongation of about 11 per cent.

The peculiar characteristic of these steels, known as "Nitralloy," is their ability to absorb nitrogen on the surface, producing a case which is much harder than that produced by the ordinary methods of case hardening with carbon. The operation is known as "nitriding." A carbon steel can be nitrided, but the operation is slow and relatively little hardness is obtained compared to that of aluminum alloy steel.

11.41 Nitriding. Before nitriding, the steel should be annealed thoroughly, then hardened by quenching from about 926° C. (1700° F.) in oil, followed by tempering at about 593° C. (1100° F.). After heat treatment the steel should be machined; sections of the metal deficient in carbon should be removed.

Heating is carried on in a current of ammonia gas at 480–593° C. (900–1100° F.) for a period of time depending upon the depth of case required. At a temperature of about 480° C. (900° F.) small penetration but maximum hardness are obtained; at 593° C. (1100° F.) increased penetration but low hardness result. A two-step method is sometimes employed in which a temperature of 480° C. (900° F.) is first maintained to get maximum hardness; then the temperature is raised to 593° C. (1100° F.) to get deeper penetra-

Alloy Steels

tion. Strangely enough the hardness gained at the lower temperature is retained and the hardness of the outside of the case does not affect penetration depth when the temperature is raised to 593° C. (1100° F.). The longer the process, the deeper the case. The length of time depends on the job and may require from 10 to 90 hours. A special reaction chamber is required, a steel chamber being satisfactory. Either a gas or an electric furnace can be used. The treated steel is cooled in the furnace. No follow-up heat treatment is necessary.

Nitriding will produce a steel with a surface hardness of 900–1100 Brinell and with a marked resistance to corrosion. The change in dimensions during nitriding is so slight that for most purposes it is negligible, and, as the operation is carried out at a comparatively low temperature, the danger of distortion, which always occurs in case hardening, is practically eliminated. The hardness of 1100 as compared with 650 as found in ordinary carbon hardening makes these steels remarkably resistant to wear and abrasion. Nitrided Nitralloy is being used for bushings, cams, gauges, cylinders, spinner rings, crankshafts, and similar parts.

11.42 Comparative Physical Properties of Ferrous Metals and Alloys. For comparative purposes, physical properties of ferrous metals and alloys

Table 11.14

PHYSICAL PROPERTIES OF FERROUS METALS AND ALLOYS *

Metal	Tensile Strength, p.s.i.	Yield Strength, (0.2%), p.s.i.	Specific Gravity	Melting Point, °F.
Low-carbon steels	50,000–120,000	30,000–90,000	7.8–7.9	2,750–2,800
High-carbon steels	100,000–200,000	75,000–175,000	7.8	2,600–2,750
Cast iron and malleable iron	25,000–120,000	Up to 60,000	7	2,100–2,400
Standard alloy steels	70,000–250,000	50,000–210,000	7.8–8.8	2,500–2,750
Stainless steels	100,000–220,000	50,000–125,000	7.4–8.0	2,500–2,800
Tool and die steels	100,000–250,000	80,000–200,000	7.5–10.0	2,600–2,800

* Strength values are approximate.

are tabulated in Table 11.14. These values may be compared with those for non-ferrous metals and alloys given in Table 12.5.

Questions

11.1. What is an alloy steel?
11.2. Describe the Society of Automotive Engineers' numbering system for steels.
11.3. Identify the steels corresponding to the following SAE numbers: 1030, 3140, 4335, 5140, 6150, 8630, 30302, 50100, 51410, and 950.
11.4. Describe the mechanical properties of high-strength low-alloy steel (SAE 950 Series).
11.5. What are the special properties of nickel steels (SAE 2300 Series)?
11.6. Why is a nickel steel valuable as a structural steel?
11.7. What are the mechanical properties of chrome-nickel steels (SAE 3100 Series)?

11.8. Discuss the mechanical properties of chrome-molybdenum steel (SAE 4100 Series).

11.9. Discuss the mechanical properties of nickel-chromium-molybdenum cast steel (SAE 8630). What is the tensile strength of this steel in as-rolled condition?

11.10. What percentages of chromium and carbon are usually contained in chromium steel?

11.11. What conditions in the service required of a given mechanical part would determine your choice between a nickel or a chromium steel?

11.12. What is "stainless" steel?

11.13. What is meant by the term "18-8"?

11.14. Discuss the utilization of chrome-nickel stainless steels.

11.15. Discuss the Navy specifications for high-carbon tool steels.

11.16. What are some of the outstanding properties and uses of manganese steel?

11.17. State the mechanical properties of structural silicon steel.

11.18. Why is silicon steel used for electrical machinery?

11.19. What are free-cutting steels?

11.20. State the type of steel or other ferrous metal that you would select as being the best suited for the following uses: (a) frog on a railway track, (b) important structural members of a long-span bridge, (c) ball bearings, (d) plates for exterior surfaces of a prominent building, (e) parts to withstand wear in a gyratory rock crusher, (f) tractor differential gear, (g) an automobile crankshaft, (h) a rear axle for a truck, (j) vats for holding corrosive liquids, (k) tank to withstand temperature of 900° C. (1652° F.) under pressure, (l) pipe for fire main on ship for pumping salt water, (m) pole pieces of an electric motor, and (n) dredge-bucket teeth.

11.21. What is the outstanding characteristic of Invar? What is its composition?

11.22. What unique property is possessed by Elinvar?

11.23. Describe in detail the process of nitriding.

References

11.1. American Society for Metals: *Metals Handbook.* 1948 ed., Cleveland, Ohio.

11.2. Bain, E. C., and Llewellyn, F. T.: "Low-Alloy Structural Steels." *Proc. Am. Soc. Civil Engrs.,* v. 62, 8, Oct., 1936, Part I, p. 1184.

11.3. Britton, S. C.: "Some Properties of Commercial Steel Sheets Containing Additions of Copper, Manganese, Chromium, and Phosphorus." *J. Iron Steel Inst.,* v. 135, 1937, pp. 161–185.

11.4. Bullens, D. K.: *Steel and Its Heat Treatment.* John Wiley & Sons, 1949, 5th ed., 3 vols.; v. 3, Engineering and Special-Purpose Steels, 607 pages.

11.5. Camp, J. M., and Francis, C. B.: *The Making, Shaping, and Treating of Steel.* Pittsburgh, Pa., Carnegie-Illinois Steel Corp., 5th ed., 1940.

11.6. Climax Molybdenum Co.: *Molybdenum in Steel.* New York, 13 sections.

11.7. Cross, H. C., and Krause, D. E.: "Phosphorus as an Alloying Element in Steels for Use at Elevated Temperatures." *Metals & Alloys,* v. 8, 1937, pp. 53–58.

11.8. Dumond, T. C.: *Engineering Materials Manual.* New York, Reinhold Publishing Co., 1951.

11.9. Epstein, S., Nead, J. H., and Halley, J. W.: "Choosing a Composition for Low-Alloy High-Strength Steel." *Trans. Am. Inst. Mining Met. Engrs.,* v. 120, 1936, pp. 309–345. Also: *Am. Inst. Mining Met. Engrs., Metals Technol.,* v. 3, 1936, *Tech. Publ.* 697, 31 pages.

11.10. Eshbach, O. W.: *Handbook of Engineering Fundamentals.* John Wiley & Sons, 2nd ed., 1952, Section 12.

Alloy Steels

11.11. Gill, J. P.: *Tool Steels*. Cleveland, Am. Soc. Metals, 1944, 577 pages.
11.12. International Nickel Co., Inc.: *Nickel Alloy Steels*. New York, 2nd ed., 1949.
11.13. Jones, J. A.: "The Present Trend in Alloy Constructional Steels." *Iron Steel Ind.*, v. 10, 1936, pp. 194–201.
11.14. Judge, A. W.: *Engineering Materials*. London, Pitman & Sons, 1943, vols. 1 and 2.
11.15. Kinzel, A. B., and Crafts, W.: *The Alloys of Iron and Chromium*. New York, McGraw-Hill Book Co., v. 1, 1937, 535 pages.
11.16. Krivobok, V. N., and Sachs, G.: *Forming of Austenitic Chromium-Nickel Stainless Steels*. International Nickel Co., New York, 1947, 309 pages.
11.17. Miner, D. F., and Seastone, J. B.: *Handbook of Engineering Materials*. John Wiley & Sons, 1954.
11.18. Promisel, N. E.: "Conservation of and/or Substitution for Critical Jet-Engine Materials." *J. Metals*, July, 1952, pp. 698–702.
11.19. *SAE 1952 Handbook*, New York, Society of Automotive Engineers, 1952.
11.20. Sauveur, A.: *The Metallography and Heat Treatment of Iron and Steel*. McGraw-Hill Book Co., 5th printing, 1938.
11.21. Seabright, L. H.: *The Selection and Hardening of Tool Steels*. McGraw-Hill Book Co., 1950, 263 pages.
11.22. Steel Founders' Society of America: *Steel Castings Handbook*. Cleveland, Ohio, 1950 ed., 511 pages.
11.23. Vanadium Corporation of America: *Vanadium Steels and Irons*. New York, 1938, 189 pages.

CHAPTER 12

Non-Ferrous Metals and Alloys

The Pure Metals

12.1 The Non-Ferrous Metals of Industrial Importance. The non-ferrous metals of greatest industrial importance comprise aluminum, copper, lead, magnesium, nickel, tin, and zinc. Those of secondary importance include antimony, bismuth, cadmium, mercury, and titanium. A number of these latter metals are chiefly important as alloy elements, and others, such as chromium, cobalt, molybdenum, tungsten, and vanadium, are used largely as alloy metals.

The non-ferrous alloys of greatest importance are the alloys of copper with tin, *the bronzes;* the alloys of copper with zinc, *the brasses;* and the alloys of aluminum, magnesium, nickel, and titanium. Many important special bronzes and brasses are made, however, in which a third alloy element is included. For this purpose tin or zinc, lead, phosphorus, manganese, aluminum, silicon, iron, titanium, and vanadium are most common.

Aside from the bronzes and brasses, copper forms more or less valuable alloys with practically all the metals listed above; aluminum is the principal metal of a number of important alloys, and the same is true of magnesium, titanium, zinc, lead, tin, nickel, and a few others.

Copper

12.2 Classification of Commercial Forms of Copper. Ores of copper are found in almost every important country of the world, and native copper is found in the region abutting upon the south shore of Lake Superior, and in a few other localities. Copper ores exist in a great variety of forms, usually as sulfide or oxide. The greater proportion of the world's supply of copper is derived from copper pyrites.

The classification of copper most common in the United States is not a particularly rational one, but one which trade conditions have imposed. The American Society for Testing Materials recognizes three general classes of American copper, which may be defined as follows:

Electrolytic copper is copper derived by the electrolysis of a copper sulfate solution with anodes of crude copper and cathodes of pure copper. (Copper migrates from the anode, leaving its impurities behind, and is deposited on the cathode.)

Lake copper is copper that has originated on the northern peninsula of Michigan, U.S.A.

Casting copper is more or less impure copper that is either fire-refined copper from virgin sources, copper electrolytically produced by deposition from impure liquors, or copper reclaimed from secondary sources.

Electrolytic copper has largely replaced all other classes whenever a pure grade of copper is demanded. A large proportion of the electrolytic copper produced is derived from copper pyrites and has previously been smelted and fire refined.

12.3 The Extraction of Copper from Its Ores. The metallurgy of copper is very complex on account of the great variety of the ores and the frequent necessity of providing for the recovery of not only copper, but also the precious metals which occur in copper ores. The number of metallurgical methods of extraction of metallic copper is therefore very large.

The chief sources of copper are ores that are essentially more or less complex sulfides, ores which, although originally sulfides, have by atmospheric agencies been altered to oxides and carbonates, and native copper ores wherein the copper exists as free metal.

Sulfide ores are usually treated by one of the following two general processes: (*a*) Roasting, smelting, and converting; and (*b*) pyrite smelting. When the ores are wholly oxidized, the copper may be recovered by a process of direct reduction.

Roasting, Smelting, and Converting. Roasting has for its principal objects the burning of the sulfur contents of the ore to sulfur dioxide (SO_2), which passes away as gas, and the changing of the metal with which the sulfur was combined into an oxide. No effort is made, however, to eliminate the sulfur entirely, or completely oxidize the metal, since some sulfur and lower oxides are desirable in the subsequent smelting operation.

Two types of furnaces are in use, the reverberatory and shelf furnaces. Finely crushed ore is roasted in reverberatory furnaces similar to those for smelting. The shelf furnace contains six circular hearths, one above the other, provided with openings alternately at the center and at the periphery to permit the descent of the ores. A vertical hollow shaft traverses the center of the furnace, carrying rabbles which are set to move the material toward the outlet opening of each hearth. The air required for combustion is forced in by a fan at the bottom, and the products of combustion (principally sulfur dioxide gas) escape through a flue provided at the top. The ore is delivered by hoppers to a drying hearth on the top of the furnace; rabbles gradually transfer it to the peripheral opening leading to the top roasting hearth, and by the motion of successive sets of rabbles it is gradually dropped from hearth to hearth, falling alternately at the center and the periphery, until it leaves the lowest hearth in a roasted condition. After a cold furnace has been brought to temperature and the ores have reached a dull-red-heat, calcination thereafter continues by the combustion of the sulfur of the ore without any extraneous fuel.

Smelting of copper ores has for its object simply the concentration of the ore by removal of the earthy portion or gangue, in order that only the metallic portion may have to be treated by the subsequent more expensive refining process. Copper ores are smelted either in a blast furnace or in a reverberatory furnace. The ultimate product of the smelting operation is a large amount of slag and a small metallic portion called *matte*, which is essentially a mixture of metallic sulfides of copper, iron, and other metals originally present in the ore.

The matte is converted into metallic copper in a Bessemer converter of side-blown type with a basic lining of magnesite brick. There are two main stages in the operation of Bessemerizing copper mattes. The first is essentially the elimination of the iron sulfide; the second, the final sulfur elimination. During the first stage the oxygen of the air blown into the molten matte forms oxides of iron, sulfur, and copper, and the last immediately reacts with the remaining iron sulfide, re-forming copper sulfide with the production of more iron oxide. The iron oxide now reacts with the silica, which has been introduced with the charge or during the blow, and produces a great quantity of ferrous silicate slag which must be poured off at the end of this stage. The sulfur oxidizes to sulfur dioxide, which is driven off. The product of the first stage of converting is a "white metal," which is practically pure copper sulfide.

In the second stage the white metal is blown to produce *blister* copper, the sulfur being eliminated by the action of copper oxide, first produced, on the copper sulfide present. The progress of the operation is judged principally by the appearance of the converter flames. Blowing in each stage requires about 60 minutes.

Pyrite Smelting. This term is applied to the smelting of a pyritous ore mainly by the heat of combustion of its own sulfide constituents. It is a process of smelting raw ore in a blast furnace, and the expense of the usual roasting treatment is therefore saved. Pyrite smelting is practiced only by a few American smelters. Ores suitable for pyrite smelting must contain a large amount of iron sulfide. Pyrite smelting requires more flux than ordinary smelting, makes more slag, causes a greater metal loss, and requires a stronger blast pressure.

With only minor exceptions, the products from the foregoing processes must be further subjected to a refining treatment before being marketed.

Non-Ferrous Metals and Alloys

Two general methods of refining are available, electrolytic refining, and fire or furnace refining. The electrolytic is now the method most commonly applied.

12.4 The Properties and Uses of Copper. The properties of copper that possess the greatest practical importance are its electrical conductivity (or conversely, resistivity), its tensile properties, and its resistance to corrosion.

Electrical Resistivity. The maximum resistivity of various classes of copper and copper products permitted under the standard specifications of the American Society for Testing Materials is as tabulated, the resistivity being expressed in international ohms per meter-gram at 20° C. (68° F.):

Low-resistance lake copper wire bars (annealed)	0.15436
High-resistance lake copper (minimum)	0.15694
Electrolytic copper wire and cakes, slabs, and billets for electrical purposes	0.15436
Electrolytic copper ingots and ingot bars, cakes, slabs, and billets not intended for electrical uses	0.15694
Hard-drawn copper wire	
Diameters 0.460 to 0.325 in.	0.15775
Diameters 0.324 to 0.040 in.	0.15940
Medium-hard-drawn copper wire	
Diameters 0.460 to 0.325 in.	0.15694
Diameters 0.324 to 0.040 in.	0.15857
Soft or annealed copper wire	0.15614

The electrical conductivity depends principally upon the purity of the copper, and the specifications for lake and electrolytic copper therefore contain the tabulated stipulations as to the minimum metal content:

Class of Copper	Minimum Metal Content
Low-resistance lake copper	99.900 (silver counted as copper)
High-resistance lake copper	99.900 (silver and arsenic counted as copper)
Electrolytic copper (all shapes)	99.900 (silver counted as copper)

Mechanical Properties. The tensile properties of hard-drawn, medium-hard-drawn, and soft or annealed copper wire of various sizes specified by the American Society for Testing Materials are indicated in Table 12.1.

The gradual increase in the tensile strength requirement and the decrease in ductility called for, as the size of wire becomes smaller, is in conformity with the well-known fact that the tensile strength increases rapidly, and ductility decreases, as the amount of cold working to which the copper is subjected in drawing increases, Fig. 12.1a. The effect of partial and complete annealing is also recognized by the slightly lower strength values and slightly higher degree of ductility called for in medium-hard-drawn wire and by the much lower strength and very much greater ductility required in the soft wire, Fig. 12.1b.

Materials of Construction

Table 12.1
ASTM SPECIFICATIONS FOR COPPER WIRE

Diameter, in.	Area, cir. mils *	Hard-Drawn Wire Minimum Tensile Strength, p.s.i.	Hard-Drawn Wire Minimum Elongation, % in 10 in.	Medium-Hard-Drawn Wire Tensile Strength Minimum, p.s.i.	Medium-Hard-Drawn Wire Tensile Strength Maximum, p.s.i.	Medium-Hard-Drawn Wire Minimum Elongation, % in 10 in.	Soft Wire Minimum Tensile Strength, p.s.i.	Soft Wire Minimum Elongation, % in 10 in.
0.460	211,600	49,000	3.75	42,000	49,000	3.75	36,000	35
0.410	168,100	51,000	3.25	43,000	50,000	3.60	36,000	35
0.365	133,225	52,800	2.80	44,000	51,000	3.25	36,000	35
0.325	105,625	54,500	2.40	45,000	52,000	3.00	36,000	35
0.289	83,520	56,100	2.17	46,000	53,000	2.75	37,000	30
0.258	66,565	57,600	1.98	47,000	54,000	2.50	37,000	30
0.229	52,440	59,000	1.79	48,000	55,000	2.25	37,000	30
			% in 60 in.			% in 60 in.		
0.204	41,615	60,100	1.24	48,330	55,330	1.25	37,000	30
0.182	33,125	61,200	1.18	48,600	55,660	1.20	37,000	30
0.165	27,225	62,000	1.14	—	—	—	37,000	30
0.162	26,245	62,100	1.14	49,000	56,000	1.15	37,000	30
0.144	20,735	63,000	1.09	49,330	56,330	1.11	37,000	30
0.134	17,956	63,400	1.07	—	—	—	37,000	30
0.128	16,385	63,700	1.06	49,600	56,660	1.08	37,000	30
0.114	12,995	64,300	1.02	50,000	57,000	1.06	37,000	30
0.104	10,815	64,800	1.00	—	—	—	37,000	30
0.102	10,404	64,900	1.00	50,330	57,330	1.04	38,500	25
0.092	8,464	65,400	0.97	—	—	—	38,500	25
0.091	8,281	65,400	0.97	50,660	57,660	1.02	38,500	25
0.081	6,561	65,700	0.95	51,000	58,000	1.00	38,500	25
0.080	6,400	65,700	0.94	—	—	—	38,500	25
0.072	5,184	65,900	0.92	51,330	58,330	0.98	38,500	25
0.065	4,225	66,200	0.91	—	—	—	38,500	25
0.064	4,096	66,200	0.90	51,660	58,660	0.96	38,500	25
0.057	3,249	66,400	0.89	52,000	59,000	0.94	38,500	25
0.051	2,601	66,600	0.87	52,330	59,330	0.92	38,500	25
0.045	2,025	66,800	0.86	52,660	59,660	0.90	38,500	25
0.040	1,600	67,000	0.85	53,000	60,000	0.88	38,500	25
0.021	—	—	—	—	—	—	38,500	25
0.020	—	—	—	—	—	—	40,000	20
0.003	—	—	—	—	—	—	40,000	20

* One circular mil = 0.0000007854 sq. in.

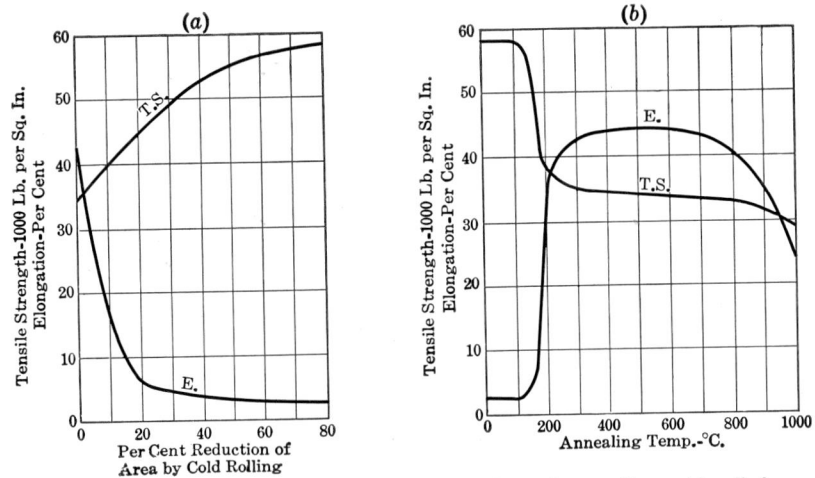

Fig. 12.1. (a) Effect of cold-rolling copper. (b) Effect of annealing cold-rolled copper at various temperatures.

The mechanical properties of wrought copper are given in Table 12.2. The modulus of elasticity of drawn copper is usually found to be in the

Table 12.2

MECHANICAL PROPERTIES OF WROUGHT COPPER *

Type	Heat Treatment	Tensile Strength, p.s.i.	Yield Strength (0.5% offset), p.s.i.	Elongation in 2 in., %	Rockwell Hardness	Shear Strength, p.s.i.	Endurance Strength at 100 Million Cycles
Electrolytic tough pitch copper (ETP)	Annealed	32,000–35,000	10,000	45–35	40F	22,000–24,000	11,000
	Half-hard	42,000	36,000	14	40B	26,000	12,000
	Hard	50,000–55,000	45,000	6–1.5	50B	28,000–29,000	13,000
	Spring	55,000–66,000	50,000	4–1.5	60B	29,000–33,000	11,000
Deoxidized copper (DHP)	Annealed	32,000	10,000	45	40F	22,000	—
	Half-hard	42,000	36,000	25	40B	26,000	14,000
	Hard	50,000	45,000	8	50B	28,000	19,000
	Spring	55,000	50,000	—	60B	29,000	18,500

* Selected from *Materials & Methods*, May, 1950, p. 99.

neighborhood of 17,000,000 pounds per square inch. Electrolytic tough pitch copper has a minimum content of 99.900 per cent copper with oxygen about 0.04 per cent. It possesses excellent hot-working and cold-working properties. It is available in rods, tubes, pipes, structural shapes, and wire. It is used for electrical conductors, contacts, and switches, for architectural trim, automobile radiators, and chemical process equipment. Deoxidized copper also is specified to have a minimum content of 99.900 per cent copper. It has phosphorus from 0.015 to 0.040 per cent. This copper also has excellent fabricating properties and is manufactured into rods, tubes, pipes, and rolled strip. Typical uses are for heat-exchanger tubes, plumbing and gas lines, and gasoline and oil lines. Creep curves for this deoxidized copper are given in Fig. 12.2.

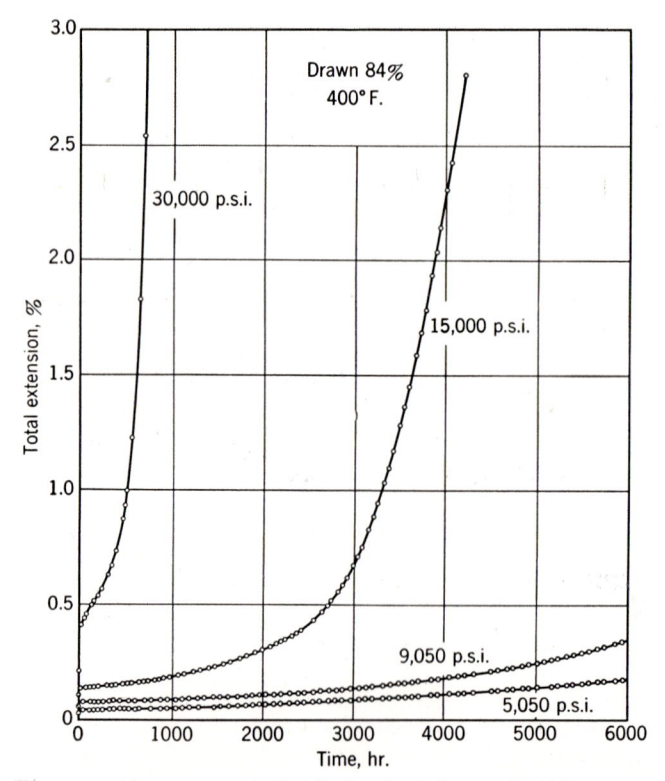

Fig. 12.2. Time-extension curves at 400° F. for hard-drawn deoxidized copper (0.019% P), 84% reduction. (ASTM type DHP.)*

Corrosion Resistance. Copper has great resistance to corrosion under a wide range of conditions. It is resistant to atmospheric and sea-water corrosion. Owing to its resistance to attack by many industrial chemicals, copper is extensively used for pipes, tubes, stills, condensers, evaporators, autoclaves, and pumps. Copper should not be used, however, in contact with oxidizing acids and most oxidizing agents or where the metal will be subjected to alternate exposure to oxidizing conditions and acid reagents. Copper is not resistant to corrosion by ammonia and carbon dioxide. Other metals that have greater strength and lower cost but poorer resistance to corrosion are often covered or lined with copper.

* A. I. Blank and H. L. Burghoff: Creep characteristics of phosphorized copper (0.019% P) at 300, 400, and 500° F., *Proc. ASTM*, v. 51, 1951.

Zinc

12.5 Commercial Forms of Zinc. Zinc occurs to some extent in almost every important political division of the world, usually as a sulfide, a carbonate, or a silicate. It is used not only as metallic zinc, in which form it is known to trade as "spelter," but also as zinc dust, which is formed in the distillation of zinc, and as zinc pigments, such as zinc oxide, leaded zinc oxide, and lithopone.

12.6 Extraction of Zinc from Its Ores. The chemical properties of zinc are so different from those of other common metals that the metallurgical methods by which metallic zinc is derived from ores are unique. Whatever the original state of the zinc in the ore, it must be in the form of an oxide before the metallic zinc is obtainable. In this form it may be reduced by carbon at high temperature, but this temperature is above the volatilizing point of the metal, so that it is always obtained as a vapor which must be condensed. Moreover, zinc vapor must be condensed at a temperature above the point of fusion if the metallic zinc is to be obtained in the more commonly useful commercial form, as spelter. Otherwise, a powder known as "zinc dust," or "zinc fume," is produced. This dust has certain special uses, but it oxidizes very readily and cannot be remelted and cast to form spelter. A further complication is introduced by the fact that zinc cannot be reduced in the presence of even minute quantities of carbon dioxide without becoming oxidized, and it is therefore essential that the reduction be accomplished in the presence of an excess of carbon and in a closed retort without access of air. Another method consists in leaching roasted sulfide and electrolyzing the solution.

12.7 Properties and Uses of Zinc. Commercial metallic zinc, or spelter, contains varying amounts of impurities up to a maximum permissible amount of about 1.5 per cent for the lowest grade. The principal impurities are lead, iron, and cadmium, according to the content of which spelters are divided into six grades by the American Society for Testing Materials, as given in Table 12.3.

Lead in moderate quantities tends to make spelter softer in rolling, but weakens the coating formed in galvanizing. In quantities above about 0.7 per cent, it causes castings to crack badly. Iron hardens spelter and renders it more brittle. An excessive amount of dross is formed in galvanizing. Cadmium hardens spelter and makes it brittle. It is therefore particularly undesirable in galvanizing, because the coating is easily cracked off. Cadmium also tends to cause cracking of castings.

Zinc exhibits a certain amount of creep at ordinary temperatures and consequently is seldom used to withstand stress in a structure or machine. Attempts have been made to utilize solid zinc corrugated sheets for roofing,

Table 12.3
ASTM SPECIFICATIONS FOR ZINC

Grade	Maximum Content of Lead, %	Maximum Content of Iron, %	Maximum Content of Cadmium, %	Maximum Content of Lead, Iron, and Cadmium, %
1a. Special high-grade	0.010	0.005	0.005	0.010
1. High-grade	0.07	0.03	0.07	0.10
2. Intermediate	0.20	0.03	0.50	0.50
3. Brass special	0.60	0.03	0.50	1.00
4. Selected	0.80	0.04	0.75	1.25
5. Prime western	1.60	0.08	—	—

Grades 1a, 1, 2, 3, and 4 shall be free from aluminum.

but these sheets tend to sag when placed on purlins spaced according to standard galvanized-iron practice.[1]

Since zinc is a plastic metal, its tensile strength as determined by test depends upon the rate of application of load. Cast zinc when slowly tested shows a tensile strength of 5000 to 10,000 pounds per square inch and is non-ductile. It becomes malleable when heated to 100–150° C. (212–302° F.) and may be rolled into sheets. Zinc which has been rolled and then annealed at 200° C. (392° F.) has a tensile strength of about 16,000 pounds per square inch and a ductility of about 5 per cent in 8 inches when load is applied at a slow rate parallel to the direction of rolling. The tensile strength perpendicular to the direction of rolling is about 20,000 pounds per square inch, but the ductility is reduced. When the load is rapidly applied, the tensile-strength values are increased to as much as 26,000 and 32,000 pounds per square inch, respectively.

Spelter is used as a galvanizing coating on iron and steel, being applied by dipping or by electrolysis. Zinc is above iron in the electromotive series and will protect iron from corrosion long after the zinc layer is broken because, when iron and zinc are in contact, the zinc becomes the anode in an electrolytic couple which prevents rusting of the steel over an area adjacent to the coating. Protection may be obtained over a distance as great as ¼ inch in seashore atmospheres where the conductivity of the moisture film connecting the iron and zinc surfaces is improved because of dissolved gases and salts in the moisture film.[2] This fact is utilized to prevent the corrosion of marine hardware, marine boilers and condensers, and also parts of the hulls of ships.

---

[1] E. A. Anderson: "Zinc in the Chemical Industries." *Mech. Eng.*, Dec., 1936, p. 799.
[2] *Ibid.*

A considerable quantity of spelter is rolled into sheet zinc. A further quantity is used in making castings, and a considerable amount in combination with copper and other metals in making brass and other alloys. Since zinc melts at 419° C. (786° F.), it cannot be used in high-temperature work.

Lead

12.8 Commercial Forms of Lead. Lead occurs in almost every part of the world, usually as a sulfide, but sometimes as oxidized decomposition products of the original sulfide. It usually occurs associated with zinc and often with silver.

Chemical lead, acid lead, and *copper lead* are the A.S.T.M. grades of lead most commonly used for corrosion resistant chemical construction. *Tellurium lead* is chemical grade lead containing 0.04 per cent tellurium, the presence of which improves the fatigue resistance. *Corroding lead* is of the highest purity and is preferred for manufacturing lead pigments and chemicals.

The principal commercial alloy of lead is *antimonial lead,* called "hard lead." It is made by adding from 1 to 12 per cent antimony to ordinary lead. Antimony hardens and strengthens lead and renders it heat-treatable; it also lowers the melting point of lead. Antimonial lead is not usually mined or refined as such, but is made by alloying.

12.9 Extraction of Lead from Its Ores. The metallurgical processes involved in the extraction of lead from its ores comprise the following operations: roasting or sintering of the ore; smelting in the blast furnace; and a number of secondary operations, including treatment of the matte which forms a portion of the products of the blast furnace, the recovery of dust from roasting and smelting furnaces and from matte converters, and the desilverizing of the lead if the silver content is sufficient to justify it.

The method of roasting lead sulfide ore consists essentially in forcing flame and air through finely divided sulfide ore with the object of partly removing the sulfur by converting the sulfide to oxide and at the same time agglomerating the material in a form suitable for use in a blast furnace.

12.10 Properties and Uses of Lead. The physical properties of lead commonly taken into account are its plasticity, its malleability, its high density, and its excellent resistance to corrosion. (See reference 12.18.) Lead gradually elongates under sustained stress at ordinary temperature. The creep limit of lead is approximately a fiber stress of 200 pounds per square inch at room temperature with some variation depending upon composition or heat treatment. Pure commercial lead shows a tensile strength of 1900 pounds per square inch and an elongation of 55 per cent when tested at the rate of 0.25 inch per inch per minute, but owing to the plasticity and creep characteristic of lead these values would vary greatly with change in rate of application of load; indeed, it is questionable whether the results of instantaneous tensile-strength tests of lead have much significance.

Because of its plasticity and malleability, lead is easily rolled into sheets or extruded in the form of tubes, pipes, rods, ribbons, and wires.

The high resistance of lead to corrosion is due to the formation of a protective adherent film that forms over the surface on contact. Such a film may vary from an oxide tarnish to a heavy coat of lead sulfate and has the characteristic of "self-healing." In general, lead is resistant to corrosion by the atmosphere, natural waters, and most mineral acids in which an insoluble product is formed. Steel pipes, tanks, etc., are coated with lead, and many water pipes and conduits for electrical conductors are made of lead. Because of danger to health, lead pipes should not be used for very soft drinking waters and those containing magnesium chloride or a high content of free carbon dioxide, but tin-lined lead pipes are safe for carrying soft drinking water. Lead is used in equipment for handling many chemicals and reagents including sulfuric acid.

Lead is often used because of its great density; it weighs approximately 707 pounds per cubic foot. Since the ability of materials to shield against gamma rays is directly related to density, lead is utilized as a shielding material in nuclear reactors against gamma rays so as to provide safe conditions for personnel.

In addition to sheet and pipe, lead is also commonly used in castings where it is generally hardened by adding antimony. In the chemical industry it is used in the form of sheet to line wood, steel or concrete vessels and as a cladding on steel for vessels operating at high temperatures or under vacuum or where vibration is a factor. Collapsible tubes are made from lead by impact extrusion. These may be lined with tin on the inside or outside or both by coating the lead disk prior to extrusion with a layer of pure tin on either or both sides.

The United States consumes more than one million tons of lead per year. About one-third of this is made into lead chemicals such as red lead for metal protective paints, white lead as an ingredient in exterior house paints, litharge for glass manufacture, storage batteries, tetraethyl lead for gasoline, various lead chemicals as stabilizers in plastics, in the ceramic industries, in addition to a host of other compounds embracing practically all industries.

TIN

12.11 Commercial Forms of Tin. Tin is used quite extensively in the form of sheet tin and as tinfoil, but it has almost no other commercial application except as a constituent of many valuable alloys. A limited but important use is in the making of boiler fuse plugs, for which purpose it must be of the highest purity. Tin is one of the important metals that are

Non-Ferrous Metals and Alloys

not abundant in the United States. The principal sources of tin are the Federated Malay States in the East Indies (referred to as the Straits or Straits Settlements), England, Australia, and Bolivia.

12.12 Extraction of Tin from Its Ore. The extraction of tin from its ore involves the mechanical, or combined mechanical, thermal, and chemical, concentration of the ore, reduction by smelting with charcoal or coke in shaft furnaces or reverberatory furnaces, and refining of the crude tin derived by smelting.

The most common refining treatment is simply a liquation process, the pure tin being melted out on a hearth and allowed to escape while the less fusible alloys of the impurities remain behind as liquation dross.

12.13 Properties and Uses of Tin. The properties of tin of commercial importance are its great malleability at ordinary temperatures and its high resistance to corrosion when pure. A large amount of the world's production of tin is used as a coating on sheet iron or steel. A smaller proportion is cold-rolled into sheet tin and used in the manufacture of roofing material, tinfoil, etc. Tin is effective as a coating as long as the surface remains unbroken, but it will not protect the iron after the surface is broken as zinc will, since tin is below iron in the electromotive series. Tin tends to creep under sustained stress at ordinary temperature.

When heated above atmospheric temperatures tin becomes brittle, until at 200° C. (392° F.) it can be powdered by hammering. Iron in considerable amounts makes tin hard and brittle and less rust-resistive. Arsenic, antimony, and bismuth, in amounts exceeding about 0.05 per cent, lower its strength considerably; copper and lead (1 to 2 per cent) increase its hardness and strength but render it less malleable.

Aluminum

12.14 Commercial Forms of Aluminum. Practicable processes for the production of metallic aluminum have been developed since 1886. Prior to that time the metal was merely a chemical curiosity, but since the discovery of electrolytic extraction methods it has assumed a position of great importance. It is recommended particularly by its lightness (sp. gr. = 2.70) combined with considerable strength, great ductility, high heat and electric conductivity, malleability, non-corrosiveness, and immunity from attack of certain acids.

Aside from its very common use as rolled, pressed, drawn, or cast metal, metallic aluminum is utilized in the form of aluminum foil, like tinfoil, and powdered aluminum as a paint pigment, in explosives, in lithographing and printing, and in the Thermit process of welding.

12.15 Extraction of Aluminum. Aluminum is one of the most abundant elements in the world; yet there are few minerals from which it has been successfully extracted. The most important are bauxite and cryolite; rocks containing aluminum sulfate, kaolin, and clay are of much less importance. Whatever the original source of the material, it is converted into alumina (Al_2O_3) before the metal is extracted.

Bauxite is a mixture of alumic and ferric hydrates containing widely varying amounts of alumina, ferric oxide, titanium oxide, silica, calcium, and magnesium carbonates, water, etc. Most bauxites carry from 55 to 65 per cent alumina.

Cryolite is a double fluoride of sodium and aluminum, represented by the formula $Al_2F_6 + 6NaF$, and containing, when pure, 13.07 per cent aluminum.

The only methods of extraction of aluminum of commercial importance consist in the electrolysis of comparatively pure alumina dissolved in a bath of molten cryolite. Alumina for the purposes of electrolysis is usually made from bauxite, but it may be prepared by treating siliceous bauxite, kaolin, or clay with sulfuric acid, and subsequently driving off the sulfuric acid from the aluminum sulfate produced, by ignition. Bauxite is treated with a soda solution, and the alumina is extracted as sodium aluminate. The alumina may be precipitated from the solution as hydroxide by carbon dioxide, and subsequently washed, filtered, and dehydrated by heating, or it may be precipitated as hydroxide by stirring the solution with pure aluminum hydroxide.

The metal derived as the product of the above operations is commercial aluminum, which is designated as 2S. Its chemical composition is given in Table 12.13, a minimum aluminum content of 99.0 per cent being required. Special grades are obtainable, containing as much as 99.97 per cent aluminum. Electrical Conductor grade (EC) contains 99.45 per cent minimum aluminum.

12.16 Properties and Uses of Aluminum. Typical mechanical properties of commercial aluminum (2S) are given in Table 12.17. The minimum values for 2S-O apply to metal in an annealed condition; and the higher values, to metal that has been cold-worked without subsequent annealing (2S-H12 to 2S-H18). The very marked effect of cold working in increasing the strength and improving the elastic properties of the metal is exhibited by these values. The ductility of annealed aluminum is high, but cold working hardens aluminum; in wire-drawing the metal must be frequently annealed to restore ductility.

The low electrical resistance of aluminum is one of its most valuable properties, since a relatively high conductivity, combined with its lightness and strength, makes it especially well adapted for long-span transmission lines. Pure aluminum is being used extensively in electrical work both as bus bars and rods in power stations and in large quantities for transmission lines with high voltages. Aluminum wires of about the same electrical conductivity as copper are enough larger so that corona losses are much less. With regard to equivalent conductivities, it has been calculated that 1 pound of aluminum is equivalent to about 1.6 pounds of copper; in 1954 electrical conductors of aluminum cost considerably less than equivalent ones of copper.

Aside from the electrical uses of metallic aluminum, large quantities are consumed in the manufacture of many articles of everyday domestic use and in many industries where tanks, cooking vats, etc., which must be heat-conductive, non-corrodible, and non-poisonous, are used. For these purposes the metal is either cast or rolled, and many articles are finished in a press. A further quantity of aluminum is finished in the form of seamless tubing which has many important applications.

Aluminum is resistant to atmospheric corrosion and is little affected by most neutral salts, most organic acids (except formic, oxalic, and trichloro-acetic acids), many organic solvents, and generally dry gases. It is highly resistant to ammonia and ammonium hydroxide. Aluminum is generally attacked by acid and alkaline salt solutions, sodium and potassium hydroxide solutions, and mineral acids such as halogen acids and intermediate concentrations of nitric and sulfuric acids.

Aluminum has the high thermal coefficient of expansion of 0.000025 per degree C. and a high thermal conductivity (0.475 gram-cal. per sec. per cm.-cube per degree C.). It therefore expands greatly upon being heated but has the ability to carry heat away rapidly. Its melting point is 659° C. (1218° F.).

Aluminum is suitable for casting purposes where lightness and softness are required rather than hardness and strength. Most of the aluminum used for these purposes, however, is alloyed with other metals which harden it and materially increase its strength. Much of the rolled and drawn aluminum is also slightly alloyed, with an improvement in strength and hardness.

Magnesium

12.17 Commercial Forms of Magnesium. Magnesium is a light metal (specific gravity = 1.74) which has considerable strength, fair ductility, and high heat conductivity. It is used principally as a constituent of light-weight alloys.

12.18 Extraction of Magnesium. Magnesium is produced by the electrolysis of magnesium chloride, which is obtained as a by-product from the process of purifying sodium chloride derived from brine wells or from sea water. A molten bath of magnesium chloride mixed with sodium and potassium chloride is electrolyzed at a temperature of about 700° C. (1292° F.). The presence of sodium and potassium chloride is necessary to prevent decomposition of the magnesium chloride during heating. The process is carried out in an air-tight container. Chlorine gas is liberated at the anode, and magnesium at the cathode, where it rises to the surface because of its lightness and is poured off. This magnesium metal contains some non-metallic impurities which may be largely eliminated by reheating in a vacuum or in contact with a flux to prevent oxidation. Owing to its relatively low boiling point (1120° C. [2048° F.]), impurities can be removed by distillation.

Formerly magnesium was obtained by an oxide process similar to the electrolytic process for the production of aluminum.

12.19 Properties and Uses of Magnesium. Magnesium has a tensile strength when cast of about 14,000 pounds per square inch, its compressive strength is about 24,000 pounds per square inch, its elongation in 2 inches is about 5 per cent, and its Brinell hardness is about 30. When rolled it has a tensile strength of about 25,000 pounds per square inch, an elongation in 2 inches of 4 per cent, and a Brinell hardness of about 40. Magnesium has the high thermal coefficient of expansion of 0.000029 per degree C. and a high thermal conductivity (0.376 gram-cal. per sec. per cm.-cube per degree C.). Thus magnesium expands a great deal upon being heated, but it has the advantage of carrying heat away rapidly. Its melting point is 651° C. (1204° F.). Magnesium in finely divided particles ignites easily. A coating of magnesium hydroxide is formed in humid air which protects it from further oxidation. Magnesium is not used alone structurally, but alloys containing magnesium are employed for structural parts principally because of their light weight.

николь

12.20 Commercial Forms of Nickel. Metallic nickel is becoming increasingly valuable in the production of materials which must possess strength and resistance to corrosion. It is used in the manufacture of nickel and other alloy steels and nickel cast iron; and a further quantity, in alloys of non-ferrous metals.

12.21 Extraction of Nickel from Its Ores. The methods of extraction of nickel from sulfur compounds, after removal of gangue, involve principally the separation of nickel from sulfur and from iron, and in most ores from copper also. The first operation consists in roasting the pyrite ore, the object of which is to remove sulfur until only enough remains to combine with nickel, copper, and a portion of the iron during the smelting operation which follows.

The second step in the process is the smelting of the roasted ore in a blast furnace. All the iron that has previously been oxidized passes into the slag; the residue of undecomposed iron sulfide forms a matte containing all the nickel and copper sulfides.

Non-Ferrous Metals and Alloys

Complete separation of the iron cannot be effected in the smelting operation because of the loss of nickel in the slag that would result, and the next step in the operation is therefore the removal of the iron sulfide by an oxidizing fusion. This operation is accomplished in a converter, and the removal of iron is complete.

Metallic nickel and copper are derived from the refined matte by repeated smelting, by electrolysis, and by volatilizing as an organic nickel compound.

12.22 The Properties and Uses of Nickel. The most important property of nickel, aside from the advantages which it may confer upon ferrous or non-ferrous metals with which it is alloyed, is its resistance to corrosion. Nickel is highly resistant to atmospheric, fresh-water, and salt-water corrosion, and it resists attack by neutral and alkaline salt solutions and by alkalies. On this account, and because of its silvery appearance, one of the commonest commercial applications of metallic nickel is in plating iron, steel, or other metals. (Chromium coatings, however, are more durable than nickel.)

The mechanical properties of nickel are excellent, sometimes equaling those of medium-carbon steel, but it is too expensive for general use. It is quite ductile and fairly malleable but is rendered brittle and incapable of being rolled by not more than 0.1 per cent of arsenic or sulfur. Most of the other impurities common to commercial nickel are not injurious to its properties, and some are beneficial in limited amounts.

Nickel is available in various forms, such as hot-rolled rods, hard- or soft-rolled sheets, hard- and soft-drawn wires, castings, and shot for alloying purposes. The hardness and tensile properties of "A" or 99 per cent nickel are shown in Table 12.4.

Table 12.4

TENSILE PROPERTIES AND HARDNESS OF 99% NICKEL *

Form of Nickel	Yield Point, p.s.i.	Tensile Strength, p.s.i.	Elongation in 2 in., %	Reduction of Area, %	Brinell Hardness (3000 kg.)
Hot-rolled rods	20,000– 30,000	70,000– 80,000	40–50	50–70	100–120
Annealed sheet	15,000– 25,000	60,000– 75,000	35–45	——	80–100
Cold-rolled sheet	85,000–105,000	90,000–110,000	1–2	——	130–160
Annealed wire	15,000– 25,000	60,000– 75,000	20–30	——	——
Hard-drawn wire	110,000–130,000	120,000–140,000	1–2	——	——
Castings	20,000– 30,000	50,000– 60,000	20–30	——	80–100

* *Circular* 100, U. S. Bureau of Standards.

The modulus of elasticity of 99 per cent pure nickel is slightly higher than that of steel (30–33,000,000 pounds per square inch), and Poisson's ratio for nickel has been stated to be 0.33. Nickel retains its tensile strength, yield point, and ductility at elevated temperatures.

Titanium

12.23 Commercial Forms of Titanium. Commercial production of titanium was begun in 1948, and production for the year 1951 in the United States was about 700 tons. Research is being conducted on the development of commercial titanium and its alloys. Titanium is an abundant element in nature, but it is not plentiful commercially because of difficulty in separating it from its ores. The chief commercial ores are rutile and ilmenite. Rutile is essentially titanium dioxide. Titanium has a silvery-white color and is extremely hard.

12.24 Manufacture of Titanium. Commercial titanium is produced by the Kroll process in the form of sponge and is then melted by arc- and induction-melting procedures to obtain a massive product. Desired shapes are obtained by hot and cold working. Commercial titanium is available in the form of plate, sheet, rod, tubing, wire, and forgings. It can be annealed satisfactorily by heating to 1200 to 1300° F.

12.25 Properties and Uses of Titanium. Mechanical properties of commercial titanium are given in Table 12.22. The mechanical properties depend upon the amount of carbon, nitrogen, and oxygen present in very small percentages as impurities. Carbon has the least effect and nitrogen the greatest of these three impurities. Modulus of elasticity is 15,000,000 pounds per square inch for commercial titanium. One of the principal properties of titanium which is of interest concerning its utilization is its comparatively light weight of 0.16 pounds per cubic inch and specific gravity of 4.5. Its strength compares favorably with that of alloy steels with little more than half the weight. It has a very high specific tensile strength; for example, for Ti100A the tensile strength is 110,000 pounds per square inch in annealed condition which corresponds to a specific tensile strength of 24,400. (Compare with values in Table 12.18.)

Titanium has a melting range of 3135° F. In spite of its high melting point, titanium is not suitable for high-temperature applications because both nitrogen and oxygen are absorbed by titanium at high temperatures and prolonged exposure results in permanent embrittlement of the metal. Above 600° F., hydrogen can also be absorbed in large quantities and may cause embrittlement. Titanium and its alloys are not recommended for continuous service above 1000° F.

Fatigue strengths of titanium and its commercial alloys compare favorably with those of steel. The notch sensitivity of titanium has not been definitely established. Titanium has excellent corrosion resistance, particularly to chlorides, sea water, and to oxidizing conditions.

Titanium is used for shrouds of aircraft which must withstand temperatures of 400–500° F. Other applications are for rivets, for marine parts

Non-Ferrous Metals and Alloys

subject to sea water, and on a limited scale for corrosion-resistant chemical equipment.

The Principal Non-Ferrous Alloys

12.26 Classification. Non-ferrous alloys are arranged in the following groups:
   a. Alloys in which copper is the chief constituent.
   b. Alloys in which aluminum is the principal metal.
   c. Alloys in which magnesium is the base metal.
   d. Alloys of nickel.
   e. Die-casting alloys.
   f. Bearing metals and fusible alloys.

THE COPPER ALLOYS

12.27 General. The copper-base alloys may be divided into two general classes, brass and bronze. Brass is an alloy of copper and zinc; minor percentages of other elements may be added. Originally the term bronze was applied only to copper-tin alloys, but common practice is to designate as bronze all copper-base alloys which have additions of any element except zinc. There is, however, no definite dividing line between brasses and bronzes.

For comparative purposes, physical properties of non-ferrous metals and alloys are given in Table 12.5. The higher tensile properties of bronze as

Table 12.5

PHYSICAL PROPERTIES OF NON-FERROUS METALS AND ALLOYS

Metal	Tensile Strength, p.s.i.	Yield Strength (0.2%), p.s.i.	Specific Gravity	Melting Point, °F.
Copper	23,000– 52,000	14,000– 50,000	8.9	1,980
Bronze	40,000–200,000	20,000–175,000	7-9	1,800–1,950
Brass	30,000– 40,000	15,000– 50,000	8.4 – 8.8	1,720–1,950
Zinc and its alloys	15,000– 45,000	10,000– 25,000	6.6 – 7.1	727– 785
Lead and its alloys	2,000– 12,000	1,000– 10,000	10.5 –11.5	300– 625
Tin alloys	2,000– 15,000	1,300– 9,800	7.3 – 7.8	360– 470
Aluminum and its alloys	13,000– 72,000	5,000– 62,000	2.6 – 2.9	940–1,225
Magnesium and its alloys	13,000– 65,000	3,000– 50,000	1.74– 1.9	815–1,200
Nickel-base alloys	60,000–100,000	30,000– 80,000	8.3 – 8.9	2,200–2,600

compared to copper and brass are indicated. Comparisons between physical properties for various non-ferrous alloys may be made, and these values may also be compared with the physical properties of ferrous metals and alloys given in Table 11.14.

12.28 Ordinary Bronzes. The influence of tin upon the properties of copper is that of a pronounced hardener and strengthener, so long as a limiting percentage of 20 or 25 per cent is not exceeded. The range of composition of ordinary commercial bronzes is not broad, all the important ones containing 80 per cent or more of copper.

A solid solution of copper and tin known as the "alpha" phase exists for tin contents up to approximately 12 per cent. For tin contents ranging from 12 to 28 per cent approximately, a "delta" phase occurs, producing a mixture of alpha and delta phases.

The bronzes exhibiting the greatest tensile strength and bending strength, and the highest yield strength, are those containing more than 80 per cent of copper. The compressive strength increases with decrease in copper content until an alloy containing about 75 per cent of copper and 25 per cent of tin is passed. Beyond these limits the strength decreases rapidly with further additions of tin. The stiffness increases until a 50 per cent tin alloy is reached, but the ductility reaches its maximum with only about 4 per cent of tin and is entirely lacking with more than 25 per cent. When the high-tin alloys are reached, the great ductility of the tin becomes a characteristic. All the alloys containing between 25 and 75 per cent of tin are extremely brittle and weak, and those containing more than 75 per cent of tin are weak and soft.

The strength and ductility of bronzes are considerably affected by heat treatment. M. Guillet found that, with bronzes containing over 92 per cent of copper, quenching between 400° C. (752° F.) and 600° C. (1112° F.) slightly increases the strength and ductility. With less than 92 per cent of copper, both strength and ductility increase decidedly as soon as the quenching temperature exceeds 500° C. (932° F.). The maximum strength of all alloys was found to be reached by quenching at about 600° C. (1112° F.), the beneficial effect becoming more marked as the copper content is reduced.

All bronzes having a relatively high tin content are at a disadvantage with those copper alloys containing small amounts of tin because tin has a high cost and is a critical metal in time of war.

12.29 Special Bronzes. Special bronzes will be treated in this article.

Aluminum Bronze. The principal commercial alloy of copper and aluminum is aluminum bronze. Typical compositions and physical properties are given in Table 12.6. The addition of iron in small percentages improves the casting qualities. If small percentages of nickel are added, the tensile strength, yield strength, and hardness are increased with some decrease in ductility. Compositions containing 9.5 per cent or more aluminum can be hardened by heat treatment. The standard quench is at 871° C. (1600° F.), with reheating to 371–538° C. (700–1000° F.) and slow cooling. Careful control in molding and pouring is necessary to produce sound castings. It may be hot rolled or hammer forged, but its hot-working temperature range is narrow. Aluminum bronze cannot be cold-worked or cold-drawn without risk of cracking.

Table 12.6
TYPICAL COMPOSITIONS AND PHYSICAL PROPERTIES OF ALUMINUM BRONZE CASTINGS *

	Type B As Cast	Type A As Cast
Copper, %	89	89.5
Aluminum, %	10	8
Iron, %	1	2.5
Tensile strength, min., p.s.i.	65,000	75,000
Yield strength, min., p.s.i.	28,000	32,000
Elongation in 2 in., min., %	20	25
Brinell hardness (3000 kg.)	120	150
Impact strength, Izod, ft.-lb.	31	34
Unit weight, lb. per cu. in.	0.270	0.273

* See SAE 68A and 68B, and ASTM-B148 Alloys 9A and 9B. Also see reference 12.2.

Aluminum bronze is heat resistant, retaining its strength and hardness at high temperatures. It is therefore utilized for hot-mill guides, valve seats for superheated steam, and valve guides in internal-combustion engines. Aluminum bronze has fatigue resistance close to that of steel. The metal is highly resistant to corrosion and has, therefore, been used for ship fittings and propeller blades. On account of its excellent resistance to corrosive attack of acid solutions it is valuable for pickling apparatus, pumps for acids, pipes, vats, etc. Aluminum bronze is attacked, however, by ammonium solutions.

In ordinary machine construction and in automobile construction it has found many special applications, and, because of the peculiar smooth surface which it acquires, it has been found to be an excellent antifriction metal. One of the disadvantages of aluminum bronze is the difficulty in producing an alloy of uniform quality. Also the metal is difficult to weld.

Aluminum-Manganese Bronze. This is the strongest and toughest type of bronze with excellent hardness, equaling nickel-alloy structural steels in tensile strength. Its high mechanical properties are attained by careful control in alloying and not by cold working or heat treatment; hot working, however, improves the tensile strength and ductility to a moderate extent. The temperature range for forging and rolling is wide. The metal is not ordinarily subject to "season cracking." (See Art. 12.30.) The composition of five different grades fall within the following limits: copper, 60–68 per cent; zinc, 20–24 per cent; aluminum, 3–7 per cent; manganese, 2.5–5 per cent; and iron, 2–4 per cent. Typical specifications for mechanical properties of five grades of aluminum-manganese bronze are given in Table 12.7.

Aluminum-manganese bronze has good wear resistance under heavy or shock loads, is capable of withstanding high fluid pressures, and is resistant

Table 12.7

MECHANICAL PROPERTIES OF ALUMINUM-MANGANESE BRONZE *

Commercial Grade Number	Form	Tensile Strength, min., p.s.i.	Yield Strength, min., p.s.i.	Elongation in 2 in., min., %	Brinell Hardness, min.
1A	Cast, forged, or rolled	115,000	75,000	12	240
1	Cast, forged, or rolled	108,000	65,000	14	220
2	Cast	100,000	55,000	16	200
3	Cast, forged, or rolled	90,000	45,000	20	175
4	Forged or rolled	85,000	40,000	25	150

* Selected from reference 12.2. (*Courtesy* American Manganese Bronze Co.)

to corrosion. Its applications include hydraulic valves for pressures up to 20,000 pounds per square inch, pump and fan impellers, tracks and rollers for sluice gates, bridge bearings, spur and bevel gears for severe service, and recoil parts on heavy ordnance which are subjected to shock loads.

Manganese Bronze. Manganese bronze is one of the most valuable copper-zinc alloys. A typical composition of regular-grade manganese bronze is copper, 56–60 per cent; manganese, 1.0 per cent maximum; aluminum, 0.05–1.0 per cent; lead, 0.4 per cent maximum; iron, 0.4–1.5 per cent, and zinc, the remainder. Its mechanical properties are given in Table 12.8.

Table 12.8

MINIMUM MECHANICAL PROPERTIES OF REGULAR GRADE MANGANESE BRONZE *

Property	Cast	Forged
Tensile strength, p.s.i.	65,000	70,000
Yield strength, p.s.i.	30,000	35,000
Elongation in 2 in., %	25	30
Brinell hardness	100	110

* Selected from reference 12.2. (*Courtesy* American Manganese Bronze Co.)

It is one of the low-price non-ferrous alloys because it contains none or little of the higher-priced metals such as tin, aluminum, and magnesium. Its electrical conductivity is 26 per cent compared to copper as 100 per cent.

Manganese bronze is one of the best copper alloys for hot working and makes excellent forgings and hot-rolled rods. Probably no metal or alloy possessing equal strength and toughness can be cast in intricate forms so successfully as manganese bronze. It should not be cold worked. Manganese bronze is particularly resistant to corrosion by sea water and is resistant to attack by dilute acids. It is very commonly used for steamship propellers and other ship fittings, for piston rods, shafts, axles, and for many kinds of castings and forgings employed in general machine, locomotive, and automobile construction. Manganese bronze is also utilized for large valves and castings for water-supply systems and hydroelectric-power plants.

A modified manganese bronze containing nickel called "turbine metal" has a close-grain structure which is highly resistant to pitting and erosion. Its tensile strength is 80,000 pounds per square inch minimum; its yield strength, 40,000 pounds per square inch; and its elongation in 2 inches, 20 per cent. It is used for runners of hydraulic turbines and high-speed pumps.

Beryllium-Copper Alloy. Beryllium-copper alloy is commonly called beryllium copper, and sometimes beryllium bronze. This alloy contains a small percentage of beryllium alloyed with copper. The addition of beryllium to copper produces effects comparable to those of carbon on iron. Like steel, beryllium bronze is hardenable by appropriate heat treatment, and the properties thus produced may extend over a wide range.

Beryllium metal, also called glucinum, has the low specific gravity of 1.84, as compared with 1.74 for magnesium, but its melting temperature of 1285° C. (2345° F.) is much higher than that of either magnesium or aluminum. It is a stable light-weight metal.

Physical properties of standard high-strength wrought beryllium-copper alloy number 25 are given in Table 12.9. This alloy contains beryllium,

Table 12.9

PHYSICAL PROPERTIES OF BERYLLIUM-COPPER ALLOY NO. 25 ROD AND BAR *

Condition	Tensile Strength, p.s.i.	Yield Strength (0.2% offset), p.s.i.	Elongation in 2 in., %	Rockwell Hardness
Solution-annealed	60,000– 85,000	—	35–50	45–80B
Hard	80,000–120,000	—	10–20	80–100B
Heat-treated from solution annealed	165,000–180,000	130,000–150,000	3–10	36–40C
Heat-treated from hard	185,000–215,000	160,000–185,000	2– 5	39–44C

Specific gravity	8.26
Melting range	1600–1800° F.
Modulus of elasticity in tension	19,000,000 p.s.i.
Electrical conductivity, % I.A.C.S. at 20° C.	22–30

* Selected from *Materials & Methods*.

1.90–2.15 per cent; cobalt, 0.25–0.35 per cent; and the remainder copper. It combines good electrical conductivity with the highest strength and hardness of any copper alloy when heat treated.

Solution annealing is conducted at 1450° F. to soften the material and force the beryllium into solution; this is followed by quenching in water to retain the structure. The alloy may be hardened by cold work. Like steel, beryllium-copper alloy can be fabricated into desired shapes because of its ductility and then hardened by heat treatment. It is heat treated at 600–650° F., followed by quenching in cold water.

An outstanding quality of beryllium bronze is its high endurance limit in fatigue. Values of endurance limit are reported to vary from 35,000 to 47,000 pounds per square inch, which compare favorably with heat-treated low-carbon steels. The unique feature is their ability to maintain this high endurance limit under corrosive conditions and at temperatures from 300 to 400° F. This alloy also has good resistance to corrosion and wear. It is non-magnetic. Beryllium bronze is also highly resistant to pitting of surface which occurs in connection with surface wear of rollers and gears. It is available in cast, wrought, and forged form. This alloy is a good spring material and is utilized for bourdon tubes. Other applications are for resistance-welding electrodes, heavy-duty switches, cams, bushings, and as molds for forming plastics.

Owing to its non-sparking characteristics, beryllium-copper alloy is utilized in manufacturing chisels and hammers for use under conditions where sparks might cause an explosion.

Gun Metal. Gun metal contains 88 per cent copper, 10–8 per cent tin, and 2–4 per cent zinc. It is a general-purpose bronze of good average mechanical properties and fairly good wearing qualities. It is resistant to corrosive action of sea water and can be readily cast and freely machined. At one time, guns were commonly cast of it. Because of its qualifications and long-established record, it is extensively used, but other bronzes have better specific properties. Gun metal is available in sand and centrifugal castings having properties meeting the following specifications: Minimum tensile strength, 40,000 pounds per square inch; minimum yield strength, 18,000 pounds per square inch in tension and 15,000 pounds per square inch in compression; minimum elongation in 2 inches, 20 per cent; and Brinell hardness from 60 to 75. Typical applications include pump casings and impellers, water-turbine runners, condenser heads, and cylinder linings. Gun metal is inferior to hydraulic bronze or valve bronze for pressure-tight service.

Nickel Bronze. Nickel bronze is a copper-tin-zinc red metal alloy to which from 1 to 10 per cent nickel is added. Addition of nickel refines the grain and increases heat-resisting qualities. A typical composition is copper, 88 per cent; tin, 5 per cent; nickel, 5 per cent; and zinc, 2 per cent. When heat treated, it has a tensile strength of 70,000 pounds per square inch and elongation in 2 inches of 15 per cent. It is used for pressure-tight service.

Non-Ferrous Metals and Alloys

Cupro-Nickel is a 70 per cent copper, 30 per cent nickel alloy used for tubes of stills, condensers, evaporators, and heat exchangers. It maintains its strength and hardness up to 800° F., and is resistant to corrosion by salt water. Cupro-nickel shows the highest resistance to stress corrosion and corrosion fatigue of any of the copper-base alloys. It can be cast and hot- or cold-formed.

Phosphor Bronze. The addition of very small percentages of phosphorus to any bronze has a remarkable effect upon its properties. The tensile strength is considerably increased, and the yield strength and endurance under repetition of stress are greatly increased. Phosphorus added in amounts up to 0.5 per cent acts principally as a deoxidizer, and the marked improvement in the properties of the bronze is principally due to the elimination of copper oxide. For percentages from 0.5 to 1.2, the phosphorus combines with copper to form the compound copper phosphide, which greatly hardens the bronze.

Phosphor bronzes intended for use as engine parts and valve metal ordinarily show only traces of phosphorus and contain about 7 per cent of tin. Gear bronze containing 89 per cent copper and 11 per cent tin is harder. Minimum requirements are: tensile strength, 35,000 pounds per square inch; yield strength, 18,000 pounds per square inch; elongation in 2 inches, 10 per cent; and Brinell hardness, 70. High-tin phosphor bronze, known as hard bronze with 15 per cent tin, or as disk bronze with 18 per cent tin, has high compressive strength but is brittle. It is used for bearing plates for contact with hardened-steel disks under heavy slow-moving loads where no shock is involved. (See ASTM-B22, classes A and B.) However, this bronze is being supplanted by aluminum-manganese bronze which is tough, will carry heavier loads, and has a low coefficient of friction.

Phosphor bronzes of proper composition may be rolled or drawn into wire and when so fabricated exhibit about the same tensile properties as medium structural steel. Working cold has the same effect as upon steel, the strength, and especially the yield strength, being raised to a marked extent. All the phosphor bronzes are remarkably resistant to corrosion and are much utilized on subaqueous construction. They withstand anthracite-mine waters and sulfuric acid solutions.

Leaded Phosphor Bronze. Leaded phosphor bearing bronzes, particularly those for railway service, contain from 10 to 30 per cent lead. These bronzes excel any other class of bearing metals in resistance to wear under severe conditions and in addition possess a very low coefficient of friction. Typical mechanical properties of bearing bronze containing 80 per cent copper, 10 per cent tin, and 10 per cent lead are given in Table 12.10. (See reference 12.2 and ASTM-B22 Class C.)

Silicon Bronze. Silicon bronze is a general-purpose corrosion-resisting alloy. Compositions for castings run from 93 to 96 per cent copper and

Table 12.10
MECHANICAL PROPERTIES OF LEADED PHOSPHOR BEARING BRONZE
(80 Cu, 10 Sn, 10 Pb)

Property	Sand Cast	Chill Cast
Tensile strength, p.s.i.	30,000	35,000
Yield strength, tension, p.s.i.	13,000	15,000
Yield strength, compression, p.s.i.	10,000	12,000
Elongation in 2 in., %	8	6
Brinell hardness	55	75

3 to 4 per cent silicon with small additions of tin, manganese, or zinc and iron. Typical minimum requirements for mechanical properties of castings are: tensile strength, 45,000 pounds per square inch; yield strength, 20,000 pounds per square inch; elongation in 2 inches, 20 per cent; and Brinell hardness (500-kilogram load), 60. Silicon bronze is a free-flowing metal, producing accurate thin section castings of smooth texture and golden-yellow color, but it requires careful foundry technique. It has excellent weldability, good machinability, and can be both hot- and cold-worked, thereby improving mechanical properties. It is available in forgings, rod, bar, and sheet form as well as sand-, centrifugal-, and permanent-mold castings. Chief applications are for welded tanks, springs, condenser tubes, and chemical equipment.

Copper-Tin-Zinc Bronze. The copper-tin-zinc alloys are among the most valuable and commonly used of all the bronzes. The range of composition of the bronzes of this class is from 50 to 95 per cent of copper, 1 to 15 per cent of tin, and 5 to 50 per cent of zinc. A very common bronze of this type, called "88-10-2," contains 88 per cent copper, 10 per cent tin, and 2 per cent zinc. ASTM specifications for sand castings of this alloy (B143-Alloy 1A) call for the following minimum tensile requirements: tensile strength, 40,000 pounds per square inch; yield strength, 18,000 pounds per square inch (0.5 per cent elongation); and elongation in 2 inches, 20 per cent.

Hydraulic Bronze. This bronze (also called red brass, composition brass, and ounce metal) is a pressure-tight, close-grained, free-machining alloy which is easily cast in intricate sections. A typical composition is 85 per cent copper, 5 per cent tin, 5 per cent zinc, and 5 per cent lead, hence its common trade name of "85-5-5-5." One per cent nickel may be added to refine the grain. The best grade hydraulic bronze meets the following minimum requirements of the ASTM Specification B62–51: tensile strength, 30,000 pounds per square inch; yield strength, 14,000 pounds per square inch; and elongation in 2 inches, 20 per cent. A Brinell-hardness value of 50 is typical (500-kilogram load). Its application is as a general-purpose pressure-tight casting metal for light to moderate pressures such as for valve bodies, condenser heads, and pipe fittings.

Valve Bronze (Navy composition "M") is a modified hydraulic bronze containing less lead. A typical composition is 89 per cent copper, 6 per cent tin, 3.5 per cent zinc, and 1.5 per cent lead. It is not as easily cast as hydraulic bronze and is not as free machining but possesses slightly higher tensile strength and hardness (Brinell hardness, 55). ASTM Specification B61–51 requires minimum values of mechanical properties as follows: tensile strength, 34,000 pounds per square inch; yield strength, 16,000 pounds per square inch; and elongation in 2 inches, 22 per cent. Valve bronze is selected for valves, cocks, flanges, manifolds, and heads and covers for pressure-tight vessels under moderate hydraulic and steam pressures. It resists corrosion by sea water fairly well.

Statuary Bronze. This is a leaded copper-tin-zinc bronze which develops a film by oxidation known as "patina," giving a sheen or glistening appearance to the surface.

Bell Metal. This bronze contains about 18 per cent tin and has resonance.

Speculum Metal. A bronze containing 33 per cent tin which is silvery in color and has a high reflective surface when polished. It is used in telescopes.

Vanadium Bronze. Vanadium has occasionally been added to bronzes in very small amounts with remarkably beneficial effects upon properties.

12.30 Ordinary Brasses. The influence of zinc upon the properties of copper is in the direction of increasing both strength and ductility, so long as certain limiting percentages are not exceeded, but these limiting percentages are much higher than for tin, zinc being a less potent element than tin in similar amounts. (See Table 12.11.)

The constitution of brasses having a composition range of zinc up to 35 per cent consists of a single-phase solid solution of copper and zinc known as the "alpha" phase. The space lattice is face-centered cubic in the alpha phase. At a composition of approximately 35 per cent zinc, the space lattice becomes body-centered cubic. Above a zinc content of 35 per cent, a second phase termed the "beta" phase occurs, producing a mixture of two phases. The effect of the beta phase is to strengthen and harden the alloy. As the zinc content increases, the beta phase becomes dominant and the brass becomes brittle and worthless structurally. For the higher percentages of zinc, the copper goes into the space lattice of zinc, the space lattice of the alloy being hexagonal.

The different ordinary (plain) brasses of importance in construction and industrial applications will be described. The mechanical properties of these brasses are tabulated in Table 12.11.

Commercial Bronze. This brass (90 per cent copper, 10 per cent zinc) is used for grillwork and marine hardware.

Table 12.11
MECHANICAL PROPERTIES OF BRASSES AND MUNTZ METAL *

Type	Heat Treatment	Tensile Strength, p.s.i.	Yield Strength (0.5% offset), p.s.i.	Elongation in 2 in., %	Rockwell Hardness	Shear Strength, p.s.i.	Endurance Strength at 100 Million Cycles
Commercial bronze (90 Cu-10 Zn)	Annealed	37,000– 40,000 †	10,000	45–50	53F	28,000–30,000	10,000
	Half-hard	45,000– 60,000	45,000	11– 6	58B	35,000–37,000	15,500–19,000
	Hard	54,000– 74,000	54,000	5– 4	70B	38,000–42,000	17,000–21,000
	Spring	72,000– 90,000	62,000	3	78B	42,000	19,000–23,000
Red brass (85 Cu-15 Zn)	Annealed	39,000– 41,000	10,000	48	56F	31,000	10,500
	Half-hard	57,000– 72,000	49,000	12– 8	65B	37,000–43,000	18,000–27,000
	Hard	70,000– 88,000	57,000	5– 6	77B	42,000–48,000	21,000–29,000
	Spring	84,000–105,000	63,000	3	86B	46,000–54,000	24,000–27,000
Low brass (80 Cu-20 Zn)	Annealed	42,000– 44,000	12,000	52–55	57F	32,000	14,000
	Half-hard	61,000– 82,000	50,000	18– 8	70B	39,000–47,000	20,000
	Hard	74,000–107,000	59,000	7– 5	82B	43,000–53,000	22,000–23,000
	Spring	91,000–125,000	65,000	3	91B	48,000–60,000	22,500–26,500
Cartridge brass (70 Cu-30 Zn)	Annealed	44,000– 48,000	11,000	66–64	54F	32,000–34,000	10,000
	Half-hard	62,000	52,000	23	70B	40,000	18,500
	Hard	76,000	63,000	8	82B	44,000	21,000
	Spring	94,000–130,000	65,000	3	91B	48,000–60,000	23,000
Yellow brass (65 Cu-35 Zn)	Annealed	46,000– 50,000	14,000	65–60	58F	32,000–34,000	13,500
	Half-hard	61,000– 88,000	50,000	23–15	70B	40,000	19,000
	Hard	74,000–110,000	60,000	8	80B	43,000–55,000	19,000–20,000
	Spring	91,000–128,000	62,000	3	90B	47,000–60,000	19,000–22,500
Muntz metal (60 Cu-40 Zn)	Annealed	54,000	21,000	45	80F	40,000	—
	Half-hard	70,000	50,000	10	75B	44,000	—

* Based on data from Copper & Brass Research Assoc. Selected from *Materials & Methods*, May, 1950, pp. 99 and 101.
† Values given are for flat products except where two values are given, the second is for wire.

Red Brass. (85 per cent copper, 15 per cent zinc.) This is the best corrosion-resisting plain brass. It is utilized for heat-exchanger tubes, plumbing lines, electrical sockets, and weatherstripping.

Low brass (80 per cent copper, 20 per cent zinc) is used for ornamental metal work and pump lines.

Cartridge brass (70 per cent copper, 30 per cent zinc) is used for automotive radiator cores and tanks, lamp fixtures, springs, and ammunition components.

Yellow brass (65 per cent copper, 35 per cent zinc) is employed for grillwork, lamp fixtures, springs, and plumbing accessories. It is the strongest of the plain brasses. Its specific gravity is 8.47. The specific tensile strength for hard yellow brass having a tensile strength of 74,000 pounds per square inch is 74,000/8.47 = 8,700. (Compare with other alloys in Table 12.5.)

Ordinary brasses in general have good resistance to industrial, rural, and marine atmospheres and some resistance to weak acids and bases. They have generally poor resistance to ammonia, ferric and ammonium compounds, and cyanides. They all have excellent characteristics for cold working. As to joining characteristics, they are excellent for soft soldering, good for silver-alloy brazing, good for oxyacetylene welding, good to fair for carbon-arc welding, and poor for resistance welding. Common fabrication processes comprise forming and bending, heading and upsetting, and roll threading and knurling. Typical available forms include rolled strip, sheet, plate, rod, tube, and wire.

Low brass, cartridge brass, yellow brass, and Muntz metal are subject at times to a type of failure called *season cracking*. It is due to a combination of unevenly strained metal and a specific corroding agent, commonly either ammonia or one of the salts of mercury. Serious failures caused by this phenomenon have occurred. Such stress-corrosion cracking is most frequently found in drawn rods, tubes, and hollow ware. Cracks in rods and tubes may be transverse, longitudinal, or spiral; in deep-drawn products the cracks may be circumferential or longitudinal. Remedies are (1) special cold deformations, and (2) thermal stress relief. Special cold deformations may eliminate residual stresses to some extent and, when suitably applied, may eliminate detrimental effects of season cracking in certain cases. However, thermal stress relieving is more reliable; it is a low-temperature operation at from 300 to 650° F. which is below the recrystallization point. The internal stresses are relieved without materially decreasing the hardness which may have been intentionally produced in the part by cold working.

Brass that is badly overstrained becomes greatly distorted (see Fig. 2.5), showing such elongation of the crystals as to give the impression of a distinctly fibrous structure under the microscope. When such strained material is annealed a recrystallization of the alloy takes place with the formation of the remarkable condition known as "twinning." This is illustrated by the photomicrographs in Fig. 2.6a, corresponding to a low annealing temperature, and in Fig. 2.6b, annealing at a much higher temperature. The marked difference in grain size should be noted. The smaller grains are associated with high tensile strength, hardness, and moderate ductility; the large grains indicate low tensile strength and soft metal.

Low brass, cartridge brass, yellow brass, and Muntz metal tend to dezincify under the following environmental conditions: (1) moderate concentrations of certain salts or acids, especially chlorides; (2) a limited amount of dissolved oxygen; (3) low velocity of water flow, particularly stagnation; and (4) elevated temperature. In the dezincification reaction, brass dissolves as an entity, followed by redeposition of copper from solution. In the brass-electrolyte-copper electrolytic cell which is formed, copper is the reactant at the cathode. The introduction of a few hundredths of a per cent of arsenic inhibits dezincification of cartridge brass and admiralty metal without impairment of the brass in other respects. Similar small additions of antimony or phosphorus are equally effective. (See reference 12.27.)

12.31 Special Brasses. Brief descriptions of several special brasses will be given.

Muntz metal is a brass containing 60 per cent of copper and 40 per cent of zinc. It can only be rolled hot and was formerly much used as a sheathing for wooden vessels. Sea water attacks it and forms zinc salts, which prevent the fouling of the bottoms of ships by living organisms such as barnacles. It is used for condenser tubes in fresh non-corroding waters. Mechanical properties of Muntz metal are given in Table 12.11.

Naval brass (also called Tobin bronze) is made by the addition of about 1 per cent of tin to Muntz metal; this addition of tin markedly improves resistance to corrosion. It is used as condenser-tube material, pump parts, motorboat shafting, and marine hardware. The tensile requirements of the American Society for Testing Materials for naval brass rods for structural purposes are shown in Table 12.12.

Table 12.12

ASTM TENSILE REQUIREMENTS FOR NAVAL BRASS RODS

Diameter or Distance between Parallel Faces	*Yield Point, p.s.i.*	*Tensile Strength, p.s.i.*	*Elongation in 2 in., %*
Up to 1 in., incl.	31,000	62,000	25.0
Over 1 to 2½ in., incl.	30,000	60,000	30.0
Over 2½ to 3½ in., incl.	25,000	56,000	35.0
Over 3½ in.	22,000	54,000	40.0

Admiralty metal (Admiralty brass) is manufactured by adding about 1 per cent of tin to cartridge brass (70% Cu-30% Zn); this addition of tin greatly increases corrosion resistance. Admiralty metal is generally accepted as the best condenser-tube metal commercially available.

Copper-Zinc-Lead Brasses. The addition of small percentages of lead softens brass and renders it more easily cut by machine tools, its free-cutting properties being improved so that automatic machines may be employed. The presence of the lead lowers the strength and decreases the ductility considerably. More than 5 per cent of lead cannot be profitably used because of the danger of segregation, and the usual addition is not in excess of 3 per cent.

Copper-Zinc-Aluminum Brasses. Aluminum is added to brass in amounts up to about 5 per cent with beneficial effects on the tensile properties. The tensile strength and elastic limit are considerably raised, the hardness is increased, and ductility is decreased. The effect of aluminum upon the tensile strength and ductility of rolled and cast brass is shown by Fig. 12.3, which is based upon tests reported by M. Guillet. The addition of aluminum

Non-Ferrous Metals and Alloys 275

is also beneficial in that it facilitates the making of good brass castings. Aluminum brass is principally used in making castings for machinery, marine work, etc., for forgings, and for rolled bars, plates, and shapes designed for any purpose requiring a strong brass, or a strong and non-corrodible metal.

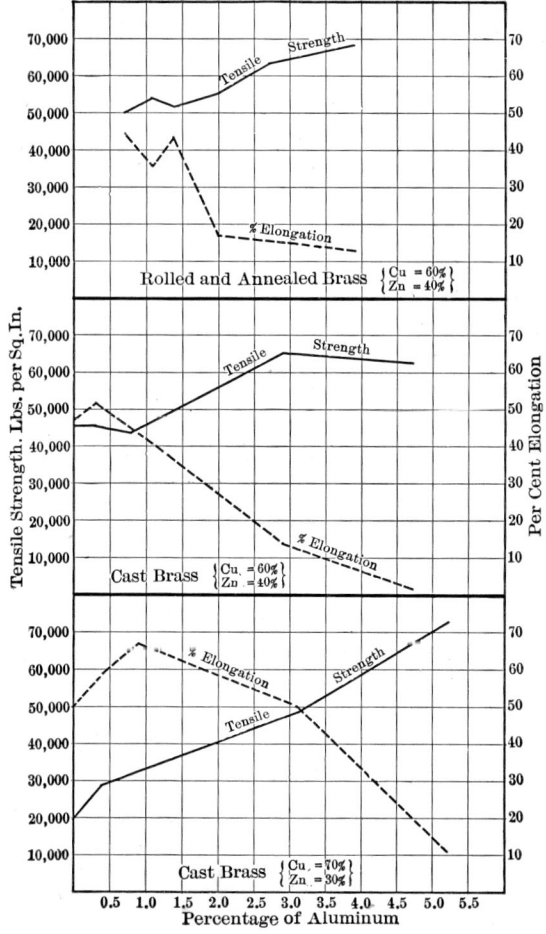

Fig. 12.3. Effect of aluminum on tensile properties of brass. (Guillet.)

Copper-Zinc-Iron Alloys. Two brass alloys containing iron have been commonly used. *Sterro metal* contains about 60 per cent of copper, 38 to 38.5 per cent of zinc, and 1.5 to 2 per cent of iron. *Delta metal* varies in composition, but it usually contains about 55 per cent of copper, 41 per cent of zinc, 3 per cent of iron, and 1 per cent of manganese, phosphorus, and other elements. These metals, particularly the delta metal, possess a considerably higher strength and better working qualities than the brass would possess without the iron addition. They are also more resistant to corrosion. They possess, to a lesser extent, the characteristic properties of manganese bronze and aluminum brass, and have been adopted for the same class of uses, principally on marine construction.

White brass contains less than 10 per cent of copper and more than 90 per cent of zinc. The metal possesses most of the characteristics of zinc but is somewhat hardened and strengthened by the small amount of copper, the coarse crystalline structure of cast zinc being largely destroyed. The material is principally used in making ornaments which are plated with bronze and sold under the name French bronze.

White brass solder contains 34 to 44 per cent of copper and 66 to 56 per cent of zinc. It is extremely weak and brittle and is used only in a powdered condition for brazing purposes.

Alloys of Aluminum

12.32 General. For construction purposes aluminum alloys are preferred instead of commercially pure aluminum (2S) because of increased hardness and strength. Aluminum alloys were introduced commercially about 1910; their applications have increased rapidly in the automotive and aircraft industries. They are also extensively used in shipbuilding and in building construction.

12.33 Composition. Aluminum alloys contain copper, silicon, magnesium, and zinc in various combinations, and limited amounts of other elements such as manganese, chromium, iron, nickel, and titanium. (See Table 12.13 for chemical composition limits.)

Aluminum alloys are divided into two groups: (1) non-heat-treatable alloys, and (2) heat-treatable alloys. The first group contain elements which either remain in solid solution under all conditions or form constituents which are insoluble in solid aluminum under all conditions; mechanical properties are changed by strain hardening under cold work. The heat-treatable alloys have alloying agents whose solubility in solid aluminum increases markedly as the temperature is raised, and have limited solubility at comparatively low temperatures. The production of high-strength alloys is based upon this difference in solubility of elements in aluminum at high temperatures as compared to ordinary temperatures. Strength is increased by "solution heat treatment" in which the fabricated part is heated to a temperature just below the melting point of any of the constituents, held for a sufficient time to allow the soluble constituents to go into solid solution, and then quenched rapidly to prevent precipitation from the supersaturated solid solution at lower temperatures. By such treatment separated constituents are distributed as very fine particles throughout the mass of the metal, and a harder and stronger alloy results.

Table 12.13
CHEMICAL COMPOSITION LIMITS OF WROUGHT ALUMINUM ALLOYS*

Alloy	Designation	Cu	Fe	Si	Mn	Mg	Zn	Cr	Ni	Ti
Commercial aluminum	2S	0.20	†	†	0.05	—	0.10	—	—	—
	3S	0.20	0.70	0.60	1.00–1.50	—	0.10	—	—	—
	52S	0.10	‡	‡	0.10	2.20–2.80	0.10	0.15–0.35	—	—
Non-Heat-Treatable Alloys										
Aluminum-copper type	14S	3.90–5.00	1.00	0.50–1.20	0.40–1.20	0.20–0.80	0.25	0.10	—	0.15
	17S	3.50–4.50	1.00	0.80	0.40–1.00	0.20–0.80	0.10	0.10	—	—
	24S	3.80–4.90	0.50	0.50	0.30–0.90	1.20–1.80	0.10	0.10	—	—
	25S	3.90–5.00	1.00	0.50–1.20	0.40–1.20	0.05	0.25	0.10	—	0.15
Heat-Treatable Alloys										
Aluminum-silicon type	32S	0.50–1.30	1.00	11.50–13.50	0.20	0.80–1.30	0.25	0.10	0.50–1.30	0.15
Aluminum-magnesium-silicon type	A51S	0.35	1.00	0.60–1.20	0.20	0.45–0.80	0.25	0.15–0.35	—	0.15
	61S	0.15–0.40	0.70	0.40–0.80	0.15	0.80–1.20	0.20	0.15–0.35	—	0.15
	63S	0.10	0.35	0.20–0.60	—	0.45–0.85	0.10	0.10	—	0.10
Aluminum-zinc-magnesium-copper type	75S	1.20–2.00	0.70	0.50	0.30	2.10–2.90	5.10–6.10	0.18–0.40	—	0.20
Aluminum-magnesium type	150S	0.25	0.80	0.50	0.15	1.00–1.80	0.25	0.10	—	—

* Composition in per cent; maximum unless shown as a range. Reference, *Materials & Methods*, Manual 71, June, 1951, p. 92.
† Iron plus silicon, 1.0% max. Aluminum, 99.0% min.
‡ Iron plus silicon, 0.45% max.

Alloys 17S (Duralumin) and 24S are relatively soft and malleable after solution heat-treatment, but they undergo a marked change in properties at room temperature due to "aging." All the other heat-treatable alloys, except forging alloy 25S, after heat treatment develop improved tensile strength and yield-point values to some extent by "natural aging" at room temperature, but if they are held at elevated temperatures in the range of 115° C. (240° F.) to 193° C. (380° F.), the increase in strength by "artificial aging" is much greater. Mechanical properties can be further modified by cold work either before or after aging. The general scheme of temper designations for aluminum alloys is given in Table 12.14.

Table 12.14
TEMPER DESIGNATIONS FOR ALUMINUM ALLOYS *
GENERAL SCHEME

-F   As fabricated.
-O   Annealed, recrystallized (wrought products only).
-H   Strain-hardened.
      -H1, plus one or more digits. Strain-hardened only.
      -H2, plus one or more digits. Strain-hardened and then partial annealed.
      -H3, plus one or more digits. Strain-hardened and then stabilized.
-W   Solution heat-treated, unstable temper.
-T   Treated to produce stable tempers other than -F, -O, or -H.
      -T2   Annealed (cast products only).
      -T3   Solution heat-treated and then cold-worked.
      -T4   Solution heat-treated.
      -T5   Artificially aged only.
      -T6   Solution heat-treated and then artificially aged.
      -T7   Solution heat-treated and then stabilized.
      -T8   Solution heat-treated, cold-worked, and then artificially aged.
      -T9   Solution heat-treated, artificially aged, and then cold-worked.
      -T10 Artificially aged and then cold-worked.

* *Alcoa Temper Designations for Cast and Wrought Products.* Effective Jan. 1, 1948, published by Aluminum Company of America.

12.34 Castings. Castings are produced by pouring liquid aluminum into molds which give the metal its final shape. Data for common aluminum casting alloys are given in Table 12.15.

12.35 Wrought Aluminum Alloys. Wrought aluminum alloys have their shape changed by mechanical working after the molten alloys have been permitted to solidify in a mold. Hot plastic slabs or billets are rolled down into bars or structural shapes in hot-rolling presses. Such working improves the quality of the metal by breaking down inclusion pockets and voids to produce a homogeneous product. Typical wrought products include sheet, plate, rods, bars, wire, tube, structural shapes, extrusions, screw-machine

Table 12.15
COMMON ALUMINUM CASTING ALLOYS

Alloy Classification	Nominal Composition, %	SAE Number	ASTM Designation	Type of Casting	Casting Properties	Responds to Heat Treatment	Machinability	Corrosion Resistance	Characteristics and Uses
Aluminum-copper	4.5 copper	38	C1	Sand	Good	Yes	Very good	Good	Widely used high-strength alloy. Internal-combustion engines, automobiles, and outboard motors.
	4 copper	39	CN21	Sand and permanent mold	Fair	Yes	Very good	Good	High mechanical strength and good bearing qualities at elevated temperatures. Pistons, valve guides, and air-cooled cylinder heads.
	10 copper plus silicon and magnesium	34	CG1	Sand and permanent mold	Good	Yes	Excellent	Fair	High strength and hardness at elevated temperatures. Cylinder heads, pistons, and camshaft bearings.
Aluminum-silicon	5 silicon	35	S1 and S2	Sand and permanent mold	Excellent	No	Fair	Very good	High fluidity when molten. Intricate architectural and marine castings. Castings requiring pressure tightness.
	12 silicon plus nickel	321	SN41	Permanent mold	Fair	Yes	Fair	Good	Good mechanical properties at high temperatures. Low coefficient of expansion. High wear resistance. Pistons.
Aluminum-magnesium	4 magnesium	320	G1	Sand	Fair	No	Very good	Excellent	Pipe fittings, carburetor cases, and food-handling equipment.
	10 magnesium	324	G3	Sand	Fair	Yes	Very good	Excellent	High strength and ductility. Good shock resistance. Structural parts of railroad cars, trucks, buses, and aircraft.
Aluminum-copper-silicon	7.5 copper, 2.5 silicon, plus zinc	33	CS22	Sand and permanent mold	Very good	No	Excellent	Fair	General casting alloy. Automotive cylinder heads and washing-machine agitators.
Aluminum-silicon-copper	5 silicon, 1 copper, plus magnesium	322	SC21	Sand and permanent mold	Excellent	Yes	Good	Good	High strength at elevated temperatures. Liquid-cooled cylinder heads.
Aluminum-zinc-magnesium	5.5 zinc, 0.6 magnesium, 0.5 chromium	310	ZG41	Sand and permanent mold	Good	Not needed	Excellent	Good	High dimensional stability and physical strength. High ductility for 2 weeks after casting. Premium-priced alloys.

Table 12.16

CHARACTERISTICS AND APPLICATIONS OF WROUGHT ALUMINUM ALLOYS

Alloy Designation	Characteristics and Applications
	Non-Heat-Treatable Alloys
2S	Excellent drawing, forming, and welding properties. Excellent corrosion resistance. General-purpose alloy. Structural and architectural applications.
3S	Slightly stronger than 2S. Very good drawing, forming, and welding properties. Excellent corrosion resistance. General-purpose alloy. Sheets used structurally as aluminum siding and for stampings.
52S	Medium mechanical properties. Good forming properties. Welding properties inferior to 3S. Excellent corrosion resistance to saline solutions. Sheet used in marine and architectural applications.
	Heat-Treatable Alloys
14S	Very high mechanical strength and hardness when tempered. Moderate corrosion resistance. General use as structural shapes and forgings. Used for machine frames and aircraft.
17S	Duralumin alloy which ages (precipitation hardens) at room temperature. High mechanical strength. Good forming properties. Moderate corrosion resistance. 14S or 61S now preferred. Used for screw-machine rod and for rivets.
24S	Ages naturally at room temperature. Higher mechanical strength than 17S. Good forming properties. Moderate corrosion resistance. General-purpose applications. Used for screw-machine products.
25S	Good forging properties. High mechanical strength. Corrosion resistance inferior to 17S. Forging alloy for aircraft propellers.
32S	Forgings only. Good forging properties and resistance to corrosion. Low coefficient of expansion. Suitable for high-temperature service. Pistons for internal-combustion engines.
A51S	Forgings only. Outstanding forging properties and higher yield strength than 25S or 17S. Corrosion resistance about equal to 17S. For large radial engine crankcases.
61S	For most structural applications it is the most generally used aluminum alloy. Medium mechanical strength. Greatest ease of fabrication of the heat-treatable alloys. Very good corrosion resistance.
63S	Lower mechanical strength than 61S. Extrusions for tubing and architectural applications such as: building panels, window frames, and bridge railings. 63S-T6 tubing used for portable irrigation systems.
75S	Highest-strength aluminum alloy. Aircraft applications.
150S	General-purpose alloy. Strength intermediate between 3S and 52S. Very good forming, drawing, and finishing characteristics. Good weldability. Outstanding corrosion resistance superior to 2S and 3S.

Non-Ferrous Metals and Alloys

Table 12.17

TYPICAL MECHANICAL PROPERTIES OF WROUGHT ALUMINUM ALLOYS *

Alloy	Designation and Temper	Tensile Strength, p.s.i.	Yield Strength (0.2%), p.s.i.	Elongation in 2 in., % †	Brinell Hardness, 500-kg. load, 10-mm. ball	Shearing Strength, p.s.i.	Endurance Limit, p.s.i.
	Non-Heat-Treatable Alloys						
Commercial aluminum	2S-O	13,000	5,000	35	23	9,500	5,000
	2S-H12	15,500	14,000	12	28	10,000	6,000
	2S-H14	17,500	16,000	9	32	11,000	7,000
	2S-H16	20,000	18,000	6	38	12,000	8,500
	2S-H18	24,000	22,000	5	44	13,000	8,500
	3S-O	16,000	6,000	30	28	11,000	7,000
	3S-H12	19,000	17,000	10	35	12,000	8,000
	3S-H14	21,500	19,000	8	40	14,000	9,000
	3S-H16	25,000	22,000	5	47	15,000	9,500
	3S-H18	29,000	26,000	4	55	16,000	10,000
	52S-O	27,000	12,000	25	45	18,000	17,000
	52S-H32	34,000	27,000	12	62	20,000	17,500
	52S-H34	37,000	31,000	10	67	21,000	18,000
	52S-H36	39,000	34,000	8	74	23,000	18,500
	52S-H38	41,000	36,000	7	85	24,000	19,000
	Heat-Treatable Alloys						
Aluminum-copper type	14S-O	27,000	14,000	18 ‡	45	18,000	13,000
	14S-T4	62,000	40,000	20 ‡	105	38,000	20,000
	14S-T6	70,000	60,000	13 ‡	135	42,000	18,000
	17S-O	26,000	10,000	22 ‡	45	18,000	13,000
	17S-T4	62,000	40,000	22 ‡	105	38,000	18,000
	24S-O	27,000	11,000	19	47	18,000	13,000
	24S-T3	70,000	50,000	16	120	41,000	20,000
	24S-T4	68,000	48,000	19	120	41,000	20,000
	24S-T36	72,000	57,000	13	130	42,000	18,000
	25S-T6	58,000	37,000	19	110	35,000	18,000
Aluminum-silicon type	32S-T6	55,000	46,000	9 ‡	120	38,000	16,000
Aluminum-magnesium-silicon type	A51S-T6	48,000	43,000	17 ‡	100	32,000	11,000
	61S-O	18,000	8,000	22	30	12,500	9,000
	61S-T4	35,000	21,000	22	65	24,000	13,500
	61S-T6	45,000	40,000	12	95	30,000	13,500
	63S-T42	22,000	13,000	20 ‡	42	14,000	9,500
	63S-T5	27,000	21,000	12 ‡	60	17,000	9,500
	63S-T6	35,000	31,000	12	73	22,000	9,500
Aluminum-zinc-magnesium-copper type sheet	75S-O	33,000	15,000	17	60	22,000	—
	75S-T6	82,000	72,000	11	150	49,000	24,000
Aluminum-magnesium type	150S-O	21,000	8,500	—	—	14,000	12,000
	150S-H22	23,500	16,500	—	—	15,000	12,500
	150S-H32	25,500	21,000	—	—	16,000	12,500
	150S-H18	33,000	31,000	—	—	19,500	13,500

* *Courtesy* Aluminum Co. of America.
† Sheet specimens, 1/16 in. thick, except marked ‡ which are round specimens, 1/2 in. in diam.

products, rivets, and forgings. The characteristics and applications of the most important wrought aluminum alloys are described in Table 12.16.

12.36 Mechanical Properties. Typical mechanical properties of wrought aluminum alloys are given in Table 12.17. The yield strength of structural aluminum alloys is rather high in proportion to tensile strength. The ductility is reduced by cold working, but is in general high. The modulus of elasticity is between 10,300,000 and 10,500,000 pounds per square inch. The modulus of rigidity (ratio of shear stress to shear strain) is approximately 3,850,000 pounds per square inch. The endurance limit is the maximum stress that can be applied to a specimen for 500 million completely reversed cycles at a speed of 10,000 revolutions per minute without fracture. Endurance limits vary from 24,000 pounds per square inch for 75S-T6 zinc-bearing aluminum alloy down to 5000 pounds per square inch for 2S-O commercial aluminum; these values are somewhat lower than for carbon steels.

The high ratio of tensile strength to specific gravity (specific tensile strength) is the most significant factor of aluminum alloys for selection for structural applications. Table 12.18 gives comparative strength ratios of various alloys and steels.

Table 12.18

COMPARATIVE STRENGTH-WEIGHT RATIOS OF COMMON ALLOYS *

Alloy	Specific Gravity	Density, lb. per cu. in.	Tensile Strength, p.s.i.	Specific Tensile Strength	Yield Strength, p.s.i.	Specific Yield Strength
Structural steel	7.8	0.28	60,000	7,700	35,000	4,500
Aluminum (clad 24S-T4)	2.8	0.10	64,000	22,800	42,000	15,000
Aluminum (clad 24S-T86)	2.8	0.10	70,000	25,000	66,000	23,600
Magnesium (AZ61X)	1.8	0.065	44,000	24,400	29,000	16,100
Brass (67% Zn-33% Cu)	8.5	0.307	75,000	8,800	55,000	6,500
Stainless steel (Austenitic 18:8 full hard)	7.8	0.28	185,000	23,700	140,000	17,900
Chrome-molybdenum steel (SAE 4140)	7.8	0.28	156,000	20,000	131,000	16,800

* *Materials & Methods, Manual* 71, June, 1951, p. 97.

12.37 Clad Products. "Clad" products are manufactured by bonding a thin layer of corrosion-resistant aluminum to a core of high-strength aluminum alloy which is less corrosion resistant. Bonding is accomplished by rolling the layers while hot which causes diffusion of the core into the aluminum layer. The resulting integral structure is shown in the photomicrograph, Fig. 12.4. The surface layer is so thin that the loss in tensile strength is only about 1 per cent. An example is clad 24S sheet or plate which is coated with 99.3 per cent minimum aluminum; the core strength of 24S is combined with excellent resistance to corrosion of high-purity aluminum.

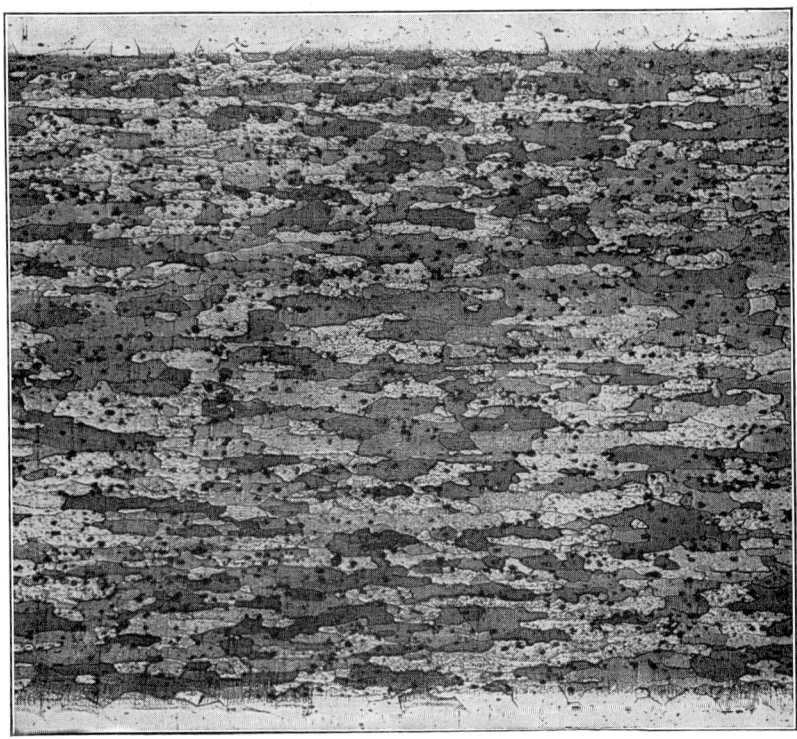

Fig. 12.4. Full cross-section of 0.040-in. Alclad 24S-T4(-T) sheet 100×. Etched: HF-HCl-HNO$_3$ solution, 15 sec. Etching differentiates between surface layers of high-purity aluminum and 24S-T4(-T) core. Diffusion zones, resulting from migration of copper and magnesium into the coating layers, are evident. (*Courtesy* A. G. H. Dietz: *Engineering Laminates.* Published by John Wiley & Sons.)

12.38 Aluminum Alloy Gears. Wrought aluminum alloy 14S-T6 is superior to cast aluminum alloys in resistance to pitting in connection with surface wear of gears and rollers. Aluminum alloy gears must be mated with ferrous or non-ferrous gears of high hardness to prevent scoring of the tooth surfaces. (See reference 12.17.)

12.39 Codification of Light-Weight Metals and Alloys. In 1952 the American Society for Testing Materials published a codification of light-weight metals and alloys, both cast and wrought. The designations are based on chemical composition limits. The full name of the base metal precedes the designation. The temper designation follows the alloy designation. (See *ASTM, Book of Standards,* 1952, Part 2.)

12.40 Aluminum-Coated Iron and Steel. Aluminum-coated iron and steel have the surface characteristics of aluminum coupled with the mechanical properties of the ferrous core. Typical core materials are cast iron, mild carbon steel, copper steel, and low-alloy high-strength steel. The coated products are produced in the form of wires, rods, and sheets. The coating of aluminum usually is about 0.5 ounces per square foot of surface which corresponds approximately to 0.001 inches per side.

The essential feature of the process is to subject ferrous metal to the action of a reducing gas such as hydrogen before placing it into the aluminum bath. This treatment removes oxygen and causes reduction of oxides on the surface of the ferrous metal and also charges the surface with enough of the reducing gas to insure a satisfactory union with aluminum at the time of immersion. This product can be subjected to metal working without cracking or detachment of the coating. The material is corrosion resistant and fireproof up to 954° C. (1750° F.).

Typical mechanical properties of hot-dipped aluminum-coated low-carbon steel are as follows: tensile strength, 45,000 pounds per square inch; yield point, 30,000 pounds per square inch; elongation in 2 inches, 15 to 25 per cent; and Rockwell B hardness, a maximum of 70.

Applications include jackets of circulating heaters and internal combustion engine mufflers and tailpipes where heat and corrosion resistance are required.

ALLOYS OF MAGNESIUM

12.41 Alloys of Magnesium. The addition of aluminum to magnesium up to about 9 per cent produces a solid solution called the "delta" phase which has much greater strength and somewhat greater ductility than magnesium. The low specific gravity of 1.8 of this alloy is of great importance. Owing to its light weight it is employed in airplane construction for structural shapes, chair frames, engine parts such as cast pistons and crankcases, and forged propellers. It is also used to some extent in automobile construction.

12.42 Castings. The chemical compositions of typical magnesium-alloy sand castings and permanent-mold castings are given in Table 12.19. The addition of manganese improves resistance against corrosion by salt water and salt-water atmosphere, and also makes the metal capable of being welded. For molding in sand, an alloy of rather high zinc content (2.5 to 3.5 per cent) is suitable because zinc gives ductility and casting fluidity.

Magnesium-zirconium casting alloys minimize uneven heat distribution through the mold so that microporosity is almost eliminated, and possess good mechanical properties; zirconium acts as a powerful grain refiner.

For press work, 8.5 per cent aluminum content is quite good. For die castings, an aluminum content of 8.3 to 9.7 per cent is specified in order to give greater fluidity than is possessed by alloys of lower aluminum percentage. Magnesium alloy containing 12 per cent aluminum has increased strength and hardness when heat treated but is too brittle for many purposes.

12.43 Wrought Magnesium Alloys. Table 12.19 gives chemical compositions of four wrought magnesium alloys and one forging alloy.

Table 12.19

CHEMICAL COMPOSITION OF MAGNESIUM ALLOYS

ASTM Designation	Forms	Aluminum, %	Zinc, %	Manganese, min., %	Tin, %
AZ31X	Extruded bars, rods,	2.5–3.5	0.6–1.4	0.20	——
AZ61X	shapes, and tubes	5.8–7.2	0.4–1.5	0.15	——
AZ80X		7.8–9.2	0.2–0.8	0.12	——
M1		——	——	1.20	——
TA54	Forgings	3.0–4.0	——	0.20	4.0–6.0
AZ63	Sand castings	5.3–6.7	2.5–3.5	0.15	——
AZ92	Permanent mold castings	8.3–9.7	1.7–2.3	0.10	——
AZ90	Die castings	8.3–9.7	0.4–1.0	0.13	——

Magnesium alloys have certain disadvantages as compared with aluminum alloys. Cold shaping at room temperature of magnesium alloys must be carefully controlled, but, if the alloy is heated to 225° C. (437° F.), molding and shaping are made much easier. The hexagonal space lattice of the crystals does not permit rapid change of shape as obtained by means of drop hammers or spindle presses, but the hydraulic press is of advantage in shaping since pressure can be applied slowly. Rolling should be carried out only at a temperature of at least 300° C. (572° F.).

Advantages of magnesium alloys are lower specific gravity and good machineability which are significant with respect to shipping charges, handling expense, and machining costs.

12.44 Physical Properties. Mechanical properties of typical magnesium alloys are given in Table 12.20. Table 12.18 gives the specific tensile strength of magnesium alloy.

The thermal conductivity of magnesium-aluminum alloys is about 0.200 (gram-cal. per sec. per cm.-cube per ° C.), which is less than for magnesium or aluminum, but greater than for cast iron, whose value is 0.147. Its

Table 12.20

TYPICAL MECHANICAL PROPERTIES OF MAGNESIUM ALLOYS

ASTM Designation	Forms	Tensile Strength, p.s.i.	Tensile Yield Strength (0.2%), p.s.i.	Elongation in 2 in., %	Compressive Yield Strength (0.2%), p.s.i.	Shearing Strength, p.s.i.	Endurance Limit, p.s.i.	Brinell Hardness	Charpy Impact Strength, ft.-lb.
AZ31X	Extruded bars	39,000	28,000	12	17,000	19,000	14,000	50	3.2
AZ61X		45,000	32,000	15	21,000	21,000	17,000	60	3.0
AZ80X		49,000	35,000	10	26,000	21,000	19,000	67	2.2
M1		38,000	28,000	8	13,000	16,000	9,000	46	2.1
TA54	Forgings	40,000	28,000	12	21,000	16,000	11,000	52	2.0
AZ63-AC *	Sand castings	29,000	14,000	6	14,000	18,000	11,000	50	3.0
AZ63-HT †		40,000	14,000	12	14,000	19,000	14,000	55	5.0
AZ63-HTA ‡		40,000	19,000	5	19,000	21,000	13,000	73	2.0
AZ92-AC	Permanent mold castings	24,000	14,000	2	14,000	19,000	11,000	65	1.0
AZ92-HT		40,000	14,000	10	14,000	20,000	14,000	63	4.0
AZ92-HTA		40,000	22,000	2	23,000	21,000	13,000	83	1.0
AZ90-AC	Die castings	36,000	23,000	4	23,000	20,000	14,000	60	2.0

* As-cast.
† Heat-treated.
‡ Heat-treated and aged.

Non-Ferrous Metals and Alloys

thermal coefficient of expansion is 0.000029 per ° C. as compared to 0.000011 for cast iron. Its melting point is about 620° C. (1148° F.), depending on composition. Magnesium alloys in a finely divided state will burn, but large sections in the solid state are not easily ignited.

Dow metal is the commercial name of a magnesium-aluminum alloy. *Electron metal* is the commercial name applied to a magnesium alloy containing about 4 per cent zinc and small percentages of copper, iron, and silicon. It has a tensile strength of about 40,000 pounds per square inch and an elongation in 2 inches of about 18 per cent. Its applications are similar to those of magnesium-aluminum alloys.

12.45 Corrosion Resistance. Electrolytic corrosion presents a difficult problem in the design of an assembly in which dissimilar metals come into contact; this is especially critical with magnesium because of its high position in the electromotive series. Galvanic corrosion is avoided by treating all faying surfaces with a coat of zinc chromate primer followed by a coat of aluminum lacquer. A ferrous metal used next to a magnesium alloy should be plated with zinc or cadmium. For magnesium alloy structures exposed to severe salt sprays, a zinc chromate primer followed by lacquers, enamels, or varnishes should be applied over a chrome pickled treatment of the metal surface.

Alloys of Nickel

12.46 Monel Metal. An important alloy of nickel with copper and small percentages of other elements is the so-called natural alloy, Monel metal, obtained by the direct smelting of a Canadian ore. The process consists of calcination of copper-nickel sulfide ore, reduction of the corresponding oxide with charcoal in acid open-hearth furnaces, and refining in basic electric furnaces. The regular Monel metal, designated as B Monel metal, is a solid solution; its chemical and mechanical properties are given in Table 12.21. It is of value chiefly because of its great resistance to corrosive liquids, acids, pickling solutions, mine waters, and the like, and because of the fact that it retains its physical properties at temperatures considerably higher than most of the common alloys, both non-ferrous and steel. The effect of temperature on the tensile properties of B Monel metal is shown in Fig. 12.5.

R Monel metal is a special alloy containing a small amount of sulfur to give free-machining properties and is adapted to the manufacture of automatic screw-machine products.

K Monel metal is a special alloy produced by the addition of 2–4 per cent of aluminum to Monel metal. It has age-hardening properties and is non-magnetic. It is used for pump rods and propeller shafts. The chemical and mechanical properties of R and K Monel metals are given in Table 12.21.

Table 12.21

CHEMICAL AND MECHANICAL PROPERTIES OF MONEL METAL AND INCONEL METAL *

	B Monel, Hot-Rolled	B Monel, Cold-Drawn, 24% Reduction, Stress Relieved	B Monel, Cold-Drawn, Annealed 1450° F., 3 hr.	R Monel, Hot-Rolled	K Monel, Hot-Rolled	K Monel, Cold-Drawn, Age-Hardened 10 hr. at 1050° F.	Inconel, Hot-Rolled
Nickel, %	66.7	66.7	66.7	66.6	65.0	65.0	81.0
Copper, %	31.3	31.3	31.3	31.1	30.1	30.1	0.1
Aluminum, %	—	—	—	—	3.2	3.2	—
Chromium, %	—	—	—	—	—	—	13.0
Iron, %	0.8	0.8	0.8	1.1	0.8	0.8	5.5
Manganese, %	0.9	0.9	0.9	1.0	0.5	0.5	0.1
Sulfur, %	0.007	0.007	0.007	0.041	0.005	0.005	0.008
Tensile strength, p.s.i.	83,750	97,250	78,350	75,600	99,900	157,650	91,150
Yield strength, p.s.i. (0.2% offset)	40,650	86,650	33,350	35,650	47,000	119,650	47,000
Elongation in 2 in., %	39.5	27.0	44.0	39.5	42.5	22.0	42.0
Reduction of area, %	67.5	66.4	65.9	68.9	63.7	37.5	66.0
Compression yield strength, p.s.i. (0.2% offset)	38,050	80,750	28,250	33,500	40,350	121,250	41,950
Brinell hardness (3000-kg. load)	145	199	123	121	163	329	159
Charpy impact, ft.-lb.	232	151	206	187	170	42	191

* C. F. Catlin and W. A. Mudge: *Proc. ASTM*, v. 38, Part II, 1938.

Inconel Metal. This nickel-chromium-iron alloy has corrosion resistance against tarnishing and is used in the food industries. It is non-magnetic, and because of its freedom from scaling and intercrystalline attack it is suitable for use at elevated temperatures. Its properties are also given in Table 12.21.

12.47 Nickel Silver. Nickel silver or German silver is brass to which nickel has been added. It is valuable chiefly because of its silvery white

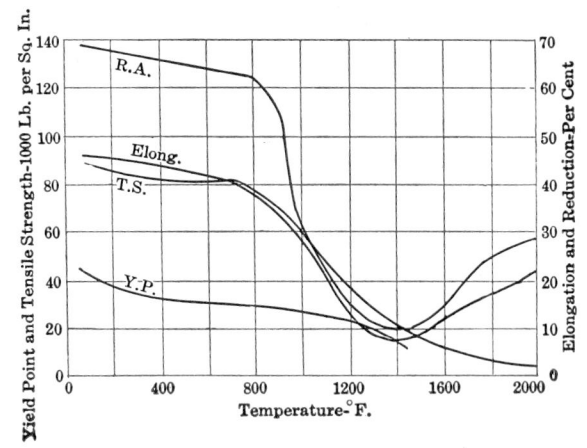

Fig. 12.5. Properties of B Monel metal at high temperatures.

color and its resistance to corrosion. The typical compositions of nickel silver are nickel 5 to 30 per cent, zinc 10 to 35 per cent, and copper 50 to 80 per cent. Nickel silver is principally used in the making of physical and scientific instruments. Tungsten up to 1 or 2 per cent is also occasionally added to form an alloy called *platinoid* which has unusually high electrical resistance and is used for electrical purposes.

Alloys of Titanium

12.48 General. Titanium alloys are preferred to commercial titanium for certain applications because of greatly increased tensile strength.

12.49 Constitution. The alpha phase of titanium has an hexagonal close-packed crystal structure up to 1625° F.; at higher temperatures, the body-centered cubic beta phase exists.

12.50 Composition. Titanium alloys contain combinations of chromium, iron, aluminum, vanadium, molybdenum, and manganese in small percentages. Elements such as chromium, iron, vanadium, molybdenum, and manganese tend to stabilize the high-temperature modification (the beta phase) of titanium and to produce alloys which are hardenable by heat treatment. Aluminum, nitrogen, and oxygen tend to strengthen the low-temperature modification (the alpha phase).

12.51 Mechanical Properties. Mechanical properties of a typical titanium alloy are given in Table 12.22. The tensile strength and yield strength is greatly increased as compared to commercial titanium; hardness is increased to some extent, and the ductility is not decreased appreciably. In view of the low specific gravity of 4.5, titanium alloys have an excep-

Table 12.22

MECHANICAL PROPERTIES OF TITANIUM AND TITANIUM ALLOY *

Type	Form	Condition	Tensile Strength, p.s.i.	Yield Strength (0.2% offset), p.s.i.	Elongation in 2 in., %	Reduction of Area, %	Rockwell Hardness
Commercial titanium RC55 (carbon 0.2% max.)	Sheet, bar, and plate	Annealed	75,000	65,000	25	55	50–54A
	Forgings	Annealed	75,000	65,000	15	30	50–54A
Ti 100A (carbon 0.02% max.)	Sheet and strip	Annealed	110,000	95,000	17.5	—	98B
	Wire	Annealed	108,000	88,000	22.5 †	47.5	—
	Wire	Cold-drawn full hard	190,000	160,000	12.5 †	25	—
Titanium alloy MST, 2.5 Fe, 2.5 V	Sheet, 0.04 in.	Annealed 1 hr. at 1300° F.	135,000	125,000	10	—	65A
	Sheet, 0.04 in.	Cold-worked	175,000	170,000	2	—	68A
	Forgings	Hot-forged 80% reduction	130,000	105,000	12	35	65A

* J. L. Everhart: Titanium and Its Alloys, *Materials & Methods*, May, 1952, p. 117.
† Per cent elongation in 4 diameters.

tionally high specific tensile strength: In annealed condition, 135,000/4.5 = 30,000, and in cold-worked condition, 175,000/4.5 = 38,900. (Compare with values in Table 12.18.)

12.52 Uses. Uses are similar to those of titanium but particularly for those applications requiring very great strength for a minimum weight. Considerable research on titanium alloys is in progress.

DIE-CASTING ALLOYS

12.53 Die Castings. Die casting consists of forming one casting after another from molten metal under pressure by means of a permanent mold. Pressures vary from 10 to over 20,000 pounds per square inch. Die castings can be formed sufficiently close to dimensions so that for many purposes machining is not required; they can be polished or chromium-plated to improve the appearance. Die castings are used a great deal in automobile construction and for small machine parts. Alloys of zinc are most common for die casting, but alloys of aluminum, magnesium, and copper are also suitable for the purpose.

12.54 Zinc Die-Casting Alloys. The chemical compositions and mechanical properties of the two most used zinc die-casting alloys are given in Table 12.23. These alloys are subject to a slight shrinkage after casting, occurring over a period of several weeks. It is possible to produce this shrinkage quickly by a stabilizing anneal; no dimensional changes occur in these alloys after such annealing for 3–6 hours at 212° F. Exposure to

Non-Ferrous Metals and Alloys

Table 12.23

CHEMICAL COMPOSITIONS AND MECHANICAL PROPERTIES OF ZINC DIE-CASTING ALLOYS *

Property	Alloy	Alloy
ASTM No. (B86–48)	XXIII	XXV
SAE No.	903	925
Aluminum, %	3.5–4.3	3.5–4.3
Copper, %	0.10 †	0.75–1.25
Magnesium	0.03–0.08	0.03–0.08
Iron, %	0.10	0.10
Lead, %	0.007	0.007
Cadmium, %	0.005	0.005
Tin, %	0.005	0.005
Zinc, %	Remainder	Remainder
Tensile strength, p.s.i.	41,000	47,000
Elongation in 2 in., %	10	7
Compressive strength, p.s.i.	60,000	87,000
Shearing strength, p.s.i.	31,000	38,000
Brinell hardness	82	91
Impact strength, ft.-lb.		
(¼ by ¼ in. bar)	43	47
Transverse deflection, in.	0.27	0.16
Endurance limit, p.s.i.	6,500	7,675

* Reference: *SAE Handbook 1952*, pp. 226–227.
† Percentages are a maximum except where a range is given.

stagnant moisture or condensation with limited access to oxygen may cause a non-uniform type of corrosion on zinc die castings, producing a white bulky film of corrosion products. The presence of small quantities of lead in zinc in a short time brings about a change in physical and dimensional stability, but this tendency is corrected by using an antidote of about 1 per cent copper. Magnesium is also used as an antidote but does not give as good strength or hardness as copper.

12.55 Aluminum Die-Casting Alloys. The American Society for Testing Materials has specifications covering ten aluminum-base alloys of different compositions for die casting. Table 12.24 gives the chemical compositions of these alloys. Mechanical properties are given in Table 12.25, and characteristics and applications are indicated in Table 12.26. Advantages of aluminum die-casting alloys for automotive engine parts are lightness of metal and good heat-conducting and -dissipating characteristics. These alloys also have less resonance and are therefore quieter than most other alloys.

12.56 Magnesium Die-Casting Alloys. Magnesium alloy AZ90 is the alloy used in most applications of magnesium die castings. Its composition is given in Table 12.19, and its mechanical properties in Table 12.20. This

Table 12.24

ASTM CHEMICAL REQUIREMENTS FOR ALUMINUM DIE-CASTING ALLOYS

Alloy	Aluminum, %	Copper, %	Iron max., %	Silicon, %	Manganese, max., %	Magnesium %	Zinc, max., %	Nickel, max., %	Tin, max., %	Other Constituents Except Aluminum, max., (total), %
G2	Remainder	0.2 max.	1.8	0.3 max.	0.3	7.5–8.5	0.1	0.1	0.1	0.2
S4	Remainder	0.6 max.	2.0	4.5– 6.0	0.3	0.1 max.	0.5	0.5	0.1	0.2
S5	Remainder	0.6 max.	2.0	11.0–13.0	0.3	0.1 max.	0.5	0.5	0.1	0.2
S9	Remainder	0.6 max.	1.3	11.0–13.0	0.3	0.1 max.	0.5	0.5	0.1	0.2
SC2	Remainder	3.0–4.0	2.0	4.5– 5.5	0.5	0.1 max.	1.0	0.5	0.3	0.5
SC5	Remainder	3.0–4.0	1.3	4.5– 5.5	0.5	0.1 max.	1.0	0.5	0.3	0.5
SC6	Remainder	3.0–4.0	1.3	7.5– 9.5	0.5	0.1 max.	1.0	0.5	0.3	0.5
SC7	Remainder	3.0–4.0	2.0	7.5– 9.5	0.5	0.1 max.	1.0	0.5	0.3	0.5
SG2	Remainder	0.6 max.	1.3	9.0–10.0	0.3	0.4–0.6	0.5	0.5	0.1	0.2
SG3	Remainder	0.6 max.	2.0	9.0–10.0	0.3	0.4–0.6	0.5	0.5	0.1	0.2

Table 12.25

MECHANICAL PROPERTIES OF ALUMINUM DIE-CASTING ALLOYS

Alloy	Tension Tests on Round Specimens — Tensile Strength, p.s.i.	Elongation in 2 in., %	Charpy Impact on Square Specimens, ft.-lb.
G2	30,000	5.0	4.5
S4	30,000	5.0	4.5
S5	37,000	1.8	2.0
S9	35,000	3.5	—
SC2	38,000	2.5	2.5
SC5	35,000	3.0	3.0
SC6	41,000	3.0	3.5
SC7	43,000	2.0	3.2
SG2	43,000	5.0	4.2
SG3	43,000	3.0	2.7

magnesium alloy has very good casting and physical properties; castings may be produced with very smooth surfaces and high dimensional accuracy which requires a minimum amount of machining. It is available only in the "as-cast" condition.

12.57 Brass Die Castings. It has been found possible to force brass into die cavities by means of high pressure at a temperature somewhat below the melting point. The copper content of brass die castings ranges from 57 to 81.5 per cent, but brass having a composition of 60 per cent copper and 40 per cent zinc with the comparatively low melting point of 904° C.

Table 12.26
CHARACTERISTICS AND TYPICAL APPLICATIONS OF ALUMINUM DIE-CASTING ALLOYS *

Alloy	Casting Properties	Machinability	Corrosion Resistance	Typical Applications
G5	Fair	Very good	Excellent	Suitable for all casting processes
S4	Very good	Fair	Good	Thin general-purpose castings; marine fittings, carburetor bodies, outboard-engine parts
S5	Excellent	Fair	Very good	General-purpose castings of intricate design with thin sections; outboard-engine frames
S9	Excellent	Fair	Very good	Same as S5 but where greater ductility is required
SC2	Good	Good	Fair	Simple castings without thin walls; brackets, frames, and levers with thick sections
SC5	Good	Good	Fair	Same as SC2 but where greater ductility is required
SC6	Very good	Good	Fair	Similar to SC7 but where higher ductility is required
SC7	Very good	Good	Fair	General-purpose castings; satisfactory for thinner sections than SC2 or SC5
SG2	Excellent	Good	Excellent	Same as SG3 but where higher ductility is required
SG3	Excellent	Good	Excellent	General-purpose castings requiring high resistance to corrosion; cover plates, instrument cases

* Selected from *Materials & Methods*.

(1655° F.) is generally used since it is less severe on dies than brasses of higher copper content and yet has good physical properties. Brass die castings have good strength and corrosion resistance. They have mechanical properties superior to those of brass sand castings for the same alloy owing to a finer grain size, and have better surface finish and soundness, and greater dimensional accuracy. Brass sand castings which require little machining are cheaper, however. Forgings have better machinability and soundness than die castings. Applications of brass die castings are for automotive gears, shock-absorber parts, bearings, pumps, and parts for electrical switchboards.

BEARING METALS

12.58 Special Bearing or Antifriction Metals. The bearing bronzes and the lead-antimony bearing metals have been already considered. Aside from the bearing bronzes, the best-known bearing metals are those composed of tin, copper, and antimony, which are called *babbitt metal*. The composition of this alloy is extremely variable, but the usual limits are tin 80 to 90 per cent, copper 3 to 10 per cent, and antimony 8 to 12 per cent. The quantity of antimony should always exceed the amount of copper in order to prevent brittleness. The ultimate constitution of babbitt metals appears to be that of a ground mass of soft tin with hard crystals of a copper-antimony compound and a tin-antimony compound scattered through it. The hard particles carry the load and resist wear, while the soft ground mass allows the metal to adjust itself to the surface of the shaft and equalize the bearing pressure.

Alloys of lead, tin, and antimony have been considerably used as bearing metals, the best compositions being those containing 10 to 15 per cent of antimony, 10 to 20 per cent of tin, and the balance lead.

Alloys of lead, copper, and antimony have occasionally been used as bearing metals where heavy loads are encountered. A typical composition is lead, 65 per cent; copper, 10 per cent; and antimony, 25 per cent.

The American Society for Testing Materials has published composition specifications for a large list of white metals or babbitts. The Society of Automotive Engineers has also published specifications for six babbitts which, it is believed, will meet all ordinary needs, and from which the summary in Table 12.27 has been made.

Table 12.27

SAE BABBITT METALS

Approximate Composition

SAE Number	Sn	Cu	Sb	Pb
10	90.0	5.0	5.0	—
11	87.0	6.0	7.0	—
12	89.0	3.5	7.5	—
13	5.0	0.5	9.5	85.0
14	9.5	0.5	15.0	75.0
15	1.0	0.5	15.0	83.0

Alloy 10 is a very fluid tin babbitt for thin linings or bronze-backed bearings. Alloy 11 is a rather hard tin babbitt which may be used under heavy pressures. It has very little "wiping" tendency. Alloy 12 is a tin babbitt which is somewhat stronger and harder than alloy 10. Alloys 13, 14, and 15 are comparatively cheap lead babbitts. Alloy 13 is used only under light loads and at low speeds; a typical application is railroad-car journal bearings. Alloy 14 is for moderate loads and speeds; applications are for bearings for blowers and pumps. Alloy 15 is for bearings under heavy loads and at high speeds; typical uses include bearings for diesel engines, automotive engines, steamships, and steel mills. Figure 12.6 shows the structure of typical babbitt metals.

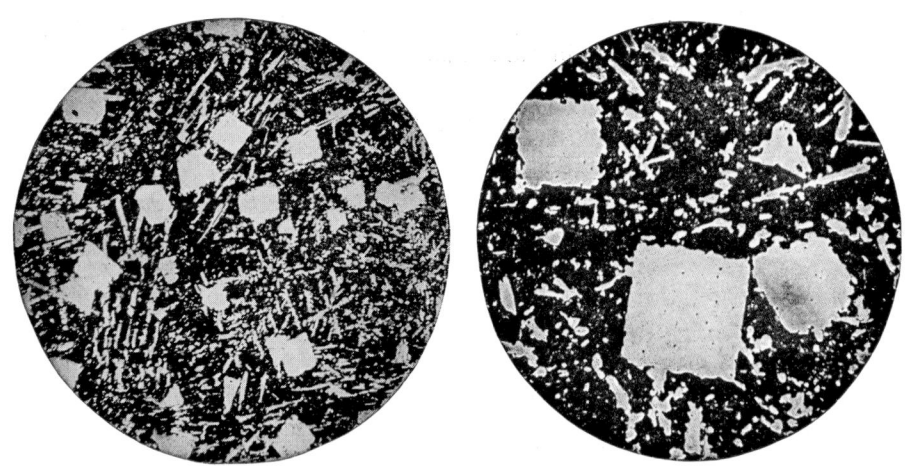

Fig. 12.6. Structure of typical babbitt metals 100×.

Powder Metallurgy

12.59 General. Powder metallurgy comprises the pressing and sintering of metal powders. It is utilized primarily for the fabrication of small structural parts. Parts of pressed and sintered metal powders have in some instances replaced competitive stampings, die castings, small sand castings, and screw-machined parts. Examples of conversions include bezel rings, notched rings, brake disks, and rotors. Precision machining may be eliminated in some cases by such conversion.

12.60 Metal Powders. Methods of converting metal into powder comprise atomization, reduction, electrolysis, and decomposition. Atomization is accomplished by blasting a stream of molten metal by a high-pressure stream of water or air to produce disintegration into small drops which freeze quickly into powder. The powder particles are sphere-like in shape. Reduction or roasting of metal oxides produces a sponge-like metal which can be easily ground to a spongy powder. By electrolysis, metals may be deposited on a cathode in fine granular form. The granular particles are easily removable. By decomposition, metal salts may be decomposed under heat and pressure to produce a metal powder.

12.61 Sintered Aluminum Powder. Sintered aluminum powder is produced by cold-pressing aluminum powder of fine particle size into briquets under a pressure of 300 to 700 pounds per square inch, sintering the briquets at a temperature of from 900 to 1100° F., followed by hot-pressing under 700 pounds per square inch pressure and finally extruding the material into rods. Its specific gravity is 2.8. It can be further worked either hot or cold into sheets, shapes, or drop forgings. Exposure to temperatures as high as 900° F. for 100 hours results in little change in room temperature properties.

The relatively high mechanical properties at room temperature and at high temperatures are indicated in Table 12.28.

Table 12.28

MECHANICAL PROPERTIES OF SINTERED ALUMINUM POWDER AT ROOM AND HIGH TEMPERATURES *

Temperature, °F.	Tensile Strength, p.s.i.	Yield Strength (0.2% offset), p.s.i.	Elongation in 2 in., %
72	50,000	34,200	10
212	40,000	34,000	10
392	32,800	30,530	8
752	21,300	20,600	4
932	14,200	13,500	2

* *Materials & Methods*, Aug., 1952, p. 89.

12.62 Copper-Alloy Infiltrated Iron. Stator blades for gas turbines have been produced of copper-alloy infiltrated iron. Iron powder is molded by a die and then sintered. It is then coined to exact dimensions of a blade. After coining, the porous blade is infiltrated with a copper alloy to the greatest density possible and heat treated to develop strength properties. Tensile strengths of 90,000 pounds per square inch with elongations of 8 per cent have been developed.

12.63 Porous Metals. Powder metallurgy is utilized to produce porous metals. Examples are filters, bearings, and blades of jet-engine turbines. *Porous filters* are manufactured by sintering spherical particles produced by atomization. Such filters of brass and bronze are used in fuel lines for filtering fuels oils, diesel oils, and gasoline.

Porous bearings are manufactured by mixing a lubricant with the powder and then, after pressing the mixture to desired shape, the lubricant is evaporated while being sintered. The resultant bearing has many small-size interconnected pores. By immersing the porous bearing in hot oil, the pores become saturated with the oil, thus forming a reservoir. The bearing surfaces require no further lubrication because oil is drawn from the pores during operating periods; during non-operating periods, the oil seeps back into the pores forming a reservoir for future use.

In order to utilize the principle of transpiration cooling, powder metallurgy is used to produce *porous blades* for jet-engine turbines which are subjected to extremely high temperatures. In transpiration cooling (also called sweat cooling), a stream of coolant either gas or liquid is forced through the permeable metal of the turbine blade in a direction opposite to the flow of heat. The coolant gets hotter while flowing through the permeable blade. When the coolant reaches the surface, it forms a protective layer. In this manner significant temperature drops up to 500° F. can be obtained. In order to obtain desired temperature drops, the permeability of the sintered powder metal must be carefully controlled. Maximum permeability for a given porosity is desirable in order to obtain high strengths. Transpiration cooling makes possible utilization of less strategic metals because blade temperatures can be reduced materially below those of the gas.

12.64 High-Temperature Alloys. By means of powder metallurgy, pressed and sintered shapes of *molybdenum-base alloys* measuring 6 inches square by 4 feet long and weighing over 400 pounds can be produced. The creep and stress-rupture properties at temperatures in excess of 1600° F. of molybdenum-base alloy compacts are exceptionally high.

Cermets also have excellent high-temperature properties. They comprise metal-bonded carbides, borides, nitrides, oxides, aluminides, and silicides. Pressing and sintering techniques of powder metallurgy are employed. A good example of a cermet is cemented titanium carbide. It has good tensile properties up to 1800° F. and excellent oxidation-resistance and thermal-shock characteristics. Applications of molybdenum-base alloys and titanium-carbide cermets are for turbine blades of jet engines.

12.65 Cemented Carbide Tools. Cemented carbide tools are extremely hard and are used as cutting tools and drawing dies. A typical example is tungsten carbide tools composed of tungsten carbide powder and from 3–13 per cent cobalt powder as a matrix. Nickel powder and iron powder are also used as matrix materials. Cemented tungsten carbide with 6 per cent cobalt has a compressive strength of 750,000 pounds per square inch and a modulus of elasticity of 88,000,000 pounds per square inch. It has a Rockwell A hardness of 90, and its specific gravity is 14.85. It is used for cutting non-ferrous metals, cast iron, and thermosetting plastics.

12.66 Non-Alloying Metals. Metals which can not be alloyed can be utilized in mixtures by means of powder metallurgy. Pressed and sintered compacts can be manufactured from powders of metals which will not form alloys. Examples are copper and lead for bearings and tungsten and silver for electrical contact points. Molybdenum and silver compacts are also used for electrical applications such as circuit breakers. The desirable features of these electrical materials are the hardness and resistance to arcing of tungsten or molybdenum and the excellent corrosion resistance and high electrical conductivity of the silver.

Questions

12.1. Name the essential steps in extracting copper from sulfide ores.

12.2. Discuss briefly the relation between the strength of copper and the mechanical treatment to which it has been subjected.

12.3. Discuss the corrosion resistance of copper.

12.4. What are the chief uses of copper?
12.5. Explain how zinc spelter protects galvanized iron from corrosion.
12.6. State the principal uses of zinc.
12.7. What are the commercial forms of lead?
12.8. What are the main properties of lead usually taken into account? What is the significance of the tensile strength of lead? Why?
12.9. What are the principal sources and properties of tin?
12.10. Describe in general the effect of cold working upon the tensile properties of aluminum.
12.11. Discuss the resistance of aluminum to corrosion.
12.12. Compare the electrical conductivity of copper and aluminum.
12.13. Compare the methods of manufacturing zinc, lead, aluminum, and magnesium.
12.14. What are the important properties and uses of magnesium? of titanium?
12.15. Describe the physical properties of nickel.
12.16. Identify the alpha phase of bronze.
12.17. How do the physical properties of bronze vary with increase in tin content?
12.18. It is desired to select a bronze for a pressure-tight casting for a vessel of thin section subject to moderate hydraulic pressure by water from a city water supply. A free-machining metal of free-flowing characteristics requiring no special skill in foundry technique is wanted. What bronze would you recommend to meet these requirements? Give reasons.
12.19. A bearing metal to be selected for a rock crusher in a quarry will be subjected to abrasive material. What bearing metal would be suitable? Why?
12.20. A bridge bearing is to be installed to withstand slow-moving, heavy loads. The metal must be strong, hard, and shock resistant. What metal would you select? State your reasons.
12.21. A bronze for manufacturing a pump runner for operation in fresh water is required. A metal of moderate strength, excellent casting qualities, good machinability, and low cost is desired. What would you recommend?
12.22. A corrosion-resisting bronze is needed for a pump impeller for handling a dilute solution of sulfuric acid. Good fatigue resistance is also desired, and a minimum tensile strength of 65,000 pounds per square inch is required. Select a bronze for this service, and give reasons for your selection.
12.23. What are the composition, properties, and uses of (*a*) phosphor bronze? (*b*) silicon bronze? (*c*) manganese bronze? (*d*) aluminum bronze? (*e*) gun metal?
12.24. What are the principal properties of beryllium bronze?
12.25. What is the composition of statuary bronze? What is meant by "patina"?
12.26. Describe the constitution of brasses.
12.27. What is the composition of cartridge brass? How does its strength compare with that of copper? Where might it be used?
12.28. What causes "season cracking"? How can it be remedied?
12.29. Describe dezincification of brass.
12.30. Compare the compositions and uses of admiralty metal, naval brass, and Muntz metal.
12.31. Describe the properties of heat-treatable aluminum alloys.
12.32. Describe the mechanical properties of wrought aluminum alloys.
12.33. What are "clad" products?
12.34. State the composition, properties, and uses of the principal alloys of magnesium.
12.35. Compare advantages and disadvantages of aluminum alloys and magnesium alloys.

Non-Ferrous Metals and Alloys

12.36. State the composition, properties, and uses of Monel metal and nickel silver.
12.37. Describe the mechanical properties of a typical titanium alloy.
12.38. Describe the composition, properties, and uses of the principal die-casting alloys.
12.39. What is babbitt metal, and why is it effective as a bearing metal?
12.40. Describe the properties of sintered aluminum powder.
12.41. How are porous bearings manufactured? How do they function?
12.42. Describe the principle of transpiration cooling of turbine blades.
12.43. What are the mechanical properties of cemented tungsten carbide?
12.44. How is powder metallurgy utilized in manufacturing high-temperature alloys?

References

12.1. Aluminum Company of America: *Alcoa Aluminum and Its Alloys.* Pittsburgh, Pa., 1947.
12.2. American Manganese Bronze Co.: *Bronze Casting Alloys, Reference Book.* Holmesburg, Philadelphia, 1945.
12.3. American Society for Metals: *Metals Handbook.* 1948 ed., Cleveland, Ohio, 1948.
12.4. American Society for Testing Materials: *Book of Standards, 1952.* Philadelphia, Pa.
12.5. Anderson, E. A.: "Zinc in the Chemical Industries." *Mech. Eng.,* Dec., 1936, pp. 799-802.
12.6. Bateman, J. H.: *Materials of Construction.* New York, Pitman Publishing Corp., 1950, 568 pages.
12.7. Brady, G. S.: *Materials Handbook.* McGraw-Hill Book Co., 7th ed., 1951, 913 pages.
12.8. Bray, J. L.: *Non-Ferrous Production Metallurgy.* John Wiley & Sons, 2nd ed., 1947.
12.9. Brown, D. I.: "Continuous Casting of Oxygen-Free Copper Raises Production." *Iron Age,* Aug. 30, 1951, p. 63. Also: "Continuous Casting Revolutionizes the Brass Industry." *Iron Age,* Sept. 6, 1951, p. 106. Also: "British Continuously Cast Large Aluminum Sections." *Iron Age,* Sept. 13, 1951, p. 166.
12.10. Desch, C. H.: *Metallography.* London, Longmans, Green & Co., 4th ed., 1938, 402 pages.
12.11. Dolan, T. J., and Brown, H. F.: "Effect of Prior Repeated Stressing on the Fatigue Life of 75S-T Aluminum." *Proc. ASTM,* v. 52, 1952, p. 733.
12.12. Dow Chemical Co.: *Dow Data Book.* Midland, Mich.
12.13. Dumond, T. C.: *Engineering Materials Manual.* New York, *Materials & Methods,* Reinhold Publishing Corp., 1951.
12.14. Eshbach, O. W.: *Handbook of Engineering Fundamentals.* New York, John Wiley & Sons, 2nd ed., 1952, Section 12.
12.15. Goetzel, C. G., and Seelig, R. P.: "Fatigue of Porous Metals." *Proc. ASTM,* v. 40, 1940, p. 746.
12.16. Gohn, G. R., and Menges, Lucille E.: "Atmospheric and Indoor Aging Studies on Some Aluminum- and Zinc-base Die-casting Alloys." *Proc. ASTM,* v. 46, 1946, p. 1064.
12.17. Gross, M. R.: Laboratory Evaluation of Materials for Marine Propulsion Gears. *Proc. ASTM,* v. 51, 1951, p. 701.
12.18. Hiers, G. O.: Corrosion-Resistant Lead Equipment. *Mech. Eng.,* Dec., 1936, pp. 793-798.
12.19. Hiers, G. O.: "Characteristics of Very Pure and Commercial Lead." *Trans. Am. Inst. Chem. Engrs.,* v. 20, 1927, pp. 131-148.

12.20. Hiers, G. O.: "Soft Solders and Their Application." *Metals & Alloys*, v. 2, 1931, p. 257.
12.21. Hoyt, S. L.: *Metals and Alloys Data Book*. New York, Reinhold Publishing Corp., 1943.
12.22. Jeffries, Z., and Archer, R. S.: *The Science of Metals*. McGraw-Hill Book Co., 1924, 500 pages.
12.23. Kelton, E. H.: Fatigue Testing of Zinc-Base Alloy Die Castings, *Proc. ASTM*, v. 42, 1942, p. 692.
12.24. LaQue, F. L.: "Nickel and Nickel-Base Alloys." *Mech. Eng.*, Dec., 1936, pp. 827–843.
12.25. Leighou, R. B.: *Chemistry of Engineering Materials*. McGraw-Hill Book Co., 4th ed., 1942, 645 pages.
12.26. Lazan, B. J., and Blatherwick, A. A.: "Strength Properties of Rolled Aluminum Alloys under Various Combinations of Alternating and Mean Axial Fatigue Stresses." *Proc. ASTM*, v. 53, 1953.
12.27. Lynes, W.: "Comparative Value of Arsenic, Antimony, and Phosphorus in Preventing Dezincification." *Proc. ASTM*, v. 41, 1941, p. 859.
12.28. Materials & Methods, Magazine, New York, Reinhold Publishing Corp.
12.29. Northern Aluminium Co.: *Extraction and Fabrication of Aluminium*. London, 1949, 113 pages.
12.30. Partridge, J. H.: *Glass-to-Metal Seals*. Sheffield, England, Soc. Glass Technol., 1949.
12.31. Peters, F. P.: "Electric-Resistance Alloys: Why Nickel-Chromium So Successfully Serves as Heating Element Material." *Trans. Electrochem. Soc.*, v. 68, 1935, pp. 29–42.
12.32. Reynolds Metal Co.: *Heat Treating Aluminum Alloys*. Louisville, Ky., 1948.
12.33. Richards, J. T.: "The Corrosion of Beryllium Copper Strip in Sea Water and Marine Atmospheres." *Proc. ASTM*, v. 53, 1953.
12.34. Sherby, O. D., Tietz, T. E., and Dorn, J. E.: "The Creep Properties of Some Forged and Cast Aluminum Alloys." *Proc. ASTM*, v. 51, 1951, p. 964.
12.35. Society of Automotive Engineers: *SAE Handbook 1952*. New York.
12.36. U. S. Naval Academy: *Engineering Materials*. Annapolis, Md., 1949.

Section III · Building Stones and Mineral Aggregates

CHAPTER 13

Building Stones and Stone Masonry

Originally Written by IRVING H. COWDREY [*]

Revised by LLOYD F. RADER

Building Stones

13.1 Stone as a Structural Material. The term "building stone" is applied to all those classes of natural rock which are employed for dimension stone and in masonry construction. Stones form, with the exception of timber, the only important class of materials that may without alteration of their natural state be used directly in the construction of engineering works.

Aside from purely structural uses, great quantities of stone are utilized on other kinds of engineering construction, such as for flagging and curbing, for paving blocks, and as crushed stone for road building, railroad ballast, and concrete aggregate (described in Chapter 14).

13.2 Classification of Rocks. *Geological Classification.* In the usual geological classification rocks are divided into *igneous rocks* formed by consolidation from a fused or semifused condition; *sedimentary rocks,* formed by the solidification of material transported and deposited by agents such as water, wind, and ice; and *metamorphic rocks,* which are formed by the gradual change of the structure and character of igneous or sedimentary rocks through the agency of heat, water, pressure, etc. Granite, greenstone, basalt, and lava are common examples of igneous rocks; sandstone, limestone and shale, of sedimentary rocks; gneiss, marble, and slate, of metamorphic rocks.

The geological classification has only a limited bearing upon the consideration of rocks as building stones. Igneous rocks are usually non-laminated and more or less crystalline in structure; sedimentary rocks are distinctly

[*] Associate Professor Emeritus of Testing Materials, Massachusetts Institute of Technology.

stratified, having, therefore, original cleavage planes; metamorphic rocks may or may not be laminated, depending upon the pressure encountered during metamorphism. Most of the metamorphic rocks which have been changed largely through the agency of pressure, water, and heat are crystalline in structure.

Physical Classification.[1] With respect to the structural character of large masses, rocks are divided into *stratified* and *unstratified*. The structure of unstratified rocks is, for the most part, an aggregate of crystalline grains firmly adhering together. Granite, trap, basalt, and lava are examples of this class.

Stratified rocks may be divided into the following classes according to physical structure:

Compact crystalline structure (marble).
Slaty structure (shale, slate).
Granular crystalline structure (gneiss, sandstone).
Compact granular structure (blue limestone).
Porous granular structure (minute shells cemented together).
Conglomerate (fragments of one stone imbedded in mass of another).

13.3 Granite. Granite is the term applied to a plutonic,[2] igneous rock, the structure of which varies from finely granular to coarsely crystalline. Its principal mineral constituents are quartz and feldspar, with varying amounts of mica, hornblende, etc. Its prevailing color is gray, though greenish, yellowish pink, and red shades are found.

Granite is more extensively used as a building stone than igneous rock of any other class. It works with difficulty, owing to its hardness and toughness, but its quarrying is usually facilitated by the existence of planes of weakness: the *rift,* extending either in vertical or horizontal planes; and secondary planes, the *grain,* along which the rock may be less readily split, at right angles to the rift. As a rule the quarry rock shows joints or fissures in the direction of the rift, and often a secondary series of joints exists in the direction of the grain. The removal of rectangular blocks of large or small dimensions is thus facilitated.

Granite is used for foundations, base courses, columns, and steps in building construction, and is suitable for any situation where strength or hardness is required. It is used to a limited extent as an ornamental stone, its suitability depending upon color and texture.

13.4 Gneiss. Gneiss has the same composition as granite, which it resembles in appearance, but differs in physical structure, the various con-

[1] I. O. Baker: *Masonry Construction.* Baker uses the term "stratified" in a broad sense to include both bedded sedimentary and banded metamorphic rocks.

[2] Plutonic rocks are igneous rocks formed by the solidification of molten material prior to its emergence on the earth's surface; volcanic rocks have cooled on the earth's surface.

Building Stones and Stone Masonry

stituents being arranged in more or less parallel bands. The rock therefore splits readily into flat slabs, which renders quarrying less expensive than that of granite and makes the stone valuable for foundation walls, street paving, curbing, and flagging. It is found in the same general localities as granite.

13.5 Limestones. The term limestone is commonly applied to all stones which, though differing from one another in color, texture, structure, and origin, possess in common the property of containing carbonate of lime (calcite) or calcite and the double carbonate of lime and magnesia (dolomite) as the essential constituent. In addition they contain as impurities oxides of iron, silica, clay, bituminous matter, talc, etc. Different limestones may be listed according to structure, composition, and mode of origin under the following heads:

Crystalline Limestone or Marble. The term "marble" is commonly applied to any limestone that will take a good polish. It is properly applied only to those limestones which have been exposed to metamorphic action and rendered more crystalline in structure.

The structure of marbles varies from finely to coarsely crystalline. Marbles are found in almost every conceivable color and are often richly streaked with several colors. All varieties of marble work well, the finer-grained white marble being especially adapted to carving. Marble has been used in this country principally for interior decoration, but many varieties are entirely suitable for exterior construction.

Compact Common Limestones. These are usually very fine-grained limestones of varying textures and colors, giving rise to many varieties. The best known and most widely used American limestone is the *Bedford limestone,* also called "Indiana limestone." This is a fine-grained, oölitic limestone which is made up of small rounded concretionary grains cemented together by carbonate of lime. It is quarried in the Bedford-Bloomington district in Indiana. Geologically it is known as the Salem limestone. It is found in two general color classifications, gray and buff. Deposits of light-gray stone are the most abundant and have been the most used. The stone can be worked with remarkable ease and hardens on exposure. The rock has little tendency to split along bedding planes. It has been extensively used for the exterior construction of buildings, for bridge piers, and for heavy cut-stone masonry in general.

13.6 Sandstones. "Sandstones are composed of rounded and angular grains of sand so cemented and compacted as to form a solid rock. The cementing material may be either silica, carbonate of lime, an iron oxide, or clayey matter." [3]

Sandstones vary greatly in color, hardness, and durability, but include many of the most valuable varieties of building stone for exterior construc-

---

[3] Merrill: *Stones for Building and Decoration,* p. 299.

tion. The qualities of sandstone as a structural material depend largely upon the character of the cementing material, the sand grains being very nearly a pure quartz for all. If the cement is siliceous, the stone is light colored, hard, and sometimes difficult to work, but very durable. If iron oxides comprise the greater part of the cementing material, the color is a red or brownish tone and the stone usually is not too hard to work well, though it does not always prove very durable. If the cementing material is lime carbonate, the stone is light colored, soft, and easy to work, but less durable than either of the above varieties. Clayey sandstones are the poorest class. They are soft and easily cut, but are particularly subject to the disintegration caused by weathering because of their high absorption. Some sandstones contain very little cementing material but owe their strength largely to the pressure under which they have been solidified. Such stones are light gray, work easily, and, if they possess sufficient cohesive strength, are very durable. Sandstones containing varying amounts of grains of feldspar or mica are inferior to ones the grains of which are entirely quartz.

13.7 Slates. Ordinary slate is a siliceous clay, compacted and more or less metamorphosed after deposition as fine silt on ancient sea bottoms. The pressure due to thousands of feet of overlying material is largely responsible for the solidification of the clay into rock having very marked cleavage planes. The most valuable characteristic of slate is its pronounced tendency to split into thin sheets having smooth regular surfaces. The non-absorptiveness of slate, its great toughness and mechanical strength, and its non-conductiveness for electric currents are other valuable attributes.

13.8 Traprock. This term has no strict geological interpretation. It is used primarily by engineers and is commonly understood to embrace all dark, fine-grained igneous rocks which show no free silica in the form of quartz crystals. In consequence of this definition, it properly includes basalt, fine-grained diorite and gabbro, and many of the felsites. Very frequently other rocks, like dark fine-grained sandstones, porphories, syenites, and even some dense shales and dolomites, have properties such that they are marketed and accepted under the broad characterization of "traprock."

13.9 Dimension Stone. Building stone reduced to blocks of definite shapes and sizes for structural uses is commonly referred to as "dimension stone." Dimension stone for construction of building walls may be cut stone or ashlar. Cut stone blocks are cut or finished accurately to definite shape and size, often to meet the dimensions given in detailed drawings. The blocks may be rectangular or specially shaped for cornices, corners, caps, etc. The setting of cut stone requires great care. Relatively small rectangular blocks having sawed or rock-face surfaces are called "ashlar." A wall built of ashlar blocks of various sizes with non-uniformly spaced joints is termed "random ashlar."

Building Stones and Stone Masonry

13.10 Production of Dimension Stone. The production of two widely used structural building stones, granite and Bedford limestone, will be described. The methods of quarrying and milling granite are typical of the processes employed for hard stone while the methods for Bedford limestone are typical for relatively soft stone.

Quarrying of Granite. Drills are required to cut granite since it is so hard. Either compressed-air hammer drills or, occasionally, steam-driven or air-driven reciprocating drills are used. Drill bits range from about 1 to 3 inches in diameter, a change to a smaller size bit being made about every 4 feet of depth. Holes are drilled 15 to 20 feet deep. A thin passageway is cut through the webs between drill holes by means of rectangular drill bars called "broaching tools." The granite is fractured into large blocks by means of blasting powder.

Small blocks are obtained by plug-and-feathers wedging. "Feathers" are iron strips curved on one side to fit the drill hole and flat on the other. Two feathers are placed in a drill hole and a "plug" or iron wedge is hammered between them. Blocks of stone are lifted out of the quarry by derricks.

Milling of Granite. Milling processes for cutting and finishing granite blocks are carried on by machine or by hand. Machine processes consist of sawing, polishing, sand blasting, and pneumatic surfacing. Granite is sawed either by gang saws or by rotary saws. Gang saws consist of a number of steel blades set parallel to each other in a frame which is drawn back and forth either in a straight line or with a swinging motion. The blades are about $\frac{1}{2}$ inch thick and have notches in the bottom edge for holding abrasive steel shot. Granite is cut into blocks or slabs by gang saws; additional cutting such as cutting the ends of blocks is done by rotary saws, 7 to 12 feet in diameter, which have detachable steel teeth. Abrasive steel shot is fed to the blade. Abrasive circular saws up to 30 inches in diameter are used for making cuts of small depth and for edging, jointing, chamfering, etc.

Machine polishing is carried on in three stages: rough grinding, fine grinding, and glossing. Rough grinding is done with steel shot or coarse silicon carbide under ironing wheels up to 6 feet in diameter and 3000 pounds in weight which are rotated on a horizontal surface of the granite. Fine grinding is carried on by means of a wheel, with emery or fine silicon carbide as abrasive, and glossing is done by a buffing wheel with putty powder. Special silicon carbide wheels are used for cutting and polishing special shapes. Granite columns are cut by turning lathes and then polished smooth.

The sand-blast process drives white silica sand as abrasive at a high velocity through a hand-controlled nozzle against the stone surface. For carving ornaments or lettering, the face is covered with a rubberlike protective coating in which a stencil of the design is cut out, leaving only those parts of the granite exposed which are to be etched. This is a very effective and economical process for etching surface ornament, relief carving, and lettering, and also for cleaning and finishing sawed surfaces.

Pneumatic surfacing machines are used for roughing, pointing, and bushing plane or flatly curved surfaces. Pneumatic tools guided by hand are employed in finishing practically every bush-hammered surface of any considerable area from rough or sawed surfaces.

Hand work is required in general for molded work, surfaces below a projection, heads, internal angles, sinkages, joints, and practically all irregular pattern stones. Hand cutting tools comprise chisels, chippers, points, plug drills, hand hammers, peen hammers, bull set hammers, bush hammers, wedges and shims, etc. Cutting granite by hammering on a tool is in reality a crushing process since the minerals of the stone are broken into small pieces or formed into dust.

Surface Finishes of Granite. "Polished" finish has a mirror gloss and brings out the full crystalline pattern and color. It is used for store fronts, base courses, monuments, thin facing, and veneer. "Honed" finish has a dull gloss without reflections, is free from scratches, and gives softer color effects than polishing. A "rubbed" surface is smooth without gloss. "Hammered" surfaces obtained by means of bush hammers may be coarse hammered using a four-cut bush hammer, medium hammered using a six-cut bush hammer, or fine hammered using an eight-cut bush hammer. This finish shows parallel ridges, is light in tone, and is suitable for general building work. "Pointed" finish is a roughly indented finish with fairly uniform texture, the size of point used and the density of distribution of indentations determining the grade: coarse, medium, or fine. It gives rugged texture effects and is economical for large surfaces. "Peen-hammered" surface is a very coarse, axed finish less regular than four-cut and has rugged texture effects. "Rock face" is rough split face with edges pitched to an approximate plane.

Quarrying of Bedford Limestone. Stripping of clay overburden and removal of poor grade rock are preliminary operations in Indiana limestone quarries in Lawrence and Monroe Counties. Since Bedford limestone is relatively soft, blocks can be cut out by means of a "channeling" machine which has a reciprocating cutting tool composed of three to five sharpened steel bars. Channeling machines, operated either electrically or by steam power, are run back and forth on a track cutting either one or two channels in the rock. (See Fig. 13.1.) Blocks about 4 feet wide and 10 feet deep are cut the length of a quarry and then are broken loose from the floor by drilling and wedging using "plug and feathers." Blocks cut to a length of 20 to 30 feet are turned over on the side and hoisted up from the quarry by derricks.

Milling of Bedford Limestone. Since Bedford limestone is soft compared to granite, different processes can be utilized in milling. Slabs and blocks are sawed out first by steel gang saws with clean silica sand or crushed

Building Stones and Stone Masonry 307

cherty rock called "chats" as abrasive. Diamond saws are satisfactory for Bedford limestone. A saw consisting of a straight steel blade with diamond teeth on the cutting edge is used sometimes for single cuts. Circular saws with diamonds set in the circumference of the steel blade, 4 to 6 feet in diameter and about ¼ inch thick, are used for cutting up blocks and slabs. Diamond saws must be cooled with water. Silicon carbide rotary saws are also used, particularly for short and shallow cuts.

Planers are generally used to obtain smooth surfaces and desired dimensions of blocks and slabs. The cutting tool is mounted on an adjustable

Fig. 13.1. Electrically operated channeling machines in operation in a Bedford limestone quarry in Indiana. (Rader.)

frame, and the stone is fed repeatedly to the tool by means of a moving bed or "platen." Sides as well as top surfaces may be planed simultaneously. Specially shaped tools are required for cutting moldings. A silicon carbide planer consisting of two vertical saws with a smaller diameter drum mounted between them is sometimes used to trim the sides and smooth the surface in a single cut.

Carving is done by hand or by means of pneumatic tools. Since Bedford stone is readily carved and does not tend to split on bedding planes, it is extensively used for carved figures, emblems, decorations, etc., for churches, chapels, libraries, and other public buildings.

Surface Finishes of Bedford Limestone. In addition to sawed surfaces whose roughness can be controlled by selection of suitable abrasives, and planed surfaces, other types of finish are frequently required to give desired architectural effects. A "tooled" surface consists of fine parallel grooves made by a planer or pneumatic tool having fine teeth. A "four-cut" surface is made with a planer tool having approximately four teeth per inch of width. A "small-fluted" surface consists of small, parallel corrugations. A bush hammer having a face with small projections produces a rough, pitted surface known as a "hammered" surface. A surface having indentations made by means of a sharp-pointed tool is called a "hand-picked" surface. Smooth or "rubbed" surfaces are obtained by hand or machine rubbing with an abrasive such as sand and water.

Properties of Building Stones

13.11 Selection of Building Stone. The selection of a proper stone for construction purposes depends to a great extent upon the climate where the stone is to be used. The range of changes of temperature, the average humidity of the atmosphere, the possibility of acid fumes in the atmosphere of many cities, and the possibility of the stone being subjected to high temperatures by fire are among the considerations which must be carefully taken into account.

The actual mechanical strength of stone is seldom of great importance, for stones in masonry structures can never be loaded to their full capacity on account of the comparative weakness of the mortar joints.

13.12 Properties of Various Stones. *Durability.* The durability of stones depends upon ability to withstand weathering agencies, and the structure, texture, and mineral composition are the real determining factors. Joint planes, cracks, or other structural imperfections afford an opportunity for water to enter and for disintegration to begin through frost action. Stones of coarse-grained texture are more subject to the disintegrating influence of temperature changes than fine-grained ones, and dense stones, owing to their practical imperviousness, are less likely to be injured through frost action than porous ones. Of the mineral compounds which make up our common rocks, sulfides are among the least resistant to weathering agencies; iron compounds in general are undesirable in large quantities; calcium and magnesium carbonates weather rather rapidly; aluminates weather less rapidly; silicates are most resistant to decay. It must not be overlooked in this connection that the three factors, structure, texture, and mineral composition, are simultaneously operative, so that a very dense, fine-grained stone made up principally of carbonate may weather well, whereas a porous or structurally imperfect stone made up principally of silica may weather poorly.

Absorption. The absorption or absorptive power of stones is represented by the weight of water that can be absorbed, expressed as a percentage of the dry weight of the stone. Absorption directly depends upon the porosity of stones, though this relation is not necessarily any fixed ratio. The gain and loss of moisture when a stone is first exposed in a damp or wet situation, and then dried, will be most rapid if the pores are large or straight, and least rapid if they are small or tortuous.

It appears from tests that the absorption of igneous and metamorphic rocks rarely exceeds ½ per cent. The sandstones absorb at least ten times as much as granites, marble, and slate, and the limestones absorb even more moisture than the sandstones.

Expansion and Contraction. Stones, like most other materials, expand upon being heated and contract when cooled. Unlike most other materials, however, they do not quite return to their original volume when cooled after heating, but show a swelling which is permanent. Experiments made at the Watertown Arsenal by heating from 0 to 100° C. (32–212° F.) and cooling through the same range showed the permanent increase in length for the various stones tested to be from 0.02 to 0.045 per cent.

The coefficient of temperature expansion per degree Fahrenheit for various building stones was found in a series of tests at the Watertown Arsenal to be quite variable, the range of values found being as follows: granites, 0.00000311 to 0.00000408; limestones 0.00000375 to 0.00000376; marbles 0.00000361 to 0.00000562; sandstones 0.00000501 to 0.00000622.

Frost Resistance. Stones can be disintegrated by frost action only when the pores are practically filled with water before exposure to freezing temperatures. As stones seldom are used under such conditions that the maximum amount of water is absorbed, instances of injury to good building stones by frost action are very rare. Experimental work on the resistance of stones to disintegration by frost indicates that the pores can be filled with water, so that the subsequent expansion upon freezing will cause rupture, only by means of high pressure or by first exhausting the air by a vacuum. It will be apparent, therefore, that only stone of the greatest absorptive power combined with low structural strength can ever be injured by frost action under the conditions encountered in practice.

Fire Resistance.[4] Practically all building stones are seriously injured if exposed to such high temperatures as may be encountered in fires, and particularly so if exposed to the combined action of fire and water. The cause of disintegration is usually considered to be the internal stresses caused by unequal expansion of unequally heated portions of the material. This explanation is rendered more forcible by the observed fact that, if highly heated stones are suddenly cooled on the exterior by application of water, the resultant disintegrating action is much more pronounced than when the cooling is slow. Probably the texture of the stone and the relative coefficients of expansion of its individual mineral constituents are also factors of importance.

Experience has shown that granites are particularly poor fire resistants. Probably on account of the irregularity of the structure and the complexity

---

[4] Ries and Watson: *Engineering Geology*, p. 446.

of the mineral composition, granites crack irregularly and spall badly. The coarse-grained granites are most susceptible to the action of fire and water, and the gneisses often suffer even more severely because of their banded structure.

Limestones suffer little from heat until a temperature somewhat above 600° C. (1112° F.) is reached, at which point the decomposition of the stone begins, owing to the driving off of carbon dioxide. The stone then has a tendency to crumble, because of the flaking of the quicklime formed. Curiously enough, the limestones do not suffer so much by sudden cooling as by slow cooling.

Marbles, owing to the coarseness of the texture and the purity of the material, suffer more than limestones at temperatures below the point where calcination begins. The cracking is irregular, and the surface spalls off as in granites.

Sandstones, especially if of a dense, non-porous structure, suffer from high temperatures and sudden cooling less than most other building stones. The cracking of sandstones that does occur appears mostly in the planes of the laminations, which should be horizontal planes as the stone is set. These cracks are therefore not so serious as irregular cracks. Sandstones in which the cementing ingredient is silica or lime carbonate are better fire resistants than those in which the grains are bound by iron oxide or clay.

Mechanical Properties of Stones. The tabulation of mechanical properties of the principal classes of building stone given in Table 13.1 has been com-

Table 13.1

MECHANICAL PROPERTIES OF BUILDING STONES

Kind of Stone	Comp. Strength, p.s.i.	Modulus of Rupture, p.s.i.	Shearing Strength, p.s.i.	Weight, lb. per cu. ft.	Modulus of Elasticity, p.s.i.
Granite	15,000 / 30,000	1,200 / 2,200	1,800 / 2,700	156 / 165	6,000,000 / 10,000,000
Limestone	4,000 / 20,000	250 / 2,700	1,000 / 2,000	145 / 170	4,000,000 / 14,000,000
Marble	10,000 / 16,000	850 / 2,300	1,000 / 1,700	168 / 178	4,000,000 / 13,500,000
Sandstone	7,000 / 20,000	500 / 2,000	1,200 / 2,500	133 / 150	1,000,000 / 7,500,000
Slate	— / —	7,000 / 11,000	— / —	170 / 180	12,000,000 / —

piled from various sources to serve as an approximate guide in the selection of a building stone.

If conditions exist which necessitate an accurate knowledge of the physical properties of the stone to be used, safety lies only in actual tests from stone

Building Stones and Stone Masonry

taken from the exact source from which it is expected to draw the supply. In any instance very large safety factors (often from 15 to 35) are allowed in design.

It will be noted, by reference to Table 13.1 that any given stone shows wide variation in properties. These variations are to be expected from the wide range of the component minerals and consequent variations in chemical composition, and in igneous rocks the rate of cooling also plays an important part. The properties of limestones are affected by their manner of formation. Marbles show variations due to the completeness of crystallization and size of the component crystals. Sandstones are affected by the character of the cementing material which holds the quartz particles together as well as by the size of the particles. Practically all stones are also affected by the type and degree of metamorphism which is present.

Stone Masonry

13.13 Stone Masonry. The actual *compressive strength* of stone masonry has not been satisfactorily determined experimentally. The tests which have been made do not form a sufficient basis for the determination of the relative strengths of the different classes of masonry, or the relative strengths of masonry of the same class constructed of different kinds of stone.

The manner of failure of masonry under compression is almost invariably by the compressive failure, followed by lateral flow, of the mortar, thus setting up tensile stresses in the stone which open transverse cracks.

It is obvious that the integrity of a masonry structure is destroyed by this failure of the mortar in the joints. In fact, it is only with the strongest mortars laid in the thinnest possible joints that the real strength of building stone can be developed.

Allowable Loads on Stone Masonry. Conservative building laws recommend approximately the values given in Table 13.2 as safe pressures for the different classes of stone masonry.

Table 13.2

ALLOWABLE LOADS ON STONE MASONRY

Kind of Masonry	Allowable Pressure, p.s.i.
Rubble, uncoursed, in lime mortar	60
Rubble, uncoursed, in Portland cement mortar	100
Rubble, coursed, in lime mortar	120
Rubble, coursed, in Portland cement mortar	200
Ashlar, limestone, in Portland cement mortar	400
Ashlar, granite, in Portland cement mortar	600

Questions

13.1. State the usual geological classification of rocks. Define each classification, and give a common example of a rock in each classification.

13.2. Name five commonly used building stones, state their geological classification, and give their relative values as to strength, durability, ease of cutting and dressing, appearance, and fire-resisting properties.

13.3. Describe the quarrying and milling of granite and Bedford limestone.

13.4. State what you would do in passing upon the quality of a building stone for use in an important structure, assuming that you could visit the quarry and observe similar stone in a structure of some age, and that you have facilities for making laboratory tests.

References

13.1. American Society for Testing Materials: "Definitions of Terms Relating to Natural Building Stone." *Designation* C119–49, *Book of Standards*, Part 3, 1952, p. 891. "Method of Test for Abrasion Resistance of Stone Subjected to Foot Traffic." *Designation* C241–51, *ibid.*, p. 869.

13.2. Bateman, J. H.: *Materials of Construction.* New York, Pitman Publishing Corp., 1950, Chap. 8.

13.3. Bowles, O.: *The Stone Industries.* McGraw-Hill Book Co., 2nd ed., 1939.

13.4. Gay, C. M., and Parker, H.: *Materials and Methods of Architectural Construction.* John Wiley & Sons, 2nd ed., 1943, 636 pages.

13.5. *Granite in Architecture* and *Architectural Granite.* Pamphlets published by National Building Granite Quarries Association, New York.

13.6. Loughlin, G. F.: "Indiana Oölitic Limestone, Relation of Its Natural Features to Its Commercial Grading." Washington, D. C., *U. S. Geol. Survey Bull.* 811, 1930, pp. 111–202.

13.7. Nord, M.: *Textbook of Engineering Materials.* John Wiley & Sons, 1952, Chap. 16.

13.8. Pletta, D. H., and Poulton, J. F.: "Volume Changes in Natural and Artificial Building Stones." *Virginia Polytech. Inst., Eng. Exp. Sta. Bull.* 34, 1938.

13.9. Ries, H.: *Building Stones and Clay Products.* John Wiley & Sons, 1912.

13.10. Ries, H., and Watson, T. L.: *Engineering Geology.* John Wiley & Sons, 5th ed., 1936.

13.11. Stone, R. W.: "Building Stones of Pennsylvania, Harrisburg, Pa." *Pa. Topographical & Geol. Survey, Bull.* M-15, 1932, 316 pages.

13.12. Terzaghi, K.: "Stress Conditions for the Failure of Saturated Concrete and Rock." *Proc. ASTM*, v. 45, 1945, p. 777.

CHAPTER 14

Mineral Aggregates

By LLOYD F. RADER

14.1 General Classification. Mineral aggregates consist of particles of minerals. They may be classified into four groups:

1. Natural aggregates.
2. By-product aggregates.
3. Processed aggregates.
4. Colored aggregates.

Natural aggregates are taken from native deposits without change in their natural state during production except for crushing, sizing, grading, or washing. Crushed stone, gravel, and sand are typical examples; other less common examples are pumice, scoria, shells, limerock, caliche, iron ore, and chats. *By-product* aggregates comprise iron blast-furnace slag and cinders. *Processed* aggregates are given specific heat treatments to produce expanded materials of lightweight characteristics; these include processed perlite, exfoliated vermiculite, burned clays, shales, and slates, and calcined diatomaceous shale. *Colored* aggregates of glass, ceramics, and marble are manufactured for decorative purposes, particularly architectural concrete.

Aggregates of low unit weight are frequently referred to as *lightweight* aggregates. Examples include pumice, scoria, lightweight slag, cinders, and the processed aggregates listed above.

14.2 Character of Particles. Particles may be naturally rounded such as pebbles, or may be angular. Gravel consists of naturally rounded pebbles. Sand consists of rock particles which have been disintegrated naturally; the grains are generally angular, but in some instances are rounded due to weathering. Crushed stone comprises angular particles which have been produced by artificial crushing of rocks. Stone sand is finely crushed rock of size corresponding to sand.

Aggregate particles have great variations in texture. For example, gravel pebbles may have a smooth texture whereas crushed blast-furnace slag particles may have rough, pitted surfaces.

Aggregate particles also have variations in porosity. Many crushed stones and gravels have low porosity. Slag, on the other hand, has many large internal voids which are not interconnected and which do not permit free passage of water. When crushed, the broken slag surfaces have vesicular cavities. Many lightweight aggregates have porous structures.

14.3 Gradation of Aggregates. Aggregates are generally classed as fine or coarse aggregates. There is no definite dividing line between the two, but for concrete work, the fine aggregate is usually less than ¼ inch in diameter. However, some aggregates known as "single aggregates" are available containing both fine and coarse sizes; an example is the Nebraska sand gravel, and another is single aggregate used for bituminous concrete.

Aggregates usually have a gradual gradation in sizes from coarse to fine. Figure 14.1 illustrates a typical gradation curve for gravel. However, "one-

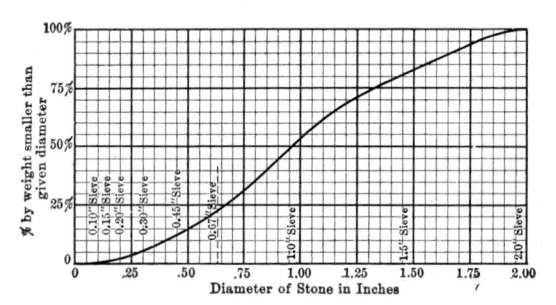

Fig. 14.1. Typical mechanical analysis of gravel.

size" gradations are also produced which have a predominance of particles in a given size range. Also aggregates with "skip gradings" are produced which are lacking in specific sizes of particles.

Feret and others have made careful study of the results of artificial mixes of aggregates. They found, if aggregates were screened into three sizes, coarse, medium, and fine, that the combination with greatest density was a mixture of approximately 2 parts coarse by weight and 1 part fine by weight with no medium-size material at all. For these tests, the coarse size was from 5 to 2 millimeters, the medium was from 2 millimeters to 0.5 millimeter, and the fine was smaller than 0.5 millimeter in size. This greatest density had an absolute volume of 0.737 in per cent of solids. Feret's work also showed that high densities could be obtained by using approximately equal proportions of coarse, medium, and fine materials. (See reference 14.11.)

Significant undersize in aggregates is defined as the material passing a test screen with openings one-sixth smaller than the nominal minimum size of the aggregate fraction. For example, the significant undersize in the 1½-inch to ¾-inch aggregate fraction would be the material passing the ⅝-inch screen.

The term "fineness modulus" is often used to denote the relative fineness of sand. Fineness modulus is defined as one one-hundredth of the sum of

Mineral Aggregates

the cumulative percentages held on the standard sieves in a sieve test of a sand. Six sieves are used in the determination, Nos. 4, 8, 16, 30, 50, and 100, the clear opening of each sieve being one-half that of the preceding one. The smaller the value of the fineness modulus the finer is the sand. For a good grade of concrete sand the fineness modulus should be between 2.25 and 3.25.

For coarse aggregate, there are nine sieves in the set, namely: the 1½-inch, ¾-inch, and ⅜-inch sizes together with the standard set for the sand analysis, Nos. 4, 8, 16, 30, 50, and 100. The fineness modulus of coarse aggregate is defined as one one-hundredth of the sum of the cumulative percentages held on the above listed sieves. The fineness modulus of an ordinary coarse aggregate for concrete ranges between 5.5 and 7.5.

14.4 Sand for Concrete Aggregate. *Grading.* Investigations have shown that for the most part the sand should be coarse rather than fine. A sand showing proper gradation in size from fairly coarse to fairly fine is preferable to either a uniformly coarse or a uniformly fine sand. ASTM specifications give the tabulated requirements:

Sieve	Percentage Passing
⅜-inch	100
No. 4 (4760-micron)	95–100
No. 16 (1190-micron)	45– 80
No. 50 (297-micron)	10– 30
No. 100 (149-micron)	2– 10

For mass dams of air-entrained concrete, a rather fine sand of fineness modulus from 2.40 to 2.50 is preferred to a coarser sand as used in non-air-entrained concrete.

Deleterious Substances. The ASTM specification for permissible limits of deleterious substances (C33–49) is given in Table 14.1. Clay, if finely divided and uniformly distributed throughout the sand, appears to have little effect unless present in large amounts. However, finishing of concrete floors, slabs, and pavements may tend to bring the fine material to the surface where it is easily worn away or scaled off. For this reason the recommended permissible limit of clay and silt in sand for concrete subject to surface abrasion is 2 per cent.

Test for Organic Matter. The sodium hydroxide or *colorimetric* test is made as follows: A 12-ounce glass prescription bottle is filled to the 4½-ounce mark with the sand to be tested, and a 3 per cent solution of sodium hydroxide is added until the total volume after shaking is 7 ounces. The bottle is stoppered, shaken thoroughly, allowed to stand for 24 hours, and the color of the solution noted. This color can be compared with standard color charts or with a standard solution of tannic acid and the relative amount of organic matter noted therefrom. In general, a color deeper than

Table 14.1
PERMISSIBLE LIMITS FOR DELETERIOUS SUBSTANCES IN CONCRETE AGGREGATES
(*ASTM Designation* C33–49)

Fine Aggregate

	Recommended * *Permissible Limits*, max., % by weight	*Maximum Permissible Limits*, % by weight
Clay lumps	0.5	1.0
Coal and lignite	0.25	1
Material finer than No. 200 sieve:		
(a) In concrete subject to surface abrasion	2	4
(b) All other classes of concrete	3	5
Other deleterious substances (such as shale, alkali, mica, coated grains, soft and flaky particles)	As specified	As specified

Coarse Aggregate

	Recommended * *Permissible Limits*, max., % by weight	*Maximum Permissible Limits*, % by weight
Soft fragments	2	5
Coal and lignite	0.25	1
Clay lumps	0.25	0.25
Material finer than No. 200 (74-micron) sieve	0.5 †	1 †
Other deleterious substances	As specified	As specified

* The recommended requirements should be specified on all work where it is economically practicable to obtain materials conforming thereto.

† When the material finer than the No. 200 sieve consists essentially of crusher dust, the recommended and maximum permissible limits specified above may be raised to 0.75 and 1.5%, respectively.

a light orange indicates an excess of harmful matter. However, it has been established that certain sands, as for example some in the vicinity of New York City, which produce a color darker than the standard color, give satisfactory compressive strengths in mortars (*ASTM Designation* C87) and give satisfactory service in concrete.

Loam or an excess of clay in sand is usually eliminated by washing, and a great deal of washed sand is used in concrete construction. Too much washing, however, tends to remove most of the fine particles and may cause the resulting concrete to be harsh and difficult to handle.

Comparison with Standard Sand. Common practice in selecting sands for concrete is to prepare mortar cubes of the commercial sand and of stand-

Mineral Aggregates

ard Ottawa sand, using the same cement for the two mixes, and to determine the percentage of the compressive strength of the standard sand mortar developed by the unknown sand mortar at 7 and 28 days. Minimum allowable percentages of the standard sand-mortar strength vary from 60 to 100 per cent, depending on the locality and the nature of the construction. This test is often applied to determine the strongest of a number of available sands. The ASTM specifications (C33–49) require the use of the compressive-strength test (Method C87) on mortar cubes of constant water-cement ratio, but some organizations employ the tensile-strength test on briquets (Method C190–49) in making comparisons with standard sand.

Bulking of Sand. When water is mixed with a given volume of dry sand, the moist sand "bulks" or increases in volume. The amount of bulking is variable, depending on the fineness of the sand and on the method used in making the measurements. Bulking increases in amount as more water is added up to a maximum and then decreases as the water content is increased, until the sand becomes saturated at which point the sand volume becomes constant. The phenomenon of bulking may be explained by increased frictional resistance between the sand grains when moistened, which tends to spread the grains apart. For further explanation, see Art. 18.19.

14.5 Stone Sand. Stone sand is a specially prepared product manufactured by crushing stone screenings or stone particles to sand size. The gradation of stone sand for use as fine aggregate in concrete is given in Table 14.2. For good workability in concrete, it is desirable that stone sand

Table 14.2

GRADATION OF STONE SAND FOR CONCRETE

Sieves, Number	Recommended Total Per Cent Passing	Allowable Range Total Per Cent Passing
4	100	100
8	95	95–100
16	70	60–75
30	45	35–50
50	20	15–25
100	8	5–10
200	5	3–6

The fineness modulus of the recommended gradation is 2.62.

have particle shapes approaching a cube; flat and elongated particles reduce workability. By means of air entrainment suitable workability can sometimes be obtained with stone sand having relatively poor particle shape. Air entrainment also improves the durability of stone-sand concrete.

Stone sand in concrete pavements may cause slipperiness. This phenomenon is probably related to the softness of the stone. The projecting points of stone sand tend to wear off under traffic, producing a mosaic surface which has no "tooth," unlike the case of hard, siliceous sands in which the small projections persist.

In construction of large dams, stone sand manufactured from the same stone as used for coarse aggregate has been utilized so that the thermal coefficient of expansion values of the fine and coarse aggregates would be similar. This procedure is considered by some engineers to be desirable in mass concrete from the standpoint of durability. Also, favorable gradations are possible for stone sand which is important in lean mass concrete for dams.

14.6 Coarse Aggregate for Concrete. *Grading.* The grading requirements for coarse aggregate for concrete specified by the American Society for Testing Materials are given in Table 14.3. All material under No. 4

Table 14.3

GRADING REQUIREMENTS FOR CRUSHED STONE, GRAVEL, AND BLAST-FURNACE SLAG FOR PORTLAND-CEMENT CONCRETE

(*ASTM Designation* C33–49)

Percentages Passing Laboratory Sieves Having Square Openings

Designated Size	4 in.	3½ in.	3 in.	2½ in.	2 in.	1½ in.	1 in.	¾ in.	½ in.	⅜ in.	No. 4 (4760- micron)
3½ in. to 1½ in.	100	90–100	—	25–60	—	0–15	—	0–5	—	—	—
2½ in. to 1½ in.	—	—	100	90–100	35–70	0–15	—	0–5	—	—	—
2 in. to No. 4	—	—	—	100	95–100	—	35–70	—	10–30	—	0–5
1½ in. to No. 4	—	—	—	—	100	95–100	—	35–70	—	10–30	0–5
1 in. to No. 4	—	—	—	—	—	100	95–100	—	25–60	—	0–10
¾ in. to No. 4	—	—	—	—	—	—	100	90–100	—	20–55	0–10
½ in. to No. 4 *	—	—	—	—	—	—	—	100	90–100	40–70	0–15
2 in. to 1 in.	—	—	—	100	95–100	35–70	0–15	—	0–5	—	—
1½ in. to ¾ in	—	—	—	—	100	90–100	20–55	0–15	—	0–5	—

* Not more than 5% passing the No. 8 (2380-micron) sieve.

sieve is commonly removed from either crushed stone or gravel, this fine part sometimes being suitable for use as fine aggregate.

The maximum size of coarse aggregate allowable depends upon the nature of the work on which the concrete is used. For thin walls and sections the size should never exceed one-quarter of the thickness of the section. In reinforced-concrete work the maximum size is usually taken as three-quarters of the clear distance between reinforcing rods. For massive concrete, however, sizes up to 3 inches or larger may be used if special methods of puddling and tamping are adopted.

Deleterious Substances. The ASTM specification for permissible limits of deleterious substances in coarse aggregate (C33–49) is given in Table 14.1. Shale particles, clay lumps, coal, lignite, porous chert, and soft fragments should not be permitted in appreciable quantities because they do not resist weathering. There is usually no trouble with the cleanliness of crushed stone if the parent rock is hard and clean.

Chert. The presence of chert particularly in limestones may cause trouble in concrete. Light, porous chert is the most detrimental; it absorbs large amounts of water and is not resistant to freezing. Detrimental chert has a specific gravity of less than 2.40 to 2.45, although somewhat denser chert may exhibit some lack of durability in concrete. Spalling of concrete may be caused by particles of chert in the aggregate. Also some cherts may react with alkalies in Portland cement.

Shape of Particles. From a standpoint of minimum void space, rounded stones are more desirable than irregular fragments; from the standpoint of ability to bond with the mortar, the rounded stones may be inferior, however, so that in general the shape of the particles will be found to be much less important than their size and hardness. Thin, flat pieces should be discarded.

Gravel vs. Broken Stone. Either gravel or broken stone may be perfectly satisfactory, and neither can be said to be wholly superior to the other. If the consistency of the concrete is such as to constitute a rather dry mix, more tamping is necessary to obtain a dense concrete with broken stone than with gravel consisting of smoother and more rounded particles.

Gravel usually has a smaller percentage of voids than broken stone, and therefore a compact concrete may be secured with a somewhat smaller amount of mortar than would be required for broken stone.

On the other hand, if properly tamped, the broken stone will to some extent interlock, forming a dense and strong concrete, the same effect being possible with a well-puddled wet mix. Also, the rough surface of the broken stone usually results in developing a greater adhesive strength or bond between the stone and the mortar. This consideration cannot be taken to be universally applicable, however, for the adhesion of cement to stone is not wholly a matter of roughness or smoothness.

Lightweight Aggregates

14.7 Lightweight Aggregates. Lightweight aggregates may be classified as (1) by-product aggregates, (2) processed aggregates, and (3) natural aggregates.

By-product aggregates include cinders and metallurgical slags. Cinders are the residue from high-temperature combustion of coal or coke, and usually are not processed. Lightweight slag is the foamed product produced by expanding molten slag by application of a limited amount of water. Two methods are employed: the jet process and the machine process. In the jet process a high-pressure jet impinges on a stream of molten slag from the blast furnace at a temperature of about 1371° C. (2500° F.), and foaming occurs in midair as well as in the dry pit into which the product falls. The resulting clinker is lightweight and has a cellular structure. In the machine process, expansion of the molten slag is achieved by agitation in a revolving machine with steam generated by contact of the slag with a controlled quantity of water. The foamed slag when cooled forms a lightweight clinker having minute, non-connecting air cells which are completely sealed. The color is white to gray or brown. Expanded-slag trade names include Celocrete, Foamed Slag, Slaglite, Superock, and Waylite.

Processed aggregates are given specific heat treatments to produce expanded or bloated characteristics. Four different types are described.

1. Burned clays, shales, and slates are sold under trade names such as Featherlite, Haydite, Lelite, Rocklite, Solite, and Tuff-lite.

Haydite is a shale product consisting of hard, porous, absorptive, gray- to brown-colored particles of fine-grained texture and of angular to round shape. The shale is crushed to a minimum size of 1 inch and burned in a rotary kiln at a temperature of 1093° C. (2000° F.) to incipient fusion. The carbon in the shale is oxidized, forming gases which escape and produce an expanded cellular structure in the shale. The shale is cooled and then ground and screened into commercial sizes of both fine and coarse aggregates.

Lelite is also a shale product, the raw shale particles are dark gray to black in color and contain some free carbon. The shale is expanded or bloated by passing through a furnace at a temperature of 1538° C. (2800° F.). The shale becomes semiplastic, and gasification of certain constituents in each particle converts the shale into a cellular mass with cell size ranging from pin head to microscopic. The particles are vitrified and form a continuous ribbon or slab emerging from the furnace. After cooling and crushing, the material is screened and stored. Lelite has good insulating properties with exceptional heat-resistant characteristics. It is chemically inert and has high refractory properties. It produces concrete weighing from 90 to 100 pounds per cubic foot when dry. It has an absorption of about 6 per cent by weight; prewetting of Lelite is recommended before adding cement, but the mixing water can be added after the cement.

Solite is manufactured from a shaly-slate material. The raw material is run through primary and secondary crushers and then placed in constantly revolving kilns fired to a temperature of 1371° C. (2500° F.). It expands on firing until it forms masses of tiny cells with vitrified partitions. These masses are cooled gradually, thereby producing a thoroughly annealed product without quenching. The cellular masses are crushed and screened to size. Solite is used both for masonry units and structural concrete.

Tuff-lite is a clay product. The clay is burned by passing it through a sintering machine. Pulverized coal is used as fuel. The sintered clay is crushed and screened to size. The finished sinter is a rather harsh vesicular material, almost black in color, resembling scoria. It is a stable aggregate and produces concrete weighing from 100 to 102 pounds per cubic foot.

2. Diatomaceous shale that is oil treated and calcined is sold as Airox, Raylite, and Diacrete. It is a soft material with vesicular structure and has a smooth impervious shell. In color it is light pink to light tan.

3. Processed perlite is made from natural siliceous volcanic rock containing water. When crushed and suddenly heated, it pops into a very lightweight material. The particles are frothy, fragile, white, and irregular in shape. It is sold under trade names such as Per Alex, Permalite, Ryolex Perlite, and Superlite.

4. Exfoliated vermiculite results from the heating of a micaceous mineral. Its most pronounced characteristic is that it expands when heated to as much as 30 times the original volume. Dried ground ore is subjected to heat and brought to a temperature of about 982° C. (1800° F.) for a time of 4 to 8 seconds. The expanded vermiculite weighs only 6 to 12 pounds per cubic foot. The particles are soft and fragile with laminated structure and are brown to buff in color. Trade names are Vermiculite, Alexite, Bee Tree, Mascrete, Unicon, and Zonolite.

Natural aggregates such as pumice and scoria are taken from volcanic deposits and crushed, sized, and graded. Pumice contains many elongated cavities and is white to bluish gray in color with impurities staining it brown. Pumice is sold under trade names of Basalite Pumice, California Red Pumice, Ingham Brand Pumice, Insulpum Agite, and Vocolite. Scoria resembles pumice but is lava whose cells are larger and more irregular in shape.

14.8 Unit Weight. Usual average values of unit weight of lightweight aggregates are given in Table 14.4. It should be noted that the lightweight aggregates fall into two groups: The extremely lightweight aggregates used

Table 14.4

UNIT WEIGHTS OF LIGHTWEIGHT AGGREGATES

Aggregate	Unit Weight, Dry, Loose Condition, lb. per cu. ft.
Perlite	6–12
Vermiculite	6–12
Cinders	50–70
Expanded blast-furnace slag	40–70
Expanded clay and shale	40–70
Diatomaceous shale	15–30
Pumice	30–60
Scoria	45–55

for insulation primarily, such as perlite and vermiculite; and the others which produce a somewhat heavier concrete suitable for both insulating and structural uses but are classed as lightweight.

14.9 Grading. The ASTM grading requirements for lightweight aggregates are given in Table 14.5.

Table 14.5

ASTM GRADING REQUIREMENTS FOR LIGHTWEIGHT AGGREGATES

Percentages Passing Sieves Having Square Openings

Size Designation	1 in.	¾ in.	½ in.	⅜ in.	No. 4 (4760- micron)	No. 8 (2380- micron)	No. 16 (1190- micron)	No. 50 (297- micron)	No. 100 (149- micron)
Fine Aggregate:									
¼ in. to dust	—	—	—	100	95–100	—	45–80	10–30	5–15
⅜ in. to dust	—	—	100	95–100	55–80	—	—	10–25	5–15
Coarse Aggregate:									
½ in. to No. 4	—	100	90–100	40–75	0–15	0–5	—	—	—
½ in. to No. 8	—	—	100	85–100	0–20	0–5	—	—	—
¾ in. to No. 4	100	90–100	—	20–55	0–10	0–5	—	—	—

PROPERTIES OF AGGREGATES

14.10 Strength Properties. Obviously, the strength properties of aggregates for use in road construction and in concrete are of importance, but since most aggregates have sufficient compressive strength, the actual crushing strength, like that of building stone, is, on the whole, of but secondary importance. The most important property of aggregates is resistance to wear or abrasion. Other properties which are sometimes measured are toughness and hardness.

Los Angeles Abrasion Loss. The resistance to wear is determined by the Los Angeles abrasion machine which consists of a cylindrical drum 28 inches in diameter and 20 inches in length, mounted longitudinally on a horizontal shaft and having a shelf 3½ inches wide extending from end to end on the inside. The drum is revolved 500 revolutions at a rate of 30 to 33 revolutions per minute. The sample consists of 5000 grams of gravel or commercially crushed stone which is graded to conform to a specified coarse or fine grading. For certain gradings, an abrasive charge consisting of steel or cast-iron spheres approximately 1⅞ inches in diameter is placed in the drum. The test charge is caused to drop from the shelf. The percentage of wear is determined from that portion which, after test, will pass a No. 12 U. S. standard sieve. (The Los Angeles test has superseded the Deval abrasion test.)

Toughness is determined from a 1-inch cylindrical specimen 1 inch long. This specimen is fractured by the impact of a 2-kilogram hammer transmitted through a standardized plunger. The vertical drop of the hammer (1 centimeter for the first impact) is increased 1 centimeter for each blow.

Mineral Aggregates

The number of blows required to produce fracture is the measure of the toughness.

Hardness is determined by pressing a 1-inch cylinder endwise against a revolving disk upon which is fed clean crushed quartz of standard size. A pressure of 1250 grams is maintained, and 1000 revolutions constitute a test. The hardness is expressed by the relation $H = 20 - \frac{1}{3}W$, where W is the loss of weight in grams.

14.11 Soundness. Soundness of aggregates is determined by use of sodium sulfate or magnesium sulfate. Samples are immersed for at least 16 and not more than 18 hours in the solution and then are dried in an oven. The procedure of alternate immersion and drying is repeated for a desired number of cycles. Aggregates which show no spalling or disintegration under this treatment are held to be "sound" and may be expected to resist disintegration under the action of frost and other common weathering agencies. Another soundness test is to subject aggregates to alternate cycles of freezing and thawing.

14.12 Specifications. Specifications for aggregates of the American Association of State Highway Officials are given below.

Type of Construction	Percentage of Wear, Los Angeles Test, Not More Than
Coarse aggregate for Portland cement concrete	40
Crushed stone and crushed slag for bituminous concrete surface course	40
Crushed stone and crushed slag for bituminous macadam and water-bound macadam surface course	40
Crushed stone, crushed slag, and crushed gravel for open-graded bituminous road-mix surface course	40
Crushed stone, crushed slag, and crushed gravel for dense-graded bituminous road-mix and plant-mix surface course	50
Crushed stone and crushed slag for bituminous concrete base course	45
Crushed stone and crushed slag for base course	50

14.13 Reactivity of Mineral Aggregates with the Alkalies in Portland Cement. Certain minerals in aggregates react chemically with the alkalies in Portland cement. Such minerals include opal, glass in felsites, and cristobalite and tridymite; the latter two are crystalline forms of silica sometimes found in volcanic igneous rocks.

Thomas E. Stanton called attention in 1940 to serious deterioration of concrete structures caused by expansion of concrete through reaction between certain minerals in aggregates and alkalies in cements in the form of sodium and potassium oxides. (See reference 14.26.) Such reaction between cements and aggregates may be explained as follows. Mixing water in the concrete acquires alkalies from the cement by preferential solubility, a solution being formed. As hydration takes place, the calcium aluminates and the silicates of the paste extract water. Thus less water is left in the solution, producing a caustic solution of greater concentration as the cement sets and hardens. During the period of curing, the caustic alkali solution reacts chemically with susceptible siliceous minerals in the aggregates. By this reaction, alkalic silica gels are formed. These gels have a great affinity for water and attract water from the cement paste, thus reducing their viscosity. Osmotic pressures are set up by the drawing of water from the paste to such an extent as to produce high enough stresses to fracture the cement paste adjacent to the reactive mineral particles. (Osmotic pressures in excess of 550 pounds per square inch have been measured.) These ruptures form small-size spaces in the concrete where the silica gels can develop. Growth of the silica gel formations causes dilation of these fractures into cracks and extension of the cracks through the mass of the concrete. At the surface, pattern cracking may be observed in some instances.

The strength and elasticity of the concrete is reduced by such ruptures. Of further importance is the fact that water can be admitted through such cracks to cause deterioration by other processes. For example, freezing and thawing may disrupt the concrete. Also solutions carrying dissolved carbon dioxide may change calcium hydroxide to calcium carbonate, thus causing volume increase.

Questions

14.1. How is the fineness modulus of a sand calculated?
14.2. Define the term "significant undersize."
14.3. Discuss the grading requirements of sand for concrete. Do the same for coarse aggregate.
14.4. Why has stone sand been utilized for construction of concrete dams?
14.5. Compare gravel with crushed stone for coarse aggregate for concrete.
14.6. Assuming that the standard method of filling and tamping a 1 cubic foot measure were used, which sand would have the greater weight per cubic foot, (1) sand dry or (2) sand containing 3 per cent water by weight? Why?
14.7. Describe the characteristics of the following: Haydite, Lelite, Solite, Tuff-lite, perlite, vermiculite, scoria, and pumice.
14.8. Write a discussion on the subject of reactivity of mineral aggregates with alkalies in Portland cement.

References

14.1. American Association of State Highway Officials: *Standard Specifications for Highway Materials and Methods of Sampling and Testing.* Washington, D. C., 6th ed., 1950.
14.2. American Society for Testing Materials: *Standards on Mineral Aggregates, Concrete, and Non-bituminous Highway Materials.* Philadelphia, 1948. Also "Tentative Descriptive Nomenclature of Constituents of Natural Mineral Aggregates." *Proc.,* 1952. Also *Symposium on Mineral Aggregates.* 1948. Also

Report on Significance of Tests of Concrete and Concrete Aggregates. 2nd ed., 1943.
14.3. Bateman, J. H.: *Materials of Construction.* New York, Pitman Publishing Co., 1950, Chap. 2, pp. 23–74.
14.4. Blanks, R. F., and Meissner, H. S.: "The Expansion Test as a Measure of Alkali-Aggregate Reaction." *Proc. Am. Concrete Inst.,* v. 42, 1946, p. 517.
14.5. Blanks, R. F.: "Good Concrete Depends on Good Aggregate." *Civil Eng.,* Sept., 1952, p. 651. Also: "Modern Concepts Applied to Concrete Aggregate." *Trans. Am. Soc. Civil Engrs.,* v. 115, 1950, p. 403.
14.6. Davis, C. E. S.: "The Effect of Soda Water and of Cooling Rate of Portland Cement Clinker on Its Reactions with Opal in Mortar." *Australian J. Appl. Sci.,* v. 2, 1, Mar., 1951.
14.7. Fahrenwald, A. W.: "New Type of Grinding Mill." *Rock Products,* Feb., 1951, pp. 93–97.
14.8. Goldbeck, A. T.: "Some Problems Concerning the Uses of Crushed Stone." *Crushed Stone J.,* Mar., 1952, p. 10.
14.9. Gray, J. E.: "Report on the Construction of Macadam Base Courses of the Non-bituminous Type, *Crushed Stone J.,* Mar., 1952, p. 15.
14.10. Highway Research Board: "Bibliography on Mineral Aggregates." Washington, D. C., 1949 (Bibliography No. 6).
14.11. Joisel, A.: "On en est La Granulométric du Beton." *La Technique Moderne-Construction,* v. 3, No. 3, June, 1948.
14.12. Josephson, G. W., Sillers, F., Jr., and Runner, D. G.: "Iron Blast-Furnace Slag —Production, Processing, Properties, and Uses." Washington, D. C., *Bull.* 479, 1949, U. S. Dept. of the Interior.
14.13. Knight, B. H.: *Road Aggregates, Their Uses and Testing.* London, Edward Arnold & Co., 264 pages.
14.14. Lenhart, W. B.: "Producing Sand for Garrison Dam." *Rock Products,* v. 54, Nov., 1951, p. 78.
14.15. Lenhart, W. B.: "Reducing Pea Gravel to Sand with Rod Mills." *Rock Products,* v. 50, Oct., 1947, p. 103.
14.16. Lenhart, W. B.: "Compact Plant Produces Many Sizes." *Rock Products,* v. 51, Oct., 1948, p. 88.
14.17. McConnell, D., Mielenz, R. C., Holland, W. Y., and Greene, K. T.: "Cement-Aggregate Reaction in Concrete." *Proc. Am. Concrete Inst.,* v. 44, 1947, p. 93.
14.18. McGrew, B.: "Crushing Theory and Practice." *Rock Products,* vols. 53 and 54, beginning in June, 1950, p. 118.
14.19. Nordberg, B.: "Canada's Most Modern Gravel Plant." *Rock Products,* v. 55, Aug., 1952, p. 160.
14.20. Parsons, W. H., and Insley, H.: "Observations on Alkali-Aggregate Reaction." *Proc. Am. Concrete Inst.,* v. 44, 1948, p. 625.
14.21. *Pit and Quarry Handbook.* 41st ed., 1948, Chicago, Complete Service Publ. Co.
14.22. Proudley, C. E.: "Rapid Determinations of Free Moisture in Aggregates." *Concrete,* v. 56, No. 8, Aug., 1948, p. 40.
14.23. Rockwood, N. C.: "Recent Progress in Sand Classification." *Rock Products,* v. 50, June, 1947, p. 100.
14.24. Runner, D. G.: *Geology for Civil Engineers as Related to Highway Engineering.* Chicago, Gillette Publ. Co., 1939, 299 pages.
14.25. Slate, F. O.: "Chemical Reactions of Indiana Aggregate in Disintegration of Concrete." *Proc. ASTM,* v. 49, 1949, p. 954.

14.26. Stanton, T. E.: "Expansion of Concrete through Reaction between Cement and Aggregate." *Trans. Am. Soc. Civ. Engrs.*, v. 107, 1942, pp. 54–84.

14.27. Streefkerk, I. H.: *Quarrying Stone for Construction Projects*. Delft, The Netherlands, Uitgeverij Waltman (distributed by Van Riemsdyck Book Service, 207–211 East 37th St., New York 16, N. Y.), 159 pages.

14.28. Trites, C. V., and Shannon, J. D.: "Acceptable Aggregates from Low-Grade Deposits." *Rock Products*, v. 53, Feb., 1950, p. 115.

14.29. Woolf, D. O.: "Reaction of Aggregate with Low-Alkali Cement." *Public Roads*, v. 27, 3, Aug., 1952, p. 50.

14.30. Woolf, D. O.: "Methods for the Determination of Soft Pieces in Aggregate." *Public Roads*, v. 26, 7, Apr., 1951, p. 148.

14.31. Woolf, D. O.: "The Identification of Rock Types." *Public Roads*, v. 26, 2, June, 1950, p. 44.

Section IV · Cementing Materials

CHAPTER 15

Gypsum Plaster

15.1 Definition and Classification. Gypsum plasters comprise all that class of plastering and cementing materials which are obtained by the partial or complete dehydration of natural gypsum and to which certain materials that serve as retarders or hardeners, or that impart greater plasticity to the product, may or may not have been added during or after calcination. Gypsum plasters may be classified as follows.[1]

- A. Produced by the incomplete dehydration of gypsum, the calcination being carried on at a temperature not exceeding 190° C. (374° F.).
    Plaster of Paris, produced by the calcination of a pure gypsum, no foreign materials being added either during or after calcination.
    Cement plaster (often called *patent* or *hard wall plaster*), produced by the calcination of a gypsum containing certain natural impurities, or by the addition to a calcined pure gypsum of certain materials which serve to retard the set or render the product more plastic.
- B. Produced by the complete dehydration of gypsum, the calcination being carried on at temperatures exceeding 190° C. (374° F.).
    Flooring plaster, produced by the calcination of a pure gypsum.
    Hard-finish plaster, produced by the calcination, at a red heat or over, of gypsum to which certain substances (usually alum or borax) have been added.

15.2 Gypsum Rocks. Pure gypsum is a hydrous lime sulfate ($CaSO_4 + 2H_2O$), the composition of which by weight is:

Lime sulfate ($CaSO_4$)	Lime (CaO)	32.6%	79.1%
	Sulfur trioxide (SO_3)	46.5	
Water (H_2O)			20.9
			100.0%

Natural deposits of gypsum are very seldom pure, the lime sulfate being adulterated with silica, alumina, iron oxide, calcium carbonate, and magnesium carbonate. The total of all impurities varies from a very small amount up to a maximum of about 6 per cent. The physical form of a

[1] Eckel: *Cements, Limes, and Plasters.*

natural gypsum is usually that of a massive rock formation. It also occurs as an earthy gypsum or gypsite and as gypsum sands.

Manufacture of Gypsum Plasters

15.3 General. Three operations are involved in the process of manufacturing plaster: crushing, grinding, and calcination. Rock gypsum is crushed to fragments about 1 inch in diameter, which are passed through an intermediate crusher and then pulverized in a finishing mill. The ground gypsum is then calcined in kettles or in rotary kilns.

15.4 Theory of Calcination. If pure gypsum is subjected to any temperature above 100° C. (212° F.), but not exceeding 190° C. (374° F.), three-fourths of the water of combination originally present is driven off. The resultant product is called *plaster of Paris* ($CaSO_4 + \frac{1}{2}H_2O$). Plaster of Paris readily recombines with water to form gypsum, hardening in a very few minutes.

If the gypsum is calcined at temperatures much above 190° C. (374° F.), it loses all its water of combination, becoming an anhydrous sulfate of lime ($CaSO_4$).

15.5 Practice of Calcination. Plaster of Paris and cement or hard wall plasters are made in practically the same manner, the difference in their properties being due to the use of comparatively pure gypsum for the first substance, and impure or adulterated gypsum for the second. Plaster is calcined in kettles or rotary kilns.

The kettle is a cylindrical steel vessel, 8 to 10 feet in diameter and 6 to 9 feet high, mounted upon a masonry foundation. The bottom is convex and made of cast iron. A masonry wall encloses the steel cylinder, leaving an open annular space between for the circulation of heat. A fire is maintained on grates below the kettle, and the heated gases pass through ports into the open annular space, then through the kettle in horizontal flues and out through the stack. A central vertical shaft propels paddles just above the bottom, thus keeping the material agitated and preventing the burning out of the bottom.

The charge, consisting of 7 to 10 tons of ground gypsum, is delivered by a chute to the charging door provided in the sheet-iron cap of the kettle. Heat is gradually applied as the charge is slowly fed in, and, as the temperature rises after charging is complete, the contents boil violently until the mechanically held water is driven off as steam. If the temperature is held at about 160° C. (329° F.), the material settles down in a quiescent state, and if the calcination is stopped at this point the resulting product is known as "first-settle" gypsum. If the temperature is raised, boiling is renewed when the water of combination begins to be driven off. If the temperature is held at about 205° C. (401° F.) the material settles down a second time and the result is "second-settle" gypsum. The kettle is discharged by blowing out through a small gate in the lower part of the side of the shell.

When the rotary calciner is employed, the raw material is used in the condition in which it comes from the intermediate crusher, and feeding from the supply bin is continuous. The cylinder of the calciner is set on a slight incline, and the lumpy material fed in at the upper end gradually traverses its length as the cylinder slowly rotates, is discharged at the lower end, and enters calcining bins lined with non-absorptive brick.

The heat attained in the rotary calciner is from 200° C. (392° F.) to 300° C. (572° F.), but time does not suffice for the complete dehydration of the gypsum, and the removal of combined water is completed in the calcining bins through the agency of the residual heat of the material itself. After about 36 hours the process is completed. Air inlets are then opened and the contents of the bin are rapidly cooled. The product of the calcining bins is conveyed to finishing mills and there pulverized to the form of the marketable article.

Flooring plaster is usually produced by the calcination of a comparatively pure gypsum in a lump form in a vertical separate-feed kiln which differs little from the separate-feed kiln used for the calcination of lime. The fuel, burned on grates outside the kiln, does not come in contact with the gypsum, but the hot gaseous products of combustion pass directly through it, heating it to a temperature of 400° C. (752° F.) to 500° C. (932° F.). Higher temperatures, or prolongation of heating beyond 3 or 4 hours, ruin the plaster by robbing it of its setting properties. Fine pulverization of the plaster must follow calcination.

A well-known variety of hard-finish plaster is the so-called *Keene's cement*. This plaster is produced by the double calcination of a very pure gypsum. After the lump gypsum has been calcined at a red heat, the resulting anhydrous lime sulfate is immersed in a 10 per cent alum solution, then recalcined, and finally pulverized in a finishing mill.

15.6 Additions Subsequent to Calcination. Plaster of Paris is seldom adulterated in any way during manufacture, but cement or hard wall plasters often require the addition of a retarder to render them sufficiently slow setting. The usual retarders are organic materials, such as glue, sawdust, blood, or packing-house tankage. As a rule the amount of retarder required does not exceed 0.2 per cent. The theory of the action of retarders is that they keep the molecules of the plaster from too close contact and thus delay crystal growth.

Certain very impure gypsums produce a plaster which is too slow-setting, or sometimes extreme rapidity of set is required. For such gypsums the addition of an accelerator is necessary. The materials used for this purpose are crystalline salts, common salt ($NaCl$) being one of the best.

Gypsum plasters destined for use as wall plasters must usually have their plasticity enhanced by the addition of some material such as clay or hydrated lime, through the agency of which the naturally "short," non-plastic material is greatly improved in working qualities and sand-carrying capacity. With the exception of those plasters made from earthy gypsum, which naturally contains 20 per cent or more of clay, it is the usual practice to add about 15 per cent of hydrated lime or, less frequently, clay, to the calcined plaster. Greater cohesiveness may also be imparted to wall plasters by the addition of finely picked hair or shredded wood fiber.

No additions are made to flooring plaster subsequent to calcination. Keene's cement is treated with an alum bath as above noted. Mack's cement, another variety of hard-finished plaster, is made by the addition to dehydrated gypsum (flooring plaster) of 0.4 per cent of calcined sodium sulfate (Na_2SO_4) or potassium sulfate (K_2SO_4).

Properties and Uses of Gypsum Plasters

15.7 Setting and Hardening. By the term "setting" is meant the initial loss of plasticity, whereas "hardening" means the subsequent gain in strength and in ability to resist indentation or abrasion. The setting of plaster of Paris and other gypsum plasters is a process of recombination of the partly or totally dehydrated lime sulfate with water to reform hydrated lime sulfate or gypsum.

A pure plaster of Paris sets within 5 to 15 minutes after the addition of water. Plasters made from impure gypsum are less quick setting, requiring from 1 to 2 hours, and the completely dehydrated classes of plasters are very slow setting, whether adulterated or not. The ultimate degree of hardness attained by impure cement or hard wall plasters greatly exceeds that of pure plaster of Paris, and the hard-burned plasters are hardest of all.

15.8 Uses of Various Gypsum Plasters. Plaster of Paris is not adapted for use as either a wall plaster or a mortar for masonry construction unless additions are made to retard its set and make it more workable. If this is done, however, it is no longer called plaster of Paris but becomes a cement or hard wall plaster.

Cement or hard wall plasters find their principal applications as wall plasters. A certain amount of hair, wood fiber, or asbestos fiber, together with hydrated lime or clay, may be mixed with the plaster at the place of manufacture. Usually wall plasters are applied in three coats: (1) scratch or first coat, (2) browning or second coat, and (3) finishing coat. Sand is ordinarily mixed with the plaster on the job, but ready-sanded plasters are available.

The American Society for Testing Materials specifies the composition of ready-sanded gypsum plasters in the accompanying table.

	Scratch or First Coat	Browning or Second Coat
Sand (by weight)	Not more than ⅔	Not more than ¾
Calcined gypsum	Not less than 20%	Not less than 15%

The remainder, in each case, may consist of materials added to control the working qualities, setting time, and the fibering. It is not economical to ship ready-sanded plaster long distances. Its advantages are quality and uniformity.

The finishing coat usually consists of prepared gypsum finishing plaster to which water is added to produce a dense and hard surface. However, sanded finishing plaster may be used; the sand may be added to cement plaster at the job site, or ready-sanded finishing plaster manufactured at the mill by adding fine sand to the gypsum plaster may be utilized.

Gauging plaster is also used for finishing coat; it is composed of 3 parts of lime putty to 1 part of calcined gypsum with or without retarder and is available in gray or white.

Wood-fiber plaster is manufactured at the plant by incorporating shredded wood fiber with plaster. It is used for scratch and browning coats for wood, metal, and gypsum lath instead of sanded-plaster coats. Wood-fiber plaster is tough, light in weight, and has good nailability. It is utilized in localities where good sand is not obtainable.

Gypsum wall plasters possess certain advantages over ordinary lime plasters, but also suffer by comparison with lime plasters in other respects. Among the advantages of gypsum plasters is the fact that the material comes upon the work ready to be mixed with sand and water and immediately applied to the lath, whereas quicklime requires careful slaking and should be allowed to season before being made up in a mortar and applied to the walls. Gypsum plasters set more rapidly and dry out in a much shorter time than lime plasters, thus often avoiding a delay in the completion of the interior finish of buildings. On the other hand, no gypsum product makes as plastic and smooth working a plaster as does the best lime, provided the lime is properly slaked, seasoned, and mixed. Lime plasters excel in sand-carrying capacity, making it possible to use more sand than with most gypsum plasters.

Lightweight aggregates such as perlite and vermiculite are frequently used in place of sand in producing gypsum wall plaster. (See Art. 14.7.) The advantages of lightweight plaster are easier work for the plasterers in lifting plaster and applying it to walls and ceilings, low dead load of walls and ceilings, good insulation, good fireproofing, and good sound-absorbing properties.

Among the other applications of hard wall plaster the following may be mentioned: Mixed with cinders or crushed stone and water to form a workable mix ("gypsum concrete"), hard wall plaster is poured in forms for floor or roof panels for buildings. Mixed with sawdust it is molded into blocks which may be nailed in place as a wall finish, and, without the sawdust, it may be molded into solid or hollow building blocks and tiles for the construction of partition walls and floors and for fireproofing. Another application of gypsum plaster is in the construction of "gypsum lath" and "wall board" wherein the plaster is laminated with thin layers of cardboard, wood, or other material in sheets which are ready to be nailed to the studding of partition walls. The wall surface if made of gypsum lath is subsequently plastered, but if made of wall board it may be finished in panels with no additional plaster by simply covering the joints with wood strips, or by decorating the surface.

Gypsum plaster and lath and gypsum blocks and tile tend to disintegrate when exposed to dampness and should not be used for exterior work in damp climates nor for moist interior locations.

Table 15.1

ASTM SPECIFICATIONS FOR GYPSUM PRODUCTS

Gypsum Plasters

Type of Plaster	Wood-Fibered	Neat	Ready-Mixed	Gauging Plaster for Finish Coat *
Content of $CaSO_4 \cdot \frac{1}{2}H_2O$, minimum, %	66.0	66.0	66.0	66.0
Content of wood fiber, minimum, %	1.0	—	—	—
Content of sand, maximum, per 100 lb. of calcined plaster	—	—	3 cu. ft.	—
Time of set, minimum, hr.	1.5	2.0	1.5	0.33
Time of set, maximum, hr.	16.0	32.0	8.0	0.67
Time of set, minimum, hr., when retarded	—	—	—	0.67
Compressive strength, minimum, p.s.i.	1200	750	400	1200

Gypsum Wall Board, Gypsum Lath, and Gypsum Sheathing Board

The composition and dimensions of plaster and wall board are specified and also their transverse strength when tested with a center load and a 14-in. span. The test specimen is 12 in. wide and 16 in. long.

Gypsum Tile or Blocks

Compressive strength, dry	75 p.s.i.
Compressive strength, saturated	Not less than 33⅓% of the dry strength

* Fineness: No residue on a No. 14 sieve and not less than 60% shall pass a No. 100 sieve. This gypsum plaster is prepared for mixing with lime putty for finish coat.

Hard-finished plasters find their principal application as wall plasters and as floor surface, especially as an imitation of tiling or marble for floors and wainscoting in hospitals, lavatories, etc. Keene's cement is, perhaps, the best-known variety of hard-finish plaster. Its set is extremely slow, and it gains in strength very gradually, but ultimately attains a great degree of hardness and a strength exceeding that of any ordinary gypsum plaster.

Gypsum often serves as a fireproofing material, although its strength is destroyed by long-continued heat. The water of crystallization is driven off and the surface reduced to a powder which, if not removed, acts as an insulator and protects the gypsum inside.

15.9 Tests for Gypsum Products. Standard methods of testing gypsum have been adopted by the American Society for Testing Materials to govern the determination of free water, fineness, chemical analysis, consistency, water-carrying capacity, dry bulk, wet bulk, time of set, and compressive strength; and in addition, definite specifications covering the physical properties of certain gypsum products have also been adopted by the Society. A few examples of these specifications are shown in Table 15.1.

Questions

15.1. Name and define four kinds of gypsum plaster.

15.2. Describe briefly the manufacture of gypsum plaster.

15.3. Write the chemical equations for the manufacture and setting of plaster of Paris.

15.4. What is Keene's cement?

15.5. In the manufacture of a gypsum wall plaster, packing-house tankage, hair, clay, and sand were added subsequent to the calcination of a pure gypsum. Give the reasons for each of these additions.

15.6. What is the theory of the action of retarders?

15.7. What materials are used to accelerate the setting of gypsum plasters?

15.8. Why is hydrated lime many times mixed with gypsum plaster to form a wall plaster?

15.9. What advantages does gypsum plaster have over lime plaster?

15.10. What are the advantages of lightweight plaster?

15.11. What is gypsum lath? wall board? gypsum concrete?

15.12. Describe the fireproofing characteristics of gypsum products.

15.13. Name the principal tests specified for gypsum products.

15.14. What is the minimum compressive strength required for neat gypsum plaster? for ready-mixed plaster? for dry gypsum blocks?

References

15.1. American Society for Testing Materials: "Standard Methods of Testing Gypsum and Gypsum Products." *Designation* C26–52, *Book of Standards,* Part 3, 1952, p. 265. Also: "Standard Specifications for Gypsum and Related Products" *Book of Standards,* Part 3, 1952, p. 247.

Materials of Construction

15.2. American Standards Association: *Standard Specifications for Gypsum Plastering,* A42.1. New York, 1942.
15.3. Bateman, J. H.: *Materials of Construction.* New York, Pitman Publ. Corp., 1950, pp. 84–90.
15.4. Eckel, E. C.: *Cements, Limes, and Plasters.* John Wiley & Sons, 3rd ed., 1928; Chaps. 1 to 5, pp. 18–148.
15.5. Lenhart, W. B.: "Gypsum Wallboard Production with Long Belt." *Rock Products,* v. 51, No. 3, Mar., 1948, p. 84.
15.6. Marani, V. G.: "Gypsum as a Fireproofing Material." *J. Cleveland Eng. Soc.,* v. 7, p. 213.
15.7. National Bureau of Standards: "Wall Plaster: Its Ingredients, Preparation, and Properties." Washington, D. C., *Circ.* 151, 1924.
15.8. Nord, M.: *Textbook of Engineering Materials.* John Wiley & Sons, 1952; Chap. 17, pp. 369–380.
15.9. Porter, J. M.: "The Technology of the Manufacture of Gypsum Products." Washington, D. C., *Nat'l Bur. Standards, Circ.* 281, 1926.
15.10. Santmyers, R. M.: "Gypsum: Its Uses and Preparation." Washington, D. C., *Information Circ.* 6163, *U. S. Bur. Mines,* Oct., 1929.
15.11. Seely, F. B., and James, R. V.: "The Plaster Model Method of Determining Stresses Applied to Curved Beams." *Univ. Illinois, Eng. Exp. Sta. Bull.* 195.
15.12. White, A. H.: "Volume Changes in Gypsum Structures Due to Atmospheric Humidity." Ann Arbor, Mich., *Univ. Mich., Dept. Eng. Research, Bull.* 2, 1926.

CHAPTER 16

Lime

16.1 Definition and Classification. *Quicklime* is the name applied to the common or commercial form of calcium oxide (CaO), obtained by the calcination of a stone in which the predominating constituent is calcium carbonate ($CaCO_3$), often replaced, however, to a greater or lesser degree by magnesium carbonate ($MgCO_3$), this product being one that will slake on the addition of water.

Hydrated lime is quicklime that has been chemically satisfied with water during manufacture.

According to the physical form of the material, quicklime for structural purposes is marketed as:

Lump lime. The size in which quicklime comes from the vertical-type kiln. Approximately 4 to 12 inches in diameter.
Granular lime. The size in which it comes from the rotary kiln. Maximum size approximately ¼ inch in diameter.
Pebble lime. Quicklime produced by calcining limestone in particle sizes approximately ¾ to 2 inches in diameter.
Crushed lime. Lump lime crushed to a specified grading.
Ground lime. Quicklime crushed and ground to a specified grading. Typical products are those passing a No. 6 sieve (or a No. 10 or No. 20 sieve).
Pulverized lime. Quicklime reduced in size to powder form by grinding. Usually all passing a No. 100 sieve.

According to relative content of calcium oxide and magnesium oxide, quicklimes are divided into four types:

High-calcium. Quicklime containing 90 per cent or more of calcium oxide (CaO). (Sometimes termed "rich," "fat," or "caustic" lime.)
Calcium. Quicklime containing not less than 75 per cent of calcium oxide.
Magnesian. Quicklime containing not less than 20 per cent of magnesium oxide (MgO or magnesia).
High-magnesian or *dolomitic.* Quicklime containing more than 25 per cent of magnesium oxide.

Hydrated lime is commonly divided into four classes: *High-calcium; calcium; magnesian; high-magnesian.* The chemical composition is practically the same as for the corresponding classes of quicklime.

Hydrated lime for structural purposes is further classified as either mason's or finishing. Each of these is manufactured in two types: normal (N) and special (S).

16.2 Limestone Rocks. An ideal, pure limestone consists entirely of calcium carbonate ($CaCO_3$), which, at a temperature of 900° C. (1652° F.) or over, becomes dissociated, the carbon dioxide (CO_2) being driven off as a gas, leaving behind a white solid, calcium oxide or quicklime (CaO).

As pure calcium carbonate consists of 56 parts by weight of CaO to 44 parts of CO_2, the theoretical proportion of quicklime obtainable by the calcination of limestone will be 56 per cent by weight.

Limestones encountered in practice depart more or less from this theoretical composition. Part of the lime is almost always replaced by a certain percentage of magnesia (MgO), making the stone to a greater or less extent a magnesian limestone. In addition to magnesia, silica, iron oxide, and alumina are usually present and, to a slight extent, sulfur and alkalies.

The physical character of the limestone has an important bearing upon the burning temperature, quite aside from the question of chemical composition. A naturally coarse, porous stone is acted upon by heat much more rapidly than a dense, finely crystalline stone, and in consequence may be burned more rapidly and at a lower temperature. Small pieces of stone may also be burned more readily than large ones.

Manufacture of Lime

16.3 Theory of Calcination. The burning or calcination of lime accomplishes three objects:

The water in the stone is evaporated.

The limestone is heated to the requisite temperature for chemical dissociation.

The carbon dioxide is driven off as a gas, leaving the oxides of calcium and magnesium.

The evaporation of any water present in the stone means that a certain portion of the heat supplied during calcination does not directly assist in the dissociation of the carbonates. This heat does not mean a thermal loss, however, because the presence of the water, and of the steam generated from it, facilitates the dissociation process.

The temperature of dissociation of pure calcium carbonate at a pressure of 1 atmosphere has been determined to be 898° C. (1650° F.); and the corresponding temperature for magnesium carbonate, somewhat lower.

Theoretically, all limestones could be properly burned at a temperature of about 880° C. (1616° F.), provided sufficient time was allowed. In practice, however, the maximum kiln output is obtained by burning at a considerably higher temperature.

16.4 Practice of Calcination. The types of kilns employed in lime burning may be described as follows:

Intermittent Kilns. For small-scale production, permanent intermittent kilns, often called "pot kilns," built of stone with a firebrick lining and provided with a grate upon which the fuel is placed, are used.

The kilns have an arched opening at the bottom through which fuel is introduced and the burned lime removed. These kilns have been largely supplanted by more modern types.

Continuous Kilns. In the vertical kiln with mixed feed, the fuel and the limestone are charged in alternate layers, the lime being removed at the bottom while fresh fuel and limestone are charged in at the top.

Vertical kilns with separate feed are so designed that the fuel and limestone do not come in contact, the fuel being burned in separate fireplaces either set in the wall of the kiln or outside the kiln shell. The limestone therefore comes in contact only with the hot gaseous products of combustion.

The fuels for lime burning are wood, bituminous coal, and producer and natural gas. Some kilns are electrically heated. Wood fuel possesses a distinct advantage over coal because of its longer flames and consequent better heat distribution throughout the mass of stone. Producer and natural gas is used because flame is more effective than hot gases in transferring heat to the stone. Some modern gas-fired vertical kilns have their burners in the center so that the flames will be efficiently distributed through the stone.

A lime kiln in operation always contains three classes of material: (a) Stone undergoing preliminary heating through the agency of the escaping hot products of combustion; (b) stone undergoing dissociation through the agency of the direct heat of the fuel; (c) calcined lime which accumulates in the lower portion of the kiln and is withdrawn in part from time to time. The total amount of lime present in the kiln cannot be drawn at one time, because, aside from the desirability of letting it cool in the kiln itself, enough must remain at all times to fill the "cooler" (that portion of the kiln below the level of the fuel grate), thus preventing unburned stone from sinking below the level of the zone in which it is subjected to the action of the flames of the fires.

Rotary Kilns. Rotary kilns are extensively used in the calcination of lime. They are subject to the disadvantage of requiring that the stone be finely crushed prior to the calcination, and the product is consequently so finely divided that it is not marketable as lump lime but can be sold only after grinding as ground or pulverized lime, or after hydrating as hydrated lime. Rotary kilns make possible improved control of feed and temperature.

Reactor Kilns. The reactor kiln consists of a vertical stack with four heating compartments and a cooling compartment in the bottom. Hot air and fuel gases are blown upward under pressure through beds of pulverized limestone in each compartment so as to produce agitation of the material. The beds of limestone are maintained in suspension by the air and gas blown through them in sufficient quantities to air-float or "fluidize" the material. The level of the limestone particles rises in the "fluidized" state to the top of an outlet pipe through which the particles flow down into the bottom of the next lower compartment. The material passes down into the lower compartments in successive order as the temperature is increased until the limestone is calcined in the lowest heating compartment. Then the calcined product flows down into the cooler at the bottom of the stack where it is air cooled and discharged. Air passed through the hot lime in the cooler is preheated for later use in the heating compartments. The limestone feed should be passing 10-mesh with fine dust removed. A lime possessing active properties can be produced in a reactor kiln with better fuel economy than for a rotary kiln.

16.5 Treatment Subsequent to Calcination. When the kiln is not provided with a cooler, the lime is spread on a cooling floor or left standing in fireproof containers for a few hours before taking it to storage, packing house, or cars. Underburned and overburned material is easily recognized by its appearance and is sorted out while being drawn into the barrows or while it lies on the cooling floor. Another method is to move the lime by means of a conveyor with workmen at the side to inspect and remove faulty particles. In some plants, soaking chambers are provided for the lime after burning so as to permit the lime particles to become uniformly heated prior to cooling.

Properties and Uses of Quicklimes

16.6 Classification of Limes. Limes may be conveniently classified, according to the purposes for which they are used, as building limes and finishing limes. Building limes must be satisfactory as regards sand-carrying capacity, yield of lime paste per unit weight of lime, and strength; finishing limes must be satisfactory with respect to rate of hydration, plasticity, sand-carrying capacity, color, yield, waste, hardness, time of setting, and shrinkage.

16.7 Chemical Composition. The approximate chemical composition of limes of various classes has been indicated in Art. 16.1, wherein limes were classified and graded according to their content of calcium oxide and magnesium oxide. Table 16.1 illustrates the range of composition found for quicklimes coming from different parts of the United States.

Lime

Table 16.1
ANALYSES OF QUICKLIMES

Class of Lime	High-Calcium Quicklimes			Calcium and Magnesium Quicklimes			Dolomitic Quicklimes		
Component	Min., %	Max., %	Ave. of (10), %	Min., %	Max., %	Ave. of (6), %	Min., %	Max., %	Ave. of (2), %
SiO_2	0.33	2.20	0.81	0.66	9.00 *	3.12	0.14	1.59	0.87
Fe_2O_3	0.08	0.43	0.23	0.17	0.59	0.41	0.19	0.39	0.29
Al_2O_3	0.02	0.42	0.22	0.18	2.57 *	0.93	0.14	0.49	0.32
CaO	91.37	98.08	94.98	78.59	84.81	81.42	55.80	64.45	60.13
MgO	0.17	4.55	1.39	1.03	16.83	9.26	31.61	40.62	36.12
H_2O	0.36	3.45	1.66	0.63	12.42 †	4.18	0.55	1.56	1.06
CO_2	0.20	1.84	0.83	0.24	1.94	0.18	0.35	3.01	1.68

* Excessively high in acid impurities.
† Incipient air-slaking shows.

16.8 Hydration or Slaking. Quicklime intended for use in mortars for masonry construction, or as a wall plaster, must first be prepared for mixing with water to form a lime paste, by being slaked. The hydration or slaking of quicklime consists in the addition of sufficient water for the formation of calcium hydroxide, the operation being represented by the formula:

$$CaO + H_2O = Ca(OH)_2$$
$$75.7 + 24.3 = 100 \text{ (parts by weight)}$$

If the quicklime were absolutely free from impurities the amount of water required for complete slaking would equal 32.1 per cent by weight of the quicklime, but the fact that the quicklime is always impure makes the amount of water actually required less than this. The formation of lime hydrate is attended by the evolution of considerable heat and an expansion to about 2½ or 3 times its former volume. Magnesian quicklimes, and particularly dolomitic quicklimes, slake more slowly than high-calcium limes, and the slaking is attended with the evolution of much less heat and far less expansion.

Lime intended for use in mortar is usually slaked in a mortar mixing box, the mixture being stirred until a thin paste, or "putty," has been formed. The putty is then covered with sand to protect it from the action of the air.

Lime paste, or putty, designed for use as a plaster should be allowed to season for several weeks.

The reaction involved in the hydration of quicklime may result in the production of either crystalline or colloidal calcium hydroxide, the relative quantity of one or the other depending upon the conditions maintained during the reaction. Crystals of calcium hydroxide form and grow slowly, whereas the colloidal hydroxide forms with great rapidity. Consequently, the more rapid the reaction the greater the proportion of colloidal hydroxide. The reaction may be most readily hastened by using warm water in slaking. The percentages of colloidal hydroxide may also be increased by violently agitating the material during the reaction. A preponderance of colloidal hydroxide is desirable from the standpoint of the mason, who judges a mortar by its plasticity, yield, and sand-carrying capacity.

The hydration of high-calcium quicklimes is attended with danger of "burning," due to too great a rise in temperature. "Burned lime" appears to be chemically inert and is useless in a mortar or plaster. Burning may best be avoided by securing an intimate contact between every particle of lime and the water. Great watchfulness and continuous stirring of the mixture are therefore necessary.

No danger of burning attends the slaking of most magnesian quicklimes, or of any dolomitic quicklime. On the contrary, the danger here is that the quicklime may never be properly slaked before being used.

"Air-slaked" lime is a very different thing from the ordinary slaked lime. Quicklime exposed to the air absorbs moisture and becomes slaked lime, the expansion accompanying hydration causing the lumps to fall into a more or less fine powder. Immediately, the slaked lime is attacked by the carbon dioxide of the air, and the resulting product is simply powdered calcium carbonate, $CaCO_3$. The quicklime at the surface becomes "air-slaked," but by so doing it immediately forms a film which protects the bulk of the material.

The rates of hydration of various quicklimes depend, first, upon the physical condition of the material, finely divided or porous quicklimes being more quickly hydrated because of their greater accessibility to water; second, upon the chemical composition of the quicklimes, high-calcium quicklimes being more quickly hydrated than magnesian or dolomitic quicklimes, and pure limes of either class being more quickly hydrated than impure ones; third, upon the temperature of burning of the quicklime, any underburned quicklime having little ability to hydrate, and overburned limes behaving similarly owing to the influence of impurities.

Quick-slaking lime should always be added to the water, not the water to the lime. Enough water should be present to cover the lime completely, and an additional supply should be available for immediate use. The mixture should be watched carefully, and at the slightest appearance of escaping steam it should be hoed thoroughly and enough water added to stop the steaming.

For medium-slaking lime, enough water should be added to the lime to half submerge it. Immediate hoeing should follow the appearance of any steam, and small amounts of water should be added when necessary to prevent the putty from becoming dry and crumbly.

For slow-slaking lime, only enough water should be added to the lime to moisten it thoroughly, and it should then be allowed to stand until the reaction has started. Small amounts of water should then be added, care being taken not to cool the mass, and there should be no hoeing until the slaking is practically complete. The slaking mass must be kept warm. In cold weather, hot water should be used if available, and the mortar box should be covered.

The ASTM specifications for structural quicklime recommend that, after slaking, the putty shall be prepared for use as follows:

White coat. After the action has ceased, run off the putty through a No. 10 sieve and store for a minimum of 2 weeks.

Base coats. After the action has ceased, run off the putty through a No. 8 sieve. Add sand up to equal parts by weight, all the hair required, and store for a minimum of 2 weeks.

Mason's mortar. After the action has ceased, add all or part of the sand required, and store for a minimum of 24 hours.

16.9 Plasticity, Sand-Carrying Capacity, and Yield. The term "plasticity" is commonly used to describe the spreading quality of the material in plastering. If it spreads easily and smoothly, it is plastic; if it sticks or drags under the trowel, or cracks, curls up, and drops behind the trowel, it is non-plastic, or "short." Magnesian limes produce mortars that work smoothly under the trowel; high-calcium mortars are likely to be sticky and work short.

Practically all lime used structurally is made up in the form of a mortar by the addition of sand to lime paste. This circumstance is due not simply to the fact that sand is cheaper than lime, but also to the fact that the great shrinkage which accompanies the setting and hardening of lime putty can thus be diminished and the consequent cracking be prevented. The extreme stickiness of some high-calcium limes is also counteracted by the sand.

It is important that the "sand-carrying capacity" of the lime be properly established. If too little sand is used, excessive shrinkage will cause a weakening of bond between the plaster or mortar and the masonry materials or plastered surface. On the other hand, too much sand produces a non-plastic and weak mortar. Common experience has shown that pure high-calcium limes excel in sand-carrying capacity, magnesian limes carry less sand, and dolomitic limes carry least of all.

The volume of paste of a definite consistency which a given amount of lime will yield when slaked is a matter of great practical importance. This "yield" of a lime can be expressed by the volume of paste of an arbitrary consistency produced per unit weight of dry quicklime. The consistency chosen is usually such that a 2-inch cylinder of putty 4 inches high will settle to a height of 3½ inches upon removal of the mold. Pure high-calcium limes yield the largest volume of paste per unit of weight; impure high-calcium and magnesian limes expand less upon being slaked and therefore show a lower yield; and dolomitic limes produce the smallest volume of paste of any class of quicklime.

Usually, between 25 and 30 pounds of quicklime will produce 1 cubic foot of putty. On this basis, the yield will be 0.033 to 0.040 cubic foot of putty per pound of quicklime.

16.10 Hardness, Time of Setting, and Shrinkage. The hardness of lime mortar, meaning by the term "hardness" resistance to impact and abrasion, has an important bearing upon the suitability of the material for use in wall plasters. Dolomitic limes produce the hardest mortars, magnesian limes are less hard, and high-calcium limes least hard.

The setting of lime and lime mortar is a chemical process involving essentially only the evaporation of the large excess of water used in forming the lime paste, followed by the gradual replacement of the water of the hydroxide by carbon dioxide in the atmosphere, causing the lime hydrate to revert to the original calcium carbonate. Dry carbon dioxide will not react with dry hydrated lime, and it is therefore necessary that excess moisture be present.

The time of setting of limes and mortars is important in connection with the use of the material in plastering operations. Lime is naturally slow setting, a circumstance which causes the loss of considerable time between the application of the different coats. The slow-setting properties of lime, as much as any other one characteristic, have been responsible for the increasing use of quick-setting gypsum plasters.

The humidity and the amount of CO_2 in the atmosphere influence the rate of setting of lime, drying the air and charging it with carbon dioxide, greatly accelerating the setting process. Magnesian limes are slower setting than high-calcium limes, and the dolomitic limes set still more slowly.

The decrease in volume, or shrinkage, of lime putty, which accompanies the process of setting and hardening, is directly explained by the volume of water lost, the net decrease in volume being slightly affected by an expansion entailed by the gain in carbon dioxide. It is the universal practice to reduce the contraction and consequent cracking of mortars and plasters by the addition of several parts of sand to one of lime paste. The only exception to this rule is that neat lime putty is sometimes spread as a thin

Lime

"skim" coat on plastered walls. In this coating, fine hair-cracks do occur, but they penetrate to so slight a depth that they do not open up appreciably.

The amount of shrinkage shown by limes is not closely related to chemical composition, but all magnesian and dolomitic limes shrink less than high-calcium limes.

16.11 Tensile and Compressive Strength of Lime Mortars. The physical properties of lime mortar vary with the chemical composition of the lime, the amount and character of the sand, the amount of water, and the conditions under which the mortar sets. Magnesian limes make stronger mortar than calcium limes and comparatively fine sand makes stronger mortar than coarse sand.

16.12 Specifications. The American Society for Testing Materials has adopted the specifications for chemical composition of quicklimes given in Table 16.2.

Table 16.2

ASTM SPECIFICATIONS FOR QUICKLIMES

Composition	Calcium Lime	Magnesian Lime
Calcium oxide, minimum, %	75	—
Magnesium oxide, minimum, %	—	20
Calcium and magnesium oxides, minimum, %	95	95
Silica, alumina, and oxide of iron, maximum, %	5	5
Carbon dioxide, maximum, %		
a. If sample is taken at kiln	3	3
b. If sample is taken at any other place	10	10

Hydrated Lime

16.13 Classification. The specifications of the American Society for Testing Materials for hydrated lime cover finishing limes and building limes as follows.

Finishing limes
　Type N, normal finishing hydrated lime.
　Type S, special finishing hydrated lime.
Building limes (Mason's hydrate)
　Type N, normal hydrated lime for masonry purposes.
　Type S, special hydrated lime for masonry purposes.

Type S, special finishing hydrated lime, is differentiated from Type N, normal finishing hydrated lime in that a limitation of 8 per cent unhydrated oxides is specified for Type S and the plasticity requirement for Type S may be determined after soaking for less than 16 hours. There is no limitation on the amount of unhydrated oxides in Type N, and the plasticity requirement for Type N shall be determined after soaking for 16 to 24 hours.

Type S, special hydrated lime for masonry purposes, is differentiated from Type N principally by its ability to develop high, early plasticity and higher water retentivity and by a limitation of 8 per cent on its unhydrated oxide content.

Building limes (Mason's hydrate) are used in the scratch and brown coats of plaster, for stucco, in mortar, and for addition to Portland cement concrete. Finishing limes are used for finish (white) coat of plaster and for all of the uses for building limes listed above.

16.14 Process of Manufacture. Hydrated lime is a dry, flocculent powder resulting from the hydration, at the place of manufacture, of ordinary quicklime. Three stages of manufacture characterize the preparation of hydrated lime.

1. The quicklime is crushed or pulverized to a fairly small size.
2. The crushed material is thoroughly mixed with a sufficient quantity of water.
3. The slaked lime is, by air separation, screening, or otherwise, separated from lumps of unhydrated lime and impurities, or the entire mass must be finely pulverized.

The degree of crushing or pulverizing practiced at various hydrated lime plants varies greatly. In some plants the quicklime is crushed to a 1-inch size; in others, to a size of ½ inch or under. A few plants, after crushing the quicklime, pulverize it so that the greater portion will pass a 50-mesh sieve.

Two methods used for hydrating quicklime are the atmospheric-pressure and the pressure-hydrated methods. In the atmospheric-pressure method, both the "batch" process and the continuous process are employed.

The batch-process hydrator consists of a revolving pan provided with plows, arranged in a horizontal spiral, which stir up and mix with lime the water which is added in the form of spray. The hydrated lime is scraped from the pan through an opening in the center into a hopper below the hydrator.

The continuous-process hydrator consists of a number of cylinders, arranged one above the other, which are provided with screw conveyors. The quicklime is fed into the upper cylinder in a continuous stream, and here water is sprayed upon it, the amount being regulated by valves. The moist lime is gradually worked by the conveyors through the upper cylinder into the lower ones, and by the time it is discharged from the lowest cylinder it is hydrated.

The pressure-hydrated method is a modern method that employs a continuous-process hydrator with the chambers under air pressure. It is efficient in hydrating the quicklime with only a relatively small amount of unhydrated oxide being left in the finished hydrate. The pressure-hydrated method is used to produce Type S, special finishing hydrated lime, and Type S, Mason's hydrate. By this method of hydration, the specification requiring that unhydrated oxides be limited to a maximum of 8 per cent can be met. In some plants, autoclave chambers are used for hydration in which elevated temperatures and pressures are maintained.

Any impurities in the lime will not slake, and any imperfectly hydrated lime can be removed from the finished product by screening or air separation.

The form of screen usually employed consists of a wire netting stretched on an inclined frame which is mechanically agitated as the material traverses its length. The usual size is from 35 to 50 meshes per linear inch. The whole structure must be enclosed to keep in the dust.

Air-separation systems usually involve the use of a Raymond impact mill or similar device in which the hydrate is subjected to the beating action of rapidly revolving blades. A current of air carries off the fine material in suspension, while the larger particles settle out. The fine material is subsequently deposited in a chamber provided for the purpose in the air duct, the precipitation being effected by the reduction in velocity of the air current. The air circuit is a closed one, the same air being circulated over again, and it is therefore a dust-proof device. The size of the particles is easily regulated by varying the velocity of the air current.

16.15 Tests. The principal physical tests for hydrated lime that have been standardized are residue, soundness, popping and pitting, and water retention. Brief summaries from the American Society for Testing Materials Standards follow:

Consistency and Plasticity. When standard consistency is required, a modified "Vicat needle" is used. Plasticity is determined by the testing of a paste of standard consistency with an "Emley plasticimeter."

Residue. The residue shall be determined as follows: 100 grams of the sample as received shall be placed on a No. 30 sieve which shall be nested above a No. 200 sieve. The material shall be washed by means of a stream of water from a faucet. The washing shall be continued until the water coming through the sieve is clear, but in no case should the washing be continued for more than 30 minutes. The 100-gram sample shall leave, by weight, a residue of not more than 0.5 per cent on a No. 30 sieve, and not more than 10 per cent on a No. 200 sieve.

Soundness. Twenty grams of the sample and 100 grams of standard Ottawa sand shall be mixed with enough water to give a plastic mortar of rather dry consistency. This shall be spread on a glass plate to form a layer ¼ inch thick by 4 inches square. The pat formed shall be aged 24 hours in air and then be soaked in water until a film of water will stand unabsorbed on its surface.

A thick cream composed of 20 grams of the sample and sufficient water shall then be spread on the surface of this pat, and the whole shall be aged for 24 hours in air. It shall then be subjected to steam above boiling water in a closed vessel for 5 hours, and after cooling it shall show no popping, checking, warping, or disintegration.

Popping and Pitting. One hundred grams of hydrated lime is mixed with water to produce a putty into which is mixed 25 grams of gypsum gauging plaster with addition of water to maintain a workable consistency. This is spread on a glass plate to make a pat 6 by 8 inches in size by approximately $\frac{1}{8}$ inches in thickness and allowed to stand overnight. The specimen and plate are placed on a rack in a steam bath. The temperature of the water in the steam bath is maintained at boiling point for 5 hours, after which the specimen is removed from the bath and examined for pops and pits.

Water Retention Test. The lime mortar consisting of 500 grams of hydrated lime and 1500 grams of standard Ottawa sand is brought to proper consistency as determined by the flow test. The flow-test apparatus comprises a flow table and mold. The mortar is subjected to a suction of 2 inches of mercury vacuum for 60 seconds, and then its consistency is determined by the flow test. The water retention value $= A/B \times 100$, where $A =$ flow after suction and $B =$ flow immediately after mixing.

16.16 Properties and Uses. Stronger and more quickly setting mortars, which shrink less upon setting and hardening, are derived from hydrated limes than from ordinary quicklime. On the other hand, mortars prepared from hydrates are generally inferior to those prepared from quicklimes from the standpoint of plasticity, sand-carrying capacity, and yield, unless the hydrated lime paste is allowed a period of seasoning before being used. Hydrates are being constantly improved in this respect.

The strength of hydrated lime mortars, both in tension and in compression, is somewhat higher than that of the corresponding quicklime mortars. This superiority is particularly noticeable in the high-calcium limes.

16.17 Hydrated Lime Versus Quicklime. Hydrated lime can be more conveniently handled than lump lime because of its powdered condition and can safely be stored or shipped by rail or water in cloth or paper bags or even in bulk. On the other hand, lump lime deteriorates rapidly in storage or transportation because of air slaking, is considered an unsafe commodity to carry by water, and wherever kept always constitutes a fire hazard.

One property of hydrated lime which often constitutes an advantage on construction work is the fact that it is ready to be immediately incorporated with sand and water to form mortar, whereas ordinary lime must be allowed to season after being slaked, thus causing delay.

The fact that hydrated lime is a physically dry material is an advantage in mixing mortars. The dry hydrate can be mixed with sand much more easily than a lime paste or putty, and a more homogeneous mixture is obtained before the excess water is added to make a plastic mortar.

On the other hand, mortars prepared from hydrated lime are very "short" and non-plastic, the volume of lime paste derived is small, as compared with that obtainable from quicklimes, and the sand-carrying capacity is low. Some hydrates are so lacking in colloidal properties that they are actually gritty.

In certain localities a service is maintained whereby prepared plasters and mortars are available to the consumer for immediate use. The advantages of such a service with respect to uniformity and quality of product are obvious. An additional feature is the highly plastic condition of the product obtained by a mechanical agitating or "whipping" process to which the slaked lime is subjected.

16.18 Expansion of Dolomitic Hydrated Limes. Considerable difficulty has been experienced in brick masonry with mortars containing dolomitic limes because of expansion. A number of brick buildings in Wisconsin and Iowa have cracked and bulged owing to the use of dolomitic hydrated lime in the masonry cement used in the mortar. One example is the Kroger building in Madison, Wisconsin; another is St. Joseph's Parochial School near Bode, Iowa.[1] Such expansion is due to the presence of free magnesium oxide in the hydrated lime used in the mortar.

Fundamentally, there is an expansion that takes place when quicklime is changed from the oxide to the hydroxide. With calcium limes, this change to the hydrate form is readily and quickly achieved when the lime is hydrated. But with dolomitic limes, the process of hydration is much slower and some free magnesium oxide is ordinarily present in hydrated dolomitic limes when the usual atmospheric pressure method of hydration is employed. Such dolomitic hydrated limes with unhydrated oxides present undergo a slow expansion caused by the slow hydration of the oxides.

Trouble has been experienced in plaster as well as in mortar. Bulges in finish (white) coat of plaster are attributed to the expansion attending the slow hydration of free magnesium oxide present in dolomitic hydrated limes used in the white coat.

Investigations have been conducted at the National Bureau of Standards by Wells, Clarke, and Levin [2] on the expansive characteristics of 80 structural hydrated limes. These were classified on the basis of chemical analysis and calculated unhydrated oxide content as high-calcium, regularly hydrated dolomitic, highly hydrated dolomitic, and magnesian limes. The

[1] J. W. McBurney: "Cracking in Masonry Caused by Expansion of Mortar." *Proc. ASTM,* v. 52, 1952, p. 1228.

[2] L. S. Wells, W. F. Clarke, and E. M. Levin: "Expansive Characteristics of Hydrated Limes and the Development of an Autoclave Test for Soundness." *Natl. Bur. Standards, Research Paper* RP 1917, v. 41, Sept., 1948.

percentage of unhydrated oxide for the high-calcium class ranged from 0 to 3.9; for the regularly hydrated dolomitic from 16.1 to 34.3; for the highly hydrated dolomitic from 1.4 to 12.6; and for the magnesian from 5.9 to 12.7. The results obtained were:

Data on the expansions of cement-lime bars prepared in proportions of 2 parts cement to 1 part lime, 1 part cement to 1 part lime, and 1 part cement to 2 parts lime, by weight, and autoclaved to 295 pounds per square inch gauge pressure for 3 hours, showed that bars prepared with the regularly hydrated dolomitic limes, which had the highest percentages of unhydrated oxide, had the highest percentage of expansion. The high-calcium limes, characterized, in general, by the lowest percentages of unhydrated oxide, gave the lowest percentage of expansion. Most of the highly hydrated dolomitic limes had percentages of unhydrated oxide and expansions that were comparable to those of the high-calcium limes. The remainder had percentages of unhydrated oxide and expansions that were greater than those of the high-calcium limes. The four magnesian limes exhibited unique behavior in that each showed lower percentage of expansion than other limes with comparable percentages of unhydrated lime.

McBurney [3] makes the following recommendations for the prevention of such expansions in mortar in brick masonry:

1. Accept for use in mortars only those masonry cements and limes which do not exceed 1.0 per cent increase in length when tested for expansion according to the ASTM Standard Method of Test for Autoclave Expansion of Portland Cement (C151–49). For slow-hardening cementitious materials, the test may be made at 48 hours instead of at 24 hours as prescribed by Method C151–49. The test bars for lime for use in cement-lime mortars shall be composed of a mixture of lime and Portland cement in the proportions specified for use on the job.

2. In the absence of tests, lime should be restricted to Type S hydrate or to putty made from high-calcium quicklime. Such a putty should be soaked for not less than 24 hours and otherwise handled as recommended by the ASTM. (See Art. 16.8, last four paragraphs.) The use of unslaked quicklime as an ingredient of mortar cannot be too strongly condemned.

3. Costly repairs such as cutting out and repointing of mortar joints should be delayed, if possible, until the hydration reaction has progressed to the stage where further expansion is negligible.

Questions

16.1. Distinguish between quicklime and hydrated lime.
16.2. Describe the essential steps in the manufacture of quicklime.
16.3. Write the chemical equation representing the manufacture of a high-calcium quicklime.
16.4. Write the chemical formula representing slaking of quicklime.
16.5. Describe proper methods of slaking quicklime. What is "burned lime"?
16.6. What is "air-slaked" lime?
16.7. Describe the chemical changes that take place in the hardening of lime mortar. Compare with the hardening of gypsum plaster.
16.8. Can lime mortar be used under water?
16.9. What is the purpose of adding sand to lime paste?

[3] J. W. McBurney: "Cracking in Masonry Caused by Expansion of Mortar." *Proc. ASTM*, v. 52, 1952, p. 1228.

16.10. State the three stages of preparing hydrated lime from quicklime.
16.11. Describe briefly the principal physical tests for hydrated lime.
16.12. Distinguish between normal and special finishing hydrated limes.
16.13. What are the uses of Mason's hydrate?
16.14. Compare the characteristics of high-calcium and dolomitic hydrated limes.
16.15. A plasterer needs a smooth mortar that trowels well. Would commercial hydrated lime meet this requirement? Give reasons for your opinion.
16.16. What are the advantages of hydrated lime as compared with quicklime?

References

16.1. American Society for Testing Materials: "Methods of Physical Testing of Quicklime and Hydrated Lime." *Designation* C110–49, *Book of Standards,* Part 3, 1952, p. 234. Also: "Symposium on Lime." Mar. 8, 1939.

16.2. Eckel, E. C.: *Cements, Limes, and Plasters.* John Wiley & Sons, 3rd ed., 1928; Chaps. 6 to 10, pp. 91–148.

16.3. Emley, W. E.: "Lime: Its Properties and Uses." Washington, D. C., *Nat'l Bur. Standards, Circ.* 30, 1920.

16.4. Knibbs, N. V. S.: *Lime and Magnesia.* London, Ernest Benn, 1924.

16.5. Leighou, R. B.: *Chemistry of Engineering Materials.* McGraw-Hill Book Co., 4th ed., 1942, 645 pages.

16.6. National Lime Association: "Lime Mortar." Washington, D. C., *Bull.* 320, 1931.

16.7. Nord, M.: *Textbook of Engineering Materials.* John Wiley & Sons, 1952; Chap. 17, pp. 369–380.

16.8. Rockwood, N. C.: Chapter 22 on lime in *Industrial Minerals and Rocks,* 2nd ed., 1949. American Institute of Mining and Metallurgical Engineers.

16.9. Searle, A. B.: *Limestone and Its Products.* London, Ernest Benn, 1935.

CHAPTER 17

Cements

17.1 Introductory. Gypsum plaster and lime are cementing materials which are comparatively simple both in composition and in chemical action. Cements, however, comprise a class of products of very complex and somewhat variable composition and constitution, whose physical characteristics are not definitely fixed, and whose actual constitution is imperfectly understood.

Cements all possess, in common, one property known as *hydraulicity*, i.e., the ability to set and harden under water. In composition they agree to the extent that they all consist essentially of lime, silica, and alumina, or of lime and magnesia, silica, and alumina and iron oxide. The hydraulic cements include hydraulic limes, pozzolan cements, slag cements, natural cements, Portland cements, Portland-pozzolan cements, and alumina cements.

Hydraulic Limes

17.2 Definition and Classification. The hydraulic limes include all those cementing materials made by burning siliceous or argillaceous limestones, whose clinker after calcination contains a sufficient percentage of lime silicate to give hydraulic properties to the product, but which at the same time contain normally so much free lime that the mass of clinker will slake on the addition of water.

17.3 Hydraulic Limestone. The ideal hydraulic limestone rock should have such a composition that, after all the silica has combined with lime during calcination, sufficient free lime remains to disintegrate the kiln product by the expansive force set up when it is slaked.

17.4 Calcination. Hydraulic limes are burned in continuous kilns. The operations involved in the process of calcination are practically the same as for common lime except that the temperature required is somewhat higher.

17.5 Slaking. The theory of slaking of hydraulic lime differs from the slaking of common quicklime in no respect except that in the former case the quicklime, which will slake, is intimately associated in lumps with lime silicate, underburned limestone, and some aluminates and ferrites, none of which can be slaked. The expansion of the quicklime in slaking breaks up the entire mass into a fine powder which will consist principally of lime silicate together with one-fourth to one-third as much hydrated lime.

Hydraulic lime is slaked at the place of manufacture. The lump lime as drawn from the kiln is spread out in thin layers and sprinkled lightly with water. It is then shoveled into heaps or bins where it is allowed to remain for about 10 days till the slaking is completed. In order that the product may be a fine, dry powder, the amount of water must be exactly right.

17.6 Uses. In spite of their designation, hydraulic limes are not suitable for subaqueous construction. They are too slow setting to render their use on general construction work practical, and their comparative weakness makes competition with natural and Portland cement impossible. They are used as an architectural decorative material and to a limited extent as masonry cement. Hydraulic limes are also used for scratch and browning plaster coats and for stucco.

Pozzolan [1] Cements

17.7 General. The oldest known hydraulic mortars were undoubtedly made by the incorporation of a volcanic tufa with slaked lime and sand. The activity of the volcanic material depends upon the presence of weakly acid silicoaluminates which combine more or less readily with lime hydrate at atmospheric temperatures. The natural or artificial materials that contain a sufficiently large percentage of available silica to combine with lime hydrate and form a cement possessing hydraulic properties are known as "pozzolans."

17.8 Pozzolanic Materials. Natural pozzolans may be classed into two groups. In the first group are materials such as pumicite, obsidian, scoria, tuff, santorin, and trass which are derived from volcanic rocks and which have a constituent of glass produced by fusion. In the second group are diatomaceous earth, opal, and clays, shales, and cherts containing substantial amounts of opaline silica. Artificial pozzolans include fly-ash, water-quenched boiler slag, and by-products from the treatment of bauxite ore.

17.9 Pozzolan Cements. Pozzolan cements include all hydraulic cementing materials which are made by the incorporation of natural or artificial pozzolans with hydrated lime without subsequent calcination. No natural

---

[1] The term "pozzolan," which is commonly applied to this class of cements by American authorities, is a corruption of the name "pozzuolana," which refers to the class of volcanic materials first utilized as hydraulic cementing material at the town of Pozzuoli, near Naples. Continental writers call them "pozzuolana" cements.

pozzolanic material is used in the United States in the manufacture of pozzolan cement. Pozzolan cements hold an unimportant place among structural materials.

Slag Cements

17.10 Definition. Slag cement may be defined as an intimate mechanical mixture of granulated blast-furnace slag of suitable chemical composition, with hydrated lime, the materials having been finely pulverized before, during, or after mixing. The mixture is not calcined.

17.11 Blast-Furnace Slag. Blast-furnace slags, such as are suitable for use in slag cements, are fusible lime silicates derived as waste products from the operation of blast furnaces in smelting iron from its ores. If the molten slag is cooled very rapidly by means of cold water, it becomes granulated or broken up into small porous particles which can be economically handled by pulverizing machinery.

Two important chemical effects are also attained by the process of granulating the slag; the slag is rendered more hydraulic, thus providing a stronger cement; and the content of undesirable sulfides always encountered in slags is reduced.

17.12 Manufacture of Slag Cements. The process of manufacture of slag cements involves the following operations: granulation of the slag, drying the slag sand, preparation of the very pure high-calcium hydrated lime, proportioning the mixture, mixing, and grinding.

The slag may be granulated by a jet of water which the stream of slag encounters as it issues from the furnace, or by the method of discharging the stream of slag from the furnace into a pit of cold water.

The slag as it comes from the bins, into which it has been discharged by the granulating device, carries from 15 to 45 per cent of water. This water is removed through the agency of heat in either a rotary cylinder or in a vertical shaft dryer. The standard proportions of slag and lime vary at different plants from as low as 25 pounds to as high as 45 pounds of lime for 100 pounds of slag sand.

The best method of grinding and mixing the slag and lime consists in grinding the slag sand in a ball mill or a tube mill, adding the hydrated lime, and mixing and pulverizing the mixture simultaneously in a tube mill or other type of cement-finishing mill.

17.13 Properties and Uses of Slag Cements. The specific gravity of slag cements usually ranges between 2.7 and 2.85. This fact affords a means of distinguishing slag cements from natural cements, which rarely fall below 2.9, and from Portland cements, which under the standard specifications must be not less than 3.1. Slag cements are usually light colored.

The use of slag cement is limited to unimportant structures or to work requiring large masses of concrete masonry where weight and bulk are more important than great strength. It is never used on comparatively light reinforced-concrete construction. Slag cement is utilized as a masonry cement because of its non-staining properties due to its low alkali content.

Natural Cements

17.14 Definition. Natural cement is the product obtained by finely pulverizing calcined argillaceous limestone, to which not to exceed 5 per cent of non-deleterious materials may be added subsequent to calcination. The temperature of calcination shall be no higher than is necessary to drive off carbonic acid gas.[2]

Two types are available: Type N natural cement for general concrete construction; and Type NA air-entraining natural cement. The latter cement is interground with an addition to produce air entrainment; furthermore, a quantity of calcium chloride not exceeding 2 per cent is sometimes added during manufacture in order to compensate for loss in strength due to air entrainment.

The distinctions between natural and Portland cements may be summarized as in the accompanying table.

	Natural Cements	*Portland Cement*
Raw material	Natural argillocalcareous rock	Artificial argillocalcareous mixture
Calcination temperature	Low	Relatively high
Chemical composition	Variable, not under control	Controllable within narrow limits
Color	Usually yellow to brown	Usually blue-gray
Specific gravity	2.7 to 3.1	3.1 to 3.2
Rate of setting	Normally rapid	Relatively slow
Strength	Low	Relatively high

17.15 Natural Cement Rocks. Natural cements are made by the calcination of a natural clayey limestone carrying from 13 to 35 per cent of clayey material, 10 to 20 per cent of which is silica and the balance alumina and iron oxide. The hydraulic properties of the cement are entirely due to the presence of this clayey material. The calcium carbonate of the limestone may be replaced to a considerable degree by magnesium carbonate, resulting in the replacement of lime by magnesia to a corresponding degree in the manufactured product.

17.16 Calcination. The rock as it is charged into the kiln consists essentially of lime and magnesium carbonate with a more or less definite percentage of clayey matter. The chemical changes that take place during calcination may be briefly mentioned as follows:

[2] Definition adopted by the American Society for Testing Materials.

Water mechanically held by the rock is first driven off; at a temperature of about 800° C. (1472° F.) magnesium carbonate is dissociated, the carbon dioxide being driven off; at a temperature of about 900° C. (1652° F.) the lime carbonate is similarly dissociated; at a temperature of 900° C. (1652° F.) to 1000° C. (1832° F.) the clay is decomposed and aluminates and ferrites of lime and magnesia are formed; lastly, at a temperature of about 1300° C. (2372° F.), silicates of lime and magnesia are formed.

The most common type of kiln in the natural cement industry in the United States is of the continuous vertical mixed-feed type, the rock and fuel being either mixed or charged in alternate layers. The usual fuel for natural cement burning is bituminous coal.

17.17 The Clinker. The clinker many times contains large proportions of free lime. Such free lime may be neutralized by slaking, usually by sprinkling or steaming the unground clinker.

The clinker is crushed in some form of crusher and then finished in one of the various types of grinders and pulverizers used in Portland cement manufacture.

17.18 Properties of Natural Cement. *Chemical Composition.* The average composition of various natural cements is indicated by the tabulated summary.

SiO_2	Al_2O_3	Fe_2O_3	CaO	MgO
22.3–29.0%	5.2–8.8%	1.4–3.2%	31.0–57.6%	1.4–21.5%

It will be apparent that the composition of natural cements is extremely variable. The wide variations in composition are accompanied by great differences in mechanical properties.

Specific Gravity. The specific gravity of natural cements is slightly below that of Portland cements, the average being about 2.95.

Time of Setting. Natural cements normally are quick setting as compared with Portland cement. The standard specifications prescribe that the initial set shall take place in not less than 10 minutes as determined by the Vicat needle or in not less than 20 minutes when the Gilmore needle is used. Final set shall be attained within 10 hours.

The addition of gypsum or plaster of Paris has a very marked effect in retarding the set of natural cements, the degree of retardation with a given percentage of gypsum depending largely upon the chemical composition of the particular cement.

Tensile Strength. In tensile strength, natural cements vary quite as much as they do in other physical properties. This variation is found not only in comparing cements from different localities, but even in comparing samples taken at different times from the output of any one locality. The standard specifications of the American Society for Testing Materials fix the following minimum requirements for tensile strength of 1:2 standard mortar briquets:

1 day in moist air, 6 days in water, 75 p.s.i.
1 day in moist air, 27 days in water, 150 p.s.i.

It is further stipulated that the cement shall show no retrogression in strength within the perod specified.

Other Physical Requirements. Tentative specifications of the American Society for Testing Materials state the following requirements for the two types of natural cement, N and NA.

Fineness, specific surface, Blaine air-permeability apparatus: Average value, not less than 6000 sq. cm. per gram; minimum value, any one sample, 5500 sq. cm. per gram.

Soundness: Autoclave expansion, as indicated by the difference between the autoclave expansion of a blend of 25 per cent of the natural cement and 75 per cent Portland cement by weight and the autoclave expansion of the Portland cement used in the blend, maximum 0.50 per cent.

Time of setting of natural cement in mortar: Not less than 30 minutes; not more than 6 hours.

Compressive strength, mortar cubes, composed of 1 part natural cement and 1 part standard sand by weight, minimum values: 1 day in moist air, 6 days in water, 500 lbs. per sq. in. 1 day in moist air, 27 days in water, 1000 lbs. per sq. in.

Type NA only: Air content of mortar made with a blend of 25 per cent Type NA natural cement and 75 per cent non-air-entraining Portland cement, 18 ± 3 per cent by volume.

17.19 Uses of Natural Cement. When economy is effected thereby, natural cement may be substituted for Portland cement in mortars and concrete for dry, heavy foundations where the stresses encountered will never be high, and for backing or filling in massive masonry in dry situations where weight and mass are more essential than strength. It should not be used in exposed situations, should not be placed under water, and is unsuitable for marine construction. It is sometimes used as an ingredient in the manufacture of masonry cements for mortar.

Portland Cement

17.20 Historical. In 1824, Joseph Aspdin, a brick mason of Leeds, England, was granted a patent on a method of manufacture of a cement for which he proposed the name *Portland cement,* because of a real or fancied resemblance of the concrete made with it to the natural limestone extensively quarried for building purposes at Portland, England.

Portland cement was manufactured first in the United States near Kalamazoo, Michigan, in 1872. At Coplay, Pennsylvania, in 1875, Portland cement was made by David O. Saylor, by calcining at a high temperature a mixture of argillaceous limestone rock with a comparatively pure limestone.

17.21 Definition. The term Portland cement is defined by the American Society for Testing Materials as follows:

> Portland cement is the product obtained by pulverizing clinker consisting essentially of hydraulic calcium silicates, to which no additions have been made subsequent to calcination other than water and/or untreated calcium sulfate, except that additions not to exceed 1 per cent of other materials may be interground with the clinker at the option of the manufacturer, provided such materials in the amounts indicated have been shown not to be harmful by tests carried out or reviewed by Committee C-1 on Cement.

The approximate proportions for Portland cement are as tabulated.

	Per Cent
Lime (CaO)	60–65
Silica (SiO_2)	20–25
Iron oxide and alumina (Fe_2O_3 and Al_2O_3)	7–12

The raw materials obtained from natural deposits must be mixed in exact proportions obtainable only in an artificial way under chemical control. Burning to an incipient fusion (sintering) insures the high density so essential to Portland cement. The presence of magnesia and sulfuric acid is unavoidable because both are contained in the raw materials and in the fuel. The percentage of each is therefore limited because an excess of either tends to cause unsoundness of cement.

17.22 Portland Cement as a Structural Material. Portland cement is by far the most important of all masonry materials in modern engineering construction and ranks second only to steel as a structural material. In monolithic concrete it is used in all types of masonry, such as foundations, footings, piers, abutments, dams, retaining walls, pavements, and roadways. When reinforced with steel, concrete is used for framework, walls, floors, and roofs of buildings, for bridges, for tunnels, subways, conduits, and innumerable other purposes. In combination with sand and lime, Portland cement serves as mortar for laying brick or stone, and as a plaster or stucco it is applied to either exterior or interior walls upon a base of structural clay tile, brick, or metal lath

Raw Materials

17.23 General. The essential constituents of Portland cement are lime, silica, and alumina. With the exception of lime, these substances are found free in nature, but not, however, in a form suitable for use in cement manufacture. Lime is always used in the form of a carbonate, and silica and alumina in the form of clay, shale, or slate.

The accompanying classification of the raw materials may be made.

Calcareous	*Argillocalcareous*	*Argillaceous*
($CaCO_3$ over 75%)	($CaCO_3$ = 40–75%)	($CaCO_3$ under 40%)
Pure limestone	Clayey limestone	Slate
Pure chalk	Clayey chalk	Shale
Pure marl	Clayey marl	Clay
Oyster shells	Blast-furnace slag	

The combination of the materials in any two of these groups which will give a mixture of proper composition might be taken as the raw material for Portland cement. The only combinations that have been used to any extent in America are:

Limestone and shale or clay.
Pure limestone and argillaceous limestone (cement rock).
Marl or chalk and clay or shale.
Oyster shells and clay or shale.
Limestone and blast-furnace slag.

17.24 Limestone. When pure, limestone forms the mineral calcite ($CaCO_3$). Commercial limestones consist essentially of calcium carbonate combined with more or less impurities consisting of magnesia, silica, iron, alkalies, and sulfur.

Carbonate of magnesia occurs very often in limestone, but much more than 5 per cent will make the limestone unsuitable for use.

Silica may be present either alone or in combination with alumina. When alone, silica does not combine with lime in the kiln, and more than a very small amount renders a limestone unfit for use. Silica combined with alumina, on the other hand, does readily combine with lime in the kiln. The argillaceous limestones are among the most important raw materials for the manufacture of Portland cement.

Iron occurs usually as either the oxide (Fe_2O_3) or sulfide (FeS_2), and less commonly as a carbonate or silicate. Except as a sulfide the iron forms a useful flux, aiding the combination of lime and silica in the kiln. As a sulfide it is injurious and to be avoided if it occurs in amounts over 2 to 3 per cent.

The alkalies soda and potash commonly occur in limestones in small percentages. Unless present in quantities above about 5 per cent, in which event they may be carried over into the cement with harmful results, they will be largely driven off in the kiln with no consequent effect upon the cement.

Sulfur may be present as iron pyrite or as lime sulfate. Either substance is extremely injurious and not more than 2 per cent can be tolerated.

17.25 Chalk. Chalk is a fine-grained limestone composed of finely cominuted marine shells. It is quarried in England as a raw material for modern cement plants of large capacity. For example, the Portland cement plant at Shoreham, Sussex, England, built in 1951 with a capacity of 350,000 tons of cement per year, is designed to handle chalk and clay as the raw materials. It is a wet-process plant.

17.26 Argillaceous Limestone, Cement Rock. The term "cement rock" is technically applied to a limestone containing about 68 to 72 per cent of lime carbonate, 18 to 27 per cent clayey matter, and not more than 5 per cent of magnesium carbonate. Cement rock is a dark gray to black slaty limestone, softer than pure limestone and consequently more easily ground. As a rule the cement rock must be mixed with a comparatively pure limestone in small percentages. Some cement rock, however, contains an excess of calcareous material, necessitating the admixture of shale or clay.

17.27 Marl. Marls are deposits of comparatively pure carbonate of lime found in beds of existing or extinct lakes and may be considered to be unconsolidated limestones. Organic matter, clay, and carbonate of magnesia are the principal impurities found in marls, with sometimes small amounts of sulfur. Marls usually analyze about 90 to 97 per cent $CaCO_3$ and $MgCO_3$, less than 1 per cent SiO_2, less than 1 per cent Al_2O_3 and Fe_2O_3 combined, the balance being made up of small amounts of organic matter, SO_3, etc. When used in the manufacture of Portland cement, marls usually require the addition of 15 to 20 per cent clay. The large percentage of water (often 50 to 60 per cent) usually present in the marl upon arrival at the plant is disregarded in the above statement of composition. Marls have the economic advantage of being naturally of fine particle size and require little or no reduction to make them suitable for burning. They may be obtained by simple methods such as dredging.

17.28 Clays, Shales, and Slates. Clays, shales, and slate may in general be considered of the same ultimate composition, differing only in the degree of consolidation. All clays are formed from the débris resulting from the decay of rocks, and hence they differ greatly in composition and physical character. Clays left where rock has disintegrated are called residual clays; those transported and deposited by stream action are sedimentary clays; and those deposited by glacial action are glacial clays. The different classes of clays differ in composition owing to differences in the manner of their deposition. Residual clays are likely to contain fragments of quartz, flint, or lime carbonate, depending upon the kind of rock disintegrated; sedimentary clays in their long water transportation usually have lost all their coarser material and so form a fine-grained homogeneous product; the glacial clays show even less homogeneity than the residual clays and are likely to contain much sand, gravel, and pebbles.

Absolutely pure clay is hydrated silicate of alumina ($Al_2O_3 \cdot 2SiO_2 \cdot 2H_2O$). Such a clay is not available for cement manufacture. It is imperative that the clay used be as free as possible from gravel and sand. The proportion of silica should not be less than 55 to 65 per cent, and the combined amount of alumina and iron oxide should be between one-third and one-half the amount of silica. The presence of gypsum or pyrite in the clay is injurious, and magnesia and alkalies should not be present in quantities exceeding about 3 per cent.

Shales are clays hardened by pressure, but they have almost invariably been formed from deposits of sedimentary clay and so do not show the irregularities in composition common to most residual or glacial clays. Shales are preferable to soft clay for mixing with limestone because, on account of the similarity in physical characteristics, segregation of the two is less likely to take place. They also carry less water and therefore require less drying. Clay, on the other hand, is better adapted for use with marl.

The slates are clays which through heavy pressure have solidified in a markedly laminated structure and acquired the property of splitting readily into thin sheets. The slates find only a limited application in the manufacture of Portland cement.

17.29 Blast-Furnace Slag. Three classes of cement which must not be confused are made with blast-furnace slag as one of the ingredients. One is the slag cement made by grinding blast-furnace slag with hydrated lime without subsequent calcination; a second is a true Portland cement made by mixing limestone and slag, grinding the mixture very finely, and calcining the product as in the usual process of Portland cement manufacture; the third is a cement made by grinding finely together true Portland cement and granulated blast-furnace slag, named Portland blast-furnace slag cement.

Blast-furnace slag is a fusible silicate formed during the smelting of iron ore by the combination of the fluxing material with the gangue of the ore. The slags used in cement manufacture are those of strongly basic character, the higher the lime the better.

Manufacture of Portland Cement

17.30 Principal Steps. The principal steps in the manufacture of Portland cement consist of quarrying, crushing, grinding, mixing, calcining, cooling the clinker, grinding the clinker, adding retarder, and packing. See Fig. 17.1.

17.31 Wet- and Dry-Process Manufacture. The treatment of the raw materials before calcination may be carried on by the *dry* or by the *wet* process. In the dry process the raw materials are dried before being ground and mixed; in the wet process the materials are ground and mixed wet.

360   Materials of Construction

The economics of manufacture favor one process over the other according to the raw materials available. If the available materials are cement rock and limestone which are naturally dry or contain so little free water that they may be dried by waste heat from the kilns so that they may be ground economically in a dry state, the dry process offers economy in the cost of

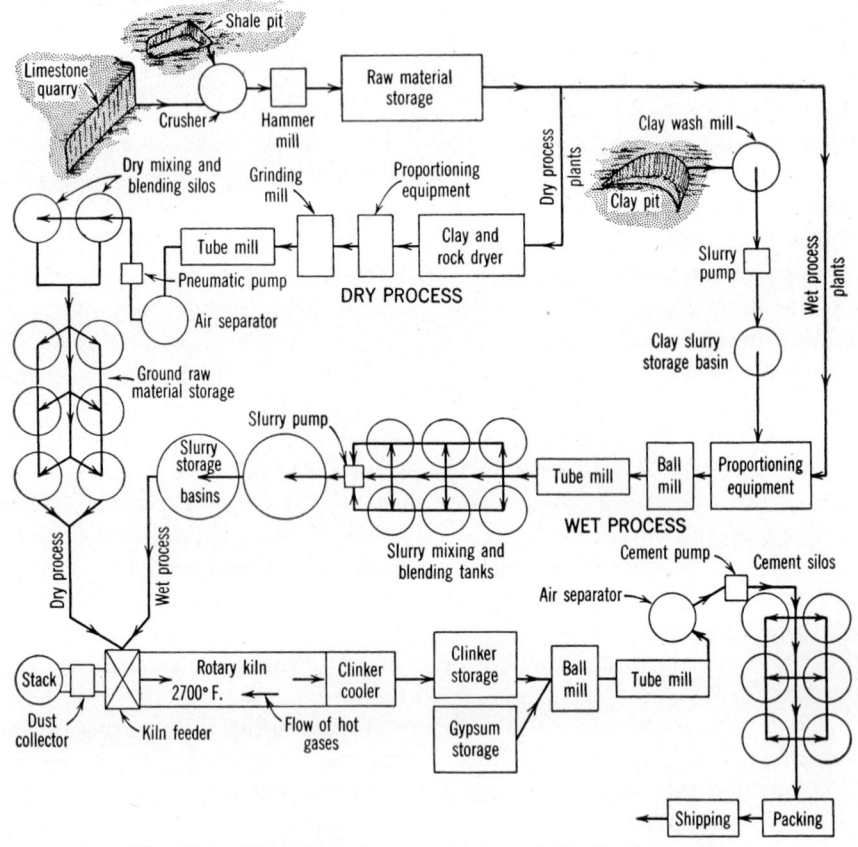

Fig. 17.1. Flow chart for manufacture of Portland cement.

grinding and burning. If, however, at least one of the components of the mixture is wet, such as a marl or a clay, the increased cost of drying the raw materials in the dry process would be relatively greater than the increased cost of burning wet materials in the wet process.

From the standpoint of chemical control of raw-material composition, there is little choice between the two processes when modern methods are employed. Under average conditions a wet-process operation is usually less complicated and better suited for the purpose of improving quality and increasing the variety of types of Portland cement which can be produced with available materials. However, for many materials, the perfection of pneumatic and mechanical blending devices for raw materials and the installation of modern blending tanks for kiln-feed control in dry-process plants makes it possible to control the uniformity of kiln feed to a degree comparable with that attained in wet-process plants.

Dust conditions differ little in the two processes. The materials are wet only during preliminary treatment in a wet-process plant, the clinker being ground dry. If the raw-material mills of a dry-process plant are provided with proper dust-collecting equipment, a dry-process plant can be kept as clean as a wet-process one.

17.32 The Dry Process of Manufacture. The raw materials employed in the dry process are usually in the form of more or less compact rock, either limestone and shale or limestone and cement rock.

Quarrying. Open quarry practice is usually followed, the rock being blasted down in benches, reduced to sizes suitable for handling by secondary blasting, loaded by power shovels onto quarry cars usually of the steel side-dump type, and removed in the cars to the crusher.

Crushing. Modern plants employ primary and secondary stages of crushing. The primary crusher is either of the jaw or gyratory type, the gyratory type being generally preferred. For example, in 1951, a 60-inch gyratory crusher was installed in one of the largest cement plants. The desired top size of the output from the primary crushers is $5/8$ inch; this output is fed into the secondary crusher which may be of gyratory type but is ordinarily of the hammermill type. Preferred practice is to operate the hammermills in closed circuit with vibrating screens to obtain a good range of particle sizes for efficient grinding. By this method of screening, it is possible to eliminate oversized particles which are detrimental to efficiency as well as removal of fine particles to reduce the dust load on the hammermills.

Storage. Storage facilities for the crushed stone and shale are ordinarily provided so that the composition can be controlled. One type of rock storage involves the use of overhead bins from which withdrawals are made by weighing feeders, whereby the materials may be proportioned. Another type employs a covered craneway for the storage of crushed stone in separate stock piles arranged according to composition. Feed bins of the raw-material grinding mills are arranged under the craneway so that they can be filled by the grab bucket. Each raw mill is provided with two feed bins from which the rock is withdrawn by separate measuring feeders so that the composition can be held within close limits.

Drying. It is often necessary to dry the rock after crushing since the presence of moisture in the rock as it comes from the quarry impairs the efficiency of grinding and pulverizing machinery. The rotary type of dryer is used almost exclusively in cement mills. Steel cylinders, 50 feet in length and 5 feet in diameter, set at a slight inclination with the horizontal, are typical. Waste gases may be utilized.

Raw Grinding. Modern practice is to use compartment mills in closed circuits, the size of the feed material being closely controlled within narrow limits. Tube mills and ball mills are also extensively employed. A typical tube mill is one 10 feet in diameter by 22 feet in length. An example of a ball mill is an installation 9 feet 6 inches in diameter by 15 feet long in a closed circuit with a 16-foot mechanical air separator. Feed is directly into the air separator and the rejects (coarse particles) are fed into the ball mill which minimizes overgrinding and by-passes acceptable material. Some cement plants perform raw grinding in two stages comprising preliminary grinding through a ball mill followed by final grinding (pulverizing) through tube mills.

Blending. After pulverization, dry raw materials are blended by the *mechanical* or the *pneumatic* method. A typical mechanical blending operation employs ten silos for raw material storage and six silos for blended material. Conveyors move mixed raw materials from the pulverizing mills into the top of any one of the storage silos. A blend is made by simultaneous drawoff from any combination of storage silos into a silo for blended material. Material is drawn from blending silos to feed the kilns. Continuous sampling is employed to check the composition of incoming materials, of the blends made, and of the kiln feed. Such a highly developed mechanical system for interchangeable handling makes possible accurate control of proportioning.

A modern pneumatic method of blending consists of pumping the dry, finely divided materials into a group of storage silos and then withdrawing the materials from the bottoms of the silos. Dry, pulverized materials when mixed with air under certain conditions have the characteristic of increasing in bulk and becoming fluent to such an extent that they may be pumped in a manner similar to the way liquids are pumped. The materials when pumped into the storage silo flow to a level surface. The pulverized materials do not flow from the silo in the order of the lowermost materials in storage, but descend uniformly from all levels above the discharge spout, thus giving a cross-section of all the thin, flat layers.

Proportioning the Raw Materials. The combining of the raw materials in such a manner as to achieve a desired ratio of calcareous to argillaceous materials is not a simple matter, for the reason that Portland cement after calcination is not a mixture of lime and clayey materials, but is what may be termed a "solid solution" of a number of components including silicates and aluminates of lime, but no free lime. The ratio of lime to clayey material previously cited very roughly expresses the relative proportions in which the two classes of material are understood to combine, and the actual proportions of two given materials which will produce a satisfactory cement can be determined only by a knowledge of the detailed composition of each of the component raw materials, and a further knowledge of the compounds which will be formed during calcination.

The application of a rule based upon complete analyses of the raw materials is not necessary once a plant is well established with fairly uniform raw materials. Usually a fixed standard total percentage of carbonate ($CaCO_3$ and $MgCO_3$) is found by experience with any given raw materials to give a satisfactory mixture, and this standard is thereafter maintained as long as the raw materials remain unchanged.

The usual method of control consists in the analysis of both raw materials at the plant before grinding, grinding and mixing according to these analyses, analyzing the mixture as a check, and correcting the mix by the addition of the constituents required by blending before calcination.

17.33 The Wet Process of Manufacture. The same classes of raw materials as used in the dry process may be employed in the wet process, but, in many cases, the materials handled by the wet process are physically soft, such as marl with clay or shale, which in their natural state carry high percentages of moisture.

Marl usually not only is saturated with moisture, but often also is covered with water to a considerable depth. Under such circumstances it is obtained by dredging, and is pumped to the mill through a pipeline. The marl usually reaches the plant in the shape of a thin mud containing about 50 per cent water. It is passed through a separator to remove stones, roots, etc., and then stored in large tanks.

The clay upon arrival at the plant is often dried in order to facilitate the determination of the correct proportion to be added to the marl. It is then ground in an edge-runner mill between millstones, or in a disintegrator.

From the storage tank the marl is pumped into either a measuring tank or a weighing hopper. The ground clay is added to the marl in the proportion determined by analysis of the materials.

The mixture is then discharged into a pug mill, which consists of a horizontal cylinder within which two shafts provided with steel blades rotate. The mixture is churned up by the revolving blades, thoroughly mixed, and discharged into large tanks, where it is sampled, analyzed, and corrected by the addition of clay or marl. In order to prevent any part of the mixture from settling, it is necessary to provide these tanks with revolving paddles which keep the mass constantly agitated. The "slurry" is then passed on to the final grinding mill.

The output of the final grinding mill is conveyed to blending basins. A typical blending basin is 20 feet in diameter by 34 feet high and is provided with revolving arms for horizontal agitation and compressed air for vertical agitation. The bottoms of the blending basins are hoppered with a slope of about 30 degrees to provide for emptying the blended slurry. This slurry is then fed to the kilns by ferris-wheel feeders which are synchronized with the kiln speed. Usually the slurry is charged into the kiln without any previous drying. It generally contains from 60 to 65 per cent of water, which must be evaporated in the upper part of the rotary kiln. This practice necessarily increases the fuel consumption of the kiln. In some plants water is removed by rotary dryers which utilize waste heat from the kilns.

17.34 Calcination. The principal objects accomplished by calcination of Portland cement mixtures are, in the approximate order of their sequence, the evaporation of water, the dissociation of carbonates of lime and magnesia, the expulsion of the alkalies, the oxidation of ferrous to ferric oxides, and the combination of lime and magnesia with silica, alumina, and ferric oxide to form the silicates, aluminates, and ferrites which make up Portland cement.

Most of the moisture is driven off at temperatures only slightly exceeding 100° C. (212° F.). Lime carbonate is dissociated at temperatures somewhat above 900° C. (1652° F.), and magnesium carbonate at temperatures probably between 800° C. (1472° F.) and 900° C. (1652° F.). The formation of silicates, aluminates, and ferrites does not take place at temperatures below about 1100° C. (2012° F.), and for most commercial cement mixtures the attainment of a temperature of about 1550° C. (2822° F.) has been found necessary in order to insure the combination of practically all the lime with the clayey constituents.

17.35 Burning the Cement Mixture. The cement mixture is calcined in a long horizontal rotary type of cement kiln which may be from 100 to 500 feet long and 8 to 12 feet in diameter. See Fig. 17.2. The steel drum of the kiln is lined with firebrick and is supported at intervals on rollers. The kiln is rotated at a speed of about 65 to 75 revolutions per hour and is inclined with the horizontal about ½ inch per foot.

Raw material is discharged into the upper end of the kiln from the supply bins either through an inclined spout or a water-jacketed screw-conveyor running through the stack flue. Usually the feeding device is belt-connected to the kiln drive so that the feeding starts and stops with the kiln.

Pulverized coal is delivered by conveyors from the coal-grinding mill to bins located above and behind the burner end of the kiln. A conveyor carries the coal from the supply bin to a point where it falls into an air injector, where it encounters an air blast which conveys it through a pipe to a nozzle projecting into the kiln.

Fuel oil, when burned in the rotary kiln, is sprayed in by a blast of air from blowers or air compressors. In order to distribute the heat properly in the kiln, two or more oil burners are necessary. Gas is also used as fuel.

Proper burning is determined by the color and appearance of the clinker, the properly burned clinker being a greenish black in color, having a vitreous luster, and showing bright, glistening specks when just cooled. Most of the lumps are the size of a walnut or smaller. Underburned clinker is brown or has brown centers and lacks the luster of well-burned clinker. Overburned clinker has hard brown centers. Overburned clinker is probably not injurious except for very low-lime cements, but overburning means a waste of fuel and increases the expense of grinding, owing to the greater hardness of overburned clinker.

Under average conditions a 10 by 340 foot kiln should turn out about 2000 barrels of cement per day with a fuel consumption of about 1,000,000

Fig. 17.2. Rotary kiln installed in a Portland cement plant. (*Courtesy* Allis-Chalmers Mfg. Co.)

British thermal units per barrel. A 12 by 500 foot kiln should turn out about 4200 barrels per day.

17.36 Treatment of the Clinker. The clinker as it issues from the kiln is very hot and must be reduced to a suitable temperature before being ground. In modern plants this is done by means of clinker coolers. Newer installations are equipped with grate clinker coolers, either of the horizontal or inclined type. Horizontal coolers provide for the movement of clinker over horizontal grates by means of a drag chain. A typical size is 4 feet 6 inches by 100 feet. Inclined-grate coolers consist of movable grates in the form of stair steps that propel the clinker down an inclined plane of about 15 degrees. A typical size is 6 by 33 feet. Air-quenching is accomplished by blowing a blast of air through the cooler clinker bed and into the kiln. Clinker chunk breakers are operated at the discharge ends of the coolers; these are either roll crushers or hammermills. Rotary type coolers are also employed but are not as efficient as grate coolers.

It is the usual practice to grind the clinker in two stages, each in a closed circuit. The first stage employs gyratory or cone-type clinker crushers which reduce the mill feed to a top size of ½ inch. The second stage usually employs tube mills in closed circuit with mechanical air separators. (In some plants the same grinding machinery as in the raw-material mill is used.) Rejects (coarse particles) from the air separators are fed back into the tube mills. Fines from the air separators are discharged into the hoppers of pumps such as Fuller-Kinyon type which transport the cement into storage. This withdrawal of fine materials from the tube mills eliminates the cushioning effect of the fines and avoids waste of power. Air separation provides a uniform method of obtaining cement of high surface area. The newer mechanical air separators are equipped with air-cooling devices which are effective in cooling the finished cement to a temperature as low as 65.5° C. (150° F.).

17.37 Addition of Retarder. The clinker produced in the rotary kiln makes a cement which is naturally very quick setting. In order to retard its set sufficiently to enable it to meet commercial requirements, it is the practice to add sulfate of lime either before grinding or between the stages of grinding and pulverizing the clinker.

The retarder is added in the form of raw gypsum ($CaSO_4 + 2H_2O$). The gypsum, in the form of lumps crushed to pass a 1-inch ring, is added to the clinker by mechanical weighing devices, the quantity being, as a rule, about 2 per cent, and never exceeding 3 per cent.

17.38 Storing and Packing. The finished cement is stored in silos from which it is withdrawn by conveyors or pumps and delivered to packing bins, or pumped directly in bulk to box cars, tank cars, special trucks, ships, and barges. Bulk cement is employed in the construction of most large concrete structures for economy, bulk shipments representing about 40 per cent of the total in the United States. Cement may be packed in wooden barrels containing 376 pounds net but generally is packed in cloth or paper bags containing 94 pounds net. The bags are sealed by wiring or sewing before filling and are filled through a self-closing valve in the bottom by means of a packing machine.

Constitution of Portland Cement

17.39 Types. Five types of Portland cement are recognized by the American Society for Testing Materials as follows:

Type 1. For use in general concrete construction when the special properties specified for other types are not required.

Type 2. For use in general concrete construction exposed to moderate sulfate action or where moderate heat of hydration is required.
Type 3. For use when high early strength is required.
Type 4. For use when a low heat of hydration is required.
Type 5. For use when high sulfate resistance is required.

17.40 Composition. The requirements of chemical composition of the American Society for Testing Materials for the five types of Portland cement are given in Table 17.1.

Table 17.1

ASTM CHEMICAL REQUIREMENTS OF PORTLAND CEMENTS

	Type 1	Type 2	Type 3	Type 4 *	Type 5 *
Silicon dioxide (SiO_2), min., %	—	21.0	—	—	—
Aluminum oxide (Al_2O_3), max., %	—	6.0	—	—	†
Ferric oxide (Fe_2O_3), max., %	—	6.0	—	6.5	†
Magnesium oxide (MgO), max., %	5.0	5.0	5.0	5.0	4.0
Sulfur trioxide (SO_3), max., %	2.0 ‡	2.0	2.5 §	2.0	2.0
Loss on ignition, max., %	3.0	3.0	3.0	2.3	3.0
Insoluble residue, max., %	0.75	0.75	0.75	0.75	0.75
Tricalcium silicate ($3CaO \cdot SiO_2$), ‖ max., %	—	50	—	35	50
Dicalcium silicate ($2CaO \cdot SiO_2$), ‖ min., %	—	—	—	40	—
Tricalcium aluminate ($3CaO \cdot Al_2O_3$), ‖ max., %	—	8	15	7	5

* Types 4 and 5 not usually carried in stock.
† The tricalcium aluminate shall not exceed 5%, and the tetracalcium aluminoferrite ($4CaO \cdot Al_2O_3 \cdot Fe_2O_3$) plus twice the amount of tricalcium aluminate shall not exceed 20%.
§ The maximum limit for sulfur trioxide content of Type 1 cement shall be 2.5% when the tricalcium aluminate content is over 8%.
‡ The maximum limit for sulfur trioxide content of Type 3 cement shall be 3.0% when the tricalcium aluminate content is over 8%.
‖ The expressing of chemical limitations by means of calculated assumed compounds does not necessarily mean that the oxides are actually or entirely present as such compounds.

The percentages of tricalcium silicate, dicalcium silicate, tricalcium aluminate, and tetracalcium aluminoferrite shall be calculated from the chemical analysis as follows:

Tricalcium silicate = $(4.07 \times \% \, CaO) - (7.60 \times \% \, SiO_2) - (6.72 \times \% \, Al_2O_3) - (1.43 \times \% \, Fe_2O_3) - (2.85 \times \% \, SO_3)$
Dicalcium silicate = $(2.87 \times \% \, SiO_2) - (0.754 \times \% \, 3CaO \cdot SiO_2)$
Tricalcium aluminate = $(2.65 \times \% \, Al_2O_3) - (1.69 \times \% \, Fe_2O_3)$
Tetracalcium aluminoferrite = $3.04 \times \% \, Fe_2O_3$

Oxide determinations calculated to the nearest 0.1% shall be used in the calculations. Compound percentages shall be calculated to the nearest 0.1% and reported to the nearest 1%.

17.41 Properties of Compounds. Five major compounds are known to be present in Portland cement after calcination: tricalcium silicate, dicalcium silicate, tricalcium aluminate, tetracalcium aluminoferrite, and magnesia. These compounds are normally present in the clinker in the form of extremely fine interlocking crystals, although some amorphous material is frequently present. Magnesia appears to exist uncombined in Portland cement. It is nearly inert though if present in excess amount it might cause unsoundness due to extremely slow hydration. The characteristics of the other four major compounds are compared in Table 17.2.

Table 17.2

CHARACTERISTICS OF MAJOR PORTLAND CEMENT COMPOUNDS *

	Tricalcium Silicate C_3S	Dicalcium Silicate C_2S	Tricalcium Aluminate C_3A	Tetracalcium Aluminoferrite C_4AF
Cementing value	Good	Good	Poor	Poor
Rate of reaction	Medium	Slow	Fast	Slow
Amount of heat liberated	Medium	Small	Large	Small

* R. W. Carlson: Development of Low-Heat Cement for Mass Concrete, *Eng. News-Record*, Oct. 20, 1932, p. 461.

The calcium silicates are the effective cementing materials; the other compounds are generally believed to have little if any cementing value. All these compounds liberate heat during hydration, the total amount of heat liberated being, in general, proportional to the rate of chemical reaction.

17.42 Tricalcium Silicate. When water is added to tricalcium silicate ($3CaO \cdot SiO_2$), a moderately rapid reaction occurs, both by hydrolysis and hydration. This reaction may be expressed approximately as

$$3CaO \cdot SiO_2 + H_2O = 2CaO \cdot SiO_2 \cdot xH_2O + Ca(OH)_2$$

One molecule of CaO splits off, and the products are crystalline calcium hydroxide and a less basic amorphous hydrated calcium silicate of composition represented by the formula $2CaO \cdot SiO_2 \cdot xH_2O$. This compound is a gel. To its formation is due the greater part of the early strength of the cement and some of the early heat evolution. Tricalcium silicate has good cementing value.

17.43 Dicalcium Silicate. In the presence of water $2CaO \cdot SiO_2$ hydrates slowly to form directly a compound of the composition $2CaO \cdot SiO_2 \cdot xH_2O$. This is similar to and possibly identical with the compound formed by the hydrolysis of $3CaO \cdot SiO_2$. Dicalcium silicate hydrates slowly, chiefly after the first week, and very little of the strength attained by the cement in 28 days is attributable to it, but the greater part of subsequent increases is due to it.

17.44 Tricalcium Aluminate. This compound hydrates very rapidly with water, chiefly in the first day, to form hydrated tricalcium aluminate; several different crystalline hydrates have been identified, the formula being $3CaO \cdot Al_2O_3 \cdot 6H_2O$. The reaction is accompanied by a considerable evolution of heat, and the mixture sets almost instantly. In the presence of gypsum the heat evolution is less, and the setting occurs more slowly. This is due to the formation of calcium sulfoaluminate, $3CaO \cdot Al_2O_3 \cdot 3CaSO_4 \cdot 31H_2O$. As long as the water contains dissolved gypsum the calcium sulfoaluminate forms in preference to the hydrated tricalcium aluminate. It is to retard the rapid hydration of the aluminate that gypsum is added to commercial cement clinker. Tricalcium aluminate has poor cementing value. All properties of cement, including volume constancy and durability, being taken into consideration, tricalcium aluminate is believed to be the least desirable of the four major cement compounds.

17.45 Tetracalcium Aluminoferrite. This compound hydrates slowly, and since it is considered to have no great cementing value it is believed to be of minor importance. The reactions of $4CaO \cdot Al_2O_3 \cdot Fe_2O_3$ with moderate quantities of water have not been completely learned. The reaction appears to be a hydrolysis resulting in the formation of hydrated tricalcium aluminate and an amorphous material of undetermined composition.

17.46 Normal Portland Cement. Type 1 Portland cement is the general-purpose cement. Common uses are in reinforced concrete buildings and bridges, tanks, culverts, footings, floors, and curbs. It is also used for concrete pavements; however, in severe climates air-entraining cement is utilized to obtain greater durability against frost action and surface scaling caused by applications of calcium chloride for melting ice on pavements. See Art. 17.59. In short, Type 1 Portland cement is selected in nearly all cases where the concrete will not be subjected to severe exposure or to special sulfate hazard, or where the heat generated by hydration will not cause an objectionable rise in temperature.

17.47 Modified Portland Cement. Type 2 Portland cement has a lower heat of hydration than Type 1 and an improved resistance to sulfate attack. It is used in structures of considerable size such as heavy retaining walls, abutments, and piers where it will minimize temperature rise when concrete is placed in warm weather. It is also selected for drainage structures where sulfate concentrations are high but not exceptionally severe.

17.48 High-Early-Strength Portland Cement. This cement (Type 3) is manufactured to meet the demand for an early use of the fabricated concrete structure instead of waiting for days, or sometimes several weeks, for the concrete to harden sufficiently. This early strength of the cement is attained by changing the proportions and adding other materials, by finer grinding, and by better burning. In many cases the composition is varied so as to give a relatively large percentage of tricalcium silicate and a correspondingly low percentage of dicalcium silicate. Double burning and triple grinding are examples of the changes in the manufacturing processes to produce this result.

17.49 Low-Heat Portland Cement. Low-heat Portland cement (Type 4) has been developed for use in concrete structures of large mass such as dams. The purpose of this cement is to reduce the amount of heat generated by the hydrating cement during the period of hardening, thereby decreasing the amount of expansion and subsequent contraction of the concrete. The heat liberated by chemical action during hydration of Type 1 normal Portland cement is dissipated rapidly in the relatively thin sections employed in most concrete work, and volume changes other than those due to stress are caused principally by variation in moisture content. In mass concrete, however, the interior of the concrete dries very slowly, if at all, and the principal volume changes are caused by variations in temperature which accompany the liberation of heat by the hydration of the cement and the dissipation of this heat from the concrete. Increase in the size of mass-concrete structures, acceleration of construction speed, and increased activity of present-day Portland cements have tended to increase the probability of cracking in large concrete masses. The problem of correcting this tendency to crack consists essentially of reducing the effects of heat of hydration of the cement.

The low-heat cement (Type 4) has a low percentage of the troublesome compound, tricalcium aluminate, and a relatively low percentage of tricalcium silicate which liberates a medium amount of heat during hydration, but has a relatively high percentage of dicalcium silicate which liberates a small amount of heat during hydration. (See Table 17.2.) Such a low-heat cement would be slow in hardening owing to the small amount of tricalcium silicate, but satisfactory ultimate strength is assured by the large amount of dicalcium silicate whose hydration occurs chiefly after the first week. Slow hardening is not undesirable in mass-concrete construction, but may even be advantageous since the entire concrete mass composed of sections cast at different times may expand and contract more nearly as a unit. The changes in chemical composition also permit fine grinding of the cement, giving the advantage of increased workability, strength, and watertightness. Such a low-heat cement might not be desirable for general construction work because of its characteristics of slow hardening.

17.50 Sulfate-Resistant Portland Cement. This is Type 5 cement which is intended for use only in structures exposed to severe sulfate action, such as waters or soils of high alkali content. It has a slower rate of hardening than Type 1 Portland cement.

Properties of Portland Cement

17.51 General. The value of cement depends primarily upon its mechanical strength when hardened.

The establishment of the existing standards for physical and mechanical properties has for its object the fixing of values readily determined in the laboratory for cements found satisfactory in practice. The results of laboratory tests of cement cannot be considered to represent the properties of the material under working conditions, the quantitative results obtained having only a relative value.

The physical properties utilized for comparative purposes are: fineness, time of setting, and soundness; the mechanical properties are the tensile and compressive strengths of standard sand mortars. (See Table 17.3.)

17.52 Setting and Hardening. When a true hydraulic cement is gauged with sufficient water and then left undisturbed, it soon loses its plasticity and reaches a state in which its form cannot be changed without producing rupture. This change in condition is known as the *setting* of cement and has usually been considered somewhat distinct from *hardening*. Setting usually takes place in a few hours or even minutes, whereas hardening may proceed for months or years.

17.53 Time of Setting. The rapidity with which a cement sets is simply a criterion by which its suitability for use under given conditions may be determined. The effect of temperature and the percentage of water used in mixing, as well as the humidity of the air, is so marked that the determination of the setting time must always be made with extreme care under standardized conditions. No analogy can be traced between the rapidity with which a cement sets and the strength it will ultimately develop.

Specification. "The cement shall not develop initial set in less than 45 minutes when the Vicat [3] needle is used or 60 minutes when the Gillmore [4] needle is used. Final set shall be attained within 10 hours." (See Table 17.3.)

In general, the higher the temperature the quicker the set will be. The percentage of water used to gauge cement influences its time of set to a very marked degree, a wet mix setting much more slowly than a dry one. It is on this account that tests for time of set are always made with a paste possessing a standard degree of plasticity (a normal consistency mix).

---

[3] *Vicat needle.* Diam. = 1 mm. Wt. = 300 grams. For initial set the needle stops 5 mm. above glass in ½ minute. For hard set the needle does not penetrate.

[4] *Gillmore needles.* For initial set $1/12$-in.-diameter needle with a weight of ¼ lb. does not penetrate. For hard set $1/24$-in.-diameter needle with a weight of 1 lb. does not penetrate.

Table 17.3

ASTM PHYSICAL REQUIREMENTS OF PORTLAND CEMENTS

	Type 1	Type 2	Type 3	Type 4 *	Type 5 *
Fineness, specific surface, sq. cm. per g.:					
Average value, min.	1600	1700	—	1800	1800
Minimum value, any one sample	1500	1600	—	1700	1700
Soundness:					
Autoclave expansion, max., %	0.50	0.50	0.50	0.50	0.50
Time of setting (alternate methods): †					
Gillmore test:					
Initial set, min., not less than	60	60	60	60	60
Final set, hr., not more than	10	10	10	10	10
Vicat test:					
Initial set, min., not less than	45	45	45	45	45
Final set, hr., not more than	10	10	10	10	10
Compressive strength, p.s.i.: ‡					
The compressive strength of mortar cubes, composed of 1 part cement and 2.75 parts graded standard sand, by weight, prepared and tested in accordance with Method C109, shall be equal to or higher than the values specified for the ages indicated below:					
1 day in moist air	—	—	1250	—	—
1 day in moist air, 2 days in water	900	750	2500	—	—
1 day in moist air, 6 days in water	1800	1500	—	800	1500
1 day in moist air, 27 days in water	3000	3000	‡	2000	3000
Tensile strength, p.s.i. ‡					
The tensile strength of mortar briquets composed of 1 part cement and 3 parts standard sand, by weight, prepared and tested in accordance with Method C190, shall be equal to or higher than the values specified for the ages indicated below:					
1 day in moist air	—	—	275	—	—
1 day in moist air, 2 days in water	150	125	375	—	—
1 day in moist air, 6 days in water	275	250	—	175	250
1 day in moist air, 27 days in water	350	325	‡	300	325
Air content of mortar, prepared and tested in accordance with Method C185, maximum per cent by volume, less than	15.0	15.0	15.0	15.0	15.0

* Types 4 and 5 are not usually carried in stock.

† The purchaser should specify the type of setting time test required. In case he does not so specify, the requirement of the Gillmore test only shall govern.

‡ The purchaser should specify the type of strength test required. In case he does not so specify, the requirements of the tensile-strength test only shall govern. The strength at any age shall be higher than the strength at the next preceding age. Unless otherwise specified, the compressive- and tensile-strength tests for Types 1 and 2 cement will be made only at 3 and 7 days. If, at the option of the purchaser, a 7-day test is required on Type 3 cement, the strength at 7 days shall be higher than at 3 days.

Normal consistency is determined by means of the Vicat apparatus, in which a standard cylinder 1 centimeter in diameter, weighing 300 grams, is allowed to penetrate neat cement paste held in a standard rubber ring. For normal consistency the cylinder should penetrate 10 millimeters in 30 seconds. The water required for normal consistency is usually between 20 and 28 per cent.

The addition of 1½ to 3 per cent of plaster of Paris or gypsum to the clinker before grinding is necessary in order to retard the set sufficiently to pass the requirements of commercial use.

17.54 Fineness of Grinding. Experiments have shown that the coarser particles of cement are inert. Even a sieve having 325 meshes per linear inch is not fine enough to separate the inert from the active material. This separation can be effected only by some suspension method which retains nothing but the impalpable powder, or flour.

The American Society for Testing Materials has adopted a method of test for fineness of Portland cement by means of the *Wagner turbidimeter* which consists essentially of a source of light of constant intensity adjusted so that approximately parallel rays of light pass through a suspension of the cement to be tested and impinge upon the sensitive plate of a photoelectric cell. The current generated by the cell is measured with a microammeter.

In testing cement, a sample is dispersed in kerosene, light is passed through the suspension activating the photoelectric cell. As the cement settles out, increased amounts of light will pass through the suspension, and the increased intensity of the light is recorded on the microammeter. The indicated reading is a measure of the turbidity of the suspension. Turbidity is in turn a measure of the surface area of the suspended sample of cement. The fineness of Portland cement as represented by specific surface is expressed as total surface area in square centimeters per gram of cement.

The *Blaine air-permeability apparatus* is also used to determine fineness of Portland cement. It consists essentially of a means of drawing a definite quantity of air through a prepared bed of cement of definite porosity. The number and size of the pores in a prepared bed of definite porosity is a function of the size of the particles and determines the rate of air flow through the bed of cement. The time required for the given volume of air to pass through the bed of cement, corrected for temperature, viscosity of the air, and specific gravity of the cement sample, is used to compute the fineness of the cement in terms of specific surface in square centimeters per gram of cement. This is a simpler and more easily performed test than the Wagner turbidimeter test. However, fineness values determined by means of the Blaine air-permeability apparatus vary from those obtained using the Wagner turbidimeter; consequently, in specifications for fineness, it is necessary to specify the type of apparatus to be used.

The maximum degree of fineness compatible with reasonable manufacturing costs is desirable. Early strength of mortar and concrete is increased by increased fineness of grinding, and soundness is improved.

17.55 Tensile Strength. Tensile strength is determined by testing briquets of cement mortar. The standard sand for the mortar is natural sand from Ottawa, Illinois, screened to pass a No. 20 sieve and retained on a No. 30 sieve. The proportions of the mortar are 1 part Portland cement to 3 parts standard sand by weight, with a standardized amount of water which depends upon that required for normal consistency of the cement. The specimen for the tensile test is a briquet with enlarged ends and a midsection exactly 1 inch square. After curing, the briquet is tested by pulling it in two in a machine built for that purpose. For specifications of the American Society for Testing Materials, see Table 17.3.

The tensile strength of cement mortar is in itself of little importance, because cement mortar and concrete are rarely called upon to withstand tensile stresses. The significance of tensile strength as revealed by laboratory tests is therefore limited to the assumption that there exists some relation between tensile strength and compressive strength. The relation between tensile strength and compressive strength is by no means constant at all ages, and it also varies with different cements and with different mixtures. The neat tensile strength is no indication of the strength of the cement in mortars and concrete, and tensile strength of neat cement has, therefore, been discontinued as a standard.

Tests of tensile strength depend upon a great many factors that influence the accuracy of the results. Perhaps the greatest of these is the personal equation. In addition to the personal factor, tensile-strength results are influenced by the temperature of the gauging water, the method of mixing and molding in general, the temperature and humidity of the air, and the manner of storage of the briquets prior to testing.

17.56 Compressive Strength. Compressive strength is determined on 2-inch cubes of cement mortar. Standard Ottawa sand is used in the proportion of 2.75 parts sand to 1 part Portland cement by weight; it is graded to pass the No. 16 sieve and be retained on the No. 100 sieve. Water is added to produce a definite consistency as measured by a flow table. Requirements for compressive strength are given in Table 17.3. The compressive-strength test is preferred to the tensile-strength test by many engineers because the conditions of testing more nearly approximate the conditions encountered by mortars and concrete in service. However, considerable difficulty is experienced at times in obtaining reproducibility.

17.57 Soundness. Soundness in a cement implies the absence of those qualities which tend to destroy its strength and durability and is one of the most important properties of cement.

Unsoundness is manifested by a lack of constancy of volume, disintegration being caused almost entirely by expansion occurring after the cement has set.

Since any amorphous hydrate shrinks during drying and expands when wet, it is evident that this behavior on the part of the amorphous hydrated constituents of gauged cements must cause shrinkage of neat cement in air and expansion in water. These changes in volume are very much lessened by mixing with inert material as in sand mortar, the degree of volume change depending upon the richness of the mortar. The result of the desiccation of the cement is the appearance of fine hair-cracks on the surface of cement or rich mortar used as a plaster or top coat. These fine hair-cracks are not an indication of defective cement, but their appearance simply is an indication of too rich a mixture.

Unsoundness is due to disruptive action caused by crystallization of certain constituents of the cement. The principal constituent so involved is lime present in the free state. Proper burning and fine grinding, at least to such a degree that the calcareous particles are of a size suitable for reaction, tend to reduce unsoundness due to the presence of free lime.

A hard-burned calcium oxide has been discovered in Portland cement which hydrates so slowly that its complete hydration in concrete may be delayed probably up to 2 years. The effect is a disintegration of the concrete in the form of characteristic cracks.

The presence of excess dehydrated magnesia may also be the cause of unsoundness. In this event, unsoundness will be observed after a much longer period, since magnesia which has been highly heated remains inert for a long time before undergoing hydration.

The presence of excess sulfates is also thought to be the cause of unsoundness. The expansion is not due in this case to the hydration of lime sulfate, but is attributed to the formation of calcium-sulfoaluminate, which is dangerous only in large quantities. The standard specifications limit the SO_3 to 2.00 per cent. (See Table 17.1.) For Type 3 cement, 2.50 per cent SO_3 is the maximum permitted.

Specification. The test for soundness of Portland cement specified by the American Society for Testing Materials is the autoclave expansion test. In this test the expansion of neat cement bars after storage in superheated steam is determined. The bars are 1-inch square, $11\frac{1}{4}$ inches long, and have $\frac{1}{4}$-inch stainless-steel reference plugs at each end which project $\frac{3}{16}$ inch beyond the end of the bar. The distance between embedded ends of the plugs is 10 inches, which is considered the effective length of the specimen.

The water-cement paste of normal consistency is mixed and tamped uniformly in the molds. The cement bars are stored for 24 hours in moist air and then measured for initial length. The bars are placed in an autoclave, heated to 215.7° C. (420.3° F.) in 1 hour, held for 3 hours by means of an automatic controller at this temperature, which corresponds to a pressure of 295 pounds per square inch, and then cooled in another hour to a steam pressure of less than 10 pounds per square inch.

The autoclave should preferably be electrically heated; the pressure chamber is a thick-walled steel cylinder with a flange. A thick steel cover is held in place during the test by steel bolts. A safety valve should be provided to guard against hazard from excess pressure.

The bars are removed from the autoclave and placed in hot water, the temperature of which is above 90° C. (194° F.). The bars are cooled at a uniform rate by addition of cold water in 15 minutes to 21° C. (70° F.), stored in this water for another 15 minutes, after which the specimens are surface dried and measured for final length. Measurements are made by means of a length comparator graduated to 0.0001 inch. Maximum autoclave expansion of 0.5 per cent is specified. A cement which expands in excess of this amount is considered unsound.

17.58 Hydrated Lime. The addition of hydrated lime to Portland-cement mortar produces a fat, viscous mortar in which the sand and cement will not separate to as great an extent as when fine aggregate is used with Portland cement alone. This tends toward the production of a mixture of greater uniformity and with less voids, thus obtaining a mortar of more uniform strength. The tensile strength of standard mortar briquets is slightly increased by addition of hydrated lime up to 15 per cent by weight but is decreased by greater additions of hydrated lime.

Air-Entraining Portland Cement

17.59 Air-Entraining Portland Cement. This cement is manufactured by intergrinding acceptable additions to Portland cement. Typical additions include:

Vinsol resin: petroleum-hydrocarbon insoluble fraction of a coal-tar hydrocarbon extract of pine wood.
Darex AEA: triethanolamine salt of a sulfonated hydrocarbon.
N-TAIR: sodium resinate produced from pine-wood stumps.
Airolon: hydroaromatic and fatty carboxyclic acids.

Three types, 1A, 2A, and 3A, are produced corresponding to Types 1, 2, and 3 Portland cements. The chemical and physical requirements are given in Tables 17.4 and 17.5. Air-entrained cements are extensively used to produce concrete of increased durability. Air-entrained concrete contains several billion microscopic air bubbles per cubic foot. The bubbles prevent the solid particles from settling or moving out of their relative

Cements

Table 17.4
ASTM CHEMICAL REQUIREMENTS OF AIR-ENTRAINED PORTLAND CEMENTS

	Type 1A	Type 2A	Type 3A
Silicon dioxide (SiO$_2$), min., %	—	21.0	—
Aluminum oxide (Al$_2$O$_3$), max., %	—	6.0	—
Ferric oxide (Fe$_2$O$_3$), max., %	—	6.0	—
Magnesium oxide (MgO), max., %	5.0	5.0	5.0
Calcium sulfate (CaSO$_4$) in hydrated portland cement mortar, at 24 ± ¼ hr., expressed as SO$_3$, grams per liter, max.	0.50	0.50	0.50
Loss on ignition, max., %	3.0	3.0	3.0
Insoluble residue, max., %	0.75	0.75	0.75
Tricalcium silicate (3CaO·SiO$_2$), max., %	—	50	—
Tricalcium aluminate (3CaO·Al$_2$O$_3$), max., %	—	8	15

position, thus reducing bleeding and segregation. Concrete made with air-entraining cement has improved workability and requires a smaller amount of mixing water for a given slump.

17.60 Air Content of Mortar. The specifications given in Table 17.5 require that an air-entraining cement shall produce mortar with an air content of 18 plus or minus 3 per cent when mixed with standard sand. The amount of water used is that required to produce mortar of such consistency to cause a flow between 2.4 and 2.9 inches as measured by the Burmister mortar-flow trough test. The weight of 500 milliliters of the mortar is determined and the air content is computed from the actual and the theoretical weights per unit volume by the following formula:

$$\text{Air content, per cent by volume} = 100 - 2W\left(\frac{182.7 + P}{5000 + 10P}\right)$$

where W = weight of 500 milliliters of mortar in grams.
P = percentage mixing water, based on weight of cement used.

17.61 Portland Blast-Furnace-Slag Cement. This type of cement is manufactured by grinding together granulated slag and Portland-cement clinker with an addition of a small percentage of gypsum to control the time of set. The proportion of slag must be between 25 and 65 per cent by weight of the total cement. The composition of the granulated slag should conform to the following formula:

$$\frac{CaO + MgO + \frac{1}{3}Al_2O_3}{SiO_2 + \frac{2}{3}Al_2O_3} \geq 1$$

Table 17.5
ASTM PHYSICAL REQUIREMENTS OF AIR-ENTRAINED PORTLAND CEMENTS

	Type 1A	Type 2A	Type 3A
Fineness, specific surface, sq. cm. per g. (alternate methods): *			
Turbidimeter test:			
Average value, min.	1600	1700	—
Minimum value, any one sample	1500	1600	—
Air-permeability test:			
Average value, min.	2800	3000	—
Minimum value, any one sample	2600	2800	—
Soundness:			
Autoclave expansion, max., %	0.50	0.50	0.50
Time of setting (alternate methods): †			
Gillmore test:			
Initial set, min., not less than	60	60	60
Final set, hr., not more than	10	10	10
Vicat test (Method C191–51T):			
Set, min., not less than	45	45	45
Air content of mortar, prepared and tested in accordance with Method C185, per cent by volume	18 ± 3	18 ± 3	18 ± 3
Compressive strength, p.s.i.: ‡			
The compressive strength of mortar cubes, composed of 1 part cement and 2.75 parts graded standard sand, by weight, prepared and tested in accordance with Method C109, shall be equal to or higher than the values specified for the ages indicated below:			
1 day in moist air	—	—	1100
1 day in moist air, 2 days in water	750	600	2200
1 day in moist air, 6 days in water	1500	1250	—
1 day in moist air, 27 days in water	3000	2500	—

* Either of the two alternate fineness methods may be used at the option of the testing laboratory. However, in case of dispute, or when the sample fails to meet the requirements of the Blaine meter, the Wagner turbidimeter shall be used, and the requirements for this method shall govern.

† The purchaser should specify the type of setting time test required. In case he does not so specify, or in case of dispute, the requirements of the Vicat test only shall govern.

‡ Unless otherwise specified, the strength tests for Types 1A and 2A cement will be made only at 3 and 7 days and for Type 3A cement only at 1 and 3 days. The strength at any age designated herein shall be higher than the strength at any preceding age.

Note: Granulated blast-furnace slag having a chemical composition within the ranges given in the accompanying tabulation generally meets the requirements of the above formula.

Silicon dioxide (SiO$_2$), %	30–40
Aluminum oxide (Al$_2$O$_3$), %	8–18
Ferrous oxide (FeO), %	0–1
Calcium oxide (CaO), %	40–50
Magnesium oxide (MgO), %	0–8
Manganic oxide (Mn$_2$O$_3$), %	0–2
Sulfide sulfur (S), %	0–2

It is claimed that Portland blast-furnace-slag cement has a lower rate of heat evolution, a higher ultimate strength at later ages, and better resistance to attack by alkaline and sea water as compared to Type 1 Portland cement. It is also cheaper. This cement is also available in air-entrained form.

Portland-Pozzolan Cement

17.62 Definition. Portland-pozzolan cement may be defined as an intimate mechanical mixture of Portland cement and pozzolan, the materials having been pulverized before, during, or after mixing.

The pozzolan may be a natural or artificial material, and may be either calcined or uncalcined prior to being mixed with Portland cement. Pozzolan is usually added in amounts ranging from 10 to 30 per cent by weight of finished cement.

17.63 Properties. Portland-pozzolan cements as a group are more grindable, produce more plastic and more impermeable concretes, and generate less heat of hydration than Portland cements as a group, but the Portland-pozzolan cements, in general, require more water to produce concrete of a given consistency and exhibit greater shrinkage of mortar upon drying. In general, for rich mixes the compressive strength of concrete is less for Portland-pozzolan cements than for Portland cements, but the former show greater compressive strength for lean mixes at the later ages if active pozzolans are employed.

Portland-pozzolan cement has heat-generation characteristics similar to low-heat cement (Type 4). Not only does it produce lower ultimate heat than Type 1 Portland cement, but it also liberates heat at more favorable rates so that heat may be extracted as fast as generated.

Portland-pozzolan cements containing active pozzolans high in silica exhibit materially greater resistance to the action of sodium and magnesium sulfates than the corresponding Portland cements; the larger the percentage of pozzolan up to 30 per cent, the greater the resistance.

17.64 Uses. The relatively high workability, impermeability, and strength of Portland-pozzolan cement *in lean mixes* of concrete favor this cement for concrete in which strength is not a primary requirement, but, because of its relatively high shrinkage, this cement is unsuitable for rich mixes in thin sections subjected to prolonged drying. Portland-pozzolan cement of proper composition is suitable for mass concrete, hydraulic structures, and structures subjected to the action of sea and sulfate waters.

Masonry Cements

17.65 Masonry Cements. Masonry cements are utilized in brick masonry and block masonry. They are composed of mixtures of various cementing materials with different other materials. Typical cementing materials are hydrated lime, hydraulic lime, pozzolan cement, slag cement, natural cement, and Portland cement. Other materials which may be incorporated in masonry cements include gypsum, limestone dust, chalk, talc, clay, resin, and diatomaceous earth. ASTM specifications recognize two types of masonry cements: Type 1 for general purpose masonry, and Type 2 for masonry where high strength is required. Compressive strength on 2-inch cubes of standard sand mortar must average as tabulated.

	Compressive Strength, Minimum, p.s.i.	
Age	Type 1	Type 2
7 days	250	500
28 days	500	1000

17.66 Masonry Mortars. Mortars for block and brick masonry may be prepared by mixing hydrated lime and fine aggregate with cement. Portland cement, masonry cements, or combinations of Portland and masonry cements are used. ASTM proportion specifications are given in Table 17.6.

Table 17.6

MASONRY MORTAR PROPORTIONS BY VOLUME (ASTM)

Mortar Type	Parts by Volume of Cement	Parts by Volume of Hydrated Lime or Lime Putty *	Aggregate, Measured in a Damp, Loose Condition
A-1	1—Portland	¼	Not under 2¼ and not over 3 times the sum of the volumes of the cement and lime used
A-2	1—Portland	Over ¼ to ½	
B	1—Portland	Over ½ to 1¼	
B	1—masonry, Type 2	None	
C	1—Portland	Over 1¼ to 2½	
C	1—masonry, Type 1	None	
D	1—Portland	Over 2½ to 4	

* Plasticizing agents other than lime may be used with the approval of the building official.

The specifications for compressive strength of 2-inch cubes of mortar of these proportions are listed in Table 17.7.

Table 17.7
COMPRESSIVE STRENGTH FOR TYPES OF MORTAR CUBES (ASTM)

Masonry Mortar Type	Average Compressive Strength at 28 Days, p.s.i.
A-1	2500
A-2	1800
B	750
C	350
D	75

Alumina Cement

17.67 Alumina Cement. Alumina cement has a high alumina content and a different chemical composition and constitution than Portland cement. The alumina cements are not quick setting but often attain strengths at 48 hours comparable to the 28-day strength of ordinary Portland cements. After 48 hours the strength increases much more slowly but continues to be about twice as great as the corresponding Portland cement strength. Tests have shown that the alumina cements resist the disintegrating action of sea water quite well.

Oxychloride Cements

17.68 General. Oxychloride cements, commonly known as *Sorel cements*, are prepared by mixing either zinc chloride and zinc oxide or magnesium chloride and magnesia. The resulting oxychlorides of zinc and magnesium respectively form very hard cements. Magnesium oxychloride has a limited application as a structural cement in the manufacture of artificial stones, tiles, grindstones, and emery wheels. It is also used in flooring cements and stuccos.

17.69 Manufacture. Magnesium oxide for use in the manufacture of magnesium cements is prepared by burning magnesite in ordinary lime kilns at a temperature of about 635° C. (1175° F.) for 24 hours. The kiln product is then ground to a fine powder and mixed dry with some inert material to be cemented, such as powdered quartz, marble, siliceous sand, or emery. The usual proportions of oxide are: for emery wheels, 10 to 15 per cent by weight; for strong building blocks, 5 to 10 per cent; and for common artificial stone, 3 to 5 per cent.

The dry ingredients, after mixing, are thoroughly dampened with magnesium chloride, passed through a pugging mill, and rammed into suitable molds.

Flooring cements, containing sawdust, wood flour, silica, talc, asbestos, pigments, etc., are prepared in a similar manner. The proportions suggested by P. H. Bates for a top coat are given in the accompanying tabulation.

Material	Per Cent by Weight
Magnesia	45
Wood flour	15
Silica	15
Kaolin	10
Asbestos	5
Color	10
	100

A magnesium chloride solution of 22° Baumé gravity is added in proportions to give a desired consistency.

Magnesite stuccos generally contain magnesium oxide, ground silica, sand, and magnesium chloride.

17.70 Properties and Uses. The time of set of oxychloride cements depends on the proportioning and ingredients but is generally between 1 and 24 hours. Full strength is attained at 1 to 4 months. Grindstones and emery wheels prepared with this cement are aged at least 1 month before being put in service. Artificial stones made with oxychloride cements will take a high polish and have high compressive strengths.

When used as flooring, only a wearing coat is ordinarily laid on concrete slabs, but on wood floors a binder course is poured with steel reinforcement and a wearing course is placed over this. The material is screeded to a depth ranging from ¼ to ⅜ inch and troweled. Typical uses are as laboratory floors and railroad and subway car floors. This flooring withstands abrasion well but deteriorates when repeatedly wet.

Questions

17.1. Distinguish between hydrated and hydraulic lime.

17.2. Distinguish between the following cements: slag, natural, Portland, Portland air-entraining, Portland-pozzolan, Portland blast-furnace-slag cement, alumina cement, and magnesium oxychloride cement.

17.3. Define Portland cement, and state its approximate percentage composition.

17.4. What raw materials are mixed together to be calcined to form Portland cement?

17.5. Describe in detail the manufacture of Portland cement by the dry and wet processes. Compare the advantages of each. How are pulverized raw materials blended?

17.6. Compare the characteristics of four major chemical compounds in Portland cement with respect to cementing value, rate of reaction, and amount of heat liberated.

17.7. Describe the chemical reactions which occur when water is added to Portland cement.

Cements

17.8. How is the time of setting of Portland cement controlled?

17.9. How do the methods of manufacture of high-early-strength Portland cement differ from those of manufacturing standard Portland cement?

17.10. State the essential differences in composition and physical properties between standard Portland cement, high-early-strength Portland cement, low-heat-of-hardening Portland cement, and high-sulfate-resisting Portland cement.

17.11. Distinguish between setting and hardening of cement.

17.12. State the ASTM specifications for the acceptance of Portland cement (type 1) for fineness, time of set, tensile strength, compressive strength, and soundness.

17.13. Name two methods of determining the fineness of cement.

17.14. Name chemical compounds which may cause unsoundness in Portland cement.

17.15. Describe the essential features of the autoclave test of cement.

17.16. What are the effects of adding hydrated lime to Portland cement mortar?

17.17. Discuss the general characteristics of Portland-pozzolan cement, alumina cement, and magnesium oxychloride flooring compound.

17.18. What type of cement would you select for the construction of a concrete pavement in an important street intersection? a concrete pavement on a highway in Wisconsin? a sidewalk in a residential district? a floor of a subway car? a long-span concrete arch bridge? a large dam? a low-stressed foundation in dry location? a precast concrete pile for use in sea water? State your reasons in each case.

References

17.1. American Society for Testing Materials: "Standard Specifications for Portland Cement." *Designation* C150–52, *Book of Standards,* Part 3, 1952, p. 1. Also: "Symposium on Use of Pozzolanic Materials in Mortars and Concretes." *Special Tech. Publ.* No. 99, Oct., 1949. Also: "Characteristics of Portland Cement." 1904–1950, *Special Tech. Publ.* 127, 1952.

17.2. American Association of State Highway Officials: *Standard Specifications for Highway Materials and Methods of Sampling and Testing.* Washington, D. C., 6th ed., 1950, Parts I and II, Sections on Cements.

17.3. Bateman, J. H.: *Materials of Construction.* New York, Pitman Publishing Corp., 1950, Chap. 3.

17.4. Bauer, E. E.: *Plain Concrete.* McGraw-Hill Book Co., 3rd ed., 1949, 441 pages.

17.5. Blanks, R. F.: "The Use of Portland-Pozzolan Cement by the Bureau of Reclamation." *Jour. Am. Concrete Inst.,* Oct., 1949, p. 89.

17.6. Bogue, R. H., and Lerch, W.: "Hydration of Portland Cement Compounds." Washington, D. C., *U. S. Bureau of Standards, Portland Cement Assoc. Fellowship, Paper* 27, **1934.**

17.7. Bogue, R. H.: *The Chemistry of Portland Cements.* New York, Reinhold Publ. Corp., 1947.

17.8. Brown, L. S.: "Tricalcium Aluminate and the Microstructure of Portland Cement Clinker." *Proc. ASTM,* v. 37, Part II, 1937, pp. 277–305.

17.9. Carlson, R. W.: "Development of Low-Heat Cement for Mass Concrete." *Eng. News-Record,* Oct. 20, 1932, pp. 461–463.

17.10. Davis, R. E., Kelly, J. W., Troxell, G. E., and Davis, H. E. "Properties of Mortars and Concretes Containing Portland-Pozzolan Cements." *Jour. Am. Concrete Inst.,* v. 32, Sept.-Oct., 1935, p. 80.

17.11. Davis, R. E.: "Use of Pozzolans in Concrete." *Jour. Am. Concrete Inst.,* Jan., 1950, p. 377.

17.12. Eckel, E. C.: *Cements, Limes, and Plasters.* John Wiley & Sons, 3rd ed., 1928, pp. 149–676.
17.13. Engelhart, G. K.: "Flotation as Applied to Modern Cement Manufacture." *Ind. Eng. Chem. (Industrial ed.)*, v. 32, No. 5, May, 1940, p. 645.
17.14. Jackson, F. H.: "Why Type II Cement?" *Proc. ASTM,* v. 50, 1950, p. 1210.
17.15. Kirk, R. E.: "The Manufacture of Portland Cement from Marl." Minneapolis, *Univ. Minnesota, Eng. Exp. Sta. Bul.,* v. 29, No. 49, 1926, 98 pages.
17.16. Lea, F. M., and Desch, C. H.: *The Chemistry of Cement and Concrete.* London, Edward Arnold & Co., 1935, pp. 1–332.
17.17. Lynam, C. G.: *Growth and Movement in Portland Cement Concrete.* London, Oxford University Press: Humphrey Milford, 1934, 135 pages.
17.18. Meade, R. K.: *Portland Cement.* Chemical Publishing Co., 2nd ed., 1939.
17.19. Meissner, H. S., and Moran, W. T.: "The Field for Low-Heat Cement." *Eng. News-Record,* Nov. 10, 1938, pp. 589–593.
17.20. Meyers, S. L.: "Thermal Expansion Characteristics of Hardened Cement Paste and of Concrete." *Proc. Highway Research Board,* v. 30, 1950, p. 193.
17.21. Morrison, R. L.: "The Properties and Methods of Utilization of Aluminate Cement." Ann Arbor, Mich., *Proc. 11th Ann. Conf. Highway Eng., Univ. Mich.,* 1925, pp. 231–249.
17.22. Nord, M.: *Textbook of Engineering Materials.* John Wiley & Sons, 1952; Chap. 18, pp. 381–406.
17.23. Nordberg, B.: "America's Largest Dry Process Cement Plant." *Rock Products,* Aug., 1952, p. 133. Also: Marquette Builds Mississippi's First Cement Plant, *Rock Products,* Aug., 1952, p. 116.
17.24. Powers, T. C.: "A Discussion of Cement Hydration in Relation to the Curing of Concrete." *Proc. Highway Research Board,* v. 27, 1947, p. 178.
17.25. Rader, L. F.: "Investigations of Mixtures of Aluminate and Portland Cements and Bonding Portland Cement Mortars." Ann Arbor, Mich., *Proc. 11th Ann. Conf. on Highway Eng., Univ. Mich.,* 1925, pp. 250–270.
17.26. Rockwood, N. C.: "Prospective Chemistry of Cement and Concrete." *Rock Products,* Aug., 1952, p. 139.
17.27. Slipecevich, C. M., Gildart, L., and Katz, D. L.: "Crystals from Portland Cement Hydration." *Ind. Eng. Chem.,* v. 35, No. 11, Nov., 1943. Also: *Highway Research Abstracts,* Apr., 1944, p. 8.
17.28. Verbeck, G. J., and Foster, C. W.: "Long-Time Study of Cement Performance in Concrete," Chap. 6, "The Heats of Hydration of the Cements," *Proc. ASTM,* v. 50, 1950, p. 1235.
17.29. White, A. H.: "Volume Changes of Portland Cement As Affected by Chemical Composition and Aging." *Proc. ASTM,* v. 28, Part II, 1928, p. 398.
17.30. White, A. H., and Kemp, H. S.: "Long-Time Volume Changes of Portland Cement Bars." *Proc. ASTM,* v. 42, 1942, p. 727.
17.31. Witt, J. C.: *Portland Cement Technology.* Chemical Publ. Co., 1947.

Section V · Concrete

CHAPTER 18

Concrete

Originally Written by RALPH G. ADAMS *
Rewritten by LLOYD F. RADER

18.1 Concrete as a Structural Material. Concrete is a mixture of inert materials of varying sizes which are bound together with a cement paste. A mixture of cement, water, and fine aggregate only is called *mortar; concrete* contains coarse aggregate in addition. The whole mass is deposited in a plastic condition and almost immediately a hardening process starts which, under proper curing conditions, may continue for years. Because it is placed in a plastic condition, concrete lends itself successfully to all kinds of construction, the only drawback being that it must be confined in forms until a proper degree of hardening has taken place.

In structures and classes of work where tensile stresses are encountered, the concrete must be reinforced with steel. Only the fabrication and items affecting the concrete mixture will be discussed here.

Concrete Materials

18.2 Cement. Portland cement (Type 1) should be specified for general concrete work and should conform to the standard specifications of the American Society for Testing Materials. Special cements may be specified for projects involving unusual requirements.

18.3 Water. There is usually very little trouble in obtaining suitable water for casting concrete. Either the city water supply is available or some proven source of drinking water is usually near at hand. Stagnant water from a small supply should not be used unless tested particularly for organic impurities. Drainage from swamps or marsh containing humic and free carbonic acid is harmful, although dissolved carbonic acid is not. Tannic acid and sugar are harmful even in very weak solutions. Effluents

---

* Professor of Testing Materials, Massachusetts Institute of Technology.

from sewage-treatment plants may be harmful to concrete as also may be those from paint works, gas plants, and fertilizer-manufacturing plants.

Sea water at normal temperatures and with a concentration of salt at about 3.5 per cent does not appreciably reduce the strength of concrete. Sea water may be used in mixing mass concrete which has no steel reinforcement, although better concrete will be obtained with fresh water and this should be procured if at all available. Owing to the danger of corrosion, sea water should not be used in concrete which carries steel reinforcement.

18.4 Aggregates. Requirements for fine and coarse aggregates for concrete are described in Chapter 14.

The Proportioning of Concrete Mixtures

18.5 Importance of Proper Proportioning. Upon important work, particularly if of large extent, a thorough study of the materials and the proper relative proportioning of those materials will generally produce better results both in decreased cost and in increased strength and durability of the final concrete. The cement is always the most expensive ingredient, and, therefore, if it is possible to reduce the amount of cement used by adjusting the proportions of the aggregate, producing thereby a leaner mix of equal or greater density and strength, economy is effected provided that the cost of handling this mix is no greater than that of a richer one.

18.6 Proportioning by Arbitrary Assignment. The oldest and probably the most popular method of proportioning is the arbitrary assignment of proportions of cement and of fine and coarse aggregate. Arbitrary assignment commonly calls for a volume of fine aggregate equal at least to one-half the volume of the coarse material. For lean mixes a greater proportion of fine aggregate is necessary. The amount of cement required depends upon the use to which the concrete is to be put and the strength desired.

It is usually customary to state concrete proportions by volume, loosely measured, giving the number of parts of cement to parts of fine and coarse aggregate. It is impossible to state, arbitrarily, the proportions used in practice for concrete in any particular situation. The following mixes are given, however, as being fairly representative of practice and of conservative building code requirements:

1:1½:3. A rich mixture used for columns and other structural parts subjected to high stresses or requiring watertightness and for structures exposed to severe weathering conditions.

1:2:3½. A standard mixture used for reinforced floors, beams, columns, arches, engine and machine foundations where vibration occurs, sewers, conduits, etc.

1:2½:4. A medium mixture used for floors on the ground, ordinary machine foundations, retaining walls, abutments, piers, thin foundation walls, building walls, sidewalks, etc.

1:3:5. A lean mixture for massive concrete, heavy walls, large foundations under steady load, stone masonry backing or filling, etc.

18.7 Effect of Water. The arbitrary assignment of the mix more or less assumes that water is put into the mix for the purpose of producing a concrete which can be easily handled. In other words, if a more fluid mixture is desired more water is added. This procedure often leads to mixes that are much too wet, under which conditions the final concrete contains a large quantity of water voids, small in size but more or less connected together. These form passages through which surface water may seep and cause disintegration and spalling due to frost action and general weathering conditions.

Water reacts with the cement particles, causing chemical changes and combinations which result in the formation of the paste that binds the fine and coarse particles together. Considering the cement in the mix as the glue or binder for the inert particles, it is reasonable to assume that an excess of water produces a dilution of the glue and hence an inherent weakness in its bond strength.

A bag of cement requires about $2\frac{1}{2}$ to 3 gallons of water to produce hydration and to carry along the chemical reactions. In a concrete mix anywhere from 4 to 12 gallons of water are added per bag of cement, depending upon conditions and the skill and knowledge of the operator. Some of this water is needed in the mix to wet the surfaces of the fine and coarse particles because the glue must have a consistency such that all cracks and minute irregularities will be completely filled. Excess water acts as a lubricant in the transporting of the aggregate to the final place in the forms and is necessary to give proper workability, but a large excess of water tends to produce segregation of the aggregate particles from the paste and produces a mix which is harsh and non-uniform.

18.8 Workability and Consistency. The term *workability* as applied to concrete mixtures indicates the ease with which the mass of plastic material may be deposited in its final resting place in the forms without segregation or honeycomb to produce a uniform, homogeneous mass. The size and gradation of the aggregate, the amount of mixing water, the duration of mixing, and the size and shape of the forms are all factors of this vague and elusive term. No measure of workability has yet been devised which satisfactorily shows the ease or difficulty of placement of the concrete.

Consistency is generally considered descriptive of the apparent workability of the mix, but it often falls far short of the actual conditions. The term consistency is descriptive of a particular condition of fluidity or lack of fluidity of any material and should always be qualified. The slump-cone test is commonly used to measure consistency.

The slump cone is a metal form in the shape of a truncated cone, 12 inches high, 4 inches in diameter at the top and 8 inches at the bottom.

The freshly mixed concrete is placed in the mold in 3 layers, each layer being puddled with 25 strokes using a ⅝-inch-diameter rammer. The form is immediately withdrawn, and the distance the mass of concrete subsides or "slumps" from the original 12-inch height is taken as a measure of the consistency of the mix.

18.9 Water-Cement-Ratio Law. Duff A. Abrams after an extensive series of tests covering a wide range of concrete mixes and consistencies developed the water-cement-ratio law. This law may be stated as follows:

"For plastic mixes using sound aggregates, the strength and other desirable properties of concrete under given job conditions are governed by the net quantity of mixing water used per sack of cement."[1]

This law indicates that for given cement and aggregates and given job conditions, the strongest concrete is that which requires the lowest water-cement ratio to give a required consistency of mix. This relationship is illustrated in Fig. 18.1 by curve A which represents results obtained by Abrams using 1918 Portland cements. For modern cements, somewhat higher compressive strengths are obtained.

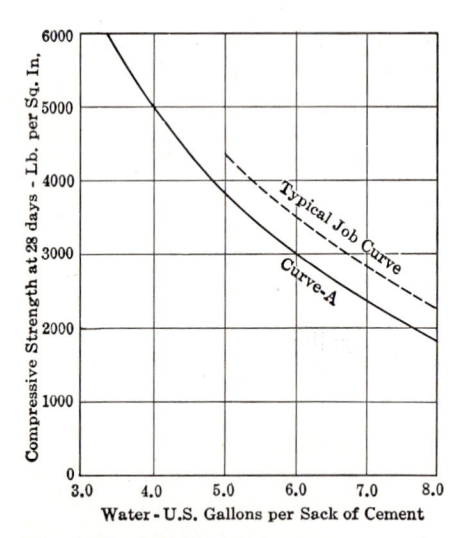

Fig. 18.1. Relation between compressive strength and water-cement ratio.

Recommended water-cement ratios for various types of structures and degrees of exposure are given in Table 18.1.

18.10 Trial-Batch Method. The method of trial batches is extensively used in selecting the desired combination of aggregates which when added to the cement paste of given water-cement ratio will produce a concrete mixture of suitable consistency. The problem consists of obtaining a desirable balance between workability and economy. Size, grading, and surface characteristics of the fine and coarse aggregates, and the relative proportions of fine and coarse aggregates, are the factors of greatest importance in determining the combination which will give the necessary workability at the lowest cost.

The following procedure is typical of the trial-batch method of proportioning. The desired water-cement ratio is selected. A definite amount

---

[1] *Design and Control of Concrete Mixtures,* Portland Cement Assoc.

Table 18.1

WATER CONTENTS SUITABLE FOR VARIOUS CONDITIONS OF EXPOSURE (GALLONS PER BAG OF CEMENT) *

Type or Location of Structure	Severe or Moderate Climate, Wide Range of Temperatures, Rain and Long Freezing Spells or Frequent Freezing and Thawing					Mild Climate, Rain or Semiarid, Rarely Snow or Frost				
	Thin Sections		Moderate Sections		Heavy and Mass Sections	Thin Sections		Moderate Sections		Heavy and Mass Sections
	Reinforced	Plain	Reinforced	Plain		Reinforced	Plain	Reinforced	Plain	
A. At the waterline in hydraulic or waterfront structures or portions of such structures where complete saturation or intermittent saturation is possible, but not where the structure is continuously submerged:										
In sea water	5	5½		6		5	5½		6	
In fresh water	5½	6		6½		5½	6		6½	
B. Portions of hydraulic or waterfront structures some distance from the waterline, but subject to frequent wetting:										
By sea water	5½	6		6		5½	6½		7	
By fresh water	6	6½		6½		6	7		7½	
C. Ordinary exposed structures, buildings, and portions of bridges not coming under above groups	6	6½		7		6	7		7½	
D. Complete continuous submergence:										
In sea water	6	6½		7		6	6½		7	
In fresh water	6½	7		7½		6½	7		7½	
E. Concrete deposited through water	†	†	5½	5½		†	†	5½	5½	
F. Pavement slabs directly on ground:										
Wearing slabs	5½	6	†	†		6	6½	†	†	
Base slabs	6½	7	†	†		7	7½	†	†	

G. Special cases:

(a) For concrete exposed to strong sulfate ground waters, or other corrosive liquids or salts, the maximum water content should not exceed 5 gal. per bag.

(b) For concrete not exposed to the weather, such as the interior of buildings and portions of structures entirely below ground, no exposure hazard is involved and the water content should be selected on the basis of the strength and workability requirements.

* Taken from Table 1 of the Report of the Joint Committee on Standard Specifications for Concrete and Reinforced Concrete, June, 1940. Water contents are based on use of plain Portland cement. When air-entraining cements or admixtures are used, the water contents will be reduced approximately ½ gallon per bag.

† These sections not practicable for the purpose indicated.

of cement is weighed and placed in the mixing pan, and the proper amount of water is added to produce a cement paste of desired water-cement ratio. Definite quantities of room-dry fine and coarse aggregates are weighed in suitable containers. Fine and coarse aggregates from the weighed quantities are added to the cement paste until a plastic mixture of desired consistency is obtained.

The remaining aggregate quantities are weighed and deducted from the original weights to determine the quantities used. The proportions by weight of cement to sand to coarse aggregate may be changed to volumetric proportions by dividing the weight of each material by its unit weight.

The slump-cone test is customarily used to determine the consistency. The tabulated limits of consistency are recommended for various classes of concrete structures.[2]

	Slump in Inches	
Type of Structure	*Minimum*	*Maximum*
Massive sections, pavements and floors laid on ground	1	4
Heavy slabs, beams, or walls	3	6
Thin walls and columns, ordinary slabs or beams	4	8

After a proportion has been established to give a certain consistency, further studies as to the ratio of fine to coarse aggregate may be made by mixing trial batches until a desirable combination is secured. Concrete mixtures having insufficient cement-sand mortar to fill the spaces between pebbles are difficult to work and result in rough, honeycombed surfaces. On the other hand, concrete mixtures in which there is an excess of cement-sand mortar will produce a low yield and the concrete is likely to be porous. A concrete mixture with proper amount of cement-sand mortar will have all spaces between pebbles filled with mortar after being lightly troweled.

Maximum yield is obtained by using a dense mixture of fine and coarse aggregates with as coarse grading and as stiff consistency as possible without producing harshness or stone pocketing. The yield of a trial batch may be determined by actual volumetric measurement or by adding the absolute volumes of the constituent materials. (See Art. 18.20.)

Proportioning by Trial Method on Job. The method of designing mixtures by trial may be applied on construction projects, using full-size routine batches composed of stock aggregates which are usually damp. This application permits continuous control. The accuracy of the method depends upon the care with which the tests and observations are made. The amount of surface moisture on the aggregates, particularly sand, is determined by test. The amount of water to be measured into the batch of concrete is adjusted so that the proper water-cement ratio will be secured. The method

[2] *Design and Control of Concrete Mixtures,* Portland Cement Assoc.

is essentially a "cut-and-try" process. If the mixture is too wet, more aggregate may be added and a greater yield obtained. If the mix is too dry, yield must be correspondingly reduced. The correction for surface moisture on the aggregates must be recalculated for each change in the amount of aggregates.

18.11 Job-Curve Method. This method is based fundamentally on the water-cement-ratio law but recognizes variations caused by different cements and aggregates. Trial batches of concrete are prepared for a series of water-cement ratios, using the cement and the fine and coarse aggregates to be employed in the project; test specimens for compressive strength are molded and tested. A job curve is plotted showing compressive strength versus gallons of water per sack of cement. A typical job curve is plotted in Fig. 18.1. If a compressive strength of 3000 pounds per square inch at 28 days were required for the project, the water-cement ratio to be selected would be scaled from the job curve as 6.7 gallons per sack of cement. A trial batch of this water-cement ratio could then be prepared and specimens molded and tested to obtain accurate properties of the concrete and the necessary quantities of materials for the design mixture.

18.12 Proportioning by Mortar-Voids Method.[3] Professor A. N. Talbot has developed a method of proportioning concrete by the determination of voids in the mortar. He found that the strength of concrete depends upon the composition of the cement paste which is assumed to occupy all the space in the concrete not filled with aggregate.

The following symbols are employed:

a = absolute volume of sand in a unit volume of concrete in place.
b = absolute volume of coarse aggregate in a unit volume of concrete in place.
c = absolute volume of cement in a unit volume of concrete in place.
v = voids (air and water) in a unit volume of concrete.
$v + c$ = volume of cement paste in a unit volume of concrete.
$\dfrac{c}{v + c}$ = cement-space ratio, or proportion of cement in the cement paste.
a_m = absolute volume of sand in a unit volume of mortar.
c_m = absolute volume of cement in a unit volume of mortar.
v_m = voids (air and water) in a unit volume of mortar.
b_0 = density, or absolute volume in a unit of bulk volume of coarse aggregate.

Typical relationships between compressive strength of concrete and cement-space ratio for different consistencies as determined by Talbot and Richart are shown in Fig. 18.2. The strength is less for the wetter consistencies. These strength values are lower than the average strengths for corresponding mixtures as reported by Abrams.

To design concrete of a given strength it is required to proportion the materials so as to give the proper cement-space ratio.

[3] Talbot: Method of Proportioning by Voids in Mortar and Concrete, *Univ. Ill., Eng. Exp. Sta., Bull.* **137**.

392 Materials of Construction

The consistency of the concrete is expressed in terms of the water content which produces the minimum voids in the mortar; this water content is called the *basic water content*. Figure 18.3 shows values of voids in mortars

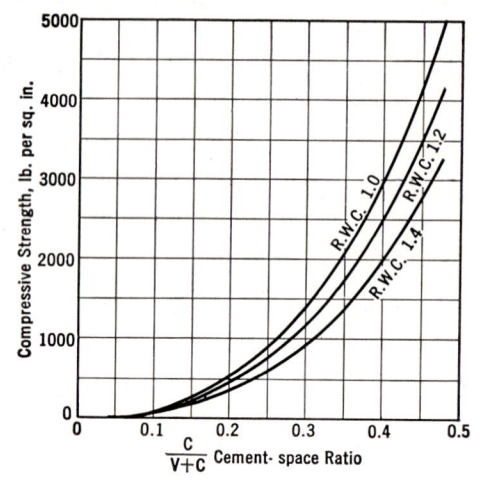

Fig. 18.2. Relations between compressive strength of concrete and cement-space ratio (Talbot and Richart.)

corresponding to different water contents for a constant ratio of sand to cement. To be workable, mortars must have water contents equal to or greater than basic water content.

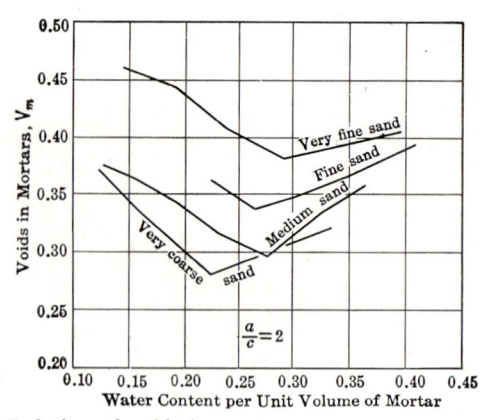

Fig. 18.3. Relation of voids in mortars to water content for $a/c = 2$.

Basic water content is determined experimentally in the laboratory for each proportion of sand to cement by a cut-and-try process. A cylindrical container of 200- to 300-cubic-centimeter capacity is suitable. A batch of sand and cement is weighed out and mixed dry. Water is added, and the mortar is mixed and tamped into the container in a uniform manner. The net weight of the mortar placed in the container is obtained, and the volume of the original batch is calculated by a simple proportion. The factors for this water content can then be calculated. This process is continued until basic water content is determined.

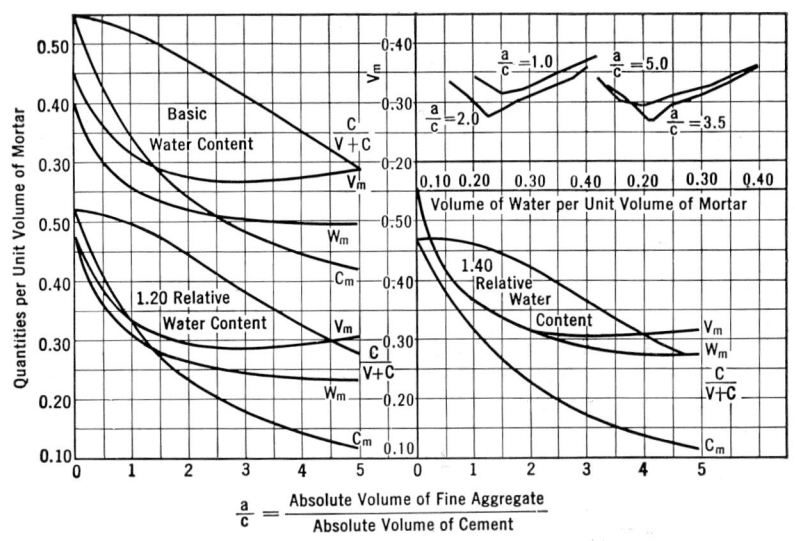

Fig. 18.4. Characteristic mortar-voids curves. (*Univ. Ill., Eng. Exp. Sta., Bull.* 137)

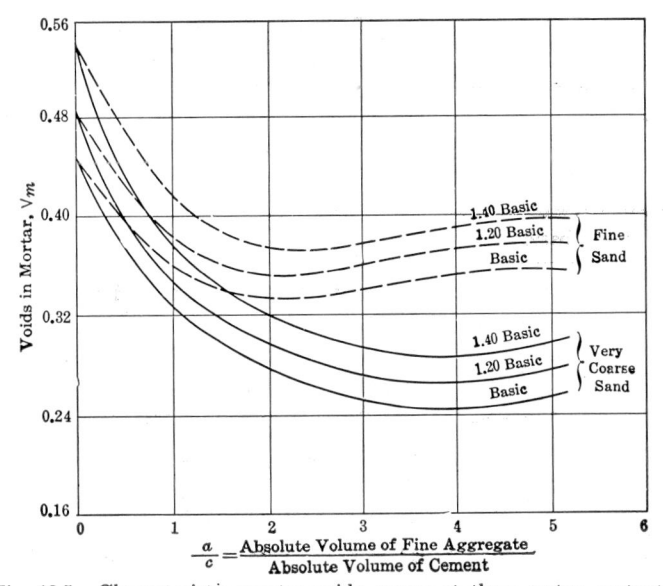

Fig. 18.5. Characteristic mortar-voids curves at three water contents.

In a similar manner the required factors are determined for mortars of different consistencies usually ranging from basic water content to 40 per cent above basic water content which is called 1.4 relative water content. This procedure is continued to obtain the required factors for a number of proportions of sand to cement. Characteristic curves can be plotted as illustrated in Fig. 18.4.

The voids in the stone also are determined. A value of the volume of stone (b) can now be assumed. For example, if the voids in the stone equal 0.45, the absolute volume of the stone (b) cannot exceed 0.55 and, after the addition of mortar, will probably be less (0.50 to 0.45).

Figure 18.3 shows the effect of fineness of sand upon the mortar voids, v_m, for various water contents for a given ratio of sand to cement, and Fig. 18.5 shows the effects of variations in consistency for various ratios of sand to cement (a/c).

Illustration of Laboratory Determination of Mortar Voids. $a/c = 3.5$; absolute volume of sand = 210 cubic centimeters and of cement = 60 cubic centimeters; weight of sand = $210 \times 2.65 = 556.5$ grams, and weight of cement = $60 \times 3.10 = 186$ grams; for 13 per cent of water use 96.5 grams water; net weight of mortar placed in container is found to be 675 grams; capacity of container = 300.5 cubic centimeters; volume of batch =

$$\frac{(556.5 + 186 + 96.5) \times 300.5}{675} = 373.5 \text{ cc.}$$

$$a_m = \frac{210}{373.5} = 0.562 \quad \text{and} \quad c_m = \frac{60}{373.5} = 0.161$$

$$w_m = \text{Water in mortar} = \frac{96.6}{374} = 0.258$$

$$v_m = 1 - (a_m + c_m) = 1 - (0.562 + 0.161) = 0.277$$

$$\frac{c}{v+c} = \frac{c_m}{v_m + c_m} = \frac{0.161}{0.277 + 0.161} = 0.366$$

This water content was found to give the minimum volume of mortar for this a/c ratio and is therefore the basic water content.

Example of Computation of Concrete Mixture. For compressive strength of 2200 pounds per square inch and consistency of 1.20 relative water content, find $c/v + c = 0.38$ from Fig. 18.2. From Fig. 18.4 for this cement-space ratio of 0.38, find $a/c = 3.0$; $v_m = 0.29$; $w_m = 0.24$.

Assume that crushed stone is to be used, for which b may be taken as 0.400:

$$v = v_m(1 - b) = 0.29(1 - 0.400) = 0.174$$

$$a + b + c + v = 1 \qquad (1)$$

$$a + 0.400 + c + 0.174 = 1$$

$$a/c = 3.0 \qquad (2)$$

Solving equations (1) and (2):

$$a = 0.320$$

and

$$c = 0.106$$

The proportion by absolute volumes is 0.106:0.320:0.400.

Material	Weight per Cubic Foot, pounds	Specific Gravity	Ratio of Absolute to Bulk Volume
Cement	94	3.10	0.485
Sand	110	2.65	0.664
Stone	104	2.70	0.616

The proportion by bulk volumes is

$$\frac{0.106}{0.485} = 0.218$$

$$\frac{0.320}{0.664} = 0.482$$

$$\frac{0.400}{0.616} = 0.649$$

or

$$1:2.21:2.98$$

Amount of mixing water $= w_m(1 - b) = 0.24(1 - 0.400) = 0.144$ cubic foot for 0.218 cubic foot of cement. The water-cement ratio is

$$\frac{0.144}{0.218} \times 7.5 = 4.95 \text{ gallons per sack}$$

This method of proportioning applies to dry as well as to plastic mixtures; when the voids in the concrete are completely filled with water as in plastic mixtures, the voids-cement ratio and the water-cement ratio are the same.

This method is scientific and is extensively used. The data obtained in the laboratory for given aggregates can be converted into field control charts for proportioning concrete.

T. H. Thornburn [4] has reported that mortar-voids curves obtained for mortars containing entrained air indicated that these curves cannot be used as a reliable basis for the design of concrete containing entrained air.

18.13 Method of Goldbeck and Gray. A method of proportioning concrete based on absolute volumes of the materials in a unit volume of concrete has been developed by A. T. Goldbeck and J. E. Gray.[5] The method makes

[4] T. H. Thornburn: "The Design of Concrete Mixes Containing Entrained Air." *Proc. ASTM*, v. 49, 1949, p. 921.

[5] A. T. Goldbeck and J. E. Gray: "A Method of Proportioning Concrete for Strength, Workability, and Durability." *Natl. Crushed Stone Assoc., Bull.* 11, revised 1953.

use of the b/b_0 ratio (same symbols as used by Talbot; see Art. 18.12). The term b/b_0 equals the dry, rodded volume (bulk volume) of coarse aggregate in a unit of concrete. The procedure of designing mixtures involves the use of data taken from Tables 18.2 and 18.3 which have been prepared by Goldbeck and Gray from test results on typical materials.

Table 18.2

DRY, RODDED VOLUME (b/b_0) OF COARSE AGGREGATE (ANY TYPE) PER UNIT VOLUME OF CONCRETE * FOR STRUCTURAL CONCRETE, PLACED WITHOUT VIBRATION

Size of Coarse Aggregate, Square Opening Laboratory Sieves	Fine Sand		Medium Sand			Coarse Sand	
	Fineness Modulus of Sand						
	2.40	2.50	2.60	2.70	2.80	2.90	3.00	3.10
	Values for b/b_0						
No. 4 to ½ in.	0.59	0.58	0.57	0.56	0.55	0.54	0.53	0.52
No. 4 to ¾ in.	0.66	0.65	0.64	0.63	0.62	0.61	0.60	0.59
No. 4 to 1 in.	0.71	0.70	0.69	0.68	0.67	0.66	0.65	0.64
No. 4 to 1½ in.	0.75	0.74	0.73	0.72	0.71	0.70	0.69	0.68
No. 4 to 2 in.	0.78	0.77	0.76	0.75	0.74	0.73	0.72	0.71
No. 4 to 2½ in.	0.80	0.79	0.78	0.77	0.76	0.75	0.74	0.73

Note: For concrete which is to be assisted in place by internal vibration under very rigid inspection, increase tabulated values of b/b_0 approximately 10%.

* *Courtesy* National Crushed Stone Association.

The steps in proportioning are:

1. Determine by ASTM procedures: (*a*) The bulk specific gravities of the fine and coarse aggregates, (*b*) the dry, rodded unit weight of coarse aggregate, and (*c*) gradation and fineness modulus of sand and gradation of coarse aggregate.

2. Compute the solid weights per cubic foot of the cement and of the fine and coarse aggregates. (Bulk specific gravity multiplied by 62.4 pounds.)

3. Knowing the size of coarse aggregate and the fineness modulus of sand, determine from Table 18.2 the proper value of b/b_0.

Table 18.3

NON-AIR-ENTRAINING STRUCTURAL CONCRETE CEMENT FACTORS (SACKS PER CUBIC YARD OF CONCRETE) REQUIRED FOR 28-DAY COMPRESSIVE STRENGTHS LISTED *

Size of coarse aggregate, square opening laboratory sieves	No. 4 to ½ in.		No. 4 to ¾ in.		No. 4 to 1 in.		No. 4 to 1½ in.		No. 4 to 2 in.		No. 4 to 2½ in.	
Slump, in.	3	6	3	6	3	6	3	6	3	6	3	6
Water,† gal. per cu. yd. of concrete												
Angular coarse aggregate	42	44	40	42	38	40	36	38	35	37	34	36
Rounded coarse aggregate	38	40	36	38	34	36	32	34	31	33	30	32
28-Day Compressive Strength,‡ p.s.i.	Cement, sacks per cu. yd. of concrete											
2000	4.6	4.8	4.4	4.6	4.2	4.4	4.0	4.2	3.9	4.0	3.8	3.9
2500	5.0	5.2	4.8	5.0	4.5	4.8	4.2	4.5	4.1	4.3	4.0	4.2
3000	5.4	5.7	5.2	5.4	4.9	5.2	4.6	4.9	4.4	4.7	4.3	4.6
3500	5.9	6.3	5.6	5.9	5.3	5.6	5.0	5.3	4.9	5.2	4.8	5.0
4000	6.5	6.9	6.2	6.5	5.8	6.2	5.5	5.8	5.4	5.7	5.2	5.5
4500	7.2	7.5	6.8	7.1	6.4	6.8	6.1	6.4	5.9	6.3	5.7	6.1
5000	8.1	8.5	7.7	8.1	7.3	7.7	6.9	7.3	6.7	7.1	6.5	6.9
Entrapped air, approximate %	2.5		2		1.5		1		1		1	

Note: For concrete to be assisted in place by internal vibration, use 3 in. slump and decrease tabulated water contents by approximately 4 gal. No reduction in cement factor is suggested.

* *Courtesy* National Crushed Stone Association.

† This is the water actually effective as mixing water.

‡ The 28-day compressive strengths shown are the minimum values to be expected and should be used for design purposes. Laboratory specimens cured under ideal conditions will generally have higher strengths.

4. Calculate the solid volume of coarse aggregate per cubic foot of dry, rodded coarse aggregate (b_0).

$$b_0 = \frac{\text{Dry, rodded weight per cubic foot}}{\text{Solid weight per cubic foot}}$$

5. Calculate $b = b/b_0 \times b_0$.

6. Knowing the kind and size of coarse aggregate and the 28-day compressive strength and slump of concrete desired, determine, from Table 18.3, the cement factor and the water content. Also select from Table 18.3 the percentage of entrapped air and calculate its solid volume per cubic yard of concrete.

7. Calculate and sum up the solid volumes of cement, coarse aggregate, water, and air.

8. Twenty-seven cubic feet minus the solid volumes of cement, coarse aggregate, water, and air equals the solid volume of sand in a cubic yard of concrete.

9. Convert solid volumes of cement, sand, coarse aggregate, and water to pounds per cubic yard of concrete, using values calculated under step 2 above.

Example of Proportioning. Determine the batch quantities for a concrete mixture designed to have a 28-day compressive strength of 4000 pounds per square inch, using crushed stone from a No. 4 sieve opening to ¾-inch in size and medium sand with a fineness modulus of 2.60. A slump of 3 inches is desired.

1. The tabulated data have been determined for the aggregates by testing and have been assumed for the Portland cement.

Material	Dry, Rodded Weight, per cu. ft.	Specific Gravity
Cement	94	3.14
Sand	—	2.63
Crushed stone	101.8	2.71

2. Solid weights per cubic foot, in pounds

   Cement: $3.14 \times 62.4 = 196$
   Sand: $2.63 \times 62.4 = 164$
   Crushed stone: $2.71 \times 62.4 = 169$

3. $b/b_0 = 0.64$
4. $b_0 = 101.8/169 = 0.603$
5. $b = b/b_0 \times b_0 = 0.64 \times 0.603 = 0.386$
6. Cement factor, sacks per cubic yard of concrete = 6.2
   Water required, gallons per cubic yard of concrete = 40

7. Solid volumes of materials, cubic feet per cubic yard of concrete

    Cement: 6.2 (sacks) × $\frac{94}{196}$ = 2.97
    Crushed stone: 0.386 × 27 = 10.42
    Water: 40/7.5 =   5.33
    Air: 0.02 × 27 =   0.54

    Total: 19.26

8. Sand: 27 − 19.26 =   7.74
9. Batch quantities, pounds per cubic yard of concrete

    Cement: 2.97 × 196 =   582
    Sand: 7.74 × 164 =   1269
    Crushed stone: 10.42 × 169 = 1761
    Water: 5.33 × 62.4 =   333

    Total: 3945

Per cent sand by solid volume of total aggregate =

$$\frac{7.74}{(7.74 + 10.42)} \times 100 = 42.6$$

The above method of Goldbeck and Gray is helpful in establishing proportions of concrete mixtures in the field. Corrections may be necessary to allow for moisture in the aggregates. Minor adjustments in the quantities can be made after the first batch to produce the desired workability.

This method can be incorporated in specifications for concrete for construction projects. The properties of the aggregates do not have to be known prior to writing the specifications. After the contract has been awarded, the exact proportions can be established for the aggregates which are to be used.

Proportioning Air-Entrained Concrete. The method of Goldbeck and Gray can also be employed for proportioning air-entraining concrete. Factors are taken from Table 18.4 instead of from Table 18.3. The same procedure in designing mixtures is followed. In changing to air-entrained concrete, there is usually a reduction in water content and in the amount of sand.

Proportioning Concrete for Pavements. Concrete for pavements should have no more sand than is necessary to form a thin layer of mortar on the finished surface of the slab. As compared to structural concrete, highway concrete should contain less sand and more coarse aggregate, and should be of a drier consistency. (See reference 18.11.)

Table 18.4

AIR-ENTRAINING STRUCTURAL CONCRETE CEMENT FACTORS (SACKS PER CUBIC YARD OF CONCRETE) REQUIRED FOR 28-DAY COMPRESSIVE STRENGTHS LISTED *

This table should always be used to proportion concrete to be subjected to freezing.

Size of coarse aggregate, square opening laboratory sieves	No. 4 to ½ in.		No. 4 to ¾ in.		No. 4 to 1 in.		No. 4 to 1½ in.		No. 4 to 2 in.		No. 4 to 2½ in.	
Slump, in.	3	6	3	6	3	6	3	6	3	6	3	6
Water,† gal. per cu. yd. of concrete Angular coarse aggregate	38	40	36	38	34	36	32	34	31	33	30	32
Rounded coarse aggregate	35	37	33	35	31	33	29	31	28	30	27	29
28-Day Compressive Strength,‡ p.s.i.	Cement, sacks per cu. yd. of concrete												
2000	4.4	4.7	4.2	4.4	3.9	4.2	3.7	3.9	3.6	3.8	3.5	3.7
2500	4.9	5.2	4.6	4.9	4.4	4.7	4.2	4.4	4.0	4.3	3.9	4.2
3000	5.6	5.9	5.3	5.6	5.0	5.3	4.7	5.0	4.5	4.8	4.3	4.7
3500	6.3	6.7	6.0	6.3	5.6	6.0	5.3	5.6	5.1	5.4	4.9	5.3
4000	7.2	7.5	6.8	7.2	6.4	6.8	6.0	6.4	5.8	6.2	5.6	6.0
4500	8.1	8.5	7.6	8.1	7.2	7.6	6.8	7.2	6.6	7.0	6.4	6.8
5000	9.2	9.7	8.7	9.2	8.2	8.7	7.7	8.2	7.4	8.0	7.2	7.7
Optimum entrained air content,§ %	6.0		6.0		5.5		5.0		5.0		4.5	

* *Courtesy* National Crushed Stone Association.

† This is the water actually effective as mixing water.

‡ The 28-day compressive strengths shown are the minimum values to be expected and should be used for design purposes. Laboratory specimens cured under ideal conditions will generally have higher strengths.

§ This optimum entrained air content provides for approximately 9% air in the mortar.

Concrete   401

18.14 Constant Water Content. Reference to Fig. 18.6 will show that for concrete produced from the same materials and possessing the same consistency, the water content (expressed as a percentage of the absolute volume of the concrete) is practically constant. These data were taken

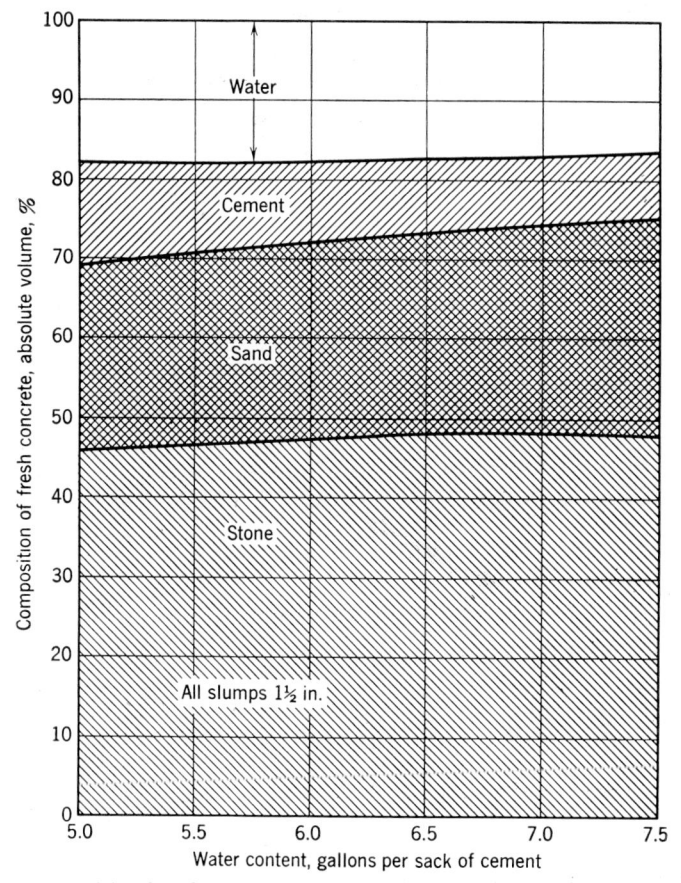

Fig. 18.6. Composition by absolute volumes of concrete mixtures for same cement and aggregates and at constant slump of 1½ in. (Rader.)

from laboratory experiments conducted by classes in the Polytechnic Institute of Brooklyn under Professor L. F. Rader beginning in 1930. It will also be noted that the absolute volume of the coarse aggregate is practically constant for these conditions. These relationships are helpful in estimating quantities of materials for mixtures when several water-cement ratios are being used. (See reference 18.26 by Professor Inge Lyse.)

The water in concrete may be classed as combined water and uncombined water. These are discussed in the next article.

18.15 Combined and Uncombined Water. An analysis of concrete mixtures of uniform consistency is shown graphically in Fig. 18.7. The abscissas have no significance, the mixtures being merely spaced equally. The ordinates of the lower diagram represent the absolute, or solid, volumes of the materials in a unit volume of concrete. In the upper diagram, the ordinates represent the absolute volume of the cement and water in the cement paste.

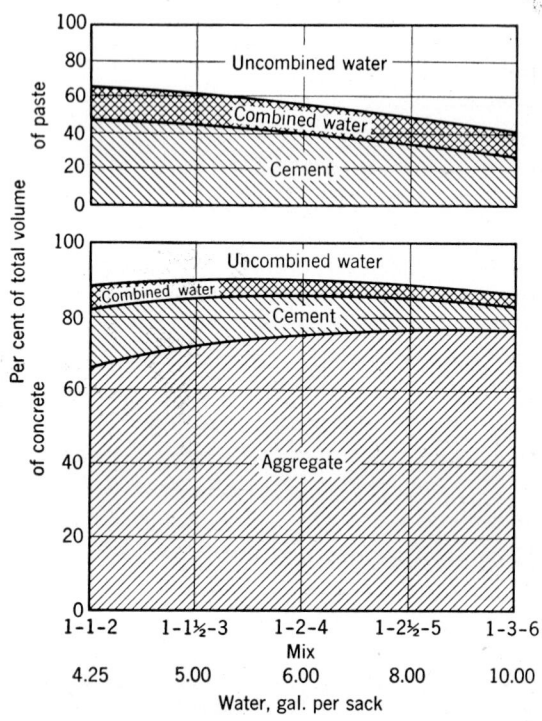

Fig. 18.7. Composition of concrete mixtures of uniform consistency (slump 3 to 4 in.) (*Courtesy* F. R. McMillan.)

In both portions of Fig. 18.7, the water is divided into combined and uncombined water. The combined water goes into chemical combination with the cement, while the uncombined water is necessary to give the concrete sufficient plasticity to be placeable.

The quantities of combined water shown in Fig. 18.7 are those existing for one particular age and under a particular set of curing conditions. The quantity of combined water may vary over a wide range, depending upon fineness and composition of cement, the water-cement ratio, the age, and curing conditions.

18.16 Summary. All methods of proportioning which have been discussed have many valuable features regarding the economy of materials, the strength, and other desirable properties which a concrete structure should possess. The choice of a particular method usually depends upon the amount of field control which the engineer can employ in checking the different phases of the work. Care should be taken in combining different methods because sometimes this leads to impossible conditions of manipulation.

Measurement of Materials

18.17 Measurement of Cement. When cement is purchased in bags or sacks, its measurement is an easy matter. A sack when properly filled contains 94 pounds and is assumed to be 1 cubic foot in volume. A barrel of cement is equal to 4 sacks and weighs 376 pounds net. Bulk cement should be measured by weight because measurement by volume is unsatisfactory owing to the fact that a cubic foot of cement may be made to vary greatly in weight depending upon the amount of compaction.

18.18 Measurement of Water. Accurate measurement of water is important since water and cement constitute the cement paste which is the binding agent and has great influence on the strength and other properties of the resulting concrete. Volumetric measurement is usually employed on modern concrete mixers, the tanks being equipped with water gauges, meters, or adjustable discharge pipes so that the proper amount may be obtained for each batch. In stationary mixing plants, water is many times measured by weight. The amount of mixing water should be corrected for surface moisture in the aggregates, particularly in sand. The amount of moisture in the aggregate can be determined by weighing the aggregate before and after drying. The amount of surface moisture in sand can be determined by means of *ASTM Designation* C70–47.

18.19 Measurement of Aggregates. Volumetric measurement of aggregates is common but is likely to be inaccurate owing to different degrees of compaction and to bulking of damp aggregates, particularly sand. Sands containing moisture tend to occupy a greater space than dry sand when shoveled about, because the films of water adhering to the sand grains increase the resistance between the surfaces of the grains and tend to spread them apart. Therefore, a cubic foot of damp sand weighs less than a cubic foot of dry sand to which the same method of placement has been applied. This swelling tendency or bulking is greater in fine sands than in coarse and is greater with small percentages of water than with large. For a moderately damp (about 7 per cent water content) fine sand the bulking is about 25 per cent.

Measuring Aggregates by Weighing. In modern proportioning plants aggregates are weighed in order to eliminate the errors incurred in volumetric measurement. Correction for the weight of moisture in the aggregates should be made. Since most specifications are written for the materials to be measured on a volumetric basis, it is necessary to know the relationship between weight and volume in order to determine the proper weights of materials for a batch. The weight per cubic foot of dry aggregate may be determined by compacting the material in a container of definite size as specified by *ASTM Designation* C29–42. Then the moisture in the aggregate in percentage by weight of dry aggregate should be determined. The weight of moist aggregate is equal to the sum of the weights of dry aggregate and moisture. Because of bulking, the weight of a cubic foot of moist aggregate will give a different result.

18.20 Quantities of Materials. In the estimation of the amounts of materials for a job, the cement factor, barrels per cubic yard of concrete, is usually obtained. This can be accurately determined by making use of the fact that the volume of concrete produced by a combination of materials is equal to the sum of the absolute volumes of the cement, the aggregate, and the water, provided that the concrete when placed has no void spaces. The absolute volume of loose material equals the unit weight of the material divided by the product of the apparent specific gravity of the material and the unit weight of water.

The following problem is illustrative of the method: To determine the amounts of materials for a 1:2:4 mix using dry materials with a water content of $7\frac{1}{2}$ gallons per sack. The weight of a cubic foot of sand is assumed to be 105 pounds, and of the gravel, 100 pounds. The apparent specific gravity of cement is about 3.1, and for the more common aggregates 2.65 is a fair value. The mix will therefore yield the following volumes:

$$\text{Cement} = 1 \text{ cu. ft.} = \frac{94}{3.1 \times 62.5} = 0.49 \text{ cu. ft.}$$

$$\text{Sand} = 2 \text{ cu. ft.} = \frac{2 \times 105}{2.65 \times 62.5} = 1.27 \text{ cu. ft.}$$

$$\text{Gravel} = 4 \text{ cu. ft.} = \frac{4 \times 100}{2.65 \times 62.5} = 2.42 \text{ cu. ft.}$$

$$\text{Water} = 7\tfrac{1}{2} \text{ gallons} = \frac{7.5}{7.5} = 1.00 \text{ cu. ft.}$$

$$\text{Total volume} = \overline{5.18} \text{ cu. ft.}$$

This calculation indicates that 1 sack of cement will yield 5.18 cubic feet of concrete. The cement per cubic yard of concrete equals $\frac{27}{5.18}$ or 5.21 sacks which equals 1.30 barrels. The sand needed per cubic yard of concrete is $\frac{5.21 \times 2}{27}$ or 0.39 cubic yard, and gravel is $\frac{5.21 \times 4}{27}$ or 0.78 cubic yard. The water needed per cubic yard of concrete is $7.5 \times 5.21 = 39.1$ gallons.

18.21 Formulas for Calculation of Factors for Concrete Mixtures. The symbols are defined as follows:

Concrete

V = volume of concrete per batch in cubic feet.
W = total weight of all ingredients per batch in pounds.
U = unit weight of concrete in pounds per cubic foot.
N = number of sacks of cement in batch.
C = weight of cement in batch in pounds.
Y = yield, or volume of concrete produced per sack of cement in cubic feet.
CF = cement factor in sacks of cement per cubic yard of concrete.

The formulas are:

$$U = W/V \quad \text{or} \quad V = W/U \tag{1}$$

$$N = C/94 \tag{2}$$

$$Y = V/N \tag{3}$$

$$CF = 27/Y \tag{4}$$

Substituting equation (3) in equation (4):

$$CF = 27N/V \tag{5}$$

Substituting equation (1) in equation (5):

$$CF = 27NU/W \tag{6}$$

Substituting equation (2) in equation (6):

$$CF = 27UC/94W \quad \text{or} \quad CF = 0.2872UC/W \tag{7}$$

Equation (7) is useful in calculating the cement factor when changes in water content are made to control the consistency and also when checking the proportioning and air content of air-entrained concrete mixtures. The unit weight of the concrete must be measured accurately.

Mixing Concrete

18.22 Mixing Machines and Machine Mixing. Concrete-mixing machines are generally of the batch type. The materials are measured separately and charged into the machine in quantities sufficient to make a batch suited to the capacity of the machine. The required amount of water is added, and the mass is mixed and then completely discharged, after which the machine is recharged.

Most concrete mixers consist of a rotating chamber into which the materials are charged and in which they are mixed with a complicated motion, due either to the shape of the mixer chamber or to the action of baffle plates placed on the inside walls of the mixing chamber.

Batch mixers are built of the tilting and non-tilting types, the latter being more common. Portable batch mixers for building construction range from 3½ to 14 cubic feet in capacity. A 27-cubic-foot size is common for portable paving mixers; the mixers are mounted on crawler tractor treads and have a boom and bucket for placing the concrete. Dual-drum mixers **mix** the materials partly in one drum and then complete the mixing in a second drum; they have an increased output as compared to single-drum mixers. Stationary batch mixers are usually of large capacity (from 1 to 6 cubic yards) and are installed at central plants and on large projects such as dams.

After all the materials are in the drum, the mixing should continue for at least 1 minute and preferably longer especially if mixes are rich in cement. An increase in the mixing time produces a stronger concrete and materially improves the watertightness of the resulting concrete. An additional 15 seconds for each ½ cubic yard additional capacity of mixer above 1 cubic yard is sometimes specified.

A great deal of concrete is mixed in stationary or central mixing plants and then dumped into truck mixers for transporting to the job. Truck mixers have a mixer unit with separate power plant mounted on the chassis frame. Common sizes range from 1 to 5 cubic yards of mixed concrete. Truck mixers may be operated to agitate the concrete slowly and tend to prevent segregation during transportation. Such agitated concrete is referred to as "central-mixed" concrete. Dump trucks may be used for transporting air-entraining concrete. (See Art. 18.37.) Truck mixers may also be operated as transit mixers. This method is to measure the materials for a batch at a stationary proportioning plant and dump the materials into the mixer body of a truck which mixes the concrete during transit or after arrival on the job site.

A machine known as the Cement Gun is also used to deposit cement mortars in the form of "Gunite." The dry mix of cement and sand is introduced into the upper chamber of the gun through a cone valve. Compressed air equalizes the pressure in this chamber with that in the lower chamber, whereupon a second cone valve admits the mixture to the lower chamber. The material is fed continuously from this chamber through a hose to the place of deposition. As it leaves the hose through a specially designed nozzle, water is added. The wet mix strikes the surface on which the mortar is deposited with considerable force, the surplus water is thrown off, and a very dense mortar is formed which is stronger than mortars placed by hand.

Deposition of Concrete

18.23 Forms. The investment in materials and the cost of labor in placing and removing forms represent quite a large percentage of the total cost of concrete work. It is evident, therefore, that the correct design and construction of forms is a very important feature of the work. Forms must be substantially built, so thoroughly braced and wired that the finished concrete shall conform to the designed dimensions and contours, and made tight to prevent leakage of cement-charged water.

The cheaper grades of lumber are generally adequate. Green timber is preferable to seasoned timber, since it is less likely to be affected by the water in the concrete. Better grades of lumber are required when a particularly smooth finish is desired or where forms are used repeatedly. Oiling of the forms is beneficial, and boards are generally planed on one side. Forms should always be wetted just prior to the deposition of the concrete.

Structural plywood is also used for forms. Common thicknesses are $9/16$, $5/8$, and $3/4$ inches. Plywood thinner than $9/16$ inch must be backed up by lumber. Standard sizes are 2, 3, and 4 feet wide by 8 feet long. Plywood is frequently selected because it produces grain marking on the surface of the concrete.

Wallboard is sometimes employed as lining for lumber forms. Both hard-finished and fiber wallboard are used. The smooth surface of hard-finished wallboard is placed next to the concrete. Fiber wallboard serves as an absorptive lining, tending to overcome surface defects caused by air and water pockets.

Steel forms are extensively used for plane surfaces of great area and with few irregularities and offsets. Steel is gradually replacing wood principally because of cheapness since the metal form can be used many times and still produce a smooth and true surface.

18.24 Transportation and Deposition in Forms. The one essential in the transportation of concrete from the place of mixing to the forms is that no opportunity be afforded for a segregation to take place between the mortar and the coarse aggregate. For this reason, chutes down which the concrete flows are often considered objectionable. Chutes may be so constructed, however, by making the slope conform to the degree of wetness of the mix, that little difficulty is encountered by reason of segregation.

On small jobs concrete is usually transported in wheelbarrows or concrete buggies. On paving jobs concrete is discharged from portable mixer into bottom-dump bucket which is moved on a boom to deposit the concrete in the forms.

For medium-sized structural jobs, concrete is often transported by pipeline, utilizing the positive displacement pump. The pipe can be readily shifted to permit delivery of concrete over a comparatively large area. For successful handling by pump and pipeline, the concrete must be uniform in consistency and not segregated.

On large construction projects, a central mixing plant is established at the site and delivery of concrete to point of deposit is made by a transporting plant. Two types of concrete-transporting and placing plants are in general use: (1) the cableway-type plant, and (2) the trestle-type plant.[6]

[6] J. R. Hardin: "Improved Techniques Lower Cost of Concrete Construction." *Civil Eng.*, Nov., 1952, p. 949.

In the cableway-type plant, concrete is transported from the mixing plant in bottom-dump buckets on flat cars, and the buckets are attached to the "hook" on the cableway for delivery of concrete to the forms. A "controllable-dump" bottom-discharge bucket has been developed which eliminates the objectionable cableway "bounce," characteristic of freely discharging buckets during dumping, that results in segregation of the concrete. The controllable-dump bucket is regulated either by opposing air cylinders or by a double-acting air cylinder. Rapid discharge is possible without segregation. The cableway-type of plant is well adapted to canyon-type sites.

The trestle-type plant is more adapted to wide river sites and low abutments. Concrete is delivered from the mixing plant in bottom-dump buckets on flat cars to either revolving cranes or hammerhead cranes for deposition in the forms.

Concrete should be deposited in nearly horizontal layers from 6 to 12 inches thick for reinforced concrete and up to 18 inches thick for mass concrete. On work where absolute continuity of the concrete is required, the deposition must be carried on continuously until completed. There will invariably be a joint or plane of weakness where 1 day's work is stopped and deposition of new concrete resumed after 12 to 15 hours. It is therefore important that the work be so planned and prosecuted that the planes of weakness lie in the direction of least stress in the finished structure.

The materials should be mixed wet enough to produce a concrete of such a consistency as will flow into the forms and about the reinforcement if such be present. At the same time, it must not be so wet as to cause difficulty through segregation of the coarse aggregate and the mortar before final deposition. Mass concrete is placed dry and vibrated with heavy-duty internal vibrators.

18.25 Vibrated Concrete. Vibration is a mechanical method of puddling concrete which is extensively used, particularly for large masses. Mixtures of stiff consistency can be effectively consolidated and those of plastic consistency can be made to flow readily into corners and pockets and around reinforcement in a more effective manner than by hand puddling. The concrete may be vibrated by means of internal vibrators placed within the mass, by means of vibrating floats placed on top of the concrete, or by vibration of the forms. Both electric and pneumatic vibrators are used.

Internal vibrators are of three general types. In one type the vibrating rod is operated through a flexible shaft by a motor. The second is a rigid-type machine consisting of a motor driving an eccentric shaft enclosed in a tube rigidly attached to the motor housing. In the third, the motor is built into the vibrating unit which is inserted into the concrete. (See Fig. 18.8.)

Vibrating floats are commonly used to consolidate and level off the surface of mass concrete. They are frequently used in combination with internal vibrators

Concrete

The method of vibrating the forms is generally used in consolidating concrete in precast units such as cast stone, building blocks, and pipe. For narrow sections that will not permit the insertion of an internal vibrator, the external type is also used. Form vibrators may consist of an electric motor with an unbalanced member, an electric magnet pulsator, or reciprocating cylinders operated by compressed air.

Fig. 18.8. Vibration of concrete with internal vibrators having motors in the units. (*Courtesy* Electric Tamper and Equipment Co.)

Frequencies of 3000 to 7000 vibrations per minute have been shown to be effective. Consistency of the concrete is a controlling factor with respect to frequency to be chosen; stiff consistencies require higher frequencies for effectiveness. The amplitude of the blow has a bearing on the type and ruggedness of the forms; light forms can be used with low amplitudes from $\frac{1}{4}$ to $\frac{3}{8}$ inch. Light blows will not displace the reinforcing steel as much as heavy blows.

The time of application depends on the consistency of the concrete and the type of structure. Internal vibrators should be applied in concrete of dry consistency in floors and slabs. At least 20 seconds of vibration per square foot of surface of each layer should be required, and the vibrators should be kept constantly moving in the concrete. In high walls the application should be timed because, if vibration is applied too long in one position, there is a tendency to force fine material away from the point of application and to bring large aggregate to the surface.

Vibratory tamping increases the unit weight of concrete over that obtained by hand tamping, but has no appreciable effect on compressive strength for consistencies where it is possible to compact by hand. Much harsher and drier mixtures can be placed by vibration. It is therefore possible to decrease the amount of sand and to obtain increased yield. Volume change may be reduced to some extent. Bond strength has been found to be greater for vibrated concrete for both plain and deformed bars.

Vibration produces compaction more rapidly than hand tamping and improves the effectiveness with which concrete can be placed, particularly in intricate forms and in thin reinforced sections. By proper placing of concrete, the durability may be increased.

18.26 Bleeding of Concrete. Bleeding (also known as weeping, or water gain) is sedimentation of both large and small particles which do not separate. The settlement causes an accumulation of water to the surface and produces compaction zones that increase in density toward the bottom of the mass. Bleeding depends upon the amount of water present and upon the surface area of the materials. Bleeding itself may be reduced by increasing this surface area, which may be done by adding fine materials such as cement, silica gel, and colloidal clay, but the addition of these fine materials may affect other properties of the concrete detrimentally.

18.27 Depositing Concrete under Water. In many classes of subaqueous concrete construction it is possible to use cofferdams or caissons from which the water may be excluded. The placing of the concrete will then not differ materially from methods common on land. When such methods are not feasible, the problem becomes one of considerable difficulty.

Cement, sand, and stone are heavy enough to sink in water, but the laitance and some cement which is not immediately hydrated will be floated away. This therefore represents a considerable loss of cement. The problem is one of placing the concrete in its final position under water without allowing the excessive formation of laitance or washing out of cement.

Many methods have been followed with a greater or less degree of success, among which the following may be mentioned:

The "tremie," a common device, consists of a large tube of wood or sheet metal, so constructed as to make its length adjustable, and provided with a hopper at the top. In use the tremie is supported vertically in the water by barges or derricks, provision being made for horizontal movement of the tube over the area occupied by the work. The lower end is allowed to rest on the bottom or is closed by a valve arrangement, and the tube is filled with concrete. The tremie is now lifted a short distance and the concrete is allowed to escape as the device is moved over the required area. A layer of concrete of any desired thickness is thus deposited, the tube being kept continuously filled to a point above the water line. This method does not entirely prevent the formation of laitance and loss of cement, but it has been found satisfactory on many large works.

Buckets, so constructed as to allow the material to flow out from the bottom, the top being closed, are used like the tremie. A derrick lowers the closed bucket into place, the bottom doors are opened, and the material escapes as the bucket is hoisted. Buckets so used are generally of large capacity, since if several yards of concrete escape at once the material compacts better with less loss of cement.

18.28 Bonding to Old Work. Since joints cannot be avoided in work not carried on continuously to completion, every reasonable precaution should be taken to make the bond of new to old work as strong as possible.

In massive work with horizontal joints, the question is one of less importance than in thin walls or situations requiring watertightness. In the former situation it will probably suffice simply to clean and wet the old work before laying new concrete. Where walls are thin, or waterproofness is required, the concrete previously placed should be roughened, thoroughly cleaned of foreign material and "laitance," and slushed with a thin grout of either neat cement or rich mortar.

Laitance is a whitish scum which is washed out of concrete when there is excess of water, as when concrete is deposited in water or when water collects in pools on the surface of freshly laid concrete. The laitance consists of the finest flocculent matter in the cement together with dirt from the aggregates. The composition of laitance is practically identical with that of the cement itself. This flocculent material remains suspended in the water for a long time, giving it a milky appearance, and settles slowly on the surface of the concrete. The laitance hardens only very slowly and never acquires much strength, so that, if not removed, it seriously interferes with the bonding of successive layers of concrete.

18.29 Finishing Concrete. Exposed concrete surfaces may be finished by a number of different methods such as wooden float, steel trowel, canvas belt, burlap, spading tool, or grinding stone. The type of finish depends largely upon the use to be made of the surface. Hand or machine methods may be employed. In hand finishing, the concrete is struck off with a template and floated. For small areas such as sidewalks the surface is hand floated; for large areas a long-handled float may be used. A smooth surface may be obtained by finishing with a steel trowel after the water film on the floated surface has disappeared. Sidewalks finished with a steel trowel are likely to be slippery when wet, however. Canvas belts and burlap can be readily used to produce a surface of rough texture.

Concrete pavements are generally finished by machine. The finishing machine spreads the concrete and screeds it to an even surface. The final finish may be obtained by floating or belting. A rough texture may be given to the surface by brooming. Concrete pavements should not be excessively worked in finishing since this tends to bring fine material to the surface where it may cause scaling or where it may easily be worn away by traffic.

18.30 Facing of Walls. The cheapest and most satisfactory method of obtaining a smooth face on concrete walls is by forcing a straight spade or slice bar along the forms, forcing the coarser aggregate back from the surface. A *rubbed finish* is sometimes obtained by removal of the forms while the concrete is still green and rubbing with a wooden float. The surface may be smoothed up by rubbing with a Carborundum stone after the forms are removed. A *tooled finish* is sometimes produced, after the concrete has partially hardened, by means of the tools used in finishing stone. A *brushed finish* is produced by brushing the green concrete with a stiff wire brush, after which a dilute solution of hydrochloric acid is applied with a brush. The acid thoroughly cleans the stone and brings out the natural colors, but it must be immediately removed by slushing with water. Otherwise acid discoloration will occur. Walls and floors may be given a smooth surface by finishing with a *grinding stone*. Special aggregates may be placed near the surface to give color effects or to produce patterns of various designs.

A layer of special mortar is sometimes placed next the forms by means of a movable sheet-steel diaphragm which is inserted in the form and kept the required distance from the face by suitable spacing blocks. The concrete and mortar are now filled in simultaneously, and the diaphragm is raised as the work proceeds, so that it is always only a few inches below the surface. In this manner the two mixes come into contact with each other before setting begins and the bond will not be imperfect.

18.31 Concreting in Freezing Weather. Low temperatures have a marked effect in increasing the setting time of cement. If water in concrete or mortar freezes before the cement has set, it is not available for the chemical action of setting and hardening and hence the concrete or mortar will not set at all until the ice melts. The above facts must be borne in mind when removing forms from concrete placed during cold weather.

If, however, the concrete has begun to set before the temperature drops considerably below the freezing point, the expansion of the water in solidifying produces an expansive force in excess of the cohesive strength of the green concrete. This action results in destruction of the bond between the cement and the aggregate and crumbling of the concrete when the ice melts.

Concrete should not be mixed or deposited at a freezing temperature, unless special precautions are taken to avoid the use of materials containing frost or covered with ice crystals, and to provide means to prevent the concrete from freezing after being placed in position and before it has thoroughly hardened.

When concrete is to be poured at or near freezing temperatures, the concrete, as it is placed in the forms, should be at a temperature between 50 and 90° F. Newly placed concrete made with normal Portland cement (Type 1) should be kept at a temperature of not less than 50° F. for 7 days or not less than 70° F. for 3 days. It is good practice to maintain a temperature of at least 40° F. for the next 4 days. Concrete made with high-early-strength Portland cement (Type 3) should be kept at not less than 70° F. for 2 days or not less than 50° F for 3 days.

This can be accomplished by heating the aggregates and the water before mixing and by proper protection and application of heat during the hardening period. The sand and stone are heated by piling them over heated iron conduits or steam pipes, and the water is heated in a large supply tank fitted with steam coils. The work may be protected from frost by covering with earth, canvas, hay, boards, etc., if the temperature falls but very little below freezing, but in case of heavy frost heat must be artificially supplied. For a building, it is practicable to house it in with sheathing or canvas. Fires are then kept going continuously in salamanders within the enclosure, thus keeping the temperature above freezing.

The effect of adding sodium chloride to concrete cured at temperatures below 32° F. is to reduce the freezing temperature and to retard the freezing of the concrete, thus permitting its setting and hardening. For curing below 32° F., the addition of salt up to 12 per cent by weight of mixing water increases the concrete strength, but higher percentages are detrimental to strength. Approximately 1 per cent of salt in the mixing water lowers the freezing point 1° F. (0.55° C.). For curing at normal temperature, the addition of salt causes a decrease in the strength of the concrete. (See reference 18.54.) The integral use of calcium chloride causes a more rapid rate of liberation of heat of hydration of the cement, thus promoting early strength development and thereby furnishing materially greater resistance of the concrete to the detrimental effect of low temperatures. (See reference 18.14.)

Air-Entrained Concrete

18.32 Scaling of Concrete Pavements. Scaling of Portland-cement concrete pavements has followed the widespread use of flake calcium chloride and common salt to remove ice or the repeated use of granular materials impregnated with these salts. The extent and severity of the scaling depend upon the amount of salts used and the frequency of applications. Concrete pavements of good quality resist such exposure better than those of poor quality, but good concrete pavements may be damaged by heavy salt applications. Concrete pavements less than 4 years old are more vulnerable to such scaling than are pavements of greater age.

18.33 Air-Entrained Concrete. Air-entrained concrete has very good resistance to the applications of calcium chloride and common salt and also

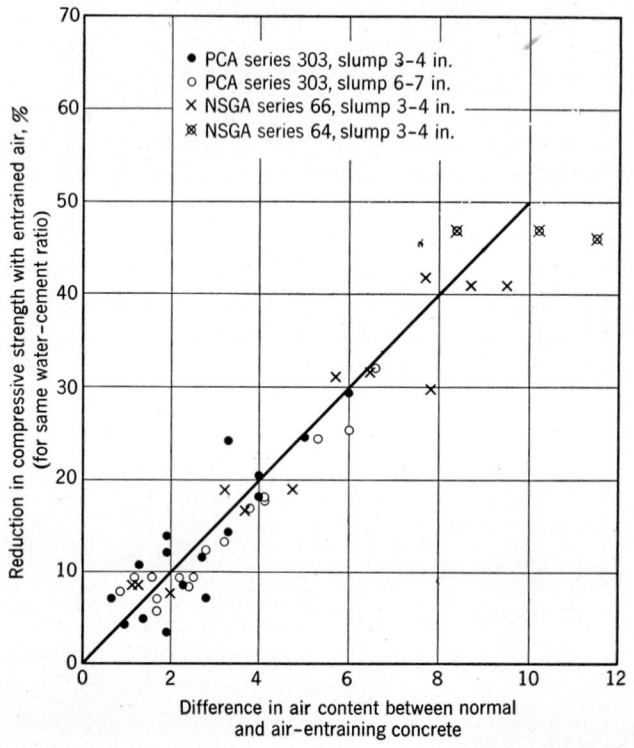

Fig. 18.9. Reduction in compressive strength with entrainment of air when water-cement ratio is maintained constant. (*Courtesy* D. L. Bloem, *Proc. ASTM*, v. 49, 1949, p. 937.)

improved resistance to deterioration by freezing and thawing. It is specified for concrete pavements by many highway departments and is also employed extensively for structural concrete. For pavement concrete, the total air content should be between 3 and 6 per cent. Research and field experience show that above the 3 per cent limit, suitable resistance to salt applications is attained and that going above 6 per cent does not appreciably improve durability but does cause some additional and unnecessary reduction in strength. See Fig. 18.9 for reduction in compressive strength. On paving jobs using air-entrained concrete, air-content determinations should be made frequently to insure that the air content remains within the specified limits.

Concrete

18.34 Methods of Determining Air Content. *Gravimetric Method.* The gravimetric method of test for weight per cubic foot, yield, and air content of concrete is a standard method of the American Society for Testing Materials (*Designation* C138-44). Satisfactory precision is obtained when determinations are carefully made; but the method is time consuming, and, under field conditions where accurate determinations may be difficult to obtain, the method has in some instances yielded erratic results.

The air content is calculated by the formula:

$$A = (T - W)/T \times 100$$

in which A = air content (percentage of voids) in the concrete.
T = theoretical weight of the concrete, in pounds per cubic foot, computed on an air-free basis.
W = weight of concrete, in pounds per cubic foot.

In computing T, theoretical weight of concrete, it is necessary to have the bulk specific-gravity values for the aggregates based on the saturated, surface-dry condition.

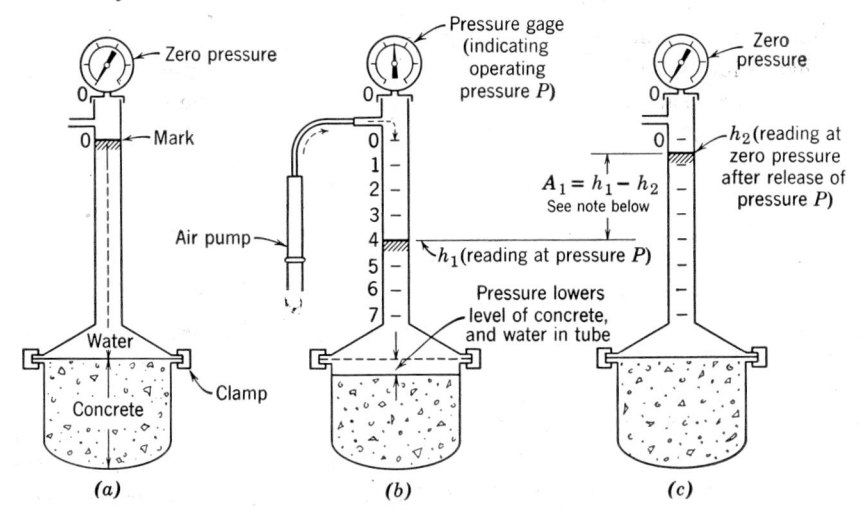

Note: $A_1 = h_1 - h_2$ when bowl contains concrete as shown in this figure; when bowl contains only aggregate and water, $h_1 - h_2 = G$ (aggregate correction factor). $A_1 - G = A$ (entrained air content of concrete)

Fig. 18.10. Illustration of pressure method of test for air content. (*Courtesy* ASTM.)

Pressure Method. The pressure method, based on Boyle's Law, utilizes the reduction in volume of the entrained air in a sample of concrete, when it is placed under pressure, as a measure of the air content of the concrete. The instrument used is called an air meter. (See Fig. 18.10.)

Rolling Method. The rolling method makes use of direct volume measurement by liquid replacement of the entrained air liberated from a sample of concrete while tumbling it into an excess of water. Isopropyl alcohol is used as the replacement liquid because of its ability to dispel effectively all foam produced during the rolling process.

Reliable results are obtainable by both the pressure and rolling methods. The pressure method requires much less time and hence is usually preferred, but the rolling method is more accurate for concrete containing aggregates of high and variable porosity such as slag.

18.35 Methods of Producing Air Entrainment. Air-entrained concrete may be produced by three methods: (1) Using air-entraining Portland cement, (2) adding an air-entraining agent to normal Portland cement and aggregates at the mixer, and (3) employing a cement mixture composed of a normal Portland cement and a blended cement which contains an air-entraining material. To be effective, an air-entraining agent must develop a stable foam during the mixing operation. Typical commercial air-entraining agents are N-TAIR, Vinsol resin, Darex AEA, and Airalon.

18.36 Effect of Adding Air-Entraining Agent. An air-entraining agent introduces into the resulting concrete minute and well-distributed air bubbles. These bubbles reduce particle interference in the fine aggregate, and hence lubricate the mortar. This wetting effect is greater on fine sands than on coarse sands. Wetting of the fine aggregate has the effect of reducing the amount of mixing water required to produce a given workability of the concrete. Because sand is responsible for the action of air-entraining agents, lean concrete mixtures need less air-entraining agent than rich mixtures since lean mixtures ordinarily have a greater proportion of fine to coarse aggregate.

18.37 Advantages of Air-Entrained Concrete. Air-entrained concrete can be readily handled and spread because the mix is very workable, cohesive, and does not readily segregate. In most cases advantage may be taken of this improved workability by reducing the water content without impairing the placeability of the mix. The mixture must be kept in the plastic range to insure entrainment of air in the concrete, and the consistency should be adjusted to give satisfactory placement under job conditions and with the equipment being used.

Air-entrained concrete is almost free from bleeding. Consequently, there is little free water on the surface for lubrication during finishing operations. This makes it necessary to carry out finishing operations without delay, or else drying will harden the surface and hinder satisfactory workmanship. The absence of free water on the surface is more critical when the temperature is high, when the relative humidity is low, or when the wind is blowing at high velocity. This condition may at first appear objectionable, but after operations have been adjusted to the material, this characteristic offers distinct advantages. It is possible to operate finishing machines closely behind the mixer; long waits and overtime at end of the day for the finishers are avoided; and early protection and curing are possible.

Ready-mixed air-entrained concrete can be successfully transported in open dump trucks, thus reducing hauling costs as compared with rotating drum trucks ordinarily used for regular concrete. Such haulage is possible because air-entrained concrete resists segregation well. R. A. Burmeister [7] of the City of Milwaukee Testing Laboratory has reported tests indicating that for 3 to 6 per cent entrained air in concrete having a cement content of 5 to 6 sacks per cubic yard of concrete and for slumps of 4 inches or less, segregation is negligible provided not more than 45 minutes elapse from the time of mixing to the time of complete discharge from the open dump truck. Segregation is severe, however, at about 6 inches slump; therefore, the consistency should be carefully controlled to a slump of 4 inches or less to utilize this method of transportation satisfactorily.

Curing of Concrete

18.38 Principle of Curing. The process of hardening of concrete is a chemical change due to the combination of water with the cement particles. This chemical process (called hydration) goes on indefinitely at a diminishing rate so long as proper temperature and moisture conditions are maintained. The control of these conditions is especially vital during the early stages of the hardening process. A mass of concrete which has been properly proportioned and poured under rigid control may be only mediocre or even poor in quality if it is allowed to dry out too rapidly.

Curing consists in supplying moisture and maintaining proper temperatures so as to have favorable conditions for hydration of the cement particularly during the early hardening period. The most favorable conditions exist when the concrete is moist and warm throughout.

T. C. Powers [8] has determined that curing procedures should be such as to keep the concrete as nearly saturated as possible until the originally water-filled space has become filled with hydration products to the desired minimum extent. Concrete sealed against evaporation must initially contain more than about 0.5 grams of water per gram of cement to assure full hydration. An average Portland cement requires about 1.4 cubic centimeters of water-filled space per cubic centimeter of cement (absolute volume), since about 2.4 cubic centimeters is the least volume that 1 cubic centimeter of cement can occupy after it has become hydrated. This amount of water is about twice the amount that can become chemically combined. For

---

[7] R. A. Burmeister: "Transporting Ready-Mixed Concrete in Open Dump Trucks." *J. Am. Concrete Inst.*, Sept., 1948, p. 41.

[8] T. C. Powers: "A Discussion of Cement Hydration in Relation to the Curing of Concrete." *Proc. Highway Research Board*, 1947, p. 178.

hydration to proceed, the amount of water present in the concrete at any given time must be greater than twice the amount that has become combined with the cement up to that time.

Figure 18.7 shows that there is a considerable amount of uncombined water available in typical concrete mixtures. Therefore, from a practical standpoint, a method of curing which prevents evaporation of the original mixing water from the mass of the concrete for a sufficient period of time will be adequate.

18.39 Methods of Curing. There are two general groups of methods for curing concrete, both of which minimize the loss of water initially placed in the concrete.

1. Application of an intermediate source of water to counteract evaporation from the concrete.
2. Application of a membrane to minimize loss of water from the concrete.

Methods in the first group comprise spraying; ponding; application of wet coverings such as burlap, cotton mats, earth, sawdust, and straw; and application of calcium chloride to the surface. Continuous spraying with water is effective but wasteful of water and often laborious. Ponding is an effective curing method but involves much labor in building earthen dikes and providing sufficient water to keep the ponds filled and is practicable only on slabs of small gradient. Vertical surfaces may be protected by burlap which should be frequently sprinkled. For pavements, immediately after the concrete has attained its initial set or has commenced to harden, it should be covered with wet burlap or wet cotton mats to prevent the formation of minute surface cracks. Typical specifications [9] for pavements, floors, and walks require that the burlap or cotton mats shall remain in place for not less than 72 hours and shall be kept wet by means of a water spray. After not less than 6 hours of such curing, the burlap or cotton mats may be replaced by wet earth, sawdust, or straw until 72 hours have elapsed after the final finishing of the surface.

A surface application of calcium chloride is sometimes made in curing concrete pavements. The principle of this method is that calcium chloride is hygroscopic or deliquescent and absorbs water from the surrounding air, thus keeping the surface moist. The chemical may be applied in flake or granular form and should be dry, free from lumps, and fine enough to pass through a mechanical spreading device. Calcium chloride should be applied only to hardened surfaces to avoid scaling.

Methods in the second group comprise waterproof paper and membrane seal coats. Waterproof paper consists of two sheets of plain kraft paper cemented together with a bituminous material in which are embedded cords

[9] Highway Research Board: *Current Road Problems* 1-R, *Curing of Concrete Pavements*, Oct., 1952.

or strands of fiber running in both directions of the paper. It is specified to be light in color. Waterproof paper is applied immediately after the final finishing operation and after disappearance of surplus water from the surface. It is kept in intimate contact with the concrete surface for 72 hours.

Membranes are of two general types: bituminous and non-bituminous. Asphalt and tar cut-back coatings and bituminous emulsions are sprayed on the surface. Bituminous coatings disfigure the concrete and absorb heat, which is objectionable in hot climates. To overcome the latter objection, a coating of whitewash is applied in not less than 3 hours nor more than 4 hours following the application of the bituminous material in order to reduce the temperature differential between the top and interior of the concrete.

Non-bituminous membranes are more commonly used and may be transparent or white pigmented. The compound should produce no darkening in the natural color of the concrete. It should, however, be of such a nature, or should be treated with a fugitive dye, so that the film will be distinctly visible for at least 4 hours after application. Typical transparent membranes are sodium silicate (water glass) and a mixture of paraffin-base wax and China-wood oil. White-pigmented curing compounds consist of finely ground white pigment mixed with a vehicle. Pigmented membranes protect the concrete against the effects of high temperatures better than transparent membranes.

Membrane materials are sprayed on the surface in the form of a fine mist to produce a uniform, water-impermeable film. They should be applied immediately after the final finishing operations and after the free water has disappeared. One or two coats may be applied; the application of two coats has the advantage of sealing imperfections in the first coat. To avoid segregation of the solids, the containers of membrane compounds should be agitated before the material is used; for white-pigmented compounds, the membrane materials should be stirred during application. White-pigmented sealing compounds should be applied in a film at a rate not less than 1 gallon per 200 square feet of surface.

Water-retention efficiency of waterproof paper and membranes is determined by ASTM test C156–52T. For waterproof paper, ASTM specifications require a moisture loss as the end of 3 days not greater than 10 per cent of the original mixing water used. Highway Research Board specifications for liquid membrane seal-coat materials require a moisture loss at the end of 3 days not greater than 8 per cent.

Integral Curing. Calcium chloride is also utilized as an integral curing agent, being added in dissolved form to the mixing water; when thus used, it tends to assist in the process of hydration and acts to accelerate the chemical reactions of the cement but does not prevent evaporation from the surface. Some engineers, although recognizing the accelerated hardening caused by the addition of calcium chloride, require surface application of water for a period up to 3 days to insure adequate curing. Such an accelerator as calcium chloride is valuable in rapid construction of all kinds, particularly for cold-weather work.

T. E. Stanton [10] in a comprehensive series of long-time tests reported a definite increase in compressive strength at 1 year for Portland-cement concrete containing additions of calcium chloride up to 5 per cent by weight.

Waterproofing

18.40 Proportioning and Curing the Mixture. Concrete can be made relatively watertight if attention is paid to the control of essential factors. The same factors that determine strength also greatly affect the watertightness of concrete. Sound aggregates of low porosity should be incorporated in pastes of low water-cement ratio to produce plastic concrete of good watertightness. Adequate curing is important since the watertightness is greatly affected by the extent to which the internal structure has been built up by hydration of the cement.

By referring to Fig. 18.7 it may be seen that rich mixtures have a smaller amount of pore space due to uncombined water in the paste than lean mixtures. The permeability is affected not only by the number of pore spaces but also by their size since flow under pressure is greatly facilitated by increase in the size of passageway. The lean mixture shown at the right with its large amount of pore space distributed through a relatively small percentage of solid paste volume will be much more permeable than the rich mixture at the left with its relatively small amount of pore space distributed through a large percentage of solid paste volume.

The beneficial effect of curing in improving watertightness by building up the amount of combined water can also easily be seen by referring to Fig. 18.7.

18.41 Use of Waterproofing Compounds. Waterproofing compounds may be classed in two general divisions: inert fillers, that is, those materials, such as clay, finely ground sand, diatomaceous silica, and hydrated lime, which serve simply as void fillers and do not have any action upon the cement nor change in themselves; and active fillers, which react with certain of the constituents of the cement to form inert insoluble compounds, or in the presence of the cement react with water and precipitate insoluble compounds.

Inert fillers are added to the dry cement before the mortar or concrete is mixed, in percentages usually amounting to 10 to 20 per cent of the

---

[10] T. E. Stanton: "A Study of Calcium Chloride as a Strength Accelerator in Portland-Cement Concrete." *Proc. Highway Research Board*, 1950, p. 232.

weight of the cement. Active fillers such as resins and stearates are also mixed with the dry cement before mixing, but the quantity is seldom more than 2 per cent by weight of the cement. Upon the addition of water to a stearate of lime, a lime soap is formed which is insoluble in water. If the stearic acid is combined with soda or potash, instead of lime, the soda soap or potash soap is readily soluble, and these must combine with the lime in the compound to form the insoluble lime soap. This is readily accomplished, since the stearates in the compounds never amount to more than a very small percentage, the greater part of the material being hydrated lime and magnesia.

All the inert fillers are fairly effective in reducing permeability, clays being slightly more effective that ground sand or feldspar. The active fillers are also usually more or less effective in reducing permeability, though often to a lesser degree than some of the inert materials. The inert fillers have little effect upon either tensile or compressive strength of mortars and concretes. The active fillers, on the other hand, usually reduce both the tensile and the compressive strength of rich mortars and only in very lean mixtures is their injurious effect upon strength no longer noted.

Hydrated lime in amounts not exceeding 10 to 15 per cent of the cement is one of the best materials for waterproofing concrete available. Its action appears to be chiefly mechanical, in that it produces a fat, viscous mortar in which separation of sand and cement is reduced to a minimum and a uniform dense concrete secured.

18.42 Layers of Waterproof Material. Layers of waterproof paper or felt, applied with a coating of coal tar or asphalt, are sometimes used as an impervious course in underground concrete walls, floors, etc. The asphalt or tar is spread hot on the concrete already placed, followed by alternate layers of paper or felt and hot asphalt or tar. Usually the waterproof course is laid 3-ply, 4-ply, or even 5- or 6-ply.

Such a course is finally coated with asphalt or tar again, and the remainder of the concrete deposited in place at once. A distinct joint in the masonry is necessarily formed in the plane of the impervious course, and this fact must not be overlooked in designing walls and floors in which a waterproof layer is incorporated.

18.43 Waterproofing Joints and Cracks. At construction joints in basins, reservoirs, dams, canal walls, and underground walls, lead or copper sheets or bituminous waterproof membranes are many times placed to stop the flow of water. Temperature cracks in concrete walls often present a problem since they may permit water to leak through. A procedure for repair is: A wedge-shaped slot is cut into the wall (when dry) from the water side, centered about the crack. The slot is kept wet for two days and then permitted to surface dry. A bonding grout of neat cement and water is scrubbed in, and a 1 to 3 cement mortar is then rammed in, beginning at the bottom of vertical cracks and working up. The new mortar is cured under wet burlap.

Protective and Special Treatments

18.44 Action of Sea Water on Concrete. Many concrete structures in sea water have remained intact and uninjured for many years; a few, constituting a small minority of all marine structures built, have been injured or destroyed. Disintegration of concrete in sea water is attributed to two main factors: (1) natural causes and (2) poor construction methods. Natural causes comprise both chemical and mechanical disintegration. Sulfates such as magnesium, calcium, and sodium sulfates are the most active chemical compounds in sea water; when found in concentrations of more than 1000 parts per million in water, the concrete will be endangered. It is believed that free lime in the cement and lime liberated by the chemical reactions of setting and hardening are acted upon by the magnesium and other sulfates in sea water, forming calcium sulfate, or calcium aluminosulfate and magnesium hydroxide. Another theory points to the tricalcium aluminate content of the cement being acted upon to form calcium sulfoaluminate. The resultant compounds are crystalline; they take up large quantities of water, producing a great increase in volume, which in turn creates cracks, scales, and spalling. Concrete with high tricalcium aluminate content has been found to be crumbly and very porous throughout the mass.

Mechanical disintegration is caused by the abrasion of débris and ice moved by tidal or wave action and the effects of freezing and thawing. When fresh concrete is placed in the forms, the lime of the cement at or near the surface is in a form to combine readily with carbon dioxide in the atmosphere. Thus, there is formed at the surface and for a slight depth in the mass, a layer of calcium carbonate which is practically insoluble in sea water. In mechanical disintegration, this skin is eroded by the abrasion of floating débris and ice, thus exposing the less resistant concrete beneath the skin to disintegration.

When water enters the concrete either through capillary action or percolation and is permitted to freeze, the accompanying expansion of the water in changing to ice opens up cracks and increases the porosity. By repeated freezing and thawing, disintegration is created.

Poor construction methods which permit such defects as laitance, honeycombing, checks, and hair cracks will augment disintegration.

18.45 Expedients Adopted to Prevent Injury by Sea Water. Foremost among the precautionary measures to be taken in the construction of marine structures of concrete is the securing of as dense and impermeable a concrete as possible

An outer shell of especially dense materials is sometimes effective on marine structures. A few inches of rich mortar (1:2 or 2½) is made to enclose and protect the inner portion of the concrete. It is necessary that this outer layer be cast at the same time as the inner portion in order that there may be a perfect bond between the two mixes.

Sometimes certain substances, such as barium chloride, are dissolved in the mixing water for the mortar of the outer shell. These, upon contact with the salts of the sea water, form insoluble sulfates which tend to close the pores in the mortar.

Sesquicarbonate of ammonia or magnesium fluosilicate is sometimes applied as a coating to the face of the finished work by brush or spray. The first substance tends to form an impervious film of carbonate of lime, and the second a film of insoluble calcium fluoride and lime silicate, thus stopping the pores. These methods remain effective only so long as the impervious coating remains intact.

The use of cement with a comparatively low tricalcium aluminate content improves the resistance of concrete to sulfate solutions. Type 2 and Type 5 Portland cements may be utilized since they are sulfate-resisting cements.

18.46 Concrete with Asphalt Admixture. Asphalt may be employed as an admixture in Portland-cement concrete. The asphalt is usually introduced in the form of an emulsion. An example is "Hydropel" which is an asphalt emulsion prepared from a hard asphalt. It supplies a thin, uniform, adsorbed film of asphalt around the cement and aggregate particles. The mixture produced has cement as the continuous phase and asphalt as the dispersed phase. Hydropel improves dispersion of the cement. When added at 1½ gallons per sack of cement, it is effective as an integral admixture, reducing capillary water absorption with subsequent reduction in expansion and contraction. The asphalt films serve as cushions, permitting plastic flow. Concrete piles containing an asphalt admixture have proved to be more resistant to impact and shattering during driving operations. Also concrete floors containing asphalt emulsion admixtures have been shown to enhance the comfort of people working on them owing to the cushioning effect. The improved comfort is related to absorption of impact energy. F. O. Anderegg [11] tested the amount of impact energy absorbed by measuring rebound of a steel ball. Steel ball bearings allowed to fall 36 inches on smooth regular concrete rebound usually 6 to 10 inches, while the rebound from smooth concrete containing asphalt emulsion admixture is 2 to 5 inches. Hydropel concrete also shows good resistance in the sodium sulfate soundness test (*ASTM Designation* C88–46T). It is resistant to deterioration by alkaline solutions and sea water.

[11] F. O. Anderegg: "Concrete Flooring with Asphalt Admixture." *Bull. ASTM,* 143, Dec., 1946, p. 11.

18.47 Additions of Cement-Dispersing Agents. Numerous patented cement-dispersing agents are available as additives to concrete immediately before or during its mixing. One of these commercial dispersing agents, Pozzolith, contains calcium lignosulfonate which when added to concrete causes dispersion of the cement particles by imparting to them a like electrostatic charge. Water that has been trapped within the cement-particle flocs is released to become a part of the mixing water. The surface area of cement particles in contact with water is increased. Pozzolith also acts as an air-entraining agent. Pozzolith is added in the proportion of ½ pound per sack of cement, and is placed in the mix dry or in solution with water. Improved cohesiveness, less bleeding, greater impermeability, and increased compressive strength for the same cement factor are obtained. The economics of adding dispersing agents and the durability of the resulting concrete are subjects of controversy.

18.48 Floor Hardening. Some concrete floors dust badly after the building is occupied. Other floors are not able to withstand heavy trucking. These faults can be laid to the mix, to excess of water, to lack of care in placing the concrete, or to quick drying out of the concrete. It is often possible to decrease the dusting or the wear by the application of a surface hardener. The usual types are magnesium fluosilicate, sodium silicate, zinc sulfate, alum, linseed oil, wax, varnishes, or paints.

Magnesium fluosilicate, in solutions from 8 to 18 per cent, decreases dusting and wear, especially for the stronger solutions. Sodium silicate, or water glass, gives excellent results, as do zinc sulfate and alum.

Linseed oil is a costly treatment but effective. Wax prevents dusting but does not harden the floor against wear. The varnishes and paints also prevent dusting but need renewal from time to time.

18.49 Vacuum Concrete Process. Extraction of a large percentage of excess mixing water which is not needed for hydration of the cement but is necessary to secure plasticity of the concrete can be accomplished by subjecting the surface of freshly deposited concrete to a partial vacuum. Simultaneously with such extraction, the surface of the concrete is subjected to the pressure of the atmosphere which tends to consolidate the mass while in a plastic state, thus filling in void and air spaces left by the removal of water. The extraction of excess mixing water from the concrete lowers the water-cement ratio and consequently increases the compressive strength of the concrete.

The excess mixing water is withdrawn through the agency of suction mats connected by suitable means to a vacuum pump. A mat consists of a tight, impermeable backing of rubber, wood, or metal, faced on the side toward the concrete with a filter fabric behind which are a series of channels through which the extracted water can flow to the suction outlet. With rigid forms, the necessary waterways are usually obtained by attaching a light expanded

Concrete 425

metal to the face of the form and then stretching the filter cloth over the expanded metal. For floors and pavements, flexible mats of sheet rubber about 3 feet by 10 feet in size are used with surface patterns on the lower side to provide waterways. The patterned surface of the rubber is covered with filter fabric which is cemented to the edges of the sheet. A band

Fig. 18.11. Vacuum concrete process applied to building construction. (*Courtesy* Vacuum Concrete Corp.)

of plain rubber around the edges of the mat provides a seal and prevents air leakage. The vacuum pump is connected by light steel tubing or by rubber hose to a manifold which provides connections for several flexible hose lines leading to the suction mats. The hose lines are connected to outlet holes in the mats by suction cups. Fig. 18.11 shows the forms, hose lines, and connections for applying a partial vacuum to a concrete wall.

The concrete is mixed and poured in the usual manner. A vacuum of 20 to 25 inches of mercury is maintained for a period ranging from 4 to 30 minutes, depending upon the type and thickness of concrete, until the concrete has lost its plasticity. It is possible to carry on this treatment without removing appreciable quantities of cement from the concrete.

The vacuum process of extracting excess mixing water has been used on concrete pavements, bridge decks, floor slabs, general concrete building construction, roofs, either precast or poured in place, and precast pipe and tile. The process has also been used in resurfacing concrete floors and pavements and in refacing walls. This treatment makes it possible to have lighter forms in construction and to strip the forms in a short time after pouring. Finishing operations may proceed immediately after treatment. The concrete should be adequately cured.

18.50 Concrete Restoration. The restoration of old concrete structures is a problem which engineers are called upon to accomplish. A recent development is the patented "Prepakt Concrete" process. Prepakt Concrete may be applied as a patch to old concrete since a high bond strength between Prepakt Concrete and cleaned hardened concrete may be obtained. Tests on beams jointed at midspan have shown such bond strength to be from 70 to 80 per cent of the strength of corresponding unjointed beams of ordinary concrete.

Prepakt Concrete is produced by placing well-graded coarse aggregate in the forms and then pumping from below, either in the dry or under water, a special mortar called Intrusion Grout to solidify the aggregate mass. Intrusion Grout consists of a mixture of Portland cement, sand, water, and two patented admixtures called Alfesil and Intrusion Aid. Alfesil consists of a very fine amorphous siliceous material which reacts with the lime that is liberated during hydration of Portland cement to form strength-producing compounds. It also acts to disperse the cement particles. Intrusion Aid is a protective colloid that prevents early setting of the grout, thus making possible the pumping of the grout into the void spaces between the aggregate particles. It also serves as an air-entraining agent. An important feature of Intrusion Aid is its expansion prior to the initial setting of the mortar which counteracts the setting shrinkage of the Portland cement. Alfesil plus Intrusion Aid hold the Portland cement and sand particles in suspension until the mortar has set; this makes possible a good mortar bond on the undersides of aggregate particles and reinforcement bars. Patches under water as well as under dry conditions can be satisfactorily constructed because the Intrusion Grout has high penetrability, displacing water as it is pumped upward in the forms without appreciable dilution of the Portland cement from the mortar.

Proportions of a typical Intrusion Grout are 2 parts Portland cement, 5 parts sand, 1 part Alfesil, and a small amount of Intrusion Aid (about 1 per cent by weight of cement and Alfesil). This mixture will produce concrete of about 4000 pounds per square inch compressive strength at 90 days.

Drying shrinkage of the concrete is reduced by packing the aggregates into the forms so as to bring the particles into contact. No clearance between coarse aggregate particles is required for workability as is true for regular concrete. A fine sand passing No. 8 sieve is used to facilitate pumping into the void spaces of the coarse aggregate. The coarse aggregate should range from a minimum size of about ⅜ inch up to any maximum size desired.

Summarizing, Prepakt Concrete is valuable in patching old concrete structures because of good bonding properties and because of reduction of setting shrinkage and drying shrinkage which decreases the tendency of the patch to crack. The method is used in rehabilitating concrete bridge piers, dams, jetties, and sea walls.

18.51 Insulating Concrete. The ingredients of insulating concrete are extremely lightweight aggregate, Portland cement, water, and air-entraining agent. Insulating concrete has a low density, a low value of thermal conductivity K, and a low compressive strength. Perlite and vermiculite are used as extremely lightweight aggregate. (See Chapter 14.) Neutralized Vinsol resin solution is a satisfactory air-entraining agent and is effective in improving workability of the mixture, overcoming segregation of fine from coarse aggregate particles, and preventing bleeding. The amount of air-entraining agent used is much greater than for paving or structural concrete of normal density. The proportions of typical mixtures of perlite insulating concrete are given in Table 18.5 together with the properties of

Table 18.5

TYPICAL MIXTURE DESIGNS OF LIGHTWEIGHT INSULATING PERLITE CONCRETE *

Dry Concrete Properties			Materials Required per Cubic Yard of Concrete			
Density, Oven-Dry, lb. per cu. ft.	Compressive Strength at 28 Days, p.s.i.	Thermal Conductivity, K	Cement, sacks	Perlite, cu. ft.	Water, gal.	Air-Entraining Agent, pt.
35	490	0.93	6.50	26	58.5	6.5
29	280	0.77	5.20	26	57	6.5
26	220	0.70	4.33	26	56.5	6.5
23.5	160	0.65	3.70	26	56	6.5
21.5	125	0.62	3.25	26	55	6.5

* *Courtesy* ASTM.

the dry concrete. These values are based on Type 1 Portland cement and perlite of average density of 8.0 pounds per cubic foot. Gradation limits for fine lightweight aggregate are given in Table 14.5 in Chapter 14; the size designation ¼ inch to dust is extensively used for insulating concrete.

Insulating concrete does not compete with structural concrete made with sand and gravel aggregates. Because of its extremely lightweight, fire-resisting, and insulating properties, insulating concrete is utilized for roof and floor fill; radiant subfloor slabs; fireproofing; curtain walls; partition and wall masonry units; and roof decks on short spans between steel joists.

Precast planks of perlite and vermiculite insulating concrete with electrically welded wire mesh fabric are used for roof construction, floors, and interior partitions. A K factor of 0.826 is typical for vermiculite insulating planks.

The compressive strength of lightweight insulating concrete is very low, ranging from 50 to 800 pounds per square inch. The modulus of elasticity of a good lightweight insulating concrete may be as low as 40,000 pounds per square inch.

18.52 Architectural Concrete.[12] *Polished Surfaces.* Concrete with special aggregates in the surface may be polished by grinding stones to bring out the colors and designs in order to produce a pleasing ornamental effect. *Art marbles,* made of colored cements and crushed marble aggregates are used to imitate marble. Precast units of various shapes and color combinations may be molded using only a thin layer of special material and backing up with cheaper materials. After hardening, the concrete surface is ground to bring out the aggregate. *Terrazzo* is art marble molded in place in walls and particularly floors of public buildings. Special aggregates are rolled into the surface of the fresh concrete; after hardening the surface is ground smooth, exposing the aggregates which may be arranged to produce designs.

Ornamental Finishes. Ornamental finishes of elaborate design can be obtained by exposing special aggregates. A typical method is to lay out the designs by cutting them into plaster-of-Paris board; another plaster-of-Paris board is cast on top of the first one to give raised areas instead of recessed. Concrete composed of gray or colored cement and colored aggregates such as crushed marble and colored glass is poured in a thin layer on top of the second plaster-of-Paris board and is backed up with cheaper concrete. The forms are removed in a day or two and the aggregate is exposed by means of wire brushes. The units are then permitted to harden before being placed in the structure.

Painted Decorations. Interior concrete surfaces may be painted or stained to produce decorative effects. Care must be taken that the concrete is of uniform texture and free from surface defects and blemishes. The concrete should be moist cured for several days and then well dried out. Lime on the surface should be neutralized by application of a coat of aqueous solu-

---

[12] *Concrete in Architecture,* a bulletin published by the Portland Cement Association.

tion of zinc sulfate. In a couple of days, a priming coat of boiled linseed oil should be applied to prevent the paint from penetrating too deeply. High-grade linseed oil paints or stains consisting of mixtures of China-wood oils and boiled linseed oils, thinned with turpentine and colored with pigments, have been applied satisfactorily. Designs may be stenciled on with paint. The painted surfaces should be protected by coats of clear varnish or shellac.

Stucco. Portland cement stucco is extensively used for exterior walls of buildings. The surface may be finished smooth or rough, and various patterns may be obtained by troweling, floating, rubbing, and sponging. Three-coat work is common, consisting of a first or scratch coat, a second or brown coat, and a finish coat. The first two coats are each about $\frac{3}{8}$ inch thick and the finish coat from $\frac{1}{8}$ to $\frac{1}{4}$ inch depending upon the texture selected. Typical proportions for all coats are 1 sack Portland cement, 3 cubic feet sand, and 10 pounds hydrated lime or lime putty to give the mortar the necessary plasticity to spread easily. A mineral oxide pigment of desired color may be added to the finish coat. White Portland cement should be used for light-colored finishes. Portland-cement stucco is readily applied directly on concrete masonry walls. In the case of wood frame construction, Portland-cement stucco should be applied to expanded metal lath that has been securely fastened.

Portland-Cement Plaster. This plaster has greater strength, hardness, and water resistance than gypsum and lime plasters. It is also more nearly vermin-proof. Portland cement plaster has, however, an objectionable tendency to crack, owing to its comparatively high drying shrinkage.

Concrete Products

18.53 General. Building units of either plain or reinforced concrete are often poured and cured in plants devoted to the manufacture of such products, to be delivered when aged to the site of construction. Among these concrete products may be listed blocks, bricks, pipes, tiles, posts, sills, lintels, copings, etc. The most widely used of these are concrete masonry blocks and concrete bricks. (See Art. 19.24.)

18.54 Concrete Masonry Blocks. Concrete masonry blocks are of varying shapes and sizes but conform generally to the requirements of modular design in which a 4-inch module or increment constitutes the standard unit. Nominal dimensions usually are in multiples of 4 inches. Actual dimensions of blocks allow for thickness of mortar joints which may be $\frac{1}{4}$, $\frac{3}{8}$, or $\frac{1}{2}$ inch thick. Typical hollow concrete masonry units are illustrated in Fig. 18.12.

Aggregates employed for concrete masonry blocks are generally gravel and sand, but lightweight aggregates are being utilized to a great extent

430   Materials of Construction

primarily to reduce the unit weight. Both Type 1 standard and Type 3 high-early-strength Portland cements are used.

Most concrete masonry blocks are manufactured by automatic-machine molding or by hand-operated machine molding using dry or moist concrete mixtures. The blocks are ejected from the machines immediately after molding. Hand puddling in molds is used to some extent, however, using wet concrete mixtures; the blocks are cured in the molds.

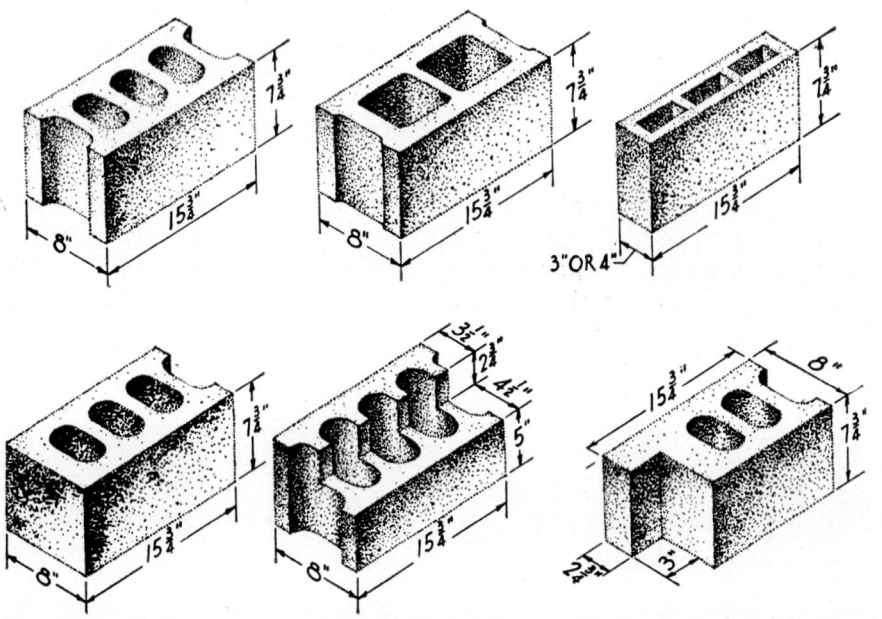

Fig. 18.12. Hollow concrete masonry units. (*Courtesy* National Concrete Masonry Assoc.)

Concrete masonry blocks are usually placed in a curing room immediately after fabrication to hasten the attainment of a reasonable strength. The curing methods generally consist of low-pressure steam curing or of water-spraying curing in "fog rooms" containing warm air. Steam, under a pressure higher than atmospheric, gives good results, as the higher temperature hastens the setting action and the moisture prevents any drying out. A new development is electric curing which is still in the experimental stage.

The strength requirement of the American Society for Testing Materials for hollow load-bearing blocks is an average compressive strength for 5 units of 1000 pounds per square inch of gross area, with no unit below 800 pounds per square inch of gross area. Water absorption is specified not to exceed 15 pounds for cubic foot of concrete for an average of 5 units. The moisture content should not exceed 40 per cent at the time of delivery to the job site.

18.55 Concrete Pipes. Concrete pipes may be plain or reinforced. They are used for sewers, drains, culverts, and irrigation pipes. Sewer pipes are manufactured in sizes from 4 to 24 inches in diameter when plain, and when reinforced with steel are made in diameters from 12 to 108 inches. Standard culvert pipes are reinforced and available in diameters from 12 to 108 inches. Extra-strength culvert pipes are also available in diameters from 24 to 108 inches. Plain concrete irrigation pipes come in diameters from 6 to 24 inches. Bell-and-spigot ends are available in sizes up to 48 inches, but tongue-and-groove ends are generally used for pipes 24 inches in diameter and larger, and are available also in the smaller sizes.

Aggregates for concrete pipes are usually gravel and sand. The maximum size of gravel is usually restricted to not over $\frac{1}{2}$ inch, but up to 1-inch maximum size may be used in large pipes having thick walls. Careful control of aggregate grading is necessary to get a dense concrete. In view of the small maximum size of the gravel, more sand than gravel is customarily used in the mix. Type 1 ordinary cement is generally employed, but Type 3 high-early-strength Portland cement is permitted by ASTM specifications.

Except for very large pipes molded by hand methods, machine-molding methods are used; three types of machines are: (1) packer-head, (2) tamping, and (3) centrifugal machines. Curing methods comprise steam curing, water-spray curing, and saturated-cover curing such as that done with burlap.

Specifications of the ASTM have requirements for strength, absorption, and hydrostatic tests. Crushing-strength tests of pipes are made by either the three-edge-bearing or sand-bearing methods. The minimum allowable crushing strength by the three-edge-bearing method varies from 1000 pounds per lineal foot for 4-inch plain concrete sewer pipe to 2400 pounds per lineal foot for 24-inch pipe. The maximum allowable percentage absorption for all pipes is 8 per cent. Pipes must not leak under hydrostatic tests. (See also Art. 19.52.)

Concrete pipes are manufactured with porous walls for use as drain pipes. They are available in diameters from 4 to 24 inches. The rate of infiltration usually required on all sizes is not less than 2 gallons per minute per inch of internal diameter per length of pipe. Pipes come in 24-, 30-, and 36-inch lengths.

18.56 Cast Stone. Cast stone consists of precast-concrete shapes for use as sills, copings, facings, steps, etc. A durable, hard, and carefully graded aggregate is selected with maximum size of coarse aggregate usually not exceeding $\frac{3}{8}$ inch. Cement is generally Type 1 regular Portland cement, but white Portland cement and alumina cement are also employed. Various types of molds are used. Adequate curing is essential and is preferably done in a water-spray type of curing room for 7 to 14 days. The ordinary finish obtained by contact with the forms is commonly used, but cast-stone units may be sawed or planed to give a distinct type of finish. Cast stone is manufactured in several different colors. It is important to produce cast stone products of high compressive strength and low absorption. Cubes 2 by 2 inches in size, cut from cast-stone shapes, should show a compressive strength of at least 5000 pounds per square inch at 28 days, and not to exceed 8 per cent absorption.

18.57 Prestressed Block-Beam Structures. Concrete block units are utilized in construction of prestressed block-beam structures. Beams assembled from concrete blocks, strung like beads on wire cables and then prestressed, are used for bridges and buildings. Concrete block for this application should develop a final compressive strength of 3750 pounds per square inch; they are cured for 28 days to eliminate shrinkage. During assembly of the blocks into beams, wood cores are placed in the cores (holes) in the blocks to prevent mortar entering the cores. Specially designed holes are provided in the blocks to hold the steel wire cables. Hydraulic jacks are employed in prestressing. As soon as the block and end plates are placed, the cables are strung and enough tension applied to extrude excess mortar and shorten the block-beam to proper length. The block-beams are cured under tension for 7 days until mortar reaches a compressive strength of 2000 pounds per square inch when final force is applied to the cables; the beams are then ready for assembly into structures. An advantage of prestressed block-beam construction is the short time required to assemble the superstructure.

18.58 Marble-Face Building Block. The marble facing of the building blocks is manufactured by mixing crushed marble with white Portland cement and colored pigments. Nickel-plated steel pans are the forms for the marble facing. The marble-facing concrete in the pans is vibrated. The pans are placed on drying racks, and, after several minutes of drying, the pans are placed in a face-down tamper machine where the concrete for the body of the block is tamped on to the back of the marble-facing in the pans. For this backup, lightweight aggregate concrete is suitable because of low weight and good insulating properties. Both single-faced and double-faced units are made. The racks for holding the pans are placed in a steam kiln to cure the concrete. The pans are stripped after 1 day in the kiln. A very smooth, dense, and impervious facing can be obtained. Various colors are employed. Typical thicknesses of blocks are 4, 6, and 8 inches. These blocks can be used as load-bearing units since a strength of 1400 pounds per square inch on the gross area of the block can be developed in well-made units. Accessories such as corners and sash blocks are also manufactured.

Physical Properties of Concrete

18.59 Compressive Strength. The compressive strength of concrete depends primarily on the water-cement ratio. Other factors such as character of the cement, conditions of mixing, deposition, curing and aging, character and grading of the aggregates, and size and shape of test specimen have a bearing on the compressive strength.

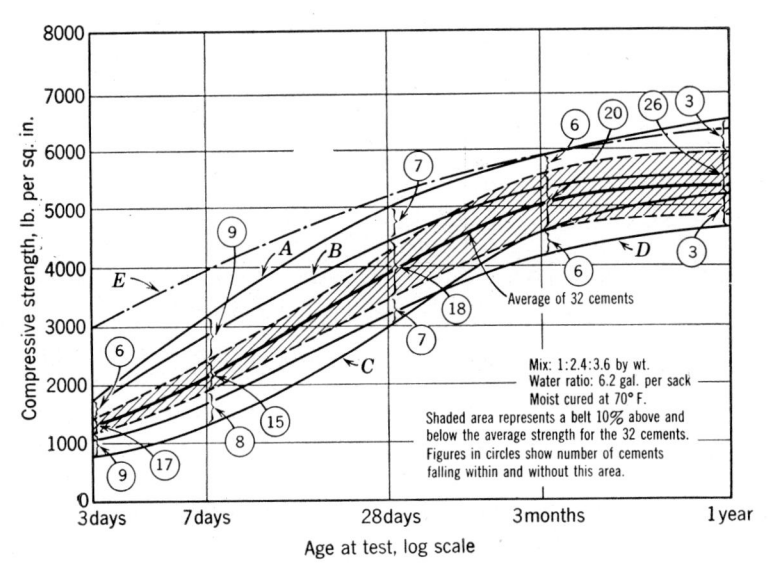

Fig. 18.13. Age versus compressive strength of concrete for 32 standard Portland cements. (*Courtesy* F. R. McMillan.)

Effect of Character of the Cement. All Portland cements behave similarly, but they do not gain their strength at the same rate. This is brought out in Fig. 18.13, which shows tests of concrete made from 32 brands of cement which were conducted in the Portland Cement Association laboratory. In this diagram, which represents age-strength relation, are shown two of the highest, two of the lowest, and the average of the 32. The shaded area represents a belt 10 per cent above and 10 per cent below the average curve. The numbers in the circles at each of the five ages represent the number of cements which fall within the band 10 per cent above or below the average, also the number which fall outside of that band on both sides.

Effects of Variations in Mix and Consistency. Figure 18.14 shows that the water-cement ratio fixes the compressive strength, regardless of variations in the cement content or in consistency.

434   Materials of Construction

Effects of Curing and Aging. Curing and aging cannot be separated; an increase in age provides for further chemical combinations if the conditions are favorable for continued reaction. Figure 18.14 shows for moist-cured

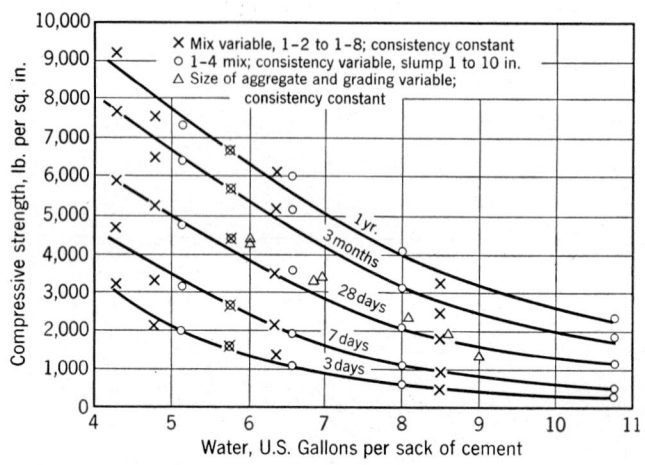

Fig. 18.14. Compressive strength of concrete of varying water contents at different ages. (Moist-room curing; 6 by 12 in. cylinders.) (*Courtesy* F. R. McMillan.)

concrete the effect of age on the relation between water-cement ratio and compressive strength. The similarity in the curves for the various ages should be noted.

Effect of Shape of Test Specimen. Compression tests of concrete are ordinarily conducted on cylindrical specimens with height equal to twice the diameter so that surfaces of rupture produced upon fracture will not intersect the end bearings. Tests conducted on short cylinders or prisms will give greater strengths than those obtained on cylinders of standard height. The ends of the cylinders should be carefully formed to give

Table 18.6

RELATION BETWEEN SIZE OF SPECIMEN AND COMPRESSIVE STRENGTH OF CONCRETE

Diameter of Cylinder, in.	Height of Cylinder, in.	Per Cent of Compressive Strength of 6 by 12 in. Cylinder
2	4	108
3	6	106.5
4	8	104
6	12	100
8	16	96
12	24	92
18	36	86
24	48	84
36	72	83.5

parallel, smooth surfaces so as to obtain uniform distribution of stress. A uniformly stressed cylinder which has been properly molded will break in the shape of a double cone with vertex in the center of the cylinder.

Effect of Size of Test Specimen. The effect of size of test specimen upon compressive strength of concrete as determined by R. F. Blanks and C. C. McNamara [13] is given in Table 18.6. It is customary to state compressive strength in terms of the values obtained on 6 by 12 inch cylinders.

18.60 Tensile Strength. In Fig. 18.15 are shown the results of tensile tests of concrete at various ages plotted in terms of the water-cement ratio.

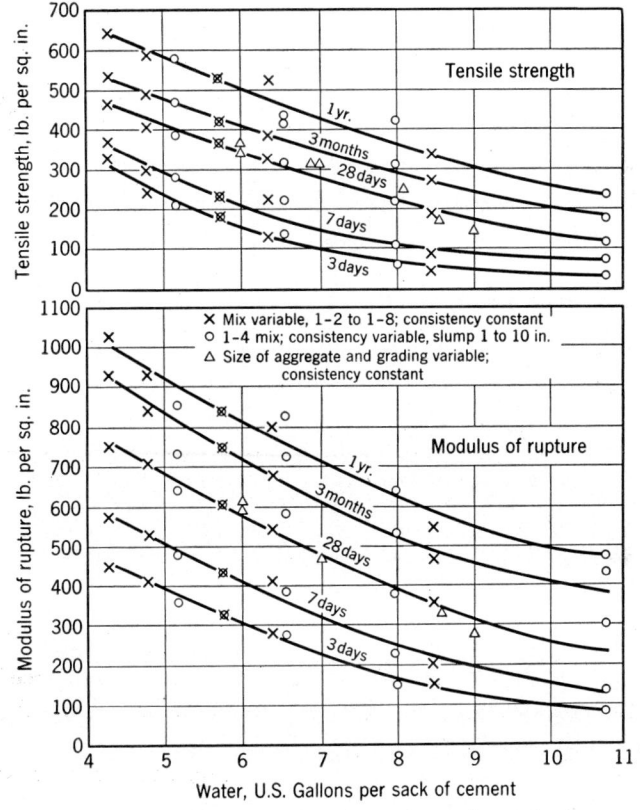

Fig. 18.15. Tensile and flexural strengths of concrete of varying water contents at different ages. (Moist-room curing; tension cylinders, 6 by 18 in.; beams, 7 by 10 by 38 in.) (*Courtesy* F. R. McMillan.)

The same characteristics of the water-cement ratio strength relation will be noted for tensile as for compressive strength. The tensile strength of ordinary concrete ranges from about 7 to 10 per cent of the compressive strength.

[13] *Proc. Am. Concrete Inst.*, v. 31, 1935.

18.61 Flexural Strength. The flexural strength of plain concrete is almost wholly dependent upon the tensile strength. Experiments show, however, that the modulus of rupture is considerably greater than the strength in tension. Results of flexural tests of concrete at various ages plotted in terms of the water-cement ratio are given in Fig. 18.15. The same general characteristics of the water-cement ratio strength relation are shown in these results as for compressive strength. Flexural strength is of importance in the design of concrete pavements.

18.62 Shearing Strength. The shearing strength of concrete is a most important property of the material, since it is the real determining factor in the compressive strength of short columns. The strength of concrete beams depends also, under certain conditions, upon the shearing strength of the material.

The average strength of concrete in direct shear varies from about one-half of the compressive strength for rich mixtures to about 0.8 of the compressive strength for lean mixtures.[14]

18.63 Elastic Properties. The elastic properties of concrete are of importance not only because of their bearing upon the deformation of concrete

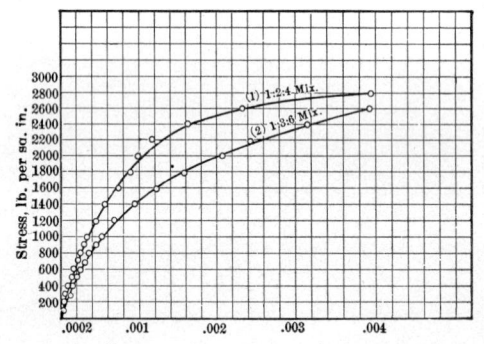

Fig. 18.16. Stress-strain diagram for concrete in compression. Age 3 months.

structures under load, but also because in the design of reinforced concrete it is necessary to know the relative stresses in the steel and the concrete under like distortions.

Figure 18.16 shows typical stress-strain diagrams for short prisms of concrete in compression.

Concrete is not perfectly elastic for any range of loading, an appreciable permanent set taking place for even very low loads, and the deformation is not proportional to the stress at any stage of the loading.

There can be, therefore, no elastic limit for concrete in the true sense of the term. There appears to be a stress, however, below which repetition of the same load does not cause appreciable increase in set, whereas beyond

[14] *Univ. Ill. Eng. Exp. Sta. Bull.* 8.

this stress repetition of load causes increased set indefinitely, finally resulting in rupture far below the normal ultimate strength. For practical purposes, therefore, it is convenient to consider this stress as the elastic limit. Experiments made by Bach, Probst, Van Ornum, and others seem to place this stress at about 50 to 60 per cent of the ultimate strength.

The elastic properties of concrete vary with the richness of the mixture and with the intensity of stress. They also vary with the age of the concrete.

18.64 Modulus of Elasticity. Since the deformation of concrete is not proportional to the stress at any stage of the loading, the modulus of elasticity is not a constant for any appreciable range of stress, decreasing as the load increases. The modulus of elasticity is customarily determined by one of three arbitrary methods: (1) the initial tangent method, in which a tangent is drawn to the curve at its origin; (2) the tangent method, in which a tangent is drawn to the curve at a point corresponding to a given stress; and (3) the secant method, in which a line is drawn through the origin and a point on the curve corresponding to a given design stress, as for example 800 pounds per square inch. The slope of the line gives the value of the modulus of elasticity in pounds per square inch.

The initial tangent modulus is of little value except for comparing the stiffness of rich and lean concretes. The tangent modulus and particularly the secant modulus are of importance for reinforced-concrete design. Values of the tangent and secant moduli vary ordinarily from 1,000,000 to 5,000,000 pounds per square inch depending upon the method used. The modulus is higher for richer mixtures and increases with the age of the concrete.

18.65 Ratio E_c/E_s. The relative moduli of elasticity of concrete and steel determine the relative stresses in the two materials when the combined concrete and steel member is deformed a given amount. So long as the bond is not destroyed, the ratio E_c/E_s (called $1/n$) fixes the relative stresses in the concrete and steel.

18.66 Stress-Strain Curves. Bach determined the true elastic curve in compression by repeatedly loading and unloading the test specimen to a given stress until the set at zero load became constant. At low stresses, the required constant set is soon obtained, but as the stresses are increased, the number of times the specimen must be loaded is correspondingly greater. The elastic deformation for a given stress is determined by subtracting the permanent set from the total deformation. The true elastic curve is obtained from a number of elastic deformations corresponding to different values of stress. The true elastic curve is useful in determining the change of shape of concrete after removal of stress but does not indicate the total amount of deformation which the material undergoes for a given stress. The total-deformation curve is of importance in reinforced-concrete design, since the unit stress carried by the steel is a function of the total deformation of the combination of steel and concrete.

Bach determined the equation for unit deformation in compression of true elastic curves to be of the exponential form,

$$\epsilon = KS_c^m$$

where $K = 1/E_c$, m is a constant varying from 1.11 to 1.16, and S_c is the compressive stress. Bach determined the modulus of elasticity in compression, E_c, from the true elastic curve using the tangent method.

18.67 Sonic Modulus of Elasticity. The sonic, or dynamic, modulus of elasticity is obtained by measuring the fundamental transverse frequency of beams and cylinders. The apparatus consists of a driving circuit, a pickup circuit, and supports for the specimen. The beam or cylinder is supported at its nodal points, $0.224L$ from each end, and subjected to a vibratory loading. The loading is produced by a plunger (driving unit) attached to the cone of a radio loud speaker and is applied generally at the center of the specimen or near one end. The period of vibration of the plunger can be varied by turning a tuning dial. When the frequency of the plunger is the same as the natural or fundamental frequency of the specimen, a condition of resonance is obtained and the specimen vibrates with maximum deflection. The pickup circuit consisting of a deflection or output meter electrically connected to an amplifier and a crystal pickup attached to one end of the specimen is used to note the resonance. The fundamental frequency of vibration of the specimen can be ascertained from the tuning-dial reading. With the fundamental frequency, density, and specimen dimensions known, the sonic modulus of elasticity can be computed.

The following formula may be used to calculate the sonic modulus of elasticity:

$$E = CWn^2$$

$$\text{For cylinder } C = \frac{0.00416L^3T}{d^4} \text{ seconds}^2 \text{ per square inch}$$

$$\text{For prism } C = \frac{0.00245L^3T}{bt^3} \text{ seconds}^2 \text{ per square inch}$$

where E = sonic modulus of elasticity, in pounds per square inch.
  W = weight of specimen, in pounds.
  n = fundamental transverse frequency, in cycles per second.
  L = length of specimen, in inches.
  d = diameter of cylinder, in inches.
  t, b = dimensions of cross-section of prism in inches, t being in the direction of vibration.
  T = a correction factor which depends on the ratio of the radius of gyration K to the length of the specimen L. (K for a cylinder is $d/4$ and for a prism is $t/2\sqrt{3}$.) For Poisson's ratio, $u = 1/6$, Pickett [15] gives the following formula for T:

---

[15] G. Pickett: "Equations for Computing Elastic Constants from Flexural and Torsional Resonant Frequencies of Vibration of Prisms and Cylinders." *Proc. ASTM*, v. 45, 1945, p. 846. See also "Test for Fundamental Frequency of Concrete Specimens." C215–47T, 1949, *ASTM Standards,* Part 3, p. 855.

$$T = 1 + 81.79\left(\frac{K}{L}\right)^2 - \frac{1314\left(\frac{K}{L}\right)^4}{1 + 81.09\left(\frac{K}{L}\right)^2} - 125\left(\frac{K}{L}\right)^4$$

A great advantage of the sonic method is that the value of E can be determined without injuring the specimen so that a series of determinations on a single specimen can be obtained. Further, the relationship between reduction in sonic E and reduction in flexural strength for individual specimens has been investigated. Reagel [16] in extensive tests covering a wide range has shown that the percentage reductions in modulus of rupture R and in sonic modulus of elasticity E can be expressed as:

$$R = 6E^{0.6}$$

This relationship is of practical application in determining the deterioration of concrete specimens in freezing and thawing tests.

18.68 Fatigue of Concrete. Plain concrete, when subjected to flexure, exhibits fatigue. The flexure-resisting ability of a concrete of a given quality is indicated by an endurance limit whose value depends upon the number of repetitions of stress. The Illinois Division of Highways found that an endurance limit of 55 per cent of the flexural stress which would cause rupture (known as the modulus of rupture) permitted indefinite repetitions of load without failure. In concrete pavement design, the allowable flexural working stress is limited to 55 per cent of the modulus of rupture strength of the concrete used so that the pavement will be able safely to resist stresses which will be periodically repeated a great many times during the life of the pavement.

18.69 Adhesion to Steel. The adhesion of concrete to steel is important in its bearing on the design of reinforced concrete. The bond strength depends principally upon the richness of the mix and the character of the surface of the steel. The adhesive strength of 1:2:4 concrete to plain round rods is in the neighborhood of 400 pounds per square inch. The adhesive strength may be greatly increased by using bars with deformations of suitable design.

C. A. Menzel reported in 1939 on research of pull-out tests, involving 1-inch round and square bars cast in concrete prisms:

> The resistance of deformed bars has more relation to concrete compressive strength than does the resistance of plain bars.
> Slip is greatly increased as steel stresses are raised.
> Bond is better with dry than with wet mixes of concrete.

An extensive investigation of bond efficiency of deformed concrete reinforcing bars, sponsored by the American Iron and Steel Institute, was re-

---

[16] F. V. Reagel: "Freezing and Thawing Tests of Concrete." *Proc. Highway Research Board*, 1910.

ported by A. P. Clark in 1946. Results were given of tests on 17 bars of different types of deformations. The main conclusions were:

For the best bond resistance of a bar, there is a definite relation between the height and spacing of the deformations.

Height of deformations are an important factor in determining the effect of the settlement of the concrete under the bar.

The pattern of the deformation does not seem to be an important factor in determining the bond resistance.

The inclination of the face of the deformations is an important factor in determining the bond resistance.

The American Society for Testing Materials specification A305–50T for minimum requirements for the deformations of deformed steel bars for concrete reinforcement gives the spacing, height, and gap of deformations for different sizes of bars. (See Table 18.7.) The deformations must be

Table 18.7

ASTM DIMENSIONAL REQUIREMENTS FOR DEFORMED STEEL BARS FOR CONCRETE REINFORCEMENT

Deformation Requirements

Deformed Bar Designation Number	Nominal Diameter, in.	Maximum Average Spacing, in.	Minimum Height, in.	Maximum Gap (Chord of 12½% of Nominal Perimeter), in.
3	0.375	0.262	0.015	0.143
4	0.500	0.350	0.020	0.191
5	0.625	0.437	0.028	0.239
6	0.750	0.525	0.038	0.286
7	0.875	0.612	0.044	0.334
8	1.000	0.700	0.050	0.383
9	1.128	0.790	0.056	0.431
10	1.270	0.889	0.064	0.487
11	1.410	0.987	0.071	0.540

placed with respect to the axis of the bar so that the included angle is not less than 45 degrees.

18.70 Durability of Concrete. Durability is the ability to resist deterioration caused by destructive forces. The main causes of deterioration of concrete are:

1. Abrasive forces causing wear of concrete.
2. Chemical attack by sea water (Art. 18.44), alkalies, acids, sewage, oils, and chloride salts.
3. Expansive forces caused by chemical reactions between certain minerals in aggregates and the alkalies in Portland cement. (See Art. 14.13.)

4. Expansive forces caused by unsound aggregates. (Standard sodium and magnesium sulfate soundness tests for aggregates have made possible detection of the more extreme unsound aggregates. Art. 14.11.)

5. Expansive forces caused by unsound cement. (Unsound cement is rarely found in practice, especially since the adoption of the autoclave expansion test.)

6. Destructive forces caused by alternate wetting and drying of concrete. (See Art. 18.74.)

7. Destructive forces caused by alternate heating and cooling of concrete. Some aggregates have coefficients of thermal expansion considerably lower than those of Portland cement pastes. When concrete made with such aggregates is subjected to extreme variations in temperatures as in a pavement, bond failures between aggregates and cement may occur. (See also Art. 18.74.)

8. Destructive forces caused by alternate freezing and thawing of moist or saturated concrete. This action will be discussed in the next article.

18.71 Freezing and Thawing of Concrete. Concrete containing moisture is deteriorated by the alternations of freezing and thawing which occur in temperate zone climates. In Wisconsin about 25 cycles occur annually; in Virginia about 40. When calcium or sodium chloride is applied to the surface of concrete pavements to remove ice, the number of cycles may be markedly increased.

Freezing and thawing tests have been devised to endeavor to obtain an indication of the resistance to deterioration which concrete structures may be reasonably expected to render under given types of exposure. A test employed by the Highway Research Board Committee on Durability of Concrete consists of the following steps:

1. After curing for 28 days, beams are immersed in water at 40° F.
2. Beams are removed from water and placed in air of cold room where temperatures of specimens are reduced from 40° F. to 0° F. in not less than 5 and not more than 7 hours. Beams are retained in freezer for 18 hours with minimum freezer temperature of minus 10° F.
3. Beams are then removed from freezer and immersed for 6 hours in water at 40° F.
4. Beams are then returned to air of freezer as in step 2.

In addition to the above method of freezing in air after soaking in water and after thawing in water, the following methods have been used:

Freezing and thawing immersed in water.
Freezing partly immersed in water and thawing partly or wholly immersed in water.
Freezing and thawing directionally to simulate conditions in a pavement.

After every 5 cycles, measurements of weight and sonic modulus of elasticity are made. Correlation is made between sonic E and modulus of rupture.

The deteriorating influence of freezing and thawing is related to three factors:

1. The permeability of the concrete.
2. The ratio of freezable water in the concrete to the air voids.
3. The rate at which the temperature falls during freezing.

The first two factors are influenced by the character of the aggregate, the quality of the cement paste, the consistency of the mix, methods of placement and curing, and the number, size, and distribution of air bubbles entrained in the hardened concrete. With respect to the third factor, high rates of freezing should be avoided in testing because it is probable that they will change the process of deterioration from that occurring at the very low rates of freezing encountered in nature.

Air-entraining concrete is more resistant to freezing and thawing than ordinary concrete. Powers [17] has stated a hypothesis to explain this; he suggests that as freezing of water begins and consequent expansion takes place, the internal pressure increases and some water is forced through the paste to the unfilled air voids. Damage is thus minimized. Assuming adequate total air volume, the distance between air spaces rather than the total volume of air would be the factor determining the degree of protection to the concrete. Thus, the effectiveness of entrained air increases as the bubble size decreases.

18.72 Durability Factor. Stanton Walker has suggested a method to indicate resistance to freezing and thawing by a single number rather than by an elaborate description. This number is a *durability factor* which is a function of the area under the curve obtained by plotting sonic modulus of elasticity, expressed as the percentage of the value at zero cycles, with respect to the number of cycles of freezing and thawing. Figure 18.17 illustrates the method of computing the factor and demonstrates its significance. The durability factor at any number of cycles is the ratio between the area under the curve above the 50 per cent E line and the total area above the same line. For example, the durability factor at 50 cycles for the concrete represented by the middle curve would be area $AFIG/ABIG$; at 100 cycles it would be $AJG/ACKG$.

By this method, the denominator in each case represents the area under a curve for concrete showing no deterioration caused by freezing and thawing. If such a resistant concrete could be produced, its durability factor at any number of cycles would be unity. Generally the factor becomes somewhat lower as the number of cycles used for measurement is increased. In most cases, 100 cycles should suffice to give a reliable index of resistance

---

[17] T. C. Powers: "A Working Hypothesis for Further Studies of Frost Resistance of Concrete." *J. Am. Concrete Inst.*, v. 16, 4, 1945.

to freezing and thawing. An alternate requirement might be to continue the cycles until the loss in sonic E reached 50 per cent.

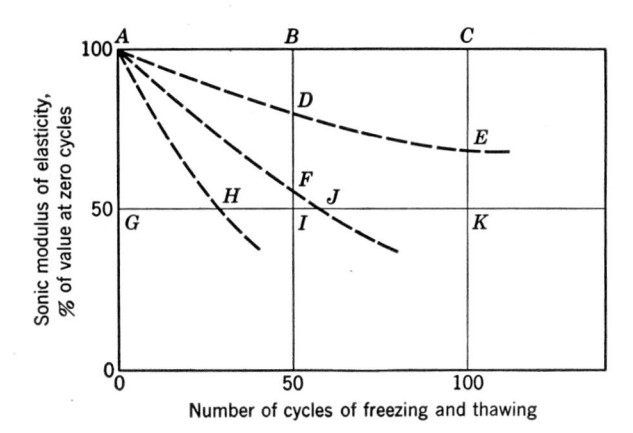

Curve	At 50 Cycles	At 100 Cycles
ADE	$\dfrac{ADIG}{ABIG}$	$\dfrac{AEKG}{ACKG}$
AFJ	$\dfrac{AFIG}{ABIG}$	$\dfrac{AJG}{ACKG}$
AH	$\dfrac{AHG}{ABIG}$	$\dfrac{AHG}{ACKG}$

Fig. 18.17. Method of calculating durability factors. (Stanton Walker.)

18.73 Effects of Water and Air Content on Concrete Properties. Test results obtained by Guy H. Larson, Materials Engineer of the State Highway Commission of Wisconsin, showing the effects of water and air content on concrete properties are given in Table 18.8. Dolomitic sand (specific gravity = 2.59) and dolomitic gravel (specific gravity = 2.68) were used in all mixes.

Mixture No. 1: paving mixture using 5.42 sacks of standard Portland cement (Type 1) per cubic yard of concrete; 1.5-inch slump. Sand comprises 40 per cent of total aggregate.

Mixture No. 2: same as mixture No. 1 except that mixing water was increased to obtain a slump of 3.5 inches.

Mixture No. 3: same quantities as in mixture No. 1 but with addition of N-TAIR air-entraining agent.

Mixture No. 4: similar to mixture No. 3 but with amount of sand reduced to 36 per cent of total aggregate and mixing water reduced to obtain a slump of 1.5 inches. Same amount of air-entraining agent used.

Table 18.8

SUMMARY OF TESTS ON PORTLAND CEMENT CONCRETE

(G. H. Larson)

Mixture No.	1	2	3	4
Batch weight, lb.				
Cement	25.9	25.9	25.9	25.9
Sand	68.0	68.0	68.0	61.0
Gravel	105.0	105.0	105.0	112.0
Water	9.3	10.7	9.3	7.7
N-TAIR, air-entraining agent, gm.	——	——	7.9	7.9
Total	208.2	209.6	208.2	206.6
Slump, in.	1.5	3.5	3.25	1.5
Unit weight, lb. per cu. ft.	151.6	151.0	147.2	148.8
Volume of batch, cu. ft.				
Actual	1.373	1.388	1.415	1.388
Theoretical air-free	1.348	1.371	1.348	1.322
Air content, %				
Gravimetric	1.8	1.2	4.7	4.7
By air meter	1.7	1.2	5.1	4.0
Yield, cu. ft. concrete per sack of cement	4.98	5.04	5.14	5.04
Cement factor	5.42	5.36	5.26	5.36
Water-cement ratio, by volume	0.742	0.805	0.724	0.632
Compressive strength, p.s.i. (4 days)	2590	2240	2280	2810
Flexural strength, p.s.i. (4 days)	510	507	448	518

Reviewing the results obtained in Table 18.8 with the different mixtures by comparing each mixture in turn with mixture No. 1, it is noted that:

a. For mixture No. 2, increasing the mixing water increased the slump, actual and theoretical air-free volumes, yield, and water-cement ratio, but decreased the unit weight, air content, cement factor, and both compressive and flexural strengths.

b. For mixture No. 3, the addition of an air-entraining agent to mixture No. 1 increased the slump, actual volume, air content, and yield, maintained theoretical air-free volume and water-cement ratio, but decreased the unit weight, cement factor, and both compressive and flexural strengths.

c. For mixture No. 4, adjusting air-entrained mixture No. 3 by reducing the sand and increasing the gravel and reducing the total mixing water so as to produce the same slump as for mixture No. 1, increased actual volume, air content, yield, and both compressive and flexural strengths, but decreased unit weight, theoretical air-free volume, cement factor, and water-cement ratio as compared to mixture No. 1.

Attention is directed to advantages of air-entrained mixture No. 4 in which proportions have been adjusted by reducing sand and water contents. This adjustment gives consideration to the increased volume of mortar resulting from the bulking effect of the entrained air. Advantage is taken of the inherent workability of the concrete resulting from the cohesiveness and "fatness" of the mortar in air-entrained concrete. These factors permit some reduction in the quantities of sand and mixing water in air-entrained concrete as compared to those commonly used in non-air-entrained concrete mixtures.

Taking as a criterion concrete mixtures normally used for cements containing no air-entraining agents, a reduction in the batch weight of the sand by an amount equivalent to about 3 per cent of the total weight of both sand and coarse aggregate should under average conditions closely compensate for the entrained air. This reduced amount of sand and about $\frac{1}{4}$ gallon less net mixing water than normally used per sack of cement are suggested for incorporation in the first trial batches. Observations of the mix should then be made to determine whether further adjustments in the sand content, or in the amount of sand and coarse aggregate, or in the water content, are necessary to obtain proper consistency and workability. Yield tests should be made and used as a basis for further correction in the mix to obtain the specified cement factor. The air content must also be checked.

18.74 Expansion and Contraction. Values of the coefficient of expansion of concrete as obtained by W. G. Mullen at the University of Maryland are given in Table 18.9. (See reference 18.30.) Saturated and dry concretes have similar values of the coefficient of expansion which are somewhat lower than those of partially dry concrete. Mullen found that the thermal coefficient of expansion of concrete is affected by the coefficient of expansion of coarse aggregate in proportion to its absolute volume as modified by some function of the moduli of elasticity of the mortar and the coarse aggregate. Concrete containing silica-type aggregates has a greater coefficient of expansion than that containing limestone-type aggregates. Concrete with traprock coarse aggregate has a coefficient of expansion intermediate between the values for limestone aggregate concrete and silica aggregate concrete. The coefficient of contraction is somewhat smaller than the coefficient of expansion.

In addition to the volumetric changes due to temperature variation, concrete is subject to other volume changes caused by the chemical processes of setting and hardening or by variation in the moisture content. Experiments show that concrete hardened in air contracts, and concrete hardened in water expands, the amount of change in volume depending upon the richness of the mixture. Experiments made by A. H. White indicate that the expansion or contraction even of old concrete, when alternately wet and dried, is far from being negligible. Pieces of concrete, presumably not leaner than 1:3:6 or richer than 1:2:4, sawn from a sidewalk after 20

Table 18.9

THERMAL COEFFICIENTS FOR CONCRETE (W. G. Mullen)

Concrete Containing 50% Coarse Aggregate by Volume

Coarse Aggregate	Fine Aggregate	Coefficient of Expansion, per °F. $\times 10^{-6}$		
		Saturated	Partly Dry	Oven-Dry
Silica	Silica	6.22	7.24	6.32
Limestone	Silica	4.02	4.28	3.71
Silica	Limestone	5.08	5.81	5.60
Limestone	Limestone	3.42	3.67	3.51

Saturated Concrete (Similar Proportions and Exposure)

Coarse Aggregate	Fine Aggregate	Coefficient of Expansion, per °F. $\times 10^{-6}$	Coefficient of Contraction, per °F. $\times 10^{-6}$
Silica	Silica	6.24	5.80
Limestone	Silica	4.00	3.71
Traprock	Silica	4.89	4.45
Silica	Limestone	4.41	4.13
Limestone	Limestone	3.14	3.10
Traprock	Limestone	3.67	3.42

years in service, showed an expansion of 0.05 and 0.06 per cent when placed in water, and the same contraction when subsequently allowed to dry in air.

18.75 Plastic Flow. Plastic flow, or time yield, of concrete is the deformation that occurs under sustained stress. This phenomenon of flow is also called creep. Plastic flow is considered to be due largely to the seepage of water from the gel when an external load is applied to the concrete. The flow of water to or from the cement gel takes place through minute capillary channels which permeate the mass. The flow along the capillaries is a function of the pressure gradient along these channels. The greater the compressive stress, the steeper the pressure gradient and the more rapid the expulsion of water. The rate of expulsion is also a function of the vapor pressure on the outside of the mass. Shrinkage due to loss of moisture and time yield due to seepage are interrelated phenomena, although they may be conveniently considered as separate and additive in their effect.

A portion of the total yielding may be due to crystalline flow which in metals is called creep and to viscous flow which refers to movement of particles one over the other, as in the flow of oil. Davis[18] suggests that

[18] R. E. Davis, H. E. Davis, and J. S. Hamilton: "Plastic Flow of Concrete under Sustained Stress," *Proc. ASTM*, v. 34, Part II, 1934, pp. 354–386.

differences in flow observed in concrete containing different mineral aggregates may be due to crystalline flow and that the existence of lateral flow accompanying axial flow when the lateral dimensions are unrestrained may be caused by viscous flow.

Davis found that, the higher the sustained stress, the greater the flow. The moisture content of the cement gel has a marked effect upon the time yield, the flow of a totally dry concrete being of small magnitude. The extent of hydration of the cement alters the time *vs.* flow relation appreciably, since concrete of greater age under given curing conditions at the time of loading shows less plastic flow. In plain concretes flow has been observed to continue even after almost 7 years under sustained stress, although the rate of flow is very small at such ages. Usually the flow practically ceases after 1 or 2 years.

Small plain concrete cylinders stored in dry air under sustained stresses within the range of ordinary working stresses for concrete may have a total change in length due to flow and shrinkage combined equivalent to 1 or 2 inches per 100 feet in 7 years. For cylinders stored under moist conditions, the total deformation due to flow and expansion may be only one-fourth to one-third of the total deformation of similar concretes stored in dry air.

Davis found the total unit time deformations of air-stored reinforced columns to be from one-third to one-half of those in corresponding air-stored plain concrete columns. These deformations cause appreciable changes in the distribution of stress between the steel and concrete in reinforced-concrete columns under load in dry air, the stress in the steel being increased. In general, the results of tests indicate that plastic flow does not seriously reduce the strength of most reinforced-concrete structures.

Washa [19] reported on plastic flow of thin reinforced-concrete slabs in 1947. For slabs of a given span, water-cement ratio, and curing method, the greatest plastic flow deflections were obtained for the slabs made with largest water content. This result was most pronounced for the longest span, and least pronounced for the shortest span. Some beams were sealed by painting with a bakelite lacquer and then with paraffin. Plastic flow, shrinkage, warpage, and weight loss all took place at a slower rate for the sealed beams than for the dry (unsealed) specimens. The ultimate shrinkage and weight loss were about the same for the two curing conditions, but the sealed specimens had higher moduli of elasticity and ultimate compressive strengths at 5 years. The sealed specimens generally had lower plastic-flow deflections and deformations.

18.76 Weight of Concrete. The weight of concrete is a factor in design, as it must be included in the dead load on any structure. The weight depends almost entirely upon the character of the aggregate and the density of the concrete. If the aggregate, both fine and coarse, is of well-graded

[19] G. W. Washa: "Plastic Flow of Thin Reinforced Concrete Slabs." *Proc. Am. Concrete Inst.*, v. 19, 3, Nov., 1947, p. 237.

stone and sand, and the concrete is deposited in a manner to insure the minimum of void space, the weight may run as high as 160 pounds per cubic foot, and for less carefully chosen materials or less perfectly executed work the weight may not exceed 140 pounds per cubic foot. For practical purposes of design it is customary to assume the weight of stone concrete to be 150 pounds per cubic foot.

The unit weights of different classes of lightweight concrete are as tabulated.

Type of Concrete	Unit Weight, lb. per cu. ft.
Lightweight structural concrete	80–120
Lightweight masonry units	75–100
Lightweight insulating concrete	20–75

18.77 High-Density Concrete for Gamma-Ray Shielding. Concrete is used for thick walls in structures built for shielding against gamma radiation. For high-energy gamma radiation, the thickness of concrete wall required varies approximately in inverse proportion to the density of the concrete. By using barytes aggregates, the density of concrete has been increased to a unit weight of about 220 pounds per cubic foot. Baryte (barium sulfate) has a specific gravity of 4.5 and a Mohs hardness of 3 to 3.5. Barytes concrete is suitable for construction of reactor cell walls of homogeneous mass where ducts, steel sleeves for remote-control operations, shielding windows, and staggered-edge doors constitute obstructions.[20] However, attention must be paid to workability of the concrete so as to avoid segregation of aggregates. Uniform concrete is essential because uniform shielding quality is important. Barytes concrete should not be submerged in water or exposed to continuous heavy washing action. A typical barytes concrete mixture is given in question 18.42. The slump should be approximately 3 inches. Vibration is helpful in obtaining uniformity of concrete. Curing should follow approved methods for ordinary concrete.

18.78 Fire-Resistant Properties. Concrete as a fire resistant has been subjected to various experimental trials; but the best proof of its value lies in the experience afforded by many very severe fires wherein concrete well demonstrated its superiority over most other materials which are used for fire protection.

The value of concrete as a protection for steelwork in case of fire is due to several considerations. In the first place, concrete is in itself incombustible; second, its temperature coefficient is practically the same as that of steel, thus giving it an advantage over materials like structural clay tile,

[20] E. G. Tirpak: "Barytes Aggregates Make Heavy Concrete for Shielding." *Civil Eng.*, Aug., 1951, pp. 453–456.

which expands much more rapidly than steel, and hence tends to fail by reason of the destruction of the bond caused by unequal expansion; and third, the rate of heat conductivity of concrete is very low, owing in part to its porosity and consequent air content, and in part to the dehydration of the water of chemical combination, the volatilization of which absorbs heat. This latter action increases the porosity, and hence the conductivity of the concrete which has suffered dehydration is still further lowered, and the penetration of the dehydrating action proceeds very slowly.

The concrete which thus becomes dehydrated is seriously injured, but the effect is seldom appreciable to a depth of more than a fraction of an inch, except in very hot and long-burning fires. Concrete called "cinder concrete," in which the usual coarse-stone aggregate has been replaced by cinders, has been found quite as effective a fire resistant as stone concrete.

In general, it is considered that a covering of concrete over steelwork, 2 inches in thickness, is sufficient to protect the steel effectually against temperatures sufficiently high to cause warping and twisting, with consequent failure of the structure.

Fire tests on concrete columns by the Bureau of Standards have shown that spalling of the concrete varies with different aggregates. Limestone, traprock and blast-furnace slag resist particularly well, whereas quartz gravels cause the greatest spalling. Quartz and granites have a sudden expansion of considerable magnitude at a temperature of 575° C. (1067° F.).

18.79 Permeability Tests. Figure 18.18 gives the results of permeability tests on mortar disks, 6 inches in diameter by 1 inch thick, the specimens

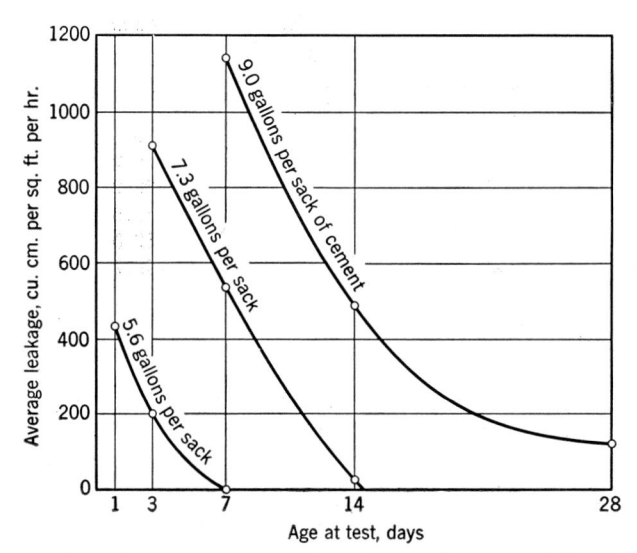

Fig. 18.18. Effect of water content and curing on the permeability of concrete (*Courtesy* F. R. McMillan.)

being subjected to a water pressure of 20 pounds per square inch for 48 hours after different periods of moist curing at 21° C. (70° F.). These results show that leakage at a given age can be reduced by using mixtures of low water-cement ratio and that, for a given water-cement ratio, the permeability can be decreased to a low value by extending curing.

Questions

18.1. State the water-cement-ratio law.

18.2. Sketch the general shape of the compressive strength versus water-cement-ratio curve.

18.3. Describe the job-curve method of proportioning concrete.

18.4. Describe the basic theory of the method of proportioning concrete by the mortar-voids method (Talbot-Richart).

18.5. Determine by the method of Goldbeck and Gray the proportions of gravel concrete to have 3500 pounds per square inch compressive strength at 28 days. A 6-inch slump is desired. The size of the gravel is No. 4 to 2 inches in size. The fineness modulus of the sand is 2.50. Both gravel and sand are igneous in type. The specific gravity of the gravel is 2.66 and of the sand 2.62. The dry, rodded weight of the gravel is 101.0 pounds per cubic foot.

18.6. Refer to question 18.5. It is desired to substitute dolomitic aggregates for the igneous ones. The specific gravity of the gravel is 2.68, and of the sand 2.59. The sieve analysis of the gravel and sand are given in the accompanying table. The dry, rodded weight of the gravel is 100.2 pounds per cubic foot. Determine the quantities for a 1-cubic-yard batch of concrete.

Sieve Number	Accumulative Percentages Retained	
	Gravel	Sand
1½-inch	0	
¾-inch	58.0	
⅜-inch	80.5	
4	96.0	0
8		6.2
16		22.2
30		50.6
50		82.0
100		98.2

18.7. Refer to question 18.5. Determine the quantities if a crushed stone having the same size but a specific gravity of 2.72 and a dry, rodded weight of 101.3 pounds per cubic foot is substituted for the gravel.

18.8. Refer to question 18.5. Determine the quantities for a cubic yard of air-entrained concrete.

18.9. Define with respect to concrete: workability, consistency, basic water content, yield, density, bulking, permeability, durability, plastic flow.

18.10. State the advantages and disadvantages of three methods of measuring sand for concrete.

18.11. The proportions of a Portland cement concrete mixture are 1:2.0:3.1 by volume. The water-cement ratio is 6.5 gallons per sack of cement. The slump was 3 inches. The materials have the properties given in the accompanying table. Calculate the yield of concrete per sack of cement, the cement factor in barrels of cement per cubic yard of

	Specific Gravity	Unit Weight, lb. per cu. ft.
Cement	3.14	94
Sand	2.65	105
Stone	2.80	104

concrete, the quantities of materials required per cubic yard of concrete, and the weight of the concrete per cubic foot.

18.12. Solve question 18.11 for a Portland cement concrete mixture composed of the same materials having proportions of 1:1.5:2.5. The water-cement ratio is 5.0 gallons per sack of cement. The slump was 2 inches.

18.13. The absolute volumes in per cent given in the accompanying table were calculated from the quantities used for a trial batch of concrete having a water-cement ratio of 6.5 gallons per sack of cement. The slump was 1½ inches.

Material	Absolute Volume, %	Specific Gravity
Cement	10.6	3.15
Sand	29.6	2.65
Stone	40.9	2.70
Water	18.9	1.00

Compute estimated quantities of materials in pounds for a trial batch of 5.5 gallons per sack water-cement ratio for the same materials and slump. The batch is to provide 1 cubic foot of concrete. *Hint:* Assume that the percentages of absolute volume of water and stone are the same for the two water-cement ratios. Refer to Art. 18.14. What would be the estimated value of the cement factor for this mixture in barrels of cement per cubic yard of concrete?

18.14. The mixture given in the accompanying table is designed to yield 1 cubic yard of concrete containing 6 sacks of cement per cubic yard with a slump of 3 inches. Cal-

Material	Weight, lb.
Cement	564
Sand	1140
Gravel	2160
Water	236
Total	4100

culate the cement factor when 33 pounds of additional water are added to the concrete to produce a slump of 7 inches. The measured unit weight is 150.1 pounds per cubic foot.

18.15. An air-entraining concrete mixture designed to yield 1 cubic yard of concrete of 4-inch slump and with 4.5 per cent entrained air has the quantities given in the

Material	Weight, lb.
Cement	470
Sand	1260
Gravel	1940
Water	230
Total	3900

452   Materials of Construction

last table on p. 451. The actual amount of air is determined to be 3.5 per cent, and the unit weight is 145.8 pounds per cubic foot. What is the cement factor?

18.16. State the type of vibrating equipment you would select for the following concreting operations: (*a*) a concrete pavement, (*b*) a reinforced-concrete beam, (*c*) a concrete dam, (*d*) a reinforced-concrete pipe 12 inches in diameter, and (*e*) a high wall for a bridge abutment.

18.17. Describe two methods of depositing concrete under water.

18.18. Describe the precautions you would employ in pouring a reinforced-concrete building in freezing weather.

18.19. Discuss the importance of curing concrete. Describe four field methods of curing concrete pavements.

18.20. Describe the cableway-type plant for transporting and placing concrete.

18.21. What are the advantages of air-entrained concrete?

18.22. Describe methods of checking the air content of air-entrained concrete.

18.23. Describe four methods of waterproofing concrete.

18.24. What effect has sea water upon concrete? How may such an effect be minimized?

18.25. Describe the essential features of the vacuum concrete process.

18.26. Discuss the physical properties of insulating concrete.

18.27. Describe the molding of concrete masonry blocks. What compressive strength is required?

18.28. Discuss the different types of concrete pipes.

18.29. Describe the construction of prestressed block-beam structures.

18.30. Distinguish between the following terms relating to concrete: (*a*) art marbles, (*b*) terrazzo, (*c*) stucco, (*d*) ornamental finishes, (*e*) cast stone, and (*f*) marble-face building block.

18.31. Write a full discussion of the elastic properties of concrete as expressed by the modulus of elasticity. Include the following points:

a. Shape of the stress-strain curve.

b. Initial tangent versus tangent versus secant modulus.

c. Values of unit stress for which modulus is commonly determined.

d. Effect of mix, age, and curing on the value of the modulus.

e. Name a value of the modulus commonly used in designing reinforced-concrete beams.

18.32. A concrete mixture was tested in compression after curing for 1 day in air and 27 days in water. The cylindrical specimen was 6 inches in diameter and 12 inches high. An ultimate compressive stress of 4160 pounds per square inch was obtained.

Load on Cylinder, lb.	Left Gauge, in.	Right Gauge, in.
500	0.0200	0.0200
5,300	0.0201	0.0202
9,710	0.0203	0.0204
15,150	0.0207	0.0206
19,800	0.0213	0.0206
24,870	0.0219	0.0206
29,230	0.0223	0.0208
32,640	0.0226	0.0209
36,450	0.0230	0.0210
39,690	0.0232	0.0212
42,840	0.0235	0.0214
46,800	0.0236	0.0219
50,870	0.0241	0.0220

Concrete

The tabulated data were obtained by means of a compressometer which had a distance between gauge points of 8 inches.

Draw the stress-strain curve, and determine the modulus of elasticity by the secant method for a design stress of 800 pounds per square inch.

18.33. A high-early-strength Portland cement concrete mixture was tested in compression after curing 1 day in air and 6 days in water. The cylindrical specimen was 6 inches in diameter and 12 inches high. The proportions of the mixture were 1:2.0:3.1 by volume, and the water-cement ratio was 6.5 gallons per sack of cement. The ultimate compressive stress was 4730 pounds per square inch. The tabulated data were obtained by means of a compressometer which had a distance between gauge points of 8 inches.

Load on Cylinder, lb.	Left Gauge, in.	Right Gauge, in.
330	0.0200	0.0200
3,880	0.0204	0.0200
8,980	0.0207	0.0200
13,340	0.0211	0.0203
18,950	0.0212	0.0205
23,690	0.0214	0.0209
27,830	0.0218	0.0209
33,400	0.0221	0.0213
38,200	0.0224	0.0217
40,620	0.0225	0.0219
44,570	0.0228	0.0220
48,770	0.0231	0.0224
52,710	0.0233	0.0228
56,590	0.0235	0.0230
59,970	0.0237	0.0233

Draw the stress-strain curve, and determine the modulus of elasticity by the secant method for a design stress of 800 pounds per square inch.

18.34. Describe how the sonic modulus of elasticity may be determined.

18.35. Discuss the subject of adhesion of concrete to steel reinforcement bars.

18.36. Discuss Powers' hypothesis explaining the resistance of air-entrained concrete to freezing and thawing action.

18.37. What is the "durability factor" for concrete as suggested by Walker?

18.38. What are typical ranges in unit weights of different classes of lightweight concrete?

18.39. Discuss the effectiveness of concrete as a fire-resistant material for construction.

18.40. Calculate the modulus of rupture of a concrete beam, 6 inches by 6 inches in cross-section, tested on a 24-inch span under center loading. The mixture is described in question 18.11. The breaking load was 3960 pounds. What would be the allowable flexural working stress for this concrete for pavement design?

18.41. Calculate the modulus of rupture of a concrete beam 8 inches by 8 inches in cross-section, tested on a 30-inch span. The load was applied at the third points of the span. The breaking load registered on the testing machine was 13,600 pounds.

18.42. The materials used for high-density concrete for construction of a shielding wall against gamma radiation have the tabulated bulk specific gravities and batch weights. The barytes were obtained from a source near Sweetwater, Tenn. Determine the quantities of materials per cubic yard of concrete in pounds. Use 62.4 pounds per cubic foot as the unit weight of water.

Materials of Construction

Material	Bulk Specific Gravity	Batch Weights, lb.
Ordinary Portland cement	3.15	658
Barytes fine aggregate	4.04	2250
Barytes coarse aggregate	4.29	3000
Water	1.00	321

18.43. Refer to question 18.42. Calculate the volumes in cubic feet of barytes fine aggregate and barytes coarse aggregate required for a cubic yard of concrete. The unit weights (dry rodded) are as follows: barytes fine aggregate 163.0 pounds per cubic foot and barytes coarse aggregate 159.0 pounds per cubic foot.

18.44. Refer to question 18.42. What is the density of this barytes concrete assuming zero per cent voids? How thick should a shielding wall of barytes concrete be to provide equal shielding qualities against gamma radiation as compared to a wall of standard concrete 12 inches thick?

References

18.1. American Association of State Highway Officials: "Standard Specifications for Highway Materials and Methods of Sampling and Testing." Washington, D. C., 6th ed., 1950, Parts I and II.

18.2. American Concrete Institute: "Entrained Air in Concrete: A Symposium." *Proc. Am. Concrete Inst.*, v. 42, 1946, p. 601.

18.3. American Society for Testing Materials: "Report on Significance of Tests of Concrete and Concrete Aggregates." Philadelphia, Pa., 1935, 123 pages. Also: *Special Tech. Publ.* 22, 1943. Also: "Symposium on Methods and Procedures Used in Identifying Reactive Materials in Concrete." June, 1948.

18.4. American Standards Association: "Modular Coordination as Related to Building Design." Report by The Producers' Council, Washington, D. C., Oct., 1945.

18.5. Bateman, J. H.: *Materials of Construction*. New York, Pitman Publ. Corp., 1950, 568 pages.

18.6. Bauer, E. E.: *Plain Concrete*. McGraw-Hill Book Co., 3rd ed., 1949, 441 pages.

18.7. Blanks, R. F.: "Effect of Alkalies in Portland Cement on the Durability of Concrete." *ASTM Bull.* 142, Oct., 1946, p. 28.

18.8. Bureau of Reclamation: *Concrete Manual*. Denver, Colo., 1942.

18.9. Callan, E. J.: "The Relation of Thermal Expansion of Aggregates to the Durability of Concrete." *Bull.* 34, *Waterways Exp. Sta.*, Vicksburg, Miss., Feb., 1950.

18.10. Davis, R. E., Davis, H. E., and Hamilton, S.: "Plastic Flow and Volume Changes of Concrete." *Proc. ASTM*, v. 37, Part II, 1937, pp. 317–331.

18.11. Goldbeck, A. T., and Gray, J. E.: "A Method of Proportioning Concrete for Strength, Workability, and Durability." *Bull.* 11, *National Crushed Stone Assoc.*, Nov., 1953.

18.12. Highway Research Board: "Bibliography on Durability of Concrete—Physical Reactions." *Bibliography* 8, 1951. Also: "Bibliography on Mineral Aggregates." *Bibliography* 6, 1949.

18.13. Highway Research Board: "Use of Air-Entrained Concrete in Pavements and Bridges." *Current Road Problems*, No. 13, May, 1946, 35 pages.

18.14. Highway Research Board: "Calcium Chloride in Concrete, Annotated." *Publ.* 217, *Bibliography* 13, 1952.

18.15. Jackson, F. H. and Kellerman, W. F.: "The Effect of Vibration on the Strength and Uniformity of Pavement Concrete." *Public Roads,* v. 18, No. 2, Apr., 1937, pp. 25–49.

18.16. Jackson, F. H.: "Age-Strength Relations for Air-Entrained Concrete." *Public Roads,* v. 27, No. 2, June, 1952, p. 31. Also: "The Durability of Concrete in Service." *Jour. Am. Concrete Inst.,* v. 18, No. 2, 1946, p. 165.

18.17. Kilcawley, E. J.: "Weathering Resistance of Concrete." Troy, N. Y., *Rensselaer Polytech. Inst. Bull.* 36, 1932, 49 pages.

18.18. Larson, G. H.: "Effect of Substitutions of Fly Ash for Portions of the Cement in Concrete." *Proc. Highway Research Board,* v. 29, 1949, p. 225. Also: v. 32, 1953.

18.19. Lea, F. M., and Desch, C. H.: *The Chemistry of Cement and Concrete.* London, Edward Arnold & Co. 1935, pp. 333–406.

18.20. Leach, C. H.: "Precast Concrete." *Rock Products,* v. 51, No. 8, Aug., 1948, p. 210.

18.21. Lerch, W.: "Significance of Tests for Chemical Reactions of Aggregates in Concrete." *Proc. ASTM,* v. 53, 1953.

18.22. Loving, M. W.: "Prestressed Reinforced Concrete Pressure Pipe." *Rock Products,* v. 51, No. 11, Nov., 1948, p. 122.

18.23. Lynam, C. G.: *Growth and Movement in Portland Cement Concrete.* London, Oxford University Press: Humphrey Milford, 1934, 135 pages.

18.24. Lyse, I.: "Cement-Water Ratio, by Weight, Proposed for Designing Concrete Mixes." *Eng. News-Record,* v. 107, No. 19, Nov. 5, 1931, p. 723.

18.25. Lyse, I.: "Simplifying Design and Control of Concrete Mixes." *Eng. News-Record,* v. 108, No. 7, Feb. 18, 1932, p. 248.

18.26. Lyse, I.: "Relation between Quality and Economy of Concrete." Bethlehem, Pa., *Lehigh Univ.,* Circ. 96, v. 8, No. 1, 1934, 19 pages.

18.27. Mather, B.: "The Testing of Aggregates in Air-Entrained Concrete." *Bull.* 30, *Waterways Exp. Sta.,* Vicksburg, Miss., 1947.

18.28. McMillan, F. R.: *Basic Principles of Concrete Making.* McGraw-Hill Book Co., 1929, 99 pages.

18.29. Mitchell, L. J.: "Thermal Expansion Tests on Aggregates, Neat Cements, and Concretes." *Proc. ASTM,* v. 53, 1953.

18.30. Mullen, W. G.: *A Study of Thermal Properties of Concrete and Concrete Aggregates,* Thesis for M.S. degree, University of Maryland, June, 1951.

18.31. Pearson, J. C.: "A Concrete Failure Attributed to Aggregate of Low Thermal Coefficient." *J. Am. Concrete Inst.,* Sept., 1941, June, 1942, and Sept., 1943.

18.32. Perry, J. R.: "Coral—A Good Aggregate in Concrete." *Eng. News-Record,* v. 135, No. 6, Aug. 9, 1945, p. 174.

18.33. Portland Cement Association: *Design and Control of Concrete Mixtures.* Chicago, Ill.

18.34. Pickett, G.: "The Effect of Biot's Modulus on Transient Thermal Stresses in Concrete Cylinders." *Proc. ASTM,* v. 39, 1939, p. 913.

18.35. Pickett, G.: "Shrinkage Stresses in Concrete—Part 2." *J. Am. Concrete Inst.,* Feb., 1946, p. 361.

18.36. Powers, T. C.: "The Air Requirement in Frost-Resistant Concrete." *Proc. Highway Research Board,* 1949, p. 184.

18.37. Preece, E. F.: "Determination and Use of the Dynamic Modulus of Elasticity of Concrete." *Proc. Highway Research Board,* v. 28, 1948, p. 233.

18.38. Price, G. B.: "Flexicore Floor and Roof Slabs." *Proc. Am. Concrete Inst.,* v. 45, 1948, p. 325.

18.39. Roberts, P. W.: "Effects on Materials in Arctic Cold." *The Military Eng.*, v. 42, No. 287, May–June, 1950, p. 176.

18.40. Scholer, C. H., and Gibson, W. E.; "Effect of Various Coarse Aggregates upon the Cement-Aggregate Reaction." *J. Am. Concrete Inst.*, June, 1948, p. 1009.

18.41. Stanton, T. E.: "Durability of Concrete Exposed to Sea Water and Alkali Soils—California Experience." *J. Am. Concrete Inst.*, May, 1948, p. 821.

18.42. Talbot, A. N., and Richart, F. E.: "The Strength of Concrete: Its Relation to the Cement, Aggregates, and Water." Urbana, Ill., *Univ. Ill. Eng. Exp. Sta., Bull.* 137, 1923, 118 pages.

18.43. Tirpak, E. G.: "Barytes Aggregates Make Heavy Concrete for Shielding." *Civil Eng.*, Aug., 1951, pp. 453–456.

18.44. Walker, S.: "Proportioning Concrete Mixtures." *Circ.* 21, *National Sand and Gravel Assoc.*, Oct., 1941.

18.45. Walker, S.: "Control of Quality of Ready-Mixed Concrete." *J. Am. Concrete Inst.*, v. 20, No. 8, Apr., 1949, p. 569.

18.46. Walker, S.: "Resistance of Concrete to Freezing and Thawing as Affected by Aggregates." *Proc. Highway Conf., Univ. Tenn. Record*, v. 47, No. 4, 1944, p. 9.

18.47. Washa, G. W.: "Tests for Air-Entraining Agents in Cement and Concrete." *ASTM Bull.* 163, Jan., 1950, p. 61 (TP11) and 168, Sept., 1950, p. 83 (TP211).

18.48. Wendt, K. F.: "The Durability of Concrete." *Selected Papers, Insitute on Concrete Roads, Univ. Wisc.*, Feb., 1949.

18.49. Wendt, K. F., and Woodworth, P. M.: "Tests on Concrete Masonry Units Using Tamping and Vibration Molding Methods." *J. Am. Concrete Inst.*, Nov., 1939, p. 121; also *Reprint* 77, *Univ. of Wisc., Eng. Exp. Sta.*

18.50. Wilson, R.: "The Coloration of Concrete." *J. Am. Concrete Inst.*, v. 26, Apr., 1930, p. 616.

18.51. Withey, M. O., and Wendt, K. F.: "Some Long Time Tests of Concrete." *J. Am. Concrete Inst.*, v. 39, Feb., 1948, p. 221.

18.52. Withey, M. O.: "Freezing and Thawing, Permeability and Strength Tests on Vibrated Concrete Cylinders of Low Cement Content." *Proc. Am. Concrete Inst.*, v. 31, 1935, p. 528.

18.53. Withey, M. O.: "Considerations Involved in the Making of Freezing and Thawing Tests on Concrete." *Proc. ASTM*, v. 46, 1946, p. 1198.

18.54. Withey, M. O., and Washa, G. W.: *Materials of Construction.* John Wiley & Sons, 1954. See pages xv–54, 55 for abstract of tests by H. E. Pulver and S. E. Johnson on effects of sodium chloride and calcium chloride solutions on strength of concrete cured at low and normal temperatures published in *The Wisconsin Engineer*, v. XVIII, No. 1, Oct., 1913, pp. 6–13.

Section VI · Brick and Clay Products—Refractory, Heat-Insulating, and Acoustical Materials

CHAPTER 19

Brick and Clay Products

19.1 General Classification. The principal clay products used structurally are building brick, masonry units, paving brick, firebrick, terra cottas, and various forms of tile.

Building brick are usually made of a mixture of clay and sand, to which coal and other foreign substances are sometimes added, which is mixed and molded in various ways, after which it is dried and burned.

Paving brick are made primarily as a material for street pavements, though certain types are suitable for building purposes.

Firebrick are of such a nature that they will withstand high temperatures. Their structural uses are largely confined to linings of flues, stacks, etc. They are discussed in Chapter 20.

Architectural terra cotta is made of selected clays and is used for decorative effect.

Tiles, made by burning various classes of clay, are used in various forms as structural-clay facing tile, building tile including both wall and floor tile, roofing tile, drain tile, and sewer pipe.

19.2 Raw Materials. The raw materials for the manufacture of structural-clay products are clay or shale. Clays are essentially a mixture of kaolinite with sand. Kaolinite is a plastic material when wet with water and becomes "set" in a fixed form upon being burned. Clays for brick making must develop proper plasticity and be capable of drying rapidly without excessive shrinkage, warping, or cracking and of being burned to the desired texture and strength. Residual, glacial, and sedimentary clays are all used for brick manufacture when they possess a sufficient plasticity for molding and burn to a body of the proper hardness and color, but sedimentary clays are usually the most satisfactory.

Sedimentary clays of importance in brick making comprise marine clays, which were deposited in ocean beds, and lacustrine clays, which were deposited in lakes or swamps. Marine deposits of clay often stretch for hundreds of miles to a depth of 30 feet or more. Their composition is remarkably uniform and, except for those which are too high limed or are excessively plastic, include the best clays obtainable for brick manufacture.

Shale is clay that has been solidified under pressure. Most shales are not soluble in water except when ground up, those suitable for the production of structural-clay products then becoming plastic with addition of water.

A very plastic clay is likely to shrink, crack, and warp in drying and be very hard after burning. The presence of coarse sand in suitable amounts tends to prevent shrinking and cracking in burning, but an excess of silica in the shape of sand destroys cohesiveness.

If a clay contains too high a percentage of such impurities as iron oxide, lime, magnesia, and alkalies, either the clay must be rejected or the impurities removed or neutralized.

Iron oxide acts as a flux and adds greatly to the hardness and strength of brick. It causes the clay to burn buff or red in color according to the amount of iron oxide present. Lime considerably in excess of iron causes the brick to burn buff and shrink strongly as vitrification is approaching. The lime must be in a very finely divided state so that it will be completely hydrated or fluxed in the process of manufacture of the brick. The presence of lumps of unhydrated lime which become hydrated after long periods is the cause of unsightly defects on brick walls called "lime pops." Magnesia and alkalies also act as fluxes. (See Table 20.1 in Art. 20.3 for composition of brick clays.)

Structural-Clay Products

19.3 Characteristics of Principal Processes. The three most common methods of manufacture of structural-clay products are the stiff-mud, the soft-mud, and the dry-press processes. The fundamental principles of preparing the clay are the same in all three processes, which differ only in details and in degree of refinement.

The flow of clay from the pit to the finished product through typical operations in a modern plant is illustrated in Fig. 19.1. Processes of manufacture of structural-clay products may be divided into the following steps:

Selection and "winning" of suitable clay.
Storage.
Preparation of clay, including cleaning, removing large pebbles, grinding, and screening.
Mixing and tempering to produce plasticity, uniformity, and homogeneity.
Shaping into units by extruding machines and cutters, molds, presses, or other appliances.
Drying, either by natural or artificial means.
Burning, usually in kilns.

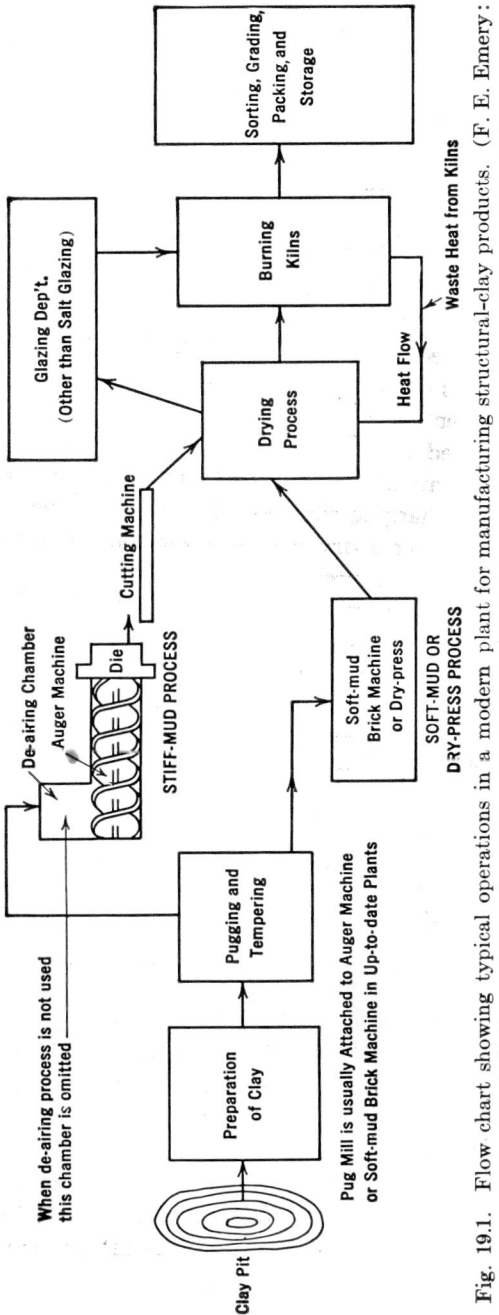

Fig. 19.1. Flow chart showing typical operations in a modern plant for manufacturing structural-clay products. (F. E. Emery: "The Manufacture of Structural Clay Products." *Civil Eng.*, v. 7, No. 11, Nov., 1937, pp. 755–759.)

Winning. "Winning" is the term applied to obtaining the clay from the pit. Clays are mostly obtained by surface digging or quarrying, and to some extent by mining, depending upon the nature and location of the deposit. In shallow banks a machine called the shale planer is sometimes used; power shovels are frequently used in excavating clay from surface pits. Many shales are so solidified that they have to be loosened by blasting. The quarrying method is suitable for some pits, the deposits being worked in benches.

Preparation of Clay. The preparation of clays is much the same in all three processes. Some clays require considerable preparation, others very little. The operations described here are typical. Clay transported from the pit or storage bins in cars or on belt conveyors is usually delivered to a granulator that consists essentially of a semicylindrical tank within which revolves a steel shaft equipped with knives so pitched that they not only break up chunks of clay and mix and granulate the material but also function as a screw conveyor, discharging the clay at the end of the machine. The clay is then ground in either a dry pan or a wet pan, which consists of two heavy rollers traveling in a circle over a metal plate.

Pugging. After the preliminary steps of preparation, the clay is tempered, the object of which is to produce a homogeneous plastic mass. This is usually accomplished in a pug mill, which is a horizontal cylinder provided with one or two power-driven shafts with blades rigidly attached. The revolving blades slice up and thoroughly mix the mass until it is ejected through an opening at one end. During the pugging operation, it may be necessary to add sand to reduce shrinkage, or more water to produce the desired plasticity.

19.4 Stiff-Mud Process. In the stiff-mud process the clay is only sufficiently moist to possess the requisite coherence under moderate pressure, which results in economy of time in drying and of fuel in burning. The clay may be pugged either in a separate pug mill or in a pug mill attached to the brick machine itself. The clay is delivered to the brick-making machine which forces the plastic mass out through a molding die in a stream called a "column." The die molds the mass into the desired shapes for brick, hollow tile, or other forms, and as the column is extruded it passes over a wire cutting table where it is cut into the desired lengths.

The brick machine of the *auger type* is usually used for molding products of uniform cross-section such as brick, building tile, and partition tile. The auger machine consists of a closed tube of cylindrical or conical shape in which, on the line of the axis of the tube, revolves a shaft to which are attached the auger and auger knives. The knives are so arranged as to cut and pug the clay and force it forward into the auger. The function of the auger is to compress and shape the clay and force it through the die. The column of clay as it issues from the die travels along the table on an end-

Brick and Clay Products

less belt which is supported on rollers. At intervals the operator throws a lever which swings downward a rigid frame, across which a series of wires are tautly stretched. By this means the column is cut into sections of desired length.

If the cross-section of the column is the same as the end of the brick, the bricks are called "end-cut" and if the cross-section corresponds to the side of a brick, they are called "side-cut." When end-cut bricks are made the clay often issues from the machine in several separate streams. Structural-clay tile, drain tile, and similar shapes are all end cut. In the size of the die and in cutting to length allowance is made for the shrinkage that results from drying and burning.

De-airing is an important development in the stiff-mud process. It is accomplished in a de-airing chamber attached to the auger machine through which the clay passes. The clay is broken up and shredded as it enters this chamber, where a vacuum of 15 to 29 inches is maintained. Some of the advantages of de-airing are greater strength in the green and in the fired body, increased workability and plasticity, and better utilization of the inferior clays. However, some clays do not respond well to the de-airing process.

19.5 Soft-Mud Process. In the soft-mud process all structural-clay products are molded by machinery, except for special products. This process is used where the clay is too wet to be forced through a die without drying and hence must be molded. In large modern plants, brick are molded under pressure in a soft-mud brick machine which tempers the clay in its pugging chamber, sands or wets the molds, presses the clay into 4 to 9 molds at a time, strikes off the excess clay, bumps the mold uniformly, and dumps the brick onto a pallet with each revolution. The pallets of brick are carried away to the dryer as fast as made. The operation of the machine is automatic, the only hand labor being that required to feed pallets and sand into the machine.

There are two classes of soft-mud brick: *sand-struck* and *water-struck*. In the sand-struck method the inside of each mold is coated with a thin layer of sand to prevent the clay from sticking. In the water-struck method, also called "slop-molding," the molds are dipped in or sprayed with water to prevent sticking. Sand-molding is the more common method, the bricks being usually cleaner and sharper than water-struck brick, although some very good grades of brick are water-struck.

19.6 Dry-Press Process. The dry-press process permits the use of non-plastic and relatively dry clays in the manufacture of high-grade products. The best results are obtained when the clay contains from 7 to 10 per cent moisture. The clay is usually prepared by granulator, dry pan, and pug mill, and then is fed into molds in the dry-press machine by a reciprocating charger located below the hopper. At each revolution of the machine the charger moves forward, and when it is directly over the molds the bottom plunger in the molds descends, allowing the molds to be filled with clay. The charger is withdrawn, the clay supply shut off, and then the top and bottom plungers move toward each other in the molds, compressing the clay between them. The pressure is now relieved and then applied a second time, the compression of the clay being greater than at first and ranging from 550 to 1500 pounds per square inch. The upper plunger is now withdrawn, and the bottom plunger raises the brick to the level of the top of the mold. The next stroke of the plunger pushes the finished brick upon the mold table, whence it is removed to the dryers.

Dry-pressed bricks are very compact, show high compressive strength, and are well formed, but they are not generally considered to be as durable as bricks produced by the stiff-mud or soft-mud processes. They are, however, extensively used as face brick. The term "pressed brick" is proper only in referring to brick made by the dry-press process.

19.7 Drying. As wet clay units come from the different brick machines, they contain from 7 to 30 per cent moisture, depending on whether the dry-press, stiff-mud, or soft-mud process has been used. Moisture in clay ware may be classified as equilibrium moisture and free moisture. Equilibrium moisture is that moisture in the material which exerts a vapor pressure equal to that exerted by the surrounding air of given temperature and humidity. Free moisture is the moisture other than equilibrium moisture and is held largely in the pore spaces. Most of the free water is removed in the drying process, and the remaining moisture during the burning process.

Mechanical dryers, which permit of automatic control of temperature, humidity, and air velocity, have come into general use. As the free water of the clay body is removed, the clay particles tend to coalesce, causing shrinkage. The general effect of such shrinkage is to increase the resistance to moisture flow in the dried layers. If the drying is carried on too rapidly as by means of hot dry air, the moisture is removed from the surface of the solid more rapidly than the interior of the solid can deliver moisture to the surface, so that the surface hardens and cracking occurs. It is desirable to dry clay ware with moist air, reducing the drying rate to the point where diffusion of water to the surface can keep up with the vaporization at the surface. This dries the clay rather uniformly throughout and minimizes the effects of local shrinkage by keeping the shrinkage uniform. These conditions may be obtained in the humidity system of drying, in which highly humidified warm air is admitted to the room and the ware is heated up until the vapor pressures of air and clay are about equal. The relative humidity of the air surrounding the clay then is decreased by raising the air temperature. This sets up a difference in vapor pressure which draws moisture gradually from the ware, and the action is continued until most of the free moisture has been removed.

Brick and Clay Products

The continuous tunnel dryer is very common for drying of bricks. The bricks are piled on cars which move slowly through the tunnel, which is heated either by hot air or by steam pipes. The tunnels are usually built of masonry and may be 100 feet or more in length.

Stationary dryers, called "hot-floor" dryers, are also extensively used. The floor of the dryer is heated from below by steam, by heat from furnaces, or by hot products of combustion from kilns.

The average time necessary for drying structural-clay products is about 3 days, and the temperature required is from 38° C. (100° F.) to 149° C. (300° F.). The heat may be supplied directly or it may be waste heat recovered from the kilns.

19.8 Burning. The burning of structural clay products in a kiln requires an average time of 3 to 4 days, after which the openings are tightly closed and the kiln is allowed to cool very slowly.

The process of burning may be conveniently divided into the following four stages:

Water Smoking. During this period which requires about 12 hours the free water in the clay is driven off under temperatures ranging from 125° C. (257° F.) to 175° C. (347° F.).

Dehydration. Dehydration consists of expelling chemically combined water by breaking down the clay molecules. It begins at about 425° C. (797° F.) and is completed at about 750° C. (1382° F.).

Oxidation. Oxidation begins during the dehydration stage. All combustible matter is consumed, carbon is eliminated, the fluxing materials are changed to oxides, and sulfur is removed.

Vitrification. Vitrification refers to the contracting and filling-up of the pore spaces of the clay. Common building bricks are not vitrified according to the definition of the term but are burned only to the incipient stage at a temperature seldom above 1200° C. (2192° F.) when the clay has been softened to a point where the larger grains stick together but not all the pores of the mass are closed. Paving bricks are completely vitrified, the mass being rendered impervious. Paving bricks require a high temperature for vitrification since they contain small amounts of fluxing materials.

19.9 Kilns. Brick kilns may be divided into two general classes, *intermittent* and *continuous kilns*. Intermittent kilns may be further subdivided into up-draft and down-draft kilns.

Up-Draft Kilns. The modern up-draft kiln has permanent sides made of brick masonry 12 to 16 inches thick, and the heat is generated in ovens outside. The flames and hot gases enter the kiln through fire passages in the walls.

Down-Draft Kilns. Kilns of this type require permanent walls and a tight roof. The floor has openings connecting with flues leading to a stack.

Most down-draft kilns are built in a circular or beehive shape, but some are rectangular.

Heat is generated in outside ovens, and the flames and gases enter the kiln through vertical flues carried to about half the height of the kiln. The heat therefore enters the brickwork at the top and is drawn downward by the chimney draft to the flues below the floor, and thence to the chimney or stack.

The down-draft kiln has a much higher efficiency than the up-draft kiln, and it is commonly used in burning structural-clay tile, terra cotta, and brick which require close control of heat and uniform burning.

Continuous Kilns. There are several types of continuous kilns. Three types of importance are: (1) the chamber type, (2) the circular type, and (3) the tunnel type. In the chamber type, a number of chambers are connected in series, and also individually connected with a stack. The stack flues and the flues between chambers are provided with dampers. While one chamber is burning, the waste products of combustion are forced to traverse the whole series of charged chambers before reaching one that is open to the stack. The material is thus preheated before being fired. The down-draft principle is utilized, the flue openings being in the floor. This type of kiln is expensive to install, but the percentage of first-class brick is also high, provided that the fuel is burned on grates or in troughs, instead of in contact with the brick.

The circular type has a circular stationary kiln divided into segmental chambers that is built around a central molding compartment. Building brick are molded in the central compartment which can be rotated so that the brick can be moved by conveyors into successive chambers of the circular kiln. Movable hoods are placed over the stationary-kiln compartments so that the brick in the kiln can be successively preheated, burned, and slowly cooled. It is economic and efficient in comparison to other continuous kilns because of low initial installation cost and low labor costs in operating.

The tunnel type of continuous kiln is built both as a straight and as a circular tunnel through which the clay products pass while being burned. The bricks are loaded on special cars which are transported through the tunnel at the proper speed through the water-smoking, dehydration, oxidation, vitrifying, and cooling zones. The heat conditions in each zone are carefully controlled. The advantages of the tunnel kiln are high heating efficiency and more uniformly burned products.

Classification and Uses of Structural-Clay Products

19.10 Building Brick and Solid Masonry Units. The standard size of building brick is $2\frac{1}{4}$ by $3\frac{3}{4}$ by 8 inches. Solid masonry units come in

Brick and Clay Products

modular sizes and may be either solid or cored; if cored, the net cross-sectional area in any plane parallel to the bearing surface shall be at least 75 per cent of the gross cross-sectional area. These brick and solid masonry units are grouped into three grades by ASTM specifications in accordance with their resistance to types of exposure.

Grade SW. Intended for use where a high degree of resistance to frost action is desired and the exposure is such that the brick may be frozen when permeated with water.

Grade MW. Intended for use where (1) the brick is exposed to temperatures below freezing but unlikely to be permeated with water or (2) a moderate and somewhat non-uniform degree of resistance to frost action is permissible.

Grade NW. Intended (1) for use as backup or interior masonry, (2) if one brick is exposed, for use where no frost action occurs, or, (3) if frost action occurs, for use where the average annual precipitation is less than 20 inches.

In emptying the kiln, the bricks are separated into various qualities according to the degree of burning and freedom from imperfections. Common brick are usually divided into three qualities:

Arch or *hard brick,* those which, owing to their position in the kiln, have been overburned, are apt to be misshapen and are used in footings and for the "filling" of brick masonry. These may also be employed in certain types of architectural construction which require the use of warped, seamed, and imperfect bricks.

Red or *well-burned brick,* which amount to about half the output of the up-draft kiln and constitute the best grade of brick for all general construction purposes.

Salmon or *soft brick,* those which have not been sufficiently burned, are too weak for first-class construction but are adequate for masonry filling and unimportant work not calling for high strength or great durability.

19.11 Facing Brick and Solid Masonry Units. These brick and units made from clay, fireclay, or shale are for placement in exposed walls and are more uniform in dimensions than building brick. There are two grades of facing brick: *SW* and *MW*. (See Art. 19.10.) The ASTM specifications cover three types of facing brick or units as follows:

Type FBX. Brick for general use in exposed exterior and interior masonry walls and partitions and for use where a high degree of mechanical perfection, narrow color range, and minimum permissible variation in size are desired.

Type FBS. Brick suitable for general use in exposed exterior and interior masonry walls and partitions where wide color ranges are desired and where a greater variation in size is permitted or desired than is specified for type FBX.

Type FBA. Brick manufactured and selected to produce characteristic architectural effects resulting from non-uniformity in size, color, and texture of the individual units.

19.12 Ceramic Glazed Facing Brick and Solid Masonry Units. These are manufactured in modular sizes and are available in two grades and two types as specified by the ASTM:

Grade S (select). For use with comparatively narrow mortar joints.

Grade G (ground edge). For use where variation of face dimension must be very small.

Type I (single-faced units). For general use where only one finished face will be exposed.

Type II (two-faced units). For use where two opposite finished faces will be exposed.

Ceramic glazed brick are made by coating unburned common brick with a thin layer of "slip," a composition of ball clay, kaolin, flint, and feldspar, and then applying a second coat of transparent glaze resembling glass. The slip gives the color to the brick, and the glaze melts upon firing the brick and forms a smooth transparent coating over the slip. Ceramic glazes may be clear or colored, and may be obtained in mottled, stippled, or smooth textures.

19.13 Chemical-Resistant Clay Masonry Units. These units are for use in masonry construction in the chemical and allied industries for contact with chemicals and are normally used with chemical-resistant mortars. They are available in two types:

Standard Brick. Intended for use where thermal shock is a service factor and minimum absorption is not required.

Minimum-Absorption Brick. Intended for use where minimum absorption is required and thermal shock is not a service factor.

For applications in contact with sulfuric acid, the brick shall show a weight loss not greater than 20 per cent for the standard type and not greater than 8 per cent for the minimum-absorption type when tested by the solubility in sulfuric acid test. (See *ASTM Designation:* C279–51T.) Similar test procedures may be used for brick in contact with other chemicals.

19.14 Structural-Clay Facing Tile. These tile are designed for use in exterior and interior unplastered walls and partitions of buildings. See Fig. 19.2. They are manufactured by the stiff-mud process from clay, fireclay, or shale. These tile are available in standard and special duty classes. Two types are specified by the ASTM:

Type FTX. Smooth-face tile suitable for general use in exposed exterior and interior masonry walls and partitions and adapted for use where tile low in absorption, easily cleaned, and resistant to staining are required and where a high degree of mechanical perfection, narrow color range, and minimum variation in face dimensions are desired.

Type FTS. Smooth- or rough-texture-face tile suitable for general use in exposed exterior and interior masonry walls and partitions and adapted for use where tile of moderate absorption, moderate variation in face dimensions, and medium color range may be used, where minor defects in surface finish, including small handling chips, are not objectionable.

19.15 Ceramic Glazed Structural-Clay Facing Tile. These tile are manufactured in grades and types similar to those for ceramic glazed facing brick and solid masonry units. (See Art. 19.12.)

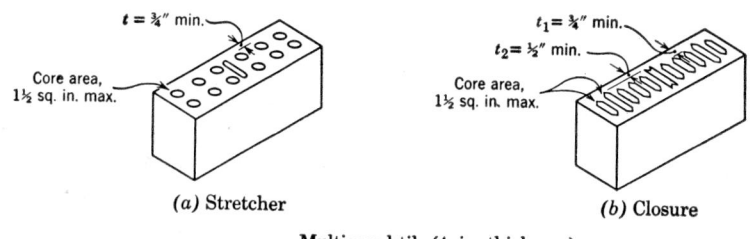

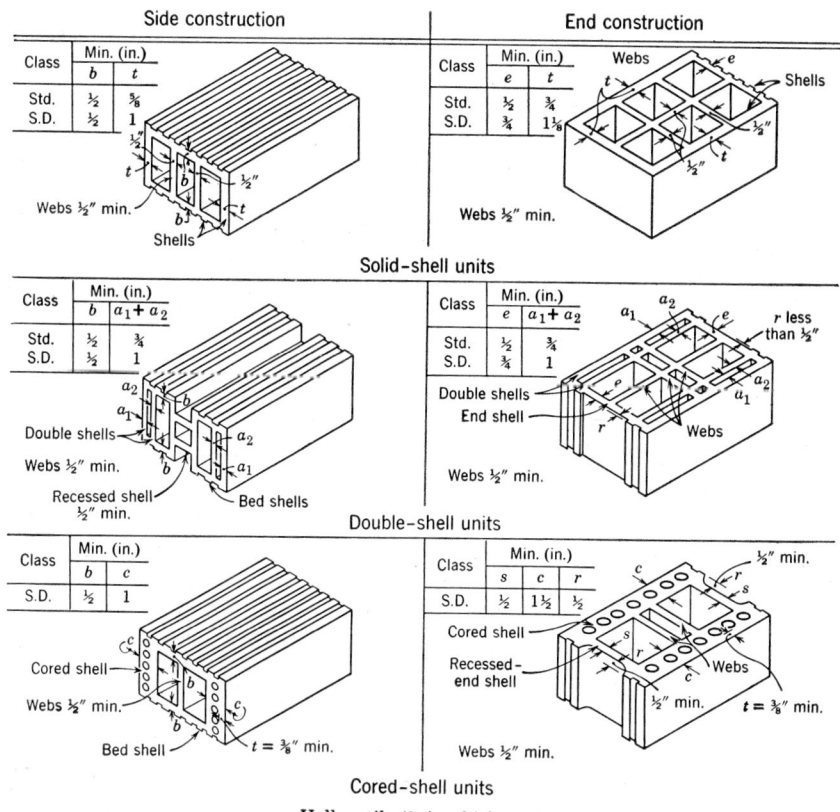

Fig. 19.2. ASTM typical shapes of hollow structural-clay building tile and facing tile in sizes for modular design with dimensions for both standard and special duty classes.

19.16 Structural-Clay Load-Bearing Wall Tile. These tile may be manufactured from surface clay, fireclay, shale, or mixtures thereof. Usually the stiff-mud process is employed. The tile are fired in tunnel or down-draft kilns. Typical shapes in sizes for modular design are shown in Fig. 19.2. End-construction tile are designed to be placed in the load-carrying wall with axes of the cells vertical. Side-construction tile are designed to be placed in the wall with the axes of the cells horizontal. Bonding tile are designed to provide recesses for header brick courses when laid up in brick-faced walls.

Two grades are specified by the ASTM:

Grade LBX. Suitable for general use in masonry construction and adapted for use in masonry exposed to weathering, provided they are burned to the normal maturity of the clay. They may also be considered suitable for the direct application of stucco.

Grade LB. Suitable for general use in masonry where not exposed to frost action or for use in exposed masonry where protected with a facing of 3 inches or more of stone, brick, terra cotta, or other masonry.

19.17 Structural Clay Non-Load-Bearing Tile. This tile is used for non-load-bearing partitions, for furring, and for fireproofing. Partition tile are generally made 12 inches long, 12 inches in height, and from 2 to 12 inches in thickness. Split furring tile is 12 by 12 inches in size with thicknesses of $1\frac{1}{2}$ or 2 inches. Fireproofing tile comes in numerous sizes similar to partition tile and also in special shapes. *ASTM* specifications have only one grade: *NB*. The stiff-mud process is used.

The finish of the outer face may be exposed-wall finish or plaster-base finish. For exposed finish, surfaces may be smooth, combed, or roughened; for plaster-base finish, surfaces may be smooth, combed, scored, or roughened. Scored tile are suitable for application of plaster or stucco.

19.18 Structural-Clay Floor Tile. Structural floor tile are made from surface clay, fireclay, shale, or mixtures thereof. There are two grades specified by the ASTM: *FT1* and *FT2*. Both grades are suitable for use in flat arches or segmental arches or in combination tile and concrete ribbed-slab construction. The finishes and surfaces are similar to those for structural clay non-load-bearing tile. (Art. 19.17.)

19.19 Roofing Tile. Roofing tile must be regular in shape and free from warping in order to avoid leakage of roofs. Consequently, it is necessary to select clays carefully to avoid distortion of the tile in drying and burning. Roofing tile are manufactured by the stiff-mud process by means of an auger machine. After drying, they are burned in a down-draft kiln. Usually roofing tile are hard burned but may be soft burned when desired for insulating purposes.

Roofing tile are made in various styles such as shingle, mission, Spanish, German, Greek, and Roman. They are available in different textures and in a variety of colors including red, buff, yellow, brown, gray, and black.

Special shapes are produced for ridges, hip rolls, and eave closures. Roofing tile are expensive in first cost but provide durable, strong, and fireproof roofs of excellent appearance at low maintenance costs.

Terra Cotta

19.20 Terra Cotta. There are two classes of terra cotta: (1) architectural terra cotta, and (2) structural terra cotta. Structural terra cotta is commonly called structural-clay tile. (See Arts. 19.14 to 19.18 for descriptions of structural-clay tile.)

Architectural terra cotta is used for decoration. It is composed of practically the same material as brick but requires a carefully selected, finely divided homogenous clay which burns to a desirable color with a slight natural glaze. It is very seldom that a single clay is used in the production of terra cotta as each shade and tint generally requires the mingling of different clays. Fireclays are often used in the manufacture of architectural terra cotta.

The clays after delivery at the factory are ground separately in wash mills or edge-runner mills, mixed with grit and water in pug mills, and deposited in layers or strata. As many as ten or twelve strata are thus piled up, and from this mass perpendicular cuts are taken and the whole is mixed together in a pug mill into a plastic mass.

The manner of molding may be by machine or by hand methods. The machine method is an extrusion process. The plastic clay is de-aired to produce a denser material and then is extruded through a die. Partition blocks, ashlar, and wall-facing blocks are usually machine made. Handmade terra cotta blocks are formed by hand molding in plaster molds. Intricate designs are modeled without a mold, and green casts are often further carved by hand before being dried and burned. Very elaborate designs of high artistic merit are sometimes executed. As it is not practicable to burn terra cotta in very large units, it is often necessary to make a complete design of many comparatively small sections.

After drying and before burning, a coating of "slip" is applied to the ware. This slip is made up of clay, feldspar, flint, etc., is opaque, and imparts the color desired for the finished product. Either a dull or a bright glazed finish may be secured.

Burning is done with extreme care to prevent either distortion or discoloration by flames or gases. Special kilns in which the ware does not come in contact with the gases are needed. In modern plants tunnel kilns are employed; the dried pieces of terra cotta are loaded on cars which are slowly moved through the kiln.

Machine-made terra cotta blocks for wall facing range in size from 8 inches by 16 inches up to 24 inches by 48 inches. The blocks may be solid and of $1\frac{7}{8}$ inch thickness, or they may be formed with hollow cores, the total thickness being $3\frac{3}{4}$ inches. Hand-made slabs range from 12 inches to 30 inches in width, from 4 to 12 inches thick, and are of various lengths; they usually are hollow and have open backs so they can be bonded to masonry walls. However, hand-made blocks with closed backs scored for bonding are also available; these generally have hollow cores to reduce dead weight. Hand-made special shapes such as copings, cornices, sills, jambs, window trim, etc., are manufactured of architectural terra cotta.

Sand-Lime Brick

19.21 General. Sand-lime brick are not made from clays, but, since their uses are identical with those of ordinary building brick, their manufacture will be discussed at this point. Solid masonry units (usually 8 by 8 by 16 inches) are also made of sand-lime mixtures.

Three grades of sand-lime brick are recognized by the American Society for Testing Materials:

Grade SW. Intended for use where exposed to temperature below freezing in the presence of moisture.

Grade MW. Intended for use where exposed to temperature below freezing but unlikely to be saturated with water.

Grade NW. Intended (1) for use as backup or interior masonry, (2) if exposed, for use where no frost action occurs; or, (3) if frost action occurs, for use where the average annual precipitation is less than 15 inches.

19.22 Materials. Almost any clean sand is suitable if the process is varied to suit its properties. A well-graded sand will make a brick of the lowest absorption and, therefore, the one least likely to disintegrate. A mixture of at least 4 parts of sand which is between the 20-mesh and the 100-mesh screen size, to 1 part of sand finer than the 150-mesh, has been found to give a brick of maximum compressive strength.

The Lime. Either high-calcium lime or dolomitic lime may be used, but high-calcium lime is preferable. The amount of lime required varies from about 8 to 12 per cent by volume. Hydrated lime is usually used.

Preparation of the Sand. The preliminary treatment of the sand depends first upon its source and second upon the details of manufacture. A soft sandstone rock must first be crushed and then screened to separate out the larger particles. Sand obtained by dredging must be dried. If an excess of clay is present, or if it is a seashore sand contaminated with the salts of sea water, washing and subsequent drying are required. If the sand does not contain a sufficient proportion of very fine quartz, it is necessary to pulverize a portion of it in a tube mill or other type of fine-grinding machine and add the pulverized material to the natural sand.

19.23 Manufacture. *Mixing.* The thoroughness of mixing is the most essential detail of the entire process. Probably the best method of thoroughly incorporating the lime with the sand and water consists in mixing the lime and sand in a tube mill and then adding water to the mix in a pug mill. The latter delivers the mix to a bin where it is allowed to stand for some hours before being delivered to the press.

Pressing the Brick. Owing to the grittiness of the mix it is not possible to make wire-cut sand-lime brick. They are therefore made in a mold in the same manner that dry-press clay brick are made, under pressures as much as 15,000 pounds per square inch.

Hardening. The bricks are not allowed to harden in air but are hardened in closed chambers subjected to steam under a pressure of 100 to 150 pounds per square inch. The hardening chamber is a horizontal cylinder of steel, provided with a removable steamtight head and tracks upon which cars carrying the bricks are run into the cylinder. The time required for hardening depends upon the steam pressure, being usually between 4 and 10 hours.

Concrete Building Brick

19.24 Concrete Building Brick. These brick are manufactured from a mixture of Portland cement and aggregates for use in brick masonry. Typical aggregates include sand, gravel, crushed stone, blast-furnace slag, bituminous or anthracite cinders, and burned clay or shale. There are two ASTM grades:

Grade A. Intended for use where exposed to temperature below freezing in the presence of moisture.
Grade B. Intended for use as backup or interior masonry.

Manufacture of Paving Brick

19.25 General. A good paving brick should be hard enough to resist the abrasive action caused by street traffic; so tough that it will not be broken by the impact of wheels; and non-absorptive, so that it will resist weathering. Its manufacture differs somewhat from that of common brick because the selection of a suitable clay is more limited and burning must be carried out at a much higher temperature, vitrification or at least incipient vitrification being required.

19.26 Raw Materials. Surface clays are generally unsuitable for paving brick because, on account of their highly siliceous character, the range of temperatures between incipient and viscous vitrification is so short that only a small portion of the kiln charge is properly burned.

Shales or rock clays are used for paving brick. Although the expense of crushing is increased owing to their rock nature, they are so impure that the range of vitrification is often as much as 400° C. (752° F.), making them an especially valuable material for paving-brick manufacture. Impure fire-clays are used to a slight extent.

Upon delivery at the plant, shales are crushed either in dry pans, rolls, or centrifugal disintegrators. The crushed clay is screened to remove all particles not passed by about a 20-mesh sieve and delivered to the pug mill where just sufficient water is added to make a stiff mud.

19.27 Molding and Drying. Practically all paving brick are made by the stiff-mud process, the machine being usually of the auger type. The size of the die is larger than for building brick. Usually side-cut brick are made.

The de-airing process is extensively used in order to obtain greater density and strength in the finished paving brick.

Paving bricks are usually laid in pavements with the wire-cut surfaces horizontal so that a rough-textured surface will be uppermost to reduce slipperiness. Paving brick laid in this manner are referred to as "vertical fiber" brick on account of the vertical position of the structure formed in the brick in forcing the clay through a die. Lugs on the ends and on one side of the brick are formed by a special compressing operation for the purpose of providing a proper spacing between the bricks in a pavement so that adequate penetration of a bituminous filler material into the joints may be obtained.

Vertical fiber lug brick have the tabulated dimensions, exclusive of lugs.

Depth, in.	*Width*, in.	*Length*, in.
2½	4	8½
3	4	8½
3½	4	8½

The practice of re-pressing paving brick after forming by wire cutting has been practically discontinued since no improvement in physical properties is obtained.

Paving brick are dried by the same methods as ordinary stiff-mud brick.

19.28 Burning, Annealing, and Sorting. Paving brick are burned in either the down-draft or the continuous kiln. The burning requires from 7 to 10 days, and the temperature attained corresponds to a bright-cherry heat, whereas only a red heat is attained in burning hard building brick. The proper temperature of vitrification for a given clay must not be exceeded, in order to avoid softening of the brick. When the brick are thoroughly burned, the kiln must be tightly closed and allowed to cool down slowly for several days. Thus the brick are annealed and acquire a great deal more toughness than when quickly cooled.

The brick must be sorted in emptying the kiln. The upper courses will be very hard burned but possibly air checked. They are excellent for foundations. From the zone of checked brick to within a few courses of the bottom, the brick should be "No. 1 pavers"; the lower courses have not been sufficiently heated to be vitrified and are classed as "No. 2 pavers." Number two pavers are excellent building brick.

19.29 Sewer Brick. Sewer brick are manufactured from selected clays or shales and are hard burned. They are used in drainage structures for carrying sewage, industrial wastes, and storm water. The stiff-mud process is employed in forming the brick. They are made in standard sizes of both building brick and paving brick, and also in the shape of blocks. Three grades of sewer brick are specified by the ASTM:

Grade SA. Brick intended for use in structures requiring imperviousness and resistance to the action of sewage carrying large quantities of abrasive material at velocities exceeding 8 feet per second.

Grade MA. Brick intended for use in structures requiring imperviousness and resistance to the action: (1) of sewage free from abrasive materials and (2) of sewage carrying abrasive materials at velocities of 8 feet per second or less.

Grade NA. Brick intended for use in structures not requiring high degrees of imperviousness nor of abrasive resistance. For example, brick of the NA grade are suitable for use in catch basins, arches, the upper portions of manholes, and for backing.

Segmental blocks are manufactured for building large diameter sewers. Liner plates of burned clay are made for lining large concrete sewers; they are available in both flat and curved shapes. Dovetail lugs are provided on one side of the clay liner plates for anchoring to the concrete.

19.30 Filter Block for Trickling Filters. Vitrified-clay filter block are produced for use in constructing trickling filter floors. One type has continuous drainage channels through the lower portion of the block and in the upper portion of the block has grilles for drainage and aeration purposes. A two-unit filter block is also made; the lower unit provides continuous drainage channels, and the upper unit contains drainage and aeration grilles.

Clay Pipes

19.31 Drain Tile. Drain tile are made from surface clays, fireclays, and shales. The materials are handled by the stiff-mud process, issuing from a special die as a hollow cylinder, which is cut to convenient lengths by wires. Two classes are specified by the American Society for Testing Materials:

Standard drain tile. Intended for ordinary land drainage where the tile are laid in trenches of moderate depths and widths.

Extra-quality drain tile. Intended for land drainage where the tile are laid in trenches of considerable depths or widths, or both, and where an extra quality is desired.

The burning of the standard drain tile is conducted at temperatures to produce a tile possessing a considerable degree of mechanical strength, but the tile is not vitrified or glazed.

19.32 Sewer Pipe. Sewer pipe is manufactured from selected surface clays, fireclays, and shales. The stiff-mud process is used. Pipes are molded vertically in cylindrical presses having double walls and of such design as to permit molding a "bell end" on one end of the pipe. Special shapes, such as elbows, Y's, and T's are made by joining parts of green pipe with slip clay.

After drying in steam chambers or in warm-air drying compartments, the ware is burned in down-draft kilns. Firing is carried on to a temperature corresponding to incipient vitrification. A special "salt glaze" is imparted to the surface of the pipe by throwing common salt into the kiln fires after a temperature of about 1150° C. (2102° F.) has been attained. The sodium vapors freed by heat pass through the kiln and by combination with the clay form a dense, hard glaze, which renders the pipe practically non-absorptive.

Sewer pipes are intended primarily for use as conductors of water, sewage, and industrial wastes, and are laid with tight cement joints. Vitrified clay sewer pipe is used for venting chemical fumes from medical and chemical laboratories. Another application is for heating ducts in basementless houses.

Extra-strength clay pipe are also manufactured; they have a salt-glaze surface. Both standard strength and extra-strength clay sewer pipes are available with a ceramic glaze.

19.33 Perforated Clay Pipe. Standard strength perforated clay pipe is similar to standard strength sewer pipe. Perforations are ¼ inch in diameter and are arranged in rows parallel to the axis of the pipe. Perforations are spaced approximately 3 inches center to center, along rows. These pipes have a salt glaze. They are used for underdrainage.

19.34 Clay Conduit. Clay conduit is utilized for carrying pipes, wires, and cables underground. Hollow rectangular blocks are ordinarily used with internal walls or webs dividing the cross-section into ducts. Circular sections are also employed. The stiff-mud process is used in forming the conduit. The units are hard-burned and salt-glazed to make them impervious.

19.35 Clay Flue Lining. Clay flue lining is manufactured in both circular and rectangular cross-sections. These units are used in lining masonry and brick chimneys. Selected fireclay is processed by the stiff-mud method. Flue lining is hard burned and is produced with a clear glaze.

Properties of Brick and Tile

19.36 General. The more important physical properties of brick are: compressive strength, flexural strength, shearing strength, and weather resistance. Of less importance, but still useful, are: absorption, porosity, density, and hardness.

These properties are of much more consequence in application to brick masonry than in individual bricks. The raw materials and the manner and

Brick and Clay Products

degree of burning influence the physical properties greatly, and, therefore, wide ranges in values are to be expected.

19.37 Crushing Strength. Since the strength of brick masonry is only a fraction of the strength of the brick, the compressive strength of individual bricks is of only relative value in that it affords a basis of comparison between different kinds of brick. Laminations and other defects are often revealed in the fracture. Bricks are usually tested flatwise as they are more often laid in that manner. The compressive strengths flatwise and edgewise are not often the same and no definite relation seems to exist between them. Half brick with approximately plane and parallel ends are used as test specimens.

19.38 Absorption. The absorption of water by brick is often considered to be indicative of its probable durability. It is sometimes claimed that the freezing of water which fills the pores of brick will constitute a disintegrating agency, but the importance of this factor is overestimated. Bricks are seldom injured by frost for the reason that water does not fill the pores completely and therefore is able to expand upon freezing without exerting any great disruptive force.

For building brick two tests are conducted: (1) the 24-hour submersion test and (2) the 5-hour boiling test. In the latter test, the bricks are immersed in water at 60 to 86° F., brought to a boil in 1 hour, boiled for 5 hours, allowed to cool to room temperature, and weighed. A saturation coefficient is computed as the ratio of absorption by 24-hour submersion in cold water to that after 5-hour submersion in boiling water.

For chemical-resistant clay masonry units, a 2-hour boiling test is employed. For structural-clay facing tile, wall tile, and floor tile, a 1-hour boiling test is specified.

19.39 Flexural Strength. This test is easily made and furnishes an approximation of the tensile strength by means of the modulus of rupture. Experiments and experience show that the failure of brick masonry under compressive stress is usually caused by failure and subsequent lateral flow of the mortar, thereby producing tensile stresses in the bricks and causing cracks to open up in the masonry. The fractured surface of a brick often affords a valuable indication of the care with which the materials have been ground and mixed, and the degree of burning is made evident to an experienced observer.

19.40 Shearing Strength. The shearing strength of bricks as shown by tests is a property of little practical importance, chiefly because it is impossible to determine the actual shearing strength. All methods of testing which have been devised are more or less subject to the same objection, i.e., the shearing stress is not acting alone, but bending is introduced, thus bringing tension and compression into play as well as shear. The shearing strength of common brick is about 1000 to 1500 pounds per square inch;

pressed brick, 800 to 1200; sand-lime brick, 500 to 1000; paving brick, 1200 to 1800; and fireclay brick, 500 to 1000.

19.41 Modulus of Elasticity. The modulus of elasticity of bricks is not a constant for any considerable range of loading. The elastic properties, as shown by the stress-strain curve for a compressive test, are quite similar to those of concrete and mortars. For ranges of loading not exceeding one-fourth of the compressive strength the modulus of elasticity of common brick is about 1,500,000 to 2,500,000 pounds per square inch; pressed brick, 2,000,000 to 3,000,000; sand-lime brick, 800,000 to 1,200,000; concrete brick, 2,000,000 to 2,500,000; and paving brick, 4,000,000 to 8,000,000.

Specified Tests and Classifications

19.42 Clay Building Brick and Solid Masonry Units. ASTM requirements are given in Table 19.1.

Table 19.1

ASTM PHYSICAL REQUIREMENTS FOR CLAY BUILDING BRICK AND SOLID MASONRY UNITS

Designation	Minimum Compressive Strength (Brick Flatwise), p.s.i., gross area		Maximum Water Absorption by 5-hr. Boiling, %		Maximum Saturation Coefficient *	
	Average of 5 Brick	Individual	Average of 5 Brick	Individual	Average of 5 Brick	Individual
Grade SW	3000	2500	17.0	20.0	0.78	0.80
Grade MW	2500	2200	22.0	25.0	0.88	0.90
Grade NW	1500	1250	No limit	No limit	No limit	No limit

* The saturation coefficient is the ratio of absorption by 24-hr. submersion in cold water to that after 5-hr. submersion in boiling water.

Table 19.2

ASTM PHYSICAL REQUIREMENTS FOR FACING BRICK AND SOLID MASONRY UNIT

(Made from Clay or Shale)

Designation	Minimum Compressive Strength (Brick Flatwise), p.s.i., gross area		Maximum Water Absorption by 5-hr. Boiling, %		Maximum Saturation Coefficient *	
	Average of 5 Brick	Individual	Average of 5 Brick	Individual	Average of 5 Brick	Individual
Grade SW	3000	2500	17.0	20.0	0.78	0.80
Grade MW	2500	2200	22.0	25.0	0.88	0.90

* The saturation coefficient is the ratio of absorption by 24-hr. submersion in cold water to that after 5-hr. submersion in boiling water.

Brick and Clay Products

Table 19.3
ASTM PHYSICAL REQUIREMENTS FOR CERAMIC GLAZED STRUCTURAL-CLAY FACING TILE, FACING BRICK, AND SOLID MASONRY UNITS

Compressive Strengths of Units

Direction of Coring	Minimum Average of Five Tests, p.s.i.	Individual Minimum, p.s.i.
Vertical	3000	2500
Horizontal	2000	1500

Table 19.4
ASTM PHYSICAL REQUIREMENTS FOR CHEMICAL-RESISTANT CLAY MASONRY UNITS

| | Minimum Modulus of Rupture (Brick Flatwise), p.s.i. || Maximum Water Absorption by 2-Hr. Boiling Test, % ||
Designation	Average of 5 Brick	Individual	Average of 5 Brick	Individual
Standard	1250	1000	6.0	7.0
Min. absorption	2500	2000	1.0	1.5

Table 19.5
ASTM PHYSICAL REQUIREMENTS FOR STRUCTURAL CLAY FACING TILE

| | Maximum Water Absorption By 24-Hr. Submersion in Cold Water, % || By 1-Hr. Boiling, % ||
Type	Average	Individual	Average	Individual
FTX	7	9	9	11
FTS	13	16	16	19

Compressive Strength Based on Gross Area

| | End-Construction Tile || Side-Construction Tile ||
Class	Minimum Average of Five Tests, p.s.i.	Individual Minimum, p.s.i.	Minimum Average of Five Tests, p.s.i.	Individual Minimum, p.s.i.
Standard	1400	1000	700	500
Special duty	2500	2000	1200	1000

Table 19.6
ASTM PHYSICAL REQUIREMENTS FOR BUILDING TILE

Structural Clay Load-Bearing Wall Tile

Grade	Maximum Water Absorption,* by 1-hr. Boiling, %		Minimum Compressive Strength (Based on Gross Area),† p.s.i.			
			End Construction Tile		Side Construction Tile	
	Average of Five Tests	Individual	Average of Five Tests	Individual	Average of Five Tests	Individual
LBX	16	19	1400	1000	700	500
LB	25	28	1000	700	700	500

* The range in percentage absorption for tile delivered to any one job shall be not more than 12.

† Gross area of a unit shall be determined by multiplying the horizontal face dimension of the unit as placed in the wall by its thickness.

Structural Clay Floor Tile

Grade	Absorption,* by 1-hr. Boiling, %	Compressive Strength (Based on Net Area),† p.s.i.			
		End-Construction Tile		Side-Construction Tile	
	Individual Maximum	Minimum Average of Five Tests	Individual Minimum	Minimum Average of Five Tests	Individual Minimum
FT1	25	3200	2250	1600	1100
FT2	25	2000	1400	1200	850

* The range in percentage absorption for tile delivered to any one job shall be not more than 12.

† Net area of a unit shall be taken as the area of solid material in shells and webs actually carrying stresses in a direction parallel to the direction of loading.

Brick and Clay Products

Table 19.6 (Cont.)

ASTM PHYSICAL REQUIREMENTS FOR BUILDING TILE (Cont.)

Structural Clay Non-Load-Bearing Tile

Grade	Absorption,* by 1-hr. Boiling, % Individual Maximum
NB	28

* The range in percentage absorption for tile delivered to any one job shall be not more than 12.

19.43 Facing Brick and Solid Masonry Units. Table 19.2 gives the ASTM physical requirements for these units.

19.44 Ceramic Glazed Facing Brick, Solid Masonry Units, and Structural-Clay Facing Tile. The requirements for these units are listed in Table 19.3.

19.45 Chemical-Resistant Clay Masonry Units. Table 19.4 gives the physical requirements for chemical-resistant units.

19.46 Structural Clay Facing Tile. The requirements are shown in Table 19.5.

19.47 Building Tile. Table 19.6 gives the ASTM physical requirements for structural-clay load-bearing wall tile, non-load-bearing tile, and floor tile.

19.48 Sand-Lime Building Brick. ASTM physical requirements for sand-lime building brick are given in Table 19.7.

Table 19.7

ASTM PHYSICAL REQUIREMENTS FOR SAND-LIME BUILDING BRICK

Designation	Minimum Compressive Strength (Brick Flatwise), p.s.i., average gross area		Minimum Modulus of Rupture (Brick Flatwise), p.s.i., average gross area	
	Average of 5 Brick	Individual	Average of 5 Brick	Individual
Grade SW	4500	3500	600	400
Grade MW	2500	2000	450	300
Grade NW	1500	1500	300	200

19.49 Concrete Building Brick. Table 19.8 shows the requirements for concrete building brick.

Table 19.8

ASTM PHYSICAL REQUIREMENTS FOR CONCRETE BUILDING BRICK

Class	Minimum Compressive Strength (Brick Flatwise), p.s.i., average gross area		Minimum Modulus of Rupture (Brick Flatwise), p.s.i., average gross area	
	Average of 5 Tests	Individual	Average of 5 Tests	Individual
Grade A	2500	2000	450	300
Grade B	1250	1000	300	200

19.50 Paving Brick. Bricks to be used as paving bricks are usually subjected to a standard "rattler" test. In this test a charge of ten bricks of block size is placed in a standard rattler, with an abrasive charge made up of 10 cast-iron balls $3\frac{3}{4}$ inches in diameter and weighing approximately $7\frac{1}{2}$ pounds each and a sufficient number of cast-iron balls $1\frac{7}{8}$ inches in diameter, weighing approximately 0.95 pound, to bring the total weight of the charge to as nearly 300 pounds as possible.

The rattler is rotated at a uniform rate, between 29.5 and 30.5 revolutions per minute, for 1800 revolutions. The loss in weight is calculated in per cent of the initial weight of the brick.

The percentage of loss in the rattler test of the respective sizes of paving brick specified shall not exceed the tabulated limits.

Size of Brick		Maximum Loss in Rattler Test, %
Transverse Dimensions, in.	Length, in.	
$2\frac{1}{2}$ by 4	$8\frac{1}{2}$	26
3 by 4	$8\frac{1}{2}$	24
$3\frac{1}{2}$ by 4	$8\frac{1}{2}$	22

The total number of pieces weighing 1 pound or more remaining after the completion of the rattler test shall not exceed 12.

19.51 Sewer Brick. *Sewer brick* are subjected to the same tests as clay building brick. The ASTM physical requirements are given in Table 19.9. It will be seen that sewer brick of the SA and MA grades are essentially high-grade building brick with high compressive strength and low absorption.

19.52 Drain Tile. *Drain tile*, whether clay or cement concrete, is usually subjected to crushing tests and absorption tests. The crushing strength is usually obtained by the three-edge-bearing method in which the lower bearing consists of two bearing strips placed 1 inch apart and the upper consists

Brick and Clay Products

Table 19.9

ASTM PHYSICAL REQUIREMENTS FOR SEWER BRICK (MADE FROM CLAY OR SHALE)

Designation	Minimum Compressive Strength (Brick Flatwise), p.s.i., average gross area		Maximum Water Absorption by 5-hr. Boiling, %	
	Average of 5 Brick	Individual	Average of 5 Brick	Individual
Grade SA	8000	5000	6	9
Grade MA *	5000	3000	12	16
Grade NA *	2500	2200	22	25

* Where resistance to frost action in the presence of moisture is required, grades MA and NA shall conform to the additional requirement that the saturation coefficient (C/B), that is, ratio of absorption by 24-hr. submersion in cold water to that after 5-hr. submersion in boiling water, shall not exceed 0.80.

of a single bearing strip, all strips extending along the full barrel length of the pipe. The sand-bearing is sometimes used in which the drain tile is bedded, above and below, in sand for one-fourth the circumference of the pipe. The absorption test is conducted on a specimen 12 to 20 square inches in area with broken edges by means of a 5-hour boiling test. Table 19.10 gives the ASTM requirements for drain tile.

19.53 Sewer Pipe. *Sewer pipe* is usually subjected to crushing tests and absorption tests. These tests are similar to those for drain tile. Table 19.11 shows the crushing-strength requirements for different grades of clay sewer pipe for the different sizes manufactured. The maximum allowable percentage absorption by the 5-hour boiling test for all sizes and grades of pipe is 8 per cent. Where the sewage shows an acid reaction, clay sewer pipe is generally preferred to cement-concrete pipe.

Brick Masonry

19.54 General. Brick masonry, for many purposes, compares favorably with most stone masonry; it is cheaper, more easily built, resists fire better, and is very durable.

19.55 Mortar Joints. Mortar is the plastic mixture of two or more materials, which is used to bind individual bricks together into a solid mass. The proper composition, preparation, and use are as important in producing good masonry as the quality of the brick themselves.

Masonry mortars are described in Art. 17.66, and proportion specifications are given in Table 17.6. (See reference 19.6 for suggested grading requirements for sands for mortars for brick masonry.)

Table 19.10

ASTM PHYSICAL REQUIREMENTS FOR DRAIN TILE

Internal Diameter of Tile, in.	Standard Drain Tile				Extra-Quality Drain Tile			
	Minimum Average Crushing Strength		Maximum Average Absorption by 5-hr. Boiling Test		Minimum Average Crushing Strength		Maximum Average Absorption by 5-hr. Boiling Test	
	3-Edge-Bearing Method, lb. per linear ft.	Sand-Bearing Method, lb. per linear ft.	Clay Tile, %	Concrete Tile, %	3-Edge-Bearing Method, lb. per linear ft.	Sand-Bearing Method, lb. per linear ft.	Clay Tile, %	Concrete Tile, %
4	800	1200	13	10	1100	1600	11	8
5	800	1200	13	10	1100	1600	11	8
6	800	1200	13	10	1100	1600	11	8
8	800	1200	13	10	1100	1600	11	8
10	800	1200	13	10	1100	1600	11	8
12	800	1200	13	10	1100	1600	11	8
15	870	1300	13	10	1100	1600	11	8
18	930	1400	13	10	1200	1800	11	8
21	1000	1550	13	10	1400	2100	11	8
24	1130	1700	13	10	1600	2400	11	8
27	1230	1850	13	10	1800	2700	11	8
30	1330	2000	13	10	2000	3000	11	8
33	1430	2150	13	10	2200	3300	11	8
36	1530	2300	13	10	2400	3600	11	8
42	1730	2600	13	10	2800	4200	11	8

Note: When the freezing-and-thawing test is made, the number of reversals (freezings and thawings) shall be as follows: for standard drain tile, 36; for extra-quality drain tile, 48.

Solid masonry units of modular sizes are laid with mortar joints of ¼-, ⅜-, and ½-inch thicknesses. The narrower joints require solid masonry units with smaller permissible variations in dimensions. (See *Standard* A62.3, 1946 of American Standards Association for tables of permissible variations.)

Table 19.11

ASTM CRUSHING-STRENGTH REQUIREMENTS FOR STANDARD-STRENGTH CLAY SEWER PIPE AND CERAMIC GLAZED-CLAY SEWER PIPE

Average Strength, min., lb. per linear ft.

Size, in.	Three-Edge-Bearing Method	Sand-Bearing Method
4	1000	1430
6	1000	1430
8	1000	1430
10	1100	1570
12	1200	1710
15	1400	2000
18	1700	2430
21	2000	2860
24	2400	3430
27	2750	3930
30	3200	4570
33	3500	5000
36	3900	5570

ASTM CRUSHING-STRENGTH REQUIREMENTS FOR EXTRA-STRENGTH CLAY SEWER PIPE AND CERAMIC GLAZED-CLAY PIPE

Average Strength, min., lb. per linear ft.

Nominal Size, in.	Three-Edge-Bearing Method	Sand-Bearing Method
4	2000 *	2850 *
6	2000	2850
8	2000	2850
10	2000	2850
12	2250	3200
15	2750	3925
18	3300	4700
21	3850	5500
24	4400	6300
30	5000	7100
36	6000	8575

* Ceramic glazed-clay pipe only.

Exterior walls are built ordinarily of standard-size brick, 2¼ by 3¾ by 8 inches in dimensions. All brick should be laid with the minimum thickness of joints consistent with proper bedding. Common brick are usually somewhat rough and uneven, but should be laid with joints from 3/16 to 3/8 inch in thickness. It is commonly specified that the height of eight courses of brick masonry shall not exceed the height of eight bricks laid dry by more than 2 inches. Pressed brick, being usually smooth and true, are laid with joints not exceeding $\frac{1}{8}$ or $\frac{3}{16}$ inch in thickness.

19.56 Bond. Bond in brickwork is the arrangement of the bricks in courses, resorted to for the purpose of tying together all parts of walls more than one brick in thickness by the action of the weight of the overlying masonry. The commonly adopted bonds for laying brick masonry are *common, English,* and *Flemish bonds.*

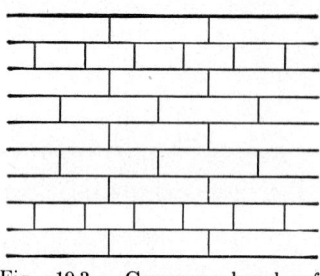

Fig. 19.3. Common bond of brickwork.

In common bond, Fig. 19.3, all the outside bricks are laid as stretchers for four to six courses, and then a course of headers is placed. This type of bond is more generally used than any other in this country.

In English bond, Fig. 19.4, heading and stretching courses alternate. This is the strongest type of bond, but it is not pleasing in appearance.

In Flemish bond, Fig. 19.5, headers and stretchers alternate in each course, each header being centrally placed with respect to a stretcher in the course below. This is a strong bond, but requires cutting brick for each course at corners.

Fig. 19.4. English bond of brickwork.

Fig. 19.5. Flemish bond of brickwork.

Mortar, unless very wet, does not adhere to dry brick nor does it set properly, for the reason that the water in the mortar is absorbed by the bricks. All bricks should therefore be wet before being laid.

19.57 Strength of Brick Masonry. The strength of brick masonry is always more a function of the mortar, the bond, and the workmanship than of the strength of the individual bricks. Where high stresses are encountered cement mortar is required, particularly if a heavy load must be carried within a short time after the masonry is laid.

From tests made upon bricks and brick masonry by J. W. McBurney at the National Bureau of Standards, Washington, D. C., the following conclusions are drawn:

1. The various measures of the strength of brick, compressive, flatwise and on edge, transverse, tensile and shearing, vary in their relation one to another for different makes of brick.
2. The factors, workmanship, strength of mortar, types of construction, and regularity of size and shape of brick being equal, compressive strength of brick, flatwise, is the most consistent measure of compressive strength of brick masonry.
3. For the soft-mud and dry-pressed brick the ratios of compressive strength flatwise to transverse strength are fairly constant. The transverse strength of these bricks is as good a measure of wall strength as the compressive flatwise strength.
4. The ratio, wall strength to brick strength, varies with variation in workmanship, strength of mortar, type of construction, and regularity of size and shape of brick.
5. Where there is a difference in strength between bricks, the ratio of wall strength to brick strength for the stronger brick is more affected by change of mortar strength than the corresponding ratio for the weaker brick.
6. All other factors being equal, the brick most regular in size and with plane, parallel faces will give the highest masonry strength.
7. The ratio, strength at first crack to maximum strength of masonry, seems influenced especially by the ratio of transverse to compressive strength and the regularity in size and shape of the bricks.

There is no recognized specification for the shape and size of brick masonry piers used in determining the compressive strength of brick masonry, but if the ratio of height to thickness, h/t, of piers is 6 or greater, the effect of shape upon the stresses obtained by test will be largely eliminated. Krefeld [1] has reported the strength correction factors given in Table 19.12 from results of tests made upon 8- by 16-inch and 12- by 16-inch piers of various heights.

Table 19.12
STRENGTH CORRECTION FACTORS FOR BRICK MASONRY PRISMS

Ratio, Height to Thickness	Strength Correction Factor	Ratio, Height to Thickness	Strength Correction Factor
1.1	0.45	5.0	0.96
1.5	0.59	6.0	1.00
2.0	0.67	8.0	1.03
2.5	0.75	10.0	1.06
3.0	0.80	12.0	1.09
4.0	0.89		

19.58 Reinforced-Brick Masonry. Reinforced-brick masonry consists of bricks, mortar, and steel reinforcement, the reinforcement rods being placed in the mortar in proper position in the structure so as to resist tensile stresses.

[1] W. J. Krefeld: *Proc. ASTM*, v. 38, Part I, 1938.

The steel bars are placed horizontally in beams and lintels and both horizontally and vertically in walls. The addition of steel reinforcement develops flexural strength and resistance to lateral loads. Tests have indicated that adequate bond strength between steel and mortar and between bricks and mortar exists when good construction methods are employed.

A variety of structures have been built with reinforced-brick masonry including arch bridges, walls, columns, floor slabs, porch floors and steps, stairways both plain and spiral, retaining walls, faces of dams, and structures of circular plan such as silos and storage bins. Reinforced-brick masonry is more costly than reinforced concrete but is sometimes selected where appearance is a factor.

19.59 Efflorescence. Efflorescence is the deposit of crystallized salts on the surface of brick masonry. The most common of these salts are calcium and magnesium sulfate, although various salts of potassium and sodium as well as of calcium and magnesium are often found. The cause of efflorescence is the presence of these salts in a more or less soluble form in the bricks themselves or in the mortar used in laying them up.

An example of soluble salts in brick is sodium vanadate. Vanadium in the clay is changed by burning to oxide form that is soluble in water. In a wall the compound salts, forming sodium vanadate, and may cause efflorescence. As to mortar, aggregates from sea water or washed by sea water in processing may contain sodium chloride and other salts which may contribute to efflorescence. Sodium chloride and calcium chloride additions to mortar to aid in curing or retard freezing will contribute toward efflorescence of masonry and for this reason should not be used. Alkalies in Portland cement may tend to cause efflorescence either as sulfates or as hydroxide which soon changes to carbonate; also lime set free on hydration may be transported to the surface of walls where it forms carbonates. Lime in mortar is essentially free from soluble salts. However, calcium hydroxide in solution may be carried to the surface of new walls when the masonry has become saturated and becomes carbonated upon exposure to air, forming minute crystals of low solubility but of high light diffractivity. Such crystals obscure the brickwork but are not harmful. On the other hand, efflorescence in the form of crystallized salts causes the growth of elongated crystals; when these crystals grow within a confined space, pressures are exerted which are too great for many masonry materials to withstand, thus resulting in surface disintegration.

Efflorescence usually appears white in color. It occurs more often in the winter but may be observed in other seasons especially following heavy rains and drops in temperature. Rain water contains considerable amounts of sulfur acids which react to produce calcium, magnesium, potassium, and sodium sulfates when rain water soaks into a masonry structure. Along ocean fronts, efflorescence may be caused by sea salts blown in by storms.

Water is the solvent for the salts and it constitutes the means whereby salts are carried to the surface where they accumulate as the water is evaporated. Without moisture in the masonry, there would be no trouble from efflorescent action. Removal of water by drainage or evaporation avoids most of the troubles. The construction of an escape mechanism such as a continuous cavity within the walls with weep holes suitably located to remove moisture quickly by drainage and ventilation has proved desirable in many instances. Covering the faces of foundation walls in contact with soil by means of a bituminous waterproofing course will tend to prevent seepage into walls. Window sills and copings should be impervious and be built with water tight joints. Flashing under architectural details such as overhanging window sills, caps, and copings should extend outward and downward about an inch to form a drip so as to protect the masonry surfaces underneath from water dripping.

Masonry of low porosity or having discontinuous pores slows down the movement of solutions and hence is affected less by efflorescence.

Sudden drops in temperature cause crystals to grow faster with a greater number of large crystals which may produce a great deal of pressure in the masonry.

Treatments on the surface of brickwork which tend to build up a crust, especially where an appreciable amount of soluble salts has accumulated, will tend to cause exfoliation as a result of efflorescent crystal pressure developing just behind the crust. Such treatments include water-repellant surface coatings of cement or mortar and of certain silicone solutions. (See references 19.3 and 19.4.)

Glass Building Blocks

19.60 General. Glass building blocks will be discussed at this point since they are frequently employed in connection with masonry construction. Glass building blocks are inserted in walls and partitions to transmit light. They are not used to withstand load in bearing walls.

19.61 Manufacture. Glass building blocks are manufactured by a process which causes a partial vacuum to be produced in the interior of the blocks. Each block is formed by fusing together two pieces that have been made by press molding. The glass is ¼ inch or more thick. After being formed, the glass blocks are annealed.

The top and bottom outside surfaces and the ends frequently have a rough surfacing material bonded to the glass for the purpose of obtaining good adherence with mortar. The outside side surfaces of the glass block may be smooth or molded with vertical ribs. The inside side surfaces have either horizontal or vertical ribs in the glass; the selection of the type of inside ribs depends upon the light source.

19.62 Physical Properties. Glass building blocks have hard surfaces and hence are not acoustical materials. Although the blocks transmit light they are not transparent and hence have the advantage of giving privacy to interior rooms. They have exhibited good fire resistance under test.

19.63 Construction Practice. Glass building blocks are laid with a ¼-inch mortar joint. A 1 part Portland cement, 1 part lime, and 4 parts sand mortar of stiff consistency is generally used. The blocks do not absorb moisture from the mortar. Cork or special cement is placed in the joints on top of panels and at sides near bottom of panels to reduce stresses in glass blocks. Panels of glass building blocks up to 144 square feet of surface area with no side longer than 20 feet are typical of good practice.

Questions

19.1. What are the requirements for a good brick-making clay?
19.2. Name and describe three processes of manufacturing structural clay products.
19.3. What is "de-airing," and what are its advantages?
19.4. Describe the essential features involved in drying structural-clay products.
19.5. Describe the four stages of burning structural-clay products.
19.6. Describe the different types of brick kilns.
19.7. Distinguish between the following bricks: vitrified brick, face brick, ceramic glazed brick, vertical-fiber paving brick, sewer brick, salmon brick, and arch brick.
19.8. Describe the manufacture of sand-lime brick.
19.9. Distinguish between terra cotta and structural-clay tile.
19.10. Distinguish between drain tile and sewer pipe.
19.11. How is the glaze on sewer pipe obtained?
19.12. What is efflorescence?
19.13. Compare building brick and paving brick with respect to: character of raw materials, temperature of burning, and structural strength.
19.14. Assuming that you are called upon to pass upon the acceptability of a given grade of building brick for a certain purpose and that you have available laboratory facilities for making tests, name and briefly describe the tests that you would make, including both superficial examinations and laboratory tests.
19.15. Discuss the significance of absorption tests of brick, and state what percentages of absorption are permissible in various kinds and grades of bricks.
19.16. What are the requirements specified for clay building brick?
19.17. What is the three-edge-bearing method of testing pipes?
19.18. Name and describe three types of bond for brickwork. What are the advantages of each type?
19.19. List the advantages and disadvantages of the following materials for the bonding cement in the mortar for a brick building: quicklime, hydrated lime, masonry cement, and Portland cement. Discuss the proportioning of these materials for masonry mortars (Table 17.6).
19.20. Upon what factors does the strength of brick masonry depend?
19.21. What is the purpose of placing reinforcement in brick masonry?
19.22. Describe the use of glass building blocks in building construction.

Brick and Clay Products

19.23. What are the reasons for facing a reinforced-concrete type of building with brick?

19.24. A builder has the choice among the following materials for the exterior walls of a house: building brick, sand-lime brick, natural limestone, natural sandstone with iron oxide cementing material, and wood. List the advantages and disadvantages of each of these materials for such a purpose.

References

19.1. American Institute of Mining and Metallurgical Engineers: *Industrial Minerals and Rocks.* 2nd ed., 1949, pp. 207–244.

19.2. American Society for Testing Materials: Installing Clay Sewer Pipe. *Designation C12–51T, Book of Standards,* 1952, Part 3.

19.3. Anderegg, F. O.: Efflorescence. *ASTM Bull.* 185, Oct., 1952, p. 39.

19.4. *Brick and Clay Record:* What to Do about Efflorescing Walls, v. 110, No. 3, Mar., 1947, p. 41.

19.5. Connor, C. C.: "Factors in the Resistance of Brick Masonry Walls to Moisture Penetration." *Proc. ASTM,* v. 48, 1948, p. 1020.

19.6. Connor, C. C.: "Some Effects of the Grading of Sand on Masonry Mortar." *Proc. ASTM,* v. 53, 1953.

19.7. Emery, F. E.: "The Manufacture of Structural Clay Products." *Civil Eng.,* v. 7, No. 11, Nov., 1937, pp. 755–759.

19.8. Federal Seaboard Terra Cotta Corp.: *Architectural Terra Cotta and Wall Ashlar.* New York.

19.9. Furnas, C. C.: *Rogers' Industrial Chemistry.* New York, D. Van Nostrand Co., 6th ed., v. 1, 1942, pp. 814–850.

19.10. Gay, C. M., and Parker, H.: *Materials and Methods of Architectural Construction.* John Wiley & Sons, 2nd ed., 1943, 636 pages.

19.11. Lent, L. B.: *Brick Engineering: Design and Construction of Brick Buildings,* v. 2, Cleveland, Ohio, Common Brick Mfrs. Assoc. Am., 1931.

19.12. McBurney, J. W.: "Cracking in Masonry Caused by Expansion of Mortar." *Proc. ASTM,* v. 52, 1952, p. 1228.

19.13. McBurney, J. W., and Eberle, A. R.: Freezing-and-Thawing Tests for Building Brick. *Proc. ASTM,* v. 38, Part II, 1938, pp. 470–483.

19.14. McBurney, J. W., Copeland, M. A., and Brink, R. C.: "Permeability of Brick-Mortar Assemblages. *Proc. ASTM,* v. 46, 1946, p. 1333.

19.15. Mulligan, J. A.: *Handbook of Brick Masonry Construction.* McGraw-Hill Book Co., 1942, 526 pages.

19.16. National Brick Manufacturers Research Foundation: "Reinforced-Brick Masonry." Danville, Ill., *Bull.* 5, Feb., 1932, 89 pages.

19.17. Nord, M.: *Textbook of Engineering Materials.* John Wiley & Sons, 1952, Chap. 19.

19.18. Plummer, H. C., and Wanner, E. F.: "Modular Size of Clay-Products Units." *J. Am. Ceramic Soc.,* v. 26, 1943.

19.19. Ries, H.: *Clays, Their Occurrence, Properties, and Uses.* John Wiley & Sons, 3rd ed., 1927.

19.20. Rueckel, W. C., and Keplinger, R. B.: "The Effect of De-Airing Dry-Press and Stiff-Mud Bodies for Clay Products Manufacture. *Proc. ASTM,* v. 34, Part II, 1934, pp. 480–489.

19.21. Searle, A. B.: *The Chemistry and Physics of Clays and Other Ceramic Materials.* London, Ernest Benn, Ltd., 2nd ed., 1933.

19.22. Structural Clay Products Institute: *The A.B.C. of Modular Masonry*, 2nd Architectural ed., Washington, D. C.
19.23. U. S. National Bureau of Standards: "Vitrified Paving Brick." *Simplified Practice Recommendation* R1–40, 1940.
19.24. Withey, M. O.: "Tests on Reinforced Brick Masonry Columns." *Proc. ASTM*, v. 34, Part II, 1934, pp. 387–405.
19.25. Withey, M. O., and Wendt, K. F.: "Tests of Mortars for Reinforced Brick Masonry." *Proc. ASTM*, v. 35, Part II, 1935, pp. 426–446.

CHAPTER 20

Refractory, Heat-Insulating, and Acoustical Materials
By GORDON B. WILKES [*]
Revised by LLOYD F. RADER

Refractory Materials

20.1 General. Refractory materials are non-metallic materials that are capable of enduring high temperatures and that are commonly used in the construction of industrial furnaces, boilers, flues, crucibles, converters, dryers, pyrometer tubes, and incinerators. There are two main requirements for a refractory material: first, the ability to withstand high temperatures; and second, the possession of suitable physical and chemical characteristics to withstand hot gases, abrasion, slag action, sudden changes of temperature, flue dust, etc.

20.2 Classification of Refractories. The *alumina-silica refractories* include all the fireclay mixtures, which constitute approximately 70 per cent of the refractory products, and high-alumina refractories.

The *silica refractories* contain from 94 to 97 per cent silica.

The *basic refractories* include magnesite, chrome spinel, other refractory spinels, and forsterite.

The *special refractories* include carbon, silicon carbide, and zirconia materials.

20.3 Manufacture of Refractories. *Fireclay Brick.* Raw fireclays may be roughly divided into two classes: (1) flint clay, which has a hard structure, is slowly affected by water, has no binding qualities and a fairly high fusion temperature; (2) plastic clay, which has a soft structure, breaks down readily upon exposure to weather, has some binding quality and generally a fusion temperature somewhat lower than the flint clays.

Table 20.1 from Ries' *Economic Geology* compares the composition of fireclays and typical brick clays.

The raw clays are mixed and crushed to size, and, generally, calcined fireclay (grog) is added to reduce the shrinkage during burning. Intricate shapes are hand molded. Standard shapes are machine molded by the

[*] Professor of Industrial Physics, Massachusetts Institute of Technology.

Table 20.1

COMPOSITION OF FIRECLAYS AND BRICK CLAYS

Material	SiO_2	Al_2O_3	Fe_2O_3	FeO	CaO	MgO	Alk.	H_2O	CO_2	SO_3
Plastic fireclay	57.62	24.00	1.90	1.20	0.70	0.30	0.70	13.20	—	0.35
Flint fireclay	59.92	27.56	1.03	—	Tr.	Tr.	0.64	10.82	—	—
Brick shale	54.64	14.62	5.69	—	5.16	2.90	5.89	4.59	4.80	—
Calcareous brick clay	38.07	9.46	2.70	—	15.84	8.50	2.76	2.49	20.46	—
Blue shale clay	47.92	14.40	3.60	—	12.30	1.08	2.70	4.85	9.50	1.44

power-press process usually. However, some standard shapes are formed by the stiff-mud process, a dense column extruded through a die being wire cut and the brick formed being repressed.

Before placing the fireclay materials in the kilns, they are usually dried, sometimes by means of a very slow floor drying at a relatively low temperature but more frequently by means of a tunnel dryer heated by the gases from the kilns to a temperature of approximately 121° C. (250° F.).

Fireclay brick may be burned in circular or rectangular down-draft kilns, but the larger producers are using tunnel kilns which burn the brick more uniformly and more quickly than the down-draft kilns. The burning temperature for firebrick is usually between 1149° C. (2100° F.) and 1371° C. (2500° F.), but in some special instances they are fired to 1621° C. (3000° F.).

High-Alumina Brick. High-alumina brick contain from 50 to 99 per cent aluminum oxide, the remainder being chiefly silica. Raw materials include diasporitic clays, bauxite, and fused crystalline alumina (corundum). The power-press method of manufacture is employed. High-alumina brick are more refractory than fireclay brick and permit insulation of furnace walls at higher temperatures than fireclay brick.

Silica Brick. Silica brick are made, ordinarily, by crushing ganister, which is practically pure silica, and adding approximately 2 per cent of lime as a binding material. The bricks are molded by the soft-mud process, dried, and fired to a temperature of 1483° C. (2700° F.). Silica brick have a very large coefficient of expansion over a portion of the temperature scale as well as a considerable permanent expansion during firing. Great care must therefore be exercised in the control of temperature during firing as well as in service. Their chief use has been found in the steel industry and by-product coke ovens.

Basic Brick. Basic brick are manufactured from ground and blended raw materials of dead-burned magnesite, chrome ore, and olivine. The brick

Refractory, Heat-Insulating, and Acoustical Materials 493

are bonded either by firing, or chemically with the bonding agent such as iron oxide being mixed with the ground materials before pressing. Pressing is accomplished in mechanical or hydraulic presses at high pressure. After drying in controlled-humidity chambers, the brick are fired in tunnel kilns. Common types of basic brick are described below:

Magnesite brick consist essentially of magnesium oxide with approximately 12 per cent of other oxides. They are used primarily in the basic open-hearth process for the manufacture of steel and in various metallurgical processes.

Chrome brick contain from 30 to 40 per cent of chromic oxide, the remainder being mainly oxides of magnesium, aluminum, and silicon. They possess high refractoriness and great resistance to the corrosive action of the usual metallurgical slags.

Chrome-magnesite brick and *magnesite-chrome brick* are made from mixtures of dead-burned magnesite and chrome ore. They possess good mechanical properties.

Spinel is a special refractory produced in an electric furnace consisting of magnesia and alumina in proportions of the formula, $MgO \cdot Al_2O_3$.

Forsterite brick are made from the mineral forsterite ($2MgO \cdot SiO_2$). They have stability of volume and good mechanical strength at high temperatures.

Some chemically bonded basic brick are sheathed with thin sheet steel on three sides but not on the ends. In service in furnaces the brick become welded together and joints are thus eliminated, forming a strong structure that is resistant to spalling.

Special Refractories. Carbon brick are neutral and practically infusible. They are utilized for lining the bosh and hearth of blast furnaces.

Silicon carbide brick are electric-furnace products consisting of 85 to 95 per cent of silicon carbide. Silicon carbide is highly refractory and has a high thermal conductivity.

Zirconia (ZrO_2) and *zircon* ($ZrSiO_4$) are two compounds of zirconium that are sometimes used as special refractories.

20.4 Tests for Refractories. The following tests for refractories have been standardized by the American Society for Testing Materials.

Fusion test is carried out by making small cones of the refractory and heating at a specified rate until they soften and bend over, the temperature at which this occurs being noted with the aid of pyrometric cones. Pyrometric cone equivalent (P.C.E.) is defined as the number of the standard cone whose tip touches the supporting plaque simultaneously with a cone of the refractory being tested in the same furnace.

Load test consists of heating full-sized brick on end with a load of 25 pounds per square inch applied to the end of the brick. The percentage change in length after being heated in accordance with a time-temperature schedule serves as a measure of the load-carrying capacity at high temperatures.

Reheat test consists of heating full-sized bricks in a furnace in accordance with a time-temperature schedule and measuring the change in dimensions.

This test indicates the permanent shrinkage or expansion to be expected from the bricks when placed in a furnace.

Panel spalling test measures the resistance of brick to structural and thermal spalling. The brick, 14 in number, are laid flat as headers to form a movable panel approximately 18 inches square. The back of the panel is insulated, and the front of the panel is subjected to heat treatments. After a 24-hour preheating, the panel is given a thermal shock treatment consisting of a number of cycles of heating it within a specified time to a specified temperature and rapidly cooling by means of a specified blast. The average percentage loss in weight for all the brick in the test panel is reported.

Thermal conductivity of refractories is measured by means of standardized apparatus. (See Art. 20.10 for formula for calculating the coefficient of thermal conductivity. See Table 20.4 for typical values.)

Cold-crushing strength and *modulus of rupture* tests are standardized. The cold-crushing strength is of minor importance, but fireclay brick should have a strength of at least 1500 pounds per square inch.

20.5 Properties of Refractories. Physical properties of refractory bricks are given in Table 20.2. For fireclay brick, ASTM specifications require

Table 20.2

PHYSICAL PROPERTIES OF REFRACTORY MATERIALS *

Type of Refractory Brick	True Specific Gravity	Pyrometric Cone Equivalent	Approximate Softening Temperature, °F.	Linear Subsidence, %	Temp., °F.	Cold-Crushing Strength, p.s.i.	Modulus of Rupture, p.s.i.
Fireclay							
Superduty	2.65–2.75	33–34	3173–3200	3–9	2640	900–4000	600–1300
High-duty (aluminous)	2.60–2.70	31–33	3074–3173	1–10	2460	1000–6000	400–2000
Intermediate-duty	2.55–2.65	29–31	2984–3056	3–10	2460	1200–6000	600–2200
Low-duty	2.55–2.65	19–26	2768–2903			2000–6000	1000–2000
High-alumina							
50% alumina	2.75–2.85	34–35	3200–3245	2–7	2640	2500–5000	1000–1500
70% alumina	3.15–3.25	36–38	3290–3335	2–5	2640	4000–6000	1200–1500
90% alumina	3.55–3.65	39–40	3389–3425	1–3	2910	4000–7000	1200–2000
99% alumina	3.70–3.90	41–42	3620	0–3	3000	5000–9000	1500–3000
Silica	2.30–2.38	31–32	3056	10	2984	1000–3000	400–1200
Basic							
Magnesite	3.40–3.60		3992	10	2984	5000–10,000	1500–3000
Chrome	3.90–4.10		3542–3998	0	2597	3000–6000	1200–2000
Chrome-magnesite †	3.90–4.10					2000–4000	750–1000
Magnesite-chrome †	3.60–3.80					2000–4000	750–1000
Forsterite	3.30–3.40		3470	0	2462	1500–4000	450–800

* Typical values for standard 9-in. straight brick.
† Chemically bonded.

Refractory, Heat-Insulating, and Acoustical Materials 495

the tabulated values of permanent shrinkage in the reheat test. The Pyrometric Cone Equivalents for the following types of fireclay brick are given in Table 20.2.

Type of Fireclay Brick	Maximum Percentage Permanent Shrinkage	Temperature of Test, °F.
Superduty	1	2912
High-duty	1.5	2462
Intermediate-duty	3	2462
Low-duty	No requirement	

Concerning resistance to slags, fireclay brick have fair resistance and high-alumina good resistance to both acid and basic slags. Silica brick possess good resistance to acid slag, but poor resistance to basic slag. The basic refractory bricks have fair resistance to acid slag, but good resistance to basic slag.

For high-temperature furnaces, it is advisable to lay the brick with as thin joints as possible. The bricks, therefore, should be uniform in shape and dimensions. A standard firebrick is 9 inches by $4\frac{1}{2}$ inches by $2\frac{1}{2}$ inches in size.

20.6 Refractory Mortars. Refractory mortars are used for bonding refractory brickwork. Such mortars are of two general classes:

1. Hot-setting bonding mortars.
2. Air-setting bonding mortars.

The main constituent is similar to that of the brick to be bonded with additions of grog to reduce shrinkage. For the hot-setting class, bond is obtained by heating the material at furnace temperatures; for the air-setting class, a chemical bonding agent such as sodium silicate is added.

Heat-Insulating Materials

20.7 General. The chief reason for the use of heat insulation is the conservation of heat, but insulation is often required for other purposes.

In many buildings the cold-water pipes are insulated, not for the purpose of saving heat but to prevent condensation of water vapor when the relative humidity is high. The roofs of textile and paper mills are usually insulated for the same reason.

Insulation may serve as a protection for structural steel in order to decrease the fire hazard. Unprotected structural steel will soften in approximately 10 minutes under a severe fire exposure, but if it is suitably protected by insulation the time before failure can be extended to an hour or more.

An insulated structure is cooler in summer as well as more comfortable in winter than an uninsulated type. The use of insulation will always tend to make a more uniform distribution of temperature regardless of whether it is applied to a building, a furnace, an oven, or a cold-storage room.

Insulation permits the use of the more convenient but more expensive fuels for heating purposes, and it also tends to make more comfortable working conditions around furnaces, kilns, ovens, etc.

20.8 Classification of Insulating Materials. Insulating materials are generally divided into three main groups in accordance with their ability to withstand temperature, but with any arbitrary grouping of this nature there is bound to be considerable overlapping.

Low-temperature insulation for use below 100° C. (212° F.). Cold storage, hot water, building insulation, etc.

Moderate-temperature insulation for use between 100° C. (212° F.) and 538° C. (1000° F.). Steam pipes, ovens, low-temperature furnaces, etc.

High-temperature insulation for use above 538° C. (1000° F.). Furnaces, kilns, etc.

20.9 Composition and Uses. *Low-Temperature Insulation.* The composition by substances of commercial forms of heat-insulating materials for building construction is given in Table 20.3.

Table 20.3

COMPOSITION OF HEAT-INSULATING BUILDING MATERIALS

Commercial Form	Metal (Aluminum and Steel)	Mineral				Cellulose				Animal Hair
		Rock, Slag, and Glass Wool	Vermiculite	Perlite	Miscellaneous	Wood Fiber	Cane Fiber	Cork	Cotton	
Reflective sheets	x									
Aggregates			x	x	x					
Loose fills		x	x			x		x		
Blankets		x				x			x	x
Bats		x								
Slabs		x	x			x	x	x		x
Boards						x	x			

Reflective insulation includes bright metal surfaces such as aluminum and steel. Their heat-resisting characteristics depend upon their bright surfaces since bright metallic surfaces have a low emissivity. (The emissivity of a black surface is 1.0 since it absorbs all the radiation striking it; other surfaces have values less than 1.0, the brighter metallic surfaces having low values, for example, aluminum foil = 0.05, polished aluminum surface = 0.045, and polished sheet steel = 0.20.) Typical commercial forms are aluminum-foil-surfaced blankets, sheet-aluminum blankets, and sheet-steel reflective insulation.

Aggregates. Light-weight aggregates such as vermiculite and perlite are utilized to produce insulating plaster and insulating concrete of low thermal conductivity. (See Table 20.4.) Miscellaneous light-weight aggregates are also used in concrete for insulating purposes. (See Art. 18.51.)

Loose fills are made with both mineral and cellulose materials. Mineral materials include rock wool, slag wool, glass wool, and vermiculite. Cellulose loose-fill materials include wood-fiber insulation and granulated cork.

Rock wool is manufactured from a variety of limestones and shales which are charged with alternate layers of coke in a cupola. Cupolas range from 2 to 6 feet in diameter and from 7 to 16 feet in height. The rock is melted by the heat produced by burning the coke under forced draft at melting temperatures ranging from 1260° C. (2300° F.) to 1871° C. (3400° F.). As the molten rock flows from the bottom of the cupola, it is blown by a steam blast into shreds and then cooled in an annealing chamber. Fiber diameters range from 5 to 10 microns.

Slag wool is similar to rock wool; it is manufactured from blast-furnace slag or from copper or lead slags. Melting temperatures are lower, ranging between 1093° C. (2000° F.) and 1566° C. (2850° F.).

Glass wool (Fiberglas) is made from silica and is composed of fleecy glass fibers. These are made by forcing molten glass through fine orifices and impinging high-pressure jets of steam or air against these streams. Rock, slag, and glass wools are available in fibrous condition (pouring wool) and in granulated form (blowing wool). They are non-flammable.

Wood fiber insulation is manufactured by placing wood chips in a pressure vessel subjected to steam pressures up to 1000 pounds per square inch for a short period of time, and then discharging them suddenly. This treatment tears the wood into fibers. It can be flame-proofed by chemical treatment.

Granulated cork is used for industrial applications such as cold storage.

Blankets are fibrous insulations made from mineral wool, wood fiber, cotton, and animal hair. They are available plain without a backing, or with a paper backing, producing a vapor barrier. They may also be faced with reflective insulation. Blanket thicknesses range from $\frac{1}{2}$ up to $3\frac{5}{8}$ inches.

Bats are manufactured from mineral wool and are similar to blankets but are thicker (2 to $3\frac{5}{8}$ inches) and smaller in size.

Slabs (blocks) are generally 1 inch or more thick and come in different sizes up to 24 by 48 inches. Materials used are indicated in Table 20.3; in addition a cellular-rubber slab is made of synthetic rubber containing cells filled with nitrogen. Mineral-wool slabs are manufactured of mineral wool with a binding agent and are formed into rigid units. Vermiculite coated with asphalt is formed into slabs with an asphalt-treated felt on each side. Slabs are also made of shredded wood with Portland cement or magnesite cement. A slab for industrial applications is made of insulating boards (cellulose) with a coating of asphalt. Corkboard slabs are made of compressed and baked cork granules; rosin in the cork binds the granules together, resulting in a slab of natural cork. Their main use is for cold-storage installations, but they are also employed as roof insulation and in molded shapes for pipe insulation.

Structural-insulating boards are manufactured from wood, cane, and other vegetable fibers by reducing the fibers to a pulp and then by means of a felting process forming the fibers into boards. Suitable sizing material is incorporated to render the boards water resistant. After drying, a rigid board of good tensile and compressive strength is produced. These boards are sold commercially in the form of building board, roof and wall sheathing, lath, planks, and tileboard. A fire-resistant finish is usually applied to structural-insulating boards. (Example: U. S. Department of Commerce fire-resistant insulation board CS42–49 with Class F finish.)

Another rather interesting development in this field of insulation is the use of chopped paper mixed with silicate of soda that is sprayed on the walls with compressed air. Any desirable thickness up to 2 inches may be applied by this method.

Moderate-Temperature Insulation. The well-known 85 per cent magnesia, consisting of 15 per cent asbestos fiber and 85 per cent of the light carbonate of magnesia, is used considerably for temperatures under 315° C. (600° F.). Above this temperature mixtures of diatomaceous earth and asbestos are frequently used as are also mixtures of expanded vermiculite and a heat-resistant binder. Mineral and rock wool are suitable, and there are a considerable number of asbestos cements that serve well for filling irregular openings and surfaces. In general the asbestos cement is not as good an insulator as the molded product and should only be used where one of the molded shapes is impracticable.

High-Temperature Insulation. A large number of insulating blocks and bricks composed chiefly of diatomaceous earth and porous clays can be used up to temperatures ranging from 760° C. (1400° F.) to 1482° C. (2700° F.). Above 1482° C. (2700° F.) some type of firebrick or refractory product, such as silica, magnesite, silicon carbide, or zirconia, is required.

The following physical properties should be considered when choosing an insulating material:

Refractory, Heat-Insulating, and Acoustical Materials

20.10 Coefficient of Thermal Conductivity. This is usually expressed in the English system of units by K_f, which indicates the number of B.t.u. per hour that will pass through an area of 1 square foot, with a thickness of 1 inch, when there is a 1° F. temperature difference between the two surfaces of the material.

$$K_f = \frac{q \times l}{A(t_2 - t_1)}$$

where q = B.t.u. per hour.
l = thickness in inches.
A = area in square feet.
t_2 = temperature of hotter surface, °F.
t_1 = temperature of cooler surface, °F.

The coefficient of thermal conductivity should not be confused with the term "conductance," which compares the insulating value of two materials without taking account of the thickness.

$$C = \frac{q}{A(t_2 - t_1)}$$

The term "transmittance" expresses the "over-all" resistance to heat flow and includes the two surface resistances.

$$U = \frac{q}{A(t_2 - t_1)}$$

where t_2 = temperature of the air on hotter side.
t_1 = temperature of the air on colder side.

The coefficient of thermal conductivity varies with the temperature, usually increasing with increasing temperatures except in metals. Values for typical heat-insulating materials are given in Table 20.4.

20.11 Water Resistance. In low-temperature work, there is frequently a tendency for water vapor to condense in the walls with a consequent lowering of efficiency of the insulation. The insulating material should be water resistant. It should be protected from the infiltration of air, particularly from the warmer side, since air passing through the wall from the colder side to the warmer side is slowly warmed and there is no tendency for condensation of water vapor under such conditions.

20.12 Fire Resistance. This factor is very important in building construction since many of the insulating materials consist of organic material. Many of the fiber boards are treated with material that renders them somewhat fire retardant.

Table 20.4
PROPERTIES OF HEAT-INSULATING MATERIALS

Material	Density, lb. per cu. ft.	Maximum Safe Temperature, °F.	Coefficient of Thermal Conductivity	Mean Temperature, °F.
Rock wool	3.5	1500	0.29	90
	10.0	1500	0.27	90
Rock-wool bats	3.0	1500	0.31	90
Glass wool	1.6	—	0.30	90
	5.4	—	0.22	90
Cellular glass slab	10.5	—	0.40	50
	10.5	—	0.55	300
Vermiculite	—	—	0.48	—
Wood fiber	3.0	212	0.31	—
Wood-fiber insulating board	16.0	212	0.33	70
Cane-fiber insulating board	13.2	—	0.34	86
Corkboard	10.6	212	0.30	90
Chopped paper, sprayed on	4.2	—	0.28	94
Cotton	2.45	—	0.24	90
Hairfelt	10–20	212	0.3	90
85% magnesia	20	650	0.5	—
Diatomaceous earth	18	1200	0.5	—
Insulating firebrick	20–60	1600–2900	0.8–2.2	400
Fireclay brick	100–130	2600–3000	6–8	—
Common-clay brick	—	—	5.0	—
Concrete, sand and gravel aggregate	142	—	12.6	—
Concrete, expanded vermiculite aggregate	20	—	0.68	—
Wood, Douglas fir, 0% moisture	34	212	0.67	75
Wood, red oak, 0% moisture	48	212	1.18	75

In addition to the above factors, a suitable insulating material must be able to withstand the temperature and other physical and chemical conditions of the particular situation.

20.13 Standard Tests. The most important of the standard tests for determining the resistance to heat transfer of various materials are the following:

Plate Test. This test is used to determine the coefficient of thermal conductivity of materials that come in flat sheet form.

Box Test. A guarded-box test serves admirably to determine the rate of heat flow through built-up wall sections.

Water-Vapor Permeability Test. This test method for determining the water-vapor permeability of sheet materials includes the desiccant method and the water method.

Structural Tests. These tests include modulus of rupture and compressive strength of preformed blocks and transverse strength, deflection, and tensile strength of structural-insulating boards.

Acoustical Materials

BY LLOYD F. RADER

20.14 General. The term acoustical materials is applied to those materials possessing special sound-absorptive properties. All materials have some noise-reducing characteristics, but only those with outstanding sound-absorptive properties are classed as acoustical materials. These materials are employed to improve auditory conditions and for noise reduction in rooms where there are disturbing noises.

Sound-absorption consists of conversion of sound energy into other forms of energy and finally into heat. Sound-absorption depends primarily upon the porosity of materials. Materials with many small interconnecting pores that penetrate deeply are especially efficient in absorbing sound. Sound waves enter these pores where a part of their energy is converted into heat because of viscous and frictional resistance and also because the sound waves may cause vibration of very fine fibers in the material. Sound insulation may be augmented by vibration of thin panels caused by the alternating pressure of sound waves which converts energy into heat.

20.15 Sound-Absorption Coefficient. The sound-absorption coefficient is a measure of the efficiency of a material to absorb energy at a definite frequency. This coefficient is the ratio of the energy absorbed by the material from an impinging sound wave to the total acoustical energy. A sabin is the unit designated to represent the equivalent of 1 square foot of absorptive surface having an absorption coefficient of 1.0. Thus an area A which has an absorption coefficient α possesses a total absorption of $A\alpha$ sabins. Values of sound-absorption coefficients for various frequencies for various types of acoustical materials are given in Table 20.5.

20.16 Types of Acoustical Materials. There are three general types of acoustical materials: (1) prefabricated units and tiles, (2) blankets, and (3) acoustical plaster and sprayed-on materials. The classification of these materials according to U. S. Federal Specification is given in Table 20.6. In Table 20.5 sound-absorption coefficients for typical materials of each type and class are tabulated for different frequencies.

20.17 Acoustical Treatment. Acoustical treatment is provided for rooms in which music or speech should be clearly heard. For music, the various component frequencies must be preserved so as to be heard without distortion. For speech, the individual speech sounds must be distinguishable

Table 20.5
SOUND-ABSORPTION COEFFICIENTS OF ACOUSTICAL MATERIALS

U.S. Federal Specification SS-A-118-a Type	Material	Thickness, in.	Nature of Surface	Weight, lb. per sq. ft.	128	256	512	1024	2048	4096
					\multicolumn{6}{c}{Absorption Coefficients (at frequencies indicated in cycles per sec.)}
			Prefabricated Units *†							
IA	Blocks, mineral granules, P.C. binder	5¾	Unpainted; joints not sealed	23.4	0.63	0.84	0.46	0.37	0.59	0.49
IB	Blocks, small mineral granules, gypsum binder	1	Integrally painted		0.12	0.30	0.74	0.76	0.71	0.67
IC	Cork granules and mineral binder	1	Factory-painted		0.11	0.26	0.66	0.90	0.74	0.79
IIA	Asbestos with non-absorbent face 3/16-in. thick	1 3/16	Perforated; painted			0.70	0.65	0.65	0.75	0.70
IIB	Compressed wood fibers	5/8	Perforated; painted	0.56	0.10	0.16	0.62	0.97	0.81	0.73
IIC	Wood fiber	3/4	Slotted; painted	0.91	0.09	0.28	0.68	0.80	0.79	0.81
III	Cork	3/4	Fissured; painted	1.13	0.12	0.27	0.72	0.79	0.76	0.77
IVA	Shredded wood, cement binder	3/4	Unpainted	1.75	0.06	0.17	0.37	0.68	0.82	0.74
IVB	Felted mineral fiber	1		0.54	0.18	0.42	0.81	0.75	0.71	0.72
IVC	Felted glass fiber	3/4	Painted	0.69	0.04	0.20	0.63	0.91	0.82	0.82

Refractory, Heat-Insulating, and Acoustical Materials

Blanket

Material	Thickness (in)							
Rock wool blanket	1	1.04	0.15	0.37	0.89	0.98	0.89	0.86

Sound-Absorptive Plaster and Sprayed-On Fibers

	Material	Thickness (in)							
I	Gypsum acoustic plaster on metal lath; finished with cork float	½		0.10	0.22	0.42	0.78	0.78	0.70
II	Porous plaster; applied with trowel	½		0.28	0.43	0.47	0.50	0.46	0.42
III	Sprayed asbestos fibers; sprayed on metal lath; finished with roller	½		0.25	0.78	0.97	0.81	0.82	0.85

Non-Acoustic Building Materials

Material	Thickness (in)							
Gypsum plaster, scratch and brown coats on metal lath, on wood studs	⅜		0.02	0.03	0.04	0.06	0.06	0.03
Lime plaster, sand finish, on metal lath			0.04	0.05	0.06	0.08	0.04	0.06
Concrete, poured			0.01	0.01	0.02	0.02	0.02	0.03
Brick wall, Unpainted	18		0.02	0.02	0.03	0.04	0.05	0.07
Brick wall, Painted	18		0.01	0.01	0.02	0.02	0.02	0.02
Wood sheathing, pine, Unpainted	¾		0.10	0.11	0.10	0.08	0.08	0.11

* Unit size, 12 in. by 12 in. except IA = 7⅜ in. by 15⅞ in. and IIA = 16 in. by 16 in.
† Mountings on hard rigid material such as concrete.

Table 20.6

CLASSIFICATION OF ACOUSTICAL MATERIALS

(According to U. S. Federal Specification SS-A-118-*a*)

Type	*Prefabricated Units*
I	Cast units having a pitted or granular-appearing surface.
	Class A. All-mineral units composed of small granules or finely divided particles with Portland cement binder.
	Class B. All-mineral units composed of small granules or finely divided particles with lime or gypsum binder.
	Class C. Units composed of small granules or finely divided particles of mineral or vegetable origin with incombustible mineral binder.
II	Units having mechanically perforated surface; the perforations to be arranged in a regular pattern.
	Class A. Units having a perforated surface which acts as a covering and support for the sound absorbent material. The facing material to be strong and durable and substantially rigid.
	Class B. Units having circular perforations extending into the sound-absorbent material.
	Class C. Units having slots or grooves extending into the sound-absorbent material.
III	Units having a fissured surface.
IV	Units having a felted-fiber surface.
	Class A. Units composed of long wood fibers.
	Class B. Units composed of fine felted vegetable fibers or wood pulp.
	Class C. Units composed of mineral fibers.

Type	*Acoustical Plaster and Sprayed-On Materials*
I	Acoustic plaster. This shall be composed of a cementitious material such as gypsum, Portland cement, or lime with or without an aggregate.
II	Acoustic materials other than acoustic plaster which are applied with a trowel.
III	Fibrous materials combined with a binder agent and which are applied by being sprayed on with an air gun or blower.

so that a speaker can be understood. Reverberation of sound is the main factor affecting the acoustics of a room, and reduction in reverberation is usually required for rooms where poor acoustical conditions are encountered.

Sound waves striking surfaces of a room are partly absorbed and partly reflected; reflected sound waves continue to move along their paths until they strike another surface where they are again partly absorbed and partly reflected. Walls of plaster, concrete, brick, and wood absorb less than 11 per cent of sound waves striking them. (See Table 20.5.) Hence, room walls built of ordinary building materials may have a great deal of reverberation, and the music and speech sounds are not dampened rapidly but are heard along with new sounds causing a great number of indistinguishable

Refractory, Heat-Insulating, and Acoustical Materials

sounds. Such rooms may be improved in acoustical conditions by installing acoustical materials with good sound-absorbing properties.

The period of reverberation is defined as the time in seconds for sound to decrease to one millionth of its initial intensity after the source is stopped. The W. C. Sabine formula for computing the period of reverberation is:

$$T = 0.05V/a$$

in which T = period of reverberation of room, in seconds.
V = volume of the room, in cubic feet.
a = total absorption of the surfaces of the room, in sabins.

Where the desirable period of reverberation is known and the volume of the room is constant, the total absorption required can be computed by the Sabine formula. The amount of absorption to be added can be calculated by subtracting the absorption of the ordinary walls from the total absorption required. The necessary area of acoustical material to be applied to walls and ceiling of a given room can be calculated by dividing the amount of absorption to be added by the net sound-absorption coefficient to be employed after subtracting the coefficient of the surface to be covered. For values of sound-absorption coefficients, see Table 20.5.

20.18 Noise Reduction. Noise reduction may be necessary to provide a quieter condition in a room where there is disturbance. Usually noise reduction requires more absorption of sound than that necessary to produce good acoustical conditions. The reduction in noise level brought about by increasing the absorption of sound in a room may be computed by the formula:

$$\text{Decibel reduction} = 10 \log_{10} \frac{a_2}{a_1}$$

in which a_2 = total absorption in the room after treatment, in sabins.
a_1 = total absorption in the room before treatment, in sabins.

(For further information, see reference 20.8.)

20.19 Painting of Acoustical Materials. Acoustical materials with small pores in the surface such as acoustical plaster and fiberboards will have their sound-absorption coefficients reduced if covered by thick coats of paint. Such materials should therefore not have applications of viscous water or oil paints, varnish, or calcimine. Where painting is required, thin coats of paints, lacquers, stains, or aniline dyes may be applied. The use of a spray gun is recommended rather than a brush. The surface pores should be cleaned by means of a solvent before painting. Some acoustical materials with large perforations or perforated facings may not be affected acoustically by painting if the holes are not covered.

Questions

20.1. Name the principal types of refractory bricks.

20.2. Compare building brick and fireclay brick with respect to: composition of clay, temperature of burning, and structural strength.

20.3. Name and briefly describe four tests for refractories.

20.4. A highly refractory material is desired for the lining of a furnace that is to be used in a metallurgical process in which a large amount of silicon is oxidized to form a slag. What materials might be chosen? Why?

20.5. What refractories are suitable for: (a) the roof of an open-hearth furnace, (b) the hearth of a basic open-hearth furnace, and (c) the lining of an acid Bessemer converter? Give reasons for your answers.

20.6. What are the chief purposes of insulation?

20.7. Name and briefly describe the characteristics and uses of typical insulating materials.

20.8. Name and describe three types of loose-fill insulation.

20.9. Name and describe four types of heat-insulating slabs.

20.10. Describe the manufacture of (1) rock wool, (2) glass wool, (3) wood-fiber insulation, and (4) structural-insulating boards.

20.11. Give two examples of reflective insulation.

20.12. Distinguish between acoustical treatment and noise reduction of rooms.

20.13. Define the unit "sabin."

20.14. Define "time of reverberation."

20.15. Determine the number of square feet of a given type of acoustical material for constructing walls and ceiling of an auditorium if it is desired to have a period of reverberation of 1.1 seconds at 512 cycles per second. The existing wall is gypsum plaster, scratch and brown coats on metal lath on wood studs. The size of the auditorium is 50 by 100 by 20 feet.

20.16. A room 10 feet wide by 20 feet long by 10 feet high has painted brick walls and a plaster ceiling. It is proposed to cover the ceiling with ⅝-inch compressed-wood-fiber prefabricated units, 12 by 12 inches in size. (Type IIB, perforated and painted.) The frequency is 512 cycles per second. Neglect window and door areas. How many decibels reduction would you estimate for this treatment? What would be the approximate time of reverberation after installing the prefabricated units?

20.17. Solve question 20.16 for a frequency of 2048 cycles per second.

References

20.1. American Institute of Mining and Metallurgical Engineers: *Industrial Minerals and Rocks.* New York, 2nd ed., 1949.

20.2. American Society for Testing Materials: "Symposium on Thermal Insulating Materials." Philadelphia, Pa., Mar., 1939. Also: *Manual of ASTM Standards on Refractory Materials,* Feb., 1952. Also: *Book of Standards,* 1952, for refractory and thermal insulating materials.

20.3. Bradley, R. S.: "Insulating Firebrick as a Furnace Lining." *Heat Treating and Forging,* v. 23, 1937, pp. 349–352.

20.4. Chesters, J. H.: *Steelplant Refractories.* United Steel Co., 1944.

Refractory, Heat-Insulating, and Acoustical Materials

20.5. Close, P. D.: *Building Insulation*. Chicago, American Technical Society, 1951, 402 pages.
20.6. Close, P. D.: *Thermal Insulation of Buildings*. New York, Reinhold Publishing Corp., 1947, 104 pages.
20.7. Harbison-Walker Refractories Co.: *Modern Refractory Practice*. Cleveland, Ohio, Caxton Co., 3rd ed., 1950.
20.8. Knudsen, V. O., and Harris, C. M.: *Acoustical Designing in Architecture*. John Wiley & Sons, 1950; Chap. 6, pp. 84–118, and Appendix 1, pp. 405–426.
20.9. Leighou, R. B.: *Chemistry of Engineering Materials*. McGraw-Hill Book Co., 4th ed., 1942; Chaps. 3 and 21.
20.10. Nord, M.: *Textbook of Engineering Materials*. John Wiley & Sons, 1952; Chap. 20, pp. 421–433.
20.11. Norton, F. H.: *Refractories*. McGraw-Hill Book Co., 2nd ed., 1942.
20.12. Rait, J. R.: *Basic Refractories*. Iliffe & Sons, Ltd., London, 1950, 408 pages.
20.13. Searle, A. B.: *Refractories for Furnaces*. Crosby Lockwood & Son, 1939.
20.14. Trinks, W.: "Why and How Insulating Refractories Insulate." *Ind. Heating*, v. 4, 1937, pp. 911–914.
20.15. Vermiculite Institute: *Standard Specifications for Vermiculite Plastering and for Vermiculite Acoustical Plastic*. 208 South LaSalle St., Chicago, Nov., 1951. (A.I.A. File No. 21-A-5.)

Section VII · Timber

CHAPTER 21

Timber[1]

By IRVING H. COWDREY [*]

Revised by LLOYD F. RADER

21.1 General. Timber has been one of the primary materials of engineering construction since the earliest times, and, despite the fact that it has been largely superseded by concrete and steel in certain classes of structures, the consumption of timber for structural and other commercial purposes is very large.

In spite of the many species of trees (something like six hundred grow in the United States alone), the kinds of timber of great commercial importance are very limited in number. The larger part of all timber used structurally is derived from only fifteen distinct groups—those commonly known as *pine, fir, oak, hickory, hemlock, ash, poplar, maple, cypress, redwood, birch, gum, spruce, cedar,* and *walnut.* These common group names usually include several species and varieties, which may show quite diverse characteristics and possess, therefore, very different values as timbers of construction.

The engineer should have some knowledge of the classes of trees and of their growth and structure in order to understand the fundamentals of the physical and mechanical properties of timbers.

Timber Woods—Growth and Structural Characteristics

21.2 Classes of Trees. All trees are primarily divided into two botanical groups according to their manner of growth:

Exogenous trees, or *exogens,* increase in diameter by the annual formation between the old wood and the bark of a layer of new wood which envelops

---

[1] The data upon which this chapter is based are taken, very largely, from the publications of the U. S. Forest Service and the textbooks of Record and Betts.

[*] Associate Professor Emeritus of Testing Materials, Massachusetts Institute of Technology.

the entire living portion of the tree. Practically all classes of commercially important timbers are derived from trees of this group.

Endogenous trees, or *endogens,* grow both diametrically and longitudinally, principally the latter, by the addition of new wood fiber intermingling with the old. Most endogens are small plants like corn, sugar-cane, wheat, and rye, but others, like the palm, the yuccas, and the bamboo, have some value as a source of structural material.

21.3 Exogenous Trees. *Conifers.* Conifers, the needle-leaved trees, form the most important portion of our timber trees, comprising principally the pines, the spruces, fir, hemlock, larch, cedar, cypress, and redwood. They are usually light and soft, hence often called "softwoods," and are for the most part "evergreens."

Broad-Leaved Trees. Broad-leaved trees comprise many varieties of oak, ash, poplar, hickory, maple, walnut, elm, chestnut, birch, beech, basswood, whitewood (tulip), gum, lignum vitae, mahogany, and many other species of lesser commercial importance. They are usually heavy and hard, hence often called "hardwoods." As a rule, they are deciduous, although many broad-leaved trees are evergreen in certain climates. The broad-leaved woods are not used for structural purposes to anywhere near the same extent as the conifers, but are specially adapted for interior finishing, cabinetwork, furniture, etc.

21.4 Endogenous Trees. This group is confined largely to tropical or semitropical regions. The palms, because of their long, straight stems and comparative immunity from the destructive action of the teredo (a marine wood-borer) are sometimes locally used as piles but have practically no other commercial uses. The bamboo grows with extreme rapidity but requires years to harden after its growth is attained. Bamboo has many commercial applications in Asia, particularly in Japan and in China, where it is even used structurally to a considerable extent.

21.5 Exogenous Growth of Wood.[2] *Pith, Wood, and Bark.* The section of any exogenous tree exhibits a central portion called the pith. It is black, brown, or gray in color, usually of small diameter, and does not increase in size after the first year.

Outside the pith the wood appears in concentric zones or rings of annual growth. The demarkation between the rings, when evident, is because of the difference in structure between the wood slowly formed toward the end of one season and that rapidly formed in the succeeding spring.

The outermost portion, or periphery, of the section is formed by material of variable and very complex structure, called the bark.

---

[2] For a much more detailed treatment of the growth and structural elements of wood, see Record's *Economic Woods of the United States,* Stevens' *Plant Anatomy,* Hough's *Handbook of Trees of the Northern States and Canada,* Snow's *Wood and Other Organic Structural Materials,* and Brown, Panshin, and Forsaith's *Textbook of Wood Technology.*

21.6 Wood Structure. In the broadest interpretation, wood may be considered to be made up of two chief structural elements, *cells* and *vessels*. The elemental cells are technically subdivided as *tracheids*, *wood fibers*, and *parenchyma*. Although there is considerable difference in form and function

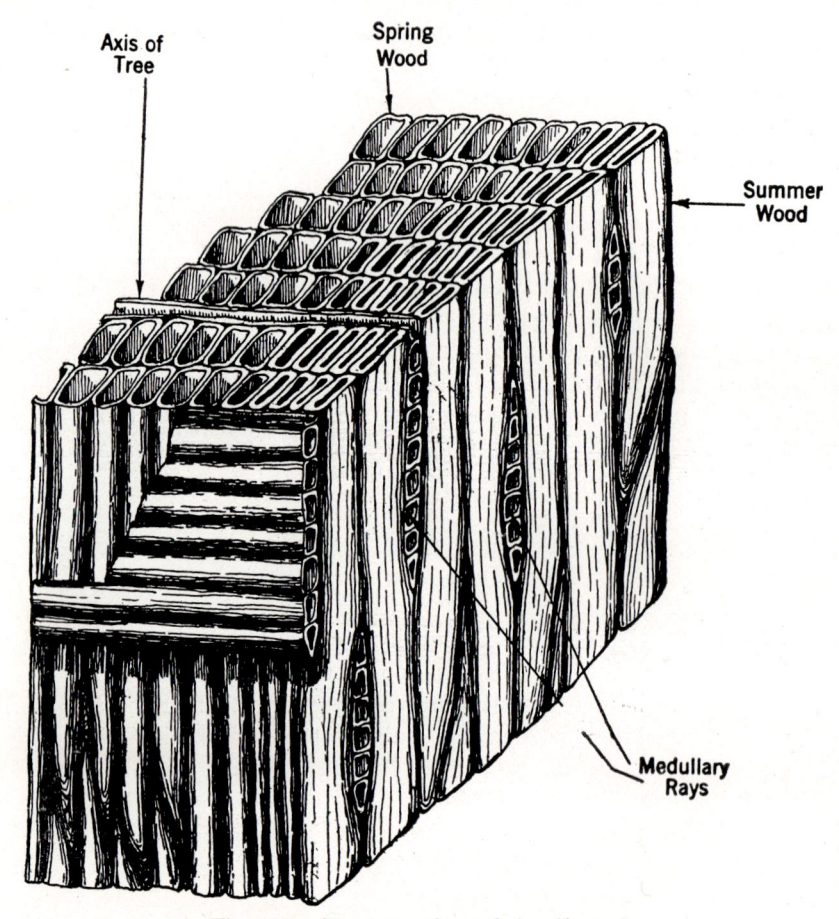

Fig. 21.1. Structure of wood (coniferous).

between these various subdivisions, such distinctions are beyond the scope of this discussion and all these elements will be here referred to simply as cells. In cross-section these cells are roughly polygonal and most commonly appear to be rectangular with rounded corners. In most timber a very large proportion of these cells will be formed with longitudinal axes approximately parallel with the axis of the tree as shown in Fig. 21.1. Other cells, arranged in groups, lie with their axes along lines perpendicular to the axis of the tree, thus passing between the previously noted cells. These radial groups of cells form what are known as *radial, pith, or medullary rays* (Fig. 21.1). Between the late growth of one year and the new growth of the following year the bond is very weak. This weakness is in part neutralized by the "dowel pin" action of the medullary rays which continue without interruption from their several origins to the bark of the tree. The medullary rays in certain woods, such as oak, are frequently of very large vertical dimension. It is to this fact that quarter-sawed oak owes its beautiful figure.

It will be noted in Fig. 21.1 that the cells found in the spring (or early growing season) differ from those of the summer growth (late season) in size, shape, and thickness of wall. In the spring wood, perhaps no more than 10 per cent of the gross area may be cell wall; in the summer wood the actual walls may constitute 90 per cent of the total section.

When wood has been cut into timber and is ready for use, these cells will, for the most part, be empty. Their behavior under stress will be similar to that of a collection of empty tubes. The strength of the individual cell will then bear some relation to the thickness of its wall. If the stress is applied parallel with the "grain," failure will in general occur when the cells crumple; therefore, the heavy-walled summer cells are able to sustain a major share of the total load. A high percentage of summer growth is then conducive to high crushing strength parallel with the grain. When the stress acts along a line perpendicular to the grain and in a radial direction, the summer wood is incapable of bearing its proportionate share of the stress as the thin-walled spring cells collapse like any tubular form under lateral pressure. Hence all woods are very weak under direct compression perpendicular to the grain.

Shrinkage (discussed more fully later) occurs mainly across the cells. There is very little change in length. Heavy cells shrink more than cells with light walls. Hence any wood containing a large percentage of heavy-walled cells will cause more trouble during its seasoning and will be difficult to kiln-dry. Timber with a very small percentage of summer growth (notably white pine) will naturally be weak, but it will present fewer drying problems and will show less tendency to warp and check during seasoning. The crossing of adjacent cells localizes and concentrates shrinkage strains. Hence timber having very large and heavy-celled medullary rays (white oak) is subject to extreme local shrinkage strains and presents a great problem in the dry kiln.

Cell walls consist essentially of cellulose in the form of fibrils which are long spiral strands; some lignin is also present. The walls are anisotropic but are cemented together by a layer of isotropic substance, essentially lignin, called the middle lamina. The cell walls are perforated with recesses, called pits, whose function is to make possible the flow of sap between cells through the middle lamina. Many of the pits occur in pairs, the recesses being opposite each other in adjacent cells.

The *vessels* are formed by the fusion of numbers of cells and are in the form of open tubes often extending the entire length of the tree. They are

Fig. 21.2. Cross-section. *a.* Ring-porous hardwood (white ash). *b.* Diffuse-porous hardwood (red gum). *c.* Non-porous wood (Eastern hemlock). (Photomicrographs 30×.) (Record.)

occasionally large enough to be perceived in the cross-section of wood on the end of a piece with the unaided eye. The absence or arrangement of these vessels, or pores, gives rise to a rough classification of wood into three divisions: namely, "ring porous," Fig. 21.2a; "diffuse porous," Fig. 21.2b; and "non-porous," Fig. 21.2c. In the non-porous woods (conifers in general) there appear tubular spaces between the cells, called "resin ducts." These differ from the vessels of porous wood in that they do not possess true walls.

21.7 Annual Growth Rings. Spring and Summer Wood. The growth of all exogenous trees is a process of formation of new wood fiber between the old wood and the inner bark. This place of formation is a thin layer called the *cambium,* which is invisible without a microscope and in which all growth in thickness of bark and wood takes place. Owing to the inability of trees to sustain their physiological activities indefinitely and the effect of the alternation of seasons in all temperate zones, this growth is intermittent, and the zones of growth in general correspond to the annual periods. The succeeding rings of growth may easily be distinguished from one another in most species because of the different structure of the wood formed rapidly in the spring and that more slowly added in the summer (Figs. 21.1 and 21.2). No wood is added during the winter months. The distinction between adjoining growth rings is sometimes augmented by the deposition of infiltrated pigments or resin in the late wood.

The rate of growth of trees is quite variable, not only in different species, but even for different specimens of the same species. This means that the growth rings are of variable thickness. The thickness of the ring is not even uniform circumferentially, because of unequal acceleration of the growth on different sides; thus the section often becomes oval, and, even if circular, the pith is eccentric (Fig. 21.3).

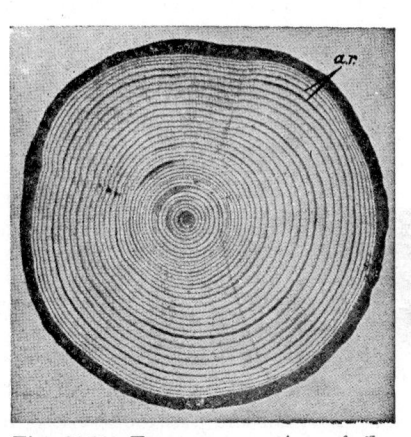

Fig. 21.3. Transverse section of the stem of a young balsam fir tree, showing annual rings of growth, *a.r.* Light rings are spring wood. Dark rings are summer wood. (*Bull.* 55, *U. S. Forest Service.*)

The maximum thickness of growth rings attained during the period of thriftiest growth rarely exceeds 0.5 inch for either conifers or broad-leaved trees. For most trees a thickness of 0.10 to 0.15 inch indicates a good thrifty growth. Trees in dense forests always grow less rapidly than trees in the open.

21.8 Sapwood and Heartwood. As the process of formation of annual rings of new wood adds layer after layer of vigorous healthy tissue over that previously formed, the old tissue gradually ceases to take an active part in the physiological activities of the tree, loses its protoplasmic contents, and dies. Decay does not usually follow immediately, however, and the dead wood continues sound and provides mechanical support for the tree.

The living elements of the tree are called "sapwood"; the dead elements, "heartwood." There is usually a sharp line of demarkation between the sapwood and heartwood, although the vigor of the living wood decreases progressively from the cambium inward. The proportion of sapwood varies considerably in different species and also between individuals of the same species. All young trees show a higher percentage of sapwood than old trees of the same species.

The distinction in color between sapwood and heartwood, which is characteristic of most woods, is due to the darkening of the dead wood by the presence of infiltrated pigment, gums, resins, etc., which permeate the cell walls and sometimes also the cellular and intercellular cavities. Certain woods, like spruce, fir, hemlock, poplar, willow, and gum, show little or no difference in appearance between the two portions.

As a rule, the heartwood is more highly valued than the sapwood of the same variety. This is because the heartwood offers greater resistance to decay than the sapwood. So far as strength is concerned, the prejudice in favor of the heartwood is entirely without justification, since the sapwood, except in very old trees, is equal to the adjoining heartwood in strength. There are, however, noteworthy instances in which the sapwood is preferable, as, for example, hickory, ash, birch, all the paper-pulp woods, and timber to be treated with preservatives.

Physical Characteristics of Wood

21.9 Slash and Rift Cut. The structure of wood as previously described gives rise to variations in the characteristics of timber depending upon the angle which the plane of cutting makes with the two systems of cells, Fig. 21.4. When the saw cut is approximately perpendicular to the axis of the tree the surface is said to be *cross cut* or *end grain*. A cut paralleling the axis of the tree and in a plane approximately radial (parallel with medullary rays) produces a surface known as *rift cut*. Rift-cut lumber is also known as edge-grain lumber in softwoods and as quarter-sawed in hardwoods. When the cutting plane is perpendicular to the medullary rays, that is, more or less tangential to the annual rings, the surface is *slash cut*. Slash-cut lumber is also called flat-grain lumber in softwoods and plain-sawed in hardwoods. Usually rift-cut lumber is not cut strictly parallel with the medullary rays, and often in slash-cut boards the material near the edges is far from being tangent to the annual rings. It is commercial practice to call lumber with annual rings from 45 to 90° with the surface rift-cut, whereas material with rings from 0 to 45° with the surface is called slash-cut.

Rift-cut lumber has the following principal advantages as compared with slash-cut lumber: (1) it shrinks and swells less in width; (2) it twists and cups less; (3) it does not surface check or split so badly in seasoning and in use; (4) it wears more evenly; (5) types of figure coming from pronounced rays, interlocked grain, and wavy grain are brought out conspicuously; (6) width of sapwood in a board depends on width of sapwood in the log; (7) it holds paint better in some species.

Slash-cut lumber, on the other hand, has the following advantages: (1) it is generally cheaper, because it requires less time and involves less waste in cutting; (2) it does not collapse so easily in drying; (3) the figure resulting from the annual rings is brought out conspicuously; (4) circular or oval knots occurring in slash-cut boards affect the strength and surface appearance less than spike knots which may occur in rift-cut boards; however, a greater percentage of the boards from a log sawed to produce all

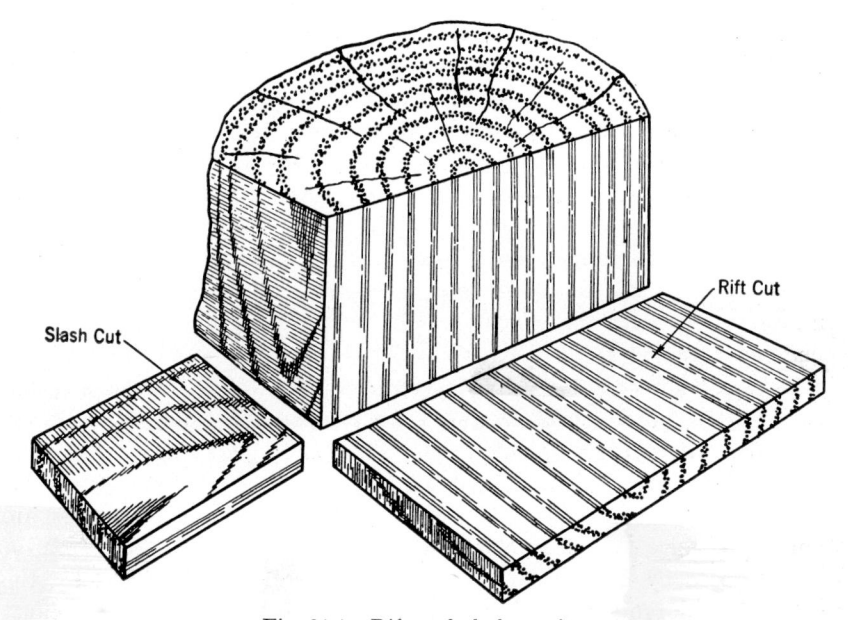

Fig. 21.4. Rift and slash cutting.

slash-cut lumber will contain knots than boards from a log sawed to produce the maximum amount of rift-cut material; (5) shakes and pitch pockets when present extend through fewer boards.

All planks or boards subject to surface wear as flooring or deck planks should be rift-cut. Rift-cut boards may often be obtained most economically by resawing large dimension stock. When the principal cells all lie with their axes closely paralleling the planes of sawing, then the resulting stick will be perfectly straight grained. A very slight distortion of the normally cylindrical layers of growth will produce a variation in the *figure* of the wood yet may have no appreciable effect on the straightness of grain. (See illustration of checks, Fig. 21.5, where the checks show the grain to be practically straight with a decided wave in the figure.)

21.10 Defects in Timber. A defect is any irregularity occurring in or on wood which may lower its strength, durability, or utility. Knots constitute one of the most common defects; they originate in the timber cut from the stem or branches of a tree because of the encasement of a limb, either living or dead, by the successive annual layers of wood. In most structural timber, limbs originate at the pith of the stem, and the knots found deep in a log are therefore small, increasing in size toward the bark. So long as the limb is growing, its layers of wood are a continuation of those of the stem. But a majority of the limbs of conifers die after a time, and, if a portion of a dead limb is subsequently encased by the growing stem, there will be no intimate connection between the new stem wood and the dead wood of the limb, and a board cut so as to intercept this portion of the log will contain an *encased knot*. A board cut from the log at such a depth that the limb is intercepted at a point where it was encased while still living will contain an *intergrown knot* which has annual rings intergrown with those of the surrounding wood. The distortion of the grain around encased knots is less than for intergrown knots. An intergrown knot is usually harder than the surrounding wood and in coniferous woods is likely to be very resinous, which may affect its retentivity of varnish or paint. A *spike knot* is one sawn in a lengthwise direction.

In structural beams the effect of knots on the bending strength largely depends upon their location. Knots in the tension side of a beam near the point of maximum stress will have a significant effect on the maximum load a beam will sustain, whereas knots on the compression side are somewhat less serious. Knots in any position have little effect on shear. Stiffness of beams is not greatly affected by knots.

In long columns, in which stiffness is the controlling factor, knots are not of importance. In short or intermediate columns the reduction in strength caused by knots is approximately proportional to the size of the knot, although large knots have a somewhat proportionately greater effect than small ones.

Knots actually increase hardness and strength in compression perpendicular to grain and are objectionable in regard to these properties only to the extent that they cause non-uniform wear or a non-uniform distribution of pressure at contact surfaces. Knots, however, are harder to work and machine than the surrounding wood, may project from the surface when shrinkage occurs, and are a cause of twisting.

Knots and other common defects found in timber are illustrated in Fig. 21.5. A *shake* is a separation along the grain usually between the rings of annual growth which may be caused by the action of wind on trees. Cracks extending between two faces of a piece of lumber are called *through shakes*. A *check* is a lengthwise separation of the wood, the greater part of which occurs across the rings of annual growth. Checks usually occur in seasoning and are the result of unequal shrinkage. A *pitch pocket* is an opening between the fibers of the wood extending along the grain, usually containing pitch or bark. "Dote," "doze," "rot," and "red heart" are terms

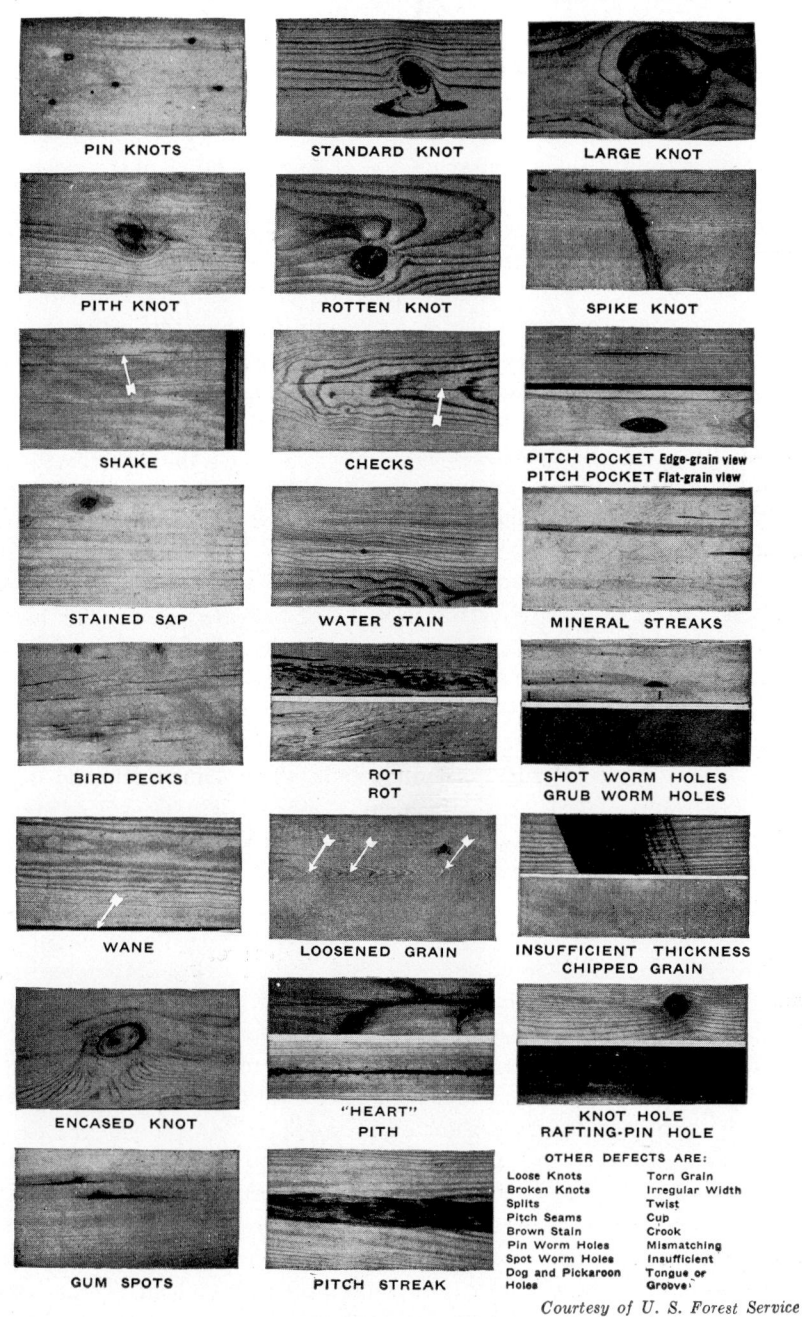

Fig. 21.5. Defects in timber.

synonymous with "decay." *Worm holes* are similar to knots or knot holes in reducing the strength of lumber, but do not involve distortion of the grain. Occasional ones of small diameter do not seriously weaken the wood. *Wane* is bark, or lack of wood or bark from any cause, on edge or corner of a piece. *Cross-grain* is grain not parallel with the axis of a piece. It may be either diagonal or spiral grain. *Compression wood* is abnormal wood formed on the lower side of branches and of leaning trunks of softwood trees which has relatively wide annual rings, a large amount of summer wood, and a dark-reddish to brown color. It tends to shrink excessively lengthwise. *Warp* is any variation from a true or plane surface and includes bow, crook, cupping, and twist. *Bow* is distortion of a board in which the face is convex or concave longitudinally; *crook* is similar distortion of the edge of a board. *Cupping* is transverse distortion of the face of a board. *Twist* is distortion of a board caused by turning of the edges so that the four corners of a board are not in the same plane.

21.11 Grading of Lumber. The purpose of grading lumber is to provide for orderly marketing. The function of grading is the establishment of utility classes in order to make it possible to obtain many individual pieces of similar characteristics. This is especially important for timber because individual pieces sawed from the same log vary a great deal with respect to density, strength, and defects such as knots and blemishes. The lumber associations have established gradings for both softwood and hardwood material.

Softwood lumber is divided into three use classifications: (1) stress-grade (structural) lumber, (2) yard lumber, and (3) factory and shop lumber. Stress-grade lumber includes joist and plank (2 to 4 in. thick and over 4 in. wide), beams and stringers (5 in. by 8 in. and larger), and posts and timbers (5 in. by 5 in. and larger). Stress-grade lumber is graded on the basis of strength and is intended for structural uses where working stresses are required. (See Art. 21.27.) Yard lumber is divided into Select and Common classes. Select has four grades: A and B (suitable for natural finishes such as shellac and varnish) and C and D (suitable for paint finishes). Common yard lumber is for general utility and is divided into five grades: No. 1 to No. 5 inclusive. No. 1 and No. 2 grades can be utilized without waste and are used in good building work; the other three grades are for use that permits some waste. Factory and shop lumber is graded with respect to its use for sash and doors or for general cut-up purposes.

"Density rules" are employed for grading structural lumber such as dense southern yellow pine, dense and close-grained Douglas fir and close-grained redwood. The rule for dense southern yellow pine is typical:

"Dense southern yellow pine shall show on either end an average of at least six annual rings per inch and at least one-third summer wood . . . as measured over the third, fourth, and fifth inches on a radial line from the pith. Wide-ringed material excluded by this rule will be acceptable, provided that the amount of summer wood as above measured shall be at least one-half." (*ASTM Designation* 245–49T).

Hardwood lumber is classed into eight grades by the National Hardwood Lumber Association: Firsts, Seconds, Selects, No. 1 Common, No. 2 Common, Sound Wormy, No. 3A Common, and No. 3B Common. Grading is based largely upon the percentage of "clear cuttings" of a given size which may be cut from the piece.

For special grading rules for different species, reference should be made to specifications of the lumber manufacturers' associations.

21.12 Weight. The specific gravity of the actual wood fiber of all species is about 1.5, so it is apparent that no wood would float in water were it not for the buoyancy of the air present in the cells, walls, and intercellular spaces.

Two factors chiefly influence the weight of wood formed at succeeding periods of growth: first, the proportion of summer wood formed; and second, the size and number of pores present in the early wood. The first is the controlling factor in most conifers; and such trees as pine, spruce, etc., form light wood as saplings when the proportion of early wood is greatest, the heaviest wood during the period of thriftiest growth when summer wood preponderates, and lighter wood again in old age when the proportion of summer wood drops below the maximum. In most broadleaved trees, on the other hand, especially those having conspicuous pores, like the oak, chestnut, ash, etc., the heaviest wood is that of the sapling and the wood becomes slightly lighter with each succeeding year's growth. This is due to the fact that the pores in the wood near the pith are very minute, but larger and larger pores are formed during succeeding periods of growth.

The weight of wood is in itself an important quality in many of its structural uses. Weight is also closely related to strength, provided that the factor of variation in moisture content is eliminated.

21.13 Moisture Content of Wood. The moisture content of a wood sample is determined from thin pieces, whose broad surfaces are perpendicular to the grain of the wood, or from chips. After careful weighing these are heated in an oven held at approximately 99° C. (210° F.) until there is no further loss of weight. The loss of weight (water content) divided by the "oven-dry weight," expressed as percentage, is known as the moisture content.

21.14 Season of Cutting. There is little difference in the moisture content of green wood in winter and in summer. The season of cutting has very little direct effect on the characteristics of the wood itself, but the method of handling after cutting may be important. Seasoning proceeds more rapidly during the summer than during the winter and is more likely to produce checking. Insects, stains, and decay-producing fungi are more vigorous in the summer, and the freshly cut wood is most subject to attack at this time. Winter cutting, therefore, has the advantage that more favorable seasoning conditions and greater freedom from stains, molds, decay, and insects simplify the problem of caring for the timber before conversion.

21.15 Seasoning of Timber.[3] The seasoning or drying of timber frequently precedes its application to structural purposes. The natural drying of timber by long outdoor exposure to the action of the air is called "seasoning"; artificial drying by exposure for a limited period to elevated temperatures in a closed chamber is called "kiln drying." In either method the loss of moisture is entirely by evaporation, and the treatment, if properly carried out, is appreciably beneficial to strength.

Two types of kilns are available for artificial drying: (1) compartment kiln in which the conditions of temperature and humidity are changed as the drying progresses, the lumber being stacked in the compartment, and (2) progressive kiln in which a low temperature with high humidity condition is maintained at the entering end of the kiln and a high temperature with low humidity condition at the exit end, the lumber being moved periodically through the kiln. Both types of kilns may have either natural or forced circulation. The advantages of forced circulation are accurate control of humidity and faster drying without danger to the stock.

In artificial drying, temperatures of 70° to 82° C. (158° to 180° F.) are usually employed. Pine, spruce, cypress, cedar, etc., are dried fresh from the saw, 4 days being allowed for 1-inch boards. Hardwoods, especially oak, ash, maple, birch, and sycamore, are air-seasoned for 3 to 6 months to allow the first shrinkage to take place more gradually and are then exposed to the above temperatures in the kiln for about 6 to 10 days for 1-inch lumber. By employing lower temperatures, 38° to 49° C. (100° to 120° F.), green oak, ash, etc., can be seasoned in dry kilns without danger to the material. Steaming the lumber is commonly resorted to in order to prevent checking and case hardening.

21.16 Shrinkage, Warping, and Checking in Drying. The shrinkage of wood in drying is due solely to the loss of moisture from the walls of the cells. Variation in the water content of the lumina of the lifeless cells and in the protoplasmic contents of the living cells does not affect the volume of the wood in any way.

---

[3] A more detailed discussion will be found in *Seasoning of Wood*, J. B. Wagner; *Timber, Its Strength and Seasoning*, H. S. Betts; and *Properties and Uses of Wood*, A. Koehler.

As moisture is evaporated, the cell walls become thinner; the lumina become larger, and the exterior cross-sectional dimensions become smaller. The contraction of a wood element in a longitudinal direction is scarcely appreciable, however. The total volumetric change of an element is roughly proportional to the original thickness of its walls. The aggregate volumetric change of a mass of thin-walled wood elements is therefore much less than that of a mass of thick-walled elements, Fig. 21.6. This explains the fact that summer wood almost invariably shrinks more than spring wood, its wood elements being thicker-walled, and for the same reason heavy wood shrinks more than lighter wood of the same species.

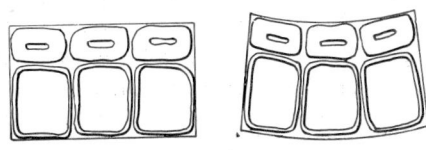

Fig. 21.6. Illustration showing that thick-walled fibers shrink more than thin-walled fibers. (*Bull* 10, *U. S. Forest Service*.)

Shrinkage from green to oven-dry condition in different species ranges as follows: [4]

	Per Cent
Volumetric	7 to 21
Longitudinal	0.1 to 0.3
Radial	2 to 8
Tangential	4 to 14

The amount of shrinkage varies in different directions, being small longitudinally in the direction of the fibers, comparatively large radially, and greatest tangentially. The difference between tangential and radial shrinkage is explained by the fact that bands of dense summerwood are continuous in a tangential direction and shrink a great deal, forcing the bands of springwood along with them. However, in a radial direction summerwood bands alternate with bands of less dense springwood, and the total shrinkage is the summation of shrinkages of summerwood and springwood which is smaller than for all summerwood.

The warping of lumber is due either to unequal drying of different portions or to unequal shrinkage on account of irregularities in structure. Any straight-grained green board exposed on only one side to air and heat will become concave on the exposed side because of the more rapid drying and consequent shrinkage of that side. Boards cut tangentially from the log tend to become convex on the side toward the pith when dried, because of the greater shrinkage of the wood in a direction parallel to the annual growth rings. If lumber is cross grained, the component of the shrinkage in a longitudinal direction causes a warping lengthwise as well as in the

---

[4] See reference 21.14. *Bull.* by Markwardt and Wilson.

transverse direction; and where the grain is spiral, boards may become badly twisted.

Checking of timber in drying is a result of the inability of the lumber to accommodate strains consequent upon unequal shrinkage. A great many small checks occur, particularly in the ends of timbers, owing to the more rapid drying from the cross-section and the consequent excess of shrinkage of the end portion over that of the balance of the timber. Similar checks occur on the sides of logs and timbers because of the precedence of the shrinkage of the outer portion over that of the inner portion, which has

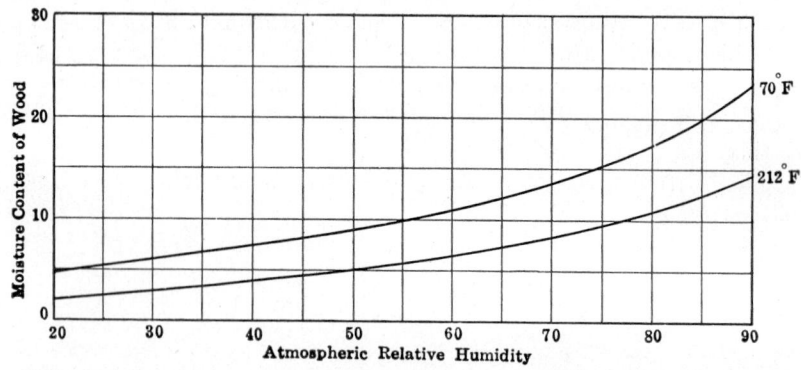

Fig. 21.7. Relation between atmospheric relative humidity and moisture content of wood.

scarcely begun to lose its moisture. Both of these classes of seasoning checks are considered temporary, because they close up and become imperceptible as the inner portion of the timber dries and shrinks. They are still there, whether visible or not, however, and always impair the structural qualities of the wood in some measure.

Another class of checks, more important than the temporary checks, because they are likely to be larger and are permanent, are those caused principally by the shrinkage of timber in a tangential direction along the rings which is greater than that along the radius. The occurrence of the rays in radial planes often contributes to the formation of these large radial checks because they form a plane of weakness at the very point where the strains are the greatest and most complex (two severe stresses existing at right angles to each other, owing to the shrinkage of the rays opposing the shrinkage of the main wood fibers). The danger of the occurrence of large checks of this nature constitutes a serious difficulty in seasoning large timbers, and especially round timbers such as poles, piles, and posts. Too rapid seasoning always increases the danger of injury by excessive checking.

Some woods, mostly hardwoods, become *case hardened* when rapidly dried in the kiln; that is, the outer part dries and shrinks, and commonly checks, while the interior is still practically in its original condition. The drying of the interior is thus retarded, but when it does occur great internal strains are set up, resulting in the formation of large or numerous radial checks which follow the rays. When these checks are comparatively small, but numerous, the wood is said to be *honeycombed*. The case hardening of timber may be avoided by air seasoning before placing it in the kiln or by admitting steam to the kiln.

Wood, when dried, has the ability to reabsorb water from the atmosphere. The amount of water thus acquired always exceeds the moisture content of the air but varies with the humidity, Fig. 21.7. The consequent shrinking and swelling of the wood is a serious handicap if exact fitting is desired. This action may be reduced, but not eliminated, by prolonged exposure to temperatures in the neighborhood of 100° C. (212° F.), or by boiling, steaming, or prolonged soaking.

Mechanical Properties of Woods

21.17 General. The intelligent use of wood for any structural purpose requires a general knowledge of the mechanical properties of different woods, in order that the one selected may conform in its structural qualities to the requirements imposed, and in order that a given purpose may be served at a minimum expense.

Wood is not like many other structural materials in that its mechanical properties are extremely variable, not only between different species and different trees of the same species, but also between specimens cut from different portions of the same tree.

21.18 Tensile Strength. Timber in construction is practically never subjected to pure tensile stresses for the simple reason that the end connections cannot be so devised that they do not involve either shear along the grain or compression across the grain. Since the resistance offered by any timber to compression across the grain, or shearing stress along the grain, never amounts to more than a small fractional part of the tensile strength, it is evident that considerations of economy in the design of structures will frequently call for iron or steel instead of timber for those members which must withstand tension.

Failure in tension across the grain involves principally the resistance offered by the thinner-walled wood elements to being torn apart longitudinally. Wood sustains in tension across the grain only a small fraction (one-tenth to one-twentieth, perhaps) of the load carried in tension along the grain.

21.19 Compressive Strength. The compressive strength of wood in a direction normal to the grain is simply a matter of the resistance offered by the wood elements to being crushed or flattened. The cells with the thinnest walls collapse first, and the action proceeds gradually.

The endwise compressive strength of wood, i.e., the strength of wood in compression along the grain, depends upon the anatomical structure and the moisture content of the wood and the manner of failure is fixed by these same factors. The individual fibers (or other elements) of wood act as so many hollow columns bound firmly together, and failure involves either buckling or bending of the individual fibers or bundles of elements.

21.20 Flexural Strength and Stiffness. The flexural or transverse strength of any material is necessarily closely related to its tensile and compressive strength. In timber beams, whose resistance to shear parallel with the grain is comparatively low, the intensity of longitudinal shear also becomes a very vital factor.

The tensile strength of all timber is greatly in excess of its compressive strength (about three times as much on the average), and the latter will usually be the determining factor in limiting the cross-breaking strength. (Compressive strength will always be the determining factor, assuming there exist no defects such as knots or uneven grain on the tension side of the beam and that the loading is not so placed as to cause high shearing stresses.) It is apparent, therefore, that the considerations which fix the compressive strength similarly affect the cross-breaking strength.

Although the compressive strength is usually the determining factor which limits the transverse strength of wood, it is often only the initial failure which occurs in compression.

The stiffness of timber used structurally as beams is often quite as important as its cross-breaking strength. In plastered ceilings, for instance, the maximum deflection permitted is usually limited to $\frac{1}{360}$ of the span, so that timber beams must be so designed as not only to carry the load imposed safely but also to do so without excessive deflection.

Stiffness of timber largely depends upon the same factors as strength. Dense woods are always stiffer than open, porous woods, and heavy woods are stiffer than light woods except so far as the weight is attributable to moisture contained.

Any attempt to predict the strength of a given piece of timber must take into account the manifold factors which may exert an influence upon this strength. The most important of these are (1) species and variety; (2) locality from which the timber has been obtained; (3) density (see density rule, Art. 21.11); (4) moisture content; (5) defects and their location. The exact weight to be given to these variables is largely a matter of judgment based on extended experience in handling timber, although some attempt has been made to reduce their effect to a more or less mathematical basis.[5]

---

[5] For a detailed description of defects allowable in various structural timbers see *ASTM Specifications* D245–49T.

Timber is commonly so used that the high stresses will be in a direction closely paralleling the grain. The seriousness of most defects lies in the fact that they tend to distort the direction of the grain and so introduce conditions that will cause the major stresses in the member to possess components across the grain of the wood.

21.21 Diagonal Grain. As previously noted, *grain* must not be confused with *figure*. The true inclination of the grain can best be determined by noting the direction of the fine checks in the surface of a timber or by lifting a few fibers with a knife point and noting the direction in which they lie. In specifications diagonal grain is described in terms of the tangent of the angle it makes with the edge of the stick. A slope of 1:20 or less is commonly accepted as straight-grained material. See Table 21.1 for strength ratios corresponding to various slopes of grain.

Table 21.1

STRENGTH RATIOS CORRESPONDING TO VARIOUS SLOPES OF GRAIN *

Maximum Strength Ratio, %

Slope of Grain	For Stress in Extreme Fiber in Bending (Beams and Stringers of Joists and Planks)	For Stress in Compression Parallel to Grain (Posts and Timbers)
1 in 6	—	56
1 in 8	53	66
1 in 10	61	74
1 in 12	69	82
1 in 14	74	87
1 in 15	76	100
1 in 16	80	—
1 in 18	85	—
1 in 20	100	—

* *ASTM Designation D245–49T.*

21.22 Moisture and Strength. All woods gain both in strength and in stiffness when thoroughly air seasoned or kiln dried. The actual net gain which, from a comparison of strength and stiffness of small specimens in the green and oven-dry condition, would appear to be attainable, cannot be even approximately realized in practice, however, because of the operation of several factors which greatly modify the effect of lessened moisture. Checking, for instance, always occurs to some extent in drying lumber and will partly or entirely counterbalance the gain due to drying, the extent of this effect depending upon the size and the variety of the timber.

In lumber 4 in. and less in thickness, the development of defects during seasoning does not offset the increase in strength from drying as much as in larger sizes, and in these smaller sizes used in dry locations, higher working stresses in extreme fiber in bending can be permitted.

Large timbers dried only by air seasoning, even though the process is prolonged for several months or even years, seldom lose sufficient moisture to benefit their strength to more than a slight degree. Such timbers, therefore, cannot be safely depended upon to show any greater strength than if

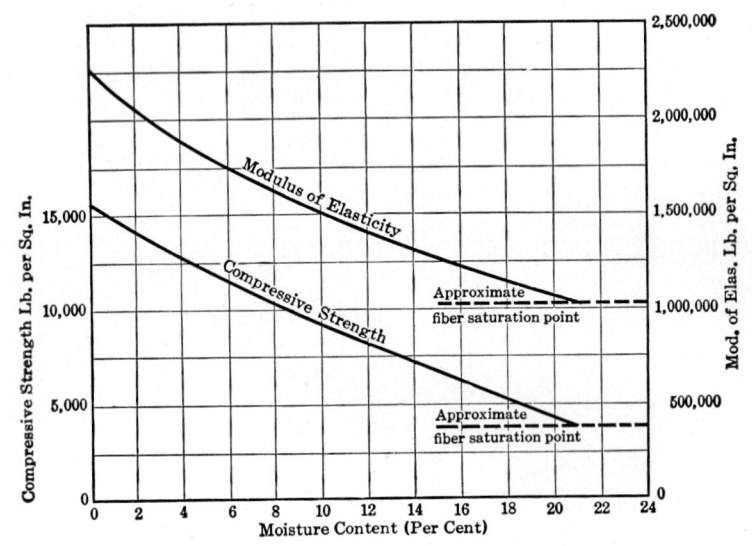

Fig. 21.8. Effect of moisture on properties of longleaf yellow pine.

they were in the original green condition. The explanation of this fact is that a great part of the moisture which is first evaporated from wood is water which exists only as "free water" in the lumina of vessels and cells, whereas only variation in the moisture content of the walls of the wood elements affects strength in any way.

The degree of moisture at which maximum absorption by the cell walls is reached is called the "fiber-saturation point" of the wood. After this point is reached added moisture does not lessen the strength of wood. At this point, also, wood ceases to swell.

The fiber-saturation point is determined experimentally by tests of the strength of very small specimens covering a large range of moisture content. When further moisture no longer lessens the strength, the fiber-saturation point is reached, Fig. 21.8. Tiemann found this point for various woods to be approximately 25 per cent.

21.23 Weight and Strength. The relation between strength and true density (dry) has been carefully studied at the Forest Products Laboratory, and after analysis of the results of many thousand tests the following expressions have been deduced.

Air-dry timber: Modulus of rupture = $26{,}200 \times (\text{sp. gr.})^{1.25}$
Green timber: Modulus of rupture = $18{,}500 \times (\text{sp. gr.})^{1.25}$

This is in general true regardless of species. Like all empirical formulas, the above are somewhat inexact. The actual data show that mean values for different species and variation in locality may deviate from the calculated value by 30 per cent. This, however, is no greater variation than may be expected from individual specimens taken at random from any lot of commercial timber. The above-noted formulas have been derived from tests on small, clear, straight-grained specimens.

21.24 Rate of Growth and Strength. The average rate of growth of timber is readily computed by counting the annual rings along a radial line and dividing by the length of the line. The indications are that for most species there is a rate of growth which, in a very general way, is associated with the greatest strength. For the species tested this appears to be as tabulated.

	Rings per Inch
Douglas fir	24
Shortleaf pine	12
Loblolly pine	6
Western hemlock	18
Tamarack	20
Norway pine	18
Redwood	30

21.25 The Time Factor in Tests of Timber. Timber differs from most other materials in that small variations in the rate of application of load have a more pronounced effect upon the strength and stiffness shown by a specimen under test. If a timber-compression block or beam is loaded rapidly, it will appear to have a higher ultimate strength, and will also appear to be stiffer, than it will if it is loaded less rapidly. This behavior is due to the fact that the deformation lags far behind the load, and if any load is permitted to remain upon a specimen for a sensible time interval the deformation increases, the amount of increase becoming greater for heavier loads. Actual failure appears to be consequent upon the attainment of a certain limiting amount of deformation or strain, rather than a limiting load or stress.

When constant loads amounting to a large fraction of the ultimate strength of timber are sustained for very long periods, the deformation may continue to increase until rupture occurs, even though the stress encountered is far below the ultimate strength of the timber as originally determined. Several

Table 21.2
MECHANICAL PROPERTIES OF A FEW IMPORTANT WOODS GROWN IN THE UNITED STATES *

Common and Botanical Name	Weight, lb. per cu. ft. Green	Weight, lb. per cu. ft. Air-Dry †	Shrinkage from Green to Oven-Dry (in % of green volume)	Modulus of Rupture, p.s.i. Green	Modulus of Rupture, p.s.i. Air-Dry	Modulus of Elasticity, 1000 p.s.i. Green	Modulus of Elasticity, 1000 p.s.i. Air-Dry	Maximum Crushing Strength, Parallel to Grain, p.s.i. Green	Maximum Crushing Strength, Parallel to Grain, p.s.i. Air-Dry	Compression Perpendicular to Grain, Proportional Limit, p.s.i. Green	Compression Perpendicular to Grain, Proportional Limit, p.s.i. Air-Dry	Maximum Shearing Strength, Parallel to Grain, p.s.i. Green	Maximum Shearing Strength, Parallel to Grain, p.s.i. Air-Dry
Hardwoods													
Ash, white (*Fraxinus sp.*)	48	41	12.8	9,500	14,600	1,410	1,680	4,060	7,280	860	1,510	1,350	1,920
Elm, American (*Ulmus americana*)	54	35	14.6	7,200	11,800	1,110	1,340	2,910	5,520	440	850	1,000	1,510
Hickory, true (*Carya sp.*)	63	51	17.9	11,300	19,700	1,570	2,190	4,570	8,970	1,080	2,310	1,360	2,130
Maple, red (*Acer rubrum*)	50	38	13.1	7,700	13,400	1,390	1,640	3,280	6,540	500	1,240	1,150	1,850
Maple, sugar (*Acer saccharum*)	56	44	14.9	9,400	15,800	1,550	1,830	4,020	7,830	800	1,810	1,460	2,330
Oak, red (*Quercus sp.*)	64	44	14.8	8,500	14,400	1,360	1,810	3,520	6,920	800	1,260	1,220	1,830
Oak, white (*Quercus sp.*)	63	47	16.0	8,100	13,900	1,200	1,620	3,520	7,040	850	1,410	1,270	1,890
Walnut, black (*Juglans nigra*)	58	38	11.3	9,500	14,600	1,420	1,680	4,300	7,580	600	1,250	1,220	1,370
Conifers													
Cedar, western red (*Thuja plicata*)	27	23	7.7	5,100	7,700	920	1,120	2,750	5,020	340	610	710	860
Cypress, bald (*Taxodium distichum*)	51	32	10.5	6,600	10,600	1,180	1,440	3,580	6,360	500	900	810	1,000
Douglas fir, coast type (*Pseudotsuga taxifolia*)	38	34	11.8	7,600	12,700	1,570	1,950	3,860	7,430	440	870	930	1,160
Fir, white (*Abies sp.*)	46	27	9.8	5,900	9,800	1,150	1,490	2,830	5,480	360	620	770	990
Hemlock, eastern (*Tsuga canadensis*)	50	28	9.7	6,400	8,900	1,070	1,200	3,080	5,410	440	800	850	1,060
Pine, longleaf (*Pinus palustris*)	55	41	12.2	8,700	14,700	1,600	1,990	4,300	8,440	590	1,190	1,040	1,500
Pine, shortleaf (*Pinus echinata*)	52	36	12.3	7,300	12,800	1,390	1,760	3,430	7,070	440	1,000	850	1,310
Pine, western white (*Pinus monticola*)	35	27	11.8	5,200	9,500	1,170	1,510	2,650	5,620	290	540	640	850
Redwood (old growth) (*Sequoia sempervirens*)	50	28	6.8	7,500	10,000	1,180	1,340	4,200	6,150	520	860	800	940
Spruce, Sitka (*Picea sitchensis*)	33	28	11.5	5,700	10,200	1,230	1,570	2,670	5,610	340	710	760	1,150
Spruce, eastern (*Picea sp.*)	34	28	12.6	5,600	10,100	1,120	1,450	2,600	5,620	290	590	710	1,070
Tamarack (*Larix laricina*)	47	37	13.6	7,200	11,600	1,240	1,640	3,480	7,160	480	990	860	1,280

* Compiled from R1903-10, June, 1952, Forest Products Laboratory.
† "Air-Dry" lumber contained 12% moisture.

Timber

series of long-time tests have shown that timbers, loaded either transversely or in compression with loads amounting to 50 to 60 per cent of the ultimate strength determined by rapid loading, will ultimately fail, the time required varying from a few weeks to several months.

This important conclusion may therefore be drawn: The strength of timber under any kind of permanent load is only about one-half its strength as found by short-time tests.

21.26 Tabulation of Mechanical Properties of Structural Timbers. Table 21.2, showing the mechanical properties of some American timber, has been compiled from the tests of the U. S. Forest Service.

Table 21.3

BASIC STRESSES FOR CLEAR MATERIAL *

(All values in pounds per square inch and for material under long-time service conditions at maximum design load.)

Species	Extreme Fiber in Bending	Modulus of Elasticity	Compression Parallel to Grain † $L/d = 11$ or less	Compression Perpendicular to Grain	Maximum Horizontal Shear
Hardwoods					
Ash, commercial white	2,050	1,500,000	1,450	500	185
Elm, white	1,600	1,200,000	1,050	250	150
Hickory, true and pecan	2,800	1,800,000	2,000	600	205
Maple, sugar and black	2,200	1,600,000	1,600	500	185
Oak, commercial red and white	2,050	1,500,000	1,350	500	185
Conifers					
Cedar, western red	1,300	1,000,000	950	200	120
Cypress, southern	1,900	1,200,000	1,450	300	150
Douglas fir, coast region	2,200	1,600,000	1,450	320	130
Fir, commercial white	1,600	1,100,000	950	300	100
Hemlock, eastern	1,600	1,100,000	950	300	100
Pine, western white, eastern white, ponderosa, and sugar	1,300	1,000,000	1,000	250	120
Pine, Norway	1,600	1,200,000	1,050	220	120
Pine, southern yellow (longleaf or shortleaf)	2,200	1,600,000	1,450	320	160
Redwood	1,750	1,200,000	1,350	250	100
Spruce, red, white, and Sitka	1,600	1,200,000	1,050	250	120
Tamarack	1,750	1,300,000	1,350	300	140

* Source: Forest Products Laboratory, U. S. Department of Agriculture. See also *ASTM Designation* D245–49T.

† L = unsupported length, and d = least dimension of cross-section.

21.27 Basic Stresses for Clear Wood. Basic stresses for material that is free from defects affecting the strength and that is used in structural sizes under such conditions that no deterioration will occur are given in Table 21.3. These stresses are working-stress values for pieces of timber having a strength ratio of 100 per cent. These basic stresses are applicable to both green and dry material and pertain to lumber exposed to the weather. Allowances have been made for the variability of the strength of clear wood and for the effect of long-continued stress, and a factor of safety has been introduced. These basic stresses have been taken from publications of the Forest

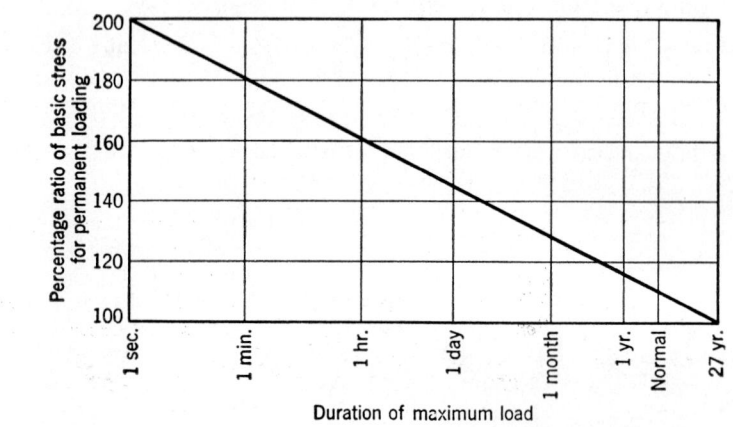

Fig. 21.9. Relation of basic stress to duration of maximum load.

Products Laboratory, U. S. Department of Agriculture. Multiplication of the basic stress by the strength ratio for the grade of lumber gives the working stress for that grade of material. Strength ratios for various grades of lumber and for various defects may be found in *ASTM Designation* D245–49T; this information is also published in the grading rules of various lumber associations.

Basic stresses given in Table 21.3 are applicable to the condition of long-time loading (except for modulus of elasticity values). Timber has the ability to absorb overloads of considerable magnitude for short periods, or smaller overloads for longer time periods. Advantage can be taken of this characteristic in many structural designs. Figure 21.9 shows the relation of basic stress to duration of maximum load.

21.28 Elastic Properties of Timber. The ratio of compressive strength to modulus of elasticity which is a ratio of strength to stiffness is much greater for timber than for steel, iron, or concrete. Wood has no well-defined yield point, but the proportional limit, or yield strength, is determined as a measure of elastic strength. Wood has a high degree of resilience.

Timber members have good resistance to shock. Wood can withstand a large deformation for a comparatively low stress. A unit volume of steel has greater elastic resistance to shock than wood as measured by area under

Timber 531

the stress-strain curve, but since a much greater volume of wood is required to resist a given stress, timber members have better elastic shock resistance than steel. Timber members are much better in this respect than cast iron or concrete. Partly on account of these elastic shock-resisting properties timber is extensively used for railroad ties, fence posts, highway guardrail posts, wagon wheels, implement handles, etc. Resistance to complete failure under shock is less for wood than steel but greater than for cast iron and concrete.

21.29 Timber Connectors. Timber connectors are devices used in conjunction with bolts to increase the efficiency of joints in wood members. These devices consist of metal rings or plates which are embedded partly in each of adjacent members to transmit the load from one member to the

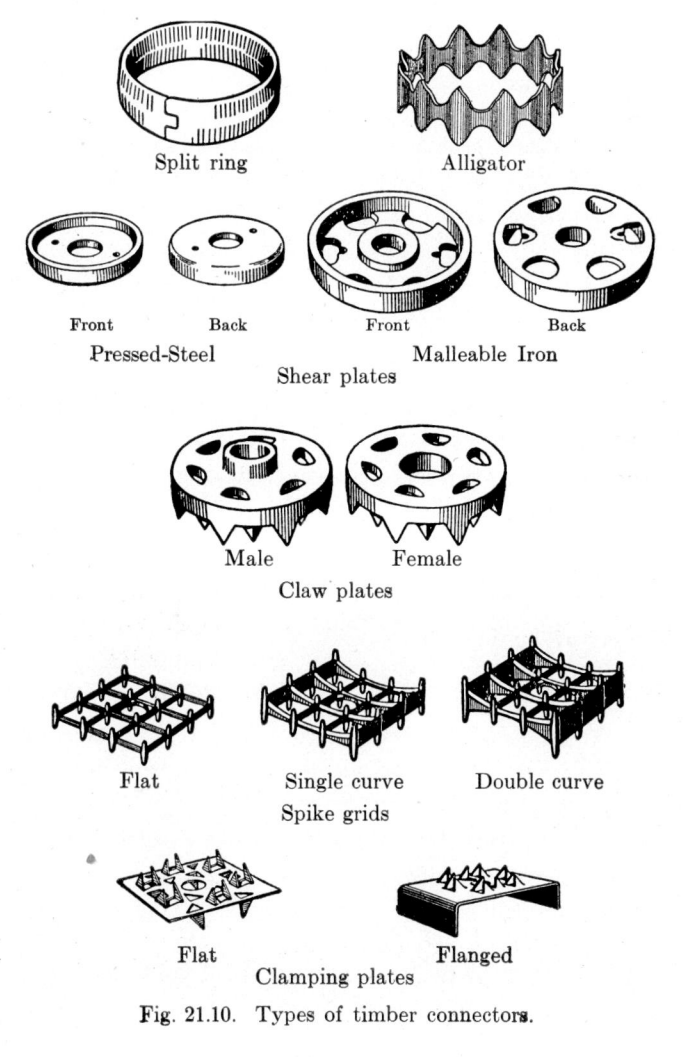

Split ring   Alligator

Front   Back   Front   Back
Pressed-Steel   Malleable Iron
         Shear plates

Male   Female
Claw plates

Flat   Single curve   Double curve
        Spike grids

Flat   Flanged
    Clamping plates

Fig. 21.10. Types of timber connectors.

other. The *split-ring* type fits into precut grooves. (See Fig. 21.10.) The *alligator* type, consisting of a circular band of sheet steel in which teeth have been cut, is pressed into the wood between the members; it is well adapted for light simple structures. *Shear-plate* connectors are placed in precut grooves and are completely embedded in the timber, being flush with the surface of the timber. For wood-to-wood connections they are used in pairs; this type is also suited for wood-to-steel connections such as attachment of timber columns to footings through steel straps, and of wood members to steel gusset plates. *Claw plates* are similar in action to shear plates but lack the advantage of being flush; both grooving and pressure are required for insertion. They are used in pairs for wood-to-wood connections, or singly for wood-to-steel connections. *Spike grids* are flat or curved connectors designed for poles and piles in piers and wharves, towers, and trestles. *Clamping plates*, either flat or flanged, are used to join wooden members that intersect at right angles, such as bridge ties and guard timbers.

Modern metal connectors are utilized in a great variety of structures including timber bridges, trusses for buildings, trestles, towers, and wharves. Their main advantage is that large loads can be transmitted between members without seriously reducing the cross-sectional area of the timber members joined.

When decay resistance or durability is required in structures built with connectors, the timbers are first shop-fabricated for assembly on the site, including the forming of grooves for ring connectors and the boring of bolt holes. After shop fabrication, the timbers are treated with a wood preservative to obtain penetration of the preservative especially in the ring grooves and bolt holes. The timbers are then transported to the field and erected. Such treated structures have given long service under outdoor exposures.

Decay, Durability, and Preservation of Timber

21.30 Decay of Timber. The decay of wood is not an inorganic process like rusting of iron or crumbling of stone but is due to the action of wood-destroying fungi. These wood-penetrating fungi consist of *hyphae*, which are branched threads or filaments of microscopic size. The masses of hyphae are known as micelia. These organisms depend on woody tissue for their food. They spread from cell to cell through the pits in the cell walls or bore through cell walls, causing disintegration of woody substance which in advanced stages is easily recognized by changes in texture, continuity, and color. The wood becomes soft, friable, spongy, stringy, punky, or pitted, depending on the type of fungus. Wood-destroying fungi may be further classed as *brown rot* or *white rot*. The former involves destruction principally of cellulose while the white rot destroys lignin and produces a white color to the attacked wood since the light-colored cellulose is left.

Four conditions are necessary for the development of decay in wood: (1) A supply of food for wood-destroying fungi, (2) suitable temperatures, (3) a small amount of air, and (4) sufficient moisture. If any one of these conditions does not exist, attack by fungi will be eliminated. Thus wood subjected to very high or low temperatures will not be attacked by fungi. Timber immersed in water will not decay because of lack of air, and lumber kept continuously in a dry condition below a critical moisture content will resist decay.

21.31 Durability of Timber. Susceptibility to decay and comparative resistance to decay vary with different classes of timber. The determining factors are as yet almost unknown. Hardness, density, specific gravity, and strength seem to have no influence one way or the other. Some very hard tropical timbers decay very rapidly; others last very long. Hard, strong oak decays much faster than light, porous cypress; tamarack and hemlock decay rapidly, while cypress and cedar are lasting; elm and birch are short lived, the locust long lived, etc.

Timber produced today has in general less resistance to decay than that logged years ago. This is because logs cut today have more sapwood than timber produced in the past from virgin stands and old trees. In view of the smaller resistance to decay of sapwood as compared to heartwood, there is greater need of preservative treatments of lumber than in past years.

21.32 Stain and Mold. Stain is produced by wood-inhabiting fungi which penetrate and discolor wood but do not produce decay. These fungi live on the sugars and starches in the cell cavities of sapwood and generally penetrate from cell to cell through the pits. *Blue stain* is the most common; it detracts from the appearance and lowers the commercial grade of the lumber. Stock containing blue stain is not suitable for natural finishes but may be readily painted. Blue stain decreases shock resistance somewhat, but other strength values are reduced only slightly. Warm, humid conditions promote the growth of staining fungi. Blue stain may develop rapidly during summer months in freshly cut logs and unseasoned lumber as well as in lumber improperly stacked for air seasoning. Dipping of unseasoned lumber in solutions of sodium carbonate, sodium bicarbonate, or chlorinated phenol is practiced to prevent blue staining. Kiln-dried lumber ordinarily is immune from staining.

Mold is a wood-staining fungi which forms a cottony growth on the surface of the wood under moist and warm conditions. Mold does not affect the strength of lumber but discolors the surface in an objectional manner which may require dressing off the surfaces of boards.

21.33 The Preservation of Timber. By far the best method of checking the growth of wood-destroying fungi is poisoning their food supply by injecting poisonous substances into the timber, so changing the organic matter into powerful fungicides. It is a widespread idea that the germs of decay are inherent in the wood, needing only an opportunity for development to bring about its destruction. On the contrary, all wood-destroying agencies start from the outside and may even be excluded by certain paints which merely coat the surface of the timber but which are poisonous enough to prevent the germination of spores.

The first deliberate attempts to preserve timber from decay date back many centuries, when wood was charred to make it more resistant. Later came the period when wood was coated with preservative paints; then came attempts to inject preservatives into the wood.

The two leading antiseptics used as preservatives for timber are creosote (dead oil of coal tar) and zinc chloride. The reliability of each preservative has been established by more than 100 years of service. Creosote has the advantage of insolubility in water, so that it will not wash out of timber. It is the best preservative for general outdoor exposure and is preferred for piling, poles, and general construction timbers. Creosoted timber, however, is discolored so that it can not be painted, and it has an objectionable odor. Zinc chloride is soluble in water, and hence it is utilized in comparatively dry situations. Its advantages are that the treated wood can be painted and is odorless.

There are a number of other preservatives that have either creosote or zinc chloride as their base. For example, mixtures of creosote with petroleum or tar are used for treatment of railroad ties because of cheapness and increased resistance to checking and mechanical wear. It is, however, more difficult to get penetration with these mixtures than with straight creosote, and the surface of the wood is more oily. Chromated zinc chloride is a mixture of 18.5 per cent sodium bichromate and 81.5 per cent zinc chloride; it is water soluble but is more resistant to leaching than standard zinc chloride and for that reason is being extensively employed. Other water-soluble salts utilized to a limited extent as preservatives are mercuric chloride (corrosive sublimate), copper sulfate, arsenic, and sodium fluoride.

Toxic organic compounds such as tetrachlorphenol, pentachlorphenol, 2-chlororthophenylphenol, copper naphthenate, and zinc naphthenate dissolved in nonaqueous, nontoxic volatile solvent such as naphtha have been recently developed for treatment of millwork, doors, window frames, and sash. The wood is soaked in the preservative, no heat being required. The volatile solvent escapes rapidly after treatment. The toxic agent remaining does not discolor the wood detrimentally nor cause swelling since the moisture content is not affected. Treated wood is paintable and odorless.

The processes by which preservatives are injected into timber may be divided into two general classes, the *pressure processes* and the *non-pressure processes*, the distinction being only in the fact that in the former force pumps, air compressors, etc., are utilized, whereas in the latter only atmospheric pressure is relied on.

The Pressure Processes. The pressure processes in general provide for some preliminary treatment, after which the preservative is introduced into the cellular spaces by pressure. The pressure varies in different plants, the maximum being between 100 and 175 pounds per square inch. There are two types of pressure processes: (1) The "full-cell" process, and (2) the "empty-cell" process. In the former it is intended that the cells of the wood shall remain practically filled with the preservative. The preliminary treatment removes most of the imprisoned air and water before impregnation. This is accomplished by exposure to steam, followed by vacuum, which more or less empties the cells, or by boiling in the preservative under vacuum. The timber is then covered with preservative under pressure which fills the cell spaces to a considerable depth.

When it is desired that the preservative shall merely form a film over the cell walls without filling the inside of the cells, the timber is first exposed to the action of compressed air or to air at atmospheric pressure, no vacuum being applied. Without abatement of pressure, the preservative is then admitted to the treating chamber under a higher pressure and is thus forced into the cells. Upon the removal of the external pressure, the imprisoned and compressed air within the cells expands and forces out a considerable portion of the preserving fluid, which may be further removed by application of a partial vacuum. This method is known as the "empty-cell" process and is often preferred for building timbers because the treated lumber is cleaner to handle and is less apt to bleed.

Douglas fir is conditioned by boiling in creosote under a vacuum of from 15 to 25 inches of mercury at temperatures below 93.3° C. (200° F.). The hot creosote maintains the lumber at temperature, and the partial vacuum causes part of the moisture to evaporate. This preliminary treatment is followed by pressure impregnation by either the full-cell or empty-cell process.

The Non-Pressure Process. This process is known as the hot-and-cold-bath treatment. The lumber is immersed in the preservative in an open tank, and the temperature is raised to about 93.3° C. (200° F.). The heat of the preserving fluid expands the air within the cells. The cooling of the bath or the rapid removal of the wood to a cold bath causes a contraction of the air still remaining in the cells, which tends to produce an infiltration of the preservative.

Superficial Treatments. Less efficient but cheaper treatment can be secured by painting the face of the timber with at least two coats of hot creosote or some similar preservative (the *brush method*). The liquid will not penetrate to any great extent, but as long as there remains an unbroken antiseptic zone around the surface the spores of the fungi cannot enter.

Thorough air seasoning before painting is necessary, since otherwise checks may form and provide a means of access to the interior of the timber for the spores of the fungi.

A still less expensive treatment than the brush treatment is the method of dipping the timber in an open vat of the preservative. Usually the timbers are carried through the bath on chain conveyors and remain submerged only a few minutes at most. *Dipping* is not only more economical of time and labor, but also gives better results than the brush method.

Timber members should be cut to final dimension before treatment with a preservative. If cutting is necessary after treatment, the cut surfaces should be brushed thoroughly with the original preservative.

21.34 Effect of Preservative Treatments on the Strength of Timber. Reduced strength of timber after treatment is due primarily to the method of conditioning or process of impregnating rather than to the effects of preservatives used. Strength of treated timber is a function of the percentage of moisture remaining in the wood. Steaming during preliminary treatment may cause considerable reduction in strength. A high degree of steaming is injurious since the amount of moisture in the wood is increased with consequent weakening of the fibers. Boiling under vacuum causes less weakening than steaming. High temperatures maintained for long periods during impregnation in order to obtain penetration of the preservative may cause considerable loss in strength. There seems to be no ground for believing that non-pressure processes are injurious to the strength of timber.

The presence of creosote in itself will not weaken wood, since it does not react chemically with wood and appears not to enter the cell walls and fibers but only to coat them.

The presence of zinc chloride will not weaken wood except by the addition of water by reason of the fact that it is in itself a water solution. Subsequent seasoning will obviate this difficulty. A too-concentrated solution may cause chemical dissolution of some of the wood fibers, but this danger can easily be avoided.

21.35 Termites. Termites attack timber by eating out the interior of the wood and leaving a shell of sound wood to conceal their activities. Owing to their superficial resemblance to ants in size, general appearance, and habit of living in colonies, termites are frequently called "white ants." There are many species of termites, but from the standpoint of their method of attack on wood the termites of the United States may be classified into two groups: (1) the ground-inhabiting or subterranean termites and (2) the dry-wood termites. Subterranean termites are found in nearly every state and are responsible for most of the termite damage; dry-wood termites are found only around the southern edge of the United States from central California to Virginia.

Subterranean termites develop their colonies and maintain their headquarters in the ground, from which they build tunnels through earth and around obstructions to obtain the wood they need for food. In order to live, these termites must have a constant source of moisture. Subterranean termites do not establish themselves in buildings by being carried into them in lumber, but by entering from ground nests after the building has been constructed. The damage may proceed so far as to cause collapse of portions of the structure before they are discovered.

Very few woods offer any marked degree of resistance to termite attack. Impregnation with an effective preservative increases resistance. The best protection against subterranean termites is to build so as to prevent their access to the building. The foundations should be of concrete or other solid material through which the termites cannot penetrate. Cement mortar should be used with brick, stone, or concrete blocks because termites can work through some other kinds of mortar. Untreated wood must be kept well away from the ground. Termite shields consisting of sheets of metal that extend out from the foundation at an angle of 45° for a horizontal distance of at least 2 inches should be placed between foundation and woodwork in order to prevent the termites from extending their tubes over the foundation to reach the sills. Metal shields should also be fitted tightly around water and sewer pipes and electrical conduits along which termites could build their tubes and gain entrance to woodwork.

Buildings infested with subterranean termites should have the infested wood replaced, preferably with treated wood, and the precautions suggested above for new buildings should be put into effect. The entrance galleries of the termites should be destroyed, and a chemical, such as orthodichlorobenzene, may be poured into a trench near the nests and then covered up with earth so that the termites will be killed by the fumes.

Dry-wood termites can live in dry wood without outside moisture or contact with the ground. They can riddle timbers with their tunnelings if allowed to work unmolested for a few years. Outdoor timbers may be protected by preservative treatment. In constructing a building in localities where dry-wood termites are prevalent, the lumber should be inspected to see that it has not become infested before arrival at the building site. If the building is constructed during the swarming season, the lumber should be watched during the course of construction, since infestation by colonizing pairs can easily take place at this season. Since paint is a good protection against the entrance of dry-wood termites, all exposed wood should be kept adequately painted. Fine screen should be placed over openings through which access might be gained to the interior unpainted parts of the building. Badly infested wood should be replaced; if only slightly damaged, further activity may be arrested by blowing finely divided Paris green, arsenical dust, or sodium fluosilicate into each nest.

538 Materials of Construction

21.36 Marine Borers. Damage to timber structures in sea water and even sometimes in fresh water may be caused by marine boring organisms. Rapidity of attack depends on the local conditions and the kinds of borers present. Attack is rapid along the Pacific, Gulf, and South Atlantic coasts of the United States. The principal marine borers encountered in the waters of the United States are the *teredo* and *limnoria*.

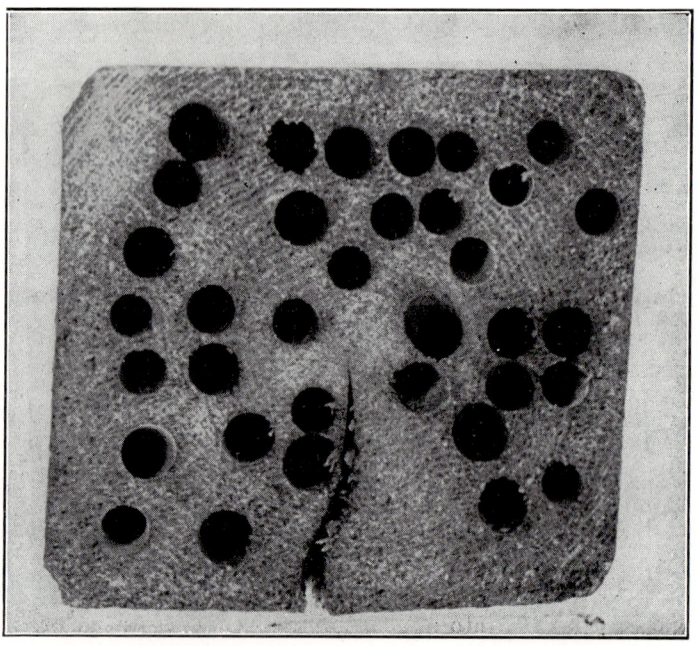

Fig. 21.11. Section of lobster pot buoy attacked by teredo at Plymouth, Mass., in 1935. (*Courtesy* Wm. F. Clapp.)

The teredo is a small mollusk and, in its early stages, a free-swimming organism. When it lodges on a suitable timber, it bores into the wood by means of a pair of boring shells on the head which grows rapidly in size during the boring process while the tail remains at the surface. The teredo bores into the interior of a timber in a direction normal to the surface and then usually turns at right angles to bore longitudinally, sometimes to a length of several feet. This organism lives upon the organic matter extracted from sea water which is pumped through its system. It lines its burrow with a shell-like deposit. The entrance holes do not grow large; the interior of a pile may be completely honeycombed even though the surface shows only slight perforations. An example of damage done by the teredo is shown in Fig. 21.11.

Limnoria are crustaceans that bore small burrows in the surface of piling. When great numbers are present, their burrows are separated by very thin walls of wood that are easily eroded by the motion of the water and objects floating upon it. This erosion causes the limnoria to bore continually deeper. Since erosion is greatest between tide levels, piling attacked by limnoria characteristically wears within such levels to an hour-glass shape. Untreated piling can be destroyed by limnoria within a year in heavily infested harbors.

Other marine borers which are frequently encountered are (1) *bankia*, which are mollusks similar to the teredo in appearance and action; and (2) *martesia*, which are wood-boring mollusks resembling clams in appearance that are active in the Gulf of Mexico and are capable of doing considerable damage by boring holes up to 1 inch in diameter and 2½ inches in length. *Sphaeroma* are similar to limnoria but are larger and do less damage; they occasionally work in fresh water.

All woods are subject to marine-borer attack. All commercially important woods of the United States should be protected in any important permanent structure where borers are active. The best practical protection for piling in sea water is heavy treatment with creosote. The treatment should be thorough with deep penetration and high absorption of the creosote in order to obtain satisfactory results in heavily infested waters. Good results may be obtained by forcing in all the creosote the piling can be made to hold by means of the pressure process. The piling should be air seasoned before treatment.

Limnoria, martesia, and sphaeroma are not always stopped even by thorough creosote treatment. The average life of well-creosoted structures is many times the average life that could be obtained from untreated structures; nevertheless, well-creosoted structures are sometimes damaged seriously.

Shallow or erratic penetration affords but slight protection. The poorly protected spots are attacked, and from them the borers spread inward and destroy the untreated interior of the pile. Low absorption also fails to make the wood sufficiently poisonous to keep the borers out or to provide a reservoir of surplus oil to compensate for depletion by evaporation and leaching. When wood is to be used in salt water, no cutting or injury of any kind should be permitted in the under-water part of the pile.

Protection against borers may be provided by surrounding treated piling by a jacket of concrete, or by clay, concrete, or cast-iron pipe sections. The pipe sections should extend from above high tide to below the mud line, and the space between the wood and the pipe should be filled with concrete.

Paint and batten methods of pile protection vary as to details but consist substantially in: (1) coating the untreated pile with a thick, viscous paint which may or may not contain poisonous materials; (2) applying burlap, roofing felt, or similar material over the paint; (3) applying a second coat of paint; (4) nailing in place a close-fitting layer of narrow battens, which are strips of sawed lumber; and (5) applying a final coat of paint to fill the crevices between the battens and coat the surface thoroughly. Experience has shown that only moderate extension of life can be expected from such treatment.

Many attempts have been made to protect piling by sheathing it with sheet copper, Muntz metal, or other corrosion-resistant metal, but they have not generally been successful. As long as a complete covering of metal can be maintained the borers cannot get in, but complete avoidance of damage to the coating has usually been found impractical.

21.37 Fire Resistance of Timber. When fire is applied to timber, moisture is vaporized, and then at temperatures above 93° C. (200° F.) extraneous materials are volatilized. Destructive distillation begins at about 149° C. (300° F.) with the production of inflammable gases which burn and cause charring of the wood. When the temperature is increased to above 204° C. (400° F.), the wood ignites, and the combustion is sufficient to support itself since the reaction is exothermic.

Small-size wooden pieces reach the point of ignition quickly when subjected to fire and speedily burn throughout the cross-section of the member. Heavy timbers, on the other hand, become charred when fire is applied; this insulates the interior of the timber members, and makes it possible in some cases for large-size members to withstand the action of severe fires. In fact, large timbers may stand up better in fires than structural steel, because thin steel members increase rapidly in temperature when heated and may collapse upon reaching the softening point.

Timber may be impregnated with chemicals to increase fire resistance. The lumber is placed in a treating cylinder, and the chemicals are pumped in under pressure. A rather large amount of chemical is required for effectiveness, 300 pounds per thousand board feet being typical. Monoammonium phosphate, diammonium phosphate, monomagnesium phosphate, and phosphoric acid are effective in retarding glowing and flaming, and do not have objectionable properties.

Lumber may be coated with fire-retardant paints to retard burning and to restrain the spreading of flames. Oil-base paints are utilized for exteriors, and cold-water paints for interiors. Sodium silicate (water glass) is an effective fire-retardant coating; it forms surface blisters on the surface of the wood as the temperature is raised to the point where the sodium silicate is decomposed, thus giving protection to the wood. Coatings are not as effective, however, as impregnated treatments against prolonged high temperatures.

Timber

Questions

21.1. Name at least eight varieties each of hardwoods and of softwoods.

21.2. Identify the following terms relating to the growth and structural characteristics of timber: pith, bark, cell, pit, vessel, medullary ray, cambium, and annual ring.

21.3. Distinguish between slash-cut and rift-cut lumber, and state the advantages of each.

21.4. Should boards for flooring be rift-cut or slash-cut?

21.5. Distinguish between springwood and summerwood and between sapwood and heartwood.

21.6. Describe the following defects of timber: encased knot, intergrown knot, spike knot, shake, check, pitch pocket, wane, cross grain, warp, bow, cupping, and twist.

21.7. In what location on a simply supported beam under equal concentrated loads at the third points would a knot have a significant effect upon the strength of the beam?

21.8. Describe the commercial grading of softwood lumber.

21.9. What is the density rule for dense southern yellow pine?

21.10. Name and describe briefly two types of kilns used in kiln drying.

21.11. Is shrinkage tangential to the annual rings greater or less than radial shrinkage? Explain why.

21.12. Discuss the importance of moisture in its effect on the properties of structural timber.

21.13. How is the moisture in green timber reduced in amount before the timber is used in construction work?

21.14. Discuss the effects of shrinkage on deterioration of timber.

21.15. What is the significance of the fiber-saturation point of wood?

21.16. What are the advantages of cutting timber in the winter?

21.17. Why are timber members ordinarily not used in tension?

21.18. Why is the determination of longitudinal shear important in designing structural-timber beams?

21.19. Explain why stiffness of structural-timber beams may be of importance.

21.20. How does the strength of timber under permanent load compare with its strength as determined by a short-time test?

21.21. What is meant by the term "basic stress"?

21.22. State typical values of maximum compressive and shearing strengths parallel to the grain for green and air-dry timber of the following varieties: hickory, red oak, Douglas fir, shortleaf pine, spruce, sugar maple, ponderosa pine, hemlock, and cypress.

21.23. Would you consider it desirable to use different unit stresses in designing small struts as compared with large structural beams of timber? Explain.

21.24. Compare the shock resistance of timber with that of steel, cast iron, and concrete.

21.25. Name and describe three types of timber connectors.

21.26. What steps may be taken to eliminate "blue stain"?

21.27. What causes the decay of wood?

21.28. Name four antiseptics used for preserving timber, and describe the pressure process of injection.

21.29. Discuss the effect of preservative treatments on the strength of timber.

21.30. Describe the action of termites in destroying timber in buildings.

21.31. How would you protect a new timber building from the destructive action of termites? What corrective measures would you employ for a house infested with termites?

21.32. Describe the action of the teredo and limnoria in attacking timber piles.

21.33. What methods are employed to protect timber piles against attack by marine borers?

References

21.1. American Society for Testing Materials: *Book of Standards,* 1952. Also: *Wood Symposium—One Hundred Years of Engineering Progress with Wood.* 1952. Published by Timber Engineering Co., Washington, D. C.

21.2. Brown, H. P., Panshin, A. J., and Forsaith, C. C.: *Textbook of Wood Technology.* McGraw-Hill Book Co., 1949, 652 pages.

21.3. Brust, A. W., and Berkley, E. E.: "The Distributions and Variations of Certain Strength and Elastic Properties of Clear Southern Yellow Pine Wood." *Proc. ASTM,* v. 35, Part II, 1935, pp. 643–673.

21.4. Clapp, W. F.: "Recent Increases in Marine-Borer Activity." *Civil Eng.,* v. 7, No. 12, Dec., 1937, pp. 836–838, and v. 17, No. 6, June, 1947, pp. 324–327.

21.5. Desch, H. E.: *Timber, Its Structure and Properties.* New York, The Macmillan Co., 2nd ed., 1947.

21.6. Dietz, A. G. H.: *Materials of Construction, Wood, Plastics, Fabrics.* D. Van Nostrand Co., 1949; Chaps. 1–10, pp. 1–189.

21.7. Forest Products Laboratory: *Wood Handbook.* Washington, D. C., U. S. Dept. Agr., 1940. Also: *Misc. Publ.* 185 "Guide to the Grading of Structural Timbers and the Determination of Working Stresses," 1934. Also: *Supplement,* 1940, revised 1943, and *Supplement* 2 "Recommendations for Basic Stresses," 1948. Also: No. R1903-10 "Strength Values of Clear Wood and Related Factors," 1952 and No. R1903-14 "Stress Grades and Working Stresses," 1953.

21.8. Gay, C. M., and Parker, H.: *Materials and Methods of Architectural Construction.* John Wiley & Sons, 2nd ed., 1943; Chap. 4, pp. 39–50 and Chaps. 18 and 19, pp. 304–371.

21.9. Hansen, H. J.: *Timber Engineers' Handbook.* John Wiley & Sons, 1948, 882 pages.

21.10. Hansen, H. J.: *Modern Timber Design.* John Wiley & Sons, 1943, 232 pages; 2nd ed., 1948, 312 pages.

21.11. Henderson, H. L.: *Air Seasoning and Kiln Drying of Wood.* Albany, N. Y., 3rd ed., 1946.

21.12. Hunt, G. M., and Garratt, G. A.: *Wood Preservation.* McGraw-Hill Book Co., 1938, 457 pages.

21.13. Kofoid, C. A., and others: *Termites and Termite Control.* Berkeley, Calif., University of California Press, 1934, 734 pages.

21.14. Markwardt, L. J., and Wilson, T. R. C.: "Strength and Related Properties of Woods Grown in the United States." Washington, D. C., *U. S. Dept. Agr., Tech. Bull.* 479, 1935.

21.15. Markwardt, L. J.: "Wood as an Engineering Material." 18th ASTM Marburg Lecture, *Proc. ASTM,* v. 43, 1943, pp. 435–492.

21.16. National Lumber Manufacturers Association: (1) *Lumber Grade-Use Guide for Softwood and Hardwood Lumber in Building and General Construction.* (2) *Wood Structural Design Data.* (3) *National Design Specification for Stress-Grade Lumber and Its Fastenings.* Washington, D. C.

21.17. Tiemann, H. D.: *Wood Technology.* Pitman Publishing Corp., 2nd ed., 1944.

21.18. Timber Engineering Co.: (1) *Design Manual for Teco Timber Connector Construction.* (2) *Installing Teco Timber Connectors in Light and Heavy Timber Structures.* (3) *Fabricating Teco Timber Connector Structures.* 1319 Eighteenth St., N.W., Washington 6, D. C.

Timber

21.19. Titmuss, F. H.: *A Concise Encyclopedia of World Timbers.* New York, Philosophical Library, 1949, 156 pages.
21.20. Wangaard, F. F.: *The Mechanical Properties of Wood.* John Wiley & Sons, 1950, 377 pages.
21.21. West Coast Lumbermen's Association: (1) *Douglas Fir Use Book.* (2) *Research Bull.* 1-6. 1410 S.W. Morrison St., Portland 5, Oregon.
21.22. Wise, L. E.: *Wood Chemistry.* New York, Reinhold Publ. Corp. 1944.
21.23. *Wood Technology Series:* 2, "Wood Structure and Engineering"; 5, "Wood Seasoning"; 6, "Construction and Housing"; 8, "Quality Control in Wood"; 9, "Wood Finishing"; 12, "Wood Preservation"; 14, "Woodworking Machinery"; 17, "Lumber." Madison, Wis., Forest Products Research Society, P.O. Box 2010, University Station.

Section VIII · Organic Plastics

CHAPTER 22

Organic Plastics

By WILLIAM HOWLETT GARDNER, PhD [*]

Rewritten and Revised by LLOYD F. RADER

22.1 Introduction. Organic plastics comprise an important group of materials of construction. Many of these plastic substances have combinations of properties which cannot be duplicated by other materials. Articles made from them have the general characteristics of lightness in weight, excellent mechanical and electrical properties, and a high degree of permanence and beauty of finish. They can be produced with precision and are easy to fabricate. Many finished articles can be turned upon a lathe, sawed, punched, and drilled to suit needed purposes. Molded parts may contain metal inserts, since most of these plastics are inert toward such materials. Several of the fabricated compositions are extremely resistant toward chemicals and toward organic liquids. Certain others are used for their special properties toward light.

22.2 Classifications. An organic plastic is a material exhibiting characteristics of plasticity which has organic substances as the binder. The term plastic is rather broadly used and is applied to any article made from plastic materials even if it has been transformed into an infusible (resinoid) state. All organic plastics contain a binder which imparts the plastic properties to the composition. Many plastics contain in addition a filler which is an inert extender. Filler is added to impart hardness, strength, and other desirable properties. Inert dyes and pigments are added for their decorative effects. Organic plastics may be divided into three general groups upon the basis of their behavior toward heat.

Thermoplastic or *heat non-convertible* compositions are those which remain permanently soft at elevated temperatures. It is necessary to cool them before they assume a rigid form. These materials can be shaped and reshaped by means of heat and pressure.

[*] Chemical Engineer, Allied Chemical and Dye Corporation.

Table 22.1

CLASSIFICATION OF THE COMMONER ORGANIC PLASTICS

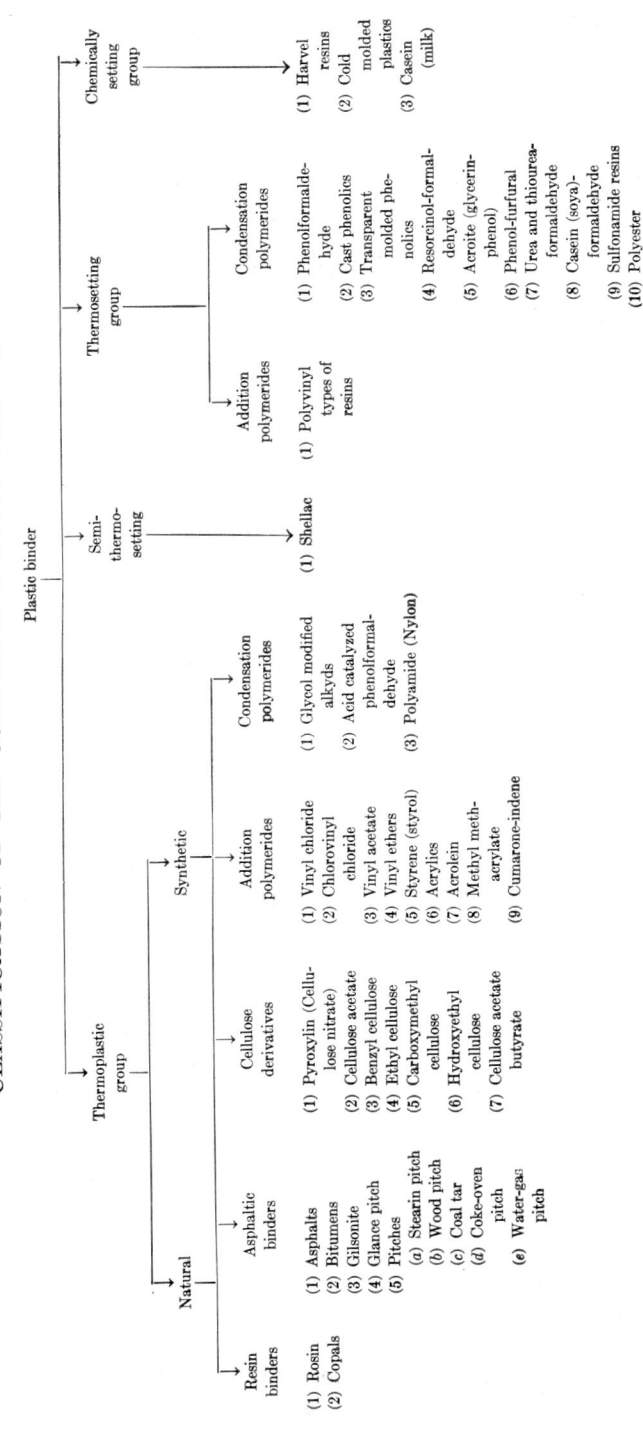

Plastic binder
├── Natural
│   ├── Resin binders
│   │   (1) Rosin
│   │   (2) Copals
│   └── Asphaltic binders
│   (1) Asphalts
│   (2) Bitumens
│   (3) Gilsonite
│   (4) Glance pitch
│   (5) Pitches
│   (a) Stearin pitch
│   (b) Wood pitch
│   (c) Coal tar
│   (d) Coke-oven pitch
│   (e) Water-gas pitch
└── Synthetic
    ├── Thermoplastic group
    │   ├── Cellulose derivatives
    │   │   (1) Pyroxylin (Cellulose nitrate)
    │   │   (2) Cellulose acetate
    │   │   (3) Benzyl cellulose
    │   │   (4) Ethyl cellulose
    │   │   (5) Carboxymethyl cellulose
    │   │   (6) Hydroxyethyl cellulose
    │   │   (7) Cellulose acetate butyrate
    │   ├── Addition polymerides
    │   │   (1) Vinyl chloride
    │   │   (2) Chlorovinyl chloride
    │   │   (3) Vinyl acetate
    │   │   (4) Vinyl ethers
    │   │   (5) Styrene (styrol)
    │   │   (6) Acrylics
    │   │   (7) Acrolein
    │   │   (8) Methyl methacrylate
    │   │   (9) Cumarone-indene
    │   └── Condensation polymerides
    │   (1) Glycol modified alkyds
    │   (2) Acid catalyzed phenolformaldehyde
    │   (3) Polyamide (Nylon)
    ├── Semi-thermosetting
    │   (1) Shellac
    ├── Thermosetting group
    │   ├── Addition polymerides
    │   │   (1) Polyvinyl types of resins
    │   └── Condensation polymerides
    │   (1) Phenolformaldehyde
    │   (2) Cast phenolics
    │   (3) Transparent molded phenolics
    │   (4) Resorcinol-formaldehyde
    │   (5) Acroite (glycerin-phenol)
    │   (6) Phenol-furfural
    │   (7) Urea and thiourea-formaldehyde
    │   (8) Casein (soya)-formaldehyde
    │   (9) Sulfonamide resins
    │   (10) Polyester
    └── Chemically setting group
        (1) Harvel resins
        (2) Cold molded plastics
        (3) Casein (milk)

Thermosetting or *heat convertible* compositions are transformed into infusible products upon heating. These compositions are thermoplastic when first heated under pressure but rapidly assume a permanent rigid state as chemical changes take place in the binder. Fabricated articles of this type of composition can be ejected from the molds without cooling.

Chemically setting compositions are those which harden by the addition of a suitable chemical to the composition just before molding or by subsequent chemical treatment following fabrication. These procedures are necessary with certain binders, or the composition would become infusible before it is formed.

The types of organic plastics which belong to each group are shown in Table 22.1. The synthetic binders which are designated as *addition polymerides* are mixtures of polymers, which have been formed by addition of like molecules. Those which are classified as *condensation polymerides* have been formed by chemical reactions in which two or more different molecules combine with the separation of water or other simple substances in the formation of these resins.

22.3 Polymerization and Condensation. *Polymerization* involves unsaturated molecules. Unsaturated molecules contain double or triple bonds between carbon atoms; these bonds are weaker than single bonds. Such unsaturated molecules are relatively unstable and when conditions become favorable, they react in a manner to break the multiple bond.

For example, a double bond may be opened up and the free valency formed may attach itself to a similar free valency which has been identically produced in another similar molecule. This double molecule has a free valency at each end, therefore it can hook up with two additional molecules. Thus by repetition of this process, a long chain is constructed involving several hundred molecules. The molecular weight of such long chains may be extremely large, even as high as 100,000. Such long chain molecules are typical of thermoplastics.

Simple unsaturated substances which can be polymerized are called *monomers*, and the large molecules formed by reactions are called polymers.

Copolymerization. Copolymers are produced by mixing monomers and then polymerizing. For example, if vinyl chloride and vinyl acetate are mixed and subsequently subjected to polymerization, the resultant material has different properties than either polyvinyl chloride or polyvinyl acetate. In this instance, the polymer has both vinyl chloride and vinyl acetate in each molecule. (It should be noted that copolymers are not just mechanical mixtures of two polymers.) The proportions of each monomer can be varied over a wide range, thus producing polymers of considerably different properties.

Condensation consists of the uniting of two unlike molecules accompanied by the splitting off of a small molecule (often a water molecule). An example is the forming of long-chain molecules of Nylon from condensation between adipic acid molecules and hexamethylenediamine molecules. The reaction is due to the tendency for two groups of atoms to unite and eliminate a water molecule.

A catalyst is usually required to produce polymerization and condensation. Irradiation by means of ultraviolet light or sunlight may be effective in causing the reaction to take place.

In addition to long-chain molecules, branched polymers and cross-linked polymers may be developed with certain molecules for both polymerization and condensation processes. Cross-linkages may occur in three dimensions giving an interlocking structure. Such cross-linked structures are typical of thermosetting materials.

In general, plastics for structural uses are produced by condensation reactions. The most important of these are the phenol and urea compounds.

22.4 Thermosetting Types of Binders. Resins made from phenol (carbolic acid) and formaldehyde are the most widely used binders for organic plastics. Articles prepared from these *phenol-formaldehyde* or *phenolic compositions* are characterized by their relative permanence, which is probably a result of their infusibility and hardness. They have excellent mechanical and electrical properties and are highly resistant to heat. The cellulose-filled products, for instance, are unaffected by temperatures up to 150° C. (302° F.), and certain mineral-filled materials will completely resist temperatures as high as 235° C. (455° F.) for short periods. These products are also highly resistant to water, oil, common solvents, mild alkalies, organic acids, and dilute mineral acids. They are disintegrated by strong sulfuric and nitric acids and by concentrated caustic solutions. Compositions show very small shrinkage upon molding, so mechanical parts can be made in this manner with a fairly high degree of precision. Rapid setting (quick-curing) materials make it possible to obtain very high rates of production in the fabrication of these articles.

Phenol-formaldehyde resins are combined with various percentages of different fillers and fabrics to give a variety of types of plastic compositions. The compositions may be divided into five general classes: namely, cellulose-filled compositions, mineral-filled compositions, molding sheet, impact-resistant materials, and special materials.

The first class is used for molding where a high finish and precision are desired. Wood flour is usually the filler employed. The molded articles have high dielectric strength, mechanical strength, and lightness, and are used extensively by the airplane, automotive, and railroad industries where weight is an important consideration in design.

The second class of compositions may have asbestos as the filler. These compositions are selected for articles designed to resist chemicals, heat, and exterior exposure. They are extensively used for outdoor electrical insulators but are not suitable for high-voltage transmission where arcing may produce carbonization with this type of plastic.

Molding sheet, the third class, is made by impregnating paper with phenolic resins. It is brittle when cold but can be softened by heat and cut into sizes suitable for molding. The sheets are 18 inches long, 40 inches wide, and $3/16$ inch thick. It is employed for molding complicated forms where a more plastic material is needed than can be obtained with the first two classes of compositions. Molded articles of these compositions are slightly inferior in mechanical properties to those made with the other phenolic compositions.

Impact-resistant articles, the fourth class, are made from impregnated paper and fabric fillers, built up in layers. These are known as *laminated plastics*. (See Art. 23.21.) The composition can be hot-pressed into plates and other simple forms. They are widely used for making articles such as heavy-service gears where unusual toughness and strength are required.

The special types, the last class, are made for individual applications, where some special property is required. Often, it is possible to sacrifice some general characteristic in order to obtain the special property. Compositions of this type include those of unusual water-resistance, special compositions for radio condensers, magneto insulation, and materials of marked opacity to X-rays for the manufacture of X-ray shields.

Transparent phenolic resins are available as plastics for molding and for casting. The cast resins are first formed into relatively simple shapes, cured by baking, and then machined to the desired form. The molding types can be handled in the conventional compression molds. The distinctive properties of these phenolic resins include hardness, heat resistance, dielectric strength, dimensional stability, and lightness in weight. Molded articles withstand temperatures up to 107° C. (225° F.) and even to 149° C. (300° F.) for short periods. Although they support combustion, they are relatively non-inflammable. They have a very high luster. One type of molding resin has a refractive index which approaches that of ruby. They are also extremely resistant to the action of ultra-violet light. Certain amber-colored resins are translucent to X-rays and are used as ports for X-ray machines. Some of the purest forms have the transparency of glass, which they surpass in strength and elasticity. They are odorless and tasteless, and water has no effect upon them.

Furfuryl-phenol plastics can be fabricated in a wide variety of ways, including both hot and cold molding. In cold molding, the plastic is formed by pressure at room temperature and cured subsequently by heat. These resins impart to finished articles properties which are similar to those of the ordinary phenol-formaldehyde binders, but in hot compression molding give a slower and more even rate of cure or set to the composition. This is an advantage with articles containing thick sections. These plastics are dark in color.

Urea-formaldehyde resins are light-colored thermosetting binders. Practically any color effect can be obtained with them. These compositions are widely used for pastel shades. Some of the resins are made by allowing both urea and thiourea to react with formaldehyde. Urea resins have very good mechanical and excellent electrical properties. They do not undergo surface carbonization in an electric arc as do phenolic plastics. They are unaffected by water if properly cured and have a high resistance to oils, solvents, and many chemicals. Weak alkalies and acids have no effect, but strong alkalies cause a slight deterioration. Strong acids produce decomposition. Urea plastics have a low burning rate, but shrink slightly under heat. The uncolored resins are unaffected by light. Severe exterior exposure to weather, however, causes a cracking of the surfaces. Cast urea resins have many of the properties of cast phenolic plastics.

Wood and paper pulp are generally used as fillers in urea-formaldehyde plastics. The fibers of these materials are so small that, when impregnated with the binder, they can be used for obtaining translucent objects. Semi-translucent and opaque compositions are also manufactured. These different compositions are not so flexible as cellulose-derivative plastics but are superior to these in many of their other properties. The compositions have unusual qualities of light diffusion when unpigmented and eliminate glare when used in thin sections. Moldings, used for indirect lighting fixtures, are superior to glass fixtures in being shatterproof.

Melamine-formaldehyde resins are also light-colored thermosetting binders with properties similar to those of urea resins. Melamine is derived from calcium carbide. The carbide is heated in nitrogen to produce calcium cyanamide which is boiled with water to form dicyanodiamide. Melamine is produced by the pyrolysis of dicyanodiamide. When reacted with formaldehyde, melamine forms a resin. Melamine resins have higher water resistance than urea resins. They are used for making high-wet-strength paper and for treating textiles to reduce shrinkage. Melamine-formaldehyde resins are used with fillers to make electrical insulating materials since melamine resins have excellent resistance to electrical arcs. Also melamine resins are combined with glass fabric to produce glass-reinforced plastics.

Polyester plastics are thermosetting and are available both as surface coatings and as molded and cast products. Since they can be molded at very low pressures, polyester plastics are utilized in making large laminated objects which can not be molded at high pressures. *Reinforced plastics* consisting of fibrous glass cloth as reinforcement in polyester plastic have a higher strength-weight ratio than any other plastic. They have good dimensional stability, exceptional resistance to rot and moisture, and great resistance to impact. Typical physical properties are given in Table 22.5.

Reinforced plastics can be nailed directly without first drilling a hole. They may not be satisfactory as a substitute for glass in some instances because they are translucent, permitting less than 50 per cent light transmission.

22.5 Thermoplastic Types of Binders. *Cellulosic Type.* *Cellulose plastics* is the general term employed for plastics made from derivatives of cellulose, such as the cellulose esters, cellulose nitrate (miscalled nitrocellulose), cellulose acetate, and cellulose acetate butyrate, and the cellulose ethers, ethyl cellulose and benzyl cellulose. These are all true thermoplastic materials. They give molded articles of the greatest toughness and resilience of any of the plastics and are extensively used for objects having thin-walled sections where other plastics may be too brittle. Non-volatile plasticizers (organic solvents) or softening agents are generally incorporated to impart the desired working qualities. These plastics have excellent electrical properties. They are strong and show good wearing qualities. They can be machined, buffed, and cut. All types of color effects can be obtained with them, including such decorative effects as mother-of-pearl and tortoise shell.

Cellulose nitrate plastics (Celluloid) are very inflammable but are much stronger than cellulose acetate plastics and are less affected by water. Ethyl celluloses have the same tensile strength as cellulose nitrates but much greater ductility and better electrical properties. Benzyl cellulose also has good ductility and superior electrical properties. Cellulose acetate and the ethers are relatively non-inflammable under ordinary conditions but burn like wood when ignited.

The cellulose plastics produce articles which are practically as clear as glass. Ethyl cellulose also shows nearly complete transmission to ultraviolet light between the wavelengths of 2800 and 4000 Angstrom units and is unaffected by sunlight. Cellulose nitrate which shows strong absorption below 2800 Angstrom units, and some absorption below 3300 Angstrom units, becomes embrittled and discolored upon exposure. Cellulose acetate which absorbs light below 2900 Angstrom units is only slightly affected. Benzyl cellulose has the disadvantages of cellulose nitrate in this respect.

Strong acids decompose all the derivatives of cellulose, but weak acids cause but slight deterioration. Ethyl cellulose resists both strong and weak alkalies. Weak alkalies have but a slight effect upon the others, but strong alkalies decompose them. They all show relatively high water absorptions but compare favorably with many of the other plastics containing fillers. Benzyl cellulose shows the least water absorption.

Non-Cellulosic Type. The *vinyl resins* all produce what might be called organic glasses. They include the colorless polymerides of methyl methacrylate, acrylics, styrene, vinyl chloride, vinyl acetate, ethylene, vinyl butyral, and similar compounds. All these are perfectly odorless, tasteless, non-toxic, and transparent plastics. They are all thermoplastic, non-burning or slow burning, very tough, and chemically inert. They show practically no water absorption.

Styrene and methyl methacrylate are among the lightest organic binders. The shock resistance of methyl methacrylate compares favorably with that of the phenolic resins. Both styrene and methyl methacrylate transmit the ultraviolet wavelengths of light. Molded articles are distorted above temperatures of 60° to 85° C. (140° to 185° F.). The most significant property of the styrene resins is their low electrical-power factors, which make them excellently suited for insulation to be used at radio frequencies.

Vinyl chloride resins have a high resilience and are superior to rubber in flexing life and in resistance to deterioration. They are used as wire and cable coatings. Copolymerides of vinyl chloride and acetate can be obtained both as filled and unfilled plastics.

Polyethylene is a vinyl resin that is very flexible and tough and that has good electrical properties. It is used as a cable covering. Its specific gravity is less than 1.0.

Polyvinyl butyral is the vinyl resin used in safety glass. When compounded with plasticizers, it is adhesive to glass, transparent, unaffected by sunlight, and tough even at low temperatures. The three commonly employed plasticizers are: dibutyl sebacate, triethylene glycol dihexoate, and triethylene glycol, esterified with certain fatty acids derived from cocoanut oil. Plasticizer is added in amounts from 20 to 30 per cent. A sheet of plastic is placed between two lights (sheets) of glass and compressed. (See Chapter 23.)

Polyvinylidene chloride (Saran) has good resistance to corrosion and chemical attack and has the property of orientation. It is used for pipes and tubing and as window screening.

Polyamide plastic (Nylon) is a thermoplastic that is manufactured by condensing adipic acid with hexamethylene diamine. The resulting polymer has a high softening point and the property of orientation. Filaments are produced by hot-extrusion and hot-melt spinning processes; these filaments are cold-drawn into fibers which produces a high degree of orientation of the molecules in the fibers. Nylon yarn has a high tensile strength, and is extensively used as a textile. Nylon is also used as an injection molding material. Molded products can be used under loads at temperatures up to 135° C. (275° F.). It has a rather high moisture absorption but is not affected by common organic solvents. Its specific gravity is 1.14.

Cumarone-indene resins soften over a narrow range of temperatures, which limits their use as plastic materials. They are very brittle, although they have excellent electrical properties which do not change with humidity. They are extensively used as binders in compositions for mastic floor tile, in the compounding of rubber, and in cold-molding compositions with other binders.

Alkyd resins made from glycerin and phthalic anhydride and modified by chemical combination with drying oils have electrical properties similar to those of shellac but are not used extensively as plastics except in thin films because of their slow rates of curing.

Natural resins other than shellac are used for blending with other binders. These compositions are applied almost entirely as filling compounds in the electrical industries. Asphalts, bitumens, pitches, and waxes have similar uses.

22.6 Chemically Setting Types of Binders. *Casein plastics* do not possess the degree of plasticity of resin binders but are extensively used for articles which can be made in shallow molds. Compositions of milk casein of a wide variety of colors can be obtained at a relatively low price. Molding is accompanied by a considerable shrinkage, and curing is effected by treating the molded articles with formaldehyde solutions. Formaldehyde, however, can be incorporated with soya-bean casein prior to molding.

Special compositions made from asphalt, drying oils, and asbestos are used for *cold molding*. Large tolerances must be allowed, depending upon the design and shape of the article, since shrinkage is from two to three times that for hot-molded plastics. Cold-molded articles are cured by baking. They do not have as good an appearance as articles made from other materials and consequently are usually used for parts hidden within an assembly. They are serviceable where resistance to heat and arcing are the primary needs; hence they are utilized for electrical insulating parts. Also cold-molding materials are used for outdoor electrical insulation because of good weather resistance. Recently phenolic resins have been substituted for asphalt in cold-molding compositions.

22.7 Semi-Thermosetting Types of Binders. *Shellac* is one of the oldest binders for molding compositions. It is still employed in large quantities for high-voltage electrical insulation where porcelain is the only extensively used competitive material. The shellac insulators are not so fragile as those made of porcelain and do not shatter. They have excellent characteristics to resist effects from arcing. The decomposition products formed under this condition are poor conductors of electricity, and surface carbonization is not excessive enough to cause serious danger of short circuits. The heat generated softens the lac, repairing any cracks which may be formed. Mixtures of shellac and phenolic resins are used for binders for insulation at intermediate voltages. These insulators have a greater resistance to heat than pure shellac compositions, which begin to deform at temperatures above 88° C. (190° F.).

Shellac compositions remain thermoplastic at elevated temperatures for relatively long periods of time as compared to thermosetting resins. Prolonged heating, however, causes chemical changes to take place which improves the electrical and mechanical properties. Fabricated insulators made of laminated paper are cured, therefore, for periods as long as 10 hours at temperatures as high as 149° C. (300° F.).

22.8 Coloring Materials. Both organic and inorganic substances are used for coloring plastic compositions. The organic pigments and dyes are generally superior for this purpose since they are more resistant to acids and alkalies. Many of the binders, for example, destroy pigments such as the iron blues, chrome greens, umbers, and ochers. Permanence in color, however, cannot always be predicted in advance of trial. The white pigments are largely limited to the lithopones and titanium oxides. These ingredients are commonly added during the incorporation of the binder with the filler. There are advantages, however, to precoloring the resins and to dyeing the fillers. Some resins are colored during their manufacture.

22.9 Manufacture of Organic Plastics. There are four main steps in the manufacture of articles made of organic plastics. They are:

1. Production of chemical intermediate materials from basic raw materials such as coal, petroleum, limestone, cotton, and salt.
2. Manufacture of synthetic resins from chemical intermediate materials.
3. Preparation of molding powders, fibers, rods, and sheets from synthetic resins coloring materials, and fillers.
4. Molding or forming of articles from molding powders, fibers, rods, and sheets.

The plastics industry is divided into two main sections: First, that manufacturing synthetic resins and preparing molding powders, fibers, rods, and sheets as indicated in steps 2 and 3 above; and second, the molders and fabricators of plastics articles as indicated in step 4 above.

22.10 Manufacture of Thermosetting Plastics. Phenolic resin moldings are typical. Phenol-formaldehyde resin is produced by condensation. Condensation takes place when formaldehyde solution (formalin) and phenol are heated together with a catalyst such as a trace of alkali or acid. In the beginning of the reaction, the product is soluble in water, but, as the reaction proceeds, liquid resin separates and a layer of water is formed on top. This process is carried out in a closed resin kettle outfitted with a condenser so arranged that volatile material can be condensed and then run back into the kettle. When the water separates from the liquid resin, the arrangement of the apparatus is changed to permit removal of the water by distillation. The resultant liquid resin is discharged into containers and hardened by cooling. This stage of resin formation is known as A stage.

Stages in Formation of Thermosetting Resins. There are three stages in the formation of thermosetting resins: A, B, and C stages.

A stage [*,1] is an early stage in the reaction of a thermosetting resin in which the material is still soluble in certain liquids and fusible.

B stage [*] is an intermediate stage in the reaction of a thermosetting resin in which the material softens when heated and swells in contact with certain liquids but may not entirely fuse or dissolve. Resins in thermosetting molding compounds are usually in this stage.

C stage [*] is the final stage in the reaction of a thermosetting resin in which the material is relatively insoluble and infusible. Thermosetting resins in a fully cured adhesive layer are in this stage.

Manufacturing Molding Powders. In manufacturing molding powders, coloring materials and fillers are mixed with melted resin and subsequently cooled and pulverized to powder form. The time and temperature of mixing are controlled to keep the resin in the B stage. During the molding operation in forming finished articles, the resin hardens and becomes a C-stage material.

A two-step process is sometimes employed in manufacturing phenolic molding powder. In this process, an insufficient supply of formalin is used in the reaction with phenol so that there are too few linkages produced to develop a completely cross-linked structure. Such a resin has thermoplastic properties and can be readily mixed with pigments and filler to produce molding powder. Hexamine is also added to the powder. When subjected to molding, the hexamine reacts to produce formaldehyde which forms additional cross-linkages and thus changes the resin into C-stage material.

22.11 Manufacture of Thermoplastic Materials. *Cellulosic Type.* Cellulose acetate is typical and will be described. It is made in large containers by digesting cotton linters in a mixture of acetic anhydride and acetic acid with a small amount of sulfuric acid as a catalyst. After digestion, the viscous material is aged ("ripened") to desired consistency and then placed in water to precipitate the solid acetate. This is followed by alternate centrifuging and washing with final drying. A plasticizer (dimethyl phthalate, etc.) is added. A solvent such as acetone or alcohol is sometimes added. The plasticized acetate is rolled into sheets, which are pressed into blocks and sliced into sheets. Coloring materials are included to produce desired color. Molding compounds are made from cut-up blocks or sheets.

Non-Cellulosic Type. Polyvinyl chloride is taken as a typical example. The type of plant used is similar to that in oil refineries. This resin is derived from acetylene. The monomer vinyl chloride is made by passing the acetylene gas into hydrochloric acid with a catalyst such as cuprous chloride. Polyvinyl chloride is produced by heating a water emulsion of vinyl chloride with a catalyst such as benzoyl peroxide in an autoclave under pressure at about 230° C. (446° F.). The material is a white, fluffy powder

---

[1] Definitions marked with an asterisk are from the ASTM *Book of Standards,* Part 6, 1952.

Organic Plastics

which when molded becomes hard and horny in appearance. When the powder is mixed with a plasticizer such as dibutyl phthalate, a tough, flexible plastic is produced. By rolling, continuous sheets of polyvinyl chloride are formed.

Molding and Fabrication of Plastics

22.12 General. Molding and fabrication are necessary to convert organic plastics into products suitable for building purposes and industrial use. Molding and fabricating processes comprise:

Compression molding.
Transfer molding.
Injection molding.
Extrusion.
Casting.
Blowing.
Laminating (see Chapter 23).
Production of plastic foams.

22.13 Compression Molding. This is the most used method of molding plastics products. Compression molding consists in placing a definite

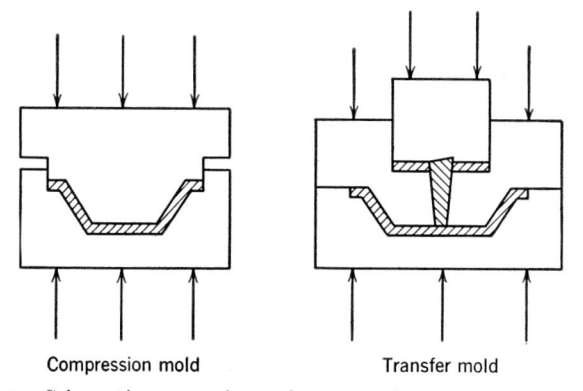

Fig. 22.1. Schematic comparison of compression and transfer molding.

amount of the plastic in the bottom part of a heated mold, closing the mold, and then subjecting it to pressure usually in a hydraulic press. The mold is heated during the pressing operation. This causes the plastic material to soften and to flow, completely filling the cavity in the mold, which has the exact shape of the desired article. For thermosetting materials, a definite time of heating is required to cure the plastic and produce a C-stage material; cooling is not necessary. However, for thermoplastic compositions, cooling is required before the pressure is released. The temperatures and pressures employed vary according to the plastic to be molded. Tempera-

556 Materials of Construction

tures range from 100° C. (212° F.) to 204° C. (400° F.); and pressures, from 1000 to 6000 pounds per square inch with pressures of 1500 to 3000 pounds per square inch being typical.

Referring to Fig. 22.1, it is shown diagrammatically that the molding pressure is developed coincident with the closing of the mold.

22.14 Transfer Molding. Transfer molding is accomplished by means of compression-molding equipment but involves principles of injection mold-

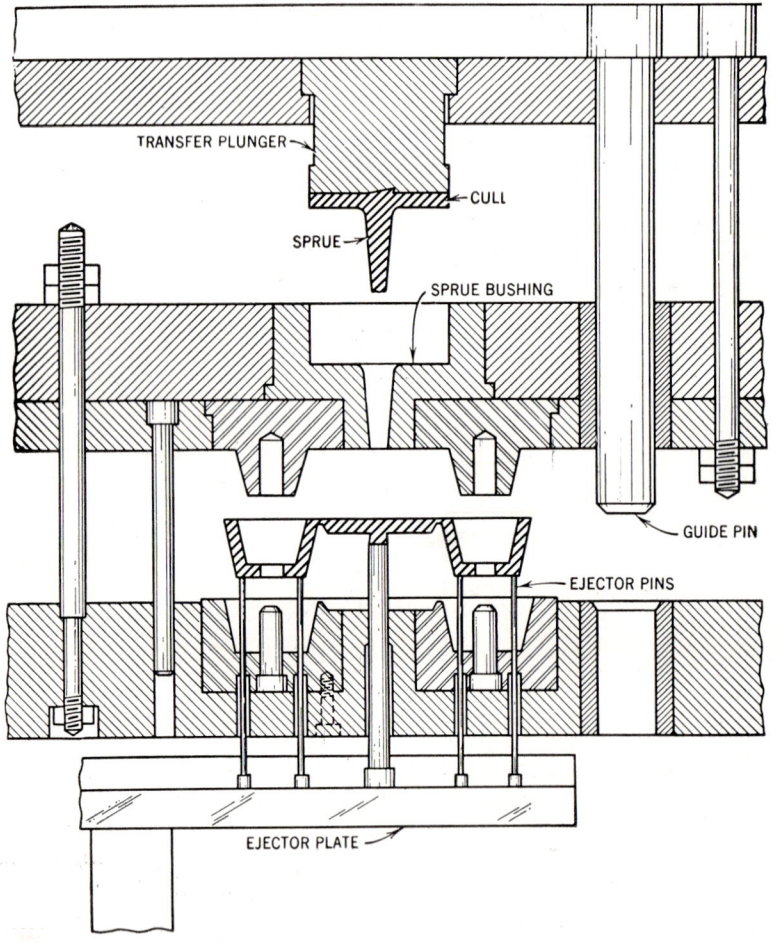

Fig. 22.2. Sectional view illustrating method of transfer molding. (*Courtesy* J. Delmonte: *Plastics Molding*. John Wiley & Sons.)

ing. A schematic representation of transfer molding is given in Fig. 22.1. The powder is first heated to a soft condition in the transfer chamber and then forced through an opening into the mold cavity. The significant difference between transfer and compression molding is that in the former the plastic material flows into a closed mold, whereas in compression molding the application of pressure occurs at the same time that the mold is closed. Transfer molding is applicable only to thermosetting plastics.

Details of transfer-mold construction and operation are illustrated in Fig. 22.2.

Transfer molding makes possible closer tolerances than compression molding; also, a smaller amount of finishing is required, and the use of complicated inserts and the production of more intricate shapes are possible.

22.15 Design and Construction of Molds. Molds for compression molding are classified according to the method of final closure. Four principal

(a) Flash type — Horizontal flash rim

(b) Semipositive type — Horizontal and vertical flash rim, Ejector pin

(c) Positive type — Small clearance

(d) Landed-positive type — Land, Plastic material

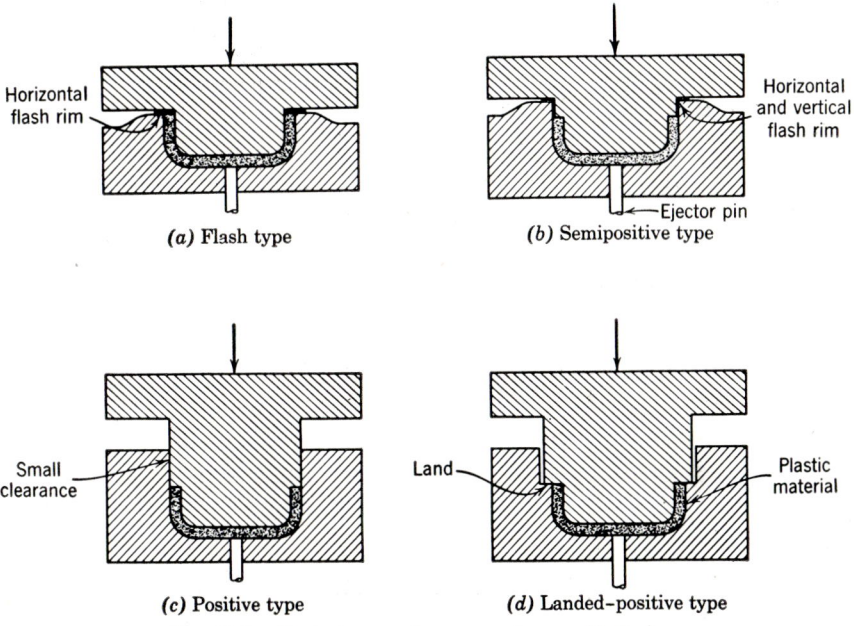

Fig. 22.3. Basic types of compression mold design.

types are the flash, positive, semipositive, and landed positive. These molds are illustrated diagrammatically in Fig. 22.3. The *flash type* of mold permits a slight excess (flash) of composition to escape during the final closure of the mold. *Positive types* permit no escape of material. They are used where the flash would lead to difficulties in obtaining the proper shape of the molded article. A disadvantage of the positive-type mold is the danger of scoring the walls of the cavity because of small clearance between plunger and cavity. *Semipositive types* incorporate features of both flash and positive types of molds and are extensively used. The plunger does not fit so closely in the cavity as is the case for the positive type, hence there is less danger of scoring. Whereas in the positive-type mold there is no flash nor "land" to arrest its motion, in the semipositive type there is both a vertical flash and a horizontal flash. The *landed-positive type* has a "land" as indicated in Fig. 22.3 and an additional cavity above the molding cavity; it can handle bulky powder without preforming.

Typical metals used for the construction of molds for forming plastics are listed in Table 22.2.

Table 22.2

METALS FOR COMPRESSION AND TRANSFER MOLDS FOR FORMING PLASTIC MOLDINGS (*Courtesy* J. Delmonte)

Mold Part	Type of Metal
Large machined mold cavity	Oil-hardening tool steel
Mold-cavity inserts prepared by hobbing	Mild, low-carbon steel, case-hardened after hobbing
Hobbed mold-cavity inserts for transfer molds subjected to little abrasion	Non-ferrous metals
Mold-cavity inserts (cast molds)	Cast iron, copper, beryllium copper, and zinc alloys
Cylinder of positive and semipositive molds and transfer pot of transfer molds	Case-hardened carbon steel with maximum hardness to resist scoring by punch
Chase (frame)	Boiler plate steel
Ejector pins and guide pins	Heat-treated and water-quenched medium-carbon steel

One of the largest items of expense in the manufacture of molded articles is the cost of molds, or dies, as they are called in the plant. Great savings can often be made in the construction of these molds and in subsequent operations by slight changes in design without affecting the usefulness or beauty of the molded articles. Engineers too frequently make the mistake of not submitting their drawings to experts on molding before having their designs finally approved.

22.16 Injection Molding. Injection molding consists in forcing softened plastic materials into a closed mold maintained at a temperature below the softening point of the composition. This method is applicable to thermoplastic materials. The plastics are heated in a plasticizing chamber and under the action of an injection plunger are forced through the chamber. (See Fig. 22.4.) Injection pressures of from 20,000 to 25,000 pounds per square inch are typical. The materials are forced past a torpedo (spreader) into a nozzle which is in contact with a sprue bushing. From the sprue bushing the materials are forced through runners and gates into the mold cavity. The mold is at considerably lower temperature than the plasticizing chamber so that the thermoplastic molding solidifies quickly. A clamping force is maintained on the mold during injection into the mold cavity and during cooling. One side of the mold is movable; after cooling, the movable

Organic Plastics 559

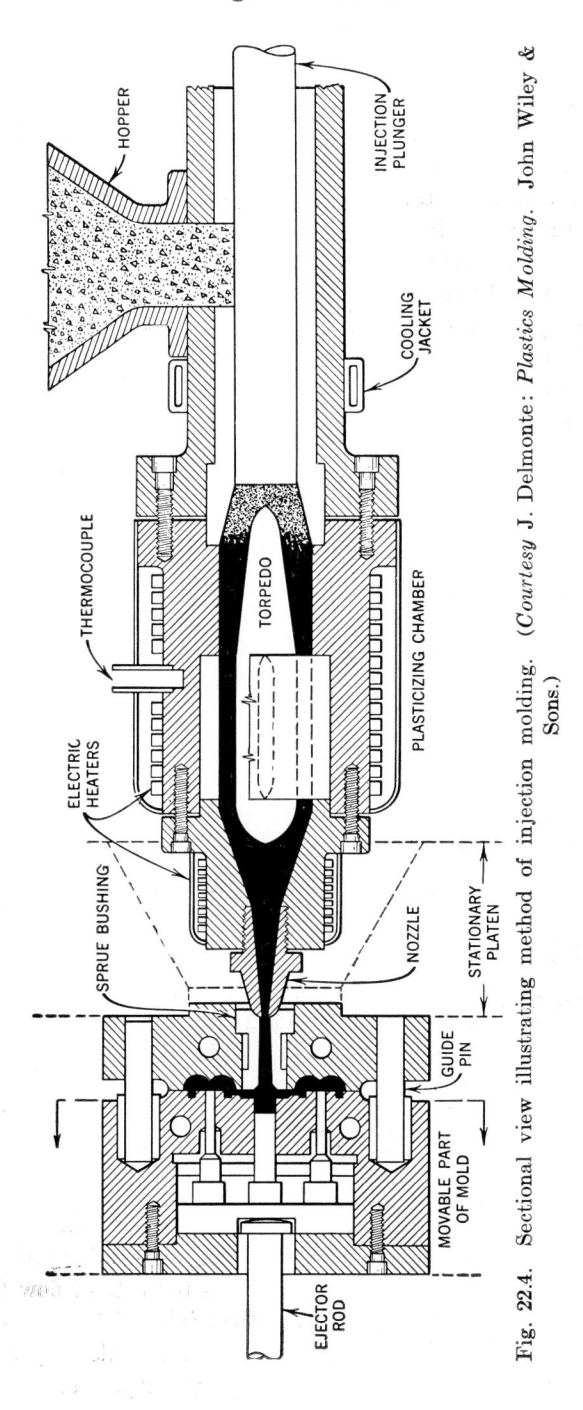

Fig. 22.4. Sectional view illustrating method of injection molding. (*Courtesy* J. Delmonte: *Plastics Molding*. John Wiley & Sons.)

part of the mold is withdrawn and the plastic molding ejected. For small moldings of 4-ounce size, six shots per minute are possible. Large objects up to 300 ounces are formed by injection molding.

A *jet-molding* method of injection molding has been developed for thermosetting plastics. It employs special induction-heating apparatus for application of intense heat to the material as it is forced through the nozzle. Injection pressures range from 15,000 to 50,000 pounds per square inch.

22.17 Extrusion. Extrusion molding is in many respects inverse of injection molding. The softened plastic is forced from a chamber by means of a screw through a die or port. Articles such as bars, rods, tubes, and conduits can be made in this manner. Typical materials used as extruders comprise cellulose acetate, polystyrene, polyvinyl chloride, and polyethylene. In modern extrusion molding, the materials are in powder form, free from moisture and solvent.

22.18 Casting. The simplest molding method is *casting* where melted resins are poured into open molds and cured without application of pressure. Cast phenolic resins are a typical example; the castings are baked in an oven at about 75° C. (167° F.) for several days until they assume a permanent set.

22.19 Blowing. Hollow molded objects are made by a special process known as *blowing*. Only certain plastics, for example, polyethylene, Celluloid, and rubber, can be adapted to this process. A hot closed-end tube of plastic from an extruding machine is passed into the space between two portions of the mold. The mold is closed, and internal air pressure or steam is used to force the plastic sheet against the sides of the mold where the plastic transfers its heat and cools. The mold is opened, and the part removed.

22.20 Plastic Foams. The production of *plastic foams* is accomplished by mixing a gas into an uncured thermosetting resin. The gas may be "whipped" into the resin, or a gas such as nitrogen may be dissolved in the resin under pressure. Then the mixture is heated to polymerize the resin and entrap the bubbles of gas. Plastic foams are formed as the core between outer and inner skins of plastic materials, wood, or metal in sandwich construction. See Chapter 23.

22.21 Flow Characteristics of Plastics. The molder of plastics needs to understand the flow characteristics of plastic materials. Comparisons between the flow characteristics of thermoplastic and thermosetting materials are shown graphically in Fig. 22.5. The most noticeable difference is in the flow rate as a function of time. Thermoplastic materials reach a constant rate of flow that continues indefinitely, whereas the rate of flow for thermosetting materials reaches a maximum and then falls off to zero with further increase in time. This action of thermosetting materials may be explained by considering their polymerization during molding. The partly cured

Organic Plastics 561

thermosetting compound loses viscosity under temperature and pressure and hence is moldable. As time continues, however, the thermosetting material polymerizes (cures) under the molding process and the rate of flow is decreased.

The temperature curve for thermosetting materials can be explained by noting that when the temperature of molding becomes too high, the

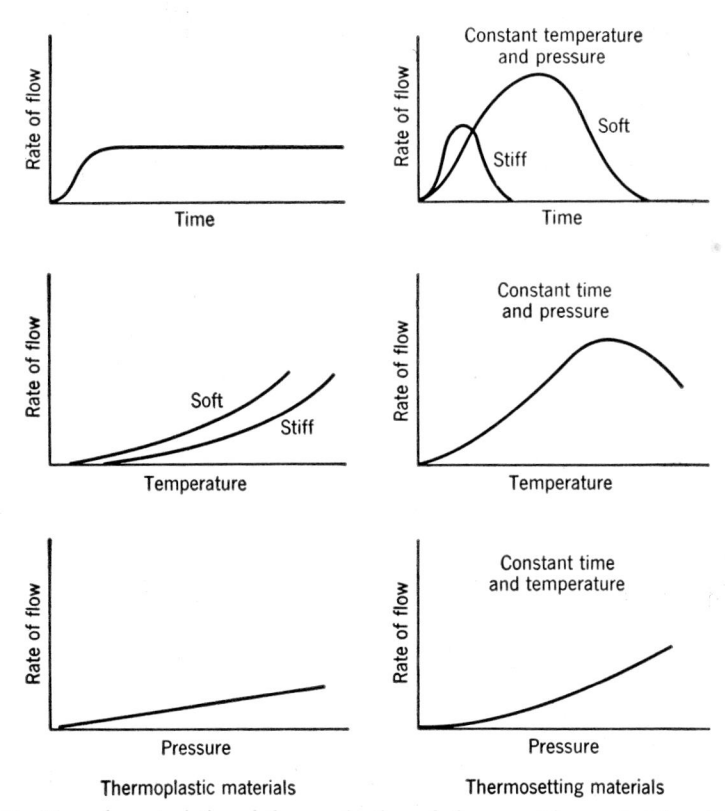

Fig. 22.5. Flow characteristics of thermoplastic and thermosetting materials. (*Courtesy* J. Delmonte: *Plastics Molding.* John Wiley & Sons.)

polymerization occurs quite rapidly, making the material incapable of flowing to its full capability.

22.22 Properties of Organic Plastics. Summaries of some of the properties of molded commercial compositions as reported by various manufacturers [2] are given in Tables 22.3 and 22.4. These tables are included only for general comparative purposes and should not be used for engineer-

[2] The Bakelite Corp.; Carbide and Carbon Chemicals Corp.; The Celluloid Corp.; Cutler-Hammer, Inc.; Durite Plastics; Hercules Powder Co.; Röhm and Haas Co.; and E. I. du Pont de Nemours & Co.

Materials of Construction

Table 22.3
MECHANICAL PROPERTIES OF MOLDED COMPOSITIONS

Type of Material	Tensile Strength, p.s.i.	Impact Strength Notched Bar, ft.-lb. per in.	Modulus of Rupture, p.s.i.	Modulus of Elasticity, p.s.i.	Specific Gravity	Heat Distortion, °C.	Hardness	Coefficient of Linear Expansion per °C.
Phenolic laminated, paper base	6,000–13,000	0.8–2.4 C*	13,000–20,000	1.0–2.0×10^6	1.34–1.55	100–140	85–125 R †	20–50×10^{-6}
Phenolic laminated, canvas base	8,000–12,000	1.6–10.4 C	12,000–19,000	1.0–2.0×10^6	1.34–1.55	100–140	95–115 R	30–70×10^{-6}
Phenolic molded, woodflour filled	6,000–11,000	0.26–0.50 C	8,000–15,000	0.8–1.5×10^6	1.25–1.52	120–140	95–120 R	35–80×10^{-6}
Phenolic molded, cellulose filled	6,000–11,000	0.40–0.80 C	8,000–15,000	0.8–1.5×10^6	1.32–1.48	120–140	95–115 R	35–80×10^{-6}
Phenolic molded, fabric filled	6,000– 8,000	0.80–6.0 C	8,000–13,000	0.8–1.5×10^6	1.35–1.40	120–140	90–115 R	35–80×10^{-6}
Phenolic molded, mineral filled	5,000– 9,000	0.26–1.0 C	8,000–18,000	1.0–5.0×10^6	1.70–2.05	120–150	100–120 R	25–50×10^{-6}
Cast phenolics	3,000– 7,000	0.30–0.50 C	3,000–14,000	0.25–0.75×10^6	1.26–1.70	40–80	70–110 R	70–160×10^{-6}
Phenolic molded, transparent	8,000	——	1,600	——	1.27	107	——	——
Furfuryl-phenol molded, woodflour filled	5,000–12,000	1.0–6.5 I ‡	10,000–16,000	——	1.3–1.4	131	35–40 B §	30×10^{-6}
Furfuryl-phenol molded, asbestos filled	4,000–12,000	1.0–6.0 I	8,000–14,000	——	1.6–2.0	136	44–46 B	20×10^{-6}
Furfuryl-phenol molded, fabric filled	5,000–10,000	20–39 I	10,000–16,000	——	1.3–1.4	——	30–35 B	——
Furfuryl-phenol laminated, paper base	10,000–20,000	5.0–20 I	20,000–30,000	——	1.3–1.4	——	——	——
Furfuryl-phenol laminated, cloth base	9,000–12,000	10.0–50 I	——	——	1.3–1.4	——	——	——
Urea molded	9,000–12,000	0.28–0.36 C	10,000–14,000	1.2–1.9×10^6	1.45–1.55	95–130	110–125 R	——
Polystyrene molded	5,000– 7,000	0.40–0.60 C	6,000– 8,000	0.40–0.60×10^6	1.05–1.07	75–80	82–92 B	65–75×10^{-6}
Acrylate molded	4,000– 8,000	0.3–4.0 C	9,000–16,000	0.4–0.6×10^6	1.18–1.19	51–60	18–20 B	80×10^{-6}
Methyl methacrylate molded	9,000–12,000	0.2–3.0 C	12,000–14,000	——	1.18–1.20	60–135	17–20 B	70–90×10^{-6}
Cellulose nitrate molded	4,900– 8,500	10–11.5 I	5,000– 8,000	0.2–0.4×10^6	1.35–1.60	71–91	7–12 B	120–160×10^{-6}
Cellulose acetate molded	4,000– 5,000	1.7–3.0 C	5,000– 7,000	0.20–0.40×10^6	1.27–1.63	50–80	85–120 R	140–160×10^{-6}
Ethyl cellulose	5,000– 9,000	3.2–9.6 I	——	0.3×10^6	1.14	100–130	——	——
Shellac	900– 2,000	——	——	——	1.1–2.7	66–90	——	——
Cold-molded composition	700– 1,700	1.5–4.5	3,500– 7,800	——	1.9–2.12	182–260	31 B	——
Hard rubber	1,500–10,000	0.5 I	——	0.33×10^6	1.12–1.80	——	——	80×10^{-6}

* C = Charpy.
† R = Rockwell
‡ I = Izod.
§ B = Brinell.

Organic Plastics 563

Table 22.4
ELECTRICAL PROPERTIES OF MOLDED COMPOSITIONS

Type of Material	Power Factors 60 cycles per sec.	Power Factors 1000 cycles per sec.	Power Factors 10^6 cycles per sec.	Dielectric Constant 60 cycles per sec.	Dielectric Constant 1000 cycles per sec.	Dielectric Constant 10^6 cycles per sec.	Loss Factor 60 cycles per sec.	Loss Factor 1000 cycles per sec.	Loss Factor 10^6 cycles per sec.	Resistivity, megohm-cm.	Dielectric Strength Step Test, v. per mil
Phenolic laminated, paper base	0.02–0.15	0.02–0.10	0.02–0.06	4.5–6.5	4.5–6.0	4.0–5.5	0.1–1.0	0.1–0.6	0.10–0.30	2×10^6–1×10^8	400–600
Phenolic laminated, canvas base	0.05–0.30	0.05–0.20	0.04–0.10	5.0–9.0	4.5–8.0	4.0–6.0	0.25–2.0	0.15–1.0	0.15–1.0	3×10^5–4×10^7	250–400
Phenolic molded, woodflour filled	0.02–0.30	0.02–0.15	0.035–0.08	4.5–10.0	4.5–10.0	4.0–8.0	0.10–3.0	0.20–1.5	0.15–0.80	10^4–10^6	200–300
Phenolic molded, cellulose filled	0.05–0.30	0.04–0.15	0.04–0.10	4.5–10.0	4.5–10.0	4.0–8.0	0.25–3.0	0.20–1.5	0.15–1.0	10^4–10^5	200–300
Phenolic molded, fabric filled	0.05–0.30	0.04–0.15	0.04–0.10	4.5–15	4.5–15	4.0–10	0.25–4.5	0.20–2.0	0.15–1.0	10^3–10^5	200–300
Phenolic molded, mineral filled	0.020–0.50	0.01–0.20	0.005–0.10	4.5–20	4.5–15	4.0–10	0.10–4.0	0.045–3.0	0.020–1.0	10^3–10^8	200–375
Cast phenolics	0.070–0.50	0.030–0.30	0.04–0.13	7.0–30	6.0–25	5.5–15	0.70–16.0	0.20–4.0	0.20–2.0	10^4–10^7	120–300
Phenolic molded, transparent	0.06	0.04	0.019	5.5	5.0	4.5				7.5×10^5	325
Furfuryl-phenol molded, woodflour filled		0.04–0.15	0.01–0.06		4.0–8.0	6–7.5				10^{10}–10^{12}	400–600
Furfuryl-phenol molded, asbestos filled		0.1–0.15	0.06–0.15		4.5–20	5–18				10^9–10^{11}	200–500
Furfuryl-phenol molded, fabric filled		0.08–0.2	0.05–0.08		4.5–6	6				10^{10}	200–500
Furfuryl-phenol laminated, paper base			0.15–0.48		4.5						900–1800
Furfuryl-phenol laminated, cloth base			0.41–0.64		4.5	6.9–7.5	0.40–1.2	0.28–0.65	0.24–0.30	1–10×10^6	300–700
Urea molded	0.050–0.13	0.035–0.07	0.035–0.040	8.10–15	8.0–9.0	2.6	0.00026–	0.00026–	Under	Over 10^{10}	275–325
Polystyrene molded	0.0001–0.0002	0.0001–0.0002	Under 0.0002	2.6	2.6		0.00053	0.00053	0.0005		500–525
Acrylate molded	0.05–0.06			3.4–3.6		2.8				1.0×10^{15}	500
Methyl methacrylate, molded	0.06–0.08		0.02	4.0–4.4		6.2				1.0×10^{15}	480
Cellulose nitrate, molded	0.062–0.149		0.07–0.09	6.7–7.3						2–30×10^{10}	660–780
Cellulose acetate, molded	0.03–0.05	0.035–0.07	0.035–0.07	4.5–7.0	4.5–6.5	4.0–4.5	0.13–0.30	0.15–0.40	0.15–0.40	10^6–10^8	300–350
Ethyl cellulose, molded	0.03–0.06	0.025		2.6–2.9	3.9						1500
Shellac, molded filled	0.004–0.018 P*			3–4			0.016–0.16 P			10^8–10^{16}	200–600
Cold-molded composition	0.2		0.07	15.0		6.0				1.3×10^{12}	85–100
Hard rubber			0.003–0.008	2.8	2.9–3.0	3.0				10^{12}–10^{15}	250–1000

* P = Paper filled.

ing design since there are several kinds and grades of each individual type of plastic. The assistance of manufacturers and of molders should be sought before making a final choice of plastic material and of the design to be used.

The properties of electrical-insulation glass-reinforced polyester are given in Table 22.5. This material has high tensile and impact strength. (See Art. 22.4.)

Table 22.5

TYPICAL MINIMUM PROPERTIES OF ELECTRICAL-INSULATION GLASS-REINFORCED POLYESTER *

Property	Standard Type	Flame-Resistant Type
Flexural strength (modulus of rupture), p.s.i., min.	20,000	34,000
After 100 hr. at 302° F.	20,000	32,000
Modulus of elasticity, p.s.i., min.	1.3×10^6	2.84×10^6
Tensile strength, p.s.i., min.	10,000	17,000
Compressive strength, p.s.i., min.	33,500	53,000
Impact strength, Izod, flatwise, ft.-lb./in., min.	12.0	19.2
After 100 hr. at 302° F.	12.0	25.0
Hardness, Rockwell M, min.	85	90
Water absorption, % max.	0.60	0.75
After 100 hr. at 302° F.	1.60	1.75

Shrinkage after 100 hr. at 302° F.: shrinkage shall not exceed 1.0% in any direction.

Dielectric strength, v./mil, min.	300	250
After 100 hr. at 302° F.	300	250
Arc resistance, sec., min.	125	40
Insulation resistance after 5 days at 125.6° F.	—	5

Warp or twist, for standard conditioning and for conditioning for 100 hr. at 302° F., shall not exceed the following:

Thickness, in.	Warp or Twist, % of length, max.
Over 1/15 to 1/4 inclusive	1.0
Over 1/4 to 3/4 inclusive	0.5
Over 3/4 to 1 inclusive	0.25

* *Materials & Methods*, Feb., 1953, p. 131.

Detailed information concerning test methods and specifications for organic plastics is given in the *Book of Standards* of the American Society for Testing Materials, Part 6, 1952.

22.23 Fields of Application. The properties of the different organic plastics fit them admirably for wide use in the aircraft industries. Molded and laminated parts have been used for a long time for control and navigation instruments and for electrical and radio equipment. The instrument board and radio room of a modern airliner are plastic exhibits in themselves. These materials are also widely used in the interior of airplanes for fittings and fixtures. Recent applications include molded plastic gasoline tanks, pipelines, direction-finder cases, and even the panes for curved windows. Styrene rings are used for illuminating dashboard instruments for night flying. This method of lighting completely eliminates glare. New methods of construction include an entire fusilage molded from laminated phenolic plastics.

In 1954, plastic sport automobiles were placed in production in the United States. Sections and parts of the bodies are stamped out of reinforced plastics (fibrous glass cloth in polyester plastic). Parts are joined together by plastic bonding materials.

Automobiles feature many applications of these materials. Shatterproof windshields and windows are examples of the use of plastics since the glass laminations are held together by polyvinyl butyral. Windshields with tinting of the plastic reduce eye glare and also the amount of radiant heat, the latter feature being advantageous in hot climates. Acrylic resins such as polymethyl methacrylate are extensively used in automobiles; examples include tail-light lenses, back-up lights, hood ornaments, instrument panels, dashboard emblems, and headlight dimmers. Nylon is used for speedometer take-off gears and for door-striker wedges; also for brake-pedal arm bushings and brake master-cylinder push-rod bushings.

Cellulose acetate and cellulose acetate butyrate are used for interiors of automobiles such as radio control knobs, radio grilles, extruded trim strips and moldings, emergency brake handles, and steering wheels molded with a metal core. Styrene is employed for dome-light lenses and molded battery cases. An application of polyethylene is for molded and extruded leaf-spring liners which seal out dirt and grit. Polyethylene is suitable for this use because of its inherent self-lubricating properties, good abrasion resistance, and resistance to extreme heat or cold.

Cellulose-filled and mineral-filled phenolics because of their high dielectric strength and good dimensional stability are utilized for electrical insulation, electrical connectors, and for waterproofing ignition parts. Rubber tires should not be overlooked in enumerating the uses of plastics.

Marine uses include many of those of the aircraft and automotive industries. In addition, certain applications are peculiar to this field, such as submarine battery jars, outboard motor parts, chimneys for hurricane-lamps, and collapsible boats.

Organic plastics have contributed greatly to the development of the electrical industries, especially in power transmission and in communication. Cheaper electricity still depends upon improvements in the insulating materials. Many of these insulators are made of organic plastics. Good mechanical strength is required in addition to electrical properties. The applications of organic plastics in these fields are too numerous to list here. It may suffice to point out that these materials are employed in the construction of such equipment as generators, motors, distributing apparatus, switchboards, panels, terminal boards, circuit breakers, electrical connections, magnetos, fuse plugs, condensers, light-bulb bases, cartridge fuses, battery cases, transformers, and various housings for both operating equipment and measuring instruments.

Globes of acrylic resins are manufactured for fluorescent light fixtures for street lighting. They afford excellent light transmission. Since they have good strength and resiliency, they can withstand severe impact without shattering. Other applications of acrylic resins are panes for press-box windows in coliseums and for skylighting in auditoriums.

Bearings for cranes, grinding wheels, gears for power-driven shovels and mixers, oil-well equipment, water meters, X-ray tube guards, pipelines, tanks, towers, stills, pumps, conveyors, helmets, and goggles are a few scattered examples of industrial uses. Railroads employ these plastics for mechanical, electrical, and architectural applications.

Cast resins and Celluloid have given the engineer materials for the construction of models which he can use for studying the distribution of stresses under different actual loadings. This is done by placing the model in the path of polarized light and analyzing the colored interference figures produced by the internal strains.

Rubber

22.24 Natural Rubber. Natural rubber is obtained from latex which is a milky emulsion tapped from the bark of hevea trees (*Hevea brasiliensis*). Solids in the latex are coagulated by adding either acetic acid or formic acid. They are then separated from the liquid by squeezing in rolls. The sheets of rubber are then washed and dried. Crude rubber is vulcanized by combining it chemically with sulfur at an elevated temperature. Vulcanization improves the physical properties of rubber to a marked degree, giving the treated rubber much greater tensile strength, a smaller permanent set, greater resistance to solvents, and less susceptibility to temperature changes.

Rubber has the outstanding property of being able to undergo great deformation without becoming damaged structurally but is not perfectly elastic according to the definition of elasticity given in Art. 1.3. This property of rubber is explained as follows: Rubber molecules are coiled when in normal position. When they are stretched by application of a tensile force, they unroll. When tension is relased, the molecules recoil quickly to their original position because the coiled state is their naturally stable state. Any permanent set is caused by slippage of one molecular chain past another when in the extended position.

When loads are applied and removed, a portion of the energy required to deform the rubber is lost in what is called "mechanical hysteresis." Owing to this property of high mechanical hysteresis, rubber compositions are utilized for absorbing shocks and reducing vibration in machines. Deterioration of rubber tires and belting operated at high speed may be produced by heat generated by mechanical hysteresis.

The mechanical, chemical, and electrical properties of hard natural rubber are excellent but are impaired by exposure to sunlight and extensive contact with oil and other organic liquids. Metal inserts must be plated with some heat-resistant coating which does not react with sulfur.

22.25 Synthetic Rubber. Synthetic rubber is the name applied to rubberlike materials that are manufactured by chemical processes. There are five commercial types of synthetic rubber of importance. These are buna S, buna N, butyl, neoprene, and thiokol.

Buna S (Government Rubber, S, called GR-S) is the copolymer of butadiene and styrene. This type comprised about 85 per cent of synthetic rubber production during World War II. It is used for tires because it can be combined with natural rubber. Buna S can be vulcanized with sulfur. It is lower in strength and flexibility than natural rubber.

Buna N (GR-A and GR-N) is the copolymer of butadiene and acrylonitrile. It is vulcanized with sulfur. It is highly resistant to solvents and oils and has very good resistance to aging and abrasion. Buna N is utilized for tank linings, conveyor belts, and hose. Because of its resistance to cold, it is selected for use in aircraft designed for flying at high altitudes. Combining buna N rubber with phenolic resins improves the strength markedly.

Butyl rubber (GR-I) consists essentially of isobutylene with small amounts of isoprene or butadiene. This synthetic rubber has the greatest impermeability to gases and therefore is used for tire inner tubes. Also it is used for diaphragms, tank linings, electrical insulation, and hose. It is highly resistant to aging and ozone, and has good resistance to oxidizing agents. Vulcanization with sulfur produces "soft" rubber.

Neoprene (GR-M) is a polymer of chloroprene. It is vulcanized with metal oxides instead of sulfur and cannot be vulcanized to "hard" rubber. Neoprene rubber possesses excellent aging resistance and has good resistance to deterioration in oil. It is used for belts, gaskets, wire insulation, and hose.

Thiokol (GR-P) *rubber* is made by copolymerization of organic compounds with polysulfides. It is particularly resistant to gasoline, fuel oils, and lubricating oils. Polysulfide rubber has good resistance to solvents in general. It is resistant to cold but not to heat. Thiokol is cheap and can be molded or extruded with the usual plastic equipment but an unpleasant odor limits it to certain types of applications. It is nevertheless extensively used for hose for gasoline, gaskets, printing rolls, and diaphragms.

Silicones

22.26 Silicones. Silicone resins, called silicones, introduced in 1945, have an inorganic structure with an organic exterior. A silicon-oxygen chain is linked to various organic groups. The resulting materials have heat-resisting properties of inorganic substances coupled with other characteristics corresponding to organic high polymers. The physical properties of silicone resins depend upon the organic component; methyl components produce better heat-resisting properties, whereas phenyl components produce resins of greater flexibility. Silicones are manufactured in the form of liquids, greases, and rubber-like solids. The liquids are used for heat-transfer media, damping fluids, and high-temperature lubricants. The greases are employed as high-temperature lubricants for bearings and valves. The rubber-like solids are used as a gasketing material for service at elevated temperatures. The hardness of silicone gaskets is not changed up to a temperature of 400° F. whereas organic synthetic rubber gaskets will harden or shrink at these temperatures. Silicones are also resistant to ultraviolet rays, ozone, water, and aging. They have good bonding properties and fair dielectric properties. Liquids have a specific gravity of 1.03 to 1.09 and gaskets 1.7 to 2.1.

Silicones are also used as components of varnish resins; these are employed as protective coatings, as bonding agents in laminates, and as electrical insulation. Thermosetting molding compositions are available containing silicones; they are used in manufacturing waterproof insulation products for high-frequency equipment and high-tension ignition systems.

Questions

22.1. Describe what is meant by an organic plastic, a binder, the resinoid state, a filler, a thermoplastic, a thermosetting resin, chemically setting compositions, addition polymerides, and condensation polymerides.

22.2. What are the important properties of organic plastics which contribute to their use as materials for construction?

22.3. Name the important groups of thermosetting plastics. What are some of their advantages and disadvantages?

22.4. Name the important groups of the thermoplastic materials. What are some of their advantages and disadvantages?

22.5. What are some of the different types of phenolic plastics? How do they differ?

22.6. Explain what is meant by a phenolic plastic, by a urea plastic, by a cellulose plastic, by an organic glass.

22.7. What types of substances are used as fillers and as coloring materials?

22.8. How are fillers incorporated with binders?

Organic Plastics

22.9. How are articles fabricated from organic plastics?
22.10. What are the different types of molds? How do they differ from one another?
22.11. What factors must be considered in designing a molded article?
22.12. List the possible items of cost in commercial molding.
22.13. Why is it desirable to submit drawings to a molding expert before having them approved?
22.14. How do the flow characteristics of thermoplastics differ from those of thermosetting plastics?
22.15. Describe the process of injection molding.
22.16. Describe the manufacture of plastic foams.
22.17. Name some applications of acrylic resins.
22.18. State typical physical properties of reinforced plastics. What are some of their applications?
22.19. What is Nylon? Name some of its applications in the automotive industry.
22.20. What types of plastics would you expect to find being used in the airplane, automotive, and railroad industries?
22.21. How might a livingroom be finished with different plastic materials?
22.22. What plastic composition or plastics would you select for manufacturing translucent Venetian blinds, for a pipeline to carry dilute sulfuric acid, for an electrical insulator to be placed near a boiler, for housing an X-ray tube, and for a float to be used in strong caustic solution? State your reasons.
22.23. Name and briefly describe five types of synthetic rubber.
22.24. Describe the properties of natural rubber.
22.25. What are silicones? What are their properties? Name several applications of silicones.

References

22.1. American Society for Testing Materials: *Symposium on Plastics.* Philadelphia, 1938. Also, section on plastics, *Book of Standards,* Part 6, 1952.
22.2. Boor, L., Ryan, J. D., Marks, M. E., and Bartoe, W. F.: "Hardness and Abrasion Resistance of Plastics." *ASTM Bull.* 145, Mar., 1947, p. 68.
22.3. Carthwright, R. P.: "The Behavior of Plastics under Various Service Conditions." *Trans. Inst. Plastics Ind. (London),* v. 7, No. 14, 1938, p. 79.
22.4. Cotterell-Butler, R.: "Plastics and Architecture." *Ibid.* v. 8, No. 15, 1939, p. 38.
22.5. Delmonte, J.: *Plastics Molding.* John Wiley & Sons, 1952, 493 pages.
22.6. Delmonte, J.: *Plastics in Engineering.* Cleveland, Ohio, Penton Publ. Co., 1949.
22.7. Engel, H. C., Hemming, C. B., and Merriman, H. R.: *Structural Plastics.* McGraw-Hill Book Co., 1950, 301 pages.
22.8. Gardner, W. H.: "Shellac, The Parent of Modern Plastics." *Paint, Oil, Chem. Rev.,* v. 99, No. 12, June 10, 1937, pp. 34–37.
22.9. Gilmore, G., and Spencer, R.: "Injection Molding Process." *Modern Plastics,* v. 27, Apr., 1950, p. 143.
22.10. Mactaggart, E. F., and Chambers, H. H.: *Plastics and Building.* London, Pitman & Sons, 1951, 181 pages.
22.11. Marin, J., and Pao, Y.: "Creep Relaxation Relations for Styrene and Acrylic Plastics." *Proc. ASTM,* v. 51, 1951, p. 1277.
22.12. Marsden, E.: "Plastics in Telephone Engineering." *Trans. Inst. Plastics Ind. (London),* v. 7, No. 13, 1938, p. 49.
22.13. *Modern Plastics Encyclopedia,* Annual editions, New York, Plastics Catalogue Corp.

22.14. Nord, M.: *Textbook of Engineering Materials.* John Wiley & Sons, 1952; Chaps. 23 and 24, pp. 466–488.
22.15. Redfarn, C. A.: *A Guide to Plastics.* London, Iliffe & Sons, 1951, 112 pages.
22.16. Schmidt, A. X., and Marlies, C. A.: *Principles of High Polymer Theory and Practice.* McGraw-Hill Book Co., 1948.
22.17. Schoenborn, E. M., and Weaver, D. S., Jr.: "Ignition Temperatures of Rigid Plastics." *ASTM Bull.* 146, May, 1947, p. 80.
22.18. *Society of Plastics Industry Handbook,* New York, 1947.
22.19. Stark, H. J.: "Effects of Vibration on Phenolic Foams." *ASTM Bull.* 189, Apr., 1953, p. 44.
22.20. Suttermeister, E., and Browne, F. L.: *Casein and Its Industrial Applications.* Am. Chem. Soc. Monograph 30. New York, Reinhold Publ. Corp., 1939; Chap. 7, pp. 181–232.
22.21. Thomas, I.: *Injection Molding of Plastics.* New York, Reinhold Publ. Corp., 1947.
22.22. Winding, C. C., and Harsche, R. L.: *Plastics Theory & Practice.* McGraw-Hill Book Co., **1947.**

Section IX · Laminates and Adhesives

CHAPTER 23

Laminates and Adhesives
By LLOYD F. RADER

23.1 General. Although there are numerous examples of early fabrication of laminated structures of wood and of metal, the development of engineering laminates into many types for various utilizations is comparatively recent. Improved synthetic resin adhesives which are resistant to attack by moisture have been a major factor in the increased production of laminates. Modern laminates make it possible to obtain certain properties more readily than by means of elemental materials and in some cases make possible the attainment of singular and novel properties.

Laminates

23.2 Definitions of Laminates. A *laminate* *,[1] is a product made by bonding together two or more layers of material or materials. The product may be *cross laminated*,* which means that some of the layers of material are oriented at right angles to the remaining layers with respect to the grain or strongest direction in tension; or it may be *parallel laminated*,* which means that all the layers of material are oriented approximately parallel with respect to the grain or strongest direction in tension. A laminate is composed of adherends and adhesive. An *adherend* * is a body which is held to another body by an adhesive.

23.3 Types of Laminates. Common types of laminated structures comprise plywood, plastic-surfaced plywood, glued-laminated wood, plastics-based laminates, sandwich-type construction, metal-clad products, thermostat metals, glass-lined metals, and composite-glass laminates.

A laminate may be classified into one or more of the following groupings:
1. Composites of one type of material.
2. Composites of materials of approximately the same density.

[1] Definitions adopted by the American Society for Testing Materials are marked with an asterisk.

3. Composites of materials of different types.

4. Sandwich construction fabricated with strong, dense skins and lightweight cores.

5. Composites consisting of heavy protective coatings bonded to core materials of poorer corrosion and wear resistance.

Adhesives

23.4 Nature of Adhesion. *Adhesion* * is defined as the state in which two surfaces are held together by interfacial forces which may consist of valence forces or interlocking action, or both. There are two types of adhesion: (1) Mechanical and (2) Specific. *Mechanical adhesion* * is adhesion between surfaces in which the adhesive holds the parts together by interlocking action. *Specific adhesion* * is adhesion between surfaces that are held together by valence forces of the same type as those that give rise to cohesion. *Cohesion* * is defined as the state in which the particles of a single substance are held together by primary or secondary valence forces. As used in the adhesive field, cohesion is the state in which the particles of the adhesive (or the adherend) are held together.

Where good adhesive action is obtained, most of the bonding strength is due to specific adhesion and a smaller part to mechanical adhesion. Thus the interlocking action of the pore spaces and uneven surfaces of the adherend by means of the adhesive binds the parts of the laminated structure together much less than specific adhesion which is due to chemical and electrical forces. These bonding forces that hold molecules and atoms together may be classed as follows: (1) electrostatic (polar) bonds, (2) covalent bonds, (3) coördinate covalent (semipolar) bonds, (4) metallic bonds, and (5) van der Waals forces. (See reference 23.17, "A General Theory of Adhesion," by R. C. Rinker and G. M. Kline.) Since these forces function over minute distances and close contact is required for proper bonding, it is necessary that the adhesive thoroughly wet the surface of the adherend. The type and composition of the surfaces of the adherends must be taken into account as well as the class and properties of adhesives in selecting combinations of materials in order to obtain good strength of laminated structure. Thus for polar surfaces, electrostatic (polar) type adhesives should be employed, while for non-polar surfaces, non-polar type adhesives should be selected for good bonding.

23.5 Types of Adhesives. From the standpoint of composition, adhesives for structural applications may be classified as natural or synthetic resin adhesives.

I. Natural adhesives.
   A. Protein adhesives.
      1. Animal.

Laminates and Adhesives 573

      2. Blood albumin.
      3. Casein.
      4. Soya-bean.
   B. Starch adhesives.
      1. Corn.
      2. Tapioca.
II. Synthetic resin adhesives.
   A. Thermosetting adhesives.
   B. Thermoplastic adhesives.

23.6 Protein Adhesives. *Animal glues* are the oldest and best known of the commonly used adhesives. They are prepared from gelatin obtained from hides and bones of animals by heating with water. Hide glues are manufactured from animal tissues and hide scraps from slaughterhouses. The tissues and scraps are washed, treated with lime, washed again to remove the residual lime, and then neutralized; this is followed by extractions with hot water ranging in temperature from 60° C. (140° F.) to 100° C. (212° F.). The extracts are evaporated in vacuum evaporators to drive off water, leaving concentrated solutions of glue which are ground into small-size fragments for marketing. Bone glues are manufactured from decalcified animal bone in a similar manner; they are usually of poorer quality than hide glues. Animal glues are good all-purpose adhesives for wood but are not moisture resistant and may be attacked by fungi; for these reasons they are being displaced by the more resistant synthetic resin adhesives.

Blood-albumin glues are produced by mixing albumin in the form of dry powder, obtained by evaporation of raw animal blood, with chemicals such as lime, ammonia, caustic soda, sodium silicate, or paraformaldehyde, and with water. They have been employed in the past as adhesives for plywood since they are water resistant; but owing to poor resistance to attack by fungi and to inferior physical properties as compared to synthetic-resin glues, blood-albumin glues have been supplanted commercially by the synthetic-resin glues. For properties of blood-albumin glues, see Table 23.1.

Casein glues consist of mixtures of casein with calcium hydroxide and one or more sodium salts; all materials are dry and finely ground. Casein is obtained from skimmed milk in which the first step is that of curdling. This curdling may be allowed to take place spontaneously by the naturally formed lactic acid, or it may be produced artificially by means of rennet or a weak acid. This type of glue may be treated with preservatives such as chlorinated phenol to improve resistance to attack by mold and fungi. Casein glues are usually marketed in powder form and need only to be mixed with water at ordinary temperature; they are available, however, in the form of emulsions that dry after application to produce water-resistant films. There is considerable variation in physical properties because casein itself is a variable product, and the use of different ingredients in varying proportions results in glues of widely differing characteristics. Only the more water-resistant glues are suitable for use in aircraft; the properties of casein glues that meet aircraft specifications are given in Table 23.1. Casein glues are used for plywood and laminated timbers

Table 23.1

PROPERTIES OF GLUES USED IN AIRCRAFT *

Property or Characteristic	Casein Glue	Blood-Albumin Glue	Synthetic-Resin Glue
Strength (dry) †	Very high to high	High to low	Very high to high
Strength (wet after soaking in water 48 hr.) ‡	About 25 to 50% of dry strength—varies with glue	About 50 to nearly 100% of dry strength	Very high; nearly 100% of dry strength
Durability in 100% relative humidity or prolonged soaking in water	Deteriorates eventually—rate varies with glue	Deteriorates slowly but usually completely in time	Very high if resin is unadulterated
Rate of setting	Rapid	Very fast with heat	Very fast with heat
Working life	Few hours to a day	Few to many hours	Few to several hours for liquid forms; several weeks for films
Consistency of mixed glue	Medium to thick; little change with temperature	Thin to thick; little change with temperature	Medium for liquid forms
Temperature requirements	Unimportant	Heat required to set most glues	Heat required for most glues
Mixing and application	Mixed cold with water; applied cold by hand or mechanical spreaders	Usually mixed cold with water; applied cold by hand or mechanical spreaders	Often applied as received or after addition of "catalyst"; liquid forms best applied by rubber-covered rolls
Tendency to foam	Slight if not mixed too rapidly	Slight to pronounced	Slight
Tendency to stain wood	Pronounced with certain woods	None, except dark glue may show through thin veneers	None, although glue may penetrate through thin or porous veneers
Dulling effect on tools	Moderate to pronounced	Slight	Moderate
Spreading capacity §			
Extremes reported ‖	35–80	30–100	30–100
Common range ‖	40–60	—	35–50

* Grades and quality only of glues that pass aircraft specifications.
† Based chiefly on joint strength tests.
‡ Based on plywood strength tests.
§ Expressed in square feet of single glue line per pound of dry glue for veneer work.
‖ Based on reports from manufacturers of various commercial products.

(see Table 23.2). Since casein glues can be applied to wood at temperatures as low as 10° C. (50° F.), they are utilized for gluing laminated timbers in the field.

Soya-bean glues are protein adhesives rather than starch because they are manufactured from protein meal, left after extraction of the oil from the soya beans. The meal is treated with calcium hydroxide and sodium hydroxide, and the dried product is mixed with water. Soya-bean glues are similar in characteristics to casein glues. They are easily applied at ordinary temperature. The major application of soya-bean glues is in the manufacture of interior-grade Douglas-fir plywood. This type of glue is cheap and has comparatively good resistance to moisture.

23.7 Starch Adhesives. The principal starch adhesives are those made from *corn* and *tapioca* (cassava). The starch is treated with acids or peroxides, is dried, and pulverized; manufactured dry glue will retain its

Table 23.2 *

USE CHARACTERISTICS OF LAMINATING GLUES †

Glue Type	Exposure Suited for	Storage Life at 80° F., months	Working Life at 70 to 75° F., hr.	Maximum Permissible Assembly Time at 70° F., min. Open	Maximum Permissible Assembly Time at 70° F., min. Closed	Permissible Moisture Content of Wood, % Min.	Permissible Moisture Content of Wood, % Max.	Setting Characteristics ‡ Cold	Setting Characteristics ‡ Room Temperature	Setting Characteristics ‡ Intermediate Temperature	Laminating Pressure, p.s.i. Min.	Laminating Pressure, p.s.i. Max.	Conditioning Period,§ days
Casein	Normal interior	12	5	15	30	2	18	Yes	Yes	Yes	100	250	5–7
Urea, powdered with catalyst	Normal interior	12	2–6	10	20	7	15	No	Yes	Yes	100	250	5–7
Intermediate-temperature-setting phenol	Interior and exterior	2–6	2–8	30–60	60–120	6	17	No	No (except with some low-density species)	Yes	100	250	1
Resorcinol	Interior and exterior	12 or more	2–5	15	50	6	17	No (except with low-density species)	Yes	Yes	100	250	1–7
Melamine ‖	Interior and exterior	6–18	2–36	30–60	60–120	7	15	No	No	Yes	100	250	

* L. J. Markwardt: "Developments and Trends in Lightweight Composite Construction," *ASTM, Special Tech. Publ.* 118, 1952.
† The values given in this table are approximations.
‡ Cold setting refers to glues that set or cure below normal workroom temperatures (minimum about 65° F.). Room temperature is considered to be 65 to 83° F. Intermediate temperature refers to glues that require heating in excessive room temperature but not above 210° F., the maximum that can be obtained ordinarily in heated chambers.
§ Where glue is completely cured by application of heat accompanied by adequate humidification before pressure is removed, merely cooling to room temperature is sufficient; where no heat is applied, a 5 to 7 day conditioning period is desirable.
‖ Includes glues both with and without separate catalyst.

properties indefinitely. To prepare the dry glue for application, it is mixed with water to form a slurry which is heated for about one-half hour at 70° C. (158° F.), and cooled. Sodium hydroxide is generally added to the slurry in order to improve gumminess of the adhesive and to increase penetrative properties into adherends such as paper or wood. Corn and tapioca glues are applied cold, preferably by means of a mechanical spreader, and are used in manufacturing interior-grade plywood and paper laminates where moderately good strength at low cost is desired. These glues have low water resistance.

23.8 Synthetic Resin Adhesives. The subject of resins is discussed in Chapter 22, "Organic Plastics." Synthetic resin adhesives are classed as thermosetting or thermoplastic adhesives. *Thermosetting adhesives* have greater applications in industry, give rigid rather than flexible bonds, and in general have better physical properties than thermoplastic adhesives. Thermosetting adhesives comprise phenol-formaldehyde resin, resorcinol-formaldehyde resin, urea-formaldehyde resin, and melamine-formaldehyde resin. *Thermoplastic adhesives* of importance include cellulose derivatives and polyvinyl acetate.

Phenol-formaldehyde resin is the most important synthetic resin adhesive. It has excellent strength and water-resistant properties which are referred to as standard. Phenol and formaldehyde are combined in such proportions as to produce a cross-linking structure. The process is one of condensation which is conducted only to the A stage in which the uncured resin is still fusible and soluble in certain liquids such as alcohol or water. This adhesive is commercially available in the A stage in three forms: a dry powder, which can be stored indefinitely; a solution in alcohol or water; and Tego film, which is a thin tissue-paper base impregnated with uncured resin. The latter is utilized in the manufacture of Douglas-fir plywood of the exterior type, a sheet of film being placed between veneers and then heated and pressed. Phenol-formaldehyde resin adhesives are applied hot at temperatures between 115° C. (239° F.) and 165° C. (329° F.). Pressures for manufacturing plywood range from 150 to 175 pounds per square inch. Properties of synthetic-resin glue used in aircraft (Table 23.1) are typical of the properties of phenol-formaldehyde resin adhesives. The use characteristics of phenolic and other thermosetting adhesives are given in Table 23.2.

Resorcinol-formaldehyde resin adhesives have characteristics similar to those of phenol-formaldehyde resins, but possess an advantage in that assembly and curing operations may be performed at room temperature, although hot pressing and curing at moderately high temperatures give improved strength and durability. This adhesive is more expensive than the phenol type but is well suited for structures for prefabricated houses and for laminated timbers and boat construction where extreme exposures must be withstood.

Urea-formaldehyde resin adhesives are manufactured by a condensation process in which urea and formaldehyde are combined in proper proportions to produce a cross-linking structure in the final infusible state. The adhesive in powder form is mixed with water, and a catalyst such as an ammonium salt may be added for the purpose of regulating the temperature for assembly and curing. The amount of catalyst is controlled by means of the pH determination. Adhesives are produced for varying curing temperatures ranging from 20° C. (68° F.) to 120° C. (248° F.). Urea-formaldehyde resin adhesives are extensively used in plywood manufacture; they are resistant to water at ordinary room temperature but will not withstand repeated wetting and drying, nor will they prove durable when wet at temperatures above 65° C. (149° F.). These adhesives should not be employed for severe outdoor exposures.

Melamine is condensed with formaldehyde to form a cross-linked thermosetting resin. This *melamine-formaldehyde resin adhesive* is prepared and handled in a manner similar to that for urea-formaldehyde resin adhesives as described above. Melamine adhesives cost more than urea-formaldehyde resin adhesives, but do have higher water resistance; in fact the melamine adhesives have durability comparable to phenol-formaldehyde resin adhesives, and if cured at high temperatures, have durability properties similar to those of resorcinol-formaldehyde resin adhesives. An outstanding characteristic of melamine-formaldehyde resins is their lack of color; their non-staining qualities account for their selection as adhesives for thin, porous wood veneers instead of dark-staining phenol- or resorcinol-formaldehyde resin adhesives. Because the melamine resin makes an outstanding light-colored surface coating, it is utilized for impregnating the surface of laminates and as an adhesive for bonding the laminate layers. Melamine-formaldehyde resin adhesives are used in laminates where thermal and electrical properties are of importance.

Cellulose nitrate and *cellulose acetate* are two cellulose derivatives used as adhesives. Cellulose nitrate adhesive contains about 12 per cent nitrogen and is available in solvent form. Bonding is accomplished by release of the organic solvent. It is a general-purpose adhesive, but because of flammability and poor moisture resistance, it has limited application for laminates. Cellulose acetate is less flammable but possesses poor weather resistance; its primary application is for bonding leather and paper. *Polyvinyl acetate* has properties similar to the cellulose types; its films are colorless, odorless, and resistant to fungus growth. It adheres well to various materials including metals, glass, rubber, plastics, leather, and paper. In emulsion form, polyvinyl acetate is suitable for bonding wood.

23.9 Preparation and Precautions. Dry hide glue is soaked in about 2¼ times its own weight of water. When the glue is softened, a process that usually requires several hours, it is melted on a water bath the temperature of which must be carefully controlled and never above 65° C. (149° F.).

578 Materials of Construction

For maximum strength, it is advisable to use the glue within 4 hours from the time of melting. For best results hide glue should never be allowed to cool and then be remelted.

Blood-albumin glue requires only the addition of cold water. (See Table 23.1.) Casein glue (see Table 23.1) is similarly mixed with cold water and applied without further preparation. This glue should never be mixed in copper, brass, or aluminum containers. Dry soya-bean glue is also mixed with cold water and applied at room temperature.

23.10 Physical Strength of Bonds. The engineer is interested in determining the mechanical strength of adhesives. Tension, tension shear,

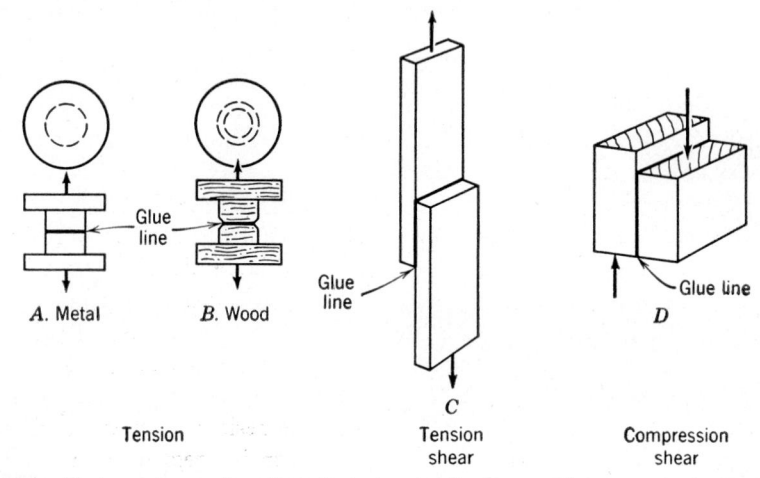

Fig. 23.1. Test specimens for strength tests of adhesives. (*Courtesy* A. G. H. Dietz: *Engineering Laminates.* John Wiley & Sons.)

and compression shear are the three types of tests employed to determine the strength of adhesives (see Fig. 23.1). Specimen A is for metal adherends. Specimen B is used for wood adherends (side-grain glued). It has a reduced glue area so as to decrease tensile stresses set up in the adherend perpendicular to the grain of the wood; by this means, failure occurs in the adhesive instead of the wood adherend. Tension shear tests shown at C are made with adherends of metal, plastic laminates, and plywood. The compression shear test illustrated at D is usually conducted with hard maple blocks.

Laminates of Wood

23.11 General. Laminates of wood comprise plywood, plastic-surfaced plywood, glued-laminated wood, and Compreg. Veneer used in manufacturing plywood will be described first.

23.12 Veneer. This term is applied to thin sheets of wood which may vary in thickness from 0.01 or 0.02 up to about 0.5 inch. They are cut by means of special machines which may use either a saw or a knife. The veneer saw is a circular saw of special form with a cutting edge about 0.05 inch thick. One face is made plane while the other is convexed to give a thickness at the center necessary for the proper stiffness. The veneer saw is efficient only for cutting moderately thick veneers and even then its use is generally limited to the working of the less valuable woods.

Sawing causes a great amount of waste in sawdust, and it is slower than other methods. Sawed veneer is equally firm and strong on both sides of the sheet, and either side may be glued or exposed to view with similar results.

Sliced veneer is cut in the form of long strips by moving a block of wood or "flitch" against a heavy knife. The veneer is forced abruptly away from the block by the knife, thus causing fine checks on the knife side. The checked or "open" side is likely to show defects in finishing, and therefore it should be the glue side whenever possible. By this method either "slash" or "quartered" surfaces may be obtained.

Rotary-cut veneer is produced in large sheets by revolving a log against a knife, "slash-cut" veneer being run out in a continuous sheet in a manner similar to the unrolling of a roll of paper. The length of the sheet (parallel to the grain) is equal to the length of the knife, and the width of the sheets (across the grain) is limited only by the width which can be handled or by the presence of defects in the log. This method is rapid and cheapest. Large quantities of Douglas-fir veneer for the manufacture of plywood are produced from large selected logs, called "peelers." Rotary-cut veneer may have an unattractive figure due to cutting around the annual rings. Variations in the rotary-cut method have been introduced to obtain veneer with improved figure.

Many of the softer woods may be cut into veneer when green without preliminary treatment. Other woods must be steamed before they can be cut satisfactorily.

The sheets of veneer are conveyed to clippers which cut the sheets to pieces of desired dimensions. The pieces are then passed through mechanical dryers of either the conveyor or roller type to dry the veneer to a definite moisture content.

23.13 Plywood. *Plywood* is the ultimate form in which veneer is used by the engineer in auto bodies, small boats, aircraft construction, and building construction. Adjacent plies are generally placed with their grain at right angles.

As has been noted under the heading Timber, wood is naturally highly variable in its properties, particularly at different angles with its grain. In the manufacture of plywood it is possible to recombine the constituent layers so that the properties in different directions may be more nearly equalized. Two salient factors must always be considered in the construction of a satisfactory plywood: (1) it must always be composed of an odd number of layers; (2) layers symmetrically located with respect to the center one must have their grain respectively parallel and should be as nearly identical in all respects as possible. Failure to observe these precautions will result in a panel that will distort very seriously.

There are two types of plywood: (1) veneer plywood and (2) lumber-core plywood. In lumber-core plywood, sheets of veneer are bonded to a central core of lumber.

The woods most commonly utilized for plywood are: Douglas fir, cherry, gum, walnut, ash, oak, elm, birch, beech, maple, poplar, basswood, cottonwood, and mahogany. Many times all plies are of the same kind of wood. Sometimes different woods are combined in order to produce a plied material of special characteristics. Stiffness and strength against bending are largely a question of thickness combined with the modulus of elasticity of the material. Moreover, the central portion of a member under bending is very lightly stressed. In consequence of these facts it is possible to have a core of light and comparatively weak wood with surface plies of stronger material and thus produce a panel in which good strength and stiffness are combined with small weight. This procedure is most applicable in moderately thick plywood.

23.14 Properties and Characteristics of Plywood. In general, it is not possible to equalize all properties in all directions. Tensile strength is equalized in three-ply work when the core is 0.5 the total thickness. Bending strength and stiffness can be approximately equalized in three-ply work when the center ply is 0.7 the total thickness of the panel.

If all layers are of equal thickness this condition is reached only when the panel is composed of fifteen plies or more. Resistance to splitting cannot be equalized in three-ply construction; it is, however, equalized in the multiple-ply type.

Wood normally shrinks as much as 5 to 8 per cent across a board, in passing from green to oven-dry conditions. Plywood under similar treatment shrinks about 0.5 per cent, and that is practically equalized in both directions of a panel. This diminution of shrinkage is produced through the shear resistance of the glue layer. The thinner the individual plies, the smaller will be these shrinkage stresses. It is obvious that very heavy plies might easily set up stresses of a magnitude sufficient to shear the glue or tear the adjacent wood fiber as the component parts tend to swell or shrink.

23.15 Douglas-Fir Plywood. Most plywood used in building construction is made from Douglas fir (*Pseudotsuga taxifolia*) which is a softwood from Oregon and Washington. Douglas-fir plywood is manufactured in

Table 23.3
RECOMMENDED WORKING STRESSES FOR PLYWOOD (DOUGLAS FIR) FOR GRADES AND THICKNESSES LISTED IN US CS45-47

In bending, tension, and compression (except bearing and 45° stresses) consider only those plies with their grain direction parallel to the principal stress.

Dry Location

Type of Stress	Exterior So2S	Exterior So1S, Exterior or Interior Concrete Form	Exterior or Interior Sheathing
Extreme fiber in bending			
Face grain ∥ to span	2,188	2,000	1,875
Face grain ⊥ to span	1,875	1,875	1,875
Tension			
∥ to face grain (3-ply only *)	2,188	2,000	1,875
⊥ to face grain	1,875	1,875	1,875
±45° to face grain	337	320	310
Compression			
∥ to face grain (3-ply only *)	1,605	1,460	1,375
⊥ to face grain	1,375	1,375	1,375
±45° to face grain	496	472	460
Bearing (on face)	405	405	405
Shear, rolling			
In plane of plies and ∥ or ⊥ to face grain	79	72	68
In plane of plies and ±45° to face grain	105	96	90
Shear			
In plane ⊥ to plies and ∥ or ⊥ to face grain	210	192	180
In plane ⊥ to plies and ±45° to face grain	420	384	360
Modulus of elasticity in bending			
Face grain ∥ to span	1,600,000	1,600,000	1,600,000
Face grain ⊥ to span	1,600,000	1,600,000	1,600,000

* For tension or compression, ∥ to grain, in 5-ply or thicker, use values for 3-ply, but in next lower grade.

Damp or Wet Location

Where moisture content will exceed 16 per cent, decrease by 20 per cent values shown for dry location for following properties:

Extreme fiber in bending, tension and compression both parallel and perpendicular to grain and at 45 degrees, and bearing. (No change in values for shear or modulus of elasticity.)

Only exterior type plywood should be used where moisture content will exceed 20 per cent.

two basic types: exterior and interior. In the exterior (waterproof) type, sheets of veneer are bonded by means of a hot-pressed phenolic-resin adhesive that is insoluble under practically any exposure (see Art. 23.8). The interior (moisture-resistant) type is generally bonded with an extended resin adhesive or sometimes with a protein glue such as blood-albumin glue; both hot and cold pressing are employed.

Douglas fir plywood is available in panels 4 feet wide by 8 feet long. Panels up to 50 feet long can be produced by scarf-jointing the panels. Thicknesses range from $3/16$ to $1\,3/16$ inches.

Working stresses recommended by the Douglas Fir Plywood Association and based on research by the U. S. Forest Products Laboratory, Madison, Wisconsin, are given in Table 23.3.

23.16 Stressed-Skin Panels. A panel with stressed covers is known as a *stressed-skin panel*. It generally consists of longitudinal framing pieces separated by headers with covers of plywood on both top and bottom. The plywood covers are adhered to the wood frames by means of resin adhesives so that the plywood acts integrally with the framing members. Stressed-skin panels are used in manufacturing factory-built houses.

23.17 Plywood Beams. Built-up timber beams with plywood webs are commonly called "plywood beams." Wood flanges are glued along the top and bottom edges of the vertical plywood webs. Vertical lumber stiffeners placed at intervals along the beam extend from top to bottom flanges. I-beams have a single web, while box-beams have two or more webs separated by flanges top and bottom. Applications of plywood beams are for roof and floor girders in frame buildings. An advantage is their low dead weight.

23.18 Plastic-Surfaced Plywood. Plastic-surfaced plywood consists of plywood faced with a plastic. It is manufactured by laying up adhesive-spread wood veneers with multiple sheets of resin-impregnated paper for surfacing, and then both the adhesive of the plywood and the resin of the plastic facing are cured by hot pressing, usually at the same time. Both softwoods and hardwoods are used for veneer. The most-used plastic is phenol-formaldehyde-impregnated paper. The adhesive for the plywood is usually a phenolic resin since it is capable of withstanding the relatively high temperatures required for curing the thermosetting resins in the plastic surfacing. Plastic surfaces containing 40 to 50 per cent resin have much better properties than those with lower resin contents. Laminates with plastic surfacings of 40–50 per cent resin content have specific gravity values from 1.35 to 1.40 They absorb moisture at a slower rate than unsurfaced exterior-grade plywood. They also possess good abrasion resistance when both wet and dry and have good weathering properties. They are available in a variety of colors and finishes.

23.19 Glued-Laminated Wood. Glued-laminated wood comprises an assembly of adhesives and wood laminas in which the grain of all laminas is approximately parallel. The laminas are held together by adhesives without dependence upon mechanical fastenings, although mechanical fastenings may also be used as auxiliary fastenings. Glued-laminated wood differs from plywood in that plywood has adjacent plies with the grain at right angles.

Both the exterior type utilizing waterproof adhesives and the interior type using water-resistant adhesives are produced. Douglas fir, yellow pine, and oak are the most-used species. The lumber must be thoroughly seasoned. Manufacture is carried on in factories employing modern methods of assembly.

This laminate permits selection of good lumber for structural members in the sections where strength and appearance are important and utilization of poorer wood in sections where the latter is satisfactory. Structural members of large cross-section and long length can be fabricated from relatively small-size pieces, thus utilizing lumber from small trees. Also pieces with a small number of defects can be utilized by cutting out and discarding those portions containing the defects. However, good lumber is required for glued-laminated wood; then too, more wood is needed in fabricating glued-laminated wood because of loss of material in dressing and scarfing the laminas. Less difficulty is encountered in seasoning small-size pieces. Glued-laminated wood members are not so apt to warp and crack as large solid-timber members. Glued-laminated wood lends itself well to fabrication of tapered and curved structural members.

Glued-laminated wood is more expensive than solid-timber construction because of more material being required, relatively high fabricating costs, and difficulties in transporting large members.

Strength. In glued-laminated wood, the adhesive lines are considered to be as strong and durable as the wood. Usually the glue film is stronger than the cohesion between the wood cells and fibers immediately adjacent to it. Separation of the component members of such a glued composite is often effected by tearing apart of the wood fibers rather than an actual rupture of the glue film. This fact has given rise to some absurd notions as to the strength of laminated members. The mere sawing of a wooden member followed by regluing will not, in general, increase its strength under any type of load. If the sawing operation has removed defective wood, knots, shakes, or other imperfections and if only the selected material has been used in the reconstructed member, the laminated member, being freed from the defects, will be stronger than the defective material from which it has been fabricated. Also, if the original material contains serious diagonal or spiral grain it may be possible to saw and recombine the layers in such a manner that the inclination of grain will be reversed in the adjacent layers.

This process again may be expected to produce a laminated member stronger than the wood from which it has been made. In the cases mentioned above, the glued-laminated material will be heavier than the original wood.

Applications. Applications of glued-laminated wood are for arches, curved truss chords, girders, and columns for various types of structures. Other applications are for keels, frames, masts, stems, and sternposts of boats and ships.

23.20 Compreg. Compreg is a laminate of wood veneers impregnated with synthetic resin. The impregnated laminas are bonded together by curing under heat and heavy pressure to develop a high density. The most satisfactory resin is water-soluble phenol-formaldehyde resin. Both plywood and parallel laminated construction can be formed from the veneers. Compreg has greatly increased mechanical properties and is highly resistant to shrinking and swelling because the resin enters the cell-wall structure and becomes chemically combined throughout the cell walls. Parallel laminated compregnated spruce has the properties given in the accompanying table. (See also reference 23.13.)

Specific gravity	1.32
Tensile strength, parallel to grain, p.s.i.	42,500
Modulus of rupture, p.s.i.	43,400
Modulus of elasticity in tension, p.s.i.	4,418,000

Laminated Plastics

23.21 Laminated Plastics. Laminated plastics are formed by impregnating sheets of fibrous materials with synthetic resins and then compressing with or without the application of heat. In the plastics industry, these are referred to simply as "laminates."

The fibrous materials (fillers) comprise paper, cotton fabric and fibers, wood, glass cloth and mat, asbestos fabric, Nylon, and perforated metal foils. Phenolic resins are the most used. Urea-formaldehyde resins are used with alpha-cellulose filler for decorative laminates where color is of importance. Melamine-formaldehyde resins are also employed where different colors, low moisture absorption, and excellent electrical properties are required. Polyester resins are utilized for low-pressure laminates. (See Art. 22.4.)

23.22 Manufacture of Laminated Plastics. The manufacture of a phenolic laminated plastic reinforced with cotton fabric will be described. The phenol-formaldehyde resin is dissolved in alcohol. Rolls of the cotton fabric are immersed in the resin solution at atmospheric pressure and room temperature and then run through a drier at about 150° C. (302° F.). The rolls of treated fabric are cut into sheets of given size, and the sheets are stacked. The stacks may have the warp threads at right angles in adjacent

Laminates and Adhesives

sheets or all parallel. The stacks are compressed in a hydraulic press at about 170° C. (338° F.) under a pressure of 1500 pounds per square inch. This heating under pressure produces bonding of one sheet to another and permits final curing of the resin.

23.23 Grades of Laminated Plastics. The most important classification of laminated plastics into grades is that of the National Electrical Manufacturers Association (NEMA Standards). The American Society for Testing Materials has specifications and methods of test for various classes of laminated plastics. (See ASTM *Book of Standards*, 1952.)

Laminated plastics are classed according to filler used.

Paper filler is the most used. Laminates containing Kraft paper have acceptable physical properties, fairly low moisture absorption, and general mechanical applications. Laminates with alpha-cellulose paper and cotton-fiber paper have good mechanical and electrical properties.

Cotton cloth is the filler next in importance to paper. It is used where high strength is required—greater than that obtained by paper filler. However, electrical properties are not as good as paper filler. Fine and medium weaves of cloth are selected where the laminate must have excellent machining properties, as when fine pipe threads must be cut. Coarse-weave-cloth filler produces a laminate of greater strength, but the machining properties are not as good. An application of woven-cotton-fabric filler is for laminates for gears and rollers. Such phenolic laminates can withstand contact-roller stresses between 11,000 and 16,000 pounds per square inch in fatigue tests of rollers up to 10 million cycles without breakdown. The filler laminas should be oriented in planes perpendicular to the contact surfaces.

Glass cloth is used for filler to obtain high impact resistance, good mechanical properties, and excellent electrical properties.

Asbestos in the form of paper, cloth, or mat is used where high heat resistance is required. Asbestos cloth has better heat resistance by about 50° F. than asbestos paper. Asbestos mat gives higher mechanical properties than either asbestos paper or cloth.

Nylon-reinforced laminates have a very low water absorption and are used where high resistance to fungus growth is necessary. Nylon is also selected for high impact resistance of laminates.

23.24 Properties. Typical physical properties of a phenolic cotton-fabric laminated plastic are given in Table 23.4.

23.25 Applications. Laminated plastics have numerous applications and are produced in large quantities. They are extensively used in electrical industries. Industrial applications include gears, bearings, pulley wheels, pump parts, and press tools. Applications for decorative purposes include wall paneling, translucent paneling, and table and counter tops.

23.26 Low-Pressure Molding. Laminated plastics are also formed by molding at low pressures. For this process the resin used is a "contact" resin. There are three general types of contact resins: (1) a mixture of an unsaturated polyester or alkyd in a solution of styrene or other monomer, (2) an unsaturated high-molecular monomer, and (3) a combination of

Table 23.4

TYPICAL PHYSICAL PROPERTIES OF PHENOLIC COTTON-FABRIC LAMINATED PLASTIC

	Phenolic Laminated Plastic Reinforced with Heavy Weave Cotton Fabric ⅛-in. Thick	
	Flatwise	*Edgewise*
Specific gravity	1.35	
Tensile strength, p.s.i.		
machine direction	11,300	
cross direction	9,740	
Compressive strength, p.s.i.	40,000	
Flexural strength (modulus of rupture), p.s.i.		
machine direction	21,100	
cross direction	19,000	
Modulus of elasticity in tension, p.s.i.		
machine direction	1,069,000	
cross direction	990,000	
Modulus of elasticity in flexure, p.s.i.		
machine direction	1,106,000	
cross direction	981,730	
Impact strength Izod, ft.-lb. per in. of notch		
machine direction	4.47	2.53
cross direction	4.28	2.40
Flexural fatigue strength, max. fiber stress to cause failure, p.s.i.	1 cycle	10^6 cycles
machine direction	20,300	4,050
cross direction	18,999	3,710
Water absorption, 24-hr. immersion at 25° C. (77° F.)	1.24%	

types 1 and 2. A typical contact resin of type 1 is polyester resin which is formed with unsaturated polyfunctional acids or alcohols by cross-linking by means of vinyl monomers using peroxide catalysts. Curing is by polymerization rather than by condensation, and no gaseous by-product nor water is produced during the reaction; hence such a resin can be cast or molded at a low pressure. Another advantage is that the resin is in liquid form and does not require a solvent to impregnate the fibrous materials.

Common fillers comprise glass fabric, cotton fabric, and paper. Low-pressure molding is carried on at pressures from 0 to 300 pounds per square inch. Low-pressure molding lends itself well to continuous laminating and to construction of large objects such as landing boats, water tanks, and aircraft-wing liners. Other applications include decorative plastics for walls, dielectrics for ultrahigh-frequency radio uses, and structural parts in aircraft manufacture.

Laminates and Adhesives

23.27 Avtex. Avtex is a resin-impregnated cotton web that is compressed under heat; its peculiar characteristic is that the cotton fibers in a given ply are oriented in the same direction to develop a high tensile strength in that direction. Unspun cotton fibers are combed and carded, cleaned, and then impregnated with phenolic resin. This is done in such a manner as to preserve the inherent strength of individual cotton fibers. After drying, the impregnated cotton web is laid up in plies either with parallel fibers or with cross plies. The plies are compressed in a heated hydraulic press. Typical physical properties are listed in Table 23.5. It should be noted that

Table 23.5

TYPICAL PHYSICAL PROPERTIES OF AVTEX

	Avtex Containing Phenolic Resin and Cotton Fibers	
	Fibers Parallel	Cross-Plied
Specific gravity	1.36	1.36
Tensile strength, p.s.i.		
parallel to fibers	27,000	20,900
at 90°	6,000	20,700
at 45°	8,000	17,900
Compressive strength, p.s.i.	27,000	50,150
Flexural strength (modulus of rupture), p.s.i.		
parallel to fibers	34,000	27,000
at 90°	10,000	28,200
at 45°	14,000	22,200
Modulus of elasticity in tension, p.s.i.	1,700,000	1,230,000
Impact strength, Izod, ft.-lb. per in. of notch		
parallel to fibers		17.4
at 90°		17.0
at 45°		20.0
Hardness, Rockwell M scale	100	100
Thermal conductivity, Btu per sq. in. per °F. per in. per hr.	1.94	1.94
Thermal expansion per °F., p.p.m., range (−)40° F. to 100° F.		12.0
Moisture absorption, %	1.8	1.8

for parallel fibers in the different plies, the high tensile strength obtained occurs parallel to the fibers, while in a direction of 90°, the tensile strength is relatively low. Applications of Avtex are for the aircraft industry.

23.28 Post-Forming. Post-forming is a process of fabrication of laminated plastics; simple bends and indentations can readily be made in sheets up to ⅜-inch thick. Post-forming is analogous to sheet metal working in metal fabrication. Laminates of phenol-formaldehyde resins and cotton-fabric fillers are suitable for post-forming. Paper-filled laminates are sometimes post-formed but are not as well adapted as cloth-filled laminates.

Post-forming comprises four steps:

1. Cutting sheets of laminated plastics to required shape.
2. Heating the laminated sheets quickly to soften the resin.
3. Forming by means of dies and tools.
4. Cooling.

Heating up to about 200° C. (392° F.) within 2 minutes is usually desirable. This can be accomplished by contact with a hot plate, by means of radiant heat from infrared bulbs, by placing in an oven, or by immersing in hot oil or molten metal. Forming is carried on by means of special dies, jigs, and tools. Low pressures up to about 60 pounds per square inch are generally sufficient. Bends can be made by means of vertically closing male and female dies. Deep drawing is done with apparatus consisting of a punch, die ring, and hold-down ring which holds down the edges of the sheet above the die ring. Dies are made of hardwood, high-pressure laminated plastic, Masonite, hard rubber, and metal. Both hand-operated and automatic tools are used. Cooling presents no great problem. Air circulation over the form may be sufficient; in some instances, water is circulated through the form. Post-forming is used principally to incorporate simple bends and indentations for strengthening members. Applications are in the electrical, aircraft, automotive, railroad, and textile industries.

23.29 Printed Circuits on Foil-Clad Plastics. Printed circuits have applications in radio and electronics. They are made by various processes which result in the reproduction of a conductive design upon a surface. A modern method comprises etching of metal-foil-clad plastics. In this method, thin metal foil is laminated to one or both sides of a large plastic sheet. An acid resist conforming to the desired conductive pattern is printed on the surface of the metal foil, and the unwanted unprinted portions of the foil are chemically etched away. After washing, cleaning of the resist, and drying, the individual circuits are punched out of the large sheet.

The acid-resist pattern is applied by either the offset-printing process or the photoetch process. The photoetch process is more expensive but gives finer quality and greater precision.

Typical materials used are as follows: $\frac{1}{16}$-inch grade XXXP paper-base phenolic laminate is used as the plastic base; it is of low cost and has good electrical properties. Metal foil selected is electrolytic copper sheet from continuous-electroplating process. The two thicknesses generally used are: (1) 0.00135 inches (1 ounce per square foot of sheet) and (2) 0.0027 inches (2 ounces per square foot). A bonding film or tape is employed to anchor the metal foil onto the plastic base.

Sandwich Construction

23.30 Sandwich Construction. Sandwich construction comprises fabrication of strong, dense skins with a lightweight core. The skins (called faces or facings) are outer layers composed of strong and relatively dense materials such as wood, plastics, metal, or other structural material. The core is made of one or more layers of lightweight and relatively weak materials such as low-density woods, expanded wood fibers, cellular plastics, cellular rubber, and foamed glass. The faces and core are bonded together.

In sandwich construction, the placing of the dense faces far apart increases effectively the moment of inertia of the section. Also the strong faces are in position on the highly stressed outer portions of the section to develop their high strength properties. These features contribute to high strength and rigidity of the assembly. Of course, the use of lightweight core materials decreases dead weight. The term "mechanical stabilization" is employed to denote balanced design for the faces and the core.

23.31 Aircraft-Type Sandwich Construction. For aircraft-type sandwich construction, a superior strength-weight ratio is important. Compactness is desired as is also a good stiffness-weight ratio. The Mosquito bomber received a great deal of attention during World War II; its fuselage was of sandwich construction composed of plywood faces with balsa core. Combinations of materials for faces and core are given in Table 23.6. Advantages of sandwich construction for aircraft are that large integral structural members can be fabricated in a few operations with a minimum of rivets, ribs, and stiffeners, and that faces are smooth because of elimination of rivets and laps; the latter is an aerodynamic advantage. This type of sandwich construction is also used in building trucks and trailers, boats, and railroad train cars.

23.32 Building-Industry-Type Sandwich Construction. For buildings, the stiffness-weight ratio is more important in sandwich construction than high strength-weight ratio. Sections are thicker for buildings than for aircraft because of the need for greater thermal resistance and because of higher structural strength and stiffness required for members for the longer spans employed. Advantages of sandwich construction for the building industry include versatility in utilizing various kinds of materials and simplification by reduction in the number of components. Combinations of materials used are listed in Table 23.6.

23.33 Sandwich Construction for Radomes. Sandwich construction of high-strength plastic is used for radar-antenna covers, called "radomes" (a coined word for "radar domes"). Radomes are mounted on aircraft. Plastic

Table 23.6
COMBINATIONS OF MATERIALS USED FOR FACES AND CORES IN SANDWICH CONSTRUCTION

Aircraft-Type Sandwich Construction

Faces	Core
Plywood	Balsa wood Paper honeycomb Cellular cellulose acetate
Polyester-impregnated glass fabric	Balsa wood Glass-fabric honeycomb Sponge rubber Resin-sponge Cellular cellulose acetate
Aluminum alloy	End-grain balsa wood Fabric honeycomb Paper honeycomb Aluminum-foil honeycomb Metal honeycomb Cellular cellulose acetate

Building-Industry-Type Sandwich Construction

Faces	Core
Plywood	Solid wood (lumber-core construction) Open-cell core of lumber, wood veneer, or paperboard rings Fabric honeycomb Paper honeycomb Low-density calcium hydrosilicate blocks Cellular glass blocks
Asbestos-cement board or lignocellulose hardboard	Laminated vegetable fiberboard Laminated insulation board, both flat grain and edge grain Low-density calcium hydrosilicate blocks Cellular glass blocks
Aluminum alloy	Fabric honeycomb Paper honeycomb Cellular hard rubber Cellular glass blocks
Thin-gauge porcelain enameled steel on $\frac{1}{8}$-in. hard board	Low-density calcium hydrosilicate
Plywood, plastic, or metal	Low-density thermosetting foamed-in-place resins

Laminates and Adhesives 591

materials meet the requirements of small interference with the reception and transmission of radio waves. Faces of glass-fabric-base plastic and a core of cellular plastic have proved satisfactory.

23.34 Fabrication. There are two general methods of fabricating sandwich construction: (1) the one-step process, and (2) the two-step process. In the one-step process, laminates are laid up to form the lower face. Adhesive is applied to the bottom side of the core pieces which are placed on the lower-face assembly. The upper side of the core pieces are coated with adhesive, and the laminates forming the upper face are laid in place on top of the core. Then the entire assembly is compressed in a molding autoclave or hot press, and all uncured impregnating resins and adhesives are cured simultaneously.

In the two-step process, the two faces are built up from laminates, compressed, and cured in advance. One of the faces with adhesive on its top side is placed on the assembly table, and core materials are fitted in place. The upper face with adhesive on its under surface is then fitted in place on top of the core. The assembly is then compressed under heat to cure the adhesive.

Edge banding is many times required to hold in the core material and insure a bond between core and faces that will resist shear.

The above description pertains to flat panels or to panels with slight curvature in one plane only. Panels with considerable curvature in one plane only can be formed by placing the facings and core in a concave mold or over a male mold and applying pressure by mating dies or by means of a blanket. For aircraft, panels of compound curvature are many times required. Fabrication of these consists of forming the facings, forming the core, and then bonding the core to the facings. Elaborate dies and molds are necessary for molding the more complex shapes. Pressure is applied by closing metal mating dies or by fluid pressure through a blanket.

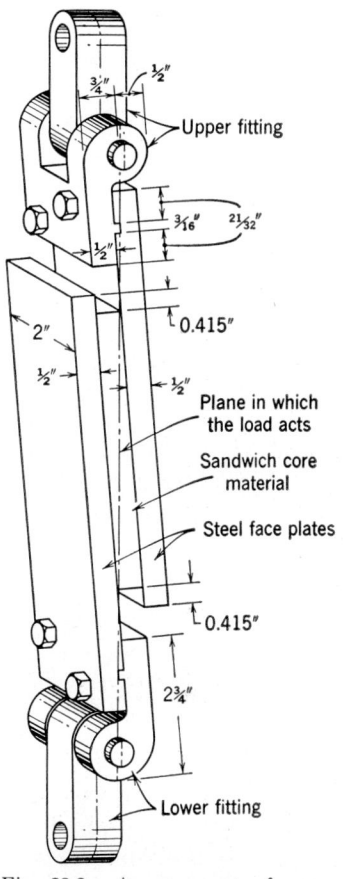

Fig. 23.2. Arrangement of apparatus and specimen for shear test. (*Courtesy* ASTM.)

592 Materials of Construction

For radomes of complex shape, foaming a plastic core in place between previously formed facings held rigidly in place so as to give the desired thickness to the sandwich has proved to be a satisfactory method.

23.35 Testing of Sandwich Construction. The testing of sandwich constructions involves testing of faces, core materials, and assembled sandwich construction. Compression tests of faces are made including stress-strain curves beyond the proportional limit. The modulus of elasticity in compression is determined. For core materials, shear modulus, compressive strength, modulus of elasticity in compression, and Poisson's ratio (ratio of lateral strain to longitudinal strain) are determined; for materials that are not isotropic, these properties are determined in three different directions.

Panels of sandwich construction are tested in flexure, in flatwise and edgewise shear, and in flatwise and edgewise compression. Figure 23.2 shows the arrangement of apparatus and sandwich specimen for shear test in flatwise plane. Apparatus for the edgewise-compression test is illustrated in Fig. 23.3. This test procedure insures a fixed-end condition at the bearing edge of each facing through the utilization of cast disk-end supports.

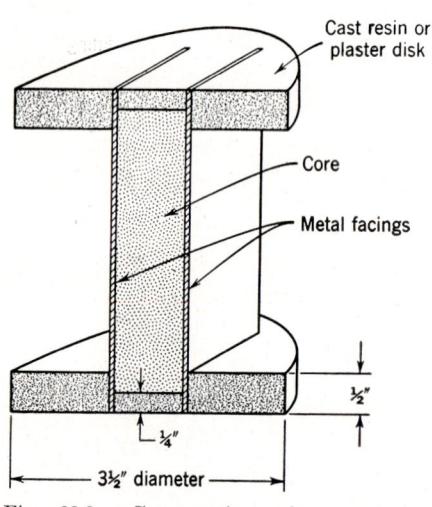

Fig. 23.3. Cross-section of compression edgewise specimen of sandwich plate with cast-resin or plaster disks at the bearing ends. (*Courtesy* ASTM.)

23.36 Structural Properties of Core. Core materials should have a high shear resistance parallel to the plane of the faces in order to develop strength and stiffness. Balsa wood placed in end-grain position (grain of wood perpendicular to faces) gives much greater shear resistance than when placed in flat-grain position. This is because in end-grain position the stresses are distributed over many fibers, whereas in flat-grain position the shear stresses would be parallel to the grain of the wood and hence have small resistance. A similar situation exists for edge-grain insulation-board core which gives a much stronger and stiffer sandwich construction than flat-grain insulation board. End-grain insulation-board core is utilized for roof decking where stiffness is desired so as to have a minimum deflection for a given roof load.

A core should have high tensile strength perpendicular to the plane of the faces in order to make it possible for the faces to develop their ultimate strength before the panel of sandwich construction buckles. Compressive

Laminates and Adhesives

strength of the core is necessary to support the faces when the panel is loaded flatwise and is being handled.

The physical properties of various core materials are given in Table 23.7. With respect to mechanical properties alone, balsa is the best low-density

Table 23.7

PHYSICAL PROPERTIES OF CORE MATERIALS *

Property	Balsa Wood	Extruded Cellular Cellulose Acetate	Cellular Hard Synthetic Rubber	Low-Density Calcium Hydro-silicate	Cellular Glass	Expanded Phenolic Foam
Density, lb. per cu. ft.	6.2	6.2	6.2	11–12	9–11	2–5
Tensile strength, p.s.i.	1,450 †	164	199		84	4–35
Compressive strength, p.s.i.	935 †	316	331	150 ‡	140	9–31
Shear strength, p.s.i.				50	64	
longitudinal direction		125	125			8–30
parallel to grain, tangentially	210					
parallel to grain, radially	175					
Modulus of rupture, p.s.i.				50	100	
Modulus of elasticity in flexure, p.s.i.				0.4×10^5	1.6×10^5	
Modulus of rigidity, p.s.i.	19,300	4,390	3,380	9,000	68,000	
Thermal conductivity, Btu-in. (sq. ft.-hr.-°F.)$^{-1}$	0.32	0.31	0.22	0.41	0.40	0.26
Coefficient of thermal expansion, in. per in.-°F.		2.5×10^{-5}			4×10^{-6}	

* Courtesy ASTM and General Electric Co.
† Grain flatwise.
‡ At 5% deformation.

structural sandwich core material, but it is variable in density, defects, and properties and also tends to absorb water vapor. Balsa is the most used core material. Extruded cellular cellulose-acetate and cellular hard synthetic rubber have a good balance between mechanical and physical properties. They have a relatively low density.

Low-density calcium hydrosilicate (called "lime-silica") is an indurated mixture of lime, silica, and asbestos; it has a microporous open-cell formation which imbibes water and transpires water vapor readily. Cellular glass, a true, durable glass, has a macroscopic sealed-cell formation which renders it virtually waterproof and vaporproof. These two inorganic cores have a dimensional stability that is superior to most organic core materials. Their somewhat higher density is a disadvantage for aeronautical and automotive applications, but these inorganic core materials can be used to advantage in building-type sandwich constructions. They are fire-resistant.

Expanded phenolic foam has low density, rather low mechanical strength, and good thermal insulating properties. It has both interconnected and independent cells.

594   Materials of Construction

Honeycomb cores can be made of materials of relatively high density and yet can achieve a low density by means of geometric arrangement. Honeycomb materials comprise resin-impregnated paper, resin-impregnated cotton fabric, metal foil such as aluminum foil, and glass-fabric-base plastic. Glass-fabric-base plastic is illustrated in Fig. 23.4. The plastic is a polyester resin, and the glass fabric is 0.003 inches thick. This honeycomb core was fabricated into sandwich construction with faces composed of polyester-

Fig. 23.4. Glass-fabric-base-plastic honeycomb, 3/16 and 1/4 in. nominal cell size. Magnification 1½×. (*Courtesy* A. G. H. Dietz: *Engineering Laminates*. John Wiley & Sons.)

impregnated glass fabric, and then tested. The strengths as obtained in these tests are given in Table 23.8. Glass fabric honeycomb core is used where high electrical-transmission efficiency is desired.

Resin-impregnated paper is the cheapest form of honeycomb. Resin-impregnated cotton-fabric honeycomb has good machinability and toughness. These two have lower mechanical properties than balsa but higher than organic cores such as extruded cellular cellulose acetate and cellular hard synthetic rubber. They are extensively used with facings of aluminum alloy and of plywood.

Aluminum-foil honeycomb has high compression and shear strengths. Its high shearing modulus enables the core to perform its function of stabilizing the faces to high stresses. Figure 23.5 shows the shear strength versus density of aluminum honeycomb core of various cell sizes and foil thick-

Table 23.8

PHYSICAL PROPERTIES OF SANDWICH CONSTRUCTION CONSISTING OF GLASS-FABRIC-BASE PLASTIC HONEYCOMB CORE AND FACINGS OF POLYESTER-IMPREGNATED GLASS FABRIC

(*Courtesy* A. G. H. Dietz: *Engineering Laminates*. John Wiley & Sons.)

Nominal cell size, in.	3/16	1/4
Fabric thickness, in.	0.003	0.003
Resin content of fabric, %	78	76
Apparent density, lb. per cu. ft.	12.9	8.4
Specific gravity	0.206	0.134
Tensile strength, flatwise, p.s.i.	379 *	271 *
Compressive strength, flatwise, p.s.i.	1248	564

* Failed in bond between honeycomb core and plastic faces.

nesses. Aluminum-foil honeycomb is not affected appreciably by aging, temperature changes, or fungus growth, and it does not absorb moisture.

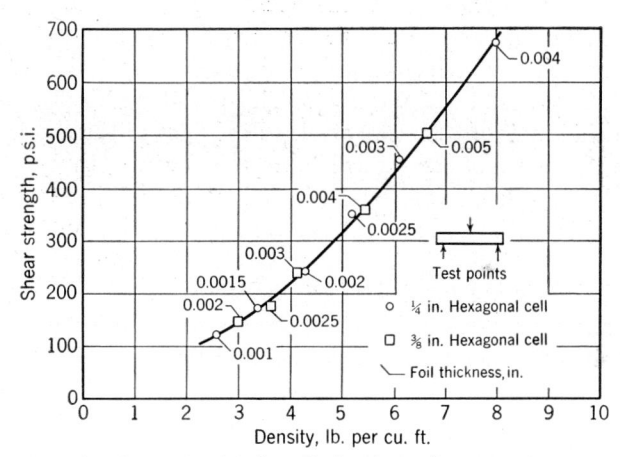

Fig. 23.5. Shear strength versus density of aluminum honeycomb core of various cell sizes. (*Courtesy* T. P. Pajak and ASTM.)

23.37 Applications. In addition to uses in the aircraft and housing industries, other applications of sandwich construction include airfield landing mat, shipping containers, refrigerator walls, boat hulls and decks, trucks and trailers, and railroad freight and passenger cars.

Composite Metals

23.38 General. Composite metals comprise composites consisting of heavy protective coatings bonded to core materials of poorer corrosion and wear resistance.

23.39 Composite Steels. Composite steels (called "clad" steels) consist of a commercial-grade steel plate to one or both sides of which is permanently joined a cladding of another metal or alloy. Plain low-carbon steel is usually used for the backing, especially where deep drawing or forming is required. For greater strength, a medium-carbon or an alloy steel is selected. If high hardness, high strength, or spring properties are desired, a high-carbon or an alloy steel is used for the backing.

Cladding materials include stainless steel, nickel, Monel, Inconel, copper, copper alloy, and cupro-nickel. Clad steels are manufactured in various thicknesses ranging from thin sheets to thick plates.

Manufacture is usually carried on by rolling using the "sandwich" process. In this method, the steel slab is cleaned on one side, and a plate of clad metal with one surface specially prepared is placed on top of the steel slab with the prepared surfaces in contact. A second assembly of a steel slab and plate of clad metal is placed on top of the first assembly with the clad surfaces facing each other in the middle and separated by a thin coating of infusible compound. The edges of the "sandwich" are sealed on all the edges to prevent contamination. Then the sandwich is placed in a soaking pit where it is heated to a temperature of approximately 1260° C. (2300° F.) [for copper about 982° C. (1800° F.)]. This is followed by rolling in a mill to bond the clad metal to the core steel. The edges of the assembly are cut off, and the two parts of the sandwich are taken apart, thus obtaining two clad-steel plates. Good bond strength and uniform thickness of clad are obtained by this method. It is suitable for sheets, strip, and plates. Other methods of manufacturing clad steel include casting, pressing, intermelting by means of electric arcs, and sintering powdered metal over the steel core. For copper and copper-alloy clad steel, the casting method followed by rolling is extensively used for making bars and wire rods. The wire rods are cleaned, heat-treated, and cold-drawn to produce wire.

Fabricating operations such as bending, flanging, forming, welding, and riveting can be performed without peeling, cracking, or buckling of the cladding. Large pressed and spun heads for tanks and pressure vessels are made from clad steel.

Typical properties of single-clad plate with 20 per cent stainless-steel clad on a low-carbon (0.08–0.10 per cent C) steel core are: tensile strength, 55,000 to 65,000; yield point, 27,500 to 32,500 pounds per square inch; elongation in 2 inches, minimum of 27 per cent; and elongation in 8 inches, minimum of 25 per cent. Stainless clad steels should not be heated above 430° C. (806° F.), and low temperature applications should be limited to *minus* 46° C. (*minus* 50° F.). Cladding thicknesses are specified as a percentage of total plate thickness and are generally either 10 or 20 per cent.

Typical applications of clad steels are storage tanks, autoclaves, penstocks, degreasers, evaporators, and heat exchangers. Since clad metal is

Laminates and Adhesives

not suitable for perforated or pierced metal-plate installations, the applications of clad steel are restricted to those types of equipment where a continuous clad surface is exposed.

23.40 Composites Containing Aluminum. *Alclad.* Cladding of corrosion-resistant aluminum to a core of high-strength aluminum alloy is described in Art. 12.37.

Aluminum-Coated Iron and Steel. This composite is described in Art. 12.40.

23.41 Bronze-Steel Laminate. Bearings are sometimes made of composite metals. An example is precast bearing bronze bonded to steel. A bronze alloy composed of 80 per cent copper, 10 per cent tin, and 10 per cent lead is cast in bar form. The interior of the bar is drilled out, and the borings are reduced to powder, which is subjected to hydrogen to eliminate oxides. The treated powder is bonded to steel to form bearings, rollers, and strip. This laminate has improved strength and impact resistance and a lower coefficient of friction than ordinary cast bronze. Graphite may be incorporated in the bronze powder if desired in order to obtain self-lubricating properties in the bearing.

23.42 Composite of Wrought Iron and Steel. Rods with interior of wrought iron and exterior of steel are made. Strands of wrought-iron fibers are combined longitudinally with mild steel, heated to a bright red heat, and rolled to desired size. The cross-section has strands of wrought iron imbedded in the steel with the surface of the rod entirely of steel. The wrought-iron fibers give toughness and ductility whereas the steel has good tensile strength and wearing surface. This composite is utilized for parts subjected to shock and vibration such as piston rods, cylinder studs, and draw-bars.

23.43 Laminated Safe Plate. Laminated plate for safes is made up of alternate layers of hard steel such as low-chromium steel and soft mild steel or wrought iron. After bonding the layers together and fabricating to desired size, the chromium-steel exterior is hardened so as to resist drilling. The soft steel or wrought-iron layers tend to clog drills and also make the laminated plate more resistant to concussion. (See Art. 11.14.)

23.44 Laminated Castings. Laminated metal castings of importance include duplex metal castings and castings coated with liquid metals.

Duplex Metal Castings. Castings of composite metals have been made in foundries for many years. Dissimilar metals are poured into the same mold to produce a composite casting. For instance, a hard cast iron can be poured first followed by a soft cast iron so as to provide a wear-resistant surface on a softer, easily machined core. An example is the manufacture of rolling-mill rolls which have a hard shell of chilled alloyed cast iron whereas the core is of softer cast iron. Another example is the use of cast steel and cast iron in a composite casting such as a grate bar. The lower part of the base is poured with cast steel to obtain high toughness and strength. This is followed by pouring cast iron into the mold and obtaining fusion at the steel-cast-iron interface. By using cast iron, resistance to warpage and machinability of the upper part of the grate bar are obtained.

Castings Coated with Liquid Metal. Composite castings are frequently manufactured by pouring a liquid metal on top of a molten cast metal in a mold so as to obtain fusion at the interface. Stainless steel, copper alloys, and aluminum alloys can be bonded to cast iron or cast steel by this method.

23.45 Sprayed Metal Laminates. Composite metals can be produced by spraying metal on to the surface of another metal. The metal is melted and sprayed in finely divided form on to the metal surfaces which are to be covered. Various types of metal are used for spraying including stainless steel, chromium-nickel alloys, aluminum, copper alloys, zinc, and tin. Usually the spraying metal is in wire form and is melted by means of an oxyacetylene flame; however, powder may be used, and melting may be accomplished by means of an electric arc. Sprayed metal has a structure composed of small scalelike particles which interlock in a plane parallel to the sprayed surface. The metal surface is prepared by blasting with angular steel grit, or a mechanical roughing tool can be employed. The roughened surface improves the bond. The stream of molten metal should be applied at an angle between 45 and 90° to the surface; spraying at an angle less than 45° may cause a wavy surface of non-uniform density known as the "shadow effect." Sprayed metal is used in rebuilding machines and equipment as well as in manufacturing new products.

23.46 Thermostat Metals. Another group of composite metals is thermostat metals. A thermostat assembly comprises two or more metals generally in strip or sheet form which possess different coefficients of thermal expansion; the assembly changes in curvature owing to stresses set up by temperature changes. *Invar* is usually selected as the component metal of small expansivity. (See Art. 11.39.) Metals of large expansivity comprise brass, nickel, nickel-iron alloys, Monel, and high-manganese nickel-copper alloys. The bond between component metals is usually effected by welding, but soldering, brazing, or casting the lower-melting alloy on the solid higher-melting alloy may be employed. There are numerous applications including heater controls, oven regulators, recording thermometers, and circuit breakers.

Glass-Lined Metals

23.47 Glass-Lined Metals. Glass-lined metals comprise fabricated metals with glass fused by means of heat to the interior surface. The purpose is to utilize the excellent chemical durability of the glass. Hypoeutectoid steel is usually the metal; its carbon content is about 0.20 per cent, and it may be killed or rimmed steel. In some cases low-alloy carbon steels are selected. After fabrication of the steel equipment, it is sand

Laminates and Adhesives

blasted, cleaned, and then sprayed with finely ground glass in slip form. A specially prepared dry fritted glass is used. The glass film is allowed to dry and then the equipment is placed in a furnace to soften and fuse the glass to the steel. Additional coatings of glass are applied until the lining is free from minute defects. A high-frequency unit is employed to test the lining and detect flaws. Applications are for equipment in the chemical industries such as equipment for nitration, sulfonation, oxidation, distillation, and polymerization processes where corrosive conditions are encountered.

Glass Laminates

23.48 Glass Laminates. Composite glass structures are formed by bonding two or more plates or sheets of glass with one or more layers of plastic or mastic material. For transparent laminates, a plasticized polyvinyl butyral resin is used as the plastic. Where transparency is not required, non-transparent plastics or mastics such as asphalt, synthetic rubber, or putty can be employed. The glass plates may be transparent, translucent, or opaque. The strength of ordinary glass composed of soda, lime, and silica can be greatly increased by heat treating which puts the outer layers of the glass in compression.

23.49 Laminated Safety Glass. This consists of a sandwich of two sheets of glass bonded together by a plastic. For automobiles, the glass plates have a normal thickness of 0.10 inch. Polyvinyl butyral resin with about 30 per cent plasticizer about 0.015 inches thick is the plastic. (See Art. 22.5.) The plastic is dusted with sodium bicarbonate and dried by passing it in rolls through dryers at about 70° C. (158° F.). The manufacturing process consists of pressing a dry sheet of plastic between clean dry glass sheets with application of heat and then transferring the laminate to an autoclave where the bonding is completed by further pressing and heating. The outstanding advantage of safety glass is that it does not shatter into splinters when broken by an impacting force. Comparison of test values for safety glass and regular glass is given in Table 23.9. The impact resistance of safety glass is much greater than that of regular glass, but the plastic interlayer in safety glass reduces the breaking-pressure resistance somewhat as compared to regular glass.

For installations in aircraft, heavy laminated safety glass is needed to provide resistance to large impact and pressure loads. For example, a double-glazed windshield consisting of a ¼-inch laminated safety glass on the outside and a lamination of heat-strengthened glass plates with ⅜-inch thick vinyl plastic forming the interior is used. Such a windshield will withstand the impact of a 14-pound bird at a velocity of about 200 miles per hour. Since it is necessary to provide joints which will be pressure- and watertight, the plastic layer is frequently extended marginally beyond the glass

Table 23.9

COMPARISON OF TEST VALUES FOR SAFETY GLASS AND REGULAR GLASS *

Tests Conducted on 12 by 12 in. Panels at 75° F.	Regular Plate Glass, ¼ in. Thick	Safety Plate Glass, ¼ in. Thick; (7/64-in. glass; 0.015-in. vinyl plastic; 7/64-in. glass)
Average breaking pressure, p.s.i. pressure loading, 5 p.s.i. per min.	14	11
Impact test, ½-lb. ball, critical distance, ft.†	2	Over 33.5

* (Courtesy of A. G. H. Dietz: *Engineering Laminates.* John Wiley & Sons.)
† Critical distance is that distance from which the steel ball was allowed to fall from rest to produce failure of 50% of specimens tested (at least 20).

plates to afford means of clamping or bolting the laminate along the edges to the aircraft. Also the extended plastic layer may be reinforced with a metal insert continuously around the edges.

23.50 Bullet-Resisting Glass. Bullet-resisting glass is a glass laminate made up of several layers of plate glass with alternate layers of vinyl-resin plastic. It is made in thicknesses from ½ to 3 inches regularly and in greater thicknesses for special installations. The inner layers of plate glass are made thicker than the outer layers. Owing to the thickness of the layers, special care in heating and cooling during manufacture is necessary.

23.51 Laminated Glass Filters. Small amounts of coloring oxides in either the glass or the plastic are sometimes used in laminated safety glass in selectively absorbing bands in the solar spectrum. An example is the use of green-colored plastic in automobile safety glass to diminish sun glare and absorb heat; a disadvantage is that transmittance of light is somewhat reduced which may be objectionable for night driving conditions. (See reference 23.7.) Colored filters are also designed to absorb ultraviolet light; an application is to reduce fading of paintings or fabrics.

23.52 Glass-Air-Cell Structures. Structures of glass plates with air cells between them are manufactured to obtain thermal insulation. Laminated safety glass may be substituted for glass to obtain better resistance to impact from objects.

Laminates of Paper

23.53 Paper Overlays. Paper overlays are applied to wood veneer and plywood.[2] Usually the paper is treated with resin such as phenol-formalde-

[2] R. J. Seidl: "Paper and Plastic Overlays for Veneer and Plywood." *Forest Products Research Soc.,* annual meeting, 1947. Also: *Housing and Home Finance Agency:* "Some Properties of Paper-Overlaid Veneer and Plywood," *Tech. Paper* 9, 1948.

hyde resin to overcome loss of properties of paper upon saturation with water.

23.54 Paper Overlays for Plywood. There are three types of paper overlays for plywood: (1) masking overlays, (2) decorative overlays, and (3) structural overlays.

Masking overlays have as their purpose the masking of minor defects such as face checking, patches, and grain pattern. Masking overlays make possible uniform paintable surfaces. Two main objectives of the utilization of masking overlays are: first, to upgrade low-grade veneer and increase the yield of plywood from a given supply of logs, and second, to extend the wood supply by broadening the base of wood species suitable for plywood.

Kraft paper made of an ordinary commercial pulpwood with a thickness of from 15 to 50 mils and with a phenolic resin content up to 25 per cent is typical of the paper used. Masking is commonly achieved by application of one sheet only. A surface of uniform texture can be obtained. This paper-overlaid plywood can be cut and worked as ordinary plywood.

The Forest Products Laboratory has developed a test for measuring the masking qualities of overlay papers. A standard plywood or veneer is made up containing both natural and simulated defects such as different-sized holes, knots, cracks of various widths, and wood of fine and coarse texture. Specimens of paper glued to the wood under standard conditions are evaluated as to comparative masking qualities. The "show-through" of defects through an overlay can be accentuated by viewing a specimen placed at a small angle to a beam of light.

Decorative overlays have as their purpose the production of attractive and serviceable surfaces. Decorative overlays consist of laminates made up of several sheets of paper impregnated with a high percentage of either phenolic or melamine resin (30 to 70 per cent). The surface sheet should be of decorative paper. The paper laminates are prepressed and then bonded to the surface of plywood. A surface of attractive design or color can be obtained. Surfaces highly resistant to abrasion and liquids can be produced. "Contact resins" can be utilized for low-pressure bonding.

Structural overlays increase strength, rigidity, and wear resistance of plywood and can be selected so as to improve the surface of the plywood and its resistance to water and water vapor. Paper thickness ranges from 3 to 10 mils; phenolic-resin content is from 30 to 60 per cent. High-strength papers are frequently selected. From one to three thicknesses of paper may be used in the overlay. The thickness of the overlay including resin is from 0.010 to 0.060 inches approximately. The bonding of the paper overlay to the wood is usually done in a single operation. The surface is hard and dense. It may or may not mask the grain. A strong and stiff laminated structure can be obtained that is resistant to water, water vapor, scuffing, and abrasion.

23.55 Paper Overlays for Veneer. The purpose of applying paper overlays to wood veneer is to make usable covering material from a single veneer. This is done by increasing the strength and rigidity of the veneer. High-strength papers, 10 to 30 mils thick, containing from 0 to 30 per cent resin are utilized. One sheet of paper is bonded to each side of the veneer, preferably with the grain of the paper at right angles to the grain of the wood veneer. Such paper-overlaid veneer is a stiff, rigid laminate that has greater dimensional stability than veneer alone. For example, an overlaid Douglas-fir veneer with paper (containing 25 per cent resin) and wood grain perpendicular expanded only about one-third as much in the cross-grain direction of the veneer as a like veneer without an overlay when the moisture content was increased. By selection of overlay paper of proper stiffness and strength, it is possible to achieve a balanced construction as far as stiffness is concerned. For example, at the Forest Products Laboratory a $\frac{1}{8}$-inch Douglas-fir veneer, covered on each side with two sheets of 14-mil kraft paper, yielded a panel of approximately equal stiffness with and across the grain of the veneer.

23.56 Paper-Overlaid Sandwich Constructions. Paper-overlaid veneer and plywood are utilized as the facings of sandwich construction. The core for such sandwiches is usually of paper honeycomb. Typical overlay facings are composed of 9-mil kraft paper containing 15 per cent phenolic-film glue bonded to veneer and plywood covers under a pressure of 175 pounds per square inch for 6 minutes at 163° C. (325° F.). A typical base paper for the honeycomb core contains 15 per cent phenolic resin.

23.57 Honeycomb Paper Cores. Honeycomb paper cores for sandwich construction are manufactured by several methods. Impregnation of the paper by a thermosetting resin is common to all methods. One method is to impregnate the paper sheets with resin and then corrugate and cure the impregnated sheets simultaneously. A corrugating machine such as is used in the production of box board can be employed. Additional resin is applied between layers to bond the corrugations together. A second method is to apply only a portion of the resin to the paper before corrugating the paper. Further application of resin is made to the corrugated sheets which are then stacked and cured and bonded together. A "flute" core is produced by these two methods. A third method is used to manufacture expanded cellular-type core. This third method is to glue sheets of paper one on top of the other by means of narrow glue lines, equally spaced at small intervals with respect to the width of the paper and running the full length of the paper sheets, producing a striped effect. The glue stripes of adjacent sheets are offset by one-half the interval between glue lines. After heating the sheets under pressure and curing, the sheets can be pulled apart and expanded into a honeycomb structure. The expanded sheets are dipped into

Laminates and Adhesives

resin and then cured. To obtain honeycomb cores of desired thickness, slices are sawed from the edges of the blocks that are formed.

Honeycomb paper cores are used in combination with facings of different materials. (See Table 23.6.) L. J. Markwardt has reported mechanical properties of honeycomb paper cores and of sandwich construction employing such cores. (See reference 23.1, *ASTM Special Technical Publication* 118.)

Questions

23.1. Define the following terms: laminate, adherend, adhesion, laminated plastic, stressed-skin panel, sandwich construction.

23.2. Distinguish between mechanical adhesion and specific adhesion.

23.3. Name and describe briefly four protein adhesives.

23.4. Describe the manufacture and properties of phenol-formaldehyde resin adhesive.

23.5. Describe mechanical tests for determining properties of adhesives.

23.6. What adhesive would you select for the following: Douglas-fir plywood for outside exposure, low-cost interior-grade Douglas-fir plywood, birch plywood for cabinet doors in a kitchen, gluing wood for household furniture, gluing thin veneers where no staining is permitted, glued-laminated wood arches for a large building, glued-laminated wood for a boat frame, gluing laminated timbers in the field, and plastic-surfaced plywood for counter tops? State your reasons.

23.7. How is veneer manufactured?

23.8. Describe physical properties of plywood.

23.9. Distinguish between exterior-grade and interior-grade Douglas-fir plywood.

23.10. How does glued-laminated wood differ from plywood?

23.11. Name some applications of glued-laminated wood.

23.12. Describe the manufacture of plastic-surfaced plywood.

23.13. What is Compreg? What are its properties?

23.14. Describe the manufacture of a typical laminated plastic product.

23.15. Name and describe briefly some typical applications of laminated plastics.

23.16. Describe low-pressure molding of laminated plastics.

23.17. What is Avtex? What special properties does it have?

23.18. What are the principal steps in post-forming of laminated plastics?

23.19. Describe the use of foil-clad plastics in making printed circuits.

23.20. Describe the fabrication of sandwich constructions by the one-step process.

23.21. Discuss the physical properties of materials used as cores in sandwich construction.

23.22. A sandwich construction is made of aluminum alloy facings and edge-grain balsa wood core. What advantage does edge-grain balsa have over flat-grain balsa core?

23.23. What type of sandwich construction is used for radomes?

23.24. Describe the testing apparatus used in conducting the edgewise compression test on panels of sandwich construction. Also the apparatus for the shear test in the flatwise plane.

23.25. Describe how glass fabric is utilized in various types of laminates.

23.26. What are the advantages of aluminum foil honeycomb?

23.27. Describe how clad steels are manufactured.

23.28. Describe the molding of duplex metal castings.

23.29. Describe the process of spraying metal in producing composite metals.

23.30. What materials are used for thermostat metals?

23.31. Describe the manufacture of glass-lined steel equipment.
23.32. What are the advantages of laminated safety glass for automobile windshields?
23.33. Name and describe three types of paper overlays for plywood.
23.34. State two main objectives of the utilization of masking overlays.

References

23.1. American Society for Testing Materials: "Symposium on Structural Sandwich Construction." *Special Tech. Publ.* 118, 1951. Also "Symposium on Adhesives." *Special Tech. Publ.* 65, 1945. Also *Book of Standards,* 1952. Also "Testing Adhesives for Durability and Permanence." *Special Tech. Publ.* 138, 1953.
23.2. Bogue, R. H.: *The Chemistry and Technology of Gelatin and Glue.* McGraw-Hill Book Co., 1922; Chap. 11 on glue, pp. 506–554.
23.3. De Bruyne, N. A., and Houwink, R.: *Adhesion and Adhesives.* New York: Elsevier Publishing Co., 1951, 517 pages.
23.4. Dietz, A. G. H.: *Engineering Laminates.* John Wiley & Sons, 1949, 797 pages.
23.5. Engel, H. C., Hemming, C. B., and Merriman, H. R.: *Structural Plastics.* McGraw-Hill Book Co., 1950, 301 pages.
23.6. Hansen, H. J.: *Timber Engineers Handbook.* John Wiley & Sons, 1947, 882 pages.
23.7. Highway Research Board: "Effect of Tinted Windshields and Vehicle Headlighting on Night Visibility." *Bull.* 68, 1953, National Research Council, Washington, D. C.
23.8. Judge, A. W.: *Engineering Materials.* London, Pitman & Sons, 1943, 2 vols.
23.9. Kommers, W. J.: "Fatigue Behavior of Wood and Plywood Subjected to Repeated and Reversed Bending Stresses." *Forest Products Lab. Rept.* 1327, Oct., 1943.
23.10. Kuenzi, E. W.: "Testing of Sandwich Constructions at the Forest Products Laboratory." *ASTM Bull.* 164, Feb., 1950, p. 21.
23.11. Learmonth, G. S.: *Laminated Plastics.* London, Leonard Hill, Ltd., 1951, 268 pages.
23.12. Leighou, R. B.: *Chemistry of Engineering Materials.* McGraw-Hill Book Co., 4th ed., 1942; Chap. 20 on glue, pp. 591–606.
23.13. Markwardt, L. J.: "Wood as an Engineering Material." *Proc. ASTM,* v. 43, 1943, p. 435.
23.14. *Modern Plastics*: "Deep-Drawn Laminates." v. 23, Mar., 1946, pp. 100-102. Also "New Thermosetting Compounds." v. 20, 1942, p. 88.
23.15. Perry, T. D.: *Modern Plywood.* New York, Pitman Publishing Co., 2nd ed., 1948.
23.16 Reid, D. G.: "Durability Tests of Metalite Sandwich Construction." *ASTM Bull.* 164, Feb., 1950, p. 28.
23.17. Rinker, R. C., and Kline, G. M.: "A General Theory of Adhesion." ASTM Symposium on Adhesives, *Special Tech. Publ.* 65, 1945.
23.18. Rinker, R. C., and Kline, G. M.: "Survey of Adhesives and Adhesion." *N.A.C.A. Tech. Note* 989, Aug., 1945.
23.19. Troxell, W. W., and Engel, H. C.: "Sandwich Materials: Metal Faces Stabilized by Honeycomb Cores." *SAE Quart. Trans.* 1, No. 3, 1947, p. 429.
23.20. U. S. Department of Agriculture, Forest Service: "Synthetic Resin Glues." *Forest Products Lab. Rept.* 1336, Jan., 1948. Also: "Buckling Loads of Flat Sandwich Panels in Compression." *Forest Products Lab. Rept.* 1525 B, C, D, and E, 1947, 1948. Also: "Approximate Methods of Calculating the Strength of Plywood." *Forest Products Lab. Rept.* R1630, revised Aug., 1950.

23.21. Veneer Association: *Veneers as Specified by the Architect for Beauty and Permanence.* Also *Veneers—Reference Data on Principal Cabinet Woods.* Veneer Association, 600 South Michigan Ave., Chicago 5, Ill.

23.22. Voss, W. C.: "Engineering Laminates—Fundamentals Underlying the Problems of Their Inhomogeneity." *Proc. ASTM*, v. 47, 1947, p. 449.

23.23. Witt, R. K., Hoppman, W. H., II, and Buxbaum, R. S.: "Determination of Elastic Constants of Orthotropic Materials with Special Reference to Laminates." *ASTM Bull.* 194, Dec., 1953, p.53.

23.24. *Wood Technology Series:* No. 4, "Veneer, Plywood, and Laminated Wood." No. 11, "Glues and Gluing." No. 13, "Electronic Heating." No. 19, "Fiber, Particle, and Hardboard." Forest Products Research Soc., P. O. Box 2010, University Station, Madison, Wis.

Section X · Organic Protective Coatings

CHAPTER 24

Organic Protective Coatings
By WILLIAM HOWLETT GARDNER, Ph.D.
Rewritten and Revised by LLOYD F. RADER

24.1 Introduction. Many materials of construction need to be protected from deterioration. A large number of organic compositions are available for this purpose. Organic protective coatings may conveniently be grouped as paints, enamels, varnishes, and lacquers.

24.2 Types of Coatings. An ordinary *paint* consists of finely divided solid particles suspended in a drying oil. The solid particles are known as *pigments* and many times consist of a mixture of both opaque and semi-opaque substances. The *drying oil* has the property of forming a tough coating when spread in a thin layer and exposed to air or heat. The aid of chemical catalysts, known as *dryers,* may or may not be required. A paint may also contain volatile solvents to reduce its viscosity for the purpose of application. The volatile solvents that are added are called *thinners.* The liquid portion of a paint is referred to as the *vehicle.*

An *enamel* is made by suspending pigments in a varnish. An enamel is characterized by an ability to form an especially smooth film. The amount of pigment in enamels is usually much less than in paints. A much higher degree of dispersion of the pigment in the vehicle is required in enamels than is generally necessary with paints.

Varnishes do not contain any pigment. They are liquid compositions which may be converted to a transparent or translucent solid film after application in a thin layer. Varnishes include two distinctly different types of coating compositions: (1) *oleoresinous varnishes* and (2) *spirit varnishes.* Oleoresinous varnishes dry as the result of chemical reactions induced by oxidation (air drying) or by oxidation and polymerization (baking). Spirit varnishes dry solely through the evaporation of volatile solvents from the film. Oleoresinous varnishes contain resins, oils, dryers, and thinners. (See Table 24.1.) They are made by dissolving the resin in heated oil, and cooking the mixture until it has attained the desired properties. Solutions of dryers and thinners are added to produce the finished compositions. Spirit

Table 24.1
COMPOSITION OF OLEORESINOUS VARNISHES AND LACQUERS

Oleoresinous Varnishes

Resins	Oils	Dryers	Thinners
Natural:	Linseed	Active dryers:	Turpentine
Congo copal	China-wood	Cobalt	Mineral spirits
Kauri copal	Tall	Manganese	Naphtha
Boea copal	Dehydrated castor	Auxiliary dryers:	Benzine
Pontianak copal	Perilla	Lead, zinc, calcium,	Coal-tar solvents
Manila copal	Oiticicia	and iron	Higher alcohols
Dammar	Soya-bean		
Sandarac	Fish	Used in the form of	
Rosin		Resinates	
Synthetic		Linoleates	
		Naphthanates	
		Tungates	
		Octyl-oxy-acetates	

Lacquers

Resins	Film-Formers	Plasticizers	Thinners
Natural:	Cellulose nitrate	Solvent type:	Solvents:
Shellac	Cellulose acetate	Dibutyl phthalate	Amyl, butyl and
Dammar	Cellulose acetate-butyrate	Tricresyl phosphate	ethyl acetates
Synthetic	Ethyl cellulose	Non-solvent type:	Latent solvents:
		Castor oil	Amyl, butyl and
		Linseed oil	ethyl alcohols
		Rapeseed oil	Diluents:
			Toluene, xylene,
			and petroleum
			naphtha

varnishes are solutions of one or more resins in volatile liquids. Varnishes composed of alcohol solutions are sometimes classed as *alcoholic varnishes*.

Lacquer is the term used to designate an organic coating which "dries" by the evaporation of solvents and thinners, leaving a film of material which was present originally in fully polymerized form. A lacquer is composed of non-volatile and volatile materials. The non-volatile portion which produces the film contains resin, film-former, and plasticizer, and, in some cases, pigment. The volatile materials or thinners comprise active solvents, latent solvents, and diluents. (See Table 24.1.)

Paint and Enamel

24.3 Function of Paint. The purposes of paints and enamels are fourfold: (1) Preserve the materials coated, (2) produce a pleasing appearance, (3) improve sanitary conditions, and (4) obtain better distribution of light.

24.4 Types of Failure. The predominant type of failure of a paint is important. It determines the type of paint which should be selected for application and which should be used in repainting. There are several types of failure: (1) checking or crazing, (2) flaking and scaling, (3) chalking, (4) washing, (5) blistering, and (6) peeling.

24.5 Pigments. The type of failure can be controlled in part by the pigments used in preparing the paint. These ingredients can be divided into three groups: (1) body pigments, (2) colored pigments, and (3) extender pigments.

Typical *body pigments* are basic carbonate white lead, red lead, zinc oxide, zinc sulfide, lithopone, titanium oxides, titanoxes, iron oxides, graphite, aluminum flakes, and lead titanate. Besides adding body to a paint, they impart to a greater or less degree opacity, firmness, hardness, imperviousness, and durability to its films. Red lead and zinc metal dust have the property of inhibiting the corrosion of iron and steel. They are used as the body pigments in anticorrosive paints to serve as the *priming coat* which is the first one applied.

Colored pigments are usually incorporated in paints for their esthetic color-giving properties. Many of them contribute to the durability of the paint films. The colored pigments may be divided most conveniently into two groups, *inorganic* and *organic pigments*. Inorganic colored pigments are listed in Table 24.2. A very large number of dyes are employed in mak-

Table 24.2

INORGANIC COLORED PIGMENTS

White: White lead, zinc oxide, lithopone, titanium oxide.
Blue: Iron blue, ultramarine, cobalt blue, sublimed blue lead.
Green: Chrome green, hydrated chromium oxide, Paris green.
Yellow: Chrome yellow (lead chromate), zinc yellow, cadmium yellow, ochre (Chinese yellow).
Orange: Mixture of chrome yellow and the red pigments of basic lead chromates.
Brown: Umber, sienna, copper oxide.
Red: Red lead, cadmium red, iron oxides, mercuric oxide, hematite ochres (Indian red and Venetian red).
Black: Lampblack, carbon black, drop black, graphite, antimony sulfide.

ing organic pigments. The most common of these are the Hansa yellows, transparent yellow lakes, blue toners, green lakes, toluidine reds, parareds, lithol reds, bordeaux lakes, madder lakes, and opaque maroons. Few, if any, of these organic pigments possess the light-fastness of many of the inorganic pigments. Organic pigments are most widely used for interior paints and enamels where fading is not so serious a factor as it is in outside paints.

Extender pigments when suspended in drying oils have little or no opacity. They include the various forms of barium sulfate, silica, diatomaceous earth,

Organic Protective Coatings

magnesium silicates, clays, gypsum, barium carbonate, calcium carbonates, and mica.

24.6 Vehicles. Vehicles for paints and enamels comprise drying oils, varnishes, lacquers, and aqueous solutions of binders. Thinners and dryers may also be added.

The principal *drying oils* are linseed oil, China-wood (tung) oil, tall oil, perilla oil, oiticicia oil, soya-bean oil, dehydrated castor oil, and fish oils. Linseed oil was practically the only common drying oil for paints until recent years. China-wood oil is used for waterproof paints and for baking compositions. Tall oil is an important oil developed as a substitute for China-wood oil and is manufactured as a by-product of the kraft paper process. It is non-crystallizing, color stable, light in color, and comparatively odorless. Dehydrated castor oil is made by catalytic dehydration and vacuum distillation. It is also a substitute for China-wood oil.

Oleoresinous varnishes are sometimes added in preparing a paint to increase the gloss, hardness, durability, and wearing qualities. They constitute the major component of the vehicle for enamels. *Lacquers* are also used as vehicles for paints and enamels.

Aqueous vehicles used for cold-water paints are of two general types. The whitewash type, or *calcimine,* contains slaked lime, salt, flour, and glue, with whiting (calcium carbonate) as the pigment. Calcimines cannot be washed without the danger of removing them. The other type, *casein paint,* is washable, and contains casein, lime, emulsified drying oils, salts, and antiseptics dissolved in water to form the vehicle for this paint. Pigments are limited to those which are alkali resistant since the vehicle contains lime. The cold-water paints are sold in both dry form and as ready-mixed paints. They are relatively inexpensive and have good covering properties and light reflection.

Thinners are added to lower the viscosity of the compositions so that objects can be properly coated by brushing, spraying, or dipping. The common thinners are turpentine, solvent naphtha, and various petroleum thinners of low-boiling range.

Dryers are added to accelerate the oxidation of the oil and the chemical reactions known as polymerization, which are responsible for the drying of the films. The principal dryers are the cobalt, manganese, and lead salts of fatty acids, rosin acids, or naphthenic acids. The general practice today is to add solutions of these catalysts to the paint.

Rubber-base water-emulsion vehicles are extensively used in interior-type paints. The rubber is latex in emulsified form. (See Art. 24.7.)

24.7 Types of Paints. Several types of paint of special properties are described in this article. *Tall-oil alkyd resin paints* are extensively used for freight car paints, metal primers, and metal and furniture enamels. They are cheap and have satisfactory properties. The coatings have air-dry or bake cycles normal to the trade and exhibit excellent adhesion, hardness, and gloss.

Oil-Resin Emulsion Paint. This type of paint is made by adding varnish or oil to a water paint. It has resistance to washing approaching that of oil paints. Alkyd-resin varnish added to casein in an aqueous medium produces good emulsion paints which are suitable for exterior use since they have good weather resistance. A modern emulsion paint has a vehicle consisting of an acrylic-resin dispersion in water. It has excellent stability, good adhesion and color retention, and long film life. It is easy to apply and is fast drying, making quick recoating possible.

Rubber-Base Interior Paint. Rubber-base interior paint has a vehicle consisting of a water emulsion with natural rubber latex. Pigments and plasticizers are added. Proteins may be included to serve as thickeners, and preservatives may be added to prevent putrefaction of the proteins. Antifreeze materials are sometimes added to overcome freezing of the emulsion in the container. Rust inhibitors are placed in the paint mixture in some cases to lessen rusting of cans. Rubber-base paints are suitable for interior surfaces including plaster walls and ceilings, woodwork, gypsum board, cement-asbestos board, cement concrete, cinder block, and brick masonry. It has good resistance to alkalies.

Rubber-base paint can be readily applied by either roller or brush. No brush marks are left. It dries quickly. It gives a so-called "satin" finish. Drippings of paint can be easily removed by means of a wet cloth. Rubber-base paint is a popular paint for home owners who wish to paint the interior surfaces of their own homes; professional painters for the most part prefer oil-base paints. Rubber-base paints do not give off fumes as do oil-base paints. Grease stains and pencil and crayon marks can be removed by scrubbing. Rubber-base paint is also scuff resistant. Rubber-base paints have certain limitations such as poor adherence to smooth, enameled or shellacked surfaces. When applied to surfaces which vary in porosity, variations in sheen may be noticeable. Two coats of rubber-base paint are frequently required to give adequate hiding power. This is particularly true of white rubber-base paints which have inferior hiding power as compared to paints of deep colors or pastel shades.

Stains. Wood stains may be divided into five classes: namely, (1) water stains, (2) oil stains, (3) non-grain-raising stains, (4) spirit stains, and (5) chemical stains. Water stains contain water-soluble dyestuffs dissolved in water; sometimes suitable organic liquids are added. Water stains are slow drying, transparent, and do not tend to fade or "bleed" into subsequently applied coatings. A disadvantage is that they tend to raise the grain of the wood. Oil stains contain oil-soluble dyes dissolved in organic liquids such as turpentine, benzol, and naphtha. They are easily applied but do not penetrate deeply. Disadvantages are tendencies to fade and to "bleed" into subsequent coatings; sealing with a surface sealer such as shellac is necessary to alleviate bleeding. Many oil stains contain pigments and are in several respects essentially highly diluted, penetrating paints. They are used in furniture finishing because desirable color and highlighting effects can be obtained with less tendency toward fading and bleeding. Other types of oil stains contain preservatives; they give greater durability.

The latest type of stain is the non-grain-raising stain. It is of the acid dye-base type with organic solvents. They dry rapidly and do not penetrate deeply. Bright, clear colors that do not tend to fade can be obtained. Spirit stains contain aniline dyestuffs dissolved in alcohol or other suitable organic liquid. Spirit stains are employed in furniture finishing; they have deep penetrating properties even through old coatings. Fading is a disadvantage. With chemical stains, the color is produced by reactions within the wood. By proper selection and application of stains, desirable esthetic effects can be obtained.

Resins

24.8 Resins. A resin is an amorphous, vitreous or semisolid, organic substance, which is insoluble in water but soluble in organic liquids or in drying oils or after being heated gives a product which is soluble in hot drying oils. Resins may be classed as *natural resins* or as *synthetic resins*. Resins are described in detail in Chapters 22 and 23 but will be discussed in this article from the standpoint of their utilization in organic protective coatings.

24.9 Natural Resins. Copals are natural resins obtained from the hardened sap of fossil deposits of trees. The Congo copals are the hardest natural resins. Other copals are the Kauri, boea, Pontianak, and manila copals. All these copals require heating to produce an oil-soluble gum. Dammar and Sandarac are natural resins obtained from the sap of living trees and are soluble in oil without the necessity of heating.

Rosin is a natural resin that is obtained as a by-product from the manufacture of turpentine. The liquid resin is obtained from pine trees by cutting a vertical slice in the bark of the tree and allowing the liquid to exude into containers. Turpentine is removed from the liquid resin by distillation, leaving rosin as the residue. Rosin is translucent, inflammable, and relatively cheap. Chemically it is essentially abietic acid. Rosin is soluble in alcohol, turpentine, and alkalies. It is used in varnishes and dryers.

Shellac is the only natural resin derived from animal life. Shellac is derived from *lac* which is the term applied to the resinous products of the Indian scale insect *laccifer lacca* Kerr. Shellac is soluble in ethyl alcohol and methylated spirits and is partly soluble in turpentine, ether, and chloroform. It is insoluble in oils and petroleum solvents. Shellac is used mainly in spirit varnishes and to some extent in cellulose nitrate lacquers. Commercial shellac is orange in color. By bleaching with sodium hypochlorite, white shellac is produced which is called bleached shellac.

24.10 Synthetic Resins. Synthetic resins comprise a heterogeneous group of materials that have been developed extensively during recent years. Most of the advances in the technology of paint and varnish manufacture have been in connection with synthetic resins.

Alkyd Resins. These are important resins for organic protective coatings. Alkyd resins are manufactured by condensation reactions between glycerin and phthalic anhydride or modifications of these materials. For use in varnishes, part of the phthalic anhydride is replaced by fatty acids from mixtures of linseed oil, China-wood oil, and castor oil. These oil-modified alkyd resins are soluble in thinners used in oleoresinous varnishes and can be incorporated in both air-drying- and baking-type varnishes. These varnishes are durable, possess good color retention, and have good gloss. They are used for automobile finishes, architectural finishes, and floor enamels. Such modified alkyd varnishes can be prepared with tall oil, producing a cheap product that gives satisfactory results for many applications. Soyabean oil is also used in alkyd-resin varnishes; they have excellent colors and good color retention. The addition of rosin to alkyd-resin varnishes reduces drying time but decreases durability, hence these resin-modified alkyd varnishes are utilized mainly for interior decorating. Substitutions for the basic ingredients of alkyd resin are sometimes made by substituting polyhydroxy alcohols such as glycol for glycerin, and dibasic acids of the aliphatic series or aromatic polybasic acids for phthalic anhydride.

Phenolic Resins. Phenolic resins are utilized where durable protection is important, particularly in deleterious atmospheres and in the presence of moisture. Phenol-formaldehyde resins constitute the main group of phenolic resins; their manufacture is described in Art. 22.10. For use in protective coatings, phenolic resins are modified during manufacture in a variety of ways to produce products of special properties. Six of these modified types are briefly described here. First, the so-called straight oil-soluble phenolic resins, first produced in 1928 by employing paraphenyl phenol instead of the ordinary unreduced phenolics. These oil-soluble resins can be combined with drying oils. The coatings produced dry primarily by polymerization rather than oxidation and are quick drying and non-heat-hardening. Second, heating phenolic resins with natural resin, ester gum, or rosin produces an oil-soluble coating material of higher melting point and good resistance to chemicals and moisture that can polymerize and harden with heat. Third, when phenolic resins are added in small amounts to ester gum or rosin, varnish resins are produced that are quick drying; these are called resin-modified products. They were introduced about 1924 as so-called 4-hour varnishes. Fourth, oil-modified phenolics are made by dispersing phenol-formaldehye resin in drying oil such as China-wood oil to give tough, flexible coatings. Introduced in 1928, they are utilized especially in baking-type varnishes. Fifth, phenolic resins are available in the form of syrups for use in reinforcing rosin or fatty acids to give quicker drying, higher melting points, and improved durability. Sixth, modified phenolics are prepared for use with cellulose nitrate in manufacturing marproof lacquers of considerable "scratch" hardness; these lacquers are highly resistant to attack by alcohol and other solvents.

Urea-Formaldehyde Resins. These resins are made by condensation of urea and formaldehyde. They form clear, white, very hard films with good chemical resistance. Urea-formaldehyde resins are used in combination with alkyd resins to produce a coating that combines the hardness qualities and chemical resistance of urea-formaldehyde resin with the toughness, adhesion, and durability of the alkyd resin. Such a product is utilized in coating kitchen cabinets, refrigerators, and hospital equipment.

Melamine-Formaldehyde Resins. Melamine when reacted with formaldehyde forms melamine resins. Melamine-formaldehyde resins have even better properties than urea resins; that is, they are faster curing and they resist higher temperatures and have better chemical resistance. They are, however, more costly than urea resins. Melamine resins may be used in coatings subjected to temperatures up to 177° C. (350° F.). Melamine resins are mixed with alkyd resins to produce coatings of superior qualities for stoves, refrigerators, washing machines, and automobiles. They do not tend to discolor.

Vinyl Resins. Vinyl resins are used for coatings of various types. In general, vinyl resins are harder, less soluble and less compatible with oils than other synthetic resins. Copolymers of vinyl acetate and vinyl chloride have excellent properties in coatings in that they are easily applied, resist aging and chemical action, and are non-flammable. They are stable in oil-resin emulsion paints. They have no color, odor, or toxicity. Such copolymer coatings are applied on refrigerators, deep freezers, and the insides of tank cars and other containers. Other vinyl resins employed in coatings are polyvinyl chloride used in chemical-resistant films, and polyvinylidene chloride polymers used in chemical- and moisture-resistant coatings. Emulsions of polyvinyl acetate are used on concrete and house exteriors, particularly in the Pacific Coast region.

Acrylic Resins. These are water white and retain their color even at elevated temperatures. They are resistant to acid, alcohol, oils, and chemical fumes. Pigments may be added to produce enamels.

Cumarone and Indene Resins. These resins can be readily combined with vegetable oils. Such mixtures are resistant to alkali and other chemicals. A disadvantage is that they tend to "yellow" when exposed to sunlight. Main applications are for concrete paint, floor sealers, aluminum paint, and container coatings.

Polyethylene Resin. This resin is flexible, tough, odorless, and tasteless. It is impermeable to moisture, has excellent electrical properties, and is highly resistant to most chemicals. Its use in films and coatings is rapidly increasing.

Polystyrene Resin. Polystyrene resin is rigid and brittle, but it can be combined with other resins to produce copolymers which are used in architectural varnishes, baking and concrete-floor enamels, and ship-bottom paints.

Chlorinated Rubber. This is a resin made by chlorinating natural rubber. For use in coatings, other resins, plasticizers, pigments, and solvents are added. Such coatings are highly resistant to acids and alkalies; they are used for painting concrete, plaster, and stucco surfaces and asbestos-cement boards. Another application is for maintenance paints for metal surfaces. Chlorinated rubber is incorporated in alkyd resin paints and enamels to facilitate drying.

Maleic Resin. Maleic resin is made from a natural resin and maleic anhydride or maleic acid. It is used to modify the properties of other resins in paint and varnish manufacture, especially where maximum viscosity and speed of drying are desired. Maleic acid is used to replace phthalic anhydride in the manufacture of alkyd resins in order to increase the hardness and reduce the air-drying and baking time.

Ester Gum. Ester gum is a resin made from rosin and glycerine. Chemically it is designated as glycerol triabietate. Ester gum is used as a component of oleoresinous varnishes and cellulose-nitrate lacquers. Before the advent of phenolic resins, it was used with China-wood oil in spar varnishes. Substitution of pentaerythritol for glycerine in esterifying rosin produces pentaerythritol-rosin ester which has a higher melting point and greater heat stability than ordinary ester gum. Varnish films made from this modified resin dry faster and are more resistant to alkali and water than those formulated from ester gum. Ester gum is also maleic modified and phenolic modified to develop improved physical properties of varnishes.

Silicone Resin. Silicone resin is described in Art. 22.26. Silicone resin is used in making varnish that is highly resistant to heat and to attack by chemicals and moisture. Coal-tar or hydrocarbon thinners are employed. By adding pigments, silicone enamels are also manufactured. Insulating varnishes for treating electrical apparatus are made with silicone resin so as to permit operation at higher temperatures and to obtain moisture-proof conditions.

Varnishes

24.11 General. The two general types of varnishes are (1) *oleoresinous varnishes* and (2) *spirit varnishes*. The composition of oleoresinous varnishes is given in Table 24.1. The natural resins include the copals, the dammars, and rosin. The synthetic resins include phenolic resins of many types, various modifications of alkyd resins, cumars, and ester gum (glycerol ester of rosin). (See Art. 24.10.)

Natural and synthetic resins that are soluble in organic liquids are also used in the manufacture of spirit varnishes. Asphalt and rubber are employed in making certain types. Shellac is the main spirit varnish in use today; it consists of lac resin dissolved in alcohol and other solvents.

Oil length is defined as the number of gallons of drying oils to 100 pounds of resin in the manufacture of a varnish. In general, a greater proportion of oil favors greater flexibility of the films and more resistance to weathering, whereas large percentages of resins give finishes which are harder and capable of being sanded and polished.

24.12 Types of Varnishes. A convenient method is to divide varnishes into two classes: (1) architectural varnishes and (2) industrial varnishes. The first group includes cabinet or rubbing varnishes; varnishes for floors, trims, and doors; flat varnishes; exterior varnishes; marine varnishes; cement and stucco sealers; and waterproofing compounds. The second group comprises an even wider variety of compositions which may be applied to different surfaces by one of several methods, such as brushing, dipping, tumbling, and spraying.

Of interest is the term *size*. A size [1] is a liquid-coating composition, usually transparent, for sealing a porous surface preparatory to application of finishing coats. *Wall sizes* consist of manila copal-rosin spirit varnishes, shellac varnishes, cheap ester-gum-drying-oil varnishes, synthetic-resin varnishes, or cumar-oil varnishes. Cumar-oil varnishes give films which are quite resistant to lime.

Lacquers

24.13 Lacquers. The composition of lacquers is shown diagrammatically in Table 24.1. The *film-forming materials* are cellulose esters or ethers. Cellulose nitrate is the most-used film-former; others include cellulose acetate, cellulose acetate butyrate, and ethyl cellulose. Ethyl cellulose makes possible flexible films and improved resistance to acids and alkalies. The viscosity of the cellulosic materials is important in manufacturing lacquers.

Resins are incorporated in lacquers to give gloss, hardness, brilliance, adhesion, and polishing characteristics. The flexibility and durability of

---

[1] ASTM standard definition.

lacquer films may also be improved by proper selection of resins. Alkyd resins are extensively used in lacquers; they contribute to durability. Maleic-modified alkyd-resin lacquers have excellent gloss, color, and durability properties and are rapid drying. Other resins used in lacquers include phenolics, urea, melamine, vinyl, acrylic, polystyrene, ester gum, and dammar. (See Art. 24.10.)

Plasticizers are softeners that are added to impart flexibility. They improve the flowing properties of wet lacquers and retard the action of the solvents. Plasticizers also intensify the luster of lacquer coatings. Typical plasticizers are listed in Table 24.1. The most used are non-volatile organic liquids. Camphor was formerly used as a plasticizer.

Thinners serve as solvents for the other ingredients and make possible the attainment of liquid lacquer of suitable viscosity for application. See Table 24.1 for typical thinners. Esters and other organic liquids listed are suitable solvents for cellulose nitrate. Alcohols are used as latent solvents; by themselves alcohols are not good solvents of cellulosic materials but when used with esters do act as solvents satisfactorily. Diluents are added to reduce the cost of the lacquer; they do not remain permanently in the dried film. Toluene is a good diluent. Diluents can dissolve the resins but not cellulose nitrate.

A lacquer coating "dries" by the evaporation of thinners, leaving a film of material which was present originally in fully polymerized form. It should be noted that a lacquer differs from an oleoresinous varnish in that oleoresinous varnish not only "dries" by evaporation of solvents but also "dries" by chemical reactions which form the polymers in the final coating.

Lacquer coatings are durable, waterproof, tough, and quick drying. They possess attributes of eye-appealing beauty, easy touch-up, and easy application. Lacquers are, however, much more expensive than oleoresinous varnishes.

Lacquers can be applied by the hot-spray process. This method makes possible reduction of viscosity by means of heat so that constant spraying under uniform conditions is possible. By using the hot-spray gun, it is not necessary to thin the lacquer so much by addition of thinners; hence a higher percentage of solids in the lacquer can be used, making possible a thicker coating per pass of the spray gun. The hot-spray lacquer process can be employed instead of baking on synthetic enamels that require expensive baking ovens; baking enamels do have the advantage that only one coat of enamel is needed.

In the usual commercial lacquer preparation there are numerous components including several different solvents. It is generally inadvisable for the purchaser to change the formulation by putting in other solvents and diluents.

Solutions containing only cellulose derivatives such as cellulose nitrate and cellulose acetate are known as *dopes*, and are classed as a special type of lacquer. They are used for imparting tautness to airplane fabrics and for coating leather. It is customary to add concentrated solutions of cellulose derivatives in the manufacture of lacquers. The solutions are referred to as *lacquer-base solutions* or *dope bases*.

The term lacquer has been used in the past to designate a variety of materials. For example, the term has been used for Japanese (Chinese) lacquer. Also there is its use with respect to Indian lacquer. Lacquer has been used as a synonym for spirit varnishes. Today the practice is to employ the word lacquer to denote organic coatings containing cellulosic film-forming materials which have been described in this article.

Special Coatings

24.14 Luminescent Coatings. Luminescent coatings contain pigments that emit light following the absorption of radiant energy and the transmutation of this energy to a longer wavelength. Stokes in 1852 determined that the emitted light is always of longer wavelength than the radiant energy absorbed in the molecule. This is explained as follows: each quantum of photons raises an electron to a higher energy level; the electron comes down to its original level of energy, either immediately or over a period of time, with the absorbed energy being released in the form of colored visible light. Luminescent light is popularly known as "cold light," since it differs from incandescent light which is due to the emission of light from intense heat.

The two types of pigments in luminescent coatings are (1) fluorescent pigments and (2) phosphorescent pigments. *Fluorescent pigments* emit light only during the time they are exposed to the exciting light source. They are usually activated by ultraviolet (black) light. The light source should radiate very little, if any, visible energy if the fluorescent coatings are to be effective. Argon glow lamps, fluorescent lamps, and high-pressure mercury-arc lamps, equipped with filters to eliminate visible light, are used as light sources. Fluorescent pigments may be either organic or inorganic in type. Typical examples of organic fluorescent pigments are synthetic dyes such as eosin, flavin, and rhodamin dyes; dye intermediates; and metallic salts of dye intermediates such as the zinc salt of 8-hydroxyquinolin. Inorganic fluorescent pigments are usually zinc sulfides or mixtures of zinc and cadmium sulfides.

Phosphorescent pigments emit light not only during exposure but also for a period of time after the exciting light is turned off. Following exposure, they may glow in the dark for a time ranging from $\frac{1}{2}$ to 12 hours.

Either "black" light or visible light may be used as the exciting light. All phosphorescent pigments are inorganic; examples are zinc sulfide, calcium sulfide, and strontium sulfide.

Applications of fluorescent coatings are for airplane and automobile instrument dials, radio and television dials, and decorations in homes, stores, and theaters. Phosphorescent coatings are used in safety installations in buildings such as exit lights and markers for alarm systems.

24.15 Fire Retardant Coatings. Ordinary paint films are highly flammable. They give off toxic gases including carbon monoxide; under confined conditions these gases may be given off in such quantities as to cause explosions.

The fire resistance of timber including chemical impregnation has been discussed in Art. 21.37. Fire-retardant coatings can also be applied to unpainted wood to reduce the rate of combustion. Chemicals incorporated in flame-retardant paints include ammonium chloride, ammonium phosphate, and borax. When subjected to flames, fire-retardant paint gives off non-toxic gases, which cool and dilute the products of combustion below the point of spontaneous ignition. A coating that is resistant to flame forms on the surface, preventing a blaze from forming. Spreading of the flames is curtailed. The coating of fire-retardant paint can be covered with applications of enamel or lacquer to produce a surface of high gloss.

Fire-retardant paints are available for metals also. The organic binder in such paint is reduced to a minimum. A pigment in the paint decomposes when heated to the flash point, perforating the film and preventing gases from accumulating in the blisters formed in the paint film. Such paint should be applied in very thin layers.

Preparation and Painting of Surfaces

24.16 Preparation of Surfaces. Surfaces should be properly prepared before organic protective coatings are applied. Cleaning of metal surfaces prior to painting is fully as important as the selection and application of protective coatings.

Structural Steel. Structural-steel members should be cleaned free from mill scale and rust while in the shop and given a prime coat before shipping to the field. Weathering of unpainted structural steel followed by wire brushing in the field usually results in partial removal only of mill scale and in a poor surface for painting. In the field, removal of scale, rust, and old paint coats is accomplished by several methods including brushing with hand or power wire brushes, hand scraping, chipping by air-driven chipping hammers with flat chisels, sand blasting, shot blasting, and cleaning with oxyacetylene flame. In the latter method, flat tips mounted on skids provide a row of small brush-like flames that are guided across the surface with a reciprocating movement, the flames impinging at an angle of about 45°. Immediately after application of the oxyacetylene flame, the steel surfaces should be power wire-brushed to remove scale, rust, and cockled paint where old paint is being removed. A primer coat should be applied to the surface promptly after cleaning before the temperature of the steel is reduced to atmospheric temperature and prior to recondensation of moisture on the steel. Second and third coatings should be applied at intervals of several days.

Sheet Steel. Sheet steel pressed into shapes for automobile bodies should have loose scale, rust, grease, oil, and dirt removed before being given a protective coating. Treatments should produce a clean, stable and less reactive surface that provides good adhesion for coatings. Acid pickling is used to remove scale and rust, and phosphoric acid is applied to remove grease and oil and to etch the metal surface, providing a roughened surface for mechanical bonding of the paint to the metal. Phosphate coatings can be used to inhibit corrosion and improve the paint retention characteristics of the metal surface.

Wood Surfaces. Wood should be thoroughly dry before paint is applied. Knots should be given an application of shellac before painting so as to prevent resin in the knots from bleeding into the paint. All glue spots should be removed. Wood surfaces of cabinets and interior woodwork should be planed to remove mill marks, scraped with a cabinet or hand scraper, and sanded before finishing materials are applied.

Plaster Surfaces. Plaster surfaces should be brushed with a zinc sulfate solution before painting. Prior to repainting, grease should be removed by benzine and the walls should be washed with soap.

Concrete Surfaces. Cement and concrete surfaces should be treated with benzine to remove grease and oil, and then a zinc sulfate solution should be applied to neutralize the lime in the concrete.

24.17 Methods of Application. Organic protective coatings for structures and houses are applied by brushing and by spraying on both exterior and interior work. Emulsion paints and cold-water paints are applied to interior walls by means of cloth or felt rollers. Spraying is used in coating automobile bodies. The spray gun is operated by means of an air compressor. An air transformer, employed to provide proper pressure for the spray gun, also filters the air and condenses moisture and oil. Two types of spray guns are the pressure gun and the suction gun. Spray booths are used in manufacturing plants to remove excess paint spray and fumes so as to decrease the fire hazard and protect the health of the workmen. Spray booths are equipped with air-ventilating systems and some have water-wash equipment designed to remove most of the overspray from the air before the air is exhausted. Electrostatic spraying is a modern method which gives a uniform coat.

Manufactured articles are coated by roller coating, by dip coating, and by flow coating. Roller coating is well adapted to flat metal sheets and composition boards. In machine dip coating, objects are attached to a traveling conveyor chain which dips them into tanks of varnish or enamel. Flow coating is used for large pieces that are suspended over a tank of enamel. The enamel is pumped through a hose manipulated by a workman to coat the object from the top down, the excess enamel draining into the tank.

Testing

24.18 Standard Tests. Numerous tests for determining physical and chemical properties of organic protective coatings have been standardized by the American Society for Testing Materials.

Paints and Enamels. Tests for paints and enamels include consistency of exterior house paints and enamel-type paints, relative dry hiding power, and measurement of dry film thickness.

Varnishes. Tests for varnishes include specific gravity, appearance, color, viscosity, flash point, non-volatile matter, skinning test in closed containers, elasticity (toughness), acid number, reactivity between paint liquids and zinc oxide, and resistance of dried films to water and to alkali.

Lacquers and Lacquer Enamels. These tests include density, drying time, gloss, homogeneity, print test, outdoor exposure, non-volatile matter, and consistency. Another test is the elongation of attached lacquer coatings.

24.19 Weathering Tests. Long-time weathering tests have been conducted on many organic protective coatings where the materials have been exposed to outdoor conditions under different climatic and environmental conditions. Valuable information has been obtained from these tests. To reduce the time and expense involved in long-time exposure tests, accelerated weathering tests have been devised. These tests are made in machines that provide radiation from electric arcs to simulate sunshine, water spray to simulate rain, and heating elements to simulate changes in seasons. Other variations comprise refrigerated water, ice baths, and exposure to oxygen. Humidity cabinets are available that provide exposure to 100 per cent humidity and to various corrosive materials such as sulfur dioxide and ammonia. Salt-fog-spray machines are also available. Chemical resistance tests can be performed by applying spots of chemical to test panels or by immersing panels in corrosive chemicals. The main difficulty with accelerated weathering tests is the lack of correlation obtained with results from long-time exposure tests. Research on correlation between accelerated weathering and long-time exposure tests is being conducted.

Questions

24.1. List the different types of components of each of the following: an ordinary paint, an enamel, an oleoresinous varnish, a spirit varnish, a cellulose nitrate lacquer, a casein paint, a calcimine, and a rubber-base interior paint.

24.2. What is meant by each of the following terms: a resin, a pigment, a thinner, a dryer, a vehicle, a plasticizer, and a dope?

24.3. For what purposes is paint used? Give examples.

24.4. Name the different types of failure of paint films.

24.5. What are the different general types of pigments? Give several examples of each type. What factors should be considered in selecting pigments for incorporation in vehicles?

24.6. Name the different types of vehicles. What are the principal drying oils?

24.7. Describe what is meant by (a) the oil length of a varnish, (b) a size, (c) a non-grain-raising stain, and (d) tall oil?

24.8. Describe the properties of the following synthetic resins with respect to their use in organic protective coatings: alkyd, phenolic, urea, melamine, vinyl, acrylic, polystyrene, chlorinated rubber, ester gum, and silicone.

24.9. Distinguish between fluorescent and phosphorescent pigments. Give examples of each.

24.10. Describe fire-retardant coatings.

24.11. How should a structural-steel bridge be prepared for painting?

24.12. Describe the method of removing old paint coats from structural-steel members with oxyacetylene flame.

24.13. Describe the use of spray guns in applying paint.

24.14. Name several accelerated weathering tests for organic protective coatings.

References

24.1. American Association of State Highway Officials: *Standard Specifications for Highway Materials and Methods of Sampling and Testing.* Washington, D. C., 6th ed., 1950; "Specifications for Bridge Paints."

24.2. American Society for Testing Materials: "Definitions Relating to Paint, Varnish, Lacquer, and Related Products." *Designation* D16–52, *Book of Standards,* 1952, Part 4. Also: "Fifty Years of Paint Testing." *Special Tech. Publ. 147,* 1953.

24.3. Baruc, J. D.: "The History of Shellac." *Paint Ind. Mag.,* Apr., 1953, p. 13.

24.4. Brady, G. S.: *Materials Handbook.* McGraw-Hill Book Co., 7th ed., 1951, 913 pages.

24.5. Browne, F. L.: "Classification of House Paints as a Guide to the Study of Formulations." *Official Digest,* Federation of Paint and Varnish Production Clubs, 172, Jan., 1938, pp. 18–31.

24.6. Doran, A. B.: "Tall Oil—Basic Material for the Paint Industry." *Paint Ind. Mag.,* Apr., 1953, p. 7.

24.7. DuBois, J. H.: *Plastics.* Chicago, American Technical Soc., 1945.

24.8. Durrans, T. H.: *Solvents.* London, Chapman & Hall, 4th ed., 1938, 238 pages.

24.9. Edwards, J. D.: *Aluminum Paint and Powder.* New York, Reinhold Publishing Corp., 1936; Chaps. 5, 6, and 7, pp. 69–179.

24.10. Gardner, H. A.: *Physical and Chemical Examination of Paints, Varnishes, Lacquers, and Colors.* Washington, D. C., Inst. of Paint & Varnish Research, 9th ed., 1939.

24.11. Gardner, H. A.: *Testing Tank Paints to Prevent Evaporation Losses; Physical and Chemical Examination of Paints, Varnishes, Lacquers, and Colors.* Washington, D. C., Inst. of Paint & Varnish Research, 10th ed., 1946.

24.12. Hickson, E. F.: "Some Properties and Tests of Traffic or Zone Paints." *J. Research Natl Bur. Standards,* v. 19, July, 1937, pp. 21–30.

24.13. Johnson, W. B.: "Oil-Resin Emulsion Paints." *Am. Painter & Decorator,* v. 26, Jan., 1949, pp. 14–17.

24.14. Jones, A.: *Cellulose Lacquers, Finishes, and Cements.* London, C. Griffin & Co., 1937, 418 pages.

24.15. Keshan, A. S.: "Color Dynamics for Modern Machinery." *Ind. Finishing,* v. 21, No. 11, Sept., 1945, p. 38.

24.16. Leighou, R. B.: *Chemistry of Engineering Materials.* McGraw-Hill Book Co., 4th ed., 1942; Chap. 19, pp. 544–590.

24.17. Martin, R. C.: *Glossary of Paint, Varnish, Lacquer, and Allied Terms.* St. Louis, Mo., American Paint Journal Co., 1937.

24.18. Mattiello, J. J.: "Protective Organic Coatings as Engineering Materials." *Proc. ASTM,* v. 46, 1946, p. 493.

24.19. Mattiello, J. J. (ed.): *Protective and Decorative Coatings.* John Wiley & Sons, 1943.

24.20. Plastics Catalogue Corp.: *Modern Plastics Encyclopedia.* New York, 1949.

24.21. Rose, K.: "A Plastics Primer for Engineers." *Materials & Methods,* v. 25, Apr., 1947, pp. 119–138.

24.22. Ross, W. A., and Critchfield, D.: *Painting Farm Buildings and Equipment.* New York, Lead Industries Assoc., 1947.

24.23. Soderberg, G. A.: *Finishing Materials and Methods.* Bloomington, Ill., McKnight & McKnight Publishing Co., 1952, 320 pages.

24.24. Stewart, J. R.: *National Paint Dictionary.* Washington, D. C., Stewart Research Lab., 3rd ed., 1948.

24.25. Storey, W. R.: "Fluorescent Paints." *Natl Painters Mag.,* v. 14, Mar., 1947, p. 16.

24.26. Von Fischer, W.: *Paint and Varnish Technology.* New York, Reinhold Publishing Corp., 1948.

24.27. Wampler, R. H.: *Modern Organic Finishes.* New York, Chemical Publishing Co., 1946.

24.28. Zimmerman, O. T., and Lavine, I.: *Handbook of Material Trade Names.* Dover, N. H., Industrial Research Service, 1953 ed., 1953, 794 pages.

Index

Numbers refer to pages

Absorption, brick, 475–479
  building stone, 308
  cast stone, 432
  concrete masonry blocks, 430
  concrete pipes, 431
  drain tile, 482
  sewer brick, 481
  sewer pipe, 481
Acicular grains, 10
Acid-resist pattern, 588
Acoustical materials, 501–506
  blankets, 501
  painting, 505, 506
  plaster, 501, 503, 504
  prefabricated units, 501, 502, 504
  sound-absorption coefficient, 501–503
  sprayed-on materials, 501, 503, 504
Acoustical treatment of rooms, 501, 504
Acrylic resins, 545, 550, 565, 566, 610, 613, 616
Active fillers for waterproofing, 420, 421
Addition polymeride, 546
Adherend, 571
Adhesion, 12
  concrete to steel, 439, 440
  definition, 572
Adhesives, 572–578
  animal glues, 572, 573
  blood albumin, 573, 574, 578
  bone glues, 573
  casein glues, 573, 574, 575, 578
  corn, 574, 576
  hide glues, 573, 577, 578
  protein, 573, 574
  soya-bean glues, 574, 578
  synthetic resin, 574, 576, 577
  tapioca, 574, 576
  thermoplastic, 576
  thermosetting, 576, 577
Admiralty brass, 274
Admiralty metal, 274
Admixtures, concrete, 420, 421, 423, 424

Aggregates for concrete, 445, 446, 500
Air content in concrete, 415, 416, 417, 443–445
  gravimetric method, 415, 444
  pressure method, 415, 444
  rolling method, 415, 416
Air-entraining concrete, 413, 414, 416, 417, 442–445 *passim*
Air furnace, 97, 184
  charge, 185
  control of melting, 185
Airolon, 376, 416
AISI steel numbering system, 217
Alclad, 282, 283, 597
Alfesil, 426
Alkalies in Portland cement, 323, 324
Alkyd resins, 552, 585, 609, 610, 612, 613, 616
"Alleghany metal," 230
Allotriomorphic crystals, 9
Alloy, eutectic, 16–18
  eutectoid, 22, 23
  solid solution, 18, 19
  two-layer, 14
Alloy cast iron, 202, 203
Alloy diagram, 15
Alloy steels, 215–245; *see* special steels
  "Alleghany metal," 230
  aluminum, 242
  chrome-molybdenum, 224, 225
  chrome-nickel, 220–223, 230–232
  chrome-vanadium, 229
  chromium, 228, 229, 237, 240
  cobalt, 236
  copper, 233
  18-8, 230
  "Enduro Nirosta," 230
  K.A. 2, 230
  manganese, 219, 220, 237
  molybdenum, 223, 224, 236
  nickel, 220
  nickel-chromium-molybdenum, 225–227

624 Index

Alloy steels, nickel-molybdenum, 228
  Nitralloy, 242, 243
  nitriding, 242, 243
  quaternary, 215
  silicon, 238, 239
  silicon-manganese, 241
  stainless, 230–232
  ternary, 215
  tungsten, 236
  vanadium, 236
Alloys, *see* special alloys
  aluminum, 276–284, 291–293
  bearing metals, 293–295
  beryllium-copper, 267, 268
  brass, 246, 271–276, 292, 293
  bronze, 246, 263–271
  copper, 263–276
  die casting, 290–293
  electrical conductivity, 24
  hardness, 23, 24
  magnesium, 284–287, 290
  nickel, 287–289
  steels, alloy, 215–245
  titanium, 289, 290
  zinc die-casting, 290, 291
Alnico, 240
Alpha iron, 9
Alternating stress, 37, 45
Alumina cement, 381, 431
Aluminum, 257–259, 277, 281
  bauxite, 258
  commercial forms, 257
  composition, 277
  corrosion resistance, 259
  cryolite, 258
  electrical resistance, 258, 259
  extraction, 257, 258
  occurrence in nature, 257
  properties, 258, 259, 281
  uses, 258, 259
Aluminum alloy gears, 283
Aluminum alloys, 276–284
  Alclad, 282, 283, 597
  aluminum bronze, 264, 265
  aluminum-copper, 277, 279
  aluminum-magnesium, 265, 266, 277, 279
  aluminum-silicon, 277, 279
  aluminum-zinc-magnesium, 277, 279
  applications, 280
  castings, 278, 279
  characteristics, 280
  chemical composition, 276, 277

Aluminum alloys, clad products, 282, 283
  mechanical properties, 281, 282
  temper designations, 278
Aluminum bronze, 264, 265
Aluminum-coated iron and steel, 284
Aluminum die-casting alloys, 291, 292, 293
Aluminum-foil honeycomb, 594, 595
Aluminum-manganese bronze, 265, 266
Aluminum paint, 257, 608
Aluminum steel, 242
  Nitralloy, 242, 243
  nitriding, 242, 243
Amorphous material, 9
Annealing, malleable cast iron, 210, 211
  steel, 140, 153
Antifriction metals, 293–295
Antimonial lead, 255
Antiseptics for wood, copper sulfate, 534
  corrosive sublimate, 534
  creosote, 534, 535, 536
  toxic organic compounds, 534
  zinc chloride, 534, 536
Arch brick, 465
Architectural concrete, 428, 429
  art marbles, 428
  ornamental finishes, 428
  painted decorations, 428, 429
  polished surfaces, 428
  Portland-cement plaster, 429
  stucco, 429
  terrazzo, 428
Architectural terra cotta, 469, 470
Argillaceous limestone, 353, 357, 358
Art marbles, 428
Asbestos in laminates, 585
Ashlar, 304, 311
Asphalt admixture, 423
Aston process, 173, 174
Austempering, 147, 148
Austenite, 132, 133, 135, 136, 137; 142–148
  passim
Autoclave test, cement, 372, 375, 376, 378
Avtex, 587

Babbitt metals, 293–295
Bainite, 143, 144, 147
Balsa wood, properties, 593, 594
Banded structure, 10, 129
Barium chloride in concrete, 423
Barytes aggregates, 448, 454
Barytes concrete, 448, 453, 454
Base coat, lime, 341

Index

Basic water content, 392
Bats, insulating, 496, 497, 500
Bauxite, 93, 258
Bearing metals, 293–295
Bedford limestone, 306–308
Bell metal, 271
Benzyl cellulose, 545, 550
Beryllium, 267
Beryllium bronze, 267
Beryllium-copper alloy, 267, 268
Bessemer process, 97, 108–114
    acid process, 109–113
    basic process, 113, 114
    casting ingots, 112, 113
    converter, 110, 111
    deoxidation, 112
    ores, 100
    oxidation, 111
    pig iron, 105
    recarburization, 111, 112, 114
Bessemer steel, 107, 108, 109, 112
    carbon-deoxidized, 112
    dephosphorized, 112
Billet-heating furnace, 124
Binders for organic plastics, 544–552
Bituminous membranes, curing concrete, 419
Blaine air-permeability test, 372, 378
Blankets, insulating, 496, 497
Blast furnace, 96, 97, 100–104
    mechanical equipment, 101, 102
    operation, 103, 104
Blast-furnace slag, 101–104 *passim*; 313, 319, 321, 323, 352, 359, 379
    granulated, 379
    lightweight, 313, 319, 321
    in Portland blast-furnace-slag cement, 377, 379
    in Portland cement, 357, 359
    in slag cement, 352, 353, 359
Blister copper, 248
Blowing, plastics, 560
Boards, structural-insulating, 496, 498, 500
Body-centered cubic structure, 9
Bolted joints, 71–75 *passim*
Bond, reinforcement in concrete, 439, 440
Bond strength, brick masonry, 486
    concrete, 439, 440
Bonds, coördinate covalent, 572
    covalent, 572
    electrostatic (polar), 572
    metallic, 572

Bonds, van der Waals forces, **572**
Boron-treated steels, 241
Bosh, 101
Brass, 246, 271–276
    Admiralty metal, 274
    alpha phase, 271
    beta phase, 271
    brazing, 167, 273
    cartridge, 272, 273
    commercial bronze, 271, **272**
    copper-zinc-aluminum, 274
    copper-zinc-iron, 275
    copper-zinc-lead, 274
    delta metal, 275
    French bronze, 276
    low, 272, 273
    Muntz metal, 272, 273, 274
    naval, 274
    ordinary, 271–274
    properties, 272, 274, 275
    red, 272
    season cracking, 273
    special, 274–276
    Sterro metal, 275
    Tobin bronze, 94, 274
    twinning, 273
    white, 276
    yellow, 272
Brass die castings, 292, 293
Brazing, 167, 273
Brick, 457–487; *see* special bricks
    absorption, 475
    building, 464, 465
    burning, 463
    ceramic glazed, 465, 466, 477, 479
    classification, 464, 465, 476–479 *passim*
    compressive strength, 475
    concrete, 471
    cutting, 461
    de-airing, 461
    drying, 462, 463
    dry-press, 461, 462
    efflorescence, 486, 487
    face, 465, 466
    flexural strength, 475
    flow chart, 459
    glazed, 465, 466, 477, 479
    kilns, 463, 464
    machine processes, 458–462
    modulus of elasticity, 476
    paving, 471–473
    preparation of clay, 460

Brick, pressed, 462
  pugging, 460
  sand-lime, 470, 471
  sewer, 473
  shearing strength, 475
  soft-mud process, 461
  stiff-mud process, 460, 461
  vitrification, 463
  winning of clay, 458, 460
Brick clays, 457, 458, 491, 492
  classification, 457
  composition, 492
  lacustrine, 457
  marine, 457
Brick kilns, 459, 463, 464
  continuous, 464
  down-draft, 463, 464
  up-draft, 463
Brick-making machines, auger type, 459, 460
  dry-press, 461, 462
  plunger type, dry-press, 461, 462
  soft-mud, 461
  stiff-mud, 460, 461
Brick masonry, 481–486
  bond, 484
  cement mortar, 481
  common bond, 484
  English bond, 484
  Flemish bond, 484
  mortar joints, 481
  reinforced, 485, 486
  strength, 484, 485
Brinell hardness test, 34
Brittleness, 4
Bronze, 246, 263–271
  alpha phase, 264
  aluminum, 264, 265
  aluminum-manganese, 265, 266
  bell metal, 271
  beryllium, 267
  copper-tin-zinc, 270
  cupro-nickel, 269
  delta phase, 264
  gun metal, 268
  hydraulic, 270
  leaded phosphor, 269, 270
  manganese, 266, 267
  nickel, 268
  ordinary, 263, 264
  patina, 271
  phosphor, 269

Bronze, properties, 263, 265, 266, 270
  silicon, 269, 270
  special, 264–271
  speculum metal, 271
  statuary, 271
  Tobin, 94, 274
  valve, 271
  vanadium, 271
Bronze-steel laminate, 597
Browning coat, plaster, 331
Building brick, 457, 461–465, 474–476, 479, 480
  arch, 465
  classification, 464, 465
  concrete, 471, 480
  hard, 465
  properties, 474–476, 479
  red, 465
  salmon, 465
  sand-struck, 461
  soft, 461
  water-struck, 461
  well-burned, 465
Building lime, 343, 344
Building stones, 301–311
  absorption, 308, 309
  classification, 301, 302
  dimension stone, 304–308
  durability, 308
  expansion and contraction, 309
  fire resistance, 309, 310
  frost resistance, 309
  gneiss, 302, 303
  granite, 302, 305, 306
  limestones, 303, 306–308
  mechanical properties, 310, 311
  milling, 305–307
  production, 305–308
  properties, 308–311
  quarrying, 305, 306
  sandstones, 303, 304
  selection of, 308
  slates, 304
  structural material, 301
  traprock, 304
Bulking of sand, 317, 403
Bullet-resisting glass, 600
Buna N, rubber, 567
Buna S, rubber, 567
Burmister mortar-flow trough, 377
Bustle pipe, 102

Index

Butyl rubber, 567
By-product aggregates, 313, 319, 320

Calcimine, 609
Calcination, gypsum, 328, 329
  hydraulic limes, 350
  natural cements, 353, 354
  Portland cement, 364, 365
  quicklime, 336–338
Calcium chloride, 418, 419, 420, 441
Calcium hydrosilicate, 593
Calcium lime, 335, 339–348 *passim*
Carbide tools, cemented, 297
Carbon brick, 491, 493
Carbon in steel, 95, 97, 107–120 *passim*; 123, 131–139 *passim*; 150–160 *passim*
Cartridge brass, 272, 273
Case hardening of steel, 152, 153
Casein paint, 609
Casein plastics, 545, 552
Cast iron, 95, 181–206
  air furnace, 184
  automotive-type, 201
  alloy, 202
  ASTM specifications, 200
  carbon in, 191
  cementite, 190–195 *passim*
  centrifugal casting, 189
  checking, 196
  chilled castings, 188
  cleaning castings, 189
  constitution, 190
  controlled, 203, 204
  cooling, 195, 196
  cope, 187
  cupola furnace, 182–184
  designing castings, 188
  drag, 187
  electric-melting furnace, 186
  flask, 187, 189
  flux, 182
  foundry pig iron, 181
  fuel, 182, 185
  gate, 189
  graphite, 191–198 *passim*
  gray, 191, 200
  hardness, 196, 197
  heat treatment, 201, 202
  high-strength, 201
  inoculated, 203, 204
  iron founding, 186–190
  ledeburite, 190

Cast iron, manganese in, 194
  metalloids, 198
  molding, 186, 187
  mottled, 191
  nodular graphite, 204, 205
  patterns, 187, 188
  pearlite, 192
  phosphorus in, 194
  physical properties, 195–201
  pouring, 188
  reverberatory furnace, 184
  segregation, 196
  shrinkage, 195
  silicon in, 193
  stress-strain diagram, 199
  sulfur in, 193, 194
  tensile strength, 197, 198
  transverse strength, 200
  tuyère, 182
  white, 191
Cast stone, 431, 432
Casting copper, 247
Castor oil, 609, 612
Catalan forge, 96
Cellular glass, 593
Cellular rubber, 593, 594
Celluloid, 545, 550, 566
Cellulose acetate, 550, 554, 565, 577, 615
  properties, 593, 594
Cellulose acetate butyrate, 550, 565, 615
Cellulose ester lacquer, 615
Cellulose nitrate, 545, 550, 577, 607, 613, 615, 617
Cellulose plastics, 550, 554, 565
Cement, *see* special kinds
  air-entraining Portland, 376–379
  alumina, 381
  high-early-strength Portland, 367, 369
  low-heat Portland, 367, 370
  masonry, 380, 381
  modified, 369
  natural, 353–355
  oxychloride, 381, 382
  Portland, 355–376
  Portland blast-furnace-slag, 377, 379
  Portland-pozzolan, 379, 380
  pozzolan, 351, 352
  slag, 352, 353
  sulfate-resisting Portland, 367, 370
Cement mortars, 372, 374, 378, 380, 381
  brick masonry, 380
Cement plaster, 327–332 *passim*

Index

Cement rock, 353, 354, 357, 358
Cementite, 131, 136, 137
Central mixing plant, concrete, 406, 407
Ceramic brick, 465, 466, 477, 479
Ceramic clay pipe, 483
Ceramic facing tile, 466, 477, 479
Cermets, 297
Chalk, 358
Channeling machine, 306, 307
Character of the fracture, metals, 30, 44
Charpy impact test, 37, 38, 53
Chemical compound, 14
Chemical-resistant clay brick, 466, 477, 479
Chemically setting compositions, 545, 546, 552
Chert, 319
Chilling of cast iron, 188
China-wood oil, 418, 609, 612, 613, 614
Chlorinated rubber, 614
Chrome brick, 493
Chrome-molybdenum steel, 224, 225
Chrome-nickel stainless steel, 230–232
  "Alleghany metal," 230
  18-8, 230–232
  "Enduro Nirosta," 230
  K.A. 2, 230
  properties, 232
  25-12, 231
Chrome-nickel steel, 64, 65, 220–223
Chromium bearing steel, 229
Chromium stainless steel, 232
Chromium steel, 228, 229, 236, 240
Chromium-vanadium steel, 229
Cinder concrete, 449
Clad products, 282, 283
Clay, 358, 360, 457, 458, 471, 491, 492
Clinker, natural cement, 354
  Portland cement, 360, 364, 365, 366
Coarse aggregate for concrete, 318
Coaxing tests, 46, 47
Cobalt steel, 236, 240
Codification of light-weight alloys, 283
Coefficient of expansion, aluminum, 259
  building stone, 309
  concrete, 446
  magnesium, 260
  malleable cast iron, 212
  plastics, 562, 587, 593
Coefficient of thermal conductivity, 259, 260, 427, 428, 494, 499, 500, 593
Cohesion, 12, 572

Cold-bending test, 31
Cold brittleness, 49
"Cold-light" coatings, 617
Cold molding, plastics, 552
Cold-water paint, 609
Cold working, steel, 127, 128, 129
  wrought iron, 177
Colored aggregates, 313
Colored pigments, 608
Colorimetric test for sand, 315, 316
Columnar grains, 10
Commercial bronze, 271
Composite metals, 595–598
  "clad" steels, 596
  sandwich process, 596
  wrought iron and steel, 597
Composition, 6
Compreg, 584
Compression molding, 555–558
Compression test, sandwich specimen, 592
Compressive strength, 1, 32
  brick, 476, 477
  brick masonry, 485
  building stones, 310
  building tile, 477, 478
  ceramic tile, 477
  concrete, 414, 427, 433–435, 444
  firebrick, 494
  gypsum plaster, 332
  masonry cement mortars, 381
  natural cement mortar, 355
  polyester, glass-reinforced, 564
  Portland cement mortar, 372, 374, 378
  refractory materials, 494
  sewer brick, 481
  steel, 32
  stone masonry, 311
  structural clay tile, 477, 478
  wood, 528, 529
  wrought iron, 177
Compressometer, 453
Concrete, 385–456
  action of sea water, 422
  adhesion to steel, 439, 440
  air-entrained, 395, 399, 413–417
  architectural, 428, 429
  asphalt admixture, 423
  bleeding, 410
  bonding to old work, 411
  cinder, 449
  coarse aggregate, 318, 319
  combined water, 402

Index

Concrete, compressive strength, 414, 427, 433–435, 444
  consistency, 387
  constant water content, 401
  contraction, 445, 446
  curing, 417–420
  depositing under water, 410, 411
  deposition, 406–408
  elastic limit, 436
  elastic properties, 436–439
  expansion, 445, 446
  facing of walls, 412
  fatigue, 439
  finishing, 411, 412
  fire-resistant properties, 448, 449
  flexural strength, 436, 444
  floor hardening, 424
  forms, 406, 407
  gravel versus crushed stone, 319
  Gunite, 406
  high-density, 448, 453, 454
  insulating, 427, 428
  laitance, 411
  low temperatures, 412, 413
  materials, 385, 386
  measurement of materials, 403, 404
  mixing, 405, 406
  mixing machines, 405, 406
  modulus of elasticity, 428, 437
  paving concrete, 399
  permeability, 449, 450
  plastic flow, 446, 447
  quantities of materials, 404
  ratio E_c/E_s, 437
  restoration, 426, 427
  sand for concrete, 315–318
  sea water, 422, 423
  shearing strength, 436
  slump test, 387, 388
  stress-strain curves, 437, 438
  tensile strength, 435
  thermal conductivity, 427, 428
  vacuum concrete process, 424–426
  vibrated, 408, 409
  water gain, 410
  waterproofing, 420–422
  weeping, 410
  weighing aggregates, 403, 404
  weight, 447, 448
  workability, 387
Concrete brick, 471, 480
Concrete masonry blocks, 429, 430
Concrete pipes, 431
Concrete restoration, 426, 427
Concreting in freezing weather, 412, 413
Condensation, 546, 547, 586, 612
Condensation polymeride, 546
Conduit, clay, 474
Cone test, hardness, 34
Consistency, cement, 373
  concrete, 387
  lime, 342
Constitution, 6–24
  alloys, 13
  cast iron, 190–195
  definition, 6
  diagram, 21, 137
  iron, 132–134
  malleable cast iron, 212
  Portland cement, 366–370
  steel, 131–137
Contact resin, 585, 586, 601
Contraction of concrete, 445, 446
Converter, 97, 110, 111, 153, 173, 248, 255, 261
Cooling curves, 13–24 *passim*
Copals, 611
Copolymerization, 546, 613
Copolymers, 613
Copper, 246–252
  annealing, 249
  blister, 248
  casting, 247
  classification, 246, 247
  cold rolling, 249
  corrosion resistance, 252
  deoxidized, 251, 252
  electrical resistivity, 249
  electrolytic, 247–252 *passim*
  extraction from ores, 247–249
  lake, 247, 249
  matte, 248
  properties, 249–252
  uses, 249–252
Copper-alloy infiltrated iron, 296
Copper alloys, 263–276
Copper steel, 233
Copper-zinc-aluminum brasses, 274
Copper-zinc-iron alloys, 275, 276
Copper-zinc-lead brasses, 274
Cored-shell tile, 467
Cores in sandwich construction, 589–595 *passim*
  structural properties, 592–595 *passim*

Corona losses in wires, 259
Corrosion, 76–81
  aluminum, 259
  aluminum bronze, 265
  cathodic protection, 80, 81
  chrome-nickel steel, 230–232
  chromium steel, 232
  copper, 252
  copper steel, 233
  electrolytic theory, 77
  endurance limit, 80
  fatigue, 80
  galvanic, 78, 79
  Inconel metal, 288
  intergranular, 79, 80
  lead, 255, 256
  magnesium alloys, 287
  manganese bronze, 266
  Monel metal, 287
  nickel, 261
  nickel steel, 232
  pipes, 79
  pitting, 79
  plastics, 551
  preventive measures, 80, 81
  primary reactions, 77, 78
  secondary reactions, 77, 78
  silicon bronze, 269
  temperature, effect of, 80
  tin, 257
  titanium, 262, 263
  transcrystalline, 80
  wrought iron, 178
  zinc, 254
Corrosion- and heat-resisting steels, 230–233
Cotton-cloth filler, laminates, 585, 586, 587
Creep, 54, 57, 69
  copper, 252
  lead, 256
  steel, 54–57
  tin, 257
  zinc, 253, 254
Creep limit, 57, 58
Creep-rupture tests, 66, 67
Creep test, 39
Creosote, 534–536
Cristobalite, 323
Crucible process, steel, 97
Cryolite, 258
Crystallization of metals, 8
Culvert pipes, 431

Cumarone-indene resins, 551, 614
Cumars, 614, 615
Cunico, 241
Cunife, 240, 241
Cupola furnace, 182–184
Cupro-nickel, 269
Cyclograph, 85

Dammar, 611, 616
Darex AEA, 376, 416
De-aired brick, 461, 472
Deformation, 1
Deformed steel bar reinforcement, 439, 440
Deleterious substances in aggregates, 315, 316, 318, 319
Delta metal, 275, 276
Dendritic structure, 10, 130, 131
Deoxidized copper, 251, 252
Desilverized lead, 255
Dezincification of brass, 273
Diatomaceous earth, 351
Diatomaceous shale, 321
Dicalcium silicate, 367, 368
Die-casting alloys, 290–293
  aluminum, 291
  brass, 292, 293
  magnesium, 291, 292
  zinc, 290, 291
Dielectric strength, plastics, 563, 564
Die steels, 233–237
  for forming plastics, 236, 237
Dies for plastics, 588
Dimension stone, 304–308
Direct reduction of steel, 106
Discaloy 24 alloy, 62, 63, 66, 67, 233
Dispersing agents for cements, 424
Dissimilar metal chart, 78
Dolomitic lime, 335, 339–342 *passim;* 347, 348
Dolomitic sand and gravel, 443, 444
Dopes, 617
Douglas-fir plywood, 580, 581, 582
Douglas-fir veneer, 602
Dow metal, 287
Drain pipe, 431
Drain tile, clay, 473, 480, 481, 482
Drift test, 32
Dryer, for paint, 606, 607, 609
Ductility, 4, 31, 55, 56
  aluminum, 281
  aluminum alloys, 281, 292, 296
  aluminum bronze, 265

Index

Ductility, aluminum manganese bronze, 266
  beryllium-copper alloy, 267
  brass, 272, 275
  chrome-nickel steel, 220, 232
  copper, 250, 251
  lead, 256
  magnesium alloys, 286
  malleable cast iron, 212
  Monel metal, 288
  naval brass, 274
  nickel, 261
  nickel steel, 220
  silicon steel, 238
  steel, 31, 55, 137, 155, 158, 159
  titanium, 290
  wrought iron, 177
  zinc, 254
  zinc die-casting alloys, 291
Dumet, 242
Duplex metal castings, 597, 598
Durability, 4
  of concrete, 440–443

Efflorescence, brick, 486, 487
18-8, 230
Elastic limit, 2
  concrete, 436
  steel, 28
Elastic properties, concrete, 436, 437
Elasticity, 2
Electric furnace, 97, 98, 120–122, 186
Electric refining of steel, 120–122
Electrical conductivity, alloys, 24
Electrical insulation, 565
  polyester, 564
  silicones, 614
Electrical iron alloys, 238–241
Electrical properties, plastics, 563, 564, 565
Electrical steels, 238–241
Electrolytic copper, 247, 249, 250, 251, 252
Electrolytic theory of corrosion, 77
Electrometallurgy, 94
Electromotive series, tin, 257
  zinc, 254
Electron metal, 287
Electron waves, 7
Elinvar, 242
Elongation, of specimen, 30
  distribution of, 31
Emulsion paint, 609, 610
Enamel, 606, 607, 620
Endurance limit, 44, 48

Endurance ratio, 47
"Enduro Nirosta," 230
Equiaxed grains, 10
Equicohesive strength, 63, 64, 70
Equilibrium diagram, 15–25 *passim*
Equilibrium moisture, brick, 462
Ester gum, 612, 614, 616
Ethyl cellulose, 545, 550, 615
Eutectic alloy, 16
Eutectoid, 22, 23
Expanded clay and shale, 320, 321
Expanded phenolic foam, 593
Expanded-slag aggregates, 319, 320
Expansion, lime, 347, 348
  of concrete, 445, 446
  plastics, 562, 587, 593
  stone, 309
  thermostat metals, 598
Extensometer test, 28, 39
Extrusion molding, plastics, 560

Face-centered cubic structure, 9
Faces, *see* Facings for sandwich construction
Facing brick, 465, 466
Facing tile, 466, 477, 479
Facings for sandwich construction, 589, 590, 591, 595
Failure of paint, 608
Fatigue, 37, 43–49, 439
  coaxing, 46, 47
  concrete, 439
  metals, 43–49
  overstressing, 46, 47
  understressing, 46, 47
  welds, 48
Fatigue cracks, 44, 45
Fatigue test, 37, 45
  repeated stress, 37, 45
  reversed stress, 37, 45
  swelling stress, 37, 45
Ferrite, 136, 137
Ferrous alloys, physical properties, 242
Ferrous metals, physical properties, 243
Fiberglas, 497
Film-former, lacquer, 607, 615
Filter block, 473
Fine aggregate, *see* Sand
Fineness modulus, 314, 315, 317
Finishing lime, 343, 344, 345
Firebrick, *see* Refractory brick
Fireclay brick, 491, 492

632 Index

Fireproofing material, concrete, 448, 449
  gypsum, 333
  tile, clay, 468
Fire resistance, building stones, 309, 310
  concrete, 448, 449
  glass building blocks, 488
  gypsum plasters, 333
  insulating materials, 499, 500
  plastics, 562
  steel, 495
  timber, 540
Fire-retardant coatings, 618
Flame hardening, 165, 166
Flash type mold, plastics, 557
Flexural strength, 32, 33
  brick, 475, 477, 479, 480, 485
  building stones, 310
  cast iron, 200, 201, 204
  concrete, 436, 444
  cores for sandwich construction, 593
  plastics, 562
  refractory brick, 494
  sandwich specimen, 592
  wood, 524, 528
Floor hardening, concrete, 424
Floor tile, clay, 468, 478
Flooring cement, 382
Flooring plaster, 327, 329
Flow characteristics of plastics, 560, 561
Flue lining, clay, 474
Fluorescent inspection, 84, 86
Fluorescent pigments, 617
Flux, 99, 100, 108, 117, 179, 182, 183, 458
Foam, expanded phenolic, 593
Forging of steel, 127
Forsterite brick, 491, 493
Fractures of metal, crystalline, 44
  cup and cone, 30
  fibrous, 30
  intercrystalline, 57
  progressive fracture, 43
  rosette, 30
  serrated, 30
  texture, 30
  transcrystalline, 56, 57
Free-cutting steels, 238
Freezing and thawing of concrete, 441, 442
Freezing of pure metal, 13, 14
French bronze, 276
Frost resistance, building stone, 309
Fuel for furnaces, 96, 97, 100, 114, 182, 185
Furfuryl-phenol plastics, 548, 549

Furnaces, air, 97, 184, 185
  arc, 121
  billet-heating, 124
  blast, 96, 97, 100–104
  Catalan forge, 96
  cupola, 182–184
  electric, 97, 98, 120–122, 186
  induction, 121
  malleablizing, 210, 211
  open-hearth, 115
  pit-furnace, 124
  puddling, 172
  regenerative, 115, 124
  reverberatory, 97, 124, 172, 184, 247, 257
  series-arc, 121
  shaft, 257
  shelf, 247
Furring tile, 468
Fusible alloys, 18
Fusion test for refractories, 493, 494

Galvanic corrosion, 78, 79
Gamma-ray inspection, 86
Gamma-ray shielding, 448
Gangue, 92, 93, 100, 103
Gap grading of aggregates, 314
Gauging plaster, 331
Gel, cement, 446, 447
Geological classification of rocks, 301, 302
German silver, 288
Ghost lines, 130
Glass-air-cell structures, 600
Glass building blocks, 487, 488
Glass cloth, laminates, 585, 586
Glass-fabric-base plastic, 594, 595
Glass laminates, 599, 600
Glass-lined metals, 598, 599
Glass-reinforced polyester, 564, 595
Glass wool, 496, 497, 500
Glucinum, 267
Glued-laminated wood, 583, 584
Glues, 572–578; *see also* Adhesives
  animal, 572, 573
  blood albumin, 573, 574, 578
  bone, 573
  casein, 573, 574, 575, 578
  hide, 573, 577, 578
  laminating, 575
  preparation and precautions, 577
  properties, 574, 575
  soya-bean, 574, 578
  strength of bond, 578

Index

Glues, synthetic resin, 574, 576, 577
Gneiss, 302
Goldbeck and Gray method, proportioning concrete, 395–400
Gradation of aggregates, 314, 315, 318
  lightweight aggregates, 322
Grain-size control, steel, 151, 152
Granite, 302, 305, 306
Granular lime, 335
Granulated cork, 496, 497, 500
Graphitic tool steels, 235
Grinding cementing materials, 362, 366
Ground lime, 335
Gun metal, 268
Gunite, 406
Gypsite, 328
Gypsum, 327, 328, 366
Gypsum block, 332
Gypsum concrete, 331, 332
Gypsum lath, 332
Gypsum plaster, 327–334
  ASTM specifications, 332, 333
  calcination, 328, 329
  cement plaster, 327, 328–330 passim
  classification, 327
  definition, 327
  fireproofing qualities, 333
  flooring plaster, 327, 329
  gypsum rocks, 327
  hard-finish plaster, 327, 329, 333
  Keene's cement, 329, 330, 333
  lightweight wall plaster, 331
  Mack's cement, 330
  manufacture, 328, 329
  plaster board, 332
  plaster of Paris, 327, 328, 329, 330
  setting, 330
  strength, 332
  tests of, 333
  uses, 330, 331
  wall board, 332
Gypsum tile, 332

Hard facing, of steel, 166, 167
Hard-finish plaster, 327, 329, 333
Hard setting, 167
Hard-wall plaster, 327–332 passim
Hardenability of steel, 143–145, 148–151
  index of, 149, 150
Hardening, of cement, 371
  of gypsum plaster, 330
  of lime mortar, 342

Hardness, 4, 23
  of aggregates, 323
  of alloys, 23
  of aluminum, 281
  of aluminum alloys, 281
  of aluminum bronze, 265
  of aluminum-manganese bronze, 266
  of beryllium-copper, 267
  of brass, 272
  of cast iron, 197, 201, 204
  of chrome-molybdenum steel, 224
  of chrome-nickel steel, 51, 221–223 passim; 232
  of copper, 251
  of lime mortar, 342
  of magnesium alloys, 286
  of malleable cast iron, 212
  of nickel, 261
  of nickel alloys, 288
  of nickel-chromium-molybdenum steels, 145, 226, 227
  of plastics, 562, 564, 587
  of steel, 51, 52, 137, 144, 146, 150, 155, 158
  of titanium, 290
  of zinc die-casting alloys, 286
Hardness tests, 34–37
  Brinell, 34
  cone test, 34
  Herbert, 36
  Knoop indenter, 35, 36
  Monotron, 36
  Rockwell, 34
  Rockwell superficial, 34, 35
  Shore scleroscope, 36
  Vickers, 35
Haydite, 320
Heat distortion, plastics, 562
Heat-insulating materials, 495–501
Heat treatment of steel, 138, 139, 140
Hematite, 99
Herbert hardness test, 36
Hexagonal lattice structure, 9
High-alloy tool and die steels, 235, 236
High-carbon tool steels, 233, 234, 235
High-chromium steels, 237, 238
High-density concrete, 448
High-manganese steel, 237
High-nickel steel, 232
High-speed tool steels, 236
High-strength low-alloy steels, 217, 218
High temperature testing, metals, 55, 73, 74
History of metals, 94–98

634 Index

Hollow clay tile, 467
Honeycomb cores, 594, 595
Honeycomb paper cores, 602, 603
Hooke's law, 2
Hot-blast stove, 102
HS No. 88 alloy, 62, 63, 233
Hydrated lime, 335, 343–348, 351, 352, 376, 421
  air separation, 345
  classification, 343
  consistency, 345
  definition, 335
  expansion, 347
  manufacture, 344, 345
  popping and pitting, 346
  properties, 346
  soundness, 345, 346
  tests, 345, 346
Hydrator for lime, 344
Hydraulic bronze, 270, 271
Hydraulic lime, 350, 351
Hydraulic limestone, 350
Hydraulic press, steel working, 127, 128
Hydraulicity, 350
Hydrometallurgy, 94
Hydropel, 423
Hydrostatic pressure tests, 88

Idiomorphic crystals, 9
Impact strength, aluminum bronze, 265
  aluminum die-casting alloys, 292
  cast iron, 204
  chrome-nickel stainless steel, 232
  magnesium alloys, 286
  malleable cast iron, 212
  nickel alloys, 288
  nickel-chromium-molybdenum steels, 227
  plastics, 562, 564, 587, 600
  steel, 53
  zinc die-casting alloys, 291
Impact test, 37, 49–52
  Charpy test, 37, 38, 50
  cold brittleness, 49
  Izod test, 37, 38, 50
  notched-bar test, 38, 50
  temperature, effect of, 50, 51
  utility tests, 37
  velocity of deformation, 52
Inconel metal, 67, 68, 69, 288
Indiana limestone, 306–308
Inert fillers for waterproofing, 420, 421

Ingot iron, 132, 155, 156
  electrical properties, 239
Ingots, casting of steel, 112, 113, 123, 124
  defects and corrections, 129, 130
Injection molding, plastics, 558–560
Insulating concrete, 427, 428
Insulating materials, 495–501
  box test, 500
  classification, 496
  coefficient of thermal conductivity, 499
  composition, 496
  conductance, 499
  fire resistance, 499
  plate test, 500
  properties, 500
  transmittance, 499
  water resistance, 499
  water-vapor permeability, 500
Insulating varnish, 614
Integral curing, concrete, 419, 420
Intergranular corrosion, 79, 80
Intergranular oxidation, 55, 56
Intermetallic compounds, 22
Intrusion Aid, 426
Intrusion Grout, 426
Invar, 241, 242, 598
Iron, *see also* special kinds
  cast, 95, 181–206
  classification, 95
  copper-alloy infiltrated, 296
  electrical iron alloys, 238–241
  galvanized, 254
  history, 96, 97
  ingot, 132, 155, 156, 239
  malleable cast, 95, 207–213
  nickel-iron alloys, 241, 242
  pig, 99–106
  wrought, 95, 172–180
Iron-carbon equilibrium diagram, 131-1
Iron carbonate, 99
Iron founding, 186–190
Iron ores, 92, 93, 99, 100
  direct reduction of, 106
Isothermal transformation diagram, 140 148
Izod impact test, 37, 38, 50

Japanese lacquer, 617
Jet-molding, plastics, 560
Jominy end-quench test, 148–151

Index

K.A. 2 stainless steel, 230
Keene's cement, 329, 330, 333
Kettle, for gypsum plaster, 328
Kilns, *see also* special kilns
  brick, 463, 464, 472, 492
  gypsum plaster, 328
  flooring plaster, 329
  Haydite, 320
  hydraulic lime, 350
  lime, 337, 338
  natural cement, 354
  Portland cement, 360, 364, 365
  sewer pipe, clay, 474
  terra cotta, 469
Knoop pyramidal indenter, 35, 36
Kraft paper, 601, 602

Lac, *see* Shellac
Lacquer, 606, 607, 609, 613, 615–617, 620
  Chinese, 617
  dopes, 617
  film-forming materials, 615
  Indian, 617
  Japanese, 617
  plasticizer, 607
  resins, 615, 616
  testing, 620
  thinners, 616
Lacquer-base solutions, 617
Laitance, 411
Lake copper, 247, 249
Lamellar structure, 10
Laminated castings, 597, 598
Laminated glass filters, 600
Laminated plastics, 548, 584–588
  Avtex, 587
  fillers, 585
  grades, 585
  low-pressure molding, 585, 586
  manufacture, 584, 585
  printed circuits, 588
  properties, 585, 586, 587
Laminated safe plate, 597
Laminated safety glass, 599, 600
Laminates, 571–605
  adherend, 571
  definition, 571
  cross laminated, 571
  of paper, 600–603
    decorative overlays, 601
    masking overlays, 601
    paper overlays, 600, 601

Laminates, of paper, structural overlays, 601
  parallel laminated, 571 [558
Landed-positive type mold, plastics, 557,
Lead, 255, 256
  antimonial, 255, 256
  commercial forms, 255
  corrosion resistance, 256
  creep, 256
  density, 256
  desilverized, 255
  extraction from ores, 255
  pigments, 608
  pipes, 256
  properties, 255, 256
  shielding against gamma rays, 256
  soft, 255
Leaded bronze, 16
Ledeburite, 132, 135, 190
Lelite, 320
Lightweight aggregates, 313, 314, 319–322
  by-product aggregates, 319, 320
  natural aggregates, 319, 321
  processed aggregates, 319, 320, 321
Lightweight concrete, 427, 428, 432, 448, 497, 500
Lightweight metals and alloys, codification, 283
Lime, 335–349, 470; *see also* Quicklime
  air-slaked, 340
  ASTM specifications, 341, 343, 345
  calcination, 337, 338
  classification, 335
  composition, 338, 339, 343
  compressive strength, 343, 346
  consistency, 345
  definition, 335
  finishing, 343
  hardness, 342
  hydrated, *see* Hydrated lime
  hydraulic, 350, 351
  kilns, 337, 338
  limestone rocks, 336
  manufacture, 336–338
  plasticity, 341, 345
  popping, 346
  putty, 339–342 *passim*
  sand-carrying capacity, 341
  sand-lime bricks, 470
  setting, 342
  shrinkage, 342, 343
  slaking, 339, 344, 345

Index

Lime, soundness, 345
  tensile strength, 343
  tests, 345, 346
  yield, 341, 342
Lime mortars, 341–348 *passim*; 380, 381
  block masonry, 380, 381
  brick masonry, 347, 348, 380, 381
  compressive strength, 343, 381
  hardness, 342
  shrinkage, 342
  tensile strength, 343
  time of setting, 342
Lime pops, 458
Limestones, argillaceous, 353, 357, 358
  Bedford, 303, 306–308
  compact common, 303
  crystalline, 303
  hydraulic, 350
  in Portland cement, 361
  Indiana, 303
  marble, 303
  properties, 310, 311
  rocks, 336
Limit of proportionality, 28
Limnoria, 538, 539
Limonite, 99
Linseed oil, 609, 612
Lithopone, 253, 553, 608
Loose fills, insulation, 496, 497
Los Angeles abrasion loss, aggregates, 322, 323
Low brass, 272, 273
Low-pressure molding, laminates, 585, 586
Low-temperature behavior, 81–83
Low-temperature properties, steels, 81, 82
Low-temperature notch-impact test, 51, 52, 81
Lumber; *see also* Timber and Wood
  factory lumber, 518
  grading of, 518, 519
  hardwood lumber, 519
  shop lumber, 518
  softwood lumber, 518, 519
  stress-grade, 518
  yard lumber, 518
Lumber-core plywood, 580
Luminescent coatings, 617, 618
Lump line, 335

Mack's cement, 330
Macroetch, 8
Macro-examination of metals, 8

Magnaglo, 84
Magnesian lime, 335, 339–343 *passim*; 347
Magnesite, 491, 492, 493
Magnesite stucco, 382
Magnesium, 10, 95, 259, 260
  extraction of, 259, 260
  history, 95
  properties, 260
  uses, 260
Magnesium alloys, 284–287
  chemical composition, 285
  corrosion resistance, 287
  physical properties, 285, 286, 287
Magnesium die-casting alloys, 291, 292
Magnesium oxychloride cements, 381, 382
Magnesium sulfate test, 323
Magnetic materials, 239, 240, 241
Magnetic-particle inspection, 84, 85
  fluorescent inspection, 84
  Magnaglo inspection, 84
Magnetic properties, steel, 160, 161
Magnetite, 99
Maleic resin, 614, 616
Malleability, 4
Malleable cast iron, 207–214
  annealing process, 210, 211
  black-heart, 211
  chemical composition, 212
  constitution, 212
  decarburization, 212
  ductility, 212, 213
  foundry methods, 209
  furnaces, 210, 211
  malleablizing process, 209, 210, 211
  manufacture, 208–212
  materials used, 208
  melting mixtures, 208
  pearlitic malleable, 213
  properties, 212
  temper carbon, 210
  tensile strength, 212
  uses, 207
  white-heart, 211
Manganese bronze, 266, 267
Manganese steel, 135, 219, 220, 237
Marble, 303, 309, 310
Marble-face building block, 432
Marine borers, 538–540
  bankia, 539
  limnoria, 538, 539
  martesia, 539
  protection from, 539, 540

Index 637

Marine borers, sphaeroma, 539
  teredo, 538
Marl, 358, 363
Martempering, 148
Martensite, 138, 139
Masonite, 588
Masonry, brick; see Brick masonry
  clay masonry unit, 465, 466, 482
  concrete block, 429, 430, 432
  stone, 311, 312
Masonry cements, 353, 355, 380, 381
Masonry mortar, 380, 381
Masonry units, structural-clay, 464–469, 476, 477, 479, 482
Mason's hydrate, 343, 344, 345
Mason's mortar, 341
Matte, 248
Mayari pig iron, 203
McVetty's creep limit, 58
Mechanical adhesion, 572
Mechanical properties, adhesives, 578
  aluminum, 258, 259, 281
  aluminum alloys, 281, 282, 292
  beryllium-copper, 267
  brass, 272, 274, 275, 282
  brick, 475, 476, 477, 479
  bronze, 263, 265, 266, 270
  building stones, 310, 311
  cast iron, 196–201
  concrete, 414, 427, 433–439, 444
  copper, 249–252
  firebrick, 494
  gypsum plaster, 332
  laminates, 581, 584, 586, 587, 593, 595, 600
  lime mortars, 343, 346
  magnesium alloys, 282, 285, 286, 287
  malleable cast iron, 212
  masonry cements, 381
  Monel metal, 288
  natural cement, 354, 355
  nickel, 261
  plastics, organic, 563, 564
  plywood, 581
  Portland cement, 372, 374, 378
  refractory materials, 494
  sintered aluminum powder, 296
  steels, 154, 155, 157–160, 220–227 *passim*; 232, 238, 243, 282
  stone masonry, 311, 312
  titanium, 262, 290
  titanium alloys, 290
  wood, 523, 524, 525

Mechanical properties, wrought iron, 176, 177, 178
Medium-alloy tool steels, 235
Meehanite cast iron, 203, 204
Melamine-formaldehyde resins, 549, 575, 577, 584, 613, 616
Melting point, ferrous metals, 243
  non-ferrous metals, 263
Membrane seal coats, 418, 419
Metal-foil-clad plastics, 588
Metal powders, 295
Metallograph, 7
Metallography, definition, 6
  history, 6
  use of microscope, 7, 8
Metals, classification, 95, 105, 107, 215–217, 246, 263
Metals Comparator, 85
Metals for molds for plastics, 558
Methyl methacrylate, 545, 551, 565
Microscope, 7, 8
Modified Portland cement, 369
Modular design, 429
  brick masonry, 482
  clay brick and tile, 465, 467
  concrete masonry block, 429, 430
Modulus, of elasticity, aluminum, 282
  beryllium-copper, 267
  brick, 476
  building stones, 310
  cast iron, 199, 204
  cemented carbide tools, 297
  concrete, 428, 437, 438, 439
  copper, 251
  definition, 3
  Elinvar, 242
  insulating concrete, 428
  laminates, 584, 586, 587, 593
  malleable cast iron, 212
  nickel, 261
  plastics, organic, 562, 564
  plywood, 581
  shearing, 33, 159, 160
  sonic, for concrete, 438, 439
  steel, 158, 160
  titanium, 262
  wood, 528, 529
  wrought iron, 177
  of rupture, see Flexural strength
Molded compositions, 561–564
Molding of organic plastics, 555–561
  blowing, 560

638 Index

Molding of organic plastics, casting, 560
  compression, 555, 556, 557
  extrusion, 560
  flash type, 557
  flow characteristics, 560, 561
  foams, 560
  injection, 558, 559
  landed-positive type, 557, 558
  positive type, 557
  semipositive type, 557
  transfer, 555, 556, 557
Molding powders, 554
Molybdenum-base alloys, 297
Molybdenum steel, 223, 224, 236
Monel metal, 287, 288
Monomer, 546, 585, 586
Monotron indentation test, 36
Mortar, air content of, 377
Mortar joints, brick masonry, 481, 482, 483
  glass building blocks, 488
Mortars, *see* special kinds
Multicored tile, 467
Muntz metal, 272, 273, 274

Natural aggregates, 313, 319, 321
Natural cement, 353–355
  air-entraining, 353, 355
  calcination, 353
  chemical composition, 354
  clinker, 354
  compressive strength, 355
  definition, 353
  natural cement rock, 353
  properties, 354, 355
  tensile strength, 354, 355
  uses, 355
Naval brass, 274
Navy composition "M," 271
Neat cement, tensile strength, 374
Neoprene, 567
Neumann bands, 12
Nick-bend test, wrought iron, 178
Nickel, 260, 261
  commercial forms, 260
  extraction from ores, 260
  hardness, 261
  properties, 261
  uses, 261
Nickel-alloy wrought iron, 179, 180
Nickel alloys, 287–289
  German silver, 288
  Inconel metal, 288

Nickel alloys, Monel metal, 287, 288
  nickel silver, 288, 289
  platinoid, 289
Nickel bronze, 268
Nickel-chromium-molybdenum steel, 225–227
Nickel-copper steel, 241
Nickel-iron alloys, 241, 242
Nickel-molybdenum steel, 228
Nickel silver, 288, 289
Nickel steel, 219, 220, 232
Nitralloy, 242, 243
Nitriding, 242, 243
Noise reduction in rooms, 505
Non-alloying metals, 297
Non-bituminous membranes for curing concrete, 419
Non-destructive tests, 83–88
  Cyclograph, 85
  fluorescent inspection, X-ray, 86
  fluorescent magnetic-particle inspection, 84
  fluorescent-penetrant inspection, 84
  gamma-ray inspection, 86
  hydrostatic pressure test, 88
  Hypersonic Analyzer, 87
  Magnaglo, 84
  magnetic analysis, 85
  magnetic-particle inspection, 84
  Metals Comparator, 85
  oil-powder inspection, 83, 84
  Reflectoscope, Supersonic, 87
  supersonic inspection, 87
  Thruray, Supersonic, 87
  X-ray diffraction, 86
  X-ray radiography, 85, 86
  Zyglo, 84
Non-ferrous alloys, classification, 263
  physical properties, 263
Non-ferrous metals, classification, 246
  physical properties, 263
Non-sparking metal, 268
Normalizing, 140
Notch-impact specimen, 37, 38, 50
Notch-impact tests, 50–53
N-TAIR, 376, 416, 444
Nuclear reactors, shielding materials, 256
Nylon, 545, 551, 565, 584, 585

Oil, drying, for paint, 606, 609
Oil-powder inspection, 83, 84
Oleoresinous varnish, 606, 607, 609, 615

Opal, 323
Open-hearth process, steel, 97, 114–119
  acid process, 118, 119
  alloy additions, 119
  basic process, 117, 118
  duplex processes, 120
  furnace and its operation, 115–117
  history, 97
  recarburization, 118, 119
  regenerative furnace, 115
  tilting furnace, 117
  turbo-hearth process, 118
  Zebra roof for furnace, 117
Ores of iron, 92, 93, 99, 100
  Bessemer ores, 100
  hematite, 99
  iron carbonate, 99
  limonite, 99
  magnetite, 99
  Mesabi Range ore, 93
  mining, 93
  strategic importance, 92, 93
  taconite, 93, 99, 100
Organic glass, 550
Organic plastics, 544–570
  chemically setting, 545, 546, 552
  classification, 544, 545, 546
  electrical properties, 563, 564
  mechanical properties, 563, 564
  molding, 555–561
  semi-thermosetting, 545, 552, 553
  thermoplastic, 544, 545, 550–552, 576
  thermosetting, 545, 547–550, 576, 577
Organic protective coatings, 606–622
  application, 619, 620
  dryers, 607, 609
  drying oils, 606, 609
  enamels, 606, 607, 620
  failures of paint, 608
  fire-retardant coatings, 618
  lacquers, 607, 615–617, 620
  luminescent coatings, 617, 618
  paints, 606, 607–611, 612–620 *passim*
  pigments, 606, 607, 608, 609, 617, 618
  plasticizers, 607, 616
  preparation of surfaces, 618, 619
  resins, 607, 611–614, 615, 616
  stains, 610, 611
  testing, 620
  thinners, 606, 607, 609, 616
  types of coatings, 606
  varnishes, 606, 607, 609, 615, 620

Organic protective coatings, vehicles, 606, 609
Ornamental finishes, concrete, 428
Ottawa sand, 316, 317, 374
Overstrain, effect on wrought iron, 177
Overstressing, in creep, 64, 65
  in fatigue, 46
Oxyacetylene gas flame, 164, 165, 618
Oxyacetylene gas welding, 164, 166, 167
Oxyhydrogen gas welding, 164
Oxychloride cements, 381, 382
  flooring cement, 382

Paint, 606, 607–611; 612–620 *passim*
  application, 619, 620
  coating, 620
  failure, 608
  function, 607
  pigments, 606, 608, 609
  spraying, 619
  stains, 610, 611
  testing, 620
  types, 609–611
  vehicles, 606, 609
Painted decorations, concrete, 428, 429
Painting, of acoustical materials, 505, 506
  of surfaces, 618, 619
Panel spalling test, 494
Paper cores, 602, 603
Paper filler, laminates, 585, 586, 588
Paper-overlaid plywood, 601
Paper-overlaid veneer, 602
Paper overlays, 600, 601, 602
Partial solid-solubility, 19, 20, 21
Partition tile, 468
Patina, 271
Paving brick, 471–473, 480
  burning, 472
  clay, 471
  de-airing process, 472
  molding, 472
  rattler test, 480
  re-pressing, 472
  vertical fiber, 472
  vitrification, 472
  wire cutting, 472
Paving concrete, 439
Pearlite, 136, 137
Pearlitic malleable cast iron, 213
Pebble lime, 335
Perforated clay pipe, 474
Period of reverberation, sound in room, 505

Perlite, 321, 331, 427, 428, 496, 497
Perlite concrete, 427, 428, 497
Permalloy, 240
Permeability, concrete, 449, 450
Permeability, electrical, 239
Perminvar, 240
Pewter, 18
Phenol-formaldehyde, 545, 547, 553, 554, 576, 584, 587, 600, 612
Phenolic compositions, 547, 548, 565, 575, 576; 584–588 *passim*; 612, 616
Phosphor bronze, 269, 270
  leaded, 269, 270
Phosphorescent pigments, 617, 618
Photomicrograph, 7
Pickett's equation, sonic modulus, concrete, 438, 439
Pig iron, 99–106
  Bessemer pig, 105
  blast furnace, 101
  calcination of ores, 100
  classification, 105
  composition, 105
  forge pig, 105
  machine-cast pig, 104
  uses, 105
Pigment, 606, 607, 608, 609, 617, 618
  body, 608
  colored, 608
  extender, 608, 609
  fluorescent, 617
  inorganic, 608
  organic, 608
  phosphorescent, 617, 618
Pipe, defect in ingots, 130
Pipe, copper, 252
  lead, 256
  steel, 126, 127
  wrought iron, 179
Pit-furnace, 124
Pitting of metals, 79
Pitting resistance, 49
Plaster board, gypsum, 332
Plaster of Paris, 327, 328, 329, 330
Plasters, cement, 327, 328–330 *passim*
  flooring, 327, 329, 330
  gypsum, 327–334; *see* Gypsum plaster
  hard-finish, 327, 329, 333
  hard wall, 327, 330, 331
  lightweight wall, 331
  strength, 332
  tests of, 333

Plasters, uses, 330, 331
Plastic foams, 560, 590
Plastic flow, concrete, 446, 447
Plastic-surfaced plywood, 582
Plasticimeter, Emley, 345
Plasticity, cement, 371, 373
  clay, brick, 458, 460
    refractories, 491
    terra cotta, 469
  concrete, 387
  definition, 3
  gypsum plaster, 333
  lime, 341, 345
  plastics, 544, 560, 561
Plasticizer, for lacquer, 607, 616
Plastics, organic; *see* Organic plastics
Plates, steel, 126
Platinoid, 289
Plywood, 579–582
  beams, 582
  Douglas-fir, 580–582
  plastic-surfaced, 582
  properties, 580
  working stresses, 581
Polarizing microscope, 8
Polyamide plastic, 545, 551
Polyester resins, plastics, 549, 550, 564 565, 584, 585, 586, 594, 595
Polyethylene, 551, 565, 614
Polymerization, 546, 586, 612
Polystyrene, 614, 616
Polysulfide rubber, 567, 568
Polyvinyl acetate, 613
Polyvinyl butyral, 551, 565, 599
Polyvinyl chloride, 550, 551, 554, 555, 613
Polyvinylidene chloride, 613
Porous bearings, 296
Porous blades for jet-engine turbines, 296, 297
Porous filters, 296
Porous metals, 296, 297
Portland blast-furnace-slag cement, 359, 377, 379
Portland cement, 355–383
  addition of retarder, 366
  air content of mortar, 377, 378
  air-entraining, 376–378
  argillaceous limestone, 358
  blast-furnace slag, 359
  burning cement mixture, 364, 365
  calcination, 364
  cement rock, 357, 358

Index

Portland cement, cementing value, 368
  chalk, 358
  clays, 358, 359
  composition, 367, 377
  compounds, 368, 369
  compressive strength, 372, 374, 378
  constitution, 366–370
  definition, 356
  dry process, 359–363
  fineness of grinding, 373, 374, 378
  hardening, 371
  heat liberation, 368
  high-early strength, 367, 369, 370
  historical, 355
  limestone, 357
  low-heat, 370
  manufacture, 359–366
  marl, 357, 358
  normal consistency, 373
  packing, 366
  properties, 371–378
  proportioning raw materials, 362, 363
  rate of reaction, 368, 370
  raw materials, 356–359
  setting, 371, 372, 378
  soundness, 374–376, 378
  sulfate-resisting, 370
  tensile strength, 372, 374
  treatment of the clinker, 365, 366
  unsoundness, 375
  wet process, 359, 360, 363, 364
Portland cement plaster, 429
Portland-pozzolan cement, 379, 380
Positive-type mold, plastics, 557
Post-forming, 587
Pot kiln, for lime, 337
Powder metallurgy, 295–297
Powers' hypothesis on frost resistance of concrete, 442
Pozzolan cement, 351, 352, 379, 380
Pozzolanic materials, 351
Pozzolith, 424
Precast planks, concrete, 428
Prepakt concrete, 426, 427
Pressed brick, 462
Pressing of steel, 127, 128
Pressure welding, 161
Prestressed block-beam structures, 432
Printed circuits on foil-clad plastics, 588
Processed aggregates, 313, 319–321
Progressive fracture, 43; *see also* Fatigue
Proportional limit, 2

Proportioning of concrete, 386–403, 443–445
  air-entrained concrete, 399, 400, 443, 444, 445
  arbitrary assignment, 386
  concrete for pavements, 399
  consistency, 387, 388
  effect of water, 387, 444
  Goldbeck and Gray method, 395–400
  mortar-voids method, 391–395
  Talbot-Richart method, 391–395
  trial-batch method, 388
  water-cement-ratio method, 388–391
  workability, 387
Protective coatings, *see* Organic protective coatings
Puddling process, wrought iron, 97, 172, 173
Pull-out tests, concrete, 439
Pulverized lime, 335
Pumice, 321, 351
Pure metal, 13
Putty, lime, 339–342 *passim*
Pyrite smelting, 248
Pyrometallurgy, 94
Pyrometric cone equivalent, 493, 494, 495

Quaternary steels, 215; *see* Alloy steels
Quicklime, 335–343; *see also* Lime
  air-slaked, 340
  calcium, 335
  chemical composition, 338, 339, 343
  classification, 335, 338
  definition, 335
  dolomitic, 335
  high-calcium, 335
  high-magnesian, 335
  hydration, 339–341
  magnesian, 335
  plasticity, 341
  sand-carrying capacity, 341
  slaking, 339–341
  specifications, 341, 343
  strength, 343
  yield, 341, 342

Radomes, 589, 591
Random ashlar, 304
Rate of strain tests, 67–71
Rattler test for paving brick, 480
Reactivity of aggregates with alkalies in cement, 323, 324
Reactor kiln, 338
Recarburization, 111, 114, 118, 119

642 Index

Red brass, 272
Red brick, 465
Reduction of area, 30, 31
Reflective insulation, 496, 497
Refractory brick, 491–495, 500
 basic brick, 492, 493
 carbon brick, 493
 chrome brick, 493
 chrome-magnesite brick, 493, 494
 cold-crushing strength, 494
 fireclay brick, 491, 492, 494, 495, 500
 Forsterite brick, 493, 494
 fusion test, 493, 494
 ganister, 492
 high-alumina brick, 492, 494
 load test, 493
 magnesite brick, 491, 493
 modulus of rupture, 494
 panel spalling test, 494
 physical properties, 494, 500
 pyrometric cone equivalent, 493, 494, 495
 reheat test, 493, 494
 silica brick, 492, 494
 silicon carbide brick, 491, 493
 spalling test, 494
 spinel, 491, 493
 zircon, 493
 zirconia, 491, 493
Refractory materials, 491–495; see Refractory brick
 classification, 491
 spinel, 491, 493
 zirconia, 491, 493
Refractory mortars, 495
Regenerative furnace, 115, 124
Reheat test for refractories, 493, 494
Reinforced brick masonry, 485, 486
Reinforced plastics, 549, 564
Relaxation test, 71, 72
Repeated stress, 37, 45
Residual stress in bolts, 72–75
Resilience, 3
Resins, 545–554, 576, 577, 611–616; see special kinds
 acrylic, 545, 550, 565, 566, 610, 613
 alkyd, 552, 585, 609–613 *passim*; 616
 contact resins, 585, 586, 601
 copal, 611
 cumar, 614, 615
 cumarone-indene, 551, 614
 dammar, 611, 616
 ester gum, 612, 614, 616

Resins, Kauri copal, 611
 maleic, 614, 616
 melamine-formaldehyde, 549, 575, 577, 584, 613, 616
 natural, 611, 612
 phenol-formaldehyde, 545, 547, 553, 554, 576, 584, 587, 600, 612
 polyester, 549, 564
 resorcinol-formaldehyde, 575, 576
 rosin, 611, 612, 614
 Sandarac, 611
 shellac, 545, 552, 553, 611, 612
 silicone, 487, 568, 614
 stages of thermosetting, 553, 554
 synthetic, 611, 612–614
 synthetic resin adhesives, 574, 576, 577
 transparent phenolic, 548
 urea-formaldehyde, 549, 575, 577, 584, 613, 616
 vinsol, 376, 416, 427
 vinyl, 545, 550, 551, 554, 565, 586, 613, 616
Resorcinol-formaldehyde resin, 575, 576
Reverberatory furnace, 97, 124, 172, 184, 247, 257
Reversed stress, 37, 45
Rivet steel, 107, 159
Riveting, 165
Road aggregates, 322, 323
 hardness, 323
 Los Angeles abrasion test, 323, 324
 resistance to wear, 322
 soundness, 323
 specifications, 323
 toughness, 322
Rock wool, 496, 497, 500
Rocks, argillaceous limestone, 353, 357, 358
 cement rock, 358
 classification, 301, 302
 gypsum, 327
 limestone rock, 336
 natural cement, 353
 road aggregates, 322, 323
Rockwell hardness test, 34
 superficial tester, 34, 35
Rods, steel, 126
Rolling mills, 124, 125
 reheating furnaces, 123, 124
 three-high, 125
 two-high, 125
 universal, 125
Roofing tile, 468, 469

Rosin, 611, 612, 614
Rotary kilns, 320, 328, 337, 364, 365
Rubber, 566–568, 614
  chlorinated, 614
  mechanical hysteresis, 567
  natural, 566, 567
  synthetic, 567, 568
Rubber-base paint, 609, 610
Rubble masonry, 311
Rusting, iron and steel, 76

S.A.E. steel numbering system, 216
Safety glass, 551, 565, 599, 600
Salmon brick, 465
Sand, bulking, 317, 403
  colorimetric test, 315, 316
  comparison with standard sand, 316
  deleterious substances, 315, 316
  fineness modulus, 314
  for concrete aggregate, 315–317
  for sand-lime brick, 470, 471
  foreign matter, 315
  measuring by weighing, 403
  moisture in sand, 317
  Ottawa sand, 316, 317, 374
  stone sand, 317, 318
Sand-bearing test for pipes, 431, 481, 482, 483
Sand-cement mortars, air-entraining, 377, 378
  brick masonry, 380
  comparison with standard sand, 316
  compressive strength, 343, 355, 372, 374, 378, 381
  expansion, 347, 348
  hydrated lime, 347, 376
  lime mortar, 342, 343
  masonry cement, 380, 381
  natural cement, 354, 355
  Portland cement, 372, 374, 376
  tensile strength, 343, 354, 372, 374
Sand-lime brick, 470, 471, 479
  grades of, 470
  manufacture, 471
  physical requirements, 479
  sand, preparation of, 470
Sandarac, 611
Sandstone, 303, 309, 310
Sandwich construction, 589–595
  aircraft-type, 589, 590
  building-industry-type, 589, 590
  cores, properties of, 592–595

Sandwich construction, fabrication, 591
  facings, 589, 590, 591, 595
  radomes, 589, 591
  testing of, 591, 592
Santorin, 351
Saran, 551
Satin finish, paint, 610
Scored tile, 468
Scoria, 321, 351
Scratch coat, plaster, 330, 331
"S" curves, 141
Season cracking of brass, 273
Sea-water action on concrete, 422
Segmental blocks for sewers, 473
Sewer brick, 473, 480, 481
Sewer pipe, 431, 474, 481, 483
Shale, 313, 320, 321, 358, 360, 458, 471, 472
Shape of aggregates, 319
Shear test, sandwich specimen, 591, 592
Shearing strength, aluminum, 281
  aluminum alloys, 281
  brasses, 272
  brick, 475, 476
  building stones, 310
  concrete, 436
  copper, 251
  cores, sandwich construction, 592, 593, 595
  definition, 1
  magnesium alloys, 286
  malleable cast iron, 212
  plywood, 581
  steel, 159, 160
  wrought iron, 178
  zinc die-casting alloys, 291
Shearing stress, 1, 33, 34, 159, 160
Sheathing board, 332
Shelf furnace, 247
Shellac, 545, 552, 553, 611, 612
Shielding materials against gamma rays, 256
Shock resistance, 37, 49–53, 81, 204, 212, 227, 232, 265, 286, 288, 291, 322, 530, 562, 564, 586, 587, 600
Shore scleroscope test, 36
Shot welding, 161
Shotting operation, wrought iron, 173, 174
Shrinkage, cast iron, 195
  clay, 462
  concrete, 446
  lime, 342, 343
  plywood, 580

Shrinkage, refractory brick, 495
  wood, 520, 521
Significant undersize in aggregates, 314
Silica brick, 491, 492
Silica gel, 324
Silicon bronze, 269, 270
Silicon carbide brick, 491, 493
Silicon-manganese steel, 241
Silicon steel, 238, 239, 240
Silicones, 487, 568, 614
Sintered aluminum powder, 295, 296
Size, 615
Skip gradings of aggregates, 314
Slabs, insulating, 496, 498, 500
Slag, blast-furnace, 313, 323, 352, 359
  granulated, 379
  lightweight, 313, 319, 321
Slag cement, 352, 353, 359
Slag pockets, 116
Slag wool, 496, 497
Slate, 304, 310, 358
Slip, 42, 466, 469
Slip-interference theory, **42**
Slip lines or bands, 10
Slurry, 360, 363
S-N diagram, fatigue, 44, **45**
Sodium chloride, 441
Sodium silicate, 419
Sodium sulphate test, 323
Solder, plumbers', 18
  tin, 18
  white brass, 276
Solid masonry units, 464–466, 476–479
Solid solution, 18–22
  intermetallic compound, 21, 22
  interstitial, 22
  solid-insolubility, 19
  solid-solubility, 19
  solid solution minimum, 19
  substitutional, 21
  superlattice, 21, 22
Solite, 320
Sonic modulus of elasticity, 438
Sorel cements, 381
Sound-absorption coefficient, 501–503
Soundness, of aggregates, 323
  of concrete, 440, 441
  of hydrated lime, 345
  of natural cement, 355
  of Portland cement, 372, 374–376, 378
Soya-bean oil, 609, 612

Space lattices, **9**
  cubic, 9
  hexagonal, 9
  tetragonal, 9
Specific adhesion, 572
Specific gravity, aggregates, 398, 404, 443
  beryllium metal, 267
  cements, 353
  ferrous metals, 243
  laminates, 586, 587, 595
  non-ferrous metals, 263
  plastics, 562
  refractory materials, 494
  timber, 526, 527
Speculum metal, 271
Spelter, 253–255 *passim*
Sperry transverse fissure test, 161
Spheroidal structure, 10
Spheroidized cementite, 146, 147
Spinel, 491, 493
Spirit varnish, 606, 615
Spot weld, 161
Sprayed metal laminates, 598
Spraying, paint, 619, 620
Stages of thermosetting resins, 553
Stainless steels, 230–233
Stains, chemical, 610, 611
  non-grain-raising, 610, 611
  oil, 610, 611
  spirit, 610, 611
  water, 610, 611
Standard alloy steels, 219
Statistical nature of fatigue properties, 47
Statistical properties of materials, 4
Statuary bronze, 271
Steam hammer, use of, 127
Stearate of lime, 421
Steel, 95–97, 107–167; *see also* special kinds and Alloy steels
  acid Bessemer, 109–112
  acid open-hearth, 118, 119
  "Alleghany metal," 230
  aluminum, 242
  annealing, 140, 153
  austempering, 147
  austenite, 132–137 *passim*; 142–148 *passim*
  bainite, 143, 144, 147
  basic Bessemer, 113, 114
  basic open-hearth, 117, 118
  billet, 124
  bloom, 124, 125

Index 645

Steel, blowholes, 129
  butt-welded pipe, 127
  carbon-deoxidized, 112
  case-hardening, 152, 153
  castings, 153–155
  cementation process, 97
  cementite, 131, 136, 137
  chrome-molybdenum, 224, 225
  chrome-nickel, 64, 65, 220–223
  chromium, 228, 229, 240
  chromium-vanadium, 229
  classification, 107
  cold-bending test, 31
  cold-drawing, 126
  cold-rolled, 127
  cold-working, 128, 129
  compressive strength, 32
  constitution, 134–137
  continuous casting, 123
  copper, 233
  corrosion, 76–81
  critical points, 134
  crucible, 97
  defects in ingots, 129, 130
  definition, 107
  deoxidation, 112
  dephosphorized, 112
  drop-forgings, 127
  ductility, 4, 30, 31, 55, 155, 158, 159
  duplex, 120
  effects of carbon on properties, 156, 157
  effects of manganese, phosphorus, silicon, and sulfur, 156, 157
  18-8 stainless, 230
  electric, 97, 120–122
  endurance ratio, 47
  "Enduro Nirosta," 230
  ferrite, 136, 137
  flame hardening, 165
  flexural strength, 32, 33
  forging, 127
  grain-size control, 151, 152
  hard facing, 166
  hardenability, 148–151
  hardening, 138, 139
  hardness, 4, 23; see Hardness
  heat treatment, 138, 139, 140
  high-carbon, 107
  high-carbon tool, 233–235
  history, 97
  hot-working, 128
  hypereutectoid, 132

Steel, hypoeutectoid, 132
  ingot iron, 132, 155, 156, 239
  ingot mold, 113
  ingotism, 130
  iron-carbon equilibrium diagram, 131–134
  isothermal transformation diagram, 140–143
  K.A. 2 stainless, 230
  killed, 122
  lap-welded pipe, 126, 127
  low-carbon, 107
  low-temperature behavior, 81–83
  magnetic properties, 160, 161
  manganese, 135, 219, 220, 237
  martempering, 148
  martensite, 138, 139
  mechanical work, 128
  medium-carbon, 107
  medium-high-carbon, 107
  modulus of elasticity, 3, 158, 160
  molybdenum, 223, 224
  nickel, 219, 220, 232
  Nitralloy, 242, 243
  nitriding, 242, 243
  normalizing, 140
  open-hearth, 97, 114–119
  pearlite, 136, 137
  physical properties, 156–160
  pipe, in ingots, 130
  pipe-making, 126, 127
  plates, 126
  pressing, 127, 128
  quenching, 138, 139
  rails, 107, 125, 126
  recarburizer, 111, 114, 118, 119
  red-shortness, 156
  rimmed, 122, 123
  rivet, 107, 159
  rods, 126
  rolling mill operations, 123–130
  S.A.E. numbering system, 216
  seamless tubes, 127
  segregation, 130
  semikilled, 123
  shearing strength, 33, 159, 160
  shock resistance, 37, 49–53, 81
  silicon, 238, 239, 240
  soaking pit, 124
  spheroidized cementite, 146, 147
  spring, 107
  stainless, 230–233

646 Index

Steel, stress-strain curves, 2, 28
  structural, 107, 126, 158, 159, 160
  teeming ladle, 112, 118, 119
  tempered martensite, 145, 146
  tempering, 140
  tensile strength test, 28–31
  thin-gauge, 127
  tool, 107, 233–236
  torsional shear, 33, 159, 160
  tungsten, 215, 236
  ultimate strength, 29
  vanadium, 215, 236
  welding, 161–167
  wire-rod, 126
  yield point, 2
  yield strength, 2
Stellite, 68, 69
Sterro metal, 275
Stiffness, 3
Stone masonry, 311, 312
Stone sand, 317, 318
Strain, 1
Strain hardening, 57
Strategic metals, 92, 93
Stratified rocks, 302
Strength-weight ratios, alloys, 282
Stress, 1
Stress-concentration factor, 4
Stress-corrosion cracking, brass, 273
Stress-relief anneal, 76
Stress rupture, 58–63
Stress-skin panels, 582
Stress-strain diagrams, 2, 3
  cast iron, 199
  concrete, 3, 437, 438
  steel, 2, 28
Structural clay products, 458–469; see Brick
Structural silicon steel, 238
Structural steel, 107, 126, 158, 159, 160
Stucco, 429
  magnesite stucco, 382
Styrene, 545, 550, 565, 585
Superlattice, 22
Supermalloy, 240
Supersonic inspection, 87, 88
Surface finishing, steels, 48
Sweat cooling, 296
Swelling stress, 37, 45
Synthetic resins, 612–614; see special kinds

Taconite, 93, 99, 100
Talbot method, proportioning concrete, 391–395
Tall oil, 609, 612
Tall-oil alkyd resin paint, 609, 610
Tego film, 576
Tempered martensite, 145, 146
Tempering, 140
Tensile properties, 1, 28
  aluminum, 263, 281, 282
  aluminum alloys, 263, 281, 282
  beryllium-copper, 267
  brass, 263, 272, 274, 275
  bronze, 263, 265, 266, 270
  cast iron, 197, 198, 243
  chrome-molybdenum steel, 224
  chrome-nickel steel, 221–223, 232
  concrete, 435
  copper, 249–251, 263
  cores, sandwich construction, 593
  die-casting alloys, 291–293
  hydrated lime, 346
  Inconel metal, 288
  laminates, 584, 586, 587, 595
  lead, 256, 263
  lime mortar, 343, 346
  magnesium, 260, 263
  magnesium alloys, 263, 285, 286
  malleable cast iron, 212, 243
  manganese bronze, 266, 267
  manganese steel, 219, 237
  Monel metal, 288
  natural cement, 354, 355
  nickel, 261
  nickel-base alloys, 263
  nickel-chromium-molybdenum steel, 226, 227
  nickel steel, 219, 220
  organic plastics, 562, 564
  plywood, 581
  Portland cement, 372, 374
  silicon steel, 238
  stainless steels, 237, 243
  steel, carbon, 238, 243
  tin, 263
  titanium, 262, 290
  titanium alloys, 290
  tool steels, 243
  wood, 523
  wrought iron, 176, 177
  zinc, 263
Tensile-strength test, 27–31

Index

Tension shear, adhesives, 578
Tension test, adhesives, 578
Teredo, 538
Termites, 536, 537
  dry-wood, 536, 537
  protection, 537
  subterranean, 536, 537
Ternary alloy steels, 215
Terra cotta, 469, 470
Terrazzo, 428
Tetragonal lattice structure, 9
Thermal coefficients, expansion, aluminum, 259
  concrete, 446
  cores, sandwich construction, 593
  Dumet, 242
  Invar, 241
  magnesium, 260
  organic plastics, 562
  thermostat metals, 598
Thermal conductivity, aluminum, 259
  concrete, 427, 428, 500
  cores, sandwich construction, 593
  formula, 499
  heat-insulating materials, 500
  magnesium, 260
  magnesium alloys, 285
  refractory materials, 494, 499, 500
  wood, 500
Thermoplastic compositions, 544, 545, 550–552, 554, 555, 561
Thermosetting compositions, 545, 546, 547–550, 553, 554, 561, 602
Thermostat metals, 598
Thinner, paint, 606, 607, 609, 616
Thiokol rubber, 567, 568
Three-edge-bearing test for pipes, 431, 480–483 *passim*
Tile, clay, building, 478, 479
  ceramic-glazed, 466, 477, 479
  drain, clay, 473, 480, 481, 482
  floor, 468, 478
  non-load-bearing, 468, 479
  properties, 474–479
  roofing, 468
  structural-clay facing, 466, 467, 477, 479
  structural-clay load-bearing wall, 467, 468, 478
  wall, 467, 468, 478
Timber, 508–543; *see also* Wood and Lumber
  basic stresses, 529, 530

Timber, decay, 532, 533
  defects, 515–518
  density rules, 518, 519
  durability, 533
  elastic properties, 530, 531
  forms for concrete, 406, 407
  grading, 518, 519
  kiln-drying, 520
  marine borers, 538–540
  mechanical properties, 523–531
  modulus of elasticity, 528, 529
  physical characteristics, 514–**523**
  preservation, 533–536
  seasoning, 519, 520
  termites, 536, 537
  time factor, 527, 529, 530
Timber connectors, 531, 532
  alligator, 531, 532
  clamping plate, 531, 532
  claw plate, 531, 532
  shear plate, 531, 532
  spike grid, 531, 532
  split ring, 531, 532
Time yield, concrete, 446, 447
Tin, 9, 256, 257
  commercial forms, 256, 257
  corrosion resistance, 257
  creep, 257
  extraction from ores, 257
  properties, 257
  uses, 257
Titanium, 262, 263, 290
  commercial forms, 262
  hardness, 290
  manufacture, 262
  properties, 262, 263, 290
  tensile strength, 290
  uses, 262, 263
Titanium alloys, 289, 290
  composition, 289
  constitution, 289
  hardness, 290
  mechanical properties, 289, 290
  tensile strength, 289, 290
  uses, 290
Tobin bronze, 94, 274
Tool steels, 107, 233–236
Torsion test, 33, 34
Torsional shear, 159, 160
  shearing modulus of elasticity, 33, **159** 160

648 Index

Toughness, 4, 37–39, 49–53, 81, 203, 204, 212, 227, 232, 265, 286, 288, 291, 322, 323, 562, 564, 586, 587, 600
  definition, 4
  of aggregates, 322, 323
Transfer molding, 555–558
Transparent curing membranes, 419
Transpiration cooling, 296, 297
Transverse strength, *see* Flexural strength
  cast iron, 200, 201
Traprock, 304
Trass, 351
Trees, broad-leaved, 509
  classes, 508
  conifers, 509
  endogenous, 509
  exogenous, 508, 509
Tremie, 410, 411
Tricalcium aluminate, 367, 369, 370, 377
Tricalcium silicate, 367, 368, 370, 377
Tridymite, 323
TTT diagrams, 141
Tubes, steel, seamless, 127
Tufa, 351
Tuff, 351
Tuff-lite, 320, 321
Tungsten steel, 215, 236
Tunnel kiln, 211, 464, 469, 492
Turbidimeter, Wagner, 373, 378
Turbine metal, 267
Turbo-hearth process, 118
Turpentine, 611
Tuyère, 102, 182, 183
Twinning, 11, 273
  of brass, 273
Two-layer alloy, 14
Two-stage process for wrought iron, 96

Ultimate strength, 28
Understressing in fatigue, 46
Universal mill, 125
Unnotched tension-impact specimen, 50
Unsoundness, of aggregates, 323
  of concrete, 440, 441
  of hydrated lime, 345
  of natural cement, 355
  of Portland cement, 375
Urea-formaldehyde resins, 549, 575, 577, 584, 613, 616
Utility impact tests, 37

Vacuum concrete process, 424–426
Valve bronze, 271
Vanadium bronze, 271
Vanadium steel, 215, 236
Varnish, 606, 607, 609, 615, 620
  alcoholic, 607
  architectural, 615
  dryers in, 606, 607
  industrial, 615
  oil length, 615
  oils in, 606, 607
  oleoresinous, 606, 609, 615
  resins in, 606, 607
  shellac, 615; *see also* Shellac
  spirit, 606, 615
  testing of, 620
  thinners in, 606, 607
  wall size, 615
Vehicles, for paint, 606, 609
  aqueous, 609
  calcimine, 609
  casein paint, 609
  dryers, 609
  drying oils, 609
  lacquers, 609
  oleoresinous varnish, 609
  rubber-base water-emulsion, 609
  thinners, 609
Veneer, 579
Veneer plywood, 580
Vermiculite, 321, 331, 427, 428, 496, 497, 500
Vermiculite concrete, 427, 428, 500
Vertical kiln, 329, 337, 350
Vicat needle, 371, 372, 378
Vickers hardness test, 35
Vinsol resin, 376, 416, 427
Vinyl resins, 545, 550, 551, 554, 565, 586, 613, 616
Volume change, concrete, 445, 446
  dolomitic hydrated lime, 347
Vulcanization of rubber, 566

Wagner turbidimeter test, 373, 378
Walker's durability factor, 442, 443
Wall board, 332
Wall size, 615
Wall tile, clay, 467, 468, 478
Water absorption, concrete, 430, 431
Water-cement ratio, 388–391
Waterproofing compounds, 420

Index

Waterproofing joints, 421, 422
Waterproofing materials, 421
Waterproof paper, 419
Water resistance, insulating material, 499
Water retention of membranes in curing of concrete, 419
Wax, 424
Wear-resisting steels, 49, 237, 238
Wear tests, 76
Weathering tests, paints, 620
Welding, 161–167, 179
  atomic-hydrogen electric-metal-arc, 164
  carbon-arc, 163
  electric-arc, 162, 163
  fusion, 162
  gas-flame, 164
  Heliarc, 164
  inert-gas electric-metal-arc, 164
  inspection of welds, 164, 165
  oxyacetylene gas, 164
  oxyhydrogen gas, 164
  pressure welding, 161
  shielded-arc, 163
  shot welding, 161
  spot welding, 161
  Thermit process, 164
  wrought iron, 179
Whipping process for slaked lime, 347
White brass, 276
White brass solder, 276
White cast iron, 191, 192, 193, 209, 210
White coat, lime, 341, 344, 347
White lead, 608
White-pigmented curing compounds, 419
White Portland cement, 431, 432
Whitewash paint, 609
Winning of clay, 458, 460
Wire-making, 126
Wood, 508–543; *see also* Timber and Lumber
  annual growth, 509–513
  antiseptics for preserving, 534
  bark, 509, 513
  cambium, 513
  case-hardened, 522, 523
  cells, 510
  checks, 516, 517, 522
  compressive strength, 523, 524
  cross-cut, 514
  defects, 515–518
  diagonal grain, 525
  diffuse porous, 512

Wood, drying, 520, 521
  end grain, 514
  endogenous growth, 509
  exogenous growth, 508, 509
  fiber-saturation point, 526
  figure, 515, 525
  flexural strength, 524, 528, 529
  grain, 515, 525
  heartwood, 513, 514
  honeycombed, 522
  knots, 515–518
  longitudinal shear, 524, 528, 529
  mechanical properties, 528, 529
  medullary rays, 510, 511
  modulus of elasticity, 528, 529
  modulus of rupture, 528, 529
  moisture, effect on strength, 525, 526
  moisture content, 519
  mold, 533
  non-porous, 512
  physical characteristics, 514–523
  pitch pocket, 516, 517
  pith, 509, 513
  plywood, 579–582; *see* Plywood
  rate of growth, effect on strength, 527
  rift-cut, 514, 515
  ring porous, 512
  rot, 516, 517
  sapwood, 513, 514
  shake, 516, 517
  shrinkage, 511, 520, 521
  slash-cut, 514, 515
  spring growth, 510, 512, 513
  stain, 533
  stiffness, 524, 525
  structure, 510–512
  summer growth, 510, 512, 513, 519
  tensile strength, 523
  veneer, 579
  vessels, 510, 512
  wane, 517, 518
  warping, 518, 520, 521
  weight, 519, 526
    relation to strength, 526, 527
Wood-fiber insulation, 496, 497, 500
Wood-fiber plaster, 331
Workability of concrete, 387
Wrought iron, 95, 172–180
  Aston process, 173–175
  composition, 175
  compressive strength, 177
  constitution, 175

Wrought iron, corrosion resistance, 178
  fatigue, 178
  history, 96
  manufacture, 172–175
  modulus of elasticity, 177
  nick-bend test, 178
  nickel-alloy iron, 180
  properties, 175–179
  puddling process, 172, 173
  removal of slag, 174
  rolling-mill operations, 175
  shearing strength, 178
  shingling, 174
  shotting, 173
  slag fibers, 175
  squeezing, 174
  tensile strength, 176, 177
  uses, 179
  welding, 179

X-ray methods, 7
X-ray diffraction, 86, 87
X-ray radiography, 85, 86

Yellow brass, 272, 273
Yield point, 2, 28
Yield strength, 2

Zebra roof for furnace, **117**
Zinc, 9, 253–255
  commercial forms, 253
  corrosion resistance, 254
  creep, 253, 254
  dust, 253
  extraction from ores, 253
  fume, 253
  galvanized coating, 254
  grades, 254
  oxide, 253
  properties, 253, 254
  specifications, 254
  spelter, 253–255
  tensile strength, 254
Zinc chloride, 534–536
Zinc die-casting alloys, 290, **291**
Zirconia, 491, 493
Zonolite, 321
Zyglo, 84